DEADLY DREAMS

The great powers of the world – China, Britain, France, the United States, and Russia – were involved in the Arrow War (1856–60). But for the fact that it was regionally contained (though it stretched from Canton to Beijing), it could be called a world war because of its global economic and diplomatic drivers. Dr. John Wong's investigation into the *casus belli* – an alleged insult to the British flag ascribed to the *Arrow*, a sailing vessel registered in Hong Kong – led him to twenty-five years of research across the globe. In *Deadly Dreams*, he identifies the origins of the war and analyzes the intricate, competing interests and passions that fueled the conflict. These include complex Chinese and British diplomacy; Chinese tea and silk exports and their world markets; British India's jealously guarded economic strategies and opium monopoly; intricate Westminster politics and British global trade; French pride and cultural priorities; Russian intrigues and territorial designs; and America's apparent aloofness and real ambitions.

This history is about economic realities, and the pursuit of personal vanity and national pride at the expense of terrific bloodshed; it is about drugs, lies, scandals, conspiracies, and strategems. Dr. Wong details how an outrageous war was started without authority, then sanctioned, and justified spiritedly (to this day). He offers penetrating insights into British offensive and Chinese defensive diplomacy, into territorial and court politics in China, into Victorian values, rhetoric and free-trade ideology. His findings shed new light on the mechanics and theories of imperialism and how they might be reassessed.

J. Y. Wong is Senior Lecturer in History in the Department of History at the University of Sydney.

Cambridge Studies in Chinese History, Literature and Institutions

General Editor, Denis Twitchett

DEADLY DREAMS

Other books in the series

Victor H. Mair Tunhuang Popular Narratives
Ira E. Kasoff The Thought of Chang Tsai
Chih-P'ing Chou Yüan Hung-tao and the Kung-an School
Arthur Waldron The Great Wall of China: From History to Myth
Hugh R. Clark Community, Trade, and Networks: Southern Fujian Province from the Third to the Thirteenth Centuries
Denis Twitchett The Writing of Official History Under the T'ang
J. D. Schmidt Stone Lake: The Poetry of Fang Chengda
Brian E. McKnight Law and Order in Sung China
Jo-Shui Chen Liu Tsung-yüan and Intellectual Change in T'ang China, 773–819
David Pong Shen Pao-chen and China's Modernization in the Nineteenth Century
J. D. Schmidt Within the Human Realm: The Poetry of Huang Zunxian, 1848–1905
Arthur Waldron From War to Nationalism: China's Turning Point, 1924–1925
Chin-Shing Huang Philosophy, Philology, and Politics in Eighteenth-Century China: Li Fu and the Lu-Wang School under the Ch'ing
Glen Dudbridge Religious Experience and Lay Society in T'ang China: A Reading of Tai Fu's 'Kuang-i chi'
Eva Shan Chou Reconsidering Tu Fu: Literary Greatness and Cultural Context
Frederic Wakeman Jr. The Shanghai Badlands: Wartime Terrorism and Urban Crime, 1937–1941
Sarah A. Queen From Chronicle to Canon: The Hermeneutics of the Spring and Autumn Annals according to Tung Chung-shu

Deadly Dreams
Opium, Imperialism, and the *Arrow* War (1856–1860) in China

J. Y. Wong

PUBLISHED BY THE PRESS SYNDICATE OF THE UNIVERSITY OF CAMBRIDGE
The Pitt Building, Trumpington Street, Cambridge, United Kingdom

CAMBRIDGE UNIVERSITY PRESS
The Edinburgh Building, Cambridge CB2 2RU, United Kingdom
40 West 20th Street, New York, NY 10011-4211, USA
10 Stamford Road, Oakleigh, Melbourne 3166, Australia

© Cambridge University Press, 1998

This book is in copyright. Subject to statutory exception
and to the provisions of relevant collective licensing agreements,
no reproduction of any part may take place without
the written permission of Cambridge University Press.

First published 1998

Printed in the United States of America

Typeset in Baskerville 10/12 pt, in Quark X Press™ [BTS]

*A catalog record for this book is available from
the British Library*

Library of Congress Cataloging-in-Publication Data
Wong, J. Y. (John Yue-wo)
Deadly dreams: opium, imperialism and the Arrow War (1856–1860)
in China / J. Y. Wong.
p. cm. – (Cambridge studies in Chinese history, literature,
and institutions)
Includes bibliographical references and index.
ISBN 0-521-55255-9
1. China – History – Foreign intervention, 1857–1861 – Causes.
2. Great Britain – Foreign relations – China. 3. China – Foreign
relations – Great Britain. I. Title. II. Series.
DS760.W87 1996
327.51–dc20   95-17248
                                                  CIP

ISBN 0-521-55255-9

HOUSTON PUBLIC LIBRARY

R01147 46003

To Grahame Harrison
True scholar, genuine friend, wonderful colleague

Contents

List of Tables xi
List of Figures xv
Poem by the late Mr Qin Esheng xvii
Foreword by Professor Wang Gungwu xix
Foreword by Professor C. A. Bayly xxi
Preface xxiii

I The confusion of imperialism

1 An attempt to peel the onion of confusion 3

II The pretext for imperialism

2 An international incident: 'That wretched question of the *Arrow*' 43

III The personalities of imperialism

3 Harry Parkes: 'If you *would* read a little international law.' – *Punch*. 69

4 Sir John Bowring: Possessed by a monomania 84

5 Commissioner Yeh: A 'monster'? 109

6 Rule, Britannia and *vox populi, vox Dei* 128

IV The rhetoric of imperialism

7 Marx, *Punch*, and a political press: The debate among the British newspapers 153

8 The *Arrow* incident and international law: The debate in the House of Lords 174

Contents

9 Triumph of the liberal conscience: The debate in the House of Commons   193
10 'Johnny' is on his knees: The 'Chinese Election'   216

V The mechanics of imperialism

11 Behind the scenes: The diplomacy of imperialism   261
12 Behind the scenes: The politics of imperialism   283
13 In the wings: The lobbies of imperialism   310

VI The economics of imperialism

14 Anglo-Chinese trade: The Chinese should buy more   333
15 China's maritime trade: The Chinese could buy more   365
16 The problem of India: The Chinese should and could buy more   386
17 The balance sheet: The Chinese are now buying more   434

VII The dynamics of imperialism

18 Conclusion   457

Chronology of major events   487
Word list   490
Abbreviations   494
Bibliography   495
Index   525

Tables

13.1	A comparison of the instructions for treaty revision to Sir John Bowring in 1854 with those to Lord Elgin in 1857	page 329
14.1	U.K. exports to China (and Hong Kong), 1827–58	334
14.2	The United Kingdom's trade deficit with China, 1827–58	336
14.3	U.K. imports from China, 1828–58	338
14.4	The top four countries (excluding the British possessions) from which the United Kingdom bought its imports, 1849–58	340
14.5	China's percentage of the United Kingdom's global imports	341
14.6	The place of China in the United Kingdom's global imports, 1849–58	342
14.7	A comparison of the United Kingdom's imports from China and from British possessions, 1854–7	342
14.8	Tea duty and average tea consumption in the United Kingdom, 1801–60	344
14.9	Tea imported into the United Kingdom, entered for home consumption and the duty derived therefrom, 1835–58	346
14.10	Tea duty added to a table of the United Kingdom's total gross income, 1842–60	348
14.11	Tea duty as a percentage of the United Kingdom's total gross revenue, 1842–60	349
14.12	A comparison of the gross tea duty with the gross land and assessed taxes of the United Kingdom, 1842–60	350
14.13	A comparison of the gross annual tea duty with the annual expenditure of the Royal Navy, 1835–57	351
14.14	Gross public expenditure of the United Kingdom, 1835–60, with the revenue from tea duty added for comparison	353
14.15	Sources of tea imported into the United Kingdom, 1854	356
14.16	Tea reexported from the United Kingdom, 1855	358

Tables

14.17	U.K. imports of raw silk worldwide, 1857	361
14.18	U.K. exports of silk stuffs and ribbons, 1858	363
15.1	Value of imports from and exports to the United Kingdom, 1827–58	367
15.2	Value of China's imports from, and exports to, the United Kingdom and India conjointly, 1827–58	368
15.3	Quantity and value of goods imported into Canton by the East India Company and its private traders in the financial year 1833–4	370
15.4	Quantity and value of goods exported from Canton by the East India Company and its private traders in the financial year 1833–4	371
15.5	Value of the British East India Company's exports from, and imports into, Canton, 1820–34	372
15.6	The United Kingdom's and China's perspectives, 1826–34	373
15.7	Bills drawn upon India and London by the Company's Select Committee at Canton, 1820–35	375
15.8	Triangular exports: From India to China, China to the United Kingdom, and the United Kingdom to India, 1827–58	377
15.9	Triangular imports: India from China, China from the United Kingdom, and the United Kingdom from India, 1827–58	379
15.10	Value of Canton's exports, 1820–34	381
15.11	Value of Canton's imports, 1820–34	381
15.12	Value of Canton's import and export trade combined, 1820–34	383
16.1	The annual balance sheet in India, 1851–8	387
16.2	Indian debt, 1801–58	387
16.3	Bengal salt, 1851–60	391
16.4	Bengal opium, 1851–60	392
16.5	Bombay salt revenue, 1851–60	395
16.6	Bombay opium revenue, 1851–60	395
16.7	Twenty major revenues of India, 1853–8	397
16.8	The place of opium in India's total gross revenue, 1821–58	397
16.9	Bengal opium (Behar and Benares) exported to China and the Straits Settlements, 1829–64	400
16.10	Malwa opium exported via Bombay to China, 1830–64	404
16.11	Value of Bengal opium and Chinese tea and silk, 1828–57	407
16.12	Opium and the United Kingdom's trade balance, 1854–7	409
16.13	Opium and U.K. exports to India, 1854–7	409

16.14	Bengal opium and U.S. cotton, 1854–7	410
16.15	The triangular trade, 1854–7	412
16.16	Sind deficit, 1851–60	424
16.17	Actual cost of troops in Sind, 1851–60	424
16.18	Major Indian exports: Indigo, cotton, and opium, 1813–61	427
16.19	Opium in the United Kingdom, 1837–55	432
17.1	Tea imported into the United Kingdom direct from China, 1838–67	435
17.2	Computed real value of tea imported into the United Kingdom from China, India and Japan, 1853–67	437
17.3	U.K. imports of raw silk into Britain from China, 1838–67	438
17.4	China's percentage of the total amount of raw silk imported into the United Kingdom, 1853–67	440
17.5	Value of U.K. exports to China (including Hong Kong), 1854–66	442
17.6	U.K. exports to China (and Hong Kong), 1854–8	445
17.7	U.K. exports to China (and Hong Kong), 1859–62	446
17.8	U.K. imports of tea compared with its exports of woollens and cottons, 1827–67	448
17.9	U.K. exports to China (and Hong Kong), 1863–6	452
17.10	Export of U.K. products to China, 1854–66	453

Figures

14.1	The declared value of U.K. exports to China (and Hong Kong), 1827–58	page 335
14.2	The United Kingdom's trade imbalance with China, 1827–58	337
14.3	The place of China in the United Kingdom's global imports, 1849–58	341
15.1	Value of Canton's exports, 1829–32	382
15.2	Value of Canton's imports, 1829–32	382
15.3	Value of Canton's import and export trade combined, 1829–30	384
16.1	Indian debt, 1801–58	389
16.2	Gross opium revenue expressed as a percentage of gross Indian revenue, 1821–8	399
16.3	Bengal opium exported to China, 1829–64	402
16.4	Bengal opium exported to China and the straits settlements, 1829–64	403
16.5	Bengal and Malwa opium exported to China, 1849–64	403
16.6	The combined amount of Bengal and Malwa opium exported to China, 1849–64	405
16.7	Major Indian exports: Indigo, cotton, and opium, 1813–61	408
17.1	Tea imported into the United Kingdom direct from China, 1838–67	436
17.2	Imports of raw silk into the United Kingdom from China, 1838–67	438
17.3	China's percentage of the total amount of raw silk imported into the United Kingdom, 1853–67	441
17.4	Value of U.K. exports to China (including Hong Kong), 1854–66	443

17.5 U.K. imports of tea compared with its exports of woollens and cottons, 1827–67 (using 1827 as the base-year figure of 100 per cent) 450

17.6 U.K. imports of tea compared with its exports of woollens and cottons, 1827–67 451

Your statements are meticulously referenced;
Your narratives are straightforward and comprehensive.
You make your views crystal clear,
You judge as if you were wielding a sword.
The quality of your work on the Opium Wars,
Rivals that of Dong Zhongshu's tomes on history.
On the occasion of your second lecture tour in China
I compose this poem as a memento.

by Qin Esheng,
at the age of eighty

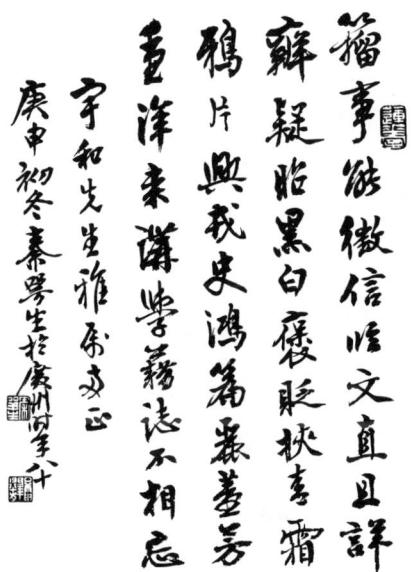

Foreword

I am delighted that Dr John Wong has finally returned to the mid-nineteenth century to complete the study of a subject he started to work on some twenty years ago – the origins of the Second Anglo-Chinese, or 'Opium', War. Having read with great interest his splendid study of Viceroy Yeh Ming-ch'en (Cambridge, 1976) and what happened to the documents of the Viceroy's yamen (Oxford, 1983), I knew he would produce an equally authoritative examination of the breakdown of Anglo-Chinese relations in 1856, which he intimated he might do during the 1970s. He was distracted from doing so for several years by a project which engaged his attention in the early 1980s, a project which honed his skills in historical detection further: the pursuit of the origins of Sun Yatsen's 'heroic image'. After that was published (Oxford, 1986), he was ready for another kind of pursuit and returned to his earlier subject with a much larger prey in mind. This time, it was the pursuit of that well-hunted but elusive animal, that beast called 'imperialism'.

Dr Wong recognizes that the beast takes many shapes and comes in many disguises. For our story, it first showed its ugly face in a most unlikely object, a Chinese lorcha named the *Arrow*. Once that was identified, the author set his sights from every angle until the shape of the animal was exposed. The part and chapter titles tell the story clearly enough: the confusion of imperialism, the pretext for it, its personalities, rhetoric, mechanics, diplomacy, politics, lobbies, economics, and dynamics. Knowing Dr Wong's record, one expects a comprehensive chase. He does not disappoint us. There is excitement in the search for villains: Harry Parkes, Sir John Bowring, Commissioner Yeh, and some minor others. There are the tense arguments in the trial scenes in Westminster, in the press, before the British voters, and finally in front of the magistrates of history themselves. There are the intrigues of diplomacy, the realities of politics, and the lobbies of vested interests. There is tough accounting: the wearisome trail through trading figures for the China coast, the British market, the Indian opium production centres, and, not least, the balance sheet.

Foreword by Professor Wang Gungwu

An anthropologist friend of mine once told me that the whole story of mankind could be found in the smallest village of the smallest tribe on the smallest island in the South Pacific – if you know how to look and what to look for. So obviously can this mammoth of an animal called imperialism be found on the tiny deck of a lorcha, in the minutiae of false reports and tardy rationalizations, in the bookkeeper's indelible black ink no less than in the glorious rhetoric of great debaters in the mother of parliaments – if you know where to look. Dr Wong has dug deep and found out where the skeletons were buried. From the broken and scattered fragments, he has given us a glimpse of what one of the many species of the beast might have looked like. Thus is the historian not content to be merely a storyteller but a scientist and anatomist who, having found various parts of limbs, skulls, and rib cages, is prepared to describe the creature's heart and brains.

At the end of the examination, I cannot say that I can see imperialism whole or know how it lived and died. But I am assured by the thoroughness of his study that this is one of its many manifestations, whether as 'a fortuitous concourse of atoms', in Palmerston's words, or, more mysteriously, the ramifications of what Douglas Hurd once called 'an Anglo-Chinese confusion'. Once again, Dr Wong has demonstrated great skill in taking apart small structures and putting them together as larger constructs. It is one of the tasks which historians are expected to perform again and again. In his new book of detection, Dr Wong has shown that patience and persistence, even a delay of a dozen years, can pay off very well.

Wang Gungwu
Vice-Chancellor
University of Hong Kong

Foreword

Studies of British empire building have characteristically concentrated on two broad periods of overseas activity. The first was the period of the 'Second British Empire' during the French Revolutionary and Napoleonic Wars. This saw a 'swing to the East' and the creation of a greater Indian Empire along with the first British footholds on the African coast. Second, much has been written about the age of 'new imperialism' in the later nineteenth century, which climaxed in the partition of Africa and the battle for concessions in China. This latter period has been the nursery of theories of imperialism since the days of Lenin and J. A. Hobson. In practice, however, empire building went on unabated through the middle decades of the nineteenth century, and did so even under ministries which formally disavowed territorial annexation, except in the case of colonies of white settlement. The 1850s and 1860s were witness to a particularly notable run of imperial adventures beginning with the consolidation of British power in the Punjab and Sind and the extension of dominion in the Malay peninsula, and ending with the so-called *Arrow* War with China, which effectively opened up this vast land to European influence and exploitation.

Curiously, the *Arrow* War and its consequences have received little attention from historians, even by comparison with its better-known precursor, the Opium War of 1839–42. The appearance of Dr John Wong's fine study is, therefore, an event of considerable importance not only for Chinese historiography, but for the study of British imperial history in general. Based on an exhaustive analysis of Chinese and English language sources, this book leaves us in no doubt about the importance of these events for China. The final humiliation of the imperial centre, symbolized by Lord Elgin's sack of the palace at Beijing, was accompanied by Britain's forcing on China of a crippling indemnity and the further opening of the country to European missionaries, traders, and diplomats. Thereafter, the 'self-strengthening movement' to reform Chinese government and the first stirrings of China's modern nationalism were inevitable.

Foreword by Professor C. A. Bayly

However, Dr Wong's study centres our attention on another actor that gained greater freedom in China after 1860 and that has received insufficient attention in earlier studies – opium. Opium was not directly mentioned in the peace of 1842, or in that of 1858, which was finally ratified in 1860. But British traders were given the right legally to import opium from India under the terms of the commercial protocol which accompanied Elgin's peace. This book convincingly shows the economic links which made Britain's imperial effort in Asia dependant on this drug. The rocky finances of the government of India, which had been thrown into even greater chaos by the rebellion of 1857–8, were underpinned by the large revenues from opium sales, as were the private business enterprises which linked Bombay, Calcutta, and Canton. More generally, opium played an important and growing part in supporting Britain's balance of trade with Asia.

In addition, therefore, Dr Wong's book makes an important contribution to the study of the theory of imperialism. He swings attention away from those general characterizations of imperial expansion which speak of 'free-trade imperialism' or, more recently, 'gentlemanly capitalism', and instead concentrates on the interconnectedness of metropolitan and peripheral concerns. The men on the 'periphery', be they Indian government officials or private traders, wanted to shoot their way into Chinese markets. In this they formed an unholy alliance with ministers who had long been irked by China's continued refusal to treat with Britain on the terms to which it felt itself entitled. The petty incident over the *Arrow* and the fate of its Union flag provided a pretext on which both interests could pick a fight. In short, Dr Wong's study illuminates an important area of British and Chinese history. It will also provoke discussion among students of the broader workings of economic imperialism.

C. A. Bayly
Vere Harmsworth Professor of
Imperial and Naval History
University of Cambridge

Preface

(I)

Upon the completion in 1971 of my manuscript on Commissioner Yeh,[1] I set out to trace the origins of the *Arrow* War. The dangers of embarking on a project which had no obvious or easy answers were quick to reveal themselves. The discovery of eagerly sought information simply raised more questions than it answered. The resolution of one problem merely produced more perplexities. Thus, the structure of an envisaged book continued to be erected, demolished, and rebuilt. Chapters were drafted, taken apart, and rewritten. Slowly but surely, I went beyond the boundaries of China into India, Great Britain, France, the United States, and Russia; and from political and diplomatic history to economic and imperial history, international law, and strategic studies. What began as an examination of an alleged insult to the British flag belonging to the boat *Arrow* led to an analysis of Chinese and British diplomacy; of Victorian passions; of the love-and-hate relations among Britain, France, the United States, and Russia; of Chinese tea and silk exports; of British India's economic strategies and opium monopoly; of Westminster politics and British global trade; and even of the cotton supplied to Lancashire mills by the Americans, who thereby made up the trade deficit caused by their heavy purchases of Chinese tea.

Consequently, the project went on for so long that some friends and colleagues thought it might never be completed; but not Professor Wang Gungwu. His wise counselling and staunch support from beginning to end is greatly appreciated. He also kindly read in 1993 what I thought was the final version and wrote me a graceful foreword. In 1994, I found myself having to

---

1. This was subsequently published as *Yeh Ming-ch'en: Viceroy of Liang-Kuang, 1852–8* (Cambridge University Press, 1976). Part of my early research activities on the *Arrow* War involved listing the diplomatic correspondence in the Chinese language between the Chinese and British authorities, resulting in the publication of my *Anglo-Chinese Relations, 1839–1860: A Calendar of Chinese Documents in the British Foreign Office Records* (Published for the British Academy by Oxford University Press, 1983).

Preface

inflict yet another revised version on him. Then Professor Christopher Bayly most kindly read what I again thought would have to be the final version of my manuscript. It occurred to me that a second foreword, from a distinguished British historian, in addition to the first by an eminent Chinese historian, might add interesting perspectives to the book. Professor Bayly most graciously agreed. My retired colleague, Grahame Harrison, has been similarly supportive. I deeply appreciate his kind advice, constant encouragement, and, in particular, his cheerful willingness to read and comment on successive drafts of chapters. To him this book is dedicated.

I am grateful to the warden and fellows of St Antony's College, Oxford, for having elected me to a postdoctoral research fellowship in 1971–4, when serious research on the project began. I am indebted to fellow Antonians Professor Patrick O'Brien, now director of the Institute of Historical Research at the University of London; and Professor Mark Elvin, now Research Professor of Chinese History at the Australian National University. Having read an earlier version of the manuscript, Professor Elvin suggested that I should show Professor O'Brien my chapters on economics. Professor O'Brien most kindly agreed and subsequently made invaluable suggestions.

I wish to thank Professor Patrick Collinson, Regius Professor of History at the University of Cambridge, and his colleague Dr Boyd Hilton. Having read the manuscript most carefully and sent helpful comments, Professor Collinson suggested that I should show the chapters on Victorian politics to Dr Boyd Hilton, who, in turn, graciously agreed to assist at a time when he really had no time. Later Dr Hilton sent me the two volumes of Greville's diaries most pertinent to my work, a present I greatly treasure. Professor Oliver MacDonagh, the first J. M. Ward Visiting Professor of History in the University of Sydney in 1995, kindly read Chapters 7–13, which have been improved as a result.

Other friends, who have generously spent time reading and commenting on various drafts in whole or in part, include Emeritus Professor Sir Harry Hinsley of the University of Cambridge; Professor Jonathan Spence of Yale University; Emeritus Professor Denis Twitchett of Princeton University; Professor Frederic Wakeman of the University of California, Berkeley; Professor David Cannadine of Columbia University; Professor Deryck Schreuder, now Vice-Chancellor of the University of Western Sydney; and colleagues and retired colleagues Emeritus Professor Marjorie Jacobs, Professor Brian Fletcher, Professor Frederick Teiwes, Professor Roy MacLeod, Dr John Reeve (now in the greener pastures of the Australian Defence Force Academy), Dr Jim Masselos, and Dr Rikki Kersten. Mr Nigel Gurney of Fisher Library and Dr Lance Eccles of Macquarie University have devoted far more time to assisting me with checking the manuscript than I had any right to expect, even of such good friends. My colleagues Dr Peter Brennan and Dr Lyn Olson have cheerfully

Preface

helped in checking my Latin expressions, and Mr Tony Cahill and Dr Ken Macnab have always patiently answered my queries about British political history.

The publisher's recommendation that I consult as far afield as Seymour Drescher's *Econocide: British Slavery in the Era of Abolition*,[2] and Robert Gavin's doctoral thesis on Palmerston's policy towards Africa[3] has greatly widened my perspective. I am grateful to Professor Gavin for sending at my request a photocopy of his thesis.

The University of Sydney in Australia, where I have been teaching since 1974, has been generous in granting me study leave. During my first study leave in 1979–80, I was elected visiting fellow of the Centre of International Studies and concurrently fellow commoner of Churchill College, Cambridge. I wish to thank Professor Sir Harry Hinsley and the master and fellows of Churchill College for having provided me with a congenial environment to further my research. My dear wife, Linda, gracefully helped me collate some of the statistics I had been copying by hand in the University Library.

I also wish to thank Professor Ramon Myers for having been instrumental in my election as a visiting scholar in 1980 at the Hoover Institution on War, Revolution, and Peace, at Stanford University; Professor Junji Banno, for my election in 1980 and again 1983 as a visiting fellow at the Institute of Social Sciences, University of Tokyo; Professor Hu Shouwei, for my election as a visiting fellow at Zhongshan University at various times in the 1970s, 1980s, and 1990s; Professor Wang Gungwu, for my election in 1993 as a visiting scholar at the Centre of Asian Studies, University of Hong Kong; Drs Cho Lee-jay and Ken Breazeale, for my election in September 1996 as a visiting fellow at the East-West Center, Honolulu; Professors Zhang Haipeng and Yang Tianshi, for my election as a visiting scholar in November 1996 at the Chinese Academy of Social Sciences, Beijing; and Professors Chen Sanjing and Lü Fangshan, for my election in December 1996 as a visiting fellow of the Academia Sinica, Taipei. These visiting appointments have greatly facilitated my research overseas. Fellow Antonians Janet Hunter, Stephen Hickey, and Andrew Purkis, as well as good friends Yuen Chuk-nang and Yiu Ngar-shui, are always warm, helpful, and hospitable each time I visit London or New York.

(II)

Needless to say it was expensive to embark on extensive overseas travels in search of public archives, private papers, and other pertinent materials for the project. I thank the following grant-giving bodies for their successive financial

2. Pittsburgh, University of Pittsburgh Press, 1977.
3. R. J. Gavin, 'Palmerston's Policy towards East and West Africa, 1830–1865'. Unpublished Ph.D. thesis, University of Cambridge, 1959.

Preface

support: The Australian Academy of the Humanities/Myer Foundation; the British Academy; the Australian Research Grants Committee; the Smuts Memorial Fund; and, through the great kindness of Judge Tan Boon Chiang, the Lee Foundation of Singapore. I appreciate, in particular, their faith in me in view of the successive grants already awarded for the project. After taking twenty-five years to research and eighteen chapters to convey my findings, I was then told that the envisaged book would be so expensive to produce that it would be priced beyond the reach of the general public. Thereupon Judge Tan and the Lee Foundation came to my rescue again, awarding me a generous subvention towards its publication.

The University of Sydney, on numerous occasions, helped meet some of the expenses of my participation in overseas conferences, which enabled me to pursue research in these places before or after the conferences. Needless to say, I owe a great debt to my colleagues for having been scholarly and forbearing in their approach towards my regular research trips during vacations.

I wish to thank the rector and fellows of St John's College within the University of Sydney for providing me with a convenient place where I drafted and redrafted some of my early chapters. The views of the then economics tutor Kieran Sharpe, of the law tutor Kyle Oliver, and of the English tutor Warwick Orr are much appreciated.

(III)

Archivists and librarians all over the world have been most helpful. In the Public Record Office in London, successive keepers Jeffrey Ede, Geoffrey Martin, Michael Roper, and their colleagues, the late Kenneth Timings, Roy Hunnisett, Norman Evans, John Walford, and Christopher Kitching, went out of their way to assist me when I did my work there in the 1970s and 1980s. On the basis that I was listing a substantial part of the Chinese documents for the office,[4] I was given free access to the repository of Chinese manuscripts put specially in the strong room attached to Room C19 in Chancery Lane, as well as the use of Room C19, whereby I was able to study each document within the context of the entire archive. Without such special consideration, my research would have taken another ten years to complete. These papers in the Chinese language, only recently made available to the public, provide additional information for a reinvestigation of the pretext for the *Arrow* War.

Liu Guilin of the First National Archives, Beijing, was extremely helpful in another way. His kind assistance enabled me to leave Beijing, after three

---

4. This was eventually published under the title *Anglo-Chinese Relations, 1839–1860*; for details, see note 1, this chapter.

Preface

bitterly cold winter months in 1981–2, with a travel bag full of microfilms of Chinese documents which would have taken years to pencil. Professor Chin Hsiao-i, director of the National Palace Museum, Taibei, was exceptionally kind and considerate.

In 1980, the staff of the state papers section in the University Library of Cambridge patiently carried many volumes of the British Parliamentary Papers so I could copy pertinent statistics.

And, after long periods of pencilling from the Parliamentary Papers, I was greatly indebted to the librarian of the Parliamentary Library of New South Wales in Australia, Dr Russell Cope, and his colleagues Dr David Clune, and Messrs Richard Baker and Greg Tillotson, for giving me permission to use their own collection in the 1990s. I was granted free access to these papers and was allowed to bring my personal computer to enter figures therefrom. Without their scholarly sympathy, my project would have taken yet another ten years to complete. In this regard, I wish to thank Zhao Huizhi and Chen Weidong for taking time off in 1990 to read out such figures for me to type into the computer, then reading them out again for me to check. I also wish to thank Mr Peter Gilbert, Director of Research Centre of the U.S. Information Office in Sydney, for his friendly assistance in my search for information that makes useful comparison between my historical research and contemporary developments.

Special thanks are also due to Mr Adrian Roberts of the Bodleian Library. Oxford; Messrs A. E. B. Owen and P. J. Gautrey of the University Library, Cambridge; Mr Howard Nelson and Dr Frances Wood of the British Library; the staff of the Newspaper Division of the British Library at Colindale; Mr S. C. Sutton of the India Office Library, London; Mr John Lust, Mrs Angela Castro, and the late Mr David Chibbett of the library of the School of Oriental and African Studies, London; Miss Felicity Ranger of the Royal Commission on Historical Manuscripts (who gave me kind permission to bring my typewriter to copy the pertinent Palmerston Papers); Dr Frank Taylor and Miss Glenise Matheson of the John Rylands University Library of Manchester (who, again, gave me permission to bring my typewriter to copy the pertinent Bowring Papers in the stacks underground); Mr C. Cooper of the Guildhall Library, London; the staff of the Bibliothèque Nationale and of the Quai d'Orsay, Paris; Mr Eugene Wu of the Harvard-Yenching Library; Drs Chü Mi and Lu Guoxin of the Library of Congress, Washington, D.C.; Mr Yang Guoxiong of Hong Kong University Library; Mrs Magdalen Lee of the East Asian Collection, Fisher Library, University of Sydney; and the staff of the Australian National Library.

I am indebted to Lord Clarendon, Sir John Keswick, and the directors of Baring Brothers for kind permission to consult the Clarendon Papers, the Parkes Papers, and the Baring Papers, respectively. The facts speak for them-

Preface

selves; and I hope that Sir John will forgive me for having been rather severe with Sir Harry Parkes.

For providing me with copies of often rare secondary sources, I wish to thank Professors Ou Hong and Hu Shouwei of Zhongshan University, Canton [Guangzhou]; Professor Wei Hsiu-mei of the Institute of Modern History, Academia Sinica, Taibei; Professor Yang Tianshi of the Institute of Modern History, Chinese Academy of Social Sciences, Beijing; Professor Luo Baoshan, formerly of Zhongshan University and now of the Guangzhou Academy of Social Sciences; Professor Zhao Huifang of the Hefei University of Technology; the late Professor Wu Deduo of the Institute of History, Shanghai Academy of Social Sciences. For advice on Russian archives, I wish to thank Professor Konstantin v. Schevelyeff of the Institute of the Far East in the Russian Academy of Sciences, and Professor Li Yuzheng of the Institute of Modern History in the Chinese Academy of Social Sciences.

For arranging or accompanying me to inspect the various sites of the *Arrow* War, Opium War, and the contemporaneous Red Turban Rebellion, I must thank Professors Hu Shouwei, Luo Baoshan, Qiu Jie, and Zhou Xingliang, all of Zhongshan University at Canton.

Other friends have devoted many hours helping me with mechanical tasks. Miss Hilary Weatherburn printed out from microfilm articles from *The Times*, *Punch*, and other publications. Miss Christine Ludlow reformatted these articles onto A4 paper, which I then photocopied and bound into volumes for easy reference. Here, I must thank the bookbinding section of Sydney Technical College and later the Sydney Book-Binders Guild for providing me with the facilities to bind these and numerous other volumes of research materials. They have saved me from drowning in a sea of notes, photocopies, and cards accumulated over a period of over twenty-five years.

(IV)

To understand the frames of mind of a business executive or public servant was, for a project like this one, essential. The fervour to open up the China market in the period under review is matched only by the present eagerness to expand trade with China, an eagerness ignited by Deng Xiaoping's adoption of an open policy since 1978. Consequently, I involved myself with both public and private sectors in the course of researching and writing this book. As honorary editor of the Australia–China Business Council, I recorded the proceedings of the annual China–Australia Senior Executive Forums in 1987 and 1988, participated in the business negotiations, and edited the forum papers for publication.[5] These papers offered me the perspectives of firms and

---

5. See J. Y. Wong (ed.), *Australia–China Relations, 1987: Business and Management, with Messages from Prime Minister R. J. L. Hawke and Premier Zhao Ziyang* (Canberra, Australia China Businessness

Preface

governments that wished to realize the supposedly huge market potential in China, perspectives not unlike those found at the time of the *Arrow* War.

I also became the honorary editor of a government publication, the *New South Wales–Guangdong Economic Committee Bulletin*. I even called an international conference to discuss Sun Yatsen's idea of the international development of China, a conference in which public servants, business executives, academics, and students interacted.[6] I continue to be active in the Australia–China Chamber of Commerce and Industry and in the Hong Kong–Australia Business Association. All this involvement has enabled me to gain some perception of the terminology, views, and methods of pertinent government departments and sections of the business community. This insight has influenced my overall approach towards the *Arrow* War, particularly the economic chapters herein.

By the time of my fifth lecture tour in China in the 1980s, the late Qin Esheng heard some of my findings on the *Arrow* War and recorded his reaction in a poem. Then he most kindly wrote the Chinese title of the book for me shortly before he died, at the age of ninety. Mr Qin was, in his time, the doyen of calligraphers in South China, a leading historian and classicist.

(V)

A few words on format are in order. With regard to romanization, initially I used pinyin when drafting the manuscript, as I have done with my book *Sun Yatsen*. After some time, however, I began adopting Wade-Giles, as I have done with my book *Yeh Ming-ch'en*, because there were so many names romanized in that system in the sources I used. In the end I decided that, on balance, less confusion might arise if I put the whole manuscript back into pinyin, but kept some of the most commonly used Wade-Giles and post office names, which are enshrined in all the primary sources and most of the secondary literature. These names include Treaty of Nanking, Treaty of Tientsin, Peking Convention, Commissioner Yeh, Prince Kung, Canton, Yangtze, Peiho, Whampoa, Shameen, Macao, Chusan, and Hong Kong. See the Word List for others.

It goes without saying that authors who have romanized their names and their works in Wade-Giles and other fashions will be cited as I find them. In the text and in the footnotes, I address people of Chinese descent by putting their surnames first. As for Japanese names, although in Japan itself surnames continue to come first, when romanised in the West the surnames invariably come last. Accordingly, I have put the personal name, Yukichi, for example,

Cooperation Committee, 1987); and idem, *Australia and China, 1988: Preparing for the 1990s, with Messages from Prime Minister R. J. L. Hawke and Premier Li Peng* (Canberra, Australia China Business Cooperations Committee, 1988).
6. See J. Y. Wong (ed.), *Sun Yatsen: His International Ideas and International Connections, with Special Emphasis on their Relevance Today* (Sydney, Wild Peony, 1987).

before the surname Fukuzawa. In the bibliography, all surnames come first in alphabetical order.

In terms of citation, when a work in the English language appears for the first time, full details are given. Subsequent citations include only an abridged English title. When a work in the Chinese or Japanese language first appears, the full Chinese or Japanese title appears in romanization with an English translation following. Subsequent citations include only an abridged and romanized Chinese or Japanese title. In the Bibliography, the Chinese and Japanese scripts replace the romanization.

As the research for, and the writing of, this work has spanned a period of twenty-five years, I must beg my readers to bear with some of the inconsistencies in the citation of newspapers. When I started, citing the date of a newspaper was considered sufficient. My research on Sun Yatsen in London, however, convinced me that to ensure quick access thenceforth I must cite the page and column as well. Ideally, I should have gone back and checked up all the newspapers I have used to add the page and column numbers to present uniform citations. Alas, this would have meant delaying the publication of a long overdue project for yet longer, which would clearly have been inadvisable.

Finally, I wish to thank all the scholars whose works I have consulted. Without the benefit of their labour, I would not have been able to ask further and different questions and build on what they have done.

I alone am to blame for all faults.

J. Y. Wong
University of Sydney
28 September 1997

Part I
The confusion of imperialism

In 1856–60, Great Britain, France, the United States, Russia, and China were involved in an international conflict; troops from as far afield as Mauritius, India, and Singapore were also involved. It was a world war (although it has never been recognized as such) in terms of the number of powers involved, if not the number of regions in conflagration. The reasons for this lack of recognition are simple: the historians of each of these nations are interested mainly in whatever aspect of the war that happened to affect their own country. Consequently, some Britons refer to it as the Second China War;[1] some French as *l'expedition de Chine*;[2] some Americans as Peter Parker and the opening of China;[3] some Russians as the founding of Vladivostok;[4] and some Chinese as the Second Opium War.[5] The fact that the finale to the war – the sack of Beijing in 1860 – is far better known than the war itself seems to have perpetuated the misconception that it was a peculiarly Chinese affair. Thus, for 140 years, national preoccupation has obscured the true nature of what was a virtual world war, and my main argument in this book is that a proper understanding of any historical event – local, regional, or international – is best achieved by crashing through the barriers of nation and discipline.

What caused the war? Imperialism, many would simply say. But what is imperialism? It has been defined as the 'advocacy of imperial interests'[6] – in

1. See D. Bonner-Smith and E. W. B. Lumby (eds.), *The Second China War, 1856–1860* (London, Navy Records Society, 1954).
2. See Henri Cordier, *L'expedition de Chine de 1857–1858: Histoire diplomatique. Notes et documents* (Paris, Félix Alcan, Éditeur, 1905), and also his *L'expedition de Chine de 1860: Histoire diplomatique. Notes et documents* (Paris, Félix Alcan, Éditeur, 1905).
3. Edward V. Gulick, *Peter Parker and the Opening of China* (Cambridge, Mass., Harvard University Press, 1973), chapter 12. One is reminded of Commodore Perry and the opening of Japan.
4. See Rosemary K. I. Quested, *The Expansion of Russia in East Asia, 1857–1860* (Kuala Lumpur, University of Malaya Press, 1968).
5. See *Di'erci yapian zhanzheng* (Source materials on the Second Opium War), 6 vs., compiled by the Chinese Historical Society (Shanghai, Renmin chubanshe, 1978).
6. *The Shorter Oxford English Dictionary, on Historical Principles* (Oxford, Clarendon Press, 1983), v. 1, p. 1030.

this case those of the British empire. Here, by attempting to pin down the origins of the *Arrow* War,[7] I aim to study the way British imperialism expressed itself in China and Britain in mid-nineteenth century: in diplomacy, rhetoric, politics, economics, strategy, and military force. To a lesser extent, the imperialist behaviour of France, the United States, and Russia is also examined. But it is the confusion that entailed British imperialism which will occupy our immediate attention.

A former British foreign secretary, Douglas Hurd,[8] once wrote a book on the *Arrow* War. He gave it the subtitle *An Anglo-Chinese Confusion*.[9] A pertinent book, based on the collective wisdom of the experts in the Chinese Academy of Social Sciences, is entitled *The Invasion of China by Imperialism*.[10] If we take the key words from both titles, we shall have a garbled phrase, 'The Confusion of Imperialism', which is the title of this part.

Few would disagree that the *Arrow* War may be fruitfully studied in the context of imperialism. But why call it a 'confusion'? The answer is that the nature of events and the pertinent records are confusing enough, as we shall see; the issues involved are indeed bewildering.

7. The reasons for naming this international conflict the *Arrow* War are given in the introduction to Part Two of this book.
8. He was foreign secretary from 1989 to 1995.
9. D. Hurd, *The Arrow War: An Anglo-Chinese Confusion, 1856–60* (London, Collins, 1967).
10. Ding Mingnan et al., *Diguo zhuyi qin Hua shi* (The invasion of China by imperialism), v. 1. (Beijing, Renmin chubanshe, 1958; reprinted, 1972).

1
An attempt to peel the onion of confusion

I. The confusing events

It all began in 1856 with Thomas Kennedy, an Irishman from Belfast who nominally captained the Chinese crew of a lorcha called the *Arrow*. The lorcha had been built in China by a Chinese, owned by a Chinese, and sold to another Chinese. But to protect the ship from the Chinese authorities, a register had been obtained by paying the necessary fees to the British government in Hong Kong and Kennedy had been employed as the nominal captain.[1]

Why was British protection necessary? An old China hand offered some clues. These vessels, he said, were well known by both the Chinese government and foreigners to be manned by inveterate smugglers. Generally these ships were very heavily armed and had a most formidable looking appearance. 'Oftentimes the peaceful inhabitants in the little towns on the coast have complained bitterly to me of the lawless and tyrannical acts of their crews', he added. 'Are these crews to be allowed to commit all sorts of offences against their own government and people and then point to the flag of England . . . as their protection and as their warrant?' he asked.[2] In the case of the *Arrow*, it was subsequently proved that she had been engaged at least in receiving stolen goods.[3]

How could British protection be purchased in this way? Apparently in those days, a Chinese could go to Hong Kong and by means of some 'mystification',[4] such as becoming the tenant of Crown lands or becoming a partner with somebody who was, obtain a colonial register for his ship and get a Briton for a captain. What sort of a Briton was he? He was 'some loose fish, some

1. See Chapter 2.
2. Robert Fortune, *A Residence among the Chinese: Inland, On the Coast, and at Sea. Being a narrative of scenes and adventures during a third visit to China, from 1853–1856, including notices of many natural productions and works of art, the culture of silks, &c, with suggestions on the present war* (London, John Murray, 1857), pp. 425–6.
3. See Chapter 2.
4. Cobden, 26 February 1857, Hansard, 3d series, v. 144, col. 1400. See next note.

3

stray person, or runaway apprentice, or idle young seaman'.[5] He had plenty of grog to drink and nothing else to do because he was not expected to take part in the working of the ship.[6] His sole value lay in his being British. Like a scarecrow, his only function was to scare off the Chinese maritime police.[7]

Nonetheless this Chinese crew was arrested on 8 October 1856, when the *Arrow* was anchored at Canton and Kennedy was away breakfasting with his fellow captains of convenience. An angry British acting consul, Harry Parkes,[8] arrived to claim the Chinese sailors, but soon came to blows with the Chinese officers. In the heat of the moment, there were loud protests about an alleged insult to the British flag.

Parkes later claimed that Kennedy was onboard the *Arrow* when the flag was allegedly pulled down, even though Kennedy himself testified that he was not.[9] Parkes also tried to put words in the mouth of his superior, the British minister plenipotentiary, Sir John Bowring,[10] in order to authorize his own demands, which he had already made to the Chinese.[11] When it was discovered that the *Arrow*'s register had in fact expired, Bowring conspired with Parkes not to tell the Chinese.[12] He even pretended to the Chinese authorities that the register was still valid.[13] And he foolishly informed Whitehall, enclosing the pertinent correspondence. He ought to have known that this was bound to embarrass the government; an annoyed secretary of state for foreign affairs instructed him to send duplicates only of despatches of great political interest.[14] But the damage was done; Bowring's correspondence created an uproar in both houses of Parliament.[15]

---

5. These were the observations of a Mr Cook. He was the U.S. marshal at Whampoa, which was a few miles downstream from Canton. His duty was to regulate the use of the Stars and Stripes. He told Richard Cobden his observations after four years in that position. See ibid.
6. Ibid.
7. Apart from the so-called yamen runners, there was not a formal civilian police force in China as we know it today. What we may describe as police duties nowadays were assumed by an army called the Green Standard. There was another army in China at that time, the Eight Banners, which had no police duties.
8. Harry Smith Parkes (1828–85) was to be appointed one of the three European commissioners to rule Canton after that city had fallen during the *Arrow* War. He was to become British consul at Shanghai in 1864, minister to Japan in 1865, and minister to China in 1883. See Stanley Lane-Poole, *The Life of Sir Harry Parkes*, 2 vs. (London, Macmillan, 1894).
9. See Chapter 2.
10. Sir John Bowring (1792–1872) was a distinguished linguist, writer, and traveller. In 1849 he was appointed consul at Canton and, in 1854, plenipotentiary in China. In May 1859, he resigned his office and returned to England. See his *Autobiographical Recollections of Sir John Bowring* (London, H. S. King, 1877).
11. See Chapter 3.
12. Bowring to Parkes, 11 October 1856, Parl. Papers 1857, v. 12, pp. 64–5, para. 4.
13. Bowring to Yeh, 14 November 1856, ibid., pp. 143–4, para. 2.
14. Clarendon to Bowring, Desp. 248 (draft), 10 December 1856, FO17/243.
15. See Chapters 8–9.

An attempt to peel the onion of confusion

Bowring also conspired with Parkes to get Rear-Admiral Sir Michael Seymour[16] to open hostilities against the Chinese. To this end, they never told the admiral that the register of the *Arrow* had in fact expired and that the ship was no longer entitled to British protection. This legal anomaly was subsequently detected by the earl of Malmesbury.[17] But there were other skeletons in the closet which the plenipotentiary and the consul necessarily concealed from the admiral, and which subsequently remained hidden despite the vigorous scrutiny by Parliament.[18]

The admiral, who had lost an eye in the recent Crimean War,[19] could see only one way to negotiate – by bombarding Canton City. The civilian casualties[20] caused an uproar in Parliament and the government lost the debate. Parliament was dissolved, an election was called. The government was returned to office, by which time large contingents of troops had been sent to China. Halfway through the war, the government lost office again. The former opposition came to power, and in a volte-face, pursued the war with renewed vigour.[21]

The Chinese officials at Canton were no better behaved. It will be seen that the British demand to enter the walled city of Canton was one of the origins of the war, because the British used the *Arrow* incident as an excuse to satisfy this exaction. Indeed, the British had made such a claim as early as 1843.[22] They repeated it year after year and finally managed, in 1847,[23] to extract a promise from the Cantonese authorities that they would be allowed entry two years thence.[24] When the time came, senior officials at Canton fabricated a 'false edict' to avoid honouring the obligation. At least they had the sense to tell the emperor[25] beforehand that they were going to issue a decree in his name. It is doubtful, however, if this precaution would have made any difference had the

16. Michael Seymour (1802–87) had served in the Mediterranean and South American stations and was promoted to rear-admiral in 1854. In the spring of 1856 he went out overland to take command of the China station. He was to be promoted vice-admiral in 1860, and admiral in 1864. From March 1863 to March 1866 he was to be commander-in-chief at Portsmouth. *Dictionary of National Biography* (hereafter cited as *DNB*) (Oxford: since 1917), v. 17, pp. 1264–5.
17. Malmesbury, 26 February 1857, Hansard, 3d series, v. 144, col. 1345.
18. See Chapter 4.
19. This happened while he was examining one of the small sea mines, which had been picked up off Cronstadt and which exploded, wounding him in the face and destroying the sight of one eye. *DNB*, v. 17, p. 1265.
20. What with the bombardment of, and deliberately setting fire to, a densely populated city, a local Chinese official estimated that several thousand houses were destroyed and that many people were killed. See Hua Tingjie, 'Chufan zhimo' (An account of contacts with foreigners), collected in Chinese Historical Society (comp.), *Di'erci yapian zhanzheng* (The Second Opium War) (hereafter cited as *Ey ya*), 6 vs. (Shanghai, Renmin chubanshe, 1978), v. 1, p. 170. For more details, see Part Three, this volume.
21. See Chapter 18.   22. Qiying to Pottinger, 9 July 1843, FO682/1976/92, encl. 2.
23. See Wong, *Anglo-Chinese Relations*, pp. 341–2.
24. Davis to Palmerston, Desp. 53, 5 April 1847, FO17/125.
25. He was Emperor Daoguang, who reigned 1821–50.

The confusion of imperialism

plot failed. But it succeeded, and the British plenipotentiary, Sir George Bonham,[26] was fooled. So have been a large number of historians.[27]

In a dramatic reversal the emperor, even before he heard that the plot had worked, took back what he had said about letting the British into Canton City for a look around, and endorsed the forgery.[28] The man who penned the 'false edict', Commissioner Xu,[29] transcribed it in his autobiography as if it were genuine. His account is included in a famous collection of materials on the *Arrow* War.[30] His collaborator, Commissioner Yeh,[31] did the same. In a subsequent memorial to the next emperor,[32] he treated the 'false edict' as if it had been true. This memorial has been included in an equally authoritative collection of primary sources.[33] Small wonder that the Chinese have always been dazzled by this unthinkable victory.

As a result of the *Arrow* incident, the British bombarded Canton. On 29 October 1856 they made a hole in the city wall and so achieved entry. Thereupon, 'the American flag was this day borne on the walls of Canton'.[34] What had happened? The U.S. consul at Hong Kong, James Keenan,[35] followed the blue-jackets into the breach, 'accompanied by a sailor from one of the U.S.

26. Samuel George Bonham (1803–63) worked for the East India Company until 1837, when he was appointed governor of Prince of Wales's Island, Singapore, and Malacca. For ten years he held this post, until in 1847 he was appointed governor of Hong Kong and plenipotentiary in China. On his return to England in 1853, a baronetcy was conferred upon him. From this time he ceased to take any part in public affairs. *DNB*, v. 2, p. 807.
27. See Chapter 4.
28. Ibid.
29. Xu Guangjin (?–c. 1858) became imperial commissioner for foreign affairs and concurrently governor-general of Guangdong and Guangxi in 1848. In 1852 he was ordered to suppress the Taiping Rebellion and thereupon was transferred to the position of governor-general of Hunan and Hubei. See *Eminent Chinese of the Ch'ing Period (1644–1912)*, ed. Arthur W. Hummel (Washington, D.C., U.S. Government Printing Office, 1943–4), pp. 319–20. See also *Qingshi liezhuan* (Biographies of Qing history) (hereafter cited as *QSLZ*), ed. Zhonghua shuji (Shanghai, 1928), *juan* 48, pp. 10a–15b.
30. Xu Guangjin, 'Sibuzhai ziding nianpu' (Autobiography of Xu Guangjin), in *Er ya*, v. 1, pp. 149–62: p. 154.
31. His full name, in pinyin, is Ye Mingchen (1809–59). He became governor of Guangdong in 1847 and imperial commissioner for foreign affairs and concurrently governor-general of Guangdong and Guangxi in 1852. He was to be captured by the British during the *Arrow* War and exiled to India, where he starved himself to death. See my *Yeh Ming-ch'en*.
32. He was Emperor Xianfeng, who reigned 1851–61.
33. *Chouban yiwu shimo* (An account of the management of foreign affairs) (hereafter cited as *YWSM* (XF)), Xianfeng period (Beijing, Zhonghua shuji, 1979), no. 679, in *juan* 17, v. 2, pp. 610–20: p. 613. This edition provides Gregorian calendar dates for the documents, and is here used in preference to the original edition, which provided only the lunar calendar dates. To enable users of the original edition to identify the documents, the *juan* number is supplied. A similar edition for the Daoguang period of the *Yiwu shimo* is not available to me, and I have therefore continued to use the original edition.
34. Notification by Commander Foote of the United States Navy, 29 October 1856, Parl. Papers 1857, v. 12, pp. 100–1.
35. See Tong Te-kong, *United States Diplomacy in China, 1844–1860* (Seattle, University of Washington Press, 1964), p. 186. The U.S. consul at Canton was Oliver H. Perry.

ships-of-war, carrying an American ensign'.[36] This act led one distinguished historian, Wei Jianyou, to conclude that the United States joined the British government in waging the war against China.[37] But before the day had elapsed, a public notice was issued by the commanding officer of the U.S. naval forces at Canton, disavowing the act as unauthorized and stating that it must not be regarded as compromising in the least degree the neutrality of his country.[38] Who was correct, the consul or the commander?

As Anglo-Chinese hostilities escalated, the U.S. naval, consular, and business communities decided to evacuate Canton on the advice of Commissioner Yeh.[39] Accordingly, they embarked on 15 November 1856.[40] But on this very day, the Chinese soldiers guarding the barrier forts fired on an U.S. warship. Commodore James Armstrong felt that the U.S. flag had been insulted. He sent his flagship there the next day and had the forts destroyed.[41] This incident reinforced the interpretation of U.S. intentions by Professor Wei, who commented that the Americans 'even used a small misunderstanding to despatch three men-of-war to attack and destroy five forts in the Barrier group of forts'.[42] On the basis of this comment, a group of China's officially chosen historians has accused the Americans of having done their utmost to assist the British imperialists attacking China[43] and of being full partners of the British in the assault on Canton.[44] At a time when the Americans were already leaving the Britons at Canton to fend for themselves, it is intriguing that an incident which completely nullified Commissioner Yeh's diplomatic coup should have occurred. Was it an accident or another conspiracy?

The French followed the example of the Americans and left Canton five days after them.[45] But later, the French joined the British as full partners of the war. What changed their minds? The Russians did not feature at all in these early conflicts. A year later, however, a Russian mission followed the Anglo-French march on Beijing. What business had the Russians to be there?

Commissioner Yeh told the emperor that in a single engagement his troops had wiped out four hundred blue-jackets, among them Admiral Seymour! This

36. Parkes to Bowring, 31 October 1856, Parl. Papers 1857, v. 12, p. 100.
37. Wei Jianyou, *Di'erci yapian zhanzheng* (The Second Opium War) (Shanghai, Renmin chubanshe, 1955), p. 49.
38. Notification by Commander Foote of the United States Navy, 29 October 1856, Parl. Papers 1857, v. 12, pp. 100–1.
39. Yeh to Perry, 10 November 1856, U.S. Senate Executive Documents, no. 22, 35th Congress, 2d Session, 'Peter Parker Correspondence', pp. 1027–8, cited in Tong, *United States Diplomacy in China*, pp. 185–6.
40. Tong, *United States Diplomacy in China*, p. 186.
41. Ibid., pp. 186–7.
42. Wei Jianyou, *Di'erci yapian zhanzheng*, p. 49.
43. *Di'erci yapian zhanzheng* (The Second Opium War), written by a collection of anonymous officially chosen historians (Shanghai, Renmin chubanshe, 1972), p. 15.
44. Ibid., pp. 15–16.
45. Tong, *United States Diplomacy in China*, p. 186.

feat was supposedly achieved on 6 November 1856.[46] British records, however, show that Seymour's report for that day says that the Royal Navy destroyed a fleet of Chinese war junks and captured the French Folly Fort with the loss of only one man, while Seymour himself watched the engagement from the Dutch Folly which the Royal Navy had previously captured.[47] If Yeh 'cried wolf' on this occasion, one wonders if he 'cried ghost' some fifteen months later, while he was prisoner on board HMS *Inflexible* and Seymour came to pay his respects![48]

II. The bewildering issues

But what lay behind all this? Where may we find the origins of the *Arrow* War? The chief antagonist of the British, Commissioner Yeh, has always been depicted by the British as a monster, as if the war were entirely his responsibility. The British prime minister, Lord Palmerston,[49] for instance, called him 'one of the most savage barbarians that ever disgraced a nation. He has been guilty of every crime which can disgrace and debase human nature'.[50] A sketch[51] of him by a British artist reinforces this impression. But some British journalists who went to see him concluded that the artist must have eaten raw beefsteaks and raw onions to conjure up such hideous fantasies.[52] While this eyewitness account was never read outside Hong Kong and was quickly forgotten, the artist's sketch has been printed and reprinted in nearly all the pertinent books,[53] perpetuating the notion that Yeh was a monster, in whose 'perverse discourtesy' and 'mulish pertinacity'[54] may be found the origins of the *Arrow* War. 'To yield to a savage of this kind were to imperil all our interests,

46. Imperial edict, 14 December 1856, incorporating Yeh's memorial, *YWSM* (XF), no. 547, in *juan* 14, v. 2, pp. 499–500.
47. Seymour to Admiralty, 14 November 1856, Parl. Papers 1857, v. 12, pp. 94–100, para. 12.
48. *Hong Kong Register* (newspaper clipping), 16 February 1858, Ryl. Eng. MSS 1230/84.
49. He was Henry John Temple (1784–1865), Third Viscount Palmerston, G. C. B., K. G. He had been secretary at war (1809–28) and secretary of state for foreign affairs (1830–4, 1835–41, and 1846–51). He became prime minister in March 1855, a position he was to hold till March 1858, and again from 1859 to 1865. He sat for Tiverton from June 1835 until his death on 18 October 1865. See Lloyd C. Sanders, *Life of Viscount Palmerston* (London, W. H. Allen, 1888); Kingsley Martin, *The Triumph of Lord Palmerston: A Study of Public Opinion in England Before the Crimea War* (revised edition, London, Hutchinson, 1963); Jasper Ridley, *Lord Palmerston* (London, Constable, 1970); and E. D. Steele, *Palmerston and Liberalism, 1855–1865* (Cambridge University Press, 1991).
50. Palmerston, 3 March 1857, Hansard, 3d series, v. 144, col. 1830.
51. The sketch was made after Yeh had been captured and was kept on board HMS *Inflexible*. See next two notes.
52. *Hong Kong Register* (newspaper clipping), 16 February 1858, Ryl. Eng. MSS 1230/84.
53. The sketch was first published in G. W. Cooke's *China: Being 'The Times' Special Correspondence from China in the Years 1857–8, with Corrections and Additions* (London, G. Routledge, 1858). For subsequent reproductions, see, e.g., Hurd, *Arrow War*, opposite p. 33.
54. *Morning Post*, 2 January 1857.

not only in the East, but in every part of the world', claimed a British newspaper.[55] But is this notion of Yeh's responsibility as untrue as the sketch?

Perhaps Yeh was not a monster, some have argued, but he was a xenophobe – his policy was to encourage popular xenophobia and therein we may find the origins of the *Arrow* War. Or may we?[56] At least one historian thinks so, alleging that Yeh was 'responsible for provoking the "second" (1856–60) Opium War'.[57]

What about British xenophobia, especially the xenophobia exhibited by Britons living far away from home and feeling isolated? To date, Western historians have been accusing the Chinese of xenophobia, and Chinese historians have been preoccupied with answering such charges. Few seem to have turned the question the other way round, paying little attention to what the eminent jurist of international law, Lord Lyndhurst,[58] had to say. His Lordship believed that Bowring was responsible for starting the war. After the crew of the *Arrow* was returned, a junk seized, and a few forts battered down, Bowring should have paused to reflect on the consequences of his actions. 'It is extraordinary that Sir John Bowring should think he had the power of declaring war', said Lord Lyndhurst, and 'to carry on offensive operations upon such a ground, upon such a pretence, is one of the most extraordinary proceedings to be found in the history of the world'.[59] If the proceedings were extraordinary, Bowring must have had his own extraordinary reasons.

The ground upon which Bowring carried on the war was the *Arrow* incident, in which Consul Parkes claimed the Union Jack had been hauled down. The British nautical practice was that a ship, when anchored, did not fly the national colours.[60] The incident occurred when the ship was at anchor and had been so for many days. Therefore its flag would not normally have been flying. Furthermore, crews of British-registered lorchas took pains to preserve the foreign appearance of their vessels by meticulously observing British nautical

---

55. Ibid., 3 February 1857.
56. This issue will be explored in Chapter 4.
57. James Polachek, *The Inner Opium War* (Cambridge, Mass., Harvard Council on East Asian Studies, 1992), p. 5.
58. He was John Singleton Copley the younger (1772–1863). He became solicitor-general in 1819, attorney-general in 1824, and Baron Lyndhurst and lord chancellor in 1827, the latter position he was to occupy in three ministries. He was said to have spoken rarely and only on great occasions, as well as to have had a 'marvellous power of digesting masses of evidence, reducing them into order, and retaining them in his memory'. As late as 1851, Lord Derby was anxious that he become lord chancellor for the fourth time, but he declined partly because, it is said, 'he was at an age, and had long been of a temper which prefers to speak on public questions unfettered by the ties of party'. Nonetheless he was present in the House of Lords at all important debates. *DNB*, v. 4, pp. 1107–14.
59. Lyndhurst, 24 February 1857, Hansard, 3d series, v. 144, cols. 1217–18. Sir James Graham expressed the same view. See Graham, 27 February 1857, ibid., col. 1561.
60. W. C. Costin, *Great Britain and China, 1883–1860* (Oxford, Oxford University Press, 1937), p. 207.

practice – Commissioner Yeh knew as much.[61] If the flag had not been hauled down, how do we resolve the issue of an alleged insult to it?

In terms of actual management of the incident, why did Parkes continue to escalate his demands? His superior, Bowring, allowed himself to be led by the nose. Why? Rear-Admiral Seymour, without sanction, readily consented to Bowring's request for military action, so readily that even Bowring was surprised.[62] Why? Successive foreign secretaries had issued the strictest injunctions to Bowring against renewing demands to enter the walled city of Canton. By using the *Arrow* incident to renew this unrelated demand, Bowring clearly contravened his instructions. Surprisingly, the foreign secretary, Lord Clarendon,[63] swallowed his own words and approved[64] Bowring's actions retrospectively. If Clarendon had good reasons for doing so, what were they?

Then something quite spectacular happened. On 6 January 1857, the British government published the report by Admiral Seymour on his naval operations on the Canton River, together with all relevant correspondence.[65] Not only documents but the private correspondence of consular officials had to observe the strictest precautions, to prevent leaks. For example, Bowring was censured for apparently having signified his permission to his secretary for Chinese affairs, Thomas Wade, 'to correspond with his friends in England on the state of affairs in China'. Sternly, Clarendon reminded Bowring of the eighth paragraph of the General Consular Instructions: 'The Consul will not on any account correspond with private persons on public affairs'.[66] Why then, should Her Majesty's government communicate to the general public information of a military nature?

Several weeks before, on 14 December 1856, a mysterious fire burnt down the foreign factories at Canton, destroying property (mainly U.S. and French) amounting to millions of dollars. At the time the factories were guarded by British forces. Who could have started the fire and for what purpose?[67]

Since 1949, mainland Chinese historians have insisted on calling the *Arrow* War the Second Opium War. Was opium ever an issue in the *Arrow* War? To date, Western historians almost unanimously deny it. Indeed, some of them

---

61. Yeh to Parkes, 24 October 1856, Parl. Papers 1857, v. 12, p. 89; cf. Yeh to Seymour, 31 October 1856, ibid., p. 103.
62. See Chapter 3.
63. He was George William Frederick Villiers (1800–70), fourth earl of Clarendon and Fourth Baron Hyde. He had been foreign secretary since 1853. He was said to be especially the guardian of peace and civilization, rather cosmopolitan than patriotic, and personally was very disinterested. See Herbert Maxwell, *The Life and Letters of George William Frederick, Fourth Earl of Clarendon*, 2 vs. (London, Edward Arnold, 1913).
64. Clarendon to Bowring, 10 December 1856, Parl. Papers 1857, v. 12, pp. 69–70; and Clarendon to Bowring, 10 January 1856, ibid., p. 157.
65. Foreign Office draft circular to H.M. Representatives abroad, 7 January 1857, FO17/261.
66. Clarendon to Bowring, Draft 64, 6 March 1857, FO17/261.
67. See Chapter 11 for a possible explanation.

An attempt to peel the onion of confusion

have even denied that opium had any role in the (first) Opium War, and have thereby argued that such a title is unwarranted.[68] If the first conflict might not be called the Opium War, then of course the second might not be called the Second Opium War. Even the Chinese authors cannot pinpoint the place of opium in the *Arrow* War. Why, then, call it the Second Opium War? Opium remained contraband in China at this time. Therefore, what were the legal, moral, and financial issues involved, if any?

The Americans invariably sided with the British in their diplomatic manoeuvres against China. What was their stake? At this time, they were the second largest buyer of tea from China, second only to the British. How did they pay for that tea? They do not seem to have sold sufficient quantities of commodities to China to balance an apparent trade deficit.[69]

As for the Chinese themselves, they believe that the British waged the war to 'conquer, enslave, plunder, and slaughter'[70] their ancestors. No doubt such a description might be suitably applied to the Mongol conquest of China in the fourteenth century. But were the British the same?

These are emotive issues to the Chinese, due to an intense resentment against the outcome of the Opium War, by which the island of Hong Kong was ceded, and of the *Arrow* War, whereby the peninsula of Kowloon was given up. The Chinese position that neither the island nor the peninsula was so ceded, despite the pertinent treaties, has perplexed many commentators. This I attribute to different perceptions of the law. The Chinese have always insisted that treaties signed under duress are not valid, a moral argument which in turn has vexed Western historians.

Equally emotive to the British was an attempt, made on 15 January 1857, to poison the European community in Hong Kong by mixing arsenic with the bread. The overdose caused immediate vomiting, so no lives were lost. The *Morning Post* in London exploded: 'Talk of international law with sanguinary savages such as these! There is but one law for such demons in human shape, and that is a law of severe, summary and inexorable justice'.[71] Who ordered and who carried out the poisoning? The *Morning Post* alleged that Yeh gave out the orders; if so, one would have expected references to it, either in Yeh's memorials to the throne or in his archives (which the British subsequently

68. See, e.g., A. J. Sargent, *Anglo-Chinese Commerce and Diplomacy* (Oxford, Clarendon Press, 1907); Peter Ward Fay, *The Opium War, 1840–1842* (Chapel Hill, University of North Carolina Press, 1975); and Frank Welsh, *A History of Hong Kong* (London, HarperCollins, 1993).
69. See H. B. Morse, *The International Relations of the Chinese Empire*, 3 vs. (Shanghai, Kelly & Walsh, 1910–18).
70. These words seem to be a direct quotation from the Chinese version of the 'Communist Manifesto' by Marx and Engels. See Wang Di, 'Minzu de zainan yu minzu de fazhan' (The nation's catastrophe and the nation's development) in *Quru yu kangzheng* (Humiliation and resistance) (Beijing, Social Science Press, 1990), p. 36. This is a collection of conference papers published to mark the 150th anniversary of the Opium War.
71. *Morning Post*, 3 March 1857.

captured in his office). But there are no such references. Parkes alleged that it was Yeh's reward of $30 per British head that prompted it;[72] but the poisoner(s) would not be able to claim the reward because there was no way of coming forward with severed heads to be counted. The real issue is: What drove the poisoners to take such action?

III. Current scholarship

Ably, Douglas Hurd has told the British side of the story of the *Arrow* War, leaving the perplexing issues alone. So has Charles Leavenworth in *The Arrow War with China*, a book fit for the eyes of the old China hands.[73] Other authors have also targeted the war in their scholarly pursuits, and some have extended their studies to cover the decades immediately before the war. The pertinent monographs include W. C. Costin's *Great Britain and China, 1833–1860*, Gerald S. Graham's *The China Station: War and Diplomacy, 1830–1860*,[74] Frederic Wakeman Jr.'s *Strangers at the Gate: Social Disorder in South China, 1836–1861*,[75] Henri Cordier's *L'expédition de Chine de 1857–1858: Histoire diplomatique. Notes et document*,[76] Karl Marx's *Marx on China: Articles from the 'New York Daily Tribune', 1853–1860*,[77] Rosemary Quested's *The Expansion of Russia in East Asia, 1857–1860*,[78] S. I. Zaretskaya's *China's Foreign Policy in 1856–1860: Relations with Great Britain and France*,[79] Earl Swisher's *China's Management of the American Barbarians: A Study of Sino-American Relations, 1841–1861, with Documents*,[80] Edward V. Gulick's *Peter Parker and the Opening of China*,[81] Tong Te-kong's *United States Diplomacy in China, 1844–60*,[82] Robert Johnson's *Far China Station: The U.S. Navy in Asian Waters, 1800–1898*,[83] Eldon Griffin's *Clippers and Consuls: American Consular and Commercial Relations with Eastern Asia, 1845–1860*,[84] Jack Beeching's *The Chinese Opium Wars*,[85] David E. Owen's *British Opium Policy in China and India*,[86] my own

---

72. Parkes to Bowring, 6 December 1856, Parl. Papers 1857, v. 12, pp. 185–6, para. 3. See also Yeh's public proclamation, 28 October 1856, Parl. Papers 1857, v. 12, p. 94.
73. London, Low, Marston & Co., 1901.
74. Oxford, Clarendon Press, 1978.
75. Berkeley and Los Angeles, University of California Press, 1966.
76. Paris, 1905.
77. London, Lawrence & Wishart, 1968 (with an introduction and notes by Dona Torr). Even before the appearance of this annotated English edition, Beijing had published a Chinese edition in 1950 entitled *Makesi Engesi lun Zhongguo* (Renmin chubanshe).
78. Kuala Lumpur, University of Malaya Press, 1968.
79. Moscow, Nauka, 1976.
80. New Haven, Conn., Yale University Far Eastern Publications, 1951.
81. Cambridge, Mass., Harvard University Press, 1973.
82. Seattle, University of Washington Press, 1964.
83. Bethesda, Md., Naval Institute Press, 1979.
84. Ann Arbor, Mich., Edwards Brothers, 1938.
85. London, Hutchinson, 1975.
86. New Haven, Conn., Yale University Press, 1934; Archon reprint, 1968.

Yeh Ming-ch'en: Viceroy of Liang-Kuang, 1852–8,[87] and later my *Anglo-Chinese Relations, 1839–1860: A Calendar of Chinese Documents in the British Foreign Office Records*.[88] James Polachek's *The Inner Opium War* is concerned mainly with the politics of the Opium War and its aftermath up to about 1850; but since the author holds Yeh responsible for the outbreak of the *Arrow* War,[89] his work is incorporated in this list.

Pertinent doctoral theses include Chiang Pai-huan's 'Anglo-Chinese Diplomatic Relations, 1856–1860',[90] Huang Yen-yü's 'Viceroy Yeh Ming-ch'en and the Canton Episode (1856–61)',[91] E. G. Biaggini's 'The Coercion of China, 1830–1860: A Study in Humbug',[92] and Franklin Bakhala's 'Indian Opium and Sino-Indian Trade Relations, 1801–1858'.[93] Master's theses include Koay Shiaw-chian's 'British Opinion and Policy on China between the First and Second Anglo-Chinese Wars, 1842–1857',[94] and Michael Spicer's 'British Attitudes towards China, 1834–1860, with special reference to the *Edinburgh Review*, the *Westminster Review*, and the *Quarterly Review*'.[95]

Chinese publications in this field are less numerous. Pertinent works include the Chinese version of *Marx on China*,[96] the Chinese version of Chiang Pai-huan's thesis mentioned above,[97] a book by Wei Jianyou, which is a serious study in a Marxist framework,[98] and another by Fang Shiming, which is not so serious a piece of work.[99] Apparently it was on the basis of the first two books, and to some extent the third, that a lucubration of propaganda, written collectively, anonymously, and without citations or bibliography, was then

87. Cambridge University Press, 1976.
88. Published for the British Academy by Oxford University Press, 1983. Works on the relations between Great Britain and China in the nineteenth century invariably use the term 'Anglo-Chinese relations'. Works on the same relations since the signing of the Joint Declaration in 1984 often use the term 'Sino-British relations'.
89. Polachek, *Inner Opium War*, p. 5.
90. Unpublished Ph.D. thesis, London School of Economics, 1939.
91. Ph.D. dissertation, Harvard University, 1940. This thesis was subsequently published as a ninety-page article under the same title in the *Harvard Journal of Asiatic Studies*, 6 (1941), pp. 37–127.
92. Unpublished D.Litt. thesis, University of Adelaide, 1944.
93. Unpublished Ph.D. thesis, School of Oriental and African Studies, University of London, 1985. This thesis is mainly about opium production in Bengal and opium sales to China, and the resultant pull of Chinese bullion. It does not attempt to explain the origins of the *Arrow* War.
94. Unpublished M.A. thesis, University of Leeds, 1967.
95. M.A. thesis, University of Sydney, 1985.
96. *Makesi Engesi lun Zhongguo* (Marx and Engels on China) (Beijing, Renmin chubanshe, 1950).
97. As mentioned, Dr Chiang completed his doctoral thesis, 'Anglo-Chinese Diplomatic Relations, 1856–60', for the London School of Economics in 1939. Later he changed his name to Jiang Mengyin, rewrote his work in Chinese, and published it in China under the title *Di'erci yapian zhanzheng* (The Second Opium War) (Beijing, Joint Publishing Co., 1965). I found out about this when I went to do research in China and met the author at Nanjing University.
98. Wei Jianyou, *Di'erci yapian zhanzheng*.
99. Fang Shiming, *Di'erci yapian zhanzheng shihua* (Popular history of the Second Opium War) (Shanghai, Xinzhi chubanshe, 1956).

produced.[100] In 1978, the Chinese Historical Society published a six-volume collection of mainly primary sources for the events of the *Arrow* War, without any assessment of the reliability of these sources, or any analysis.[101] In the 1980s, my two books, also mentioned here, were translated into Chinese.[102] In June 1995, I learned that Emeritus Professor Xia Li of Shanghai Normal University was writing a book on the *Arrow* War, in continuation of what his late colleague Wei Jinyou had done in the 1950s.[103]

The publication in 1978 of the six-volume work on the sources of the *Arrow* War was a monumental event. The appearance of a similar collection in 1954 on the Opium War had enabled Professor Chang Hsin-pao to complete his standard work on the subject ten years later.[104] But eighteen years have now elapsed since the publication of the materials on the *Arrow* War, and we are still waiting for a standard reference.

I have hinted at the kind of disarray that has existed in the Chinese versions of events and in the pertinent documents. In terms of attributing the origins of the war, the emperor blamed Yeh for having angered the British by failing to reply to two despatches.[105] I find that these despatches were received on 24 and 28 December 1857,[106] more than fourteen months after the *Arrow* incident had occurred. Other allegations, however, are less obviously false. One of Yeh's subordinates attributed the origins of the war to Yeh's having done little to cultivate the friendship of foreigners, having been sparing in his words when replying to foreign despatches, and sometimes not having replied at all.[107] This assessment is restricted by a worldview which in those days hardly went beyond Canton and knew nothing of the politics, mechanics, economics, and dynamics of imperialism.

Other Chinese commentators were to make the same mistake. Writing

100. Anon., *Di'erci yapian zhanzheng* (The Second Opium War) (Shanghai, Renmin chubanshe, 1972).
101. Chinese Historical Society (comp.), *Di'erci yapian zhanzheng*.
102. My *Yeh Ming-ch'en* was translated by Professor Ou Hong and published by Zhonghua shuju, Beijing, in 1984. My *Anglo–Chinese Relations* has also been translated by Professor Ou Hong, and will be incorporated into the book which I am writing at the moment in Chinese and which is entitled 'The Opium Wars and the Cession of Hong Kong' (Taibei, Academia Historica, forthcoming).
103. Zhou Yumin to Wong, 2 June 1995. Professor Zhou teaches history in the same University in Shanghai. I have read some of Professor Xia's work, which is very scholarly. We may look forward to a learned piece of work.
104. Chang Hsin-pao, *Commissioner Lin and the Opium War* (Cambridge, Mass., Harvard University Press, 1964).
105. Qing Veritable Records, Xianfeng period, *juan* 241, folios 26a–b, Imperial edict, 27 January 1858.
106. Mu-ke-de-na et al. to Emperor, 7 January 1858, *YWSM* (XF), no. 682 in *juan* 17, v. 2, pp. 621–2. This memorial was despatched at a prescribed speed of 600 *li* (about 200 miles, or 322 km) per day. It was not included in the Qing Veritable Records.
107. Hua Tingjie, 'Chufan shimo' (An account of contacts with foreigners), collected in *Er ya*, v. 1, p. 164.

shortly after the war and under a pseudonym, one author claimed that if Yeh had yielded to the British demands, the war could have been avoided.[108] His work shows that his understanding of the British demands involved solely those raised immediately after the *Arrow* incident, the most important of which was entry into Canton City. In other words, he interpreted the issue entirely as a clash of personalities. A treatise published in 1869 asserted that the origins of the war lay with the Chinese rebels who, defeated by Yeh, surrendered to the British in Hong Kong. The British then drilled them for battle day and night for several months, and subsequently followed their advice and attacked Canton.[109] This story, however fantastic,[110] was accepted by a subsequent author, Xie Fucheng,[111] and was in turn adopted in a Ph.D. thesis.[112]

The same author also wrote a famous account of the Canton City question – especially what happened in the spring of 1849. As one-time Chinese minister to England, France, Italy, and Belgium in 1890–3, he has been held up as a respectable and therefore reliable scholar.[113] His account, even his phraseology, have been freely adopted by the standard histories of the Qing dynasty such as the *Qing shigao*[114] and *Qingdai tongshi*.[115] His version has been popularized by the *Apocryphal History of the Qing Dynasty*.[116] His treatise has been included in a two-volume collection of sources on modern Chinese history,[117] and has been further enshrined in Western scholarship by a doctoral thesis subsequently published as a ninety-page article in a reputable journal.[118] His story was that, in 1849, Sir George Bonham was frightened into abandoning the attempt to enter Canton City by the shouting of a hundred thousand Cantonese militiamen gathered on the banks of the Pearl River, on the waters

108. Qixianhe shang diaosou (pseud.), 'Yingjili Guangdong rucheng shimo' (An account of the British entry into the city of Canton), in *Er ya*, v. 1, p. 220.
109. Li Fengling, 'Yangwu xuji' (A supplementary account of foreign affairs), in *Er ya*, v. 1, p. 223.
110. Some work on the rebels (see my *Yeh Ming-ch'en*, chapters 5–10) and on the *Arrow* War itself have made it clear how fantastically untrue the story is.
111. Xie Fucheng, 'Shu Hanyang Yexiang Guangzhou zhi bian' (Grand Secretary Yeh and the Canton episode), in *Er ya*, v. 1, p. 228.
112. Huang Yen-yü, 'Viceroy Yeh Ming-ch'en and the Canton Episode, 1856–1861', Ph.D. dissertation, Harvard University, 1940. Again, this dissertation was subsequently published as an article with the same title in the *Harvard Journal of Asiatic Studies*, 6 (1941), pp. 37–127. All references hereafter are to the article, not the thesis.
113. Huang, 'Viceroy Yeh', p. 41.
114. Zhao Erxun et al. (eds.), *Qing shigao* (A draft history of the Qing dynasty) (Mukden [Shenyang], n.p., 1937), *juan* 400, pp. 2b–4a.
115. Xiao Yishan, *Qingdai tongshi* (History of the Qing) (Taibei reprint, 1963), v. 3, pp. 459–60. Other authors have done the same. For details, see Huang, 'Viceroy Yeh', p. 45.
116. *Qingchao yeshi daguan* (A review of the apocryphal history of the Qing dynasty) (Shanghai, Zhonghua shuju, 1930; Taibei reprint, 1959), v. 2, p. 176.
117. Zuo Shunsheng (ed.), *Zhongguo jinbainianshi ziliao* (Source materials for the study of modern Chinese history in the last hundred years, part one) (Taibei, Zhonghua shuju, 1958), pp. 51–63.
118. Huang, 'Viceroy Yeh'.

of which Bonham and Commissioner Xu were meeting to discuss the matter.[119]

But in which part of the Pearl River did the two men meet? The primary sources in both English and Chinese agree that the parties met on board HMS *Hastings* near the Bogue,[120] which is close to the mouth of the river, where little could be heard from either shore if a steamer as big as the *Hastings* were moored in waters safe enough for it to anchor. A field trip to the Bogue in December 1979 convinced me that Xie's story was sheer imagination.[121] That part of the 'river' is more like the sea. It is not possible to see the other bank, only a couple of islands in the distance. The author of an authoritative five-volume work on the history of the Qing dynasty probably had the same doubts, but he took a different approach. He invented a second meeting, which supposedly took place upstream in the peaceful waters just outside the walled city of Canton, where shouts in unison from two large crowds totalling a hundred thousand and gathered on both banks of the river might be heard.[122]

IV. The search for information

I became interested in the *Arrow* War as long ago as 1968, when I began my research on Commissioner Yeh.[123] My continuing research showed that Parkes's assertion about the flag was dubious,[124] but the incident was nonetheless used as an excuse for war. This led me to investigate the origins of the war, which I felt must lie elsewhere.

To begin with, I scrutinized the papers presented to the British Parliament for debate over the *Arrow* War, papers subsequently bound into one volume entitled 'China',[125] a very rich source indeed. Chronologically speaking, the first issue involved 'insults in China',[126] meted out by the villagers around

119. Xie Fucheng, 'Shu Hanyang Yexiang Guangzhou zhi bian (Grand Secretary Yeh and the Canton episode), in *Er ya*, v. 1, p. 227.
120. For the English sources, see Parl. Papers 1857, v. 12, pp. 205–67. For the Chinese sources, see Canton Archive, now catalogued as FO931/778–810, and those collected in *Chouban yiwu shimo*, Daoguang period, *juan* 79 (henceforth cited as *YWSM* [DG]).
121. I wish to thank the History Department of Zhongshan (Sun Yatsen) University in Canton for having arranged the trip for me.
122. Xiao Yishan, *Qingdai tongshi*, v. 3, pp. 459–60. A brief reference to this particular invention has been made at the beginning of this chapter. For more details, see Chapter 5.
123. That research was completed in the University of Oxford in 1971 and was later published as *Yeh Ming-ch'en*.
124. See J. Y. Wong, 'The "Arrow" Incident: A Reappraisal', *Modern Asian Studies*, 8, no. 3 (1974), pp. 373–89.
125. Parl. Papers 1857, v. 12, 'China' (639 pages).
126. The blue book listed under this heading is no. 2175, entitled 'Correspondence Respecting Insults in China', in Parl. Papers 1857, v. 12, pp. 325–560.

An attempt to peel the onion of confusion

Canton, and labelled 'popular xenophobia' by John Nolde.[127] But the so-called insults largely stopped as early as 1849, and it seems farfetched to attribute the origins of a war to insults suffered some eight years previously. Furthermore, 'every one' of these insults had been atoned for by the Chinese authorities paying appropriate reparations.[128] The second issue concerned the Cantonese authorities' refusal to admit the British into their walled city, particularly after 1849.[129] John Nolde has interpreted this refusal as 'official xenophobia'.[130] But can it be true that London decided to wage war over such a trifling matter? If not, was there a hidden agenda? The third issue was the relationship between the *Arrow* incident and the undeclared war waged on the Chinese,[131] as well as the subordinate issue of the register of the *Arrow*[132] and the purpose of such a register.[133] Two other blue books were included in this bound volume, because they offered some background information about the other issues.[134] This documentation seems to have convinced Nolde and others that the *Arrow* War was caused by Chinese xenophobia. I could not help feeling that builders of the British Empire had better things to do than getting overly worked up by minor irritations of this kind, unless vital interests were involved.

Next I turned to Hansard, where I learned much, but could not find any important policy speeches which I thought convincingly explained the origins of the war. That was my fault. The significance of these speeches was not immediately apparent to me. It was not until much later, revisiting Hansard, that I began to see the crucial links between these speeches and the other sources in this maze of materials.

I went back to the original sources from which the editors of the blue books selected their papers: the British Foreign Office records, particularly FO17,

127. John J. Nolde, 'Xenophobia in Canton, 1842-1849', *Journal of Oriental Studies*, 13, no. 1 (1975), pp. 1-22.
128. Malmesbury, 26 February 1857, Hansard, 3d series, v. 144, cols. 1346-7.
129. The blue books listed under this heading are no. 2173, entitled, 'Correspondence Relative to Entrance into Canton, 1850-5'; no. 2164, 'Correspondence Relative to the Operations in the Canton River, April 1847'; and no. 2172, 'Further Correspondence Relative to the Operations in the Canton River', in Parl. Papers 1857, v. 12, pp. 1-50. The blue books listed under the heading 'Bombardment of Canton' are also relevant. See notes 131-4, this chapter.
130. Nolde, 'Xenophobia in Canton', p. 1.
131. This issue was listed under the heading 'Bombardment of Canton' and involved two blue books, no. 2163, entitled 'Papers Relating to the Proceedings of Her Majesty's Naval Forces at Canton, with Appendix'; and no. 2192, entitled 'Further Papers Relative to the Proceedings of Her Majesty's Naval Forces at Canton', in Parl. Papers 1857, v. 12, pp. 51-324.
132. See blue book no. 2166, entitled 'Correspondence Respecting the Registration of Colonial Vessels at Hong Kong', in Parl. Papers 1857, v. 12, pp. 579-94.
133. See blue book no. 2189, entitled 'Correspondence Respecting Consular Interference for the Prevention of Smuggling in China', in Parl. Papers 1857, v. 12, pp. 571-7.
134. See blue book no. 115, entitled 'Correspondence between the Foreign Office and the East India and China Association of Liverpool in 1846, 1847 and 1848', in Parl. Papers 1857, v. 12, pp. 561-9.

which contained the official correspondence between Whitehall and the British minister plenipotentiary in the Far East, and FO228, which included the official correspondence between the plenipotentiary and the British consuls stationed, after 1842, at the five treaty ports in China.[135] These records had been put to great use by W. C. Costin,[136] and I felt that I could not surpass his work in any major way. The full significance of these sources was not apparent to me until I had gone further in my research.

Next I searched the British Admiralty records, so effectively used by Gerald Graham.[137] I obtained some insight into the war, but few answers to its origins. Thought provoking, however, was Graham's finding that both Admiral Stirling[138] and Sir John Bowring had been trying to use the perceived Russian threat to China to goad their government into taking control of China before the Russians.[139] There were times when I thought that British strategic considerations vis-à-vis Russia might have been one of the origins of the *Arrow* War. Could that suspicion be justified?

In 1972 I went to Russia on the off chance that I might get into the archives there. Russia then still eyed foreigners with great suspicion. It was a fruitless exercise, but not a sad loss. All agree that the Russians were not entangled at the beginning of the dispute. If they could be said to have been involved in any origin of the war, it would have been the British perception of them as a threat to British interests in China. I tried again even as late as May 1997, on the off chance that Russian archives might indeed have some pertinent documents. Through the good office of Professor Li Yuzheng,[140] who has extensive contacts among the archivists in Russia, inquiries were made with the Foreign Office Archives in Moscow. The results were equally diasppointing, *glasnost* not withstanding. In July 1997, Professor Konstantin v. Schevelyoff of the Institute of the Far East in the Russian Academy of Sciences, Moscow, kindly offered to help. But he was able to send me a list of three secondary works only.

I had better luck with the Quai d'Orsay in Paris and the Library of Congress in Washington. Their records reveal the intricacy of the tripartite diplomacy regarding the *Arrow* War and show beyond doubt that the British government took the initiative to invite the French and U.S. governments to a joint

135. These ports were opened by the Treaty of Nanking, 1842. They were Canton (Guangzhou), Amoy (Xiamen), Foochow (Fuzhou), Ningpo (Ningbo), and Shanghai.
136. Costin, *Great Britain and China*.
137. Gerald S. Graham, *The China Station: War and Diplomacy, 1830–1860* (Oxford, Clarendon Press, 1978).
138. Rear-Admiral Sir James Stirling (1791–1865) was commander-in-chief in China and the East Indies from January 1854 to February 1856. He was to become vice-admiral in 1857 and admiral in 1862. *DNB*, v. 18, pp. 1267–8.
139. Graham, *China Station*, pp. 289–90.
140. She is a Fellow of the Institute of Modern History in the Chinese Academy of Social Sciences, Beijing.

approach towards China.[141] To pinpoint the origins of the war, therefore, I went back to the records in England.

This time I went through the British newspapers, of which there were scores in the mid-nineteenth century. I focused on the more important, among them *The Times*, in search of significant policy statements, leaks, scandals, and the like that might throw some light on the official documents. I subsequently found that Koay Shiaw-chian[142] and E. G. Biaggini[143] had both used these papers systematically. They sought to build up a picture of press reaction to events in China in this period.[144] I found some revealing statements which, by themselves, could not explain the origins of the war. On the other hand, they enabled me to obtain much insight into Victorian politics, which I subsequently found were inextricablely related to the war.

Then I turned to the original diplomatic correspondence between British representatives in the Far East and the Chinese authorities. A fairly complete set was preserved in London.[145] Both sides wrote to each other in Chinese, the Chinese authorities of this time refusing to learn any English. I gained some insight into the disposition and temperament of the diplomats involved, the possible misunderstandings caused by language barriers, cultural differences, divergent expectations, and so on; but I had no major breakthrough in terms of pinpointing the origins of the *Arrow* War.

I buried my head in the Canton Archive, which consisted of seventy-seven boxes of Chinese manuscripts captured at Canton when it fell during the *Arrow* War. Some of this unique treasure consisted of military intelligence, maps, and financial accounts. There were also official reports, submissions, imperial edicts, private letters, confidential notes, and depositions. I learned the importance of the local rebellions in terms of their possible effects on the conduct of China's foreign relations and was able to confirm one accepted conclusion and overthrow another.[146] But I was not much closer to the origins of the war itself.

I heard in 1980 that the records of China's central government housed in the Beijing Palace Museum were opened for the first time to researchers, including foreign scholars. Thanks to the help of the Chinese ambassador to Australia, I obtained in Beijing microfilm copies of government papers which complemented the local records captured at Canton. They added significantly to the understanding of Russia's role in the war which I had acquired from the

---

141. See Chapter 11.
142. Koay Shiaw-chian, 'British Opinion and Policy on China between the First and Second Anglo-Chinese Wars, 1842–1857', unpublished M.A. thesis, University of Leeds, 1967.
143. E. G. Biaggini, 'The Coercion of China, 1830–1860: A Study in Humbug', D.Litt. thesis, University of Adelaide, 1944. See next note.
144. Biaggini researched his doctorate for the London School of Economics. Subsequently he submitted his manuscript to the University of Adelaide in Australia for a D. Litt. in 1947.
145. See my *Anglo-Chinese Relations*.
146. See Chapter 5.

archives in London, Paris, and Washington. Together with the three-volume collection of primary Chinese documents on Sino-Russian relations published in Beijing,[147] and the Russian Collection published in Taiwan,[148] they filled an important gap which my trip to Russia in 1972 had failed to bridge.

I also went to Canton, Nanjing, Shanghai, and other places for local records and private papers of the Chinese officials. As may be imagined, Canton was rich with the oral history of the *Arrow* War, some of which had been enshrined in the writings of distinguished scholars, and on the basis of which Huang Yen-yü wrote his doctoral thesis.[149] Compared with the primary sources mentioned thus far, or with the eyewitness account prepared by the magistrate of Nanhai,[150] these subsequently recorded pieces of oral history are sensational and inaccurate.

I travelled all over the United Kingdom in search of private papers of the pertinent British politicians, diplomats, and military officers, to find their hidden agenda, if any. I was greatly enlightened. A particularly important clue was found in a private letter from Sir John Bowring to Lord Clarendon, the foreign secretary. Bowring referred to the importance of China for the Indian revenue,[151] which completely changed the direction of my research. It was, of course, Bowring who had wanted to use the *Arrow* incident to 'write a bright page in our history'.[152] At last, I had pinpointed an important link between Bowring's actions and his intentions.

Consequently, I began searching the India Office records. These had been very competently used by David Owen.[153] His story about the phenomenal growth in the volume of opium production in India was of great interest to me. Although his book was written chiefly on the subject of Indian opium, he dismissed Indian opium as a cause of either the Opium War or the *Arrow* War. He preferred to attribute their causes to British trade expansion, with which his book did not deal.

But I took David Owen's trade argument seriously. I was granted special permission to consult the private company records of the leading British firms of the time: Jardine Matheson[154] and Baring Brothers.[155] I am grateful to the

147. *Qingdai Zhong–E guanxi dangan shiliao xuanbian* (Selected sources on China–Russia relations during the Qing period, 3d series [1851–62]), 3 vs. Compiled by the Ming-Qing section of the Palace Museum (Beijing, Zhonghua shuju, 1979).
148. *Siguo xindang* (New archives on China's relations with Great Britain, France, America, and Russia), 4 vs. (Taibei, Institute of Modern History, Academic Sinica, 1966).
149. As mentioned, this thesis was submitted in 1940 under the title 'Viceroy Yeh Ming-ch'en and the Canton Episode (1856–61)'.
150. Hua Tingjie, 'Chufan shimo', collected in *Er ya*, v. 1, pp. 163–96.
151. Bowring to Clarendon, 4 October 1855, MSS Clar. Dep. C37 China.
152. Bowring to Parkes, 21 October 1856, Parkes Papers, para. 11.
153. Owen, *British Opium Policy*.
154. These papers are deposited at the University Library, Cambridge.
155. These are kept in the head office of the company, in the City of London. I am grateful to the archivist, Dr M. J. Orbell, for his assistance during my research on these papers.

company authorities for this privilege. Before me, Michael Greenberg had used the Jardine Matheson Papers to write his famous *British Trade and the Opening of China, 1800-42*.[156] His major contribution was to have substantiated an observation made by Alexander Michie about the importance of the triangular trade among India, China, and Britain.[157] Thus, my task would become one of verifying this concept and determining the degree to which it might have contributed to the outbreak of the *Arrow* War. As for the papers of Baring Brothers, Christopher Platt was to use them to write a history of the company. Sadly, this project never materialized.[158] The records of both companies revealed the strong desire to open up China for trade, and the expansion of business by individual British companies in China in the nineteenth century, but little about the wider picture of total British trade with China at the time of the *Arrow* War.

As a result, I began to scrutinize the statistics, prepared by the Board of Trade and other government departments in London, on Anglo-Chinese trade in the context of British global trade; on opium revenue within the framework of the entire balance sheet of British India; and on India-China trade in the context of China's trade with all maritime countries. These statistics were presented to Parliament annually in the form of blue books, which were subsequently bound into large volumes, whose columns of figures I collated, analysed, compared, and reorganized. I discoverd that a close reading of all the other sources invariably indicated that a thorough search of the pertinent raw statistics would be pivotal in explaining the origins of the *Arrow* War. One crucial question was this: On the basis of these statistics, what perceptions would the British policy makers have formed?

Cold statistics aside, there was clearly a great deal of Victorian passion involved in the press and parliamentary debates over the prosecution of the war. I discovered that in 1895 some influential Britons in Hong Kong, probably because of the bread poisoning during the war, were still so resentful of Commissioner Yeh and his class that they wanted similarly to exile to India anybody they regarded as a miscreant.[159] This depth of feeling about four decades after the events gives some indication of the tension at the time of the *Arrow* War.

It is a tension I often felt in pursuing the origins of that war. Studied

156. Cambridge University Press, 1951.
157. Alexander Michie, *An Englishman in China during the Victorian era: As illustrated in the Career of Sir Rutherford Alcock . . . many years Consul and Minister in China and Japan* (Taipei reprint, 1966, of an edition published in Edinburgh in 1900).
158. Apparently this was caused by a disagreement between the author and the company on the format of the book. Professor Platt, a fellow Antonian, most kindly lent me his copious notes so that I might familiarize myself with the archive before I actually tackled the original documents myself.
159. *China Mail*, editorial, Hong Kong, 22 October 1895, p. 3, col. 5.

together, the diverse sources began to give new meaning to each other; new issues emerged. What had initially seemed to be 'a fortuitous concourse of atoms'[160] slowly fell into place as my research progressed. At last, I venture to set out my findings in this volume.

V. Technology and imperial decision making

I have identified three junctures at which the *Arrow* incident might not have been allowed to develop into a war. First, Harry Parkes could have handled the incident to prevent it from becoming a quarrel. He did not. Second, Bowring could have stopped Parkes from using the quarrel to open hostilities against the Chinese. He did not. Third and most critically, the British government in London could have decided not to escalate hostilities which were in any case unauthorized. They did not. Why?

The first logical stage in our investigation is to explore the relationship between the problems of imperialism and the technology at its disposal. In this respect, Daniel Headrick's work is essential,[161] showing as it does how until the development of the international telegraph system, decisions made at the centres of power were often overtaken by events at the periphery.

It is all too easy to forget that the age of sail reigned up to about the middle of the nineteenth century. It was not until 1837 that marine technology made it possible to use steam on long-haul routes, whereupon the Peninsular & Oriental Steam Navigation Company (P&O) was formed, to which a contract was awarded by the British government in 1840 to provide a mail service to Alexandria, and in 1845 to extend that service to India and China.[162] P&O's best time in 1851 from Southampton to Calcutta was thirty-seven days, which was hailed as 'a decided improvement over the long and uncertain voyages made by sail round the Cape of Good Hope'.[163]

By the time of the *Arrow* War, mail by steamer had been introduced between Canton and Hong Kong, but not yet telegraph. Despatches between the two places took about twelve hours; and there were two mails each day, morning and afternoon. If the mail was missed by a few minutes, then a despatch, however urgent, had to wait for the next mail and thereby take twenty-four

---

160. These words are borrowed from Lord Palmerston, who used them in a quite different context. For details, see Part Four.
161. See his two books, *Tools of Empire: Technology and European Imperialism in the Nineteenth Century* (New York, Oxford University Press, 1981) and *Invisible Weapon: Telecommunications and International Politics, 1851–1945* (New York, Oxford University Press, 1991).
162. Parl. Papers 1847, v. 36, 'Peninsular & Oriental Steam Packet Company', pp. 6ff, quoted in Freda Harcourt, 'Black Gold: P&O and the Opium Trade, 1847–1914', *International Journal of Maritime History*, 6, no. 1 (June 1994), p. 10.
163. Harcourt, 'Black Gold', p. 11.

hours later.[164] Allowing time to prepare for responses, the earliest one might expect a reply would be thirty-six to forty-eight hours later. When rapid developments occurred, as in the case of the *Arrow* incident, even thirty-six hours was too long to wait. This gave Parkes a great deal of freedom to initiate actions which Bowring felt obliged to approve retrospectively.

Communications from London to Hong Kong could be by telegraph as far as Trieste, overland between ports in the Mediterranean and the Red Sea,[165] and the rest of the journey by steamer. Journalists used this combined service. But Clarendon and Bowring had to rely solely on the 'monthly mail service'[166] by steamer because of the confidential nature of their correspondence. Bowring's first despatch about the *Arrow* incident reached London on 1 December 1856,[167] just under two months from 8 October. The journalists fared worse. Apparently they missed the mail, and their message by steamer and then telegraph did not reach London until 29 December.[168] Thus, the return mail carrying either the instructions from, or reports to, Whitehall could be four months out of date.

Under the circumstances, the British government had to invest its agents with considerable powers of discretion, or affairs would become paralysed. Disowning them was almost out of the question. Much of the confusion of events arose from this technological state of affairs. The *Arrow* War seems a prime example of Daniel Headrick's thesis.

On the other hand, communications between Canton and Beijing did not even have the benefit of steam. The sea route was too unreliable and even perilous in times of typhoons. There was a long-established land route, whereby the official couriers on horseback might be required to gallop nonstop a prescribed of 400, 500, or 600 li[169] every twenty-four hours. The most urgent imperial edict could reach Canton in about fifteen days, although normal reports from Canton took about thirty-two days.[170] Thus, successive imperial commissioners for foreign affairs stationed at Canton also had a great deal of freedom. Like Parkes and Bowring, Xu and Yeh did not hesitate to use that freedom. Had the telegraph service been in operation between Canton and Beijing as well as between Hong Kong and London, undoubtedly the suggestion by Xu and Yeh to send Bonham a false edict,[171] and the proposal by Parkes and Bowring to bombard Canton,[172] would have been equally given short shrift.

164. See Bowring's complaints about missing the mail in Chapter 4.
165. The Suez Canal had not yet been constructed.
166. Harcourt, 'Black Gold', p. 12.
167. Bowring to Clarendon, Desp. 326, 13 October 1856, FO17/251.
168. *The Times*, 29 December 1856.
169. A li is about one-third of a mile.
170. See Chapter 5.
171. Ibid.   172. See Chapters 2–4.

The confusion of imperialism

When Whitehall heard about the *Arrow* dispute, unauthorized hostilities had already begun. Lord Palmerston argued that the government must support its agents abroad, and he did so in the strongest terms both in Parliament and during the subsequent election. Others agreed, among them Lord Methuen in the House of Lords and Lloyd Davies in the House of Commons, insisting that unless the government upheld the actions of Bowring, Britain could not be faithfully and effectually served.[173] The British electorate endorsed that view.[174]

But was it really true that the British government had no choice but to support its agents on this specific occasion? Here, interesting comparisons may be made with almost parallel developments in Sino-American relations at practically the same time. Chinese soldiers, having been pounded by the Royal Navy on account of the *Arrow* quarrel, mistakenly fired at a U.S. Navy boat bearing the American flag – an undoubted insult to the flag. What the U.S. Navy did was simply to attack and capture the forts from which its boat had been fired upon, burst the guns, burn the gun-carriages, and leave.[175] Washington did not pursue the matter with the Chinese any further. London could have done the same.

Sir James Graham, who had twice held the position of first lord of the Admiralty,[176] actually thought that the government should have taken a similar course of action: namely, express sympathy for the difficult circumstances under which Bowring had to operate, but ask him to patch up the differences with the Chinese.[177]

Viewed in this light, the argument that Palmerston had no choice but to continue Bowring's undeclared war cannot stand. Indeed, a breakthrough in this study is the discovery that Whitehall had begun secret negotiations with France in order to wage war on China even before the *Arrow* incident (see Chapter 11), which makes Palmerston's pronouncements sound very much like political stunts.

VI. My approach

My first step is to determine whether the Union Jack had been hauled down as alleged. This is done in Chapter 2. The second is to examine the manner in

173. Methuen, 26 February 1857, Hansard, 3d series, v. 144, col. 1322; Davies, 26 February 1857, ibid., v. 144, col. 1448.
174. '"The necessity of upholding our representatives at a distance" carried a great deal of weight with the constituencies', commented the *Guardian*, 18 March 1857.
175. Seymour to Admiralty, 24 November 1856, Parl. Papers 1857, v. 12, pp. 170–1, paras. 4–5. The Chinese soldiers fired from the forts which they had reoccupied after the British had earlier captured and then abandoned them.
176. The Rt. Hon. Sir James Robert George Graham (1792–1861) was first lord of the Admiralty, 1830–4; home secretary, 1841–6; and again first lord of the Admiralty, 1852–5. See C. S. Parker, *Life and Letters of Sir James Graham, Second Baronet of Netherby, 1792–1861*, 2 vs. (London, John Murray, 1907).
177. *Globe*, 19 March 1857, p. 1, col. 6: 'Sir James Graham'.

24

which Parkes handled the *Arrow* incident and to explain why he behaved the way he did. This is done in Chapter 3. The third is to study Bowring's management of what was now the *Arrow* quarrel and to find reasons for his conduct. This is done in Chapter 4. The rationale for Yeh's response is explored in Chapter 5. Local conditions at Canton are examined in Chapter 6. It is hoped that in this way a full picture may be presented of the complexities attending the events of this period.

News of the *Arrow* quarrel sparked off fierce controversy in the British press. This is dealt with in Chapter 7. Fiery debates also raged in both houses of Parliament. These are analysed in Chapters 8 and 9. The government lost the debate and called the famous 'Chinese Election', by which the government was returned to office. This is examined in Chapter 10.

My object being the origins of the *Arrow* War, I tend to concentrate on aspects of these events that may enlighten the subject. The predominant interpretation in mainland China since 1949 has been that of Marx, who was reporting for the *New York Daily Tribune* at the time. For that purpose, he judiciously digested the London newspapers and sat through all the parliamentary debates. One major object of Chapters 7-10 is, therefore, to assess the validity of Marx's views.

The other is to pinpoint, among the hundreds and thousands of public speeches and statements, the one that may reveal the British government's real intentions. In the end perseverance paid dividends. I find that during a fierce debate the prime minister, suffering from a terrible cold and dreadful gout, in the heat of the moment said that Britain's peaceful approaches to China for revising the Treaty of Nanking (1842) had failed, and asked what he was expected to do under the circumstances.[178] This is an important clue which opens up an entirely new avenue of inquiry, this time into what happened behind the scenes. Thus Chapter 11 deals with the question of treaty revision, involving secret negotiations among the major powers of the time: Britain, France, the United States, and Russia. The *Arrow* quarrel would be a suitable casus belli, but many Britons were genuinely uneasy about using it so. Chapter 12 addresses how the British government attempted to overcome this. The lobbying of other interest groups in Britain is dealt with in Chapter 13.

Why did Britain want to revise the Treaty of Nanking? The main reason given in the parliamentary and press debates was the expectation that the China market for British manufactures and Indian commodities would thereby greatly increase. What gave rise to this hope? In support of their arguments, politicians often quoted some isolated figures, apparently from the annual statistical returns presented to Parliament. To obtain the same sort of comprehensive impressions that these politicians should have acquired from these

---

178. Palmerston, 3 March 1857, Hansard, 3d series, v. 144, col. 1828.

annual returns, it is important to study the raw statistics systematically in order to quantify the perceptions of the politicians. Chapter 14 deals with the bilateral trade between Britain and China up to the time of the *Arrow* War. Chapter 15 attempts to determine the place of British merchants in China's total maritime trade. An important commodity in this trade was Indian opium; Chapter 16 deals with the drug and related issues. Did the war justify British expectations? Chapter 17 tries to provide an answer.

My overall conclusions are delivered in Chapter 18.

To put the confusing events and issues in perspective, a chronology of major events is compiled, leading to some interesting revelations. For instnce, questions about those responsible for the bread poisoning in Hong Kong have never been answered. Now the chronology enables us to put isolated incidents such as this one into context, and thereby offers new clues. It shows that on 12 January 1857, Seymour commanded his troops to begin setting fire at 6:50 A.M. to the suburbs near the Factory Gardens. The winter winds were so high and dry that the fire swiftly burned down countless houses. 'The whole atmosphere was now one mass of smoke, through which the sun appeared like a large yellow ball'. The Chinese 'continued working all day at their fire-engines, despite shot and shell and Minié balls' fired at them by the Royal Navy.[179] Many civilians perished in the fire. What would the dutiful sons do if their aged parents had been burnt to death? It was under this sort of circumstances that on 15 January 1857, someone secreted arsenic into the bread of a baker's shop in Hong Kong, in sharp contrast to the fact that nothing like it had happened since Yeh announced on 28 October 1856 his reward for the death of Britons. Very probably, it was an aggrieved filial son that tried to poison the entire British community in Hong Kong in retaliation for the tragic death of his parent(s). This immediately puts in perspective the views of the *Morning Post*, which described the poisoner(s) as 'demons in human shape'.[180] That paper seems to think that it was all right for the blue-jackets to burn Chinese civilians alive in their own homes, but those who 'fought fire with fire', so to speak, were not human beings.

Ultimately, it seems that behind all these squabbles, scuffles, scandals, battles, lies, conspiracies, killings, and murders lay big money and narcotics – government sponsored.[181] Let me anticipate some of my findings and interpretations. The story that the British flag had been insulted was probably invented by the nominal captain of the *Arrow* to goad the young acting consul, Harry Parkes, well known for his rashness, into immediate action. Parkes adopted the story because he wanted to humiliate the Chinese officers on account of a

179. J. Mongan's Memorandum of Operations at Canton, 5–13 January 1856, dated 14 January 1857, Parl. Papers 1857, v. 12, pp. 313–15, para. 7.
180. *Morning Post*, 3 March 1857.
181. See Chapter 12.

personal grievance, as alluded to above. Sir John Bowring allowed himself to be led on by Parkes because he wished to use the incident to gain entry into Canton City. Commissioner Yeh was determined to deny Bowring that satisfaction because the Cantonese mob simply would not permit him to do so.

The alleged insult to the Union Jack caused a sensation in Britain. Arguments and counter-arguments dominated the press and parliamentary debates, as well as the 'Chinese Election'. There seems to have been no real precedent for the newspaper jingoism of 1857, nor for the nascent power of the press at the time. As for the journalism of Karl Marx for the *New York Daily Tribune*, it will be seen that he did not have a good understanding of the nuances of the British political press and Victorian liberalism. Nor did he have any way of knowing what diplomacy went on behind the scenes. Consequently, it is quite inappropriate to see the *Arrow* War through his eyes and unscholarly to quote his words as authority when interpreting that conflict, as many Chinese historians have done.

It transpires that opium was a very important source of revenue for British India and was sold almost exclusively to China. The profits were used partly to sustain the government of India, partly to purchase U.S. cotton for the Lancashire mills, and partly to buy Chinese tea and silk (which furnished the means whereby remittance was made from India to London). Tea and silk almost alone made China the fourth, and for one year at least the third, largest trading partner of the United Kingdom in terms of imports during the years preceding the *Arrow* War. The annual duty levied on Chinese tea in the United Kingdom was alone sufficient to pay for the equivalent of a good part of the annual expenditure of the Royal Navy – a navy that kept the global British empire afloat – during the years immediately before the *Arrow* War.

Although opium had an important role to play in the United Kingdom's global trade and its national as well as international finance, it had not been legalized by the Chinese authorities,[182] despite Britain's victory in the Opium War. There were constant rumours that the Chinese government, emboldened since the so-called defeat of the British over the Canton City question in 1849, was about to launch another crackdown on opium. Were opium to be suppressed in China, the prosperous flow of global trade would be broken. Some of the Lancashire mills would close, the United Kingdom's budget would have to be revised downwards, and British India would have difficulty remaining afloat. To forestall this, the British government tried to persuade the Chinese

182. Some provincial Chinese authorities in the late 1850s began levying an illicit duty on opium as a means of finding desperately needed money to fight the Taipings. On this basis, Professor John Fairbank once argued that opium had in fact been legalized before the Treaties of 1858 which concluded the first phase of the *Arrow* War. See his article entitled, 'The Legalization of the Opium Trade before the Treaties of 1858'. *Chinese Social and Political Science Review*, 17 (July 1933), no. 2, pp. 215–63. For details about the final legalization of opium in China as a result of the *Arrow* War, see Part Six, this volume.

authorities to revise the Treaty of Nanking so as to legalize the drug. The final and complete rejection of this request was contained in Commissioner Yeh's despatch dated 30 June 1856, about three months before the *Arrow* incident occurred on 8 October. As Lord Palmerston said, what was he supposed to do under the circumstances?

VII. Economic causation versus strategic interpretation

Although my findings have led me to explain the *Arrow* War in terms of economic causation, I must pay equal attention to other interpretations of imperial expansion. Among them, the most relevant to the concerns of the present study is perhaps strategic consideration.

It will be seen in Chapter 11 that, in 1855, Admiral Sir James Stirling had used strategic arguments in an attempt to persuade the Admiralty to take control of China. He did so at a sensitive time – during the Crimean War, when he was commander-in-chief in China and the East Indies. Having led a party of intending colonists to establish the first European settlement in Western Australia, of which he became its first governor,[183] Stirling seems to have extended his colonizing zeal to China, blaming Russian ambitions. But London ignored his long submission.

Bowring also used the perceived Russian threat as a strategic argument for action. He did so likewise during the Crimean War, in fact nine months before the *Arrow* incident. At that time, Russia was the only power that managed to maintain a listening-post in Beijing. It was disguised as an ecclesiastical mission, presumably with direct access to the court, and was suspected of advising the Manchus to foil British designs.[184] Bowring's plea was ignored by Whitehall.

But it was Bowring's appeal to do something about treaty revision that finally moved Clarendon. Bowring made such an appeal about four and a half months before the *Arrow* incident.[185] Upon receiving Bowring's despatch on 17 July 1856, Clarendon minuted: 'Approve – copies to Admiralty . . . I trust [Admiral Sir Michael Seymour] will have sufficient force to be at liberty to take Sir John Bowring to the Northern Ports in company with the Minister and Naval Force of the U.S. and . . . the French Admiral . . . as the joint action of the three Treaty Powers at this moment is of great importance'.[186]

Subsequently on 22 July 1856, he formally requested the Admiralty to order

---

183. *DNB*, v. 18, pp. 1267–8. See also the *Australian Dictionary of Biography*, v. 2, *1788–1850*, ed. A. G. L. Shaw and C. M. H. Clark (Melbourne, Melbourne University Press, 1967), pp. 484–8.
184. Bowring to Clarendon, Desp. 11, 5 January 1856, FO17/244.
185. Bowring to Clarendon, Desp. 166, 16 May 1856, FO17/247.
186. Clarendon's minutes of 17 July 1856 on Bowring's Desp. 166 of 16 May 1856, FO17/247.

Seymour to convey Bowring northwards for a demonstration of force 'for the purpose of revising certain Treaty provisions'.[187] He did so without knowing that Commissioner Yeh had just rejected, on 30 June 1856, Bowring's official request to revise the Treaty of Nanking.[188] When news of that rejection reached London on 30 August 1856,[189] Clarendon thundered that the time had come when 'the vast resources of that vast Empire [must be] opened up'.[190] Cabinet met and decided to approach France and the United States for joint military action against China.

Thus, London had been actively planning a war over treaty revision for several months before news of the *Arrow* incident reached London; indeed even before the incident occurred. Clearly, what prompted Whitehall to coercion was treaty revision and not a perceived Russian threat, nor even the *Arrow* quarrel, which now assumed a different significance. Instead of the incident in any way constituting a cause of the war, as believed hitherto, it was rather the public justification for a war which the government had been scheming secretly for months.[191]

What was involved in this treaty revision? It was not so much a request for revising existing terms as a demand for a completely new treaty to be signed, in order to

1. obtain access generally to the whole interior of China;
2. obtain free navigation of the Yangtze River;
3. effect the legalisation of the opium trade;
4. provide against the imposition of transit duties on foreign goods;
5. provide for the suppression of piracy on the China coast;
6. regulate the emigration of Chinese labourers;
7. secure the permanent residence at Beijing of a representative of the British Crown, and if that could not be obtained;
8. provide for regular correspondence between H. M. representative and the Chinese chief authority at Beijing;
9. provide for ready personal intercourse between H. M. representative and the governor of the province in which he might be residing; and
10. provide that in the construction of the treaty to be concluded, all doubts were to be resolved by reference to the English version and that alone.[192]

It will be seen that the advocacy of British economic interests in China was paramount in the minds of the policy makers. During the debates on the *Arrow*

187. Hammond to Admiralty, 22 July 1856, Adm. 1/5677.
188. Yeh to Bowring, 30 June 1856, FO682/1989/9.
189. See FO endorsement, dated 30 August 1856, on Bowring to Clarendon, Desp. 202, 3 July 1856, FO17/248.
190. Clarendon to Cowley, 24 September 1856, FO17/261, p. 75. Lord Cowley was the British ambassador to Paris. Also, see Graham's treatment of the subject in *China Station*, p. 298.
191. For details, see Chapter 11.
192. Clarendon to Bowring, Desp. 2, 13 February 1854, FO17/210.

quarrel, the lord advocate[193] said: 'With interests so grave at stake it would be better, and even more just, even if a false move had been made, to proceed rather than to go back'.[194] What were those grave interests? Richard Cobden[195] elaborated on a crucial one: 'Since 1842 we have not added to our exports to China at all, at least as far as our manufactures are concerned. We have increased our consumption of tea; but that is all'.[196] Sir Erskine Perry[197] agreed: 'The sole principle of policy which ought to govern our intercourse with China was that which had reference to the mutual benefit of trade'.[198] These were complaints about the imbalance of bilateral trade between Great Britain and China, which could be rectified by giving British goods access to China beyond the five treaty ports already opened by the Treaty of Nanking.

Small wonder that the lord advocate almost welcomed the *Arrow* quarrel having been used as an excuse to open hostilities with China.[199] It was in this context that Disraeli[200] accused Lord Palmerston of attempting 'by force to

193. Both Hansard (3d series, v. 144, 'The Ministry') and the *DNB* spelt his surname Moncreiff. However, *Who's Who of British Members of Parliament: A Biographical Dictionary of the House of Commons, Based on Annual Volumes of 'Dod's Parliamentary Companion' and Other Sources* (hereafter cited as *BMP*), ed. Michael Stenton, 4 vs. (Hassocks, Harvester, 1976), would have it as Moncrieff. Either way, the Rt. Hon. James Moncrieff (1811–74) became an advocate at the Scottish bar (1833), solicitor-general for Scotland (1850–52), and lord advocate (1851–2, 1852–8, 1859–66, and in 1868). He was to be appointed lord of session as Lord Moncrieff in 1869, and made Baron Moncrieff in January 1874 (*BMP*, v. 1, pp. 273–4). He is also briefly mentioned in his father's biography in the *DNB* (v. 13, pp. 615–16: p. 616).
194. The lord advocate, 27 February 1857, Hansard, 3d series, v. 144, col. 1517.
195. Richard Cobden (1804–65) was a cotton printer in Lancashire, a director of the Manchester Chamber of Commerce, a champion of free trade, and well known as a leading member of the Anti–Corn Law League. He was the author of the pamphlets entitled *England, Ireland, and America*, and *Russia, by a Manchester Manufacturer*. He sat for Stockport (1884–7), the West Riding of Yorkshire (July 1847 to April 1857), and Rochdale (May 1859 till his death on 2 April 1865). See Nicholas C. Edsall, *Richard Cobden: Independent Radical* (Cambridge, Mass., Harvard University Press, 1986); and Wendy Hinde, *Richard Cobden: A Victorian Outsider* (New Haven, Conn., Yale University Press, 1987).
196. Cobden, 26 February 1857, Hansard, 3d series, v. 144, col. 1412.
197. Thomas Erskine Perry (1807–58) was the second son of James Perry, proprietor of the *Morning Chronicle* newspaper. He was educated at Trinity College, Cambridge, was called to the bar in 1934 and joined the home circuit, was appointed a judge of the supreme court at Bombay in 1841, and made chief justice there in 1847. He resigned in 1852. He was first elected for Devonport in May 1854 and sat until appointed a member of the Council of India in 1858. *BMP*, v. 1, p. 308.
198. Perry, 26 February 1857, Hansard, 3d series, v. 144, col. 1460. He was to vote for Cobden's motion, and thereby incurred great hostility in his own constituency. See Chapter 13, this volume.
199. The lord advocate, 27 February 1857, Hansard, 3d series, v. 144, col. 1517.
200. Benjamin Disraeli (1804–81) entered Lincoln's Inn in 1824 and Parliament in 1837. After the split in Peel's party, Disraeli set about building up anew a Conservative Party out of the demoralized fragments of the old one. He became chancellor of the Exchequer in Derby's ministry in 1852. He was to occupy that position again in 1858 and 1866. In February 1868, Derby retired, and Disraeli became prime minister. Later he was elevated to be the first earl of Beaconsfield. See W. F. Monypenny and G. E. Buckle, *The Life of Benjamin Disraeli*, 6 vs. (London, John Murray, 1910–20). For the reconstruction of the Conservative Party by Derby

increase our commercial relations with the East', using the dispute as the springboard.[201]

Herein lie the pivotal origins of the *Arrow* War – the expansion of British economic interests in China and thereby globally. I shall substantiate this interpretation not only by pinpointing the relevant public comments by ministers and other politicians (Chapters 7–10) and analysing the documentary evidence pertaining to the formulation of policies official and secret (Chapters 11–13), but by qualifying these economic interests as perceived by politicians. This is achieved by scrutinizing the statistics presented to Parliament annually (Chapters 14–17). These statistics were quoted liberally by speakers during the parliamentary debates at the outbreak of the *Arrow* War, among them Palmerston,[202] testifying to their reliance on these figures for perceptions of the of British interests involved.[203]

VIII. Contrasts with established views

An array of theories has emerged to explain the origins of the *Arrow* War, sometimes conjointly with the Opium War. The most commonly accepted is the 'insult to the flag'. Some historians have entitled their books 'The Opium Wars',[204] implying that opium was the cause of both wars, although they have yet to prove their case in the second. Others think that the *Arrow* War was a war for 'diplomatic recognition',[205] an interpretation which is an extension of the notion of 'war over kowtow' originally used to interpret the Opium War.[206] A more modern theory is the 'imperialism of free trade',[207] which has been developed into the 'Molasses War' hypothesis to explain, backwards in time, the Opium War.[208] 'Cantonese xenophobia',[209] 'insults in China'

and Disraeli, see Robert Stewart, *The Politics of Protection: Lord Derby and the Protectionist Party, 1841–1852* (Cambridge University Press, 1971).
201. Disraeli, 3 March 1857, Harvard, 3d series, v. 144, col. 1836.
202. Palmerston, 3 March 1857, Harvard, 3d series, v. 144, col. 1828.
203. See Chapters 8–9.
204. See, e.g., Jack Beeching, *The Chinese Opium Wars* (London, Hutchinson, 1975). See also Jiang Mengyin, *Di'erci yapian zhanzheng*.
205. Douglas Hurd, for example, wrote, 'The British and French, and to a lesser extent the American Governments, came slowly to the conclusion that it was not enough to defend the letter of the existing Treaties; they must be prepared to use force to get themselves recognised, in practice as well as theory, as the equals of the Government in Beijing' (*Arrow War*, p. 27).
206. John Quincy Adams, 'Lecture on the War with China', delivered before the Massachusetts Historical Society, December 1841, and reprinted in *Chinese Repository*, 11 (January–December 1842), pp. 274–89: p. 288.
207. J. Gallagher and R. Robinson, 'The Imperialism of Free Trade', *Economic History Review*, 2d series, 6, no. 1 (1953), pp. 1–15. See also D. C. M. Platt, *Finance, Trade, and Politics: British Foreign Policy, 1815–1914* (Oxford, Clarendon Press, 1968), pp. xxx–xl and 265–7.
208. Chang, *Commissioner Lin*, p. 15.
209. See, e.g., Nolde, 'Xenophobia at Canton'.

generally,[210] and the 'clash of two cultures',[211] as well as its baby, the 'measles',[212] are among other paradigms.

Let us begin with the 'insult to the flag'. The argument has always been that for the sake of national honour and pride, the British government had no choice but to avenge this insult. I have found that this so-called insult was at best 'alleged' and probably unreal. Most important, the *Arrow* incident took place well after Whitehall had started actively planning a war with China by seeking French allies. Thus, if the incident was a casus belli at all, it simply happened at a time when it might be so used.

Second, the 'clash of two cultures'. This interpretation points to the many differences between China and the West in language, culture, tradition, and concepts of justice and propriety. It concludes that these differences were so great, and the conflicts generated by them so numerous, that war was inevitable. While this theory was used originally to interpret the Opium War, it has been extended for the *Arrow* War.[213]

I have sympathy for such a theory, particularly in view of the diplomatic correspondence between the British and Chinese authorities for the period covering the two wars and the intervening years.[214] These documents offer insight into the almost daily bickerings between the two sides. But this theory is too general to explain the specific issues that led to the war. I venture to suggest that the gulf in the 1980s between China and the United Kingdom was perhaps no smaller than it had been at the time of the Opium and *Arrow* Wars. Yet the United Kingdom decided in 1984 to return to China in 1997 the spoils of those two wars – the island of Hong Kong and the peninsula of Kowloon.[215] Can we say that the 'clash of two cultures' led to the British decision to surrender the spoils peacefully? Fundamentally it is a question of power. In the nineteenth century, the United Kingdom had the power to advance its imperial interests. Even as late as 1943, Britain was still able to declare that, short of war, nobody should have any illusion about snatching anything from its hands.[216] Now the shoe is on the other foot.

---

210. Parl. Papers 1857, v. 12, pp. 325–560. This document of 236 pages bears the serial number 2175 and the title 'Correspondence Respecting Insults in China'.
211. The doyen of this school of thought is H. B. Morse. See his magnum opus, *The International Relations of the Chinese Empire, vol. 1, The Period of Conflict, 1834–60*, 3 vs. (Shanghai, Kelly & Walsh, 1910–18), chapters 3–7.
212. See Carmen Blacker, *The Japanese Enlightenment: A Study of the Writings of Fukuzawa Yukichi* (Cambridge University Press, 1969).
213. See Morse, *International Relations*, v. 1, chapters 3–7.
214. See my *Anglo-Chinese Relations*.
215. The New Territories, which were leased in 1898 for ninety-nine years, would also be returned.
216. See Roger Louis, *Imperialism at Bay, 1941–1945: The United States and the Decolonization of the British Empire* (Oxford, Oxford University Press, 1977), p. 433.

On the other hand, if we were to examine the specific clashes of a cultural nature, as we shall in Chapters 2–6, we would find a great deal of substance in this theory. But for the theory to be credible in terms of historical causation, definite evidence should be provided. In addition, many have regaled their readers with the middle kingdom mentality of the Chinese. Less frequently mentioned is the superiority complex of many Europeans, who found it difficult to accept that there could be great civilizations beside their own. It took two sides to have a clash.

I do not have much sympathy for the 'measles' paradigm. This was advocated by one of the most influential thinkers of Japan, Yukichi Fukuzawa (1835–1901). His writings were adopted as textbooks nationwide, and therefore the impact was both profound and far-reaching. He argued that Western civilization spread like measles, and there was nothing Asians could do to stop the epidemic. This is all very well as a philosophical point of view; but the author then went on to assert that neither the Opium War nor the *Arrow* War was caused by opium. He alleged that those wars erupted because the Chinese resisted, sealing themselves in to avoid contagion, and thus succeeding only in defeat – by blocking air circulation they suffocated themselves.[217] In view of the findings in this book, we cannot but marvel at the paradigms we are capable of producing.

Next, let us examine the attempt to interpret the *Arrow* War as a 'war for diplomatic recognition', which has been put forward by former British foreign secretary Douglas Hurd.[218] As mentioned, this interpretation has its origin in an earlier theory – 'the war over kowtow', which was used to interpret the Opium War. At the time of the Opium War, the former president of the United States, John Quincy Adams,[219] concluded: 'The cause of the [Opium] war is the kotow [*sic*]! – the arrogant and insupportable pretensions of China, that she will hold commercial intercourse with the rest of mankind, not upon terms of equal reciprocity, but upon the insulting and degrading forms of the relation between lord and vassal'.[220]

The editor of the *Chinese Repository* (published in Macao), who decided to print important extracts from this lecture, gave the reasons for his decision as follows: 'While, however, we differ from the lecturer with regards to the influence the opium trade has had upon the war, for it has been without doubt

---

217. See Yukichi Fukuzawa, 'Datsu–A–ron' (Dissociation from Asia), *Jiji shinpo* (News of the times), 16 March 1885, reprinted in Bunso Hashikawa, 'Japanese Perspectives on Asia: From Dissociation to Coprosperity', in Akira Iriye (ed.), *The Chinese and the Japanese: Essays in Political and Cultural Interactions* (Princeton, N.J., Princeton University Press, 1980), pp. 328–9. See also Blacker, *Fukuzawa*.
218. Hurd, *Arrow War*, p. 27.
219. He had been president during the years 1825–8.
220. John Quincy Adams, 'Lecture on the War with China', p. 288.

the great proximate cause, we mainly agree with him as to the effect that other remoter causes springing from Chinese assumption, conceit, and ignorance have also had upon it'.[221]

In other words, the man on the spot thought that opium was the immediate cause of the Opium War and the lack of diplomatic recognition the underlying cause. It will be seen that the battle for diplomatic recognition continued after the Opium War and took the form of a British demand to enter the walled city of Canton.[222] But that demand was only a means to an end. The end was the protection and extension of British imperial interests in China and India.[223]

Now, the 'xenophobia' theory. It has been suggested that 'Cantonese xenophobia',[224] official and popular, caused the *Arrow* War. It will be seen in Chapter 6 that Cantonese hostility towards the British certainly existed after the Opium War. But this hostility was not 'popular xenophobia'. Furthermore, it became active only when the Cantonese people were provoked by daredevil thugs like Charles Compton, who kicked them around like footballs.[225] On the other hand, the alleged 'official xenophobia' is said to be expressed in the refusal by the Cantonese authorities to admit foreigners to their city. It will be seen that this refusal cannot be taken as evidence for 'official xenophobia' either. The objections to foreigners entering the city came from the Cantonese masses, who had long been antagonized by British troops during the Opium War, and thereafter by unruly merchants like Compton, all part of the 'onward progress of that European ascendancy which acts with the pressure of a constant spring'.[226] The Cantonese masses intimidated their officials into keeping the city gates firmly closed to foreigners.

In the end, the Royal Navy blasted open the gates. Who caused the conflict – the host or the gatecrashers? Imperialism might be taboo to some historians and 'Cantonese xenophobia' a handy scapegoat. But it would be more accurate to say that xenophobia might be found among the British merchants and diplomats rather than their antagonists.

Similarly with the general 'insults in China',[227] which allegedly caused the *Arrow* War, it will be seen that such an interpretation cannot stand the test of documentary analysis in Chapter 6. Furthermore, it was already discredited by Richard Cobden in the House of Commons, as we see in Chapter 9.

A very influential paradigm of the *Arrow* War concerns the imperialism of

221. Ibid., p. 289, editor's note.
222. See Part Three.
223. See Part Six.
224. See, e.g., Nolde, 'Xenophobia at Canton'.
225. Memorandum on an interview between Lord Palmerston and the China Deputation, 28 June 1847, FO17/135.
226. Davis to Palmerston, Desp. 10, 26 January 1847, FO17/123; Palmerston to Davis, 11 March 1847, FO17/121.
227. Parl. Papers 1857, v. 12, pp. 325–560.

free trade. This was advocated jointly by John Gallagher and Ronald Robinson in 1953,[228] and was greatly refined by Christopher Platt in 1968.[229] But this theory has problems of its own. True, 'British policy is British trade'.[230] Indeed, all the 'great Offices of State' in the United Kingdom 'were occupied with commercial affairs'.[231] One can readily accept that during the period under review, free trade was an important ideology. One may also see that free-trade ideology was a contributing influence on British foreign policy in general.[232] It is doubtful, however, that with specific reference to the origins of the *Arrow* War, free trade was the sole or even a pivotal factor in the British policy-making process, as Platt would have us believe.

In addition, Platt argues that the Opium and the *Arrow* Wars had nothing to do with opium, maintaining that they were fought to open up China for free trade.[233]

The goal was indeed an important consideration. But if free trade had been so pivotal in British imperial policy, the British opium monopoly in India would have been abolished and British attempts to monopolize the opium supply to China would have been abandoned. However, despite an extended parliamentary inquiry in the 1830s, and an even more extended royal commission in the 1890s, the opium monopoly in India was preserved. In addition, the British authorities in India tried successfully to monopolize the supply of opium to China, indeed to nip free competition in the bud.[234] The rationale was to protect and extend imperial interests. It was in the interests of the imperial government to force the Chinese government to legalize opium – a feat achieved as a result of the *Arrow* War.[235] Thus, the war was not only about free trade in general but, more important, about the opium monopoly in particular.

In extreme form, free-trade imperialism appears as the 'Molasses War' theory. Chang Hsin-pao has argued: 'The economic force behind the free traders was too great to be restricted or contained... Had there been an effective alternative to opium, say molasses or rice, the conflict might have

228. Gallagher and Robinson, 'Imperialism of Free Trade'.
229. See Platt, *Finance, Trade, and Politics*, pp. xxx–xl and 265–7.
230. These were the words of the younger Pitt, quoted in Platt, *Finance, Trade, and Politics*, p. xiii.
231. This was the view of Joseph Chamberlain as expressed to the Birmingham Chamber of Commerce in November 1896. An extract of Chamberlain's speech may be found in ibid., p. xvi.
232. In the course of thinking through the issues involved, I was once attracted to the idea of the 'imperialism of free trade', and even wrote an article in support of such an idea, entitled 'The Building of an Informal British Empire in China in the Middle of the Nineteenth Century', *Bulletin of the John Rylands University Library of Manchester*, 59, no. 2 (Spring 1977), pp. 472–85. The present volume represents my current thinking, and the ideas in it supersede my previous views.
233. Platt, *Finance, Trade, and Politics*, p. 265.
234. See Chapter 16.
235. See Chapters 16–17.

been called the Molasses War or the Rice War'.[236] We have to agree that molasses and rice are not opium. Neither of them had any hope of reaching the same sort of profit margin attained by the drug, as we see in Chapter 16. There is no point in trying to tailor opium to fit the paradigm of free-trade imperialism. Indeed, how may Professor Chang explain the fact that the leading champions of free trade in Britain at this time – Richard Cobden, Thomas Milner-Gibson,[237] and John Bright[238] – all opposed the *Arrow* War, as we see in Chapters 9 and 10? Indeed, it was the resolution moved by Cobden and seconded by Milner-Gibson which led to the defeat of the government over the issue of the *Arrow*. Clearly the mere adoption of a paradigm, however influential, cannot explain an international conflict as complex as the *Arrow* War.[239]

In a milder form, the free-trade imperialism theory appears in the observation called 'triangular trade' from India to China, from China to the United Kingdom, and from the United Kingdom to India.[240] I have found that this trade was not unidirectional, as understood hitherto; it also worked in reverse. Until one considers the total trade among these three countries, as well as the United Kingdom's global trade, the origins of the *Arrow* War remain obscured.[241]

Having dominated academic debate for about four decades, free-trade imperialism seems to be superseded recently by a new concept, gentlemanly

---

236. Chang, *Commissioner Lin*, p. 15.
237. Thomas Milner-Gibson (1806–84) went to Charterhouse and Trinity College, Cambridge. In 1839 he obtained royal licence to assume the additional surname of Milner before that of Gibson, in order to testify his respect for the memory of Robert Milner of Ipswich. He found in free trade and its development the cardinal point of his political creed, became one of Cobden's most influential allies and a prominent orator of the Anti–Corn Law League. In 1841 he won a seat for Manchester. In 1846 Lord John Russell appointed him vice-president of the Board of Trade with the object of carrying out a free-trade policy and strengthening the government by an alliance with the League. Thus, Gibson will always be remembered as the first official exponent of free trade. He held that position until 1848. From 1859 to 1866, he was president of the Board of Trade, with Cabinet rank. *DNB*, v. 7, pp. 1164–5.
238. The Rt. Hon. John Bright (1811–88) was a cotton spinner and manufacturer, being a partner in the firm of John Bright and Brothers, of Rochdale. Later he was appointed president of the Board of Trade in 1868, chancellor of the Duchy of Lancaster in 1873, elected lord rector of Glasgow University in 1880, and D. C. L. of Oxford in 1886. See William Roberston, *The Life and Times of the Right Honourable John Bright* (London, 1889). For a more recent biography, see James L. Sturgis, *John Bright and the Empire* (London, Athlone, 1969).
239. Unfortunately, this paradigm has gained even wider currency recently because of its promotion in a textbook widely used in colleges and even high schools in the English-speaking world. See I. C. Y. Hsü, *The Rise of Modern China* (New York, Oxford University Press, 1995), p. 192.
240. See, Alexander Michie, *An Englishman in China during the Victorian Era* (Taibei, 1966; reprint of an edition published in Edinburgh in 1900), v. 1, p. 196; Owen, *British Opium Policy*, p. 207; Greenberg, *British Trade*, chapter 1.
241. See Chapter 15.

An attempt to peel the onion of confusion

capitalism.[242] Part Five of this book shows that the origins of the *Arrow* War may not be found among the gentlemanly capitalists either. It was the government that decided on war, then publicized the conflict, whereupon the merchant princes began lobbying for certain demands on China. The government even rebuffed some commercial associations for making quite inappropriate suggestions.[243] Furthermore, by concentrating on Europe, this interpretation ignores the vast trade already existing in East Asia at this time.[244]

Jack Beeching seems to be among the few British authors who use the term 'opium wars' to describe both the Opium War and the *Arrow* War.[245] He does not explain why; presumably he has followed the Chinese habit of doing so. In fact, that habit dates only from 1949 and occurs in mainland China only. Before that date, just the first conflict was called the Opium War; the second was called Ying-Fa Lianjun (Anglo-French Allied Forces),[246] a term which continues in use in Taiwan today.[247] Mainland Chinese historians have never explicitly addressed the reasons for changing the name to the Second Opium War. In private, one of them has told me that the rationale lies in Marx's view that the second war was a continuation of the first. Since the first has been called the 'Opium War', then to be logical the next has to be called the 'Second Opium War'.[248] Thus, the word of Marx has become the authority for interpreting the *Arrow* War as an opium war.

It will be seen in this book that opium, indeed, had a great deal to do with the *Arrow* War. I nonetheless decline to adopt the term 'Second Opium War' as the English title for this book; however, because my research substantiates the importance of opium in the *Arrow* War, and because this war has been known since 1949 to more than a billion Chinese by no other name, I have allowed it to be used in the Chinese title. Short of a better alternative, I prefer the title *Arrow* War, because the *Arrow* incident was the apparent excuse for war, and there is a tradition of naming wars after such excuses. It has the added merit of illustrating how, in the age of European expansion, a small diplomatic incident could be magnified to justify the use of force in order to press for

---

242. See P. J. Cain and A. G. Hopkins, *British Imperialism: Innovation and Expansion, 1688–1914* (London, Longman, 1993).
243. See Chapter 13.
244. See Chapters 14–16. This neglect of the existing East Asian trade has been pointed out systematically by Shigeru Akita, 'British Informal Empire in East Asia, 1880s–1930s: A Japanese Perspective', in Janet Hunter (ed.), *Japanese Perspectives on Imperialism in Asia* (London, London School of Economics, 1995), pp. 1–29.
245. See his book entitled *The Chinese Opium Wars*.
246. See, e.g., Zuo (ed.), *Zhongguo jinbainian shi ziliao chubian*, part 1, 'Yapian zhanzheng yu Ying-Fa lianjun' (The Opium War and Anglo-French allied forces).
247. See, e.g., Wang Zengcai, *Zhong-Ying waijiaoshi lunji* (Essays on Anglo-Chinese diplomacy history) (Taibei, Lianjing chuban sheye gongsi, 1979), p. 252.
248. One may find an implicit exposition of this rationale in *Er-ya*, v. 1, preface, p. 1.

unrelated demands. Commissioner Yeh tried throughout to argue the case over the specific casus belli. For Sir John Bowring, the whole affair was merely a pretext for wider demands on China.

The other and more dominant interpretation of the *Arrow* War by mainland Chinese historians is just as problematic. Marxist ideology apparently continues to play an important role in China in the study of the Opium and *Arrow* Wars despite the capitalistic approach taken by Deng Xiaoping in his economic policies. Quoting Marx, a Chinese historian in 1990 still attributed the origins of both wars to the determination of Western colonialists to 'conquer, enslave, plunder, and slaughter'[249] the Chinese. It will be seen that such a paradigm is not only simplistic but can be misleading. Indeed, it hardly accounts for the moral indignation of many Britons over the aggressive actions of their representatives in China, as well as for national pride, political opportunism, economic imperatives, and self-interest – which were all voiced in a wonderful array of imperial rhetoric. The debates in the British press and Parliament reflect the nuances of a kind of political dialogue which does not exist, and has never existed, in China.

Given the state of Chinese scholarship in this field, it is not surprising that the *Arrow* War is imperfectly understood in China. This distorts the nature of modern Chinese history in general, and of the Opium War in particular. The Opium War has been regarded as an independent and isolated event which ushered in China's so-called semicolonial era.[250]

This volume shows that the Opium War may not be so regarded. Instead, the *Arrow* War was the ultimate event which resolved militarily the fundamental differences that had existed from the very beginning of Anglo-Chinese relations. The results were far-reaching. China had been an independent and sovereign state. Even after its defeat in the Opium War, it was still able to reject the important British demand for legalizing the opium trade. The Chinese and British representatives signed the Treaty of Nanking as equals. Given the endless conflicts and negotiations between the British and the Chinese after the Opium War, the Treaty of Nanking was not a conclusion of peace, but a mere truce.

At the end of the *Arrow* War some twenty years later, however, the Chinese

---

249. See Wang, 'Minzu de zanlan yu minzu de fazhan', p. 36.
250. Mao Tse-tung, 'The Chinese Revolution and the Chinese Communist Party', *The Selected Works of Mao Tse-tung* (Beijing, Foreign Languages Press, 1967), v. 2, p. 314. Hu Sheng, *Cong Yapian zhanzheng dao Wusi yundong* (From the Opium War to the May Fourth Movement) (Shanghai, Renmin chubanshe, 1982); Professor Hu is the president of the Chinese Academy of Social Sciences. For the influence of the works by Mao and Hu on Chinese historiography, see Gong Shuduo et al., 'Jianguo sanshiwu nian lai Yapian zhanzhengshi yanjiu zonshu' (A survey of the works on the Opium War published during the thirty years since the establishment of the People's Republic of China), *Jindaishi yanjiu* (Modern Historical Studies), no. 3 (1984), pp. 148–66.

An attempt to peel the onion of confusion

representative, Prince Kung, 'came up and closed his hands in front of his face, according to the Chinese salute; but Lord Elgin[251] returned him a proud and contemptuous look, and merely bowed slightly, which must have made the blood run cold in poor Kung's veins'.[252] The so-called semicolonial era really began, not with China's defeat in the Opium War (as has been generally assumed by Chinese scholars),[253] but with Britain's victory in the *Arrow* War. If the historians in mainland China have thought through the implications of their rationale for using the term 'Second Opium War' – namely, that the second was the continuation of the first – then they should have come to the same conclusion, although for different reasons.

IX. In sum

It is not just inappropriate paradigms that have confused the issue. The events themselves have contributed to the confusion. In investigating the origins of the *Arrow* War, we find the great dynamism of territorial conquest in India, a conquest sustained to a large extent by the fast-growing net revenue from opium sold in China. In a sense, the drug addicts in China helped make the extension of British rule in India possible.[254] It will be seen that Britain was able to fight Russia,[255] then Persia, then China itself,[256] and even after the China war had started, the Indian mutineers as well,[257] all in rapid succession and within the same decade. Such were the dynamics of imperialism. Such too, was the strangeness of Chinese politics that the Chinese should have contributed

251. James Bruce, eighth earl of Elgin and twelfth earl of Kincardine (1811–63), was formerly governor of Jamaica (1842–6) and governor-general of Canada (1846–54). When Lord Palmerston formed his first ministry in February 1855, he offered Elgin the chancellorship of the duchy of Lancaster with a seat in the Cabinet. But Elgin declined, reportedly wishing to maintain an independent position in Parliament. In 1857, he was appointed plenipotentiary to settle the *Arrow* dispute. After his mission to China he, in the spring of 1859, accepted Palmerston's offer of postmaster general. In 1861, he was appointed governor-general of India, where he died in 1863. Much insight into the man may be obtained in Theodore C. B. Walrond (ed.), *Letters and Journals of James, Eighth Earl of Elgin* (London, John Murray, 1872).
252. Sir James Hope Grant, *Incidents in the China War of 1860*, compiled from the private journals of Sir Hope Grant by H. Knollys (London, William Blackwood, 1875), p. 209.
253. Mao, 'The Chinese Revolution', *Selected Works*, v. 2, p. 314. Mao's views on this score have been, and still are, widely accepted by Chinese historians on the mainland as a guiding principle in writing modern Chinese history. Consequently, numerous monographs have been devoted to the Opium War, but none to the *Arrow* War except those by Professors Jiang Mengyin and Wei Jianyou. Oddly enough, although the historians in Taiwan do not so revere Mao, they also seem to have concentrated on the Opium War at the expense of the *Arrow* War.
254. See Chapter 16.
255. The Crimean War.
256. The *Arrow* War.
257. The Indian Mutiny, from 10 May 1857.

financially to these British endeavours.[258] Perhaps this was no stranger than the British merchants' selling lead and shot to the Chinese at the beginning of the *Arrow* War, commodities which were then fired back at the British servicemen.[259]

All this seems so unreal and yet so true. So do Kennedy's allegations about the flag; Parkes's passion; Bowring's obsession; 'Monster' Yeh and the false edict; the chants of 'Rule, Britannia'; the cries of 'Vox populi, Vox Dei'; the attempted manipulation of the press; Clarendon's 'law of force' versus Cobden's 'justice and humanity'; Palmerston's 'national interests, national rights, national dignity'[260] as against the unmentionable traffic in opium; and the bread poisoning; all these strands combined to weave deadly dreams.[261]

258. I hope to investigate the Chinese responses to the dynamics of imperialism in a separate book.
259. See Chapter 17.
260. Lord Palmerston's election speech at Tiverton, as printed in *The Times*, Monday, 30 March 1857.
261. I am grateful to Professor Mark Elvin, who, in August 1994, suggested to me the title of *Deadly Dreams*. (It may be remembered that he also suggested the main title of my previous book, *The Origins of an Heroic Image*.)

Part II
The pretext for imperialism

The acting British consul, Harry Parkes, claimed that the Union Jack had been hauled down from the mast of a ship called the *Arrow* on 8 October 1856.[1] This was the famous *Arrow* incident. Commissioner Yeh denied Parkes's claim.[2] The dispute led to war. It is important, therefore, to find out what actually happened. Let us begin then with a brief history of the *Arrow* and of the *Arrow* incident, then examine the conditions in which the incident was documented, and decide how much weight may be attached to each piece of evidence. In this way, we may better assess the realities of the casus belli.

1. Parkes to Bowring, Desp. 150, 8 October 1856, FO228/213; see also Parkes to Yeh, 8 October 1856, enclosed in ibid.
2. Yeh to Parkes, 24 October 1856, Parl. Papers 1857, v. 12, p. 89; see also Yeh to Seymour, 31 October 1856, Parl. Papers 1857.

2
An international incident:
'That wretched question of the *Arrow*'

I. The history of the *Arrow*

The *Arrow* was a lorcha, a kind of Western schooner with Chinese rigging. According to one of her sailors, she was built in China in 1854 by a Chinese subject called Su Acheng.[1] She was subsequently sold to another Chinese subject, Fong Ah-ming,[2] who had lived in Hong Kong for about ten years and who registered the ship there on 27 September 1855. On the basis of this registration, Consul Parkes maintained that the *Arrow* was a bona fide British vessel.[3]

By her colonial registration, the *Arrow* was granted permission to fly the British flag and claim British protection.[4] Her crew consisted entirely of Chinese sailors, with the exception of the captain, who, as mentioned, was an Irishman of age twenty-one by the name of Thomas Kennedy. He candidly admitted that he had been put on board merely as nominal master of the vessel.[5] Thus, here was a vessel built in China, owned by a Chinese subject, manned by a Chinese crew, and sailing in Chinese waters, but claiming British protection. This ambiguity could easily give rise to misconceptions as to her

1. Yeh to Parkes, 14 October 1856, enclosed in Parkes to Bowring, Desp. 158, 14 October 1856, FO288/213. The name Su Acheng is here romanized according to the Chinese characters given in Yeh to Seymour, 31 October 1856, FO682/100.1. See next note.
2. Extract from *China Mail*, 11 December 1856, Parl. Papers 1857, v. 12, pp. 190–1. I have not been able to discover the Chinese characters for Fong Ah-Ming. Probably this is the Cantonese version of Fang Aming. Some Chinese local gazetteers (*Nanhai xianzhi* 2.60b, *Panyu xianzhi* 22.32b, and *Guangzhou fuzhi* 82.311) recorded that the owner was Xiao Cheng, which almost certainly refers to the same person as Su Acheng. If this were the case, then these gazetteers might have mistaken the builder for the owner.
3. S. Lane-Poole, *The Life of Sir Harry Parkes* (London, MacMillan 1894), v. 1, p. 228, quoting one of Parkes's private letters dated 14 November 1856.
4. In March 1855, the local legislature of Hong Kong passed an ordinance to this effect (Hansard, 3d series, v. 144, col. 1160).
5. See Parkes to Bowring, Desp. 153, 10 October 1856, FO228/213.

43

nationality.[6] If she were at sea flying British colours, she could be identified as a British vessel. But if she sailed into a port in China, lowered her flags in accordance with British nautical practice,[7] dropped anchor, and her British captain left, she could be mistaken for a Chinese boat.

On 3 October 1856, the *Arrow* entered the harbour of Canton,[8] having recruited on 27 September 1856 two assistant navigators, Li Mingtai and Liang Jianfu.[9] These two men had belonged to a gang of pirates who plundered two Chinese cargo ships on 6 September 1856. These cargo ships were the property of a member of the Chinese gentry called Huang Liankai. He was with his ships when the pirates closed in on them. An exchange of fire ensued, which lasted from 7 A.M. to 4 P.M. He and his men were overcome and four of his sailors were killed. He jumped overboard and escaped. On 8 October 1856, he arrived at Canton and immediately detected Li Mingtai among the crew of the *Arrow*. He recognized Li to be the pirate who, during the battle, had worn a red turban and red girdle, who was without one or two of his front teeth and had cheered on his fellow pirates to keep up their fire. At once he reported to the harbour authorities.[10]

A squad of marine police was despatched to the *Arrow*. The commanding officer, Captain Liang Guoding, subsequently claimed that when he and his men arrived at the ship, they did not see any flag on the masts, or any foreigner on board, but only Chinese sailors, whereupon they took the entire crew into custody[11] as they would have done with the sailors of any suspect Chinese vessel. When the captain of the *Arrow* returned, he found that all his crew 'had been taken out, and were in the Mandarin boats alongside'. He asked the Chinese officers to leave behind two of the *Arrow*'s sailors to look after the vessel, 'and they did so'.[12]

6. The fact that her owner was resident in Hong Kong does not mean that she belonged to a British subject. The attorney-general of the colony pointed out that hardly any one of the 60,000 Chinese inhabitants there could be legally called a British subject (Hansard, 3d series, v. 144, col. 1161). Most of the Chinese inhabitants, apart from the indigenous peasant minority, were itinerant workers who went there to make a living, as did so many merchants and labourers in China (see also FO233/185-8 series, which are Chinese documents concerning the administration of Hong Kong between 1845 and 1906).
7. Costin, *Great Britain and China*, p. 207.
8. Parkes to Bowring, Desp. 153, FO228/213.
9. Yeh to Parkes, 10 October 1856, enclosed in ibid., Desp. 154, 10 October 1856, and containing the deposition of Wu Aren. The names Liang Mingtai, Liang Jianfu, and Wu Aren are here romanized according to the Chinese characters found in Yeh to Seymour, 31 October 1856, FO682/1989/15.
10. Yeh to Parkes, 10 October 1856 (enclosed in ibid., Desp. 154, 10 October 1856, FO228/213), containing the deposition of Huang Liankai. The Chinese original of this despatch has now been tracked down. It may be found in FO228/904, pp. 318a–19b.
11. Yeh to Parkes, 14 October 1856, enclosed in Parkes to Bowring, Desp. 158, 14 October 1856, FO228/213.
12. Kennedy's deposition, 9 October 1856, enclosed in Parkes to Bowring, Desp. 155, 11 October 1856, FO228/213.

II. How the evidence of both sides was taken

Let us verify the claims of the Chinese officers. Even English documents support their assertion that no foreigner was on board the *Arrow* when they reached the vessel. Captain Kennedy admitted that he was at the time breakfasting in another vessel called the *Dart*.[13] His friends, the captain of the *Dart*, John Leach, and the captain of the *Chusan*, Charles Earl, who were eating with him, testified to the same effect.[14] The other claim of the Chinese officers, that no flags were flying, was challenged by Kennedy and his friends, who professed to have watched the incident from a distance.[15] The testimonies of these three men were supported by those of the two Chinese sailors, who, at Kennedy's request, were left behind to guard the *Arrow* after the rest of the crew had been taken away. This discrepancy between the evidence of the two sides now calls for an examination of the circumstances in which the depositions on the British side were made.

After twelve members of his crew of fourteen were led away by the Chinese officers, Kennedy lost no time in reporting his version of the incident to Consul Parkes. He claimed that Chinese officers had boarded his vessel, arrested his sailors, and hauled down the Union Jack, which he insisted had been flying on the mizenmast. Parkes's immediate reaction, as he afterwards told his superior, Sir John Bowring,[16] and Commissioner Yeh, was hesitation to 'rely solely on the master's account of so gross an outrage'. He at once despatched 'people' to make inquiries. The result of these inquiries led him, so he implied, to conclude that 'the British lorcha *Arrow*, while lying with her colours flying in the river near the Dutch Folly', had been boarded by Chinese officers, who carried away nearly all of her crew, 'and added to this act of violence, the significant insult of hauling down the national ensign'.[17]

These statements provoke a number of questions. First, Parkes had a reputation for impatience and swift action – does his hesitation to believe Kennedy's story mean that he had doubts about the honesty of the captain? Second, who were the 'people' he sent to make inquiries – were they his Chinese employees or junior consular officials? Third, whom did his agents question – Chinese bystanders, if any, or British captains like John Leach? This third query is directly related to the second because a serious problem of

13. Ibid.
14. Leach's deposition, 9 October 1856, enclosed in Parkes to Bowring, Desp. 155, 11 October 1856, FO228/213; Earl's deposition, 16 October 1856, enclosed in Parkes to Bowring, Desp. 160, 16 October 1856, FO228/213.
15. Leach's deposition, 9 October 1856, enclosed in Parkes to Bowring, Desp. 155, 11 October 1856, FO228/213; Earl's deposition, 16 October 1856, enclosed in ibid., Desp. 160, 16 October 1856. The distance was estimated by Kennedy to be between 50 and 100 yards.
16. He was also the governor of Hong Kong and superintendent of trade.
17. Parkes to Bowring, Desp. 150, 8 October 1856, para. 1, FO228/213. The Dutch Folly (Haizhu) is an island in the middle of the Pearl River at Canton.

The pretext for imperialism

language and communication is involved. None of Parkes's papers, official or private, provide any answer to these questions. Furthermore, Parkes never managed to bring forward any of the 'witnesses' whom his agents were supposed to have questioned. Nor did he ever produce a written report from his agents as to the nature and result of their investigation.

Not only were Parkes's assertions not documented, but the language he used in his communication to Yeh on the subject was highly emotional. His letter began, 'I hasten to bring to your Excellency's notice an insult of a very grave character, which calls for immediate reparation . . . , confident that your superior judgment will lead you at once to admit that an insult so publicly committed must be equally publicly atoned'.[18] The letter ended with a blatant threat to use force to obtain satisfaction. Kennedy's story and the subsequent report of Parkes's agents could hardly have accounted for this agitated state of mind. Parkes's anger and his dubious statement about the flag are the two key factors in our analysis, because it was Parkes who took the depositions on the following day (9 October 1856). It is therefore of some importance to discover why the young consul was so explosive.

Shortly after Parkes had heard from his agents that the twelve sailors of the *Arrow* were detained in Chinese war junks nearby, he went to one of them to claim the men. His descriptions of the episode are interesting. To Bowring he simply reported that the Chinese marines refused to accede to his demand, adding that they intimated 'very distinctly that they would oppose with force any attempt on my part to take the men under my charge'.[19] These few words suggest that more must have been involved. If Parkes had not made it clear that he was going to take away the men by force, why was it necessary for the Chinese marine police to make it equally clear that they would resist such an action by force?

His despatch to Yeh gave more details. He 'required' the Chinese officer in charge of the naval vessel 'to bring his prisoners to the British Consulate, there to await examination; but this he refused to do, and upon my claiming them and insisting upon their being delivered to me, he made a display of force, and threatened me with violence if I attempted to take them with me'.[20] This was as much of the episode as Parkes would have liked to be known officially. He disclosed more details in a private letter: 'They refused to do so [give up the sailors], laughed at me . . . threatened me with violence, and I was actually struck one blow, though to this circumstance I have never made official allusion, as I wished to keep every personal feature out of view'.[21]

18. Parkes to Yeh, 8 October 1856, enclosed in ibid.
19. Parkes to Bowring, Desp. 150, 8 October 1856, para. 2, FO228/213.
20. Parkes to Yeh, 8 October 1856, para. 3, enclosed in ibid.
21. Lane-Poole, *Parkes*, v. 1, p. 229, quoting one of Parkes's private letters dated 14 November 1856.

An international incident

Thus, it seems that although the Chinese officers had expressed their determination to resist, Parkes apparently tried to push his way through. A scuffle ensued, in which Parkes was physically assaulted.

Parkes had demanded in his communication to Yeh that 'an insult so publicly committed must be equally publicly atoned'.[22] The insult referred to has always been taken to mean that to the Union Jack. If we read the full text of Parkes's communication, we may find that this was not the case:

British Consulate
Canton 8 October 1856

Sir,

I hasten to bring to your Excellency's notice an insult of a very grave character, which calls for immediate reparation.

This morning shortly after eight o'clock a Chinese war boat boarded an English lorcha, the 'Arrow', lying at anchor in the river near the Dutch Folly, and regardless of the remonstrances of her master, an Englishman, seized, bound and carried off twelve of her Chinese crew, and hauled down the English colours which were then flying. Hesitating to rely solely on the master's account of so gross an outrage, I at once despatched people to make enquiries, and found that the facts were as he had stated, and that the war boat said to be under the command of Leang-kwo-ting [Liang Guoding], a captain (Show-pe) [Shoubei] in the imperial service, after leaving the lorcha, had dropped down the river, and was lying off the Yung-tsing [Yongqing] Gate, with the crew of the lorcha still on board as prisoners.

On receiving this intelligence, I proceeded in person to the war boat accompanied by H. M. Vice-Consul, and explained to the officer whom I found in charge called Le-yung-shing [Li Yongsheng] the gravity of the error committed by the said war boat in boarding and carrying off by force of arms the crew of an English vessel and the gross indignity offered to the national flag by hauling down the lorcha's ensign. I also required him to bring his prisoners to the British Consulate, there to await examination; but this he refused to do, and upon my claiming them and insisting upon their being delivered to me, he made a display of force, and threatened me with violence if I attempted to take them with me.

I have therefore to lay the case before your Excellency, confident that your superior judgment will lead you at once to admit that an insult so publicly committed must be equally publicly atoned. I therefore request your Excellency to direct that the men who have been carried away from the 'Arrow' be returned by the Captain Leang-kwo-ting [Liang Guoding] to that vessel in my presence; and if accused of any crime, they may then be conveyed to the British Consulate, where in conjunction with proper officers deputed by your Excellency for the purpose, I shall be prepared to investigate the case.

At the same time that I address your Excellency on this subject, I am submitting, both to H. M. Plenipotentiary and Commodore in command of H. M. naval forces in this river, a report of what has occurred, and I should add that the said lorcha being at

22. Parkes to Yeh, 8 October 1856, para. 4, enclosed in Parkes to Bowring, Desp. 150, 8 October 1856, FO228/213.

present detained here, in consequence of the seizure of her crew, has a claim upon your Excellency's government for the expenses which this delay occasions her.

I have &c.

[signed] Harry Parkes[23]

In this despatch we find a specific description of how this insult should be publicly atoned. Before the scuffle, Parkes merely requested the return of the Chinese sailors 'to the British Consulate';[24] afterwards, he wanted the Chinese captain to return them to the *Arrow* in his presence.[25] If the public insult Parkes had in mind had been the hauling down of the Union Jack, the reparation should have been the rehoisting, with due ceremony, of the flag by the Chinese officers involved, instead of the return of the sailors by the arresting officer in Parkes's presence. Parkes's overweening desire to avenge his humiliating physical defeat never abated and was apparent in every communication he subsequently addressed to Commissioner Yeh. Even when Yeh eventually had all twelve sailors delivered to the British Consulate, Parkes still refused to receive them because they were not given up in the public manner 'required in my letter of the 8th'.[26]

Thus, the humbling experience apparently produced Parkes's emotional tumult just described, and it probably prompted him to make those dubious statements about the flag. More important, it changed his attitude towards the *Arrow* incident. As mentioned, he was initially doubtful about the truth of Kennedy's story. After the scuffle, he wrote to Bowring as if he were absolutely certain that the Union Jack had been flying over the *Arrow*.

It is pertinent to see how the telegraphic service reported the *Arrow* incident: 'A lorcha under the British flag at anchor off Canton was boarded on the 8th of October by a Chinese force, and 12 of the crew seized. Consul Parkes proceeded on board, and was insulted and threatened with violence. The remonstrances made to Yeh were treated with contempt'.[27] There was absolutely no reference to the crucial allegation that a flag had been pulled down. Even the much more detailed overland mail could enable *The Times* to comment only: 'There are, indeed, matters in dispute, such as whether the lorcha out of which the men were taken was carrying British colours, and whether the Consul was entirely justified in the steps that he took'.[28]

23. Ibid. When romanized, Captain Leang should be spelled Liang. The Chinese version of this document has now been located in FO228/904, pp. 316a–17b, which has enabled me, inter al., to identify the Chinese characters involved.
24. Parkes to Yeh, 8 October 1856, para. 3, enclosed in Parkes to Bowring, Desp. 150, 8 October 1856, FO228/213.
25. Parkes to Yeh, 8 October 1856, para. 4, enclosed in Parkes to Bowring Desp. 150, 8 October 1856, FO228/213.
26. Parkes to Seymour, 22 October 1856, Parl. Papers 1857, v. 12, pp. 85–6, para. 6.
27. *The Times*, 29 December 1856.
28. *The Times*, 2 January 1857.

But there was something which neither the British journalists in Canton and Hong Kong nor even Bowring and Admiral Seymour were expected to know. It was the letter in Chinese which Parkes sent to Yeh, and which has now come to light. Herein, the critical passage about the insult to the flag is substantially different from the English version. What, in the English version, is 'an insult so publicly committed must be equally publicly atoned'[29] has become, in the Chinese version, 'the arrest of the lorcha's crew and the hauling down of her flag have been witnessed by all. This public insult to our nation must be equally publicly atoned'.[30] Why was Parkes vague to his English-speaking readers about the alleged insult, but specific to Yeh? He wanted 'to keep every personal feature out of view'[31] of his superiors, while requiring a public humiliation of Captain Liang to be 'witnessed by all'.

There is another passage in Parkes's letter which may be regarded as somewhat vague in the English version, but quite specific in the Chinese. Compare the second paragraph of Parkes's English letter with this: 'At 8:30 this morning, some Chinese marine boats sailed to the Dutch Folly area. Their officers boarded a lorcha of our nation. Although the English captain of the lorcha was there to stop them, they nonetheless arrested and took away twelve of his sailors'.[32] One wonders where Parkes obtained this information. It could not have been from the captain of the *Arrow*, otherwise he would contradict himself when he testified the next day in the British consulate that he was not on board when the arrests took place, and that when he hurried back to his ship, all his crew had already been taken out and 'were in the Mandarin boats alongside'.[33] Despite this deposition, with which Parkes was familiar,[34] Parkes persisted in alleging to Yeh that the Chinese officers, 'in the face of the remonstrances of her master, an Englishman, seized, bound, and carried away' the *Arrow*'s sailors.[35]

29. Parkes to Yeh, 8 October 1856, para. 4, enclosed in Parkes to Bowring, Desp. 150, 8 October 1856, FO228/213.
30. Parkes to Yeh, 8 October 1856, FO228/904, pp. 316a–17b: p. 317a. The retranslation is mine.
31. Lane-Poole, *Parkes*, v. 1, p. 229, quoting one of Parkes's private letters dated 14 November 1856.
32. Parkes to Yeh, 8 October 1856, FO228/904, pp. 316a–17b: p. 317a. The retranslation is mine.
33. Kennedy's deposition, 9 October 1856, enclosed in Parkes to Bowring, Desp. 155, 11 October 1856, FO228/213.
34. Parkes to Bowring, Desp. 151, 9 October 1856, FO228/213. The deposition was taken at the British consulate at Canton and sworn before the vice-consul, Charles A. Winchester. It is not clear whether Parkes and Winchester jointly took the statement which was then sworn before Winchester, who formally signed the document, or whether Winchester took it alone. Most probably the former, because Parkes wrote to Bowring, 'I have also taken in the course of the day several depositions confirmatory of the facts set forth in my letter of yesterday' (FO228/213, Parkes to Bowring, Desp. 151, 9 October 1856). In any case, Parkes showed himself to be fully aware of the contents of Kennedy's deposition by stating, in a private letter, that the 'master was away at the moment'. Lane-Poole, *Parkes*, v. 1, p. 228.
35. Parkes to Yeh, 21 October 1856, enclosed in Bowring to Clarendon, Desp. 76, 27 October 1856, FO17/251.

If Parkes could claim that the captain was on board the *Arrow* when initially he did not actually know, and continued to make that claim even after the captain himself had testified to the contrary, then was Parkes similarly capable of claiming that the flag was flying when it was not?

He gave Yeh twenty-four hours to reply.[36] Yeh half-apologized, saying that of course Chinese criminals hiding in British ships would be claimed through the consul; but the *Arrow* was not British-owned, no British flag was flying, and no foreigner was on board when the incident took place.[37] Parkes insisted that unless the public atonement was to be conceded, 'it is in vain for you to again address me on the subject'.[38]

Now let us look at the depositions by Kennedy and others in some detail. Parkes said that the day after the *Arrow* incident, he took 'depositions confirmatory of the facts set forth in my letter of yesterday'.[39] One of the witnesses testified that he had heard the deposition of Thomas Kennedy read over to him before he made his own statement, and that he fully confirmed Kennedy's story.[40] How irregular. It seems, therefore, that Parkes had set out to take testimonies to confirm his earlier assertions which, in turn, had been based on Kennedy's verbal report. Furthermore, he could shape the depositions to his satisfaction when he took them.

His role was particularly important when he took the testimonies of the two Chinese sailors left to guard the *Arrow*. These sailors spoke little or no English, and Parkes had to interrogate them closely in Chinese, then translate their answers into English and finally put them together as formal statements. In so doing, Parkes could compose the depositions in the manner he desired.[41] This is a time-consuming task and probably explains why he was unable to send the depositions to Hong Kong until two days later, on 11 October, although he continued to communicate with Bowring every day during the intervening period.[42]

One can see, therefore, that the circumstances surrounding Parkes's evidence do not really inspire confidence.

III. An assessment of the evidence on both sides

An examination of the evidence on both sides should enable us to decide how much weight we can attach to any part. First, let us consider Parkes's side.

36. Ibid.   37. Yeh to Parkes, 21 October 1856, Parl. Papers 1857, v. 12, p. 82.
38. Parkes to Yeh, 22 October 1856, Parl. Papers 1857, v. 12, p. 83.
39. Parkes to Bowring, Desp. 151, 9 October 1856, FO228/213.
40. Leach's deposition, 9 October 1856, enclosed in Parkes to Bowring. Desp. 155, 11 October 1856, FO228/213.
41. To date, I have not been able to locate the Chinese originals of these depositions. Unlike Parkes's letters to Yeh, therefore, I have not been able to compare the two versions.
42. Parkes to Bowring, Desp. 155, 11 October 1856, FO228/213. See next note.

An international incident

On 9 October 1856, Parkes took four depositions: by Kennedy, John Leach, and the two Chinese sailors. Leach made his deposition immediately after Kennedy, having, as he stated, 'heard the deposition of Thomas Kennedy read over to me', and saying that the purpose of his testimony was to 'fully confirm the statements contained in it'.[43] He added no detail other than that given by Kennedy and frequently used the same language and expressions. Therefore his testimony can be regarded as only an abridged repetition of Kennedy's. It is not unduly sceptical to suppose that his chief concern was to support whatever Kennedy had said.[44] One can also see the hand of Parkes in shaping this document, as, to say the least, it is most unusual for an officer to read the testimony of the first witness over to the second for confirmation. In this light, the statement by John Leach can hardly be regarded as reliable independent testimony.

It is equally difficult to put much faith in the depositions of the two Chinese sailors. We cannot know what pressures they were under by the time their statements were made – the day after the incident – or what instructions Kennedy gave before they faced their inquisitor.[45] The phraseology and details of the statement by the first sailor are on the whole different from Kennedy's, which is to be expected. Although he was present, unlike Kennedy and Leach, the crucial passage of his testimony in which the insult to the flag is alleged adds no detail to Kennedy's statement, except that the Chinese officer 'flung [the ensign] on the deck without unreeving it from the halyards'.[46] This embellishment hardly adds a significant element of conviction. Moreover, there is no mention in this evidence of the Blue Peter, which all other sources agree should normally also have been flying if the Union Jack was flying[47] (and, supposing the validity of Kennedy's allegations, would have been pulled down with it). The only other support for Parkes's case is his own brief declaration about the second Chinese sailor: 'Leung A-yung, on being examined by the Consul deposed to the same facts as Chin A-shing. He distinctly saw the flag hauled down by one of the soldiers. He and another man were busily engaged in a sampan unmooring the lorcha[48] at the moment when the mandarins boarded'.[49]

43. Leach's deposition, 9 October 1856, enclosed in ibid.
44. If Kennedy had been telling the truth, then of course it follows that this was probably what Leach would have said.
45. Parkes had already acquired a considerable reputation as a harsh but successful interrogator of Chinese of all classes. For an analysis of the character of Parkes, see G. Daniels, 'Sir Harry Parkes: British Representative in Japan, 1856–83', unpublished D.Phil. thesis, University of Oxford, 1967, Chapter 1.
46. Chin A-shing's deposition, 9 October 1856, enclosed in Parkes to Bowring, Desp. 155, 9 October 1856, FO228/213. See next few notes.
47. Costin, *Great Britain and China*, p. 207; Clarendon, 24 February 1857, Hansard, 3d series, v. 144, col. 1200.
48. This business of unmooring the lorcha under the circumstances is most peculiar and will be dealt with shortly in this chapter.
49. Parke's account of his interrogation of Leang A-yung, 9 October 1856, enclosed in Parkes to

The pretext for imperialism

As we shall see, it is impossible to discount the possibility that Leung A-yung was simply saying what he had been told to say. It thus seems that the evidence of Captain Leach and the two Chinese sailors cannot be relied upon as trustworthy. Since it is apparent that Parkes built his case against the Chinese on four documents, three of which are of little value, the basic consideration in evaluating Parkes's case is simply whether Kennedy's version is true.

Here, an important point deserves attention. Charles Earl, the U.S. captain of the lorcha *Chusan*, who was breakfasting with Kennedy and Leach when the incident occurred, did not make any statement along with them on 9 October. His presence and activities on the preceding day, it is to be noted, were mentioned in the depositions of the other two captains and could not have escaped Parkes's notice. One would expect both Parkes and Kennedy to have been anxious to acquire a deposition from him to strengthen their case, but Earl did not make one. Was he unable or did he decline to do so? It is not true that he was unavailable, because we know he was still at Canton as late as 16 October 1856. Possibly he declined. It is not clear why he eventually changed his mind and made a deposition on 16 October to corroborate Kennedy's story.[50] Douglas Hurd has emphasised the importance of Earl's statement. He has argued that since Leach and the two Chinese sailors were interested parties, their statements could not be taken seriously; but Earl was a significant witness because he was an American and therefore disinterested.[51] This view is not convincing. Although an American, Earl was apparently another captain of convenience, like Kennedy and Leach.[52] He was breakfasting with them during the incident, and he also went to the scene with them afterwards.[53] Clearly he was quite as involved as Leach, and if Leach's statement cannot be taken seriously, neither can his.

After Bowring received Earl's deposition, he failed to send it to London as he had the others.[54] He did not even mention it in his correspondence.[55] When he

Bowring, Desp. 155, 9 October 1856, FO228/213. This claim about unmooring the *Arrow* was not corroborated by any other evidence. I have not been able to find the Chinese characters of Chin A-shing or Leung A-yung. Consequently they are given here in their original form, which appears to be Cantonese.

50. Earl's deposition, 16 October 1856, enclosed in Parkes to Bowring, Desp. 160, 16 October 1856, FO228/213. This issue will be explored later in this chapter.
51. Hurd, *Arrow War*, p. 30. Hurd further maintains that Earl gave evidence seven months after the incident, giving as reference FO17/269. If one compares his reference with that in my footnotes, it is clear that Hurd has not read the documents himself (see my previous note and following notes).
52. Earl identified himself as the captain of 'the English lorcha "Chusan"' which, like the *Arrow*, was probably another Chinese-owned vessel registered in Hong Kong and thereby claimed to be 'English'.
53. Earl's deposition, n.d., enclosed in Bowring to Clarendon, Desp. 224, 7 May 1857, FO17/268. See also encl. 2, in ibid., which was Parkes to Bowring, 16 October 1856, and in which Parkes said that the deposition was taken 'today'.
54. Consequently Earl's statement is not among the Parliamentary Papers.
55. There is no allusion to it in Bowring's letters to Lord Clarendon until seven months later (see

52

finally did so,[56] it was already seven months after he and his countrymen had waged an undeclared war on Canton because of the incident.[57]

Next, Yeh's side. The assurances given by the Chinese commanding officer to Commissioner Yeh that the flag had not been insulted are open to similar doubts. If Kennedy had been telling the truth, Captain Liang and his men would have had good reason to lie. Here, three questions are critical. First, would the Chinese marine police, who had been checking the shipping in the harbour of Canton without incident since the Treaty of Nanking (1842), knowingly board a British ship?[58] It is improbable that they would have done so if the Union Jack were flying above the *Arrow*. Second, and assuming that the flag had been flying, would such experienced officers deliberately haul it down? Third, what could have been their motive to insult the flag? There was no conceivable motive. Unlike the nationalistic student protesters of the 1920s, or the hotheads among the Red Guards of the 1960s, these officers were not known to be either nationalistic or thoughtless. Even the Cantonese, who were often seen by the British as antiforeign, became hostile only when provoked. And the Cantonese police had a long history of being instructed by the Cantonese authorities to control the crowd whenever trouble appeared to be brewing.[59] There is not an iota of evidence to suggest that the Cantonese marine police were anything like the avant garde of antiforeignism. On the balance of probabilities, therefore, it seems unlikely that the Chinese officers would have knowingly boarded the ship or that they would have deliberately insulted the flag.

W. C. Costin cast doubt on the Chinese case when he wrote, 'The evidence in the possession of the Imperial Commissioner Yeh on the question of *ownership* was provided by a member of the crew lying bound with thongs before his interested inquisitors at the time he made his statement'.[60]

Such doubt cannot be sustained. It was not, of course, the question of ownership which was at issue. Neither British documents nor British historians have disputed that the *Arrow* was Chinese-owned. Why, then, did Costin denigrate the Chinese evidence over a nonissue? Did he try to denigrate, by implication, the Chinese evidence about the flag instead? If so, we must remember that the Chinese evidence about the flag had been

next note) or in his correspondence with his sons in England (Ryl. Eng. MSS 1228 and 1229 series).
56. Bowring to Clarendon, Desp. 224, 7 May 1857, FO17/268.
57. War remained undeclared to the very end.
58. In 1843, Great Britain and China signed the so-called Supplementary Treaty, a treaty supplementary to the Treaty of Nanking. In it, China signed away its sovereign right to search British vessels in Chinese waters for Chinese nationals suspected of having broken Chinese law. To apprehend such suspects, the Chinese authorities had to request their extradition through the British consul.
59. See Chapter 6.
60. Costin, *Great Britain and China*, p. 207. Emphasis added.

The pretext for imperialism

offered freely by the Chinese officer in charge and not by one of the detained sailors.[61]

The problem, then, is to determine who was telling the truth as to whether the Union Jack and the Blue Peter had been flying and were pulled down: the British officer (Kennedy), or the Chinese officer (Liang Guoding).

Costin wrote: 'That she was flying the British flag was in itself probable, as she appears to have had flying also the "Blue Peter" – the signal that she was shortly departing. For when in port it was not the custom to fly the national flag'.[62] Here, Costin conceded on the one hand that 'in port it was not the custom to fly the national flag'; but on the other, he insisted that the British flag was proboably flying, since – presumably on Earl's sole testimony – the Blue Peter 'appeared' to have been flying.

Costin's strained defence makes the case all the more thought provoking. It confirms Yeh's observation that 'it is an established regulation with the lorchas of your honourable nation, that when they come to anchor they lower their colours, and do not re-hoist them until they again get under way. We have clear proof that when this lorcha was boarded her colours were not flying; how then could they have been taken down?'[63] No reply was ever received from Parkes, Bowring, or Seymour to this statement.[64]

Thus, as Yeh stated, Costin admitted, and the British authorities did not deny, it is most unlikely that the Union Jack was flying unless the *Arrow* was already leaving port. It seems, however, at least improbable that she was literally 'under way'. If that were the case, it is very strange that Kennedy was not aboard the ship. It is also strange that the ship's departure was never mentioned in the depositions which he, Leach, and Earl had made. It will be remembered that Leung A-yung allegedly testified that he and another crewman were unmooring the *Arrow* at the time the Chinese officials boarded. It is most unlikely that the crew would have unmoored the boat in the absence of the captain, as this would mean leaving without him.[65] One therefore feels almost certain that the second sailor had been told, as an afterthought, to testify that he was unmooring the lorcha when the flag was hauled down, so as to give the impression that the ship was preparing to leave and that her national ensign was already in place. On the contrary, Kennedy said in his statement that the *Arrow* was 'anchored' in the river when the incident occurred.

61. This is evident throughout Yeh's diplomatic correspondence on the subject. See FO228/213 passim.
62. Costin, *Great Britain and China*, p. 207.
63. Yeh to Parkes, 24 October 1856, Parl. Papers 1857, v. 12, p. 89; see also Yeh to Seymour, 31 October 1856, in ibid.
64. Derby, 24 February 1857, Hansard, 3d series, v. 144, col. 1166. See the preceding note.
65. The only alternative is that the crew tried to up-anchor when the Chinese harbour police came in sight, but this possibility is remote because the crew would have no way of knowing that the police were actually coming to get them.

An international incident

If the vessel was not sailing out of port, her colours would not under normal circumstances be up. This probably explains why the foreign secretary, Lord Clarendon, on receiving the reports on the *Arrow* incident, was obliged to argue that 'even if the flag had not been actually flying at the moment, it is obvious that the national character of the lorcha was well known to the authorities'.[66] It also helps to explain why Parkes first hesitated to accept Kennedy's story. Therefore, instead of taking immediate action, Parkes sent his agents to make inquiries while he checked the ship's register. There he found that the *Arrow*'s papers were still in his possession.[67] He could have come to only one conclusion: the vessel could not possibly have lifted anchor. By law, a British captain had to deposit his papers with the British consul when his ship entered port, and was not allowed to sail again until he had regained the papers from the consulate with the proper stamps. This enabled the consul to control the ships and to check frauds. If the papers were still in the consulate, how dared the boat set sail?

Kennedy gave the time of the incident as between 8 and 8:30 A.M.[68] The consulate did not open until 10 A.M.[69] Even if Kennedy had planned to arrive punctually at the consulate at 10 A.M. to go through the formalities, it would be at least 10:30 before he could be on board again. It is therefore inconceivable that the vessel would be unmoored before 8 A.M. while he was away for breakfast with his fellow captains of convenience, because, when he returned with the register, the ship would have been drifting for two or three hours on the ebb tide[70] and would have been out of sight of Canton.

It is significant that a local newspaper, the *Friend of China*, reported that the Portuguese master and crew of lorcha no. 83, who watched the incident from nearby, had corroborated the testimony of the Chinese officers that no flags were flying on board the *Arrow*.[71] In his reply, Lord Clarendon, the foreign secretary, was unable to challenge this allegation when made in Parliament. All he could do was to declare that 'the *Arrow* was at sea, the 'Blue Peter' was up, the British flag was flying, and there can be no doubt, whatever, that a deliberate insult was intended to both that vessel and to the British flag'.[72] But, as we have seen, there remains considerable doubt about these assertions. Costin, being unable to produce any evidence other than the statement 'averred on oath by Kennedy',[73] argued that the

66. Clarendon to Bowring, 10 December 1856, Parl. Papers 1857, v. 12, pp. 169–70.
67. Lane-Poole, *Parkes*, v. 1, p. 228, quoting Parkes's letter to his wife, 14 November 1856.
68. Kennedy's deposition, 9 October 1856, enclosed in Parkes to Bowring, Desp. 155, 11 October 1856, FO228/213.
69. Parkes's letter to Patterson, 27 October 1852, quoted in Lane-Poole, *Parkes*, p. 169.
70. Earl's deposition, 16 October 1856, enclosed in Parkes to Bowring, Desp. 160, 16 October 1856, FO228/213.
71. Derby, 24 February 1857, Hansard, 3d series, v. 144, col. 1166.
72. Clarendon, 24 February 1857, Hansard, 3d series, v. 144, col. 1200.
73. Costin, *Great Britain and China*, p. 207.

Hoppo[74] must have been apprised of the *Arrow*'s status by the consul who held her papers.[75] Costin's argument seems to suggest that he was not too familiar with the manner in which Chinese institutions functioned. It was, of course, not the Hoppo who despatched the marine police to the *Arrow*. The Hoppo and the commanding officer of the marine police were two separate and independent functionaries.[76]

Whether or not Parkes performed his duty of apprising the Chinese authorities of the *Arrow*'s status is an open question. On 3 October he had accepted the register of the *Arrow*, which was already out of date. By 8 October it was eleven days out of date, yet he had taken no steps to enforce its renewal, although Hong Kong was within twelve hours by steam. Despite his doubts about Kennedy's sincerity, and the expired colonial register, Parkes felt himself duty-bound to demand the return of the crew. His unwise scuffle with the Chinese officers apparently unbalanced his attitude considerably. He subsequently wrote Bowring a self-contradictory report that the *Arrow* was boarded 'while lying with her colours flying'.[77]

IV. Why give false evidence?

A plausible reason for the Chinese officers to have given false depositions has always been clear to historians: it was illegal and outrageous to haul down the Union Jack. There had been cases in which lorchas similar to the *Arrow* were stopped by Chinese patrol boats for routine checks and were found to be engaged in smuggling salt – one of the most serious offences in China because salt was a government monopoly. However, since these lorchas were intercepted when they were actually sailing and had their British flags flying, the Chinese officers detained the vessels but did not show any disrespect to the British ensign.[78] Therefore one may assume that Chinese officers would not normally do anything improper to foreign flags.

Equally, if one can no longer be confident that the depositions on Parkes's side are to be trusted, it is necessary to enquire what reason, if any, Kennedy and the others might have had to lie. There are two clues as to why their evidence may be called into question: the validity of the *Arrow*'s papers and the nature of her activities. As mentioned, her register was already out of date

74. The Hoppo was the chief superintendent of the customhouse at Canton. Apparently it was a foreign corruption of Hubu (Ministry of Finance), which was a misunderstanding. The superintendent was sent not by the Ministry of Finance but by the imperial household in Beijing.
75. Costin, *Great Britain and China*, p. 207.
76. See Wong, *Yeh Ming-ch'en*, Chapter 3.
77. Parkes to Bowring, Desp. 150, 8 October 1856, para. 1, FO228/213.
78. See, e.g., Bowring to Yeh, 21 November 1855, FO682/1987/46; and Yeh to Bowring, 12 December 1855, FO682/1988/31. Both documents are in Chinese.

when it was handed to Parkes on 3 October 1856. It was not until 10 October, two days after the *Arrow* incident, that Parkes made any reference to the register: 'I should mention that the 'Arrow' is sailing under a colonial certificate of registry, renewable annually, bearing the date Hong Kong, 27 September 1855'. Even then, Parkes did not point out explicitly that the register had expired. Instead, he went on to describe Kennedy as 'a very respectable man of his class'.[79] In other words, his class was not respectable, but Kennedy was an exception.

What was this class of 'nominal captains'? They were 'nearly always runaway apprentices or idle young seamen', who had 'plenty of grog to drink, and have nothing else to do'.[80] In what way was Kennedy an exception to his class? Parkes did not specify. We do know, however, that 'Mr Kennedy and another witness [John Leach] both [stated] their ages at not above twenty-one. When we hear of young men of twenty-one being placed in positions of this sort, I think we may draw a very natural inference'.[81] Indeed, Kennedy's captaincy was so nominal that he did not even know who the owner of the *Arrow* was.[82]

On receiving Parkes's letter, Bowring made inquiries at the harbourmaster's office in Hong Kong. Thereupon he found that the register had expired and wrote to Parkes about it.[83] Parkes summoned Kennedy for an explanation and then gave Bowring the following reply: 'If the statement of the master is to be believed, it was because the lorcha was then at sea, and had not been in the waters of the colony since the 1st September last, that timely application had not been made for its renewal'.[84] The manner in which this reply was worded again shows Parkes's reservations about the sincerity of the young Irishman. Nevertheless, Parkes assured his superior in this letter that the *Arrow* was engaged in respectable business – the trading of rice between Hong Kong, Macao, and Canton.[85]

This assurance makes the case all the more dubious. The three places were very close to one another. Macao was 'within three or four hours' sail of Hong Kong'[86] and Canton 'within 12 hours by steam'.[87] If the *Arrow* left Hong Kong on 1 September 1856 (as claimed by her captain) and reached Canton on 3 October, what was she doing in the intervening thirty-two days? Bowring

79. Parkes to Bowring, Desp. 153, 10 October 1856, para. 3, FO228/213.
80. Cobden, 26 February 1857, Hansard, 3d series, v. 144, cols. 1399–1400. Cobden added that his information about these young captains of convenience was obtained through talking to an experienced U.S. captain.
81. Ibid., col. 1400.
82. Derby, 24 February 1857, Hansard, 3d series, v. 144, col. 1165.
83. Bowring to Parkes, Desp. 127, 11 October 1856, para. 3, FO228/213.
84. Parkes to Bowring, Desp. 156, 12 October 1856, para. 3, FO228/213.
85. Ibid.
86. Palmer, 3 March 1857, Hansard, 3d series, v. 144, col. 1736.
87. Derby, 24 February 1857, Hansard, 3d series, v. 144, col. 1170.

The pretext for imperialism

eventually found an answer, though too late to have any effect on the militant approach he had by then already sanctioned. On 1 April 1857 Bowring went to Macao to spend three days as the guest of the Portuguese governor. There he read in a French newspaper that the *Arrow* had been engaged in transactions with pirates, a fact known to the Portuguese authorities in Macao. Bowring asked his Portuguese host to verify the allegations and was dismayed to receive an affirmative answer. The governor further furnished Bowring with a copy of a deposition, dated 16 November 1856, to the effect that the Portuguese lorcha no. 27 had been attacked and captured by a group of pirates. The date of this occurrence is not specified in the document, which gives the impression that it was in September 1856 or not long before. One of the sailors, Jose do Rosario, who had been taken prisoner by the pirates, had at different times seen the *Arrow* receiving booty from them. He had also overheard a conversation between the pirates and the crew of the *Arrow*, whereby he learned that the *Arrow* was going to Macao. When he eventually managed to escape and return to Macao, he found the *Arrow* there. It was already 10 p.m. on the evening of 30 September 1856; he waited until the following morning to report to the authorities. Subsequently, a brig of war was sent to where the *Arrow* had moored but found that she had already left during the night.[88]

The revelation of the *Arrow*'s activities caused considerable embarrassment to Bowring. It took him a full week to muster sufficient courage to report this new information to London, stressing his willingness 'to punish any subject of Her Majesty, and to proceed with the utmost severity against all parties employing the British flag for purposes so nefarious'.[89]

This outburst by Bowring makes nonsense of Parkes's remark, often quoted to establish the trustworthiness of Kennedy's sworn statement, that the master of the *Arrow* was 'a very respectable man of his class'.[90] If Kennedy's crew had been using the vessel to receive stolen goods for pirates, it is hardly surprising that he should have been extremely anxious to prevent their arrest even for offences with which, as it turned out, neither he nor the *Arrow* was connected.[91] Therefore, when he saw from a distance that the Chinese police were boarding his vessel, he hurried back and tried to exploit his extraterritorial rights.[92] He

88. Bowring to Clarendon, Desp. 169, 8 April 1857, FO17/267; and enclosure: C. J. Antonio do Rozario's deposition, 16 November 1856.
89. Ibid. It is perhaps not surprising that Kennedy was in fact ordered to 'surrender his credentials' to the proper authorities in November 1856, less than two months after the incident. Parkes Papers, Bowring to Parkes, 28 November 1856.
90. Parkes to Bowring, Desp. 153, 10 October 1856, FO228/213.
91. Kennedy's deposition, 9 October 1856, enclosed in Parkes to Bowring, Desp. 155, 11 October 1856, FO228/213. It will be remembered that it was a pirate whom the *Arrow* had recruited not long before as one of its sailors that led to the arrest of the crew in Canton.
92. These rights, conferred by the Ango-Chinese Supplementary Treaty of 1843, forbade Chinese authorities from arresting Chinese offenders in British service – they could claim them only through the British consul.

urged the Chinese to believe that the *Arrow* was a foreign vessel by assuring them that he was the captain and by hoisting the Union Jack, as he afterwards stated, 'again'.[93] His performance failed to impress the Chinese officers. His only alternative was to try diplomatic channels. It is entirely possible that he fabricated the story about the insult to the flag to convince Parkes of the exceptional gravity of the situation, hoping the young consul would take immediate action before his crew were examined. As we know, Parkes did try 'to claim the men before they should be conveyed to a distance'.[94] Subsequently, nine and then ten of these dozen Chinese sailors were returned to Parkes as demanded, but he sent them back 'just as a man might send back goods . . . because they were not full weight'.[95] Parkes had his own outraged dignity to think of.

In the light of this analysis, it may be useful to examine further the depositions of John Leach and Charles Earl, who, like Kennedy, appear to have been captains of convenience. Leach's deposition, given on 9 October 1856, was perfunctory; Earl's silence on the same day might be interpreted as a similar reticence. Indeed, should Leach and Earl have been engaged in the same kind of illegal transactions as Kennedy, their reluctance to give evidence is understandable. They may have wished to avoid attracting attention to their own activities.

By 16 October 1856, when Earl finally corroborated Kennedy's story, not only Kennedy but also Parkes was anxious that he do so. As mentioned, Bowring had told Parkes on 11 October that the *Arrow*'s register had expired and therefore no longer entitled the ship to fly the British flag;[96] the startled Parkes had tried to defend Kennedy and to cover himself by saying, 'If the statement of the master is to be believed, it was because the lorcha was then at sea'.[97] Also by 16 October, the British had begun hostilities against China.[98] As Parkes was responsible for initiating these hostilities, he would be most anxious to prove to his superiors that the British flag had indeed been insulted. Under the circumstances, it is quite possible that Parkes cajoled Earl to give evidence to corroborate Kennedy's story. Earl agreed, probably because he now considered himself safe from the Chinese authorities since the British had started hostilities. Britain had defeated China before and seemed certain to do so again. Not surprisingly, Earl's evidence contained embellishments which

---

93. Kennedy's deposition, 9 October 1856, enclosed in Parkes to Bowring, Desp. 155, 11 October 1856, FO228/213.
94. Parkes to Bowring, Desp. 150, 8 October 1856, FO228/213.
95. Malmesbury, 26 February 1857, Hansard, 3d series, v. 144, cols. 13501.
96. Bowring to Parkes, Desp. 127, 11 October 1856, FO228/213.
97. Parkes to Bowring, Desp. 156, 12 Ocootber 1856, FO228/213.
98. The hostilities took the form of the Royal Navy's seizing, at the initiative of Parkes, a Chinese war junk. See Parkes to Bowring, 15 October 1856, Parl. Papers 1857, v. 12, pp. 70–1, para. 2.

appear tailor-made to affirm that the British flag had been insulted, and which were absent from Kennedy's own deposition:

> I saw them pull alongside the 'Arrow'. I passed the remark to Kennedy that the Mandarins were going alongside of his craft, he answered that he supposed they were going down as passengers. I then saw them go on board, and immediately after a Mandarin Chinaman hauling down the English Ensign. The 'Blue Peter' was also hauled down. I said to Kennedy, 'There comes your flag down', to which he replied, 'It is time for me to be on board'. I accompanied him, and John Leach, and when we got to the 'Arrow', I found her deck crowded with Mandarins and their people, and the lorcha's crew all except one man in the Mandarin boat. Kennedy told the boy to hoist the flag, *but I do not know whether it was in the cabin or on the deck*. The boy made some reply, which I took as a refusal to hoist it, and then Kennedy hoisted it himself. I do not understand Chinese, but I asked Kennedy at the time what the boy said to him, and he replied that the boy told him that the Mandarins had hauled down the flag, and he durst not hoist it.[99]

It is noteworthy that Earl should have added, apparently under questioning, that he did not know whether the flag was in the cabin or on the deck – if the flag had been hauled down, it would have been on the deck as Chin A-shing attested. W. C. Costin, in the course of defending the British case, ignored this business of Kennedy's asking the boy to hoist the flag.[100]

V. The law lords: Was the British flag flying?

The law lords used to constitute the highest legal authority in the British Empire. On the basis of Bowring's reports (with enclosures), what do they have to say as to whether the British flag was flying?

The distinguished jurist of international law, Lord Lyndhurst, said that the question was immaterial. The point was that the *Arrow* had no right to hoist the flag because her register had expired. Bowring had admitted as much.[101]

The lord chancellor[102] asserted that the flag was flying, claiming that both the English and Chinese evidence pointed to that conclusion. This assertion is extraordinary in more ways than one. First it alleges that even the Chinese officers indicated that the flag had been flying. Second, it suggests that his lordship was ignorant that the ship would not normally be flying the national ensign while at anchor. He then added that when the first complaint was made

---

99. Earl's deposition, n.d., enclosed in Bowring to Clarendon, Desp. 224, 7 May 1857, FO17/268. Emphasis added.
100. Costin, *Great Britain and China*, p. 207.
101. Lyndhurst, 24 February 1857, Hansard, 3d series, v. 144, col. 1217.
102. He was Robert Monsey Rolfe (1790–1868), who was appointed solicitor-general in 1834, created Baron Cranworth in 1850, and, on the formation of Lord Aberdeen's cabinet in December 1852, became lord chancellor. Though destitute of eloquence or wit, his speeches in Parliament were always listened to with respect. *DNB*, v. 17, pp. 158–61.

An international incident

to Commissioner Yeh of the alleged insult to the flag, Yeh did not deny it in his reply of 10 October 1856.[103] He ignored the fact that Yeh afterwards denied it repeatedly. If we compare his views with those expressed in an unsigned legal document tendered for the guidance of Lord Clarendon,[104] we shall find them so remarkably similar that he is likely to have been the author. And when we read Chapters 8 and 9, we shall realize that Clarendon seems to have relied heavily on this document during the debates in both houses of Parliament and found that he could not answer most of the questions raised by the opposition.

Not surprisingly, Earl Grey[105] thought the issue not as clear-cut as the lord chancellor had made it out, because the evidence was contradictory. On balance, he was inclined to believe that the flag was *not* flying.[106] The earl of Carnarvon[107] agreed, saying that the government were simply 'assuming that the flag was hoisted, a fact which was by no means satisfactorily established'.[108] Lord St Leonards[109] reiterated that there were serious discrepancies in the accounts about the flag, but was inclined to think that it was not flying.[110]

Lord Wensleydale[111] disagreed. Repeating the lord chancellor's argument,

103. The lord chancellor, 24 February 1857, Hansard, 3d series, v. 144, col. 1222.
104. See Doc. 22, which bears no title, author, or date, but may be attributed to late February 1857, in *British Documents on Foreign Affairs: Reports and Papers from the Foreign Office Confidential Print, Part 1, Series E, Asia, v. 17, Anglo-French Expedition to China, 1856–1858*, ed. Ian Nish (Frederick, Md., University Publications of America, 1994), pp. 18–19.
105. Henry George, Third Earl Grey (1802–94) was educated at Trinity College, Cambridge. From the start he took up an independent position in party politics. He was secretary of state for the colonies (1846–52), and led the debates in the Lords for the government. In Lord Aberdeen's coalition ministry of March 1852, Grey was not included. Thereafter, he played the part of critic to both parties, and in consequence received the support of neither. He is best known for the work he did for the colonies. See J. M. Ward, *Earl Grey and the Australian Colonies, 1846–1857: A Study of Self-Government and Self-Interest* (Melbourne, Melbourne University Press, 1958).
106. Earl Grey, 24 February 1857, Hansard, 3d series, v. 144, col. 1228.
107. He was Henry Howard Molyneux Herbert, fourth earl of Carnarvon (1831–90). In February 1858 he was to become under-secretary for the colonies in Lord Derby's second administration. In June 1866 he again joined Lord Derby's ministry as colonial secretary. He opposed Derby's Reform Bill in 1867 and resigned. In 1874 he once again became colonial secretary. *DNB*, v. 9, pp. 646–53.
108. Carnarvon, 26 February 1857, Hansard, 3d series, v. 144, col. 1317.
109. He was Edward Burtenshaw Sugden (1781–1875). He was appointed solicitor-general and knighted on 4 June 1829. He held the great seal of Ireland in Sir Robert Peel's first and second administrations. He became lord chancellor in Derby's first ministry in 1852 and was raised to the peerage (1 March 1852) as Baron St Leonards of Slaugham, Sussex. It is said that within his limits he as nearly as possible realized the ideal of an infallible oracle of law. 'His judgments, always delivered with remarkable readiness, were very rarely reversed, and the opinions expressed in his textbooks were hardly less authoritative'. *DNB*, v. 19, pp. 152–4.
110. St Leonards, 26 February 1857, Hansard, 3d series, v. 144, col. 1329.
111. He was James Parke (1782–1868). He was called to the bar in 1813, sworn of the Privy Council in 1833, and placed on the Judicial Committee. In 1834 he was transferred from the King's Bench to the Court of Exchequer. His judgments were regarded as models of lucid statement and cogent reasoning. 'His fault was an almost superstitious reverence for the dark technicalities of special pleading'. By patent of 23 July 1856 he was raised to the peerage by the title of Baron Wensleydale of Walton in the county of Lancaster. 'Wensleydale was no party

The pretext for imperialism

he said that the flag was pulled down when it was flying, 'for it was proved by three witnesses, and, in the first instance, not denied by Yeh'.[112]

Earl Granville[113] elaborated on these three witnesses: 'two of my fellow-countrymen, [whose] evidence is corroborated by a Chinese sailor on board the *Arrow*'.[114] Contradicting this evidence was the 'deposition of a Chinese sailor – a criminal, bound under the authority of Yeh corroborated by the evidence of the Chinese Mandarin himself'.[115] Thereupon he pointed out how untrustworthy the Chinese had been in the past.[116] He concluded, 'At all events, when I have the evidence of two of my countrymen on oath, all I can say is that until these individuals are shown to be unworthy of credence, I, for one, shall continue to attach some authority to their statements.'[117] We must not use today's standards to eye Granville's pronouncements. Rather, his comments ought to be seen in the context of his own times.[118] The individuals to whom he referred have been shown to be unworthy of credence in this chapter. Would Earl Granville have changed his mind if he had been able to interview them? He might, given the Victorian liberal conscience; but perhaps only in private, because he was the lord president of the Privy Council. The extent to which the liberal conscience affected members of Palmerston's cabinet will be explored in Chapter 12.

No unanimous verdict was passed by their lordships about the flag. But since the government attributed a cause of the war to the alleged insult to the flag, this chapter assumes an importance to it that it may not have otherwise had.

VI. In sum

Although any conclusion drawn about the *Arrow* incident must be tentative because it can be based only on conflicting verbal testimonies, Parkes's case, as presented, has serious weaknesses. There is no firm evidence that the Union

    politician, and except on legal questions, rarely spoke in parliament'. *DNB*, v. 15, p. 226.
112. Wensleydale, 26 February 1857, Hansard, 3d series, v. 144, col. 1337.
113. He was Granville George Leveson-Gower, Second Earl Granville (1815–91). In 1840 he became under-secretary of state for foreign affairs. By the death of his father, in 1846, he succeeded to the peerage. In 1848 he was made vice-president of the Board of Trade and also paymaster of the forces, and was admitted to the Cabinet in the autumn of 1851. In December 1852, in the administration of Lord Aberdeen, he accepted the office of president of the Council. From 1855 he was entrusted with the leadership of the House of Lords when the liberals were in office. See Lord (Edmond George) Fitzmaurice, *Life of Granville George Leveson Gower, Second Earl Granville*, 2 vs. (London, 1905).
114. Granville, 26 February 1857, Hansard, 3d series, v. 144, cols. 1366–7.
115. Ibid., col. 1367.
116. Ibid., cols. 1367–8.
117. Ibid., col. 1368.
118. For a perceptive study of the attitudes of those times, see Victor G Kiernan, *The Lords of Human Kind: European Attitudes towards the Outside World in the Imperial Age* (London, Weidenfeld & Nicolson, 1969).

Jack was flying at all, and the only truly independent witnesses – the Portuguese crew of lorcha no. 83 – declared that it was not. It is clear that the *Arrow*'s papers were null and void and that the ship had been engaged in illegal activities. Her captain therefore had good reasons to lie. In fact, if the *Arrow* dispute had not been rapidly transformed into a quarrel over insults and apologies (to Parkes personally, and to the British flag so far as his contemporaries and posterity have been given to understand), the Chinese authorities would sooner or later have found out the truth about the *Arrow*. Parkes's case then, was at best flimsy. Even the foreign secretary, Lord Clarendon, who endorsed the actions of Parkes and Bowring, and vehemently defended them in Parliament, publicly called the *Arrow* incident 'a miserable case'.[119]

As mentioned, the report to London by telegraphic service of the incident made no reference to the alleged insult.[120] This is against journalists' instinct to report sensational stories. How does one interpret their silence? Were they so sceptical about the allegation that they preferred to keep quiet? Later, the more detailed overland mail to London arrived. But *The Times* merely commented that there was a dispute as to whether the *Arrow* 'was carrying British colours'.[121] It did not say that there was a dispute as to whether the Union Jack had been insulted. How does one interpret the reluctance of this newspaper to believe, as Parkes and Bowring had so readily believed, Kennedy's story?

The comment by Parkes's biographer is short, pungent, and most interesting. For the widely consulted *Dictionary of National Biography* he wrote, 'The seizure of the *Arrow* and imprisonment of the crew were unquestionably an affront to the British flag'.[122] Not a word is said about the alleged hauling down of the flag which was supposed to have been flying. Similarly, the biography of Bowring in the same publication makes absolutely no reference to the alleged insult to the flag.

The essence of the case was summarized very well by Lord Elgin in a letter to his wife on 9 December 1857. Referring to the ultimatum about to be delivered to Commissioner Yeh, he wrote: 'I have hardly alluded in my ultimatum to that wretched question of the "Arrow" which is a scandal to us, and is so considered, I have reason to know, by all except the few who are personally compromised'.[123] The 'all' referred to here is exemplified by the *Daily Press*, an English newspaper in Hong Kong, which wrote: 'The Earl of Elgin has certainly managed to disconnect himself from that unfortunate

---

119. Clarendon, 24 February 1857, Hansard, 3d series, v. 144, col. 1196.
120. *The Times*, 29 December 1856.
121. *The Times*, 2 January 1857.
122. *DNB*, v. 15, p. 299.
123. T. Walrond (ed.), *Letters and Journals of James, Eighth Earl of Elgin* (London, John Murray, 1872), p. 209.

aggression . . . The *Arrow* subject has been exhausted – its defenders left the field long ago'.[124]

But before the defenders left the field, Parkes and Bowring, between them, had used the incident to wage an undeclared war in China. The British government simply assumed that the British flag had been pulled down, and this assumption has been generally accepted by historians. Gerald Graham, for example, took it for granted that the *Arrow*, 'flying the British flag, was suddenly boarded by Chinese police officers, while lying at anchor'.[125] Immanuel Hsü stated that the *Arrow* was lying 'with the British flags flying' and that during the subsequent 'turmoil the British flag was hauled down'.[126]

Supposing that the Union Jack had indeed been flying, would the Chinese harbour police have pulled it down? After all, Chinese soldiers[127] did subsequently insult the U.S. flag by firing on a U.S. Navy boat that was sounding the river near the barrier forts. This happened on 15 November 1856, when hostilities between Britain and China had been raging for about a month. The Chinese soldiers fired from the barrier forts, which they had just reoccupied after the British earlier captured and then abandoned them.[128]

Here a distinction should be made between the soldiers trained specifically for policing the shipping in Canton harbour and soldiers in action – soldiers who were rushed from Canton to reinforce the forts and who were on battle alert. One should also recall the actions, a fortnight before, of the U.S. consul at Hong Kong, James Keenan, which must have greatly excited the Chinese soldiers. Keenan had joined the British attack on Canton on 24 October 1856. When the city wall was breached on 29 October, he had the U.S. flag carried beside him and stormed the city with the British forces. 'He went in furthest and came out last', we are told. He displayed the Stars and Stripes on the city wall and atop Yeh's official residence. During the retreat, he fired on the Chinese.[129] Naturally but mistakenly, many Chinese soldiers thought that U.S. forces were helping the British against them.[130] Thus, two weeks later they had no difficulty recognising the U.S. flag aboard a ship sounding the waters around them and fired on it.[131]

124. *Daily Press*, 6 January 1858 (newspaper clipping), Ryl. Eng. MSS 1230/67.
125. Graham, *China Station*, p. 300.
126. Immanuel C. Y. Hsü, *The Rise of Modern China* (New York, Oxford University Press, 1990), p. 205.
127. As mentioned, what is conveniently referred to here as 'military police' was in fact the Green Standard, an army.
128. Seymour to Admiralty, 24 November 1856, Parl. Papers 1857, v. 12, pp. 170–1, para. 4.
129. Parker to Lewis Cass, Macao, 22 May 1857, U.S. Senate Executive Documents, no. 22, 35th Congress, 2d Session, 'Peter Parker Correspondence', pp. 1385–6, quoted in Tong, *United States Diplomacy in China*, p. 186.
130. See Yeh's letters to Armstrong on 20 and 28 November 1856, quoted in Tong, *United States Diplomacy in China*, p. 186, n. 47.
131. The incident was particularly frustrating for Yeh, who had by this time successfully persuaded the U.S. consul at Canton, Oliver Perry, and the U.S. naval officer commanding the

An international incident

Thus, it is explicable that Chinese soldiers fired upon the Stars and Stripes after hostilities began.[132] It remains improbable that those policing the harbour in peacetime could have pulled down the Union Jack.[133] But assuming, for the sake of argument, that the harbour police *did* pull down the British flag, then it becomes a question of intention, which will be explored in Chapter 8.

Before we leave this chapter, it may be instructive to note a certain passage in Jasper Ridley's biography of Lord Palmerston. It states that the *Arrow* was owned by a notorious Chinese pirate. The pirate found a twenty-four-year-old Ulsterman who had never been a seaman, and made him the nominal captain of the *Arrow*; and they set out with the Ulsterman and twelve Chinese on board, and the British flag at the mast, to rob the ships trading in the Canton river. It was intercepted in Chinese territorial waters and boarded by Chinese coastguards, who hauled down the British flag and arrested the thirteen members of the crew. The Ulsterman was immediately released, but the twelve Chinese were imprisoned at Canton.[134]

It has yet to be proved that the *Arrow* was owned by a pirate, although it was engaged in piratical activities (receiving pirates' loot); we *do* know that the Ulsterman was not twenty-four years old, that he was not arrested together with his crew, and that the lorcha was not intercepted at sea, nor engaged in piracy on the Canton River.

Mention, too, might be made of a passage in a venerable source. Referring to the *Arrow* incident, it alleges that 'Chinese local authorities had arrested as pirates Chinese subjects, while trying to escape by running up a British flag, which they had no right to fly'.[135] Neither English nor Chinese sources ever

    U.S. Navy at Canton, Captain Andrew H. Foote, to withdraw all U.S. personnel from that increasingly dangerous port. It was on the day that the Americans were leaving Canton that the U.S. warship, coming up to Canton from Macao and sounding the river on the way, was fired upon by the Chinese soldiers guarding the barrier forts. See Tong, *United States Diplomacy in China*, pp. 185–7.

132. Even then, Yeh took no more chances. He instructed his agents to draw pictures of flags on all foreign vessels in Canton waters, presumably for the edification of his soldiers. For an example of such drawings, see the intelligence report with drawings of British and French flags (and one other, unidentified), c. 1857, FO931/1873 (old reference FO682/327/5/34).

133. A comparable situation might be found in Hong Kong in the early 1990s. A significant trade of smuggled goods was being conducted between the territory and mainland China. Numerous incidents of Chinese patrol boats intruding into Hong Kong waters in pursuit of smugglers were recorded. Upon closer examination, it was found that the guilty parties were invariably Chinese soldiers recruited from the peasantry. The Chinese customs police, who had some formal education and some knowledge of international law, never ventured into the waters of Hong Kong, however hotly they might have been pursuing the smugglers. See *Ming Pao* (Hong Kong), Thursday, 1 October 1992, p. 6. After vigorous protests from Hong Kong authorities, such intrusions stopped almost as suddenly as they had started.

134. Jasper Ridley, *Lord Palmerston*, pp. 464–5. The author seems very much at home when dealing with Palmerston and British politics, but can be off the mark when writing about events in China.

135. Charles Parker, *Life and Letters of Sir James Graham, Second Baronet of Netherby, 1792–1861*, 2 vs. (London, John Murray, 1907), v. 2, p. 302.

indicate that the *Arrow*'s crew tried to escape, let alone running up a British flag while allegedly attempting to do so. There has been so much imaginary writing in the English language alone that, small wonder, Douglas Hurd has called the *Arrow* war a 'confusion'.

Eventually what happened to the captain of the *Arrow*, who appears to have been the source of all this heartburn? Admit the Royal Navy's deafening bombardments of Canton in an attempt to uphold the infallability of his story, he was quietly ordered to 'surrender his credentials' to the Hong Kong authorities the month following the *Arrow* incident, in November 1856. [136]

136. Bowring to Parkes, 28 November 1856, Parkes Papers.

Part III
The personalities of imperialism

The available evidence suggests that neither the British nor the Chinese government had expected that the *Arrow* incident would lead to war. In this respect, Chapters 3-5 will show how crucial were the personalities of Parkes and Bowring, and of Yeh in response. The *Arrow* War might have been waged in a different manner and under a different name if Whitehall had had an opportunity to examine the military action proposed by Parkes and endorsed by Bowring. But Whitehall did not, because it was about four months by return mail from Hong Kong.[1] Thus, it was obliged, for political reasons, to approve retrospectively the actions of its men. It was the 'tyranny of distance'[2] which allowed the personalities of imperialism to manifest themselves so fully.

These personalities involved not only the British officials, but also the British crowd at Canton. This crowd included some reckless British merchants, as well as drunken sailors and thugs. Propelled by the ascendancy of Britain as a world power, this crowd was exceptionally aggressive and bellicose, so much so that the British authorities often despaired of making them behave sensibly. It was 'Rule, Britannia' in the worst possible form. The British crowd was met by a fiercely defiant Cantonese populace, whom the Chinese officials had lost hope of controlling since the Opium War, and whose wishes they had been cajoled to respect: 'Vox populi, vox Dei.' This unusual aspect will be dealt with in Chapter 6.

As the personalities of imperialism are examined one after another, some repetition of the course of events is unavoidable, although every attempt has been made to keep it to a minimum.

1. See Chaper 1.
2. This term is borrowed from Geoffrey Blainey's *Tyranny of Distance: How Distance Shaped Australia's History* (Melbourne, Macmillan, revised edition, 1982).

3
Harry Parkes:
'If you *would* read a little international law'

I. Introduction

Not all international incidents lead to war.* The *Arrow* incident did, partly because of the manner in which it was handled by the men on the spot, including, first, the young acting British consul, Harry Parkes.

Born in 1828, Harry Smith Parkes was orphaned at five and sailed for China when he was only thirteen, to join his two sisters who had already settled there with their cousin, the wife of the Reverend Charles Gutzlaff. Arriving at Macao in October 1841, Parkes applied himself to the study of Chinese. He was attached to Sir Henry Pottinger's[1] suite during the Opium War; and although only a lad of fourteen, yet because of his language skills he was often sent ashore to find forage for cattle and other provisions. He was present at the negotiations for peace at Nanjing, when he witnessed the final humiliation of the Chinese mandarins at the signing of the treaty on 29 August 1842. In September 1843 he entered the British consulate at Canton, and was again present at the signing of the supplementary treaty at the Bogue on 8 October 1843.

Apart from two brief visits home – in 1849 and 1855 – Parkes spent all his time in the East and consequently acquired 'all the special prejudices, bogies and obsessions of any group long isolated from the culture and influence of their homeland'.[2] He believed that 'toughness in either words or deeds was all

---

* The quote is from *Punch*, 24 January 1857. An earlier version of this chapter appeared as an article in *Modern Asian Studies*, 9, no. 3 (1975), pp. 303–20. It has been completely rewritten, incorporating some of my new discoveries and further thoughts.
1. Sir Henry Pottinger (1789–1856) was political agent in Sind (1836–40) when he arranged with the Sind Amirs for the passage of Bombay troops on their way to Afghanistan. He was made a baronet for his toils. In 1840 he accepted Lord Palmerston's offer of the post of plenipotentiary in China and defeated the Chinese in the Opium War. In 1843 he was appointed the first British governor of Hong Kong. In 1846 he became governor of the Cape of Good Hope and, in 1847, governor of Madras. That post he held till 1854, when he returned to England in broken health. *DNB*, v. 16, pp. 224–6.
2. Daniels, 'Parkes', pp. 3–4.

that was needed for success in China'.³ During his first visit home, he complained that there were 'no *coolies* to help pack' or carry his luggage.⁴ On the second, he brought with him a commercial treaty with Siam which he had helped Sir John Bowring to obtain.⁵ He presented this treaty in person to the Queen.⁶ Before he left for China again in 1856, he was interviewed by Lord Palmerston.⁷ Richard Cobden formed this impression of Parkes: 'a gentleman of considerable ability, no doubt, and a good linguist (I believe some of us saw him not long ago when he came over with the Siamese treaty), but still a young man, without experience' and, more important, 'without having gone through the gradations of civil employment calculated to give him that moderation, prudence, and discretion which he may one day possess.'⁸

Parkes arrived at Canton as the acting British consul in June 1856. Three months later, the *Arrow* incident erupted.⁹ We have seen how he may have manipulated witnesses in order to obtain the depositions he wanted. In the next section, we shall see how he manipulated his immediate superior, Bowring, in order to obtain sanction for what he desired.

II. Parkes's manipulation of Bowring

Let us go back to the time of the *Arrow* incident to begin our analysis. Case studies might be illuminating; and the questions of the register of the *Arrow*, of the requirement of an apology from Yeh, and of Parkes's interpretation of Commissioner Yeh's letters, as well as of Bowring's instructions, are good examples.

First, the *Arrow*'s register. Parkes maintained that the *Arrow*'s register had been deposited with him on 3 October 1856.¹⁰ This statement posed problems

3. Ibid., p. 10.
4. Lane-Poole, *Parkes*, v. 1, p. 143.
5. G. F. Bartle, 'Sir John Bowring and the Chinese and Siamese Commercial Treaties', *Bulletin of the John Rylands Library*, 44, no. 2 (March 1962), pp. 286–308; N. Tarling, 'The Mission of Sir John Bowring to Siam', *Journal of the Siam Society*, 50, no. 2 (December 1962), pp. 91–118; and idem, 'Harry Parkes's Negotiations in Bangkok in 1856', in ibid., 53, no. 2 (July 1965), pp. 153–80.
6. Lane-Poole, *Parkes*, v. 1, p. 195.
7. Ibid., p. 223.
8. Cobden, 26 February 1857, Hansard, 3d series, v. 144, col. 1401.
9. For details of that incident, see Chapter 2.
10. See Parkes to Bowring, Desp 155, 11 October 1856, para. 5, FO228/213; and ibid., Desp. 156, 12 October 1856, para. 3. Costin wrote that 'the *Arrow*'s papers were on that morning of the 8th October lawfully deposited at the British Consulate' (*Great Britain and China*, p. 206). This date could be a clerical error for two reasons. First, Parkes himself twice professed that the *Arrow* had arrived on 3 October 1856. Second, if Costin maintained that the *Arrow* had been in Canton harbour for some days but her papers, without Parkes's notice, had not been lodged with the British Consulate until a grave incident had taken place, then he was in fact charging the consul with negligence. This, obviously, was not what Costin intended to do. Since Costin gave no reference for the source on which he based his statement, it seems more likely that he

for him. The register had expired five days previously, on 27 September.[11] Thus, it seems that he was guilty either of negligence or connivance in having accepted invalid papers,[12] probably the former.[13] He made no allusion to the register in his reports to Bowring on 8 and 9 October. When he did so on 10 October, he did not point out that it had expired.[14] He referred to the register again on 11 October, but again he did not specifically mention its expiry. Instead, he threw in a good word for the *Arrow*: 'I should here mention that the "Arrow" is well known as a trader to the legal ports. She entered from Macao with rice on the 3rd instant, reported her arrival at the Consulate, and deposited her papers, which have remained to this time in my possession'. He added, 'She was to have left for Hong Kong on the 8th instant, the day on which her crew were seized',[15] implying that she would have renewed her register in Hong Kong but for the incident.

That last sentence suggests that by this time, if not earlier, Parkes had become aware of the expiry, which meant that the *Arrow* was no longer entitled to fly the British flag. Should he have informed his superiors that the British did not have a case? Apparently he decided otherwise and, on 13 October, wrote a special despatch devoted entirely to emphasizing the enormous pressure Yeh was under because of the local and Taiping rebellions. Yeh had transferred his commander-in-chief of Guangdong's land forces to the western city of Wuzhou to protect the province from an expected invasion by the rebels in Guangxi, Parkes wrote. To the north, the Taipings had captured ten of the thirteen districts in Jiangxi province and threatened daily to descend on Guangdong, he added. There was nothing new in this despatch, and Parkes said almost as

meant that the papers were in the hands of the consul on that day, without any comment as to when they had been lodged.
11. Bowring to Parkes, Desp. 127, 11 October 1856, para. 3, FO288/213.
12. Parkes's biographer, Lane-Poole, argued that the *Arrow* 'was on the point of returning to Hong Kong to renew it; and if a vessel happen to be at sea or in some other port at the moment that her annual register expires, it would surely be monstrous to deprive her of the protection of her flag, say, in-ocean, on a mere quibble of dates' (Lane-Poole, *Parkes*, v. 1, pp. 233–4). This view dangerously implicates the man he was trying to defend. According to this argument, Parkes indeed noticed the date of the register and was therefore guilty of connivance. Besides, the *Arrow* was not in mid-ocean when her register expired. As mentioned, she left Hong Kong on 1 September, and since then had visited Macao and Canton only. The three coastal cities were so close to one another that she could easily have renewed her register, and Parkes should have ordered the captain to do so before the *Arrow* would be allowed to set sail again.
13. Parkes had the reputation of 'flitting about like a meteor' (Bowring to Parkes, 19 July 1851, Parkes Papers). When he was previously acting consul at Canton in 1852, he complained loudly about the monotonous life there, saying that the officers of visiting British gunboats were among the few variations to life (*Parkes*, v. 1, pp. 169–70). It so happened that prior to the *Arrow* incident some officers were at Canton, among them his great friend Commander Bate (see Parkes's correspondence with Bate, in Parkes Papers). Thus, negligence seems a more likely explanation than connivance.
14. Parkes to Bowring, Desp. 153, 10 October 1856, para. 3, FO288/213.
15. Parkes to Bowring, Desp. 155, 11 October 1856, para. 5, FO228/213.

much when he began thus: 'No recent intelligence of importance appears to have been received'.[16] But its strategic value cannot be overlooked. Parkes was keeping up his argument for military action, painting a picture of Yeh as weakened. Obviously he was trying to assure his chief that it would be safe to proceed with the coercive measures he had initiated, on the grounds that Yeh was not expected to resist under the circumstances. Why was Parkes so determined to make the *Arrow* incident a pretext for war? It was one thing to avenge a personal grievance by humiliating Captain Liang.[17] It would be quite another to fake a casus belli.

The second issue for consideration is the demand for an apology from Yeh. Throughout Parkes's initial communication to Yeh, on 8 October, one will not find the word 'apology'. When Yeh, in response to this letter, returned nine[18] of the twelve sailors on 10 October, Parkes apparently did not give Yeh in writing his reasons for refusing to accept them.[19] Instead, Parkes sent Yeh a list of demands among which was a new one: an apology for the alleged insult to the flag.[20] Meanwhile, Parkes made an indirect suggestion to Bowring that such an apology be demanded from Yeh. He was afraid that his hint might not be easily picked up, and he repeated it again on the following day.[21] His worry proved unnecessary. Bowring noted the suggestion and replied on 11 October: 'You will inform the Imperial Commissioner that I require an apology for what has taken place'.[22] The consul was still not satisfied: 'I trust that I read these instructions aright in believing them to mean that I am to require in writing from the Imperial Commissioner an apology for what has occurred.'[23] Lane-Poole maintained that the idea of an apology originated with Bowring.[24] As a biographer producing a book at the special request of the Parkes family,[25] his motive is understandable; for he did recognize that this fresh demand created a major difficulty in settling the *Arrow* dispute.[26] Here again, the key question is this: Did Parkes continue to increase his demands to make it impossible for Yeh to retreat with dignity?

The third issue is Parkes's insistence that 'an insult so publicly committed must be equally publicly atoned'.[27] As pointed out in Chapter 2, the insult

16. Parkes to Bowring, Desp. 157, 13 October 1856, FO228/213.   17. See Chapter 2.
18. Parkes to Bowring, Desp. 153, 10 October 1856, para. 1, FO228/213.
19. Such a reply is missing among Parkes's enclosures to Bowring, nor has such a document ever been referred to in the sources available.
20. Parkes to Bowring, Desp. 153, 10 October 1856, para. 2, FO288/213.
21. Parkes to Bowring, Desp. 155, 11 October 1856, para. 3, FO228/213.
22. Bowring to Parkes, Desp. 127, 11 October 1856, para. 5, FO288/213.
23. Parkes to Bowring, Desp. 156, 12 October 1856, para. 2, FO228/213.
24. Lane-Poole, *Parkes*, v. 1, p. 237.
25. Ibid., p. v.
26. Ibid., p. 244.
27. Parkes to Bowring, Desp. 150, 8 October 1856, FO228/213, and encl.: Parkes to Yeh, 8 October 1856, para. 4.

mentioned here referred to Parkes's public humiliation at the hands of the Chinese officers captained by Liang Guoding. That would seem to be why Parkes required the said captain to return the *Arrow*'s crew 'to that vessel in my presence'.[28] This demand was made in a letter to Yeh on the very day of the *Arrow* incident. While enclosing a copy of this letter in his own report to Bowring, Parkes did not seek retrospective authorization for his demand.[29] Perhaps he hoped that Bowring would offer it, since the demand had already been made. But Bowring did not. Parkes was not prepared to give up. He boldly interpreted Bowring's instructions to include the additional demand 'made in my letter to the Imperial Commissioner of the 8th instant . . . for the restoration of matters to their original position, in the same public manner in which they had been disturbed'.[30] An unwary Bowring replied, 'The requirement that the conditions of the Treaty be strictly fulfilled, necessarily implies the return of the arrested Chinamen to the ship . . . As to the *modus faciendi*, I shall leave that to be arranged by the Commodore and yourself'.[31] A gleeful Parkes then turned to Admiral Seymour and said that this particular demand had been 'authorised by Her Majesty's Plenipotentiary'.[32]

The fourth issue is the manner in which the consul explained the situation in Canton to his chiefs and how he interpreted Bowring's instructions so that he could incorporate his own views. Let us begin with the point about the *Arrow*'s ownership and, for that purpose, examine Parkes's first letter to Yeh penned on 8 October 1856. Instead of demanding the sailors on the grounds that, by treaty, Chinese culprits under British protection had to be claimed through the consul, Parkes required the Chinese captain to return the sailors to the *Arrow* in his presence. The word 'treaty', it is to be noted, was never used in this despatch. The reason Parkes gave for claiming the sailors was that they were part of the crew of a British vessel. This started Yeh off on the wrong tack. Not surprisingly, Yeh's first step was to ascertain whether the *Arrow* was a British or a Chinese vessel. On cross-examining the sailors, he discovered that she was owned by a Chinese subject, though nominally captained by a Briton.[33] The way Yeh argued his case seems to suggest that his concept of the nationality of a ship was based on her ownership. He was not alone in holding such a view. As we shall see in Chapter 8, British law also regarded the ownership of a vessel the decisive factor in determining her nationality.

But Parkes proceeded to elaborate on Yeh's position, regarding it as 'a declaration on his [Yeh's] part that he will respect neither British flag nor

28. Ibid.
29. Parkes to Bowring, Desp. 150, 8 October 1856, FO228/213.
30. Parkes to Bowring, 12 October 1856, para. 2, Parl. Papers 1857, v. 12, pp. 65–6.
31. Bowring to Parkes, 13 October 1856, para. 1, Parl. Papers 1857, v. 12, p. 66.
32. Parkes to Seymour, 22 October 1856, para. 3, Parl. Papers 1857, v. 12, pp. 85–6.
33. See Chapter 2.

British register, whenever any Chinese states to him that a vessel so provided is not British-owned'.[34] This led Bowring to tell Parkes – as if Parkes needed to be told – that he required 'an assurance that the British flag shall, in future, be respected'.[35]

For the sake of clarity, it might be useful to list Parkes's demands, which had increased to the following: an apology, an assurance of respect for the British flag (i.e., the safety of the people under its protection), observance of treaty provisions, compensation for the *Arrow*'s delay, and the public humiliation of the Chinese naval officer Captain Liang. These demands constituted the second stage in the development of the *Arrow* quarrel, and will be dealt with below.

III. Escalating demands

Yeh contended that there had been no violation of the treaty on his part. The treaty had stipulated that any Chinese subject in British service or territory charged with offences against Chinese law had to be claimed through the British authorities. But if the *Arrow* was not a British vessel, so Yeh argued, the treaty did not apply. In the same vein, he contended that compensation for her delay was out of the question, as the Chinese government never compensated a Chinese subject for the detention of a Chinese vessel on legal grounds. He was convinced that the British flag had not been insulted, and he obviously considered it spineless and wrong to plead guilty to a crime which had never been committed. Therefore he replied on 21 October as follows:

In response to your communication of 15 October 1856, in which you complained about my non-compliance with your demands, I have to state to you that the arrest by Chinese authorities of the Chinese sailors of a Chinese vessel has nothing to do with foreign powers.

If, in the future, should offenders of the law be found to have been hiding in foreign vessels, the consuls concerned will be informed so as to take joint action.[36]

Here, Yeh made an important concession, and even offered a half-apology. Although he was aware that the *Arrow*, like so many lorchas of her kind, used British registration to conceal her dubious transactions, he was prepared to overlook the matter. Instead, he reaffirmed the international principle of claiming extradition through the appropriate consuls.

This conciliatory gesture only prompted Parkes to reply that the continued

34. Parkes to Bowring, Desp. 155, 11 October 1856, para. 3, FO228/213.
35. Bowring to Parkes, Desp. 127, 11 October 1856, para. 5, FO228/213.
36. These two opening paragraphs of Yeh's reply have been translated by me from the Chinese original in FO228/904, pp. 332a–b, Yeh to Parkes, 21 October 1856.

retention of the twelve sailors signified the commissioner's approval of a violation of the treaty.[37] It is obvious that Yeh did not see any logic in such an argument, but to avoid a foreign war, he returned all twelve sailors. However, the consul declined to receive them on the grounds that they had not been delivered 'in the manner required in my letter of the 8th'.[38] This last condition would have appeared totally inexplicable to Yeh, who must have wondered why the consul insisted on this public display of his authority.

As mentioned, Parkes repeatedly insisted to Yeh that Captain Kennedy had been on board the *Arrow* when the incident occurred, while he knew perfectly well that he had not. Indeed the depositions of Kennedy et al. – which include the demand to rehoist the flag and the boy's alleged refusal due to fear of Captain Liang – may have been tailored by Parkes to extend the 'incident' to encompass the time Kennedy was on board. Parkes resorted to more and more threatening language each time he repeated his assertion.[39] However, Yeh 'preserved an indomitable obstinacy throughout, which, while it surprised us all, left the Admiral no alternative but to pursue the course he had commenced'.[40]

Then came this interesting private letter from Parkes:

Most fervently do I desire a speedy solution, for the responsibilities and anxiety now devolving on me are very heavy; but Yeh must bend or we must bend, and as his pride had gradually risen to an unbearable height – past such as used to animate the mandarins before the war – it is not altogether to be wondered at that he will not yield without a struggle.[41]

Did Parkes really desire a speedy solution? Probably not. He was merely trying to look like the injured party while really warmongering. He described Yeh as unbearable, suggesting that Yeh must not be borne. He cited the Opium War as the corrective which had curbed the proud mandarins before. And he concluded his long sentence by affirming the need for war. In short, this statement is a classic example of saying one thing while meaning quite another.

IV. Leading the Royal Navy on

The most striking feature of Parkes's very first letter to Yeh concerning the *Arrow* incident is his thinly disguised threat to use force by saying he was simultaneously referring the matter to Commodore Elliot, commander of the British naval forces in the Pearl River, and to his superior, Sir John Bowring.

37. Parkes to Yeh, 21 October 1856, Parl. Papers 1857, v. 12, p. 27.
38. Parkes to Seymour, 22 October 1856, Parl. Papers 1857, v. 12, p. 32.
39. See Chapter 2, Section 3.
40. Lane-Poole, *Parkes*, v. 1, p. 231.
41. Ibid., pp. 232–3.

Thus, he neither waited for a reply from Yeh nor asked for authorization from Bowring, but immediately wrote to Commodore Elliot to seek naval assistance,[42] thus preempting possible reluctance on Bowring's part.

Yeh directed the prefect of Canton to examine the twelve sailors of the *Arrow* immediately. It was found that two of them were pirate suspects, and a third was a key witness. Yeh decided to keep these three, but ordered that the remaining nine be returned to their vessel.[43] His despatch to this effect reached Parkes at noon on 10 October 1856.[44] But by this time, Parkes had received a reply from Commodore Elliot, in which the latter, without authorization from Admiral Seymour, intimated his 'intention of moving Her Majesty's ship "Sybille" up to Whampoa at once'.[45] With his hand thus strengthened, Parkes refused to receive the nine sailors 'because they were not delivered in the manner I had demanded'.[46] It should be noted that Parkes's refusal was based not on the reduced number of sailors returned, but on the lack of public ceremony.

That evening, Commodore Elliot arrived at Canton in a steam passage-boat, the shallowness of the river having prevented the *Sybille* from crossing the second bar. Parkes gave no details of his discussions with Elliot, but expressed to Bowring his belief that the commodore fully concurred in his view that 'if any reparation be due for so gross an insult, it is only by active measures on our part that such reparation can be obtained'. Furthermore, he suggested that such measures should take the form of 'reprisals on one or more of the war-boats of the Chinese force by which violence was committed'.[47] Again, Parkes did not seek retrospective authorization from Bowring.

Bowring transmitted Parkes's suggestion to Seymour, who subsequently instructed Elliot to this effect.[48] Action was taken on 14 October 1856 after an ultimatum of forty-eight hours had expired[49] – the seizure of a merchant vessel chartered by the Chinese government.[50] The seizure failed to produce the

42. Parkes to Elliot, 8 October 1856, enclosed in Parkes to Bowring, Desp. 150, 8 October 1856, FO228/213.
43. Yeh to Parkes, 10 October 1856, enclosed in Parkes to Bowring, Desp. 153, 10 October 1856, FO228/213.
44. Parkes to Bowring, Desp. 153, 10 October 1856, para. 1, in ibid.
45. Ibid., para. 5.
46. Ibid., para. 2.
47. Parkes to Bowring, Desp. 155, 11 October 1856, FO228/213.
48. Seymour to Elliot, 11 October 1856, enclosed in Bowring to Clarendon, Desp. 326, 13 October 1856, FO17/251.
49. Parkes to Bowring, Desp. 158, 14 October 1856, and Desp. 159, 15 October 1856, FO228/213. The ultimatum did not specify what action would be taken beyond the threat that unless Yeh yielded to the demands, Parkes would 'concert with the naval authorities the measures necessary for enforcing redress'.
50. Bowring to Parkes, 17 October 1856, Parkes Papers. It is apparent from this private letter that both Parkes and Bowring conceded that the junk seized was a merchant vessel, although they continued to refer to it in their official correspondence as an imperial war junk.

desired effect on the imperial commissioner. Parkes went to see Elliot, but was told that no further action could be taken without previous sanction from Hong Kong.

After waiting in vain for instructions, the consul proceeded to Hong Kong[51] 'to learn the real views' of his chiefs and to voice his 'opinion on the present position of affairs'.[52] A conference took place among Parkes, Bowring, and Seymour. At this conference Parkes went to great lengths to advocate the necessity of coercion. Then he produced a plan of action. First, the four barrier forts between Whampoa and Canton should be attacked and destroyed. If Yeh failed to respond, the forts at Canton itself should be obliterated. If Yeh remained obstinate, his official residence should be bombarded. Parkes's proposals were adopted.[53] The admiral even offered to send a gunboat specially to take Parkes back to Canton overnight.[54] Why were Bowring and Seymour so easily convinced by Parkes of the need for military action? Was it not unusual for the admiral to put a gunboat at the special service of a young acting consul?

Once back in Canton, Parkes sent Yeh a twenty-four hour ultimatum to accede to his demands.[55] Yeh still tried to argue.[56] Thereupon Parkes categorically said, 'I hold such clear and conclusive proofs of the facts which Your Excellency attempts to deny, namely, that the lorcha had the British ensign flying when boarded, and had an Englishman on board, that no doubt or question in respect thereto can for a moment be admitted.'[57] It will be remembered from Chapter 2 that initially Parkes asserted only in his Chinese language despatch to Yeh that Kennedy was on board the *Arrow* when the incident occurred. He left that part of his allegation deliberately vague in the English version of his letter, a copy of which he had to send to Bowring. Now he repeated this assertion in the English version, a copy of which was sent, in addition, to Seymour. Thus, it seems most probable that Parkes had assured Bowring and Seymour in that tripartite meeting in Hong Kong two days previously that Yeh had deliberately broken treaty obligations by sending his marine police to violate a vessel whose British nationality was clearly demonstrated by the Union Jack flying on its mast and a British captain being on board. Under the circumstances, Seymour's unusual step of sending a gunboat

51. There is conflicting evidence on the date at which Parkes arrived at Hong Kong. One source indicated it to be 20 October 1856. See Bowring to Clarendon, 23 October 1856, Parl. Papers 1857, v. 12, pp. 73–5, para. 2. Another source suggested the date to be a day earlier, 19 October. See Bowring to Parkes, 19 October 1856, Parkes's Papers. For the significance of these conflicting dates, see Chapter 4.
52. Parkes to Bowring, 20 October 1856, Parl. Papers 1857, v. 12, pp. 78–9, para. 2.
53. Ibid. This is a memorandum by Parkes on his meeting with Seymour and Bowring at Hong Kong.
54. See Bowring to Parkes, 20 October 1856, Parkes Papers.
55. Parkes to Yeh, 21 October 1856, Parl. Papers 1857, v. 12, p. 81.
56. Yeh to Parkes, 21 October 1856, Parl. Papers 1857, v. 12, p. 82.
57. Parkes to Yeh, 22 October 1856, Parl. Papers, 1857, v. 12, p. 83, para. 2.

to convey Parkes back to Canton is explicable. The admiral must have wanted to protect somebody who appeared to him to have stood up very bravely to the outrageous behaviour of the Chinese authorities.

As we have seen, there was certainly no Englishman on board the *Arrow* at the time of the incident, and probably the flag was not flying. Nonetheless, at 8:30 on the morning of 22 October 1856, Yeh offered to return ten of the twelve sailors of the *Arrow* to Parkes, keeping only the two pirate suspects. Parkes insisted that '*all* the men taken away must be returned'.[58] Shortly before noon, all twelve men were returned; but again, Parkes refused them, this time for want of delivery in the manner demanded.[59] The more conciliatory Yeh was, the more aggressive Parkes became. Why? What was his ultimate goal?

Parkes also played on the sense of honour and love of action of the British servicemen. The first letter he wrote to Commodore Elliot, for example, began: 'An outrage, involving a gross insult to our flag, has been committed...'.[60] This aroused a strong reaction among the British officers. One of them, Commander Bate, wrote, 'I am so savage about it – I hauled down the pennant at sunset yesterday... the question is, are we prepared to bite? If we fail now, goodbye to the *very little* prestige we have at Canton.'[61] Parkes then went with the commodore to seize what they thought was an imperial war junk. During subsequent military actions against the Chinese, he was always in the front line. Once he so narrowly escaped death in an explosion that he emerged with burned whiskers. The naval officers were impressed by his courage, and Seymour began to form a very high opinion of him.[62] When successful operations against the Chinese forts at Canton failed to produce the desired results, Seymour readily accepted Parkes's further proposal to intensify the pressure by shelling Yeh's official residence.

Parkes's previous suggestion to destroy the forts of Canton itself was made with the full knowledge that civilian lives and property would be endangered, because the forts were surrounded by houses. The decision to bombard Yeh's residence, which was in the new part of the walled city of Canton,[63] was made

58. Parkes to Bowring, 22 October 1856 at 7 P.M., Parl, Papers 1857, v. 12, pp. 80–1, para. 5.
59. Ibid., para. 6.
60. Parkes to Elliot, 8 October 1856, enclosed in Parkes to Bowring, Desp. 150, 8 October 1856, FO228/213.
61. Bate to Parkes, 18 October 1856, Parkes Papers. Bate was at this time a naval commander; later he was promoted to captain. The Admiralty Records, unlike the Parkes Papers, unfortunately do not contain any information which may throw light on the attitude of individual servicemen towards the *Arrow* incident, but Bate's reaction may have been fairly typical of British officers of the time.
62. Bowring to Parkes, 18 April 1857, Parkes Papers, in which Bowring transmitted a copy of a letter of the same date 'from H. E. the Naval Commander-in-Chief, expressing his appreciation of your services performed in several instances with personal danger to yourself'.
63. The walled city of Canton was divided into two parts, the old city (*laocheng*) and new city (*xincheng*).

with the same knowledge. Anxious to avoid an armed confrontation, Commissioner Yeh ordered his troops guarding the forts not to resist.[64] On the other hand, he refused to evacuate his official residence during the first two days of the bombardment (27-8 October 1856), in an attempt to convince his juniors that there was no need to panic. On the third day, the blue-jackets made a breach in the city wall and fought their way against snipers into Yeh's yamen.[65] There, they found his papers lying about on a table, and tea poured out.[66] The commissioner had apparently just left. His decision to move had been prompted by a fierce fire which had nearly engulfed his yamen the previous evening. It had been started by the blue-jackets with the aim of destroying the surrounding houses and thus clearing the way to the commissioner's yamen.[67]

Even the shelling of his official residence, however, failed to intimidate Yeh. From 3 November 1856 onwards, therefore, the bombardment was extended to government offices in the old part of the walled city of Canton. Civilian casualties multiplied. The masses were incensed. Angry bands of citizens paraded in the city to express their indignation. Yeh began to organize his troops to wage a protracted war of resistance.[68] His firmness greatly surprised his enemies. When Parkes drew up his plan for coercive action, he had thought that occupation of the barrier forts alone would be sufficient to bring Yeh to his knees. 'I cannot conceive it possible that His Excellency will then withhold compliance with our demands,' he had confidently predicted to his superior.[69] In this he was mistaken; he had grossly underestimated his opponent. By the middle of November, the 300 British sailors in Canton found themselves dangerously exposed. On 14 November 1856, the consul had to make the following admission: 'Our position is certainly an embarrassing one, but it is one from which we cannot recede, and it is only by maintaining it and working on the fears of the people that we can be successful or escape defeat which would be most injurious to our interests.'[70]

Thereupon Parkes suggested that a mission be sent to Beijing. Bowring was opposed to the proposal for two reasons. First, he was convinced that Beijing would not believe the British story. Second, he thought that November was not a suitable time to go to the Peiho.[71] He remembered that when he was there

---

64. Hua Tingjie, 'Chufan shimo', in *Er ya*, v. 1, p. 165.
65. A yamen was the official complex of a mandarin, comprising his office, a court of justice, the offices of his clerks, his residence, and servants' quarters. It was spelled 'yamun' in some documents.
66. Mrs Parkes to Mrs McClatchie, 11 December 1856, in Lane-Poole, *Parkes*, v. 1, p. 254.
67. Hua Tingjie, 'Chufan shimo', in *Er ya*, v. 1, p. 165.
68. Ibid.; see also Seymour to Admiralty, 14 November 1856, Parl. Papers 1857, v. 12, pp. 94-100.
69. Parkes to Bowring, 20 October 1856, Parl. Papers 1857, v. 12, p. 27.
70. Parkes to his sister, 14 November 1856, in Lane-Poole, *Parkes*, v. 1, p. 232.
71. Peiho (Baihe) - White River - which flows from Beijing down to Tianjin before entering the sea.

last, in November 1854, he was compelled to leave because the river was about to freeze.[72] 'Still,' he said, 'I shall not resist strong convictions contrary to my own.'[73] Parkes's proposal was never carried out because apparently the admiral also had concerns about the weather in the north.

Since a northern expedition was impossible, Parkes suggested the occupation of Canton itself and, for that purpose, urged his superiors to request military reinforcements from Singapore and India. Bowring and Seymour seemed reluctant to go so far for the time being. By January 1857, however, it was obvious that Yeh could not be subdued by the small force at their disposal, and they applied for more troops.[74]

From this account it is clear that Parkes initiated the idea of military action. It was embodied in his very first letter to Yeh on 8 October 1856 and set in motion by his letter to Commodore Elliot of the same date.[75] The first concrete suggestion was conveyed in his letter of 11 October to Bowring, in which he proposed to seize one or more Chinese war junks. Then he planned all subsequent military operations against the Chinese and participated in most of them. Step by step he had brought Great Britain into a state of undeclared war with China.

Now let us hear the views of the law lords on Parkes's actions.

V. The House of Lords on Parkes's conduct

Lord Derby[76] found Parkes to be a man very rapid in his movements. On the day of the *Arrow* incident, Parkes made presentations in the first place to Bowring; in the second place to Yeh; and in the third place as if to provide for all contingencies, without waiting for the slightest explanation, called upon Commodore Elliot to resort to coercion.[77] Undoubtedly Commissioner Yeh did not apologize. However, he did most courteously offer an explanation and an 'almost apology for that which was not a violation of the treaty'.[78] 'But Consul Parkes made up his mind not to consent to what was proposed'.[79] Instead, Parkes went to Hong Kong and laid down 'the whole of the campaign as it was to be conducted in case of the continued refusal of the Chinese

---

72. Bowring to Parkes, 12 November 1856, Parkes Papers; see Bowring to Clarendon, Desp. 173, 10 November 1854, FO17/271.
73. Bowring to Parkes, 14 November 1856, Parkes Papers.
74. Lane-Poole, *Parkes*, v. 1, p. 257.
75. Contrast the opposite view taken by Lane-Poole, in ibid., p. 237.
76. He was Edward George Geoffrey Smith Stanley, fourteenth earl of Derby (1799–1869). He had been prime minister in 1852. Now in opposition, he was the leader of the Conservative Party. He was to become prime minister again in 1858 and 1866. See Wilbur Devereux Jones, *Lord Derby and Victorian Conservatism* (Oxford, Basil Blackwell, 1956).
77. Derby, 24 February 1857, Hansard, 3d series, v. 144, col. 1181.
78. Ibid., col. 1183.
79. Ibid., col. 1184. Here, Derby was quoting Yeh word for word.

government'.[80] He coolly and deliberately recommended the bombardment of first the barrier forts, second the town forts which were surrounded by civilian dwellings, and third Yeh's residence inside the densely populated city. These recommendations were made barely twelve days after the first cause of the quarrel.[81]

Derby fell short of asking the obvious question: Who authorized Parkes to start an undeclared war? Nonetheless the foreign secretary, Lord Clarendon, came close to offering an answer: 'I fear that we must come to the conclusion that in dealing with a nation like the Chinese, if we intend to preserve any amicable or useful relations with them, we must make them sensible of the law of force'.[82] Earl Grey was noticeably upset by this frank admission, adding: 'I heard with extreme pain . . . [a] doctrine which I have heard out of doors, but which I never expected to hear repeated, or even by implication sanctioned, in this House'.[83] Earl Granville immediately interjected: 'It is far from being my recollection of the speech of my noble Friend that he maintained such a doctrine'.[84] In response, Earl Grey said that he acquitted Clarendon of having in plain words put forward any such monstrous doctrine.[85]

Lord St Leonards also reacted strongly to Lord Clarendon's feared advocation of the 'law of force'. In a very short time after their seizure, he said, the twelve men were returned by the Chinese; moreover, Commissioner Yeh promised that the occurrence should not happen again, and that in the future the usual reference should be made to the British consul. 'Mr Parkes, however, demanded that the men should be publicly restored; and upon this simple question of form, apparently introduced for the purpose of embarrassing the question, the rupture took place'.[86] Lord St Leonards concluded that 'it would startle the common sense of a body of Englishmen to be told that Mr Parkes rejected these twelve men, sent them back, and took what he called "active measures" thereupon'.[87]

Lord Malmesbury[88] used even stronger language: 'I do not know that I have ever met anything which I should consider more grotesque than the conduct of Consul Parkes throughout these transactions'.[89] Parkes had sent back the

---

80. Ibid. 81. Ibid., col. 1185.
82. Ibid., col. 1203.
83. Grey, 24 February 1857, Hansard, 3d series, v. 144, col. 1233.
84. Granville's interjection, 24 February 1857, Hansard, 3d series, v. 144, col. 1223.
85. Grey, 24 February 1857, Hansard, 3d series, v. 144, col. 1233.
86. St Leonards, 26 February 1857, Hansard, 3d series, v. 144, col. 1331.
87. Ibid., col. 1332.
88. He was James Howard Harris, third earl of Malmesbury (1807–89). He was secretary of state for foreign affairs in 1852. He was to occupy that position again in 1858. On the formation of Lord Derby's third administration in June 1866, he declined the foreign office in consequence of ill health and accepted the post of lord privy seal. He wrote *The Memoirs of an Ex-Minister* (London, Longmans, Green, 1884).
89. Malmesbury, 26 February 1857, Hansard, 3d series, v. 144, cols. 1350–1.

sailors 'just as a man might send back goods which he had bought from his grocer because they were not full weight. Mr Parkes should have remembered that these men were human beings'.[90] He concluded that the government should not lose a moment in removing Parkes as unfit for his position.[91]

VI. In sum

Richard Cobden suspected that there must have been an understanding between Parkes and Palmerston that a more aggressive policy might be followed if a suitable opportunity presented itself: 'I perceive a great change in the tone of the correspondence between him and other Ministers with whom he had to deal. When Lord Clarendon came into office, there seems to be some slackening of the rein'.[92] If there had been such an understanding, when and how had Palmerston and Parkes arrived at it? Parkes's official biographer, Stanley Lane-Poole, said that when Parkes was in London in the early part of 1856, Palmerston gave him a special audience. During that interview, 'Lord Palmerston played the part of Hephaistos to the consular Achilles',[93] so that when Parkes returned to China to take up his post as acting consul at Canton in June of that year, he came out 'girt with the armour of the gods – of Downing Street'.[94] According to Greek mythology, Hephaistos was the god of fire who made Achilles' armour. By this classical allusion, Lane-Poole probably meant that Parkes subsequently returned to China armed with Palmerston's ideas. It was unusual for a Victorian prime minister of Palmerston's stature to make time for a young man in the 'cinderella service',[95] who was not yet a full consul. We shall never know the content of Palmerston's conversation with Parkes, but Lane-Poole informs us that Palmerston gave Parkes a copy of his own instructions to Sir John Davis in 1847, when Palmerston was foreign secretary. Therein, Palmerston wrote, 'We shall lose all the vantage ground we have gained by our victories in China, if we take a low tone... We must especially take care not to descend from the relative position which we have acquired... The Chinese must learn and be convinced that if they attack our people and our factories, they will be shot'.[96]

With reason, Lane-Poole maintained that Parkes was solely responsible for the policy of 1856. To the Chinese it was Parkes 'who was the head and front

90. Ibid., col. 1351.
91. Ibid.
92. Cobden, 26 February 1857, Hansard, 3d series, v. 144, cols. 1416–17.
93. Lane-Poole, *Parkes*, v. 1, p. 223.
94. Ibid., but see also pp. 144–5, 195–6.
95. This term is borrowed from the title of D. C. M. Platt's book, *The Cinderella Service: British Consuls since 1825* (London, Longman, 1971).
96. Ibid., p. 223. The original draft of this document is classified as FO17/121, Palmerston to Davis, Desp. 1, 9 January 1847, and deposited in the Public Record Office in London.

of the offence', the plenipotentiary at Hong Kong being a mere 'diplomatic expression', he wrote.[97] Parkes's close friend, Commander Bate, actually congratulated him on having been 'the instrument, under Providence, of breaking through the old regime'.[98] Lord Elgin identified Parkes completely with the dispute, describing him as 'the impersonification of the *Arrow* case'.[99] When subsequent British reinforcements eventually brought about the occupation of Canton and Parkes was appointed one of three commissioners to rule that city, the *Daily Press* in Hong Kong commented: 'He [Parkes] was the head and front of that ill-judged squabble ... and it is a poor way to convince [the Cantonese] that all their present indescribable misery is attributable to Yeh's impracticable obstinacy when active employment is given to the very man who originated the quarrel, which, whilst we discard and repudiate, we found a *casus belli*'.[100]

Thus, friends and critics agreed that Parkes was responsible for having made the *Arrow* incident the pretext for war. But Lane-Poole claimed that Parkes 'gave the Chinese commissioner Yeh every opportunity for withdrawing from an untenable position without apology, indemnity, or humiliation'.[101] The opposite has been shown to be true. It is also interesting to read the comments of some historians who have tried to defend Parkes. H. B. Morse said that he was 'the true embodiment of the clarity of thought and energy in decision and action which characterises the best type of the English official'.[102] Douglas Hurd wrote, 'He was strikingly good-looking with fair hair and blue eyes, and, though never physically strong, seemed impervious to fear. He was forthright in speech, and deeply religious'.[103] Clearly, these defences are irrelevant to the charge of his having falsified a pretext for war.

97. Lane-Poole, *Parkes*, v. 1, p. 249.
98. Bate to Parkes, 23 February 1856, Parkes Papers.
99. Elgin to Clarendon, 14 January 1858, MSS Clar. Dep. C85.
100. *Daily Express*, 6 January 1858 (newspaper clipping), Ryl. Eng. MSS 1230/67.
101. *DNB*, v. 15, p. 299.
102. Morse, *International Relations of the Chinese Empire*, v. 1, p. 426.
103. Hurd, *Arrow War*, p. 13.

4
Sir John Bowring:
Possessed by a monomania

I. Why was Bowring led on by his young consul?

In the preceding chapter we saw how Sir John Bowring was led on by young Consul Parkes until the *Arrow* incident was transformed into an undeclared war. Hostilities led to the destruction of the foreign factories in Canton, and the British community there withdrew to Hong Kong.[1]

Bowring was full of regret. He was above all apprehensive of the reaction at home. 'I hope it will be my good fortune to terminate this work of war at Canton as satisfactorily as the work of peace in Siam,' he warily wrote in private to the foreign secretary, Lord Clarendon, 'before all I hope for your approval and I do not believe it will be wanting'.[2] To his son he expressed great anxiety about the course his government would take. He even exclaimed, 'Will they not help us, speedily, effectually in these our great straights [*sic*]?'[3] The suspense eventually became so unnerving that he began to doubt whether he would continue to be 'allowed to manage matters . . . I always fear the character of the instructions from home'.[4]

Not surprisingly, his relationship with Parkes rapidly deteriorated as he came to blame the consul for his difficulties. He ordered Parkes, now redundant as acting consul at Canton, to resume his duties as consul at Xiamen (Amoy) on the grounds that 'a long time must elapse before any resumption of trade can take place at Canton'. He added, 'I take this opportunity of cordially thanking you for the great services you have rendered during the exciting and often embarrassing events which have taken place during the period in which you have had charge of the Canton consulate'.[5]

1. See Wong, *Yeh Ming-ch'en*, chapter 10.
2. Bowring to Clarendon, 14 November 1856, MSS Clar. Dep. C57 China.
3. John Bowring to Edgar Bowring, 22 December 1856, Ryl. Eng. MSS 1228/169; John Bowring to Edgar Bowring, 10 January 1857, Ryl. Eng. MSS 1228/170.
4. John Bowring to Edgar Bowring, 28 February 1857, Ryl. Eng. MSS 1228/176.
5. Bowring to Parkes, 10 March 1857, Parkes Papers.

Parkes protested against the decision; but Bowring insisted, giving as a further reason the growing importance of Xiamen.[6] Parkes played for time. He endlessly delayed making arrangements to go to Xiamen, and when he could no longer do so, he applied for leave of absence for one month.[7] Then the admiral intervened and Bowring retracted.[8]

The question is: Why had Bowring allowed himself to be led on by the young consul? Some historians have implied that the answer lies in Bowring's personality. In Lane-Poole's judgment, the plenipotentiary was a man of a nervous, fidgety nature and may have relied a good deal upon Parkes's counsel.[9] But in what specific way could such reliance be attributed to Bowring's personality? Lane-Poole did not specify.

Other historians have made similar inferences. Gerald Graham, after reading Bowring's *Autobiographical Recollections*,[10] concluded that Bowring was 'versatile, scholarly, vain and flamboyant'.[11] G. F. Bartle described Bowring as vain and conceited.[12]

Bowring's contemporaries seem to have noted his versatility above all else. When Sir George Bonham recommended Bowring to succeed him as plenipotentiary in the Far East, he had to assure Lord Clarendon that Bowring could, under proper instructions and restraints, 'manage affairs as they now are'.[13] While Bowring's appointment was being considered in the Foreign Office, Henry Addington, the permanent under-secretary for foreign affairs,[14] informed Clarendon that there might be a question as to his carrying sufficient ballast to countervail his superfluity of sail: 'He would probably be over the Great Wall before we had time to look around us'.[15] Ironically, Parkes's opinion was similar. When he heard of Bowring's expedition to the Peiho[16] in 1854, he criticized it as 'somewhat akin to flightiness; he attempts too much, and consequently does too little'.[17] Is it possible that Parkes's perception of Bowring contributed to the consul's daring attempts to lead on the plenipotentiary?

6. Bowring to Parkes, 11 March 1857, Parkes Papers.
7. Bowring to Parkes, 18 April 1857, Parkes Papers.
8. Bowring to Parkes, 1 and 4 May 1857, Parkes Papers, see also Bate to Mrs Parkes, Monday (c. 27 April 1857), Parkes Papers.
9. Lane-Poole, *Parkes*, v. 1, p. 248.
10. London, 1877.
11. Graham, *China Station*, p. 282.
12. See, G. F. Bartle, 'The Political Career of Sir John Bowring (1793–1872) between 1820 and 1849', unpublished M.A. thesis, University of London, 1959.
13. Bonham to Clarendon, 5 August 1854, MSS Clar. Dep. C8 China.
14. Henry Unwin Addington (1790–1870) was permanent under-secretary of state for foreign affairs 1842–1854, when he retired and was sworn a privy councillor. *DNB*, v. 1 p. 121.
15. Addington to Clarendon, 26 August 1854, MSS Clar. Dep. C8 China.
16. Again, Peiho – White River – enters the sea near Tianjin.
17. Parkes to Mrs Lockhart, 18 October 1854, in Lane-Poole, *Parkes*, v. 1, p. 189.

The personalities of imperialism

But there were other sides to Bowring. He appears to have been genuinely religious, the best known of the hymns he penned being 'In the Cross of Christ I Glory'. He had helped to found the *Westminster Review* in 1824 and then edited Bentham's *Life and Works* in eleven volumes. Indeed, he was a Utilitarian, a member of the Bentham school of sociopolitical thinkers. Bentham was not a practising Christian; his approach to morality was based on the utilitarian principle of pleasure and pain, not on revealed religion.[18] Thus, Bowring's interest both in hymn writing and in Bentham unveils a conflict between the rational side and the mystical side of this complicated man.

In India, the Benthamites set out to 'reform' what they saw as barbarous Indian customs such as *sati*, creating a lot of anti-British feeling.[19] In China, Bowring became obsessed, not with objectionable Chinese customs such as foot binding, but with entry into the walled city of Canton, creating a great deal of hostility among the Cantonese.

Bowring was also an accomplished linguist, credited with a command of six European languages. After he went to China, he made an effort to learn Chinese.[20] Bartle remarked that 'few British representatives in the East, indeed, have equalled him in his desire to understand the customs and languages of the people amongst whom he had gone to live'.[21] Nevertheless he must have continued to rely on Parkes's expertise in the Chinese language; the extent of his own knowledge in that respect appears to have been restricted to a few Chinese characters that dotted some of his private correspondence.[22] When in 1858 he went to see Commissioner Yeh, who had been captured during the *Arrow* War, it was reported that he, 'after his fashion, blundered out a few words which he thought were Chinese, but had eventually to fall back on

18. Jeremy Bentham (1748–1832) was a famous writer on jurisprudence. In 1760 he went up to Queen's College, Oxford, and was induced to sign the Thirty-Nine Articles by one of the fellows who reproved his presumption in showing hesitation. In 1763, he graduated B.A. at the age of sixteen, and in the same year he began to eat his terms at Lincoln's Inn, subsequently called to the bar in 1817. He took no measures to ensure his success in law; instead he pursued the study of politics and jurisprudence which became the occupation of his life. In some ways his greatest work is 'The Introduction to Principles of Morals and Legislation', which is a clear exposition of the principle of utility. *DNB*, v. 2, pp. 268–81.
19. See, e.g, Nancy G. Cassels, 'Bentinck: Humanitarian and Imperialist – The Abolition of Suttee', *Journal of British Studies*, 5, no. 1 (November 1965), pp. 77–87. Cassels then went further to attribute these ill feelings as one of the causes of the Indian Mutiny. For more recent interpretations of the mutiny, see C. A. Bayly, *The New Cambridge History of India, vol. 2, part 1, Indian Society and the Making of the British Empire* (Cambridge University Press, 1988).
20. Evidence of this attempt may be found in an odd Chinese character here or there in his letters to Parkes among the Parkes Papers. The attempt does not appear to be very successful. But at least he tried and must be admired for his courage, especially as none of the contemporary Chinese officials appears to have made a similar attempt to learn English.
21. G. F. Bartle, 'Sir John Bowring and the *Arrow* War in China', *Bulletin of the John Rylands Library*, 43, no. 2 (1961), pp. 293–316.
22. See his private letters to his son, Lord Clarendon, and Lord Palmerston.

the interpreter'.[23] E. G. Biaggini considered him to be an honourable man, though muddle-headed.[24] W. C. Costin described him as 'a much-travelled man of wide experience' who had 'a high conception of his duty and his position'.[25]

In 1831, he was involved in a commission examining and reporting on the public accounts of France. He visited Paris, the Hague, and Brussels and examined the finance departments of their various governments. The first report made by the commission led to a complete change in the English Exchequer and was the foundation of all the improvements which have since been made. The second report, dealing with the military accounts, was carried into immediate effect. In the same year, he and George Villiers (afterwards the earl of Clarendon) were appointed commissioners to investigate the commercial relations between Britain and France, and presented two reports to Parliament.

In terms of political and diplomatic experience, he had been a member of Parliament in 1833–7 and again in 1841–9. During the latter period, he served on a parliamentary commission enquiring into Britain's commercial relations with China. This experience prompted Lord Palmerston to rescue him from financial ruin, due to business failures, by appointing him consul at Canton in 1849. In 1853, he became acting British plenipotentiary in the Far East; and in 1854, the plenipotentiary. By the time of the *Arrow* incident on 8 October 1856, therefore, Bowring had considerable diplomatic experience in addition to his political background.[26] One would not have expected a man of Bowring's stature, experience, and sense of honour, duty, and position to have been led on by a young subordinate; but he was. Why? I am not proposing anything so concrete as 'secret instructions', merely that the prestige of Palmerston's views, conveyed with Parkes's intemperate enthusiasm, may have swayed the older man and ultimately – disastrously – carried the day.

II. The *Arrow* incident and the Canton City question

Upon receiving Parkes's communication about the *Arrow* incident, Bowring made some enquiries and found that the *Arrow* 'had no right to hoist the British flag; the licence to do so expired on the 27th September'.[27] He at once instructed the consul to 'send back the register to be delivered to the Colonial Office'.[28] Then he further discovered that the *Arrow*'s register had not even

---

23. *Hong Kong Register* (newspaper clipping), 16 February 1858, Ryl. Eng. MSS 1230/84.
24. Biaggini, 'Coercion of China'.
25. Costin, *Great Britain and China*, p. 134.
26. See Bowring, *Autobiographical Recollections* (London, privately printed, 1877).
27. Bowring to Parkes, Desp. 127, 11 October 1856, FO228/213.
28. Ibid.

been duly presented at the harbour-master's office according to the regulations.[29] This omission had in fact rendered the vessel liable to confiscation and had deprived it of all its claims to protection. Now he had to decide whether or not he should pursue the *Arrow* dispute any further, because there was no longer any basis for British intervention. He opted for further action, and informed Parkes of his willingness to consider regranting the register of the *Arrow* if applied for, but adding, 'There can be no doubt that after the expiry of the licence, protection could not be legally granted'.[30] It is obvious, therefore, that he was lying when he addressed Commissioner Yeh thus: 'Whatever representations may have been made to your Excellency, there is no doubt that the lorcha *Arrow* lawfully bore the British flag under a register granted by me'.[31] Why did he do so?

A vital clue may be found initially in Bowring's private letters. On 16 October 1856, Bowring wrote such a letter,[32] and three official despatches, in rapid succession.[33] The private letter was addressed to Parkes; the despatches were addressed to Parkes, Lord Clarendon, and Commissioner Yeh. The private letter contained information absent from the despatches. In it, Bowring instructed Parkes secretly: 'You may say that I deem the matter so grave that I might probably be willing to visit the imperial commissioner *at his yamun in the City*.'[34] Here, Bowring was introducing an entirely new and unrelated element into the dispute, namely, the right of entry into Canton City.

He went on, 'Cannot we use the opportunity and carry the City question? If so, I will come up with the whole fleet. I think we have now a stepping-stone from which with good management we may move on to important sequences'.[35] It was, of course, on this very day that Parkes took Captain Charles Earl's evidence about the *Arrow* incident and sent it immediately to Bowring.[36] Bowring, however, did not forward this evidence to London.[37]

The seizure of a Chinese junk on 14 October 1856 would, under normal circumstances, have been sufficient to save Bowring face. This was a view subsequently expressed by Lord Lyndhurst in the House of Lords and Sir

29. Bowring to Parkes, Desp. 126, 13 October 1856, FO228/213.
30. Bowring to Parkes, Desp. 130, 13 October 1856. FO222/213. This was the second letter he wrote to Parkes on that day.
31. Bowring to Yeh, 14 November 1856, Parl. Papers 1857, v. 12, pp. 143–4. There is no evidence that by 14 November 1856 the *Arrow* had renewed her register. Even if she had, Bowring was still being dishonest in making such a statement because on 8 October 1856, she did not lawfully bear, if at all, the British flag.
32. Bowring to Parkes, 16 October 1856, Parkes Papers.
33. Bowring to Clarendon, Desp. 337, 16 October 1856, FO17/251; and encl. 3: Bowring to Parkes, 16 October 1856; and encl. 5: Bowring to Yeh, 16 October 1856.
34. Bowring to Parkes, 16 October 1856, Parkes Papers.
35. Ibid.
36. Parkes to Bowring, Desp. 160, 16 October 1856, FO228/213, and encl: Earl's deposition, 16 October 1856. This issue will be explored later in this chapter.
37. Bowring to Clarendon, Desp. 224, 7 May 1857, FO17/268.

James Graham in the House of Commons.[38] But at this critical juncture, Bowring decided to change the nature of the dispute by attempting to introduce the demand to enter Canton. Hereafter, the word *Arrow* all but disappeared from Bowring's correspondence. It had been merely a 'stepping-stone ... to important [con]sequences'.[39]

Parkes was greatly emboldened by these secret instructions, but was frustrated by the lack of further official action to back them. He waited in vain, so he decided to travel downstream from Canton to Whampoa to see Commodore Elliot. The commodore told him that no further action could be taken without instructions from Hong Kong.[40] Instead of returning to Canton, Parkes travelled 'at once', and without previous sanction or warning, direct to Hong Kong to call on Bowring at Government House.[41]

When did Parkes arrive at Hong Kong? On 20 October 1856, so Bowring told Lord Clarendon. In his official despatch of 23 October, Bowring wrote, 'Mr Consul Parkes, wisely judging that a conference with the naval Commander-in-chief and myself would be very useful, came down to Hong Kong on the morning of the 20th instant', and that a meeting was held on the same day with Admiral Seymour.[42] In fact, Parkes had arrived the day before, according to a private note marked 'confidential' and dated Hong Kong 19 October 1856. This note further shows that Parkes had had lengthy discussions with Bowring on that previous day, whereupon Bowring went to see the admiral. 'I have just seen the admiral', this confidential note from Bowring to Parkes begins. 'It will be necessary to be very cautious, as we shall not obtain the aid of the naval authorities beyond a certain point. I do not think the admiral will *make war*, and we must consider not what we might but what we *can* do'. The note continued, 'We are to have a meeting at 10 tomorrow'.[43]

Here is a conspiracy. Bowring was hiding from his superior in London, Lord Clarendon, and from his colleague the admiral in Hong Kong, that he had had detailed discussions with Parkes *before* the conference on 20 October, in which the admiral, Bowring, and Parkes participated.[44] He had a collaborator in Parkes, who in turn was careful to conceal, in his own official despatches, that he had arrived at Hong Kong on 19 October. Writing to Bowring officially on 20 October, he said that he had proceeded from Canton to Whampoa only

38. Lyndhurst, 24 February 1857, Hansard, 3d series, v. 144, cols. 1217–18; Graham, 27 February 1857, Hansard, 3d series, v. 144, col. 1561.
39. Bowring to Parkes, 16 October 1856, Parkes Papers.
40. Parkes to Bowring, 20 October 1856, Parl. Papers 1857, v. 12, pp. 78–9, para. 2.
41. Ibid.
42. Bowring to Clarendon, 23 October 1856, ibid., pp. 73–7, para. 2.
43. Bowring to Parkes, 19 October 1856, Parkes Papers.
44. Seymour to Bowring, 23 October 1856, at 9 A.M. on *Coromandel*, off the barrier forts, Parl. Papers 1857, v. 12, pp. 86–7. The document distinctly refers to the conference 'at which Her Majesty's Consul at Canton was present'.

'yesterday evening',[45] thus giving the impression that he could not possibly have arrived at Hong Kong before the morning of 20 October.

Why was a conspiracy necessary? Possibly Bowring feared that the admiral might suspect he was being used to settle personal accounts. At this tripartite conference Parkes, discreetly assisted by Bowring, set out to convince the admiral of the necessity of further coercion against Yeh and suggested the specific actions to be taken.[46] Thereupon 'it was decided that Mr Parkes should give in writing a succinct account of what had occurred, and that such suggestions as obtained the general concurrence of Sir Michael Seymour and myself should be embodied in a despatch, to be acknowledged by me, and which should serve as a general outline of proceedings intended to be taken'.[47]

This meticulous procedure seems to suggest that Bowring was nervous about the serious consequences of such a course of violent action and tried to shed as much of the possible blame onto the originator of the plan. Sure enough, he was subsequently attacked most fiercely by the British press and Parliament.[48] What appears very curious was that a secretary was not brought in to do the job that Parkes was asked to do – namely, to keep minutes of the meeting. Possibly, Bowring was so nervous about the conspiracy that he did not wish anybody not directly involved to know anything about the meeting, including his own secretary, W. Woodgate.[49] It also seems that he was nervous about the admiral subsequently not doing what had been verbally agreed upon and wanted to have, as it were, a written contract. Thus, when Parkes submitted his proposals in writing, Bowring had them 'read in the presence of his Excellency the naval Commander-in-chief', to obtain his 'general concurrence'.[50]

Such concurrence was forthcoming. Bowring was jubilant. He could not help writing Parkes another private note saying, 'I doubt not the success of the attack on the forts if Yeh's obstinacy compel that measure and it is now almost to be hoped that he will *chercher querelle*, – as we are so *strong* and so *right*'.[51] He continued, 'I hope you will not lose sight of the City question. You will not demand it of course, – but you will have an opportunity of saying what may help its settlement. I am quite ready to go into the City – and if Yeh will give me an official reception it will be my care to protect myself – but you will of

---

45. Parkes to Bowring, 20 October 1856, Parl. Papers 1857, v. 12, pp. 78–9, para. 1.
46. Ibid., para. 9. See also Seymour to Bowring, 23 October 1856, Parl. Papers 1857, v. 12, pp. 86–7.
47. Bowring to Clarendon, 23 October 1856, Parl. Papers 1857, v. 12, p. 73, para. 2.
48. See Part Four, this volume.
49. W. Woodgate was the registrar of the British superintendency of trade. He was a relative of a former superintendent, Sir George Bonham, who recommended his appointment. He died in service at the age of thirty-seven. See P. D. Coates, *China Consuls* (Hong Kong, Oxford University Press, 1988), p. 499.
50. Bowring to Parkes, 22 October 1856, Parl. Papers 1857, v. 12, p. 80.
51. Bowring to Parkes, 21 October 1856, para. 2, Parkes Papers. Roughly translated from French, *chercher querelle* means 'pick a quarrel'.

course hint at the gravity of the consequence of any insult to the highest British authority'.[52]

He concluded, 'The Admiral has left me in excellent dispositions, and we must write a bright page in our history'.[53] Why did the admiral readily adopt Parkes's plan to escalate hostilities? Parkes and Bowring had deliberately kept him in the dark about the expiry of the *Arrow*'s register.[54] Thus, if Parkes and Bowring assured him that the British flag had been insulted, and British sailors under British protection had been arrested against treaty provisions, he would have been duty-bound to take action. Had not Palmerston instructed Davis that if the Chinese were to 'attack our people and our factories, they will be shot'?[55]

On the morning of 23 October, the four barrier forts were captured and dismantled without any British casualties. The admiral at once wrote to inform Bowring, the despatch reaching Hong Kong late in the evening the same day.[56] Before this news arrived, Bowring had already penned a private letter to Parkes, which began: 'Yeh's letter to me are [*sic*] of the same character as to you – so I take for granted the admiral will have "done the deed"'. It ended, 'I wish we could carry the City Question – that would be the crowning affair as regards *local* matters'.[57] After the news had reached him, Bowring responded immediately, not to the admiral who had given him the news, but to the acting consul in private: 'I hear from the admiral that the Four Forts have been taken most satisfactorily'. He continued, 'No doubt Yeh will now be for giving way. I hope however you will be able to turn our position to the best account – and if you can arrange for my official reception I will come up'.[58] This is important, as Bowring clearly hopes Yeh will *not* give way before Parkes can include entry to Canton among the requirements of his submission.

Having considered the news overnight and weighed the balance, Bowring felt he had to act quickly and revealed to Seymour his secrets, albeit dressed up as treaty obligations: 'If your Excellency and the consul should concur with me in opinion that the circumstances are auspicious for requiring the fulfilment of Treaty obligations as regards the City of Canton, and for arranging an official

---

52. Ibid., para. 3.
53. Ibid., para. 11.
54. The first to discover this was the earl of Malmesbury. See Malmesbury, 26 February 1857, Hansard, 3d series, v. 144, col. 1344.
55. Palmerston to Davis, Desp. 1, 9 January 1847, FO17/121.
56. Bowring to Clarendon, 23 October 1856, Parl. Papers 1857, v. 12, p. 73, para. 5. For the actual despatch, see pp. 86–7, Seymour to Bowring, 23 October 1856, at 9 A.M. on *Coromandel*, off the barrier forts; or see Adm. 125/97 for the same despatch.
57. Bowring to Parkes, 23 October 1856, Parkes Papers. This was the first letter Bowring wrote to Parkes this day. The word 'local' was underlined in the original, suggesting that Bowring might have planned with Parkes above and beyond the capture of Canton.
58. Bowring to Parkes, 23 October 1856, Parkes Papers. This was the second letter Bowring wrote to Parkes on this day.

The personalities of imperialism

meeting with the Imperial Commission[er] within the city walls I shall willingly come to Canton'.[59]

As if afraid that the admiral might not agree, Bowring immediately tried to seek support from Consul Parkes by writing to him officially, 'I have conveyed to Sir Michael Seymour an opinion that if his Excellency and yourself agree on the fitness of the opportunity, it would be well if the *vexata quæstio* of our entrance into the City should now be settled; at least, as far as to secure us an official reception there'. He continued, 'This would be a crowning result to the successful operations of Her Majesty's naval forces'.[60]

Having drafted these two official despatches, Bowring settled down to pen a private note to Parkes. He began, 'I hope Mr Woodgate will get off two official letters whose main object is to recommend that the present opportunity – we may never have one so auspicious – be used for settling the City Question – at all events as far as *our* reception at the imperial commissioner's yamun is concerned'. Bowring's underlining of the word 'our' suggests that he intended to take Parkes along. His second paragraph reads, 'I think there will be much, and reasonable disappointment if this be not conceded'. He went on: 'Of course I will come up as soon as you have arranged an official reception and have desired the admiral to send down a steamer for me'.[61]

Woodgate promptly finished copying out Bowring's two official despatches. Thereupon, Bowring wrote a second private note to Parkes: 'I shall of course be anxious to ascertain how far the admiral and you concur in the opinion that the City Question may now becomingly be pressed. Of course entrance must not be *asked* unless insisted on'.[62]

While Bowring was writing these official despatches and private letters on 24 October, the admiral put into effect the second part of Parkes's plan of coercion. At noon, some of the forts in Canton harbour were attacked and occupied.[63] Amid the excitement, Bowring's official despatch of the morning reached Parkes at 8 p.m. Immediately Parkes replied that no opportunity 'has yet been afforded for approaching by peaceable argument the *vexata quæstio* to which your Excellency's despatch of today refers'.[64] News of the attack and Parkes's reply missed the overnight steamer for Hong Kong.[65]

Not surprisingly, the next day, 25 October, Bowring again wrote to Parkes

59. Bowring to Seymour, 24 October 1856, Parl. Papers 1857, v. 12, p. 87.
60. Bowring to Parkes, 24 October 1856, Parl. Papers. Roughly translated from Latin, *vexata quæstio* means 'vexing question'.
61. Bowring to Parkes, 24 October 1856, Parkes Papers. This was the first private letter of the day to Parkes.
62. Bowring to Parkes, 24 October 1856, Parkes Papers. This was the second private letter of the day to Parkes.
63. Parkes to Bowring, 24 October 1856, Parl. Papers 1857, v. 12, p. 88; Seymour to Bowring, 25 October 1856, Parl. Papers 1857, v. 12, p. 91, para. 1.
64. Parkes to Bowring, 24 October 1856, Parl Papers 1857, v. 12, p. 91 para. 2.
65. See Bowring to Parkes, 25 October 1856, Parkes Papers.

privately: 'I have not a word from you by this morning's steamer'. Nonetheless he added, 'In reference to the reception in the City I think it may very properly be pointed out to the people that if we had had access none of the mischiefs which have befallen them would have happened – and the only way to prevent their occurrence is the establishment of friendly personal intercourse'. One might note the irony of presenting this argument for friendliness in the wake of such aggression. He continued, 'There is no reason whatever that the admiral should not see Yeh and a meeting might be very useful'.[66] Here, one may detect an element of fear that the admiral might get into the walled city before Bowring himself, thus depriving him of the rare glory of being the first British official to achieve this.

On this same day Parkes introduced a thinly veiled demand to enter the city: 'His Excellency [the admiral] having been compelled to take much trouble in order to redress a wrong committed by your Excellency, it will be necessary to guard against the recurrence of such difficulties, by providing freer means of communication between your Excellency and Her Majesty's officers'.[67] Of course he informed Bowring of this new demand in a way that clearly shows he was trying to cover his chief from possible criticism at home: 'It may indeed with truth be said, that want of personal access to the Government of Canton, which is denied to us by the gates of this City being closed against us, has been the occasion of the present trouble'.[68] The occasion of the trouble was, indeed, no longer the *Arrow* incident.

On 26 October both the news of the capture of the Canton forts and Parkes's new demand reached Hong Kong. Bowring was elated. At once he replied to Parkes privately: 'The City Question is and will be the prominent one in the public eye – and if between us all we can manage it – great glory – and great good – will be the result. The Admiral's letters are equally brave and wise and gratify me much'.[69] He attempted self-justification: 'Of course the magnitude of our demands grows with the growth of our success. All diplomacy is the exemplification of the Sybil's story – all wise diplomacy'.[70] As before, Bowring did not acknowledge the admiral's despatch until the following day.[71]

But 26 October being a Sunday, the Royal Navy took a rest.[72] There was no news for Bowring via steamer on 27 October. He found it increasingly difficult to remain in Hong Kong and could not help writing another private letter to Parkes, saying, 'Tho' I believe my proper place is here until the admiral has

66. Ibid.
67. Parkes to Yeh, 25 October 1856, Parl. Papers 1857, v. 12, p. 90, para. 3.
68. Ibid., para. 2.
69. Bowring to Parkes, 26 October 1856, para. 1, Parkes Papers.
70. Ibid., para. 2.
71. Bowring to Seymour, 27 October 1856, Parl. Papers 1857, v. 12, pp. 91–2.
72. Seymour to Bowring, 26 October 1856, Parl. Papers 1857, v. 12, p. 92.

The personalities of imperialism

done his work I often wish I am in the consulate'.[73] He was probably concerned that he might be deprived of the privilege of being the first British official to enter Canton City.

Sunday made no difference to pagan Yeh, who replied to Parkes's thinly veiled demand to enter the city: 'But I, the Minister, also know full well what you the said consul have in view'. He explained, 'For a certainty, it is nothing less than a desire on your part to imitate the course taken by the Envoy Davis in the spring of 1847'.[74]

In the spring of 1847, Sir John Davis had forced his way up to Canton and exacted a promise from the imperial commissioner, Qiying,[75] to let the British into the city in two years' time.[76]

But Yeh was defiant. Parkes was furious: 'Your Excellency has never yet offered the satisfaction demanded in the matter of the "Arrow", and you now refuse to entertain the proposal for direct personal intercourse made to you by the naval Commander-in-chief in my letter of the 25th'.[77] Parkes is not quite accurate here. In his 'letter of the 25th', it is not at all clear that the admiral was the person who made the proposal. Parkes had simply left it vague by saying 'it will be necessary . . .'.[78] In fact a casual observer will read it to mean that it was the writer of the letter, Parkes himself, who was making that proposal. Now that the proposal was rejected, Parkes tried to seek cover under the admiral's authority. He reported this unexpected development to Bowring.[79]

Suddenly, Bowring found himself terribly exposed. He had confidently predicted that Yeh would succumb after the destruction of the Canton forts. That was why he had decided to raise openly the Canton City question. Now that this move had elicited 'only a defiant reply',[80] Bowring found he had nowhere to hide. He was obliged, belatedly, to report this unhappy development to London. In so doing, he pretended that Yeh was the first to raise the subject: '*October 27*, 1856. – A little before midnight I received the despatch from Mr Parkes, dated same day, conveying a communication from the imperial commissioner and the consul's reply. To Mr Parkes I replied, as per inclosure, requesting him should a proper opportunity offer, to remind the imperial commissioner, who had referred to the proceedings of Sir John Davis in 1847,

73. Bowring to Parkes, 27 October 1856, Parkes Papers.
74. Yeh to Parkes, 26 October 1856, Parl. Papers 1857, v. 12, pp. 92–3.
75. Qiying (?–1858) was a Manchu. He was one of the signatories to the Treaty of Nanking and was well known for his conciliatory diplomacy when he was imperial commissioner for foreign affairs from 1844 to 1848. See J. K. Fairbank, *Trade and Diplomacy on the China Coast: The Opening of Treaty Ports, 1842–54* (Cambridge, Mass., Harvard University Press, 1953).
76. For details, see Chapter 5.
77. Parkes to Yeh, 27 October 1856, Parl. Papers 1857, v. 12, p. 93.
78. Parkes to Yeh, 25 October 1856, Parl. Papers 1857, v. 12, p. 90, para. 3.
79. Parkes to Bowring, 27 October 1856, Parl. Papers 1857, v. 12, p. 92.
80. Parkes to Bowring, 27 October 1856, Parl. Papers 1857, v. 12, p. 92.

that if, instead of being shamefully violated, the engagements entered into by the Chinese authorities had been honourably kept, the present calamities would never have occurred'.[81]

This did not fool members of the British Parliament. John Russell[82] seized on Bowring's despatch to Seymour of 24 October 1856, whereby Bowring officially revealed his intention to attach the Canton City question to the *Arrow* dispute. Russell observed that by that stage Yeh had already proposed an arrangement for the future which was deemed 'very proper' in Parkes's despatch of 22 October; and all seemed on the eve of adjustment. To him, Bowring's new demand aggravated a quarrel 'which might otherwise have been amicably settled'.[83]

Bowring knew only too well that he was acting against his instructions. He had done it before;[84] now he was doing it again and was determined to persist in this course of action to the bitter end.

III. The Canton City question and an undeclared war

On the morning of 29 October 1856, Bowring wrote another private letter to Parkes: 'If things go on well of course some arrangement will be made for my having an official interview with Yeh (within the City)'. He added a postscript: 'You will of course if you arrange a meeting with Yeh make all becoming arrangements'.[85] Then the steamer arrived. 'I had scarcely despatched my note of this morning when yours of yesterday came in', he wrote. 'It appears impossible that any amount of obstinacy should not cede to the measures taken'.[86] The measures taken included the bombardment of Yeh's residence from the HMS *Encounter*, at ten-minute intervals, until 5 P.M. on 27 October.[87]

81. Ibid.
82. John Russell (1792–1878) was third son of John Russell, sixth duke of Bedford. He became home secretary in 1835 and colonial secretary in 1839. His tenure of the Colonial Office was distinguished by the conversion of New Zealand into a British colony and the formal claim to the whole of Australia. In July 1846, he succeeded in forming an administration for the first time. In 1852 he resigned. In 1865 he became prime minister for the second time. See John Prest, *John Russell* (London, Macmillan, 1972).
83. Russell, 'John Russell's Address to the Electors of London', *Globe*, Thursday 12 March 1857, p. 2, col. 6. Russell might be forgiven for thinking that Parkes's pronouncement on 22 October 1856 meant that an adjustment was close at hand – he had underestimated Parkes's own determination to humiliate Yeh; but of course he had no way of knowing Parkes's private grievance as outlined in Chapter 2.
84. For more details, see Chapter 6.
85. Bowring to Parkes, 29 October 1856, Parkes Papers. This was the first private letter to Parkes this day.
86. Bowring to Parkes, 29 October 1856, Parkes Papers. This was the second private letter to Parkes on this day.
87. Parkes to Bowring, 28 October 1856, Parl. Papers 1857, v. 12, p. 93, para. 1.

Next morning Yeh ordered a general mobilization, offering thirty dollars for every British head taken.[88]

The British response was to recommence firing the same day, 'about 1 P.M. from guns placed by the admiral in the Dutch Folly, which opened on the wall of the City just opposite that fort, and between it and the residence of the Commissioner'.[89] Confident that Yeh would yield to these further measures, Bowring reiterated in an official despatch what he had already told Parkes in private: 'I need not add, that whenever the success of Her Majesty's forces shall have prepared the way for becoming official intercourse with the authorities, I shall be most happy to proceed to Canton'.[90]

While Bowring was frantic with his pen, the Royal Navy was busy with its guns. The bombardment of Canton City resumed on 29 October. By 1 P.M. the city wall was breached. Upon hearing this, Parkes went to the admiral at 2 P.M. and stayed by his side. Thus, when the blue-jackets successfully stormed the city, Parkes had the great satisfaction of sharing 'with his Excellency the gratification of an entry into the Yamun of the imperial commissioner'.[91]

Bowring was lost for words.

Privately he acknowledged, *without comment*, Parkes's personal letter.[92] This is in stark contrast to the praise which, up to this point, Bowring had been heaping on his subordinate. After the destruction of the barrier forts,[93] he had written, 'How excellently all has been conducted'.[94] After one of the forts at Canton, the Dutch Folly, had been captured,[95] he wrote, 'It is quite a comfort to see how excellently everything is being managed with you'.[96] After the Royal Navy had opened fire on Yeh's residence,[97] he wrote,'You have a great deal to think of, – and a great deal to do and you may depend on my helping you in every possible way'.[98]

In his official reply to Parkes about the 'successful entry', however, Bowring could not avoid saying something, and he did so in a postscript: 'I have received your despatch dated yesterday, containing the gratifying intelligence that the City had been entered by Her Majesty's marine forces, the Yamun of the imperial commissioner visited by the admiral and yourself, and our great object of hostile action thus satisfactorily accomplished'.[99] The great object of

88. Ibid., para. 4; and Yeh's public proclamation, 28 October 1856, Parl. Papers 1857, v. 12, p. 94.
89. Parkes to Bowring, 28 October 1856, Parl. Papers 1857, v. 12, p. 93, para. 5.
90. Bowring to Parkes, 29 October 1856, Parl. Papers 1857, v. 12, p. 95.
91. Parkes to Bowring, 29 October 1856, Parl. Papers 1857, v. 12, pp. 98–9.
92. See Bowring to Parkes, 30 October 1856, Parkes Papers.
93. Parkes to Bowring, 23 October 1856, Parl. Papers 1857, v. 12, p. 87.
94. Bowring to Parkes, 24 October 1856, Parkes Papers.
95. Parkes to Bowring, 25 October 1856, Parl. Papers 1857, v. 12, pp. 88–9.
96. Bowring to Parkes, 26 October 1856, Parkes Papers.
97. Parkes to Bowring, 28 October 1856, Parl. Papers 1857, v. 12, pp. 93–4.
98. Bowring to Parkes, 29 October 1856, Parkes Papers. This is the second letter bearing this date.
99. Bowring to Parkes, 28 October 1856 (postscript), Parl. Papers 1857, v. 12, p. 98.

hostile action was, indeed, *not* retaliation for the alleged insult to the flag, but entry into Canton City.

The admiral had also written to inform Bowring of his entry into the city and into Yeh's official residence.[100] Bowring acknowledged receipt with this brief remark: 'I am, indeed, sorry to find that all these demonstrations do not move the imperial commissioner to enter upon becoming negotiations'.[101] To London, Bowring reported the event without comment: 'In the course of the day, 30th, a second despatch was received from Mr Parkes (also dated 29th instant) announcing that the City and the public offices had been entered by Her Majesty's marine forces, with the casualty of only five marines wounded'.[102] But he commented on the commanding officer of the landing party for no apparent reason, 'The *General* is a nuisance – a hero of the *braggadochio* school. I should not wonder if he proclaimed that he made the breach and headed for the forlorn hope'.[103] It was a different story writing to his son: 'The *vexata quæstio* left unsolved by all my predecessors I have satisfactorily settled, and with a very small loss our naval forces have entered the City of Canton'.[104]

Thus, it seems that we have found an answer to the question of why Bowring was willingly led on by Parkes over the *Arrow* incident. It was because Bowring was personally obsessed with entering Canton City and was determined to use the *Arrow* incident as an excuse for satisfying that obsession. But why was Bowring obsessed with entering the city and with his official reception there? And why was Yeh so determined to deny him satisfaction? These questions are addressed in Chapter 5. Seymour's brief entry into the city fell far short of Bowring's dreams of his own glorious reception there. Would the dispute end with Seymour's hasty visit to Yeh's ruined yamen in the absence of the host?

IV. The tables turned

Seymour now wrote to Yeh: 'The lives and property of the entire City population are at my mercy, and could be destroyed by me at any moment' unless Yeh agreed to receive him. The Admiral did not refer to the *Arrow* incident at all in this despatch.[105]

Yeh did not respond immediately. Bowring instructed Parkes: 'If the im-

100. Seymour to Bowring, 30 October 1856, Parl. Papers 1857, v. 12, pp. 98-9.
101. Bowring to Seymour, 31 October 1856, Parl. Papers 1857, v. 12, p. 157.
102. Bowring to Clarendon, 30 October 1856, Parl. Papers 1857, v. 12, p. 74.
103. Bowring to Parkes, 31 October 1856, Parkes Papers. The general referred to here was Major-General Thomas Ashburnham (see Clarendon to Elgin, Draft 4, 20 April 1857, FO17/274). He is not in the *DNB*.
104. Bowring to Edgar Bowring, 31 October, Ryl. Eng. MSS. 1228/162.
105. Seymour to Yeh, 31 October 1856, Parl. Papers 1857, v. 12, p. 101, para. 4.

perial commissioner grant an official interview to the admiral, you are authorized to make becoming arrangements for my official reception by the Viceroy'.[106] The viceroy and the imperial commissioner were one and the same person, Yeh,[107] who continued to dwell on the rights and wrongs of the *Arrow* incident and refused to grant the unrelated demand for an official reception inside the city.[108] The embarrassed admiral wrote, 'I must positively decline any further argument on the merits of the case of the lorcha 'Arrow'. . . . Should you persist in your present line of policy, you leave me but one course to pursue; and you will learn when it is too late that we have power to execute what we undertake'.[109]

True to his word, Seymour resumed offensive operations that day 'against the Government buildings in the City, from the "Encounter", "Sampson", and the Dutch Folly'.[110] Thereafter, day after day, the Royal Navy threw 'shot and shell to reach the most distant of the City forts and Government buildings'.[111] On 6 November, the *Barracouta* and *Coromandel*, together with armed boats of the squadron, dispersed twenty-three war junks and captured the French Folly Fort nearby.[112] The engagement lasted nearly an hour, with the Chinese putting up 'a very hot resistance'.[113] Even Parkes conceded that the engagement was 'exceedingly creditable to the bravery not only of our men, but of the Chinese also'.[114] He was quick to add that the position was one 'from which it would be infinitely dangerous to us to recede'.[115]

Bowring went further, proposing to Seymour that if Yeh still refused to yield, the Bogue forts, at the mouth of the Pearl River, should be destroyed.[116] This coercive measure went well beyond what Parkes had originally proposed in Hong Kong.

The Bogue forts were part of the headquarters of the provincial commander of the marine forces. They consisted of two strongholds that guarded the mouth of the Pearl River. In the west were the Hengdang (or, according to the local dialect, Wangtung) Islands forts,[117] in which were 'mounted upwards of

---

106. Bowring to Parkes, 1 November 1856, Parl. Papers 1857, v. 12, pp. 101–2, para. 4.
107. See my *Yeh Ming-ch'en*, chapter 3.
108. Yeh to Seymour, 31 October 1856, Parl. Papers 1857, v. 12, pp. 101–2, para. 7.
109. Seymour to Yeh, 1 November 1856, Parl. Papers 1857, v. 12, p. 106.
110. Seymour to Bowring, 3 November 1856, Parl. Papers 1857, v. 12, p. 108. After the British had captured the Dutch Folly Fort, they used it to bombard Canton.
111. Seymour to Bowring, 6 November 1856, Parl Papers 1857, v. 12, p. 119.
112. Ibid. See also Seymour to Admiralty, 14 November 1856, Parl. Papers 1857, v. 12, pp. 148–54, sect. 22.
113. Parkes to Bowring, 6 November 1856, Parl. Papers 1857, v. 12, pp. 118–19, para. 2.
114. Ibid., para. 3.
115. Ibid.
116. Bowring to Seymour, 8 November 1856, Parl Papers 1857, v. 12, pp. 119–20.
117. Military map, Parl. Papers 1857, v. 12, p. 281.

200 guns'.[118] In the east were the Aniangxie (or, in the local dialect, Annunghoy) forts,[119] also with 200 guns.[120]

The admiral accepted Bowring's proposal. With himself on board the *Niger*, and accompanied by the *Calcutta*, *Nankin*, *Encounter*, *Barracouta*, *Hornet*, and *Coromandel*, the Hengdang Islands forts of the Bogue were attacked and captured on 12 November. 'The Chinese troops stood to their guns up to the moment our men entered the embrasures', reported Seymour. The next day, the Aniangxie forts, on the opposite side of the Bogue entrance, were also attacked and captured.[121] Parkes hoped that Yeh would 'bend to this striking illustration of our power'.[122] Bowring prayed that this exhibition of power would 'compel the submission of that intractable' official.[123] The admiral told Bowring and London that he had 'no other operation in immediate contemplation'.[124] But Yeh remained adamant.

Thereupon both Seymour and Parkes wrote to Bowring, suggesting that the latter's 'presence at Canton would be desirable'.[125] Bowring went overnight to Canton, arriving there at 9 A.M. on 17 November. A despatch from Yeh awaited him. Bowring reported to Clarendon that 'it is a reiteration of often-repeated averments, and a renewed declaration that he [Yeh] is unwilling to concede to the demands of the admiral'.[126]

Bowring endeavoured to accomplish his objective by a further appeal to Yeh:[127] 'I am still willing and desirous of meeting you in your own yamun . . . If you consent . . . I shall request his Excellency, the Naval Commander-in-chief, to suspend hostile operations'.[128] But nothing seems to have shaken Yeh. Bowring wrote, 'I have exhausted all the means by which I could influence either his hopes or fears, as far as diplomatic representations can go, and I must leave further action to Her Majesty's naval authorities'.[129] Yeh still tried to argue about the rights and wrongs of the *Arrow* incident.[130] On this tricky matter Bowring declared that it was 'useless to continue correspondence

---

118. Seymour to Bowring, 14 November 1856, Parl. Papers 1857, v. 12, pp. 144–5, para. 3.
119. I visited these forts in 1979. I am grateful to the authorities of Zhongshan University at Canton for organizing this field trip for me.
120. Seymour to Bowring, 14 November 1856, Parl. Papers 1857, v. 12, pp. 144–5, para. 4.
121. Ibid.
122. Parkes to Bowring, 14 November 1856, Parl. Papers 1857, v. 12, pp. 146–7, para. 5.
123. Bowring to Seymour, 15 November 1856, Parl. Papers 1857, v. 12, p. 148.
124. Seymour to Bowring, 6 November 1856, Parl. Papers 1857, v. 12, pp. 144–5, para. 6; and Seymour to Admiralty, 14 November 1856, Adm. 125/97, pp. 185–225, sect. 27.
125. Bowring to Clarendon, 18 November 1856, Parl. Papers 1857, v. 12, pp. 157–8, para. 1
126. Ibid., para. 2.
127. Ibid., para. 3.
128. Bowring to Yeh, 18 November 1856, Parl. Papers 1857, v. 12, p. 161.
129. Bowring to Clarendon, 18 November 1856, Parl. Papers 1857, v. 12, pp. 157–8, para. 4.
130. Yeh was doing this as late as 21 November 1856. See Yeh to Bowring, 21 November 1856, Parl. Papers 1857, v. 12, p. 167.

leading to no result' and left Canton without further ado.[131] His language to his son was even less restrained: 'I came hither on a request from the admiral and the consul . . . but the insult is I cannot get entrance'.[132]

On 4 December, the Royal Navy recaptured the French Folly Fort and demolished it. Shelling of the city continued on this day, exploding two magazines.[133]

Such shelling could lead to the outbreak of fires. As early as 28 October, which was the second day of the bombardment of Canton, 'fire broke out on the spot'. Fearing that this fire might affect the foreign community living in the so-called factories at the waterfront, Seymour ordered that the adjoining Chinese houses be forcibly pulled down.[134] A second fire broke out in the evening of 29 October, consuming 'a large number of the houses of the people'.[135] But at 11 P.M. on 14 December 1856, a mysterious fire broke out in the U.S. factory of the foreign factory area, destroying U.S., French, and other foreign possessions. Nobody knew how the fire could have started in a place already safely separated from the rest of Canton and so heavily guarded by British servicemen, who then drove away Cantonese citizens who had sent fire engines from every street nearby, killing several of these volunteers and wounding scores of others. Even more mysterious was that 'all the foreign establishments, with the exception of the English factory, have been burnt to the ground'.[136] But once houses within the factory area were burned down, the smouldering ruins could flare up to engulf those still standing.

That was exactly what happened: the next day the English factory itself caught fire and was burned down, leaving only one house, the clubhouse (used as barracks and stores), and the church still standing.[137] O. T. Lane of the British consulate was standing near the back corner of a burned house, when the wall fell and crushed him. The admiral was in his immediate vicinity and was almost enveloped in the same ruin.[138] He reported, 'I shall withdraw the force, and carry on future operations from on board ship'.[139]

The admiral reconsidered his position the following day. 'The great importance of holding our position at Canton being evident',[140] he ordered a ditch to

131. Bowring to Clarendon, 18 November 1856, Parl. Papers 1857, v. 12, p. 159, paras. 1–2.
132. Bowring to Edgar Bowring, 21 November 1856, Ryl. Eng. MSS 1288/163.
133. Seymour to Bowring, 4 December 1856, Parl. Papers 1857, v. 12, p. 181, paras. 2–4.
134. Parkes to Bowring, 28 October 1856, Parl. Papers 1857, v. 12, pp. 93–4, para. 6
135. Parkes to Bowring, 31 October 1856, Parl. Papers 1857, v. 12, p. 100, para. 6.
136. Seymour to Bowring, 15 December 1856, Parl. Papers 1857, v. 12, pp. 194–5, para. 1. The mystery of this fire will be explored in Chapter 11.
137. Seymour to Admiralty, 29 December 1856, Parl. Papers 1857, v. 12, pp. 287–91, paras. 4–5.
138. Winchester to Bowring, 16 December 1856, Parl. Papers 1857, v. 12, p. 293, para. 10. Winchester was the British vice-consul at Canton.
139. Seymour to Bowring, 16 December 1856, Parl. Papers 1857, v. 12, p. 293, para. 2.
140. Seymour to Admiralty, 29 December 1856, Parl. Papers 1857, v. 12, pp. 287–91, para. 7.

be dug around the Factory Gardens to protect a garrison of 300.[141] To safeguard his position afloat, he had a boom of spars, strengthened with chains, extended both above and below his steam vessels against attacks by unmanned fire rafts. All Chinese boats were kept outside the booms, and the tributaries within the booms blocked up. He also garrisoned, with 140 blue-jackets, the Dutch Folly,[142] from which '[a] few shot and shell are occasionally fired into the City'.[143] The Royal Navy was also kept busy patrolling the river to keep open communications with Hong Kong.[144]

This strategy turned the Royal Navy into an easy target. And in response to the throwing of rockets and stinkpots at his ships, the admiral decide to set fire to the suburbs on each side of the Factory Gardens.[145]

Below the gardens, the houses had, in anticipation, been completely cleared out. This portion was burnt to the wall of the New City, into which the fire, aided by a strong breeze, extended for a considerable distance. Above the gardens, the houses along the riverfront were also destroyed.[146] The deliberate kindling of fires began at about 6:50 A.M. on 12 January 1857.[147] The fires quickly spread, assisted by the dry winter winds:

The whole atmosphere was now one mass of smoke, through which the sun appeared like a large yellow ball, but towards evening the fires to the west of the garden had been partially got under [control] by the indefatigable efforts of the Chinese, who continued working all day at their fire-engines, despite shot and shell and Minié balls [fired by the Royal Navy], but those on the east raged more furiously than ever.[148]

Despite all these efforts, the admiral was obliged to withdraw from the Dutch Folly and the Factory Gardens,[149] which were in forward positions against the city,[150] and move to the Bird's-Nest Fort and the Macao Passage Fort, which 'will give me a most commanding position'[151] against an attack by war junks.[152] Worse still, he found it increasingly difficult to maintain his communication with Hong Kong.[153] So he accepted the offer of 500 troops

141. Ibid., para. 8.   142. Ibid., para. 9.
143. Ibid., para. 12.
144. Ibid., para. 10.
145. Seymour to Admiralty, 14 January 1857, Parl. Papers 1857, v. 12, p. 313, para. 1.
146. Ibid.
147. J. Mongan's Memorandum of Operations at Canton, 5–13 January 1856, dated 14 January 1857, Parl. Papers 1857, v. 12, pp. 313–15, para. 6.
148. Ibid., para. 7.
149. Seymour to Admiralty, 14 January 1857, Parl. Papers 1857, v. 12, p. 313, para. 2.
150. The Dutch Folly, 'being only 400 yards from the City wall, renders it a most important position for offensive operations' (Seymour to Admiralty, 29 December 1856, Parl. Papers 1857, v. 12, pp. 287–91, para. 9). The Factory Gardens were even closer.
151. Seymour to Admiralty, 14 January 1857, Parl. Papers 1857, v. 12, p. 313, para. 2.
152. J. Mongan's Memorandum of Operations at Canton, 5–13 January 1856, dated 14 January 1857, Parl. Papers 1857, v. 12, pp. 313–15, para. 4.
153. Seymour to Admiralty, 14 January 1857, Parl. Papers 1857, v. 12, p. 313, para. 2; see also Seymour to Bowring, 23 January 1856, Parl. Papers 1857, v. 12, p. 320.

The personalities of imperialism

from the governor of Singapore, and applied to the governor-general of India for another 5,000.[154]

Meanwhile Hong Kong itself was threatened. 'Kidnapping, assassination and incendiarism,' wrote Bowring to Lord Clarendon, 'keep us on the *qui vive*'.[155] He could not wait till the New Year was over to call, on 3 January 1857, a meeting of the Executive Council, which resolved 'that the present imperfectly protected condition of the Colony, menaced as it is by the approach of hostile troops, causes much solicitude, and that his Excellency the Naval Commander-in-chief be requested, without delay, to augment the naval forces for its defence'.[156] Armed with this resolution, Bowring wrote to the admiral urging him to return for a conference.[157] To add further weight to the request, Bowring quoted a despatch from Lord Stanley, formerly secretary of state for the colonies, to Bowring's predecessor, Sir Henry Pottinger, dated 15 November 1843: 'Her Majesty's Government concur generally with you in opinion that we must depend on our naval superiority for the complete security of our commercial establishment in that island (Hong Kong)'.[158] Seymour obliged, and upon his arrival at Hong Kong 'found the colony in a state of great uneasiness. The respectable Chinese had been ordered away by the Mandarins on pain of death to all their relatives, and fears were entertained of incendiarism on the part of the immense population remaining, many being supposed to be in the pay of the Chinese Government'.[159]

Then, on 15 January 1857, 'a most diabolical attempt was made at Hong Kong ... to poison the European inhabitants, by mixing arsenic with the bread: most providentially the quantity of poison was so large as to cause immediate vomiting'.[160] There was a general panic leading to prompt and efficacious remedies.[161] Consequently, no lives were lost, but great sufferings were occasioned. Lady Bowring became so ill, and was so considerably weakened, that she died prematurely in 1858.[162] It was with much anxiety that Bowring's aunt wrote to him: 'I trust the power which protected you will still

---

154. Seymour to Admiralty, 14 January 1857, Parl. Papers 1857, v. 12, p. 313, paras. 14–15.
155. Bowring to Clarendon, 30 December 1856, MSS Clar. Dep. C57.
156. Hong Kong Executive Council Resolution, 3 January 1857, FO17/280, p. 61, enclosed in Bowring to Seymour, 3 January 1857, FO17/280, p. 60. These documents were subsequently tabled in Parliament; see Parl. Papers 1857, v. 12, pp. 319–20.
157. Bowring to Seymour, 3 January 1857, Parl. Papers 1857, v. 12, p. 319, para. 2.
158. Ibid., para. 3.
159. Seymour to Admiralty, 14 January 1857, Parl. Papers 1857, v. 12, p. 313, para. 9.
160. Ibid., para. 4.
161. Bowring to Edgar Bowring, 20 January 1857, Ryl. Eng. MSS 1228/172.
162. Ibid.; see also Bowring to Edgar Bowring, 16 and 24 July; 1 and 7 August; 9 September; 13, 16, and 25 October; 25 November 1857; and 14 January 1858 – all in Ryl. Eng. MSS 1228/172. See also Bowring to Clarendon, 19 May 1858, MSS Clar. Dep. C85; and the draft biography of Sir John Bowring, Ryl. Eng. MSS 1230/262.

be with you and shield you from all harm. Should my life be spared I shall be thankful to see you all home again'.[163]

The tables had been turned. An undeclared war had started. Bowring was very worried. As Sidney Herbert later said in the House of Commons, Bowring had deliberately contravened specific instructions to refrain from pursuing the question of entry into Canton City:

> During the whole of this period every successive Secretary of State was showing his wisdom by writing the most peremptory instructions, so as apparently to restrain the exuberant activity of the Governor of Hong Kong. The noble Lord the Member for Tiverton (Viscount Palmerston) wrote two or three letters in great detail, filled with wisdom, and cautious against risking immense interests, and paying a great price for something almost worthless. Then came Earl Granville; then the earl of Malmesbury; then the duke of Newcastle, who sent Earl Grey's despatch; and next the earl of Clarendon; each of them writing more strongly than the others, and each urging this man to give up his project, which he seemed to dream of as the one thing by which the British power in the East was to be consolidated.[164]

Thus, we are all the more intrigued as to why Bowring, to his own detriment, was so determined to be received by Yeh inside the city; and why Yeh was so equally determined, ultimately to his own peril, to frustrate that desire.

V. The House of Lords on Bowring's conduct

Lord Derby found much fault with Bowring's proceedings. Bowring had told Parkes that the *Arrow* had no right to hoist the British flag, the licence to do so having expired on 27 September 1856.[165] Bowring added, 'But the Chinese had no knowledge of the expiry'.[166] Then Bowring did something even more foolish. He wrote to Yeh, 'Whatever representation may have been made to your Excellency, there is no doubt that the lorcha *Arrow* lawfully bore the British flag under a register granted by me'.[167] Derby thundered, 'What honourable or honest man could sanction, or could have written or put forward claims such as those advanced by Sir John Bowring?'[168] 'What, because your adversary may be ignorant, are you to suppress facts?' He continued, 'The Chinese authorities did not know it. No; but Sir John Bowring knew it'.[169] On this subject, Lord Clarendon preferred to remain silent.[170]

163. Lane to Bowring, 30 March 1857, Ryl. Eng. MSS 1230/211.
164. Herbert, 2 March 1857, Hansard, 3d series, v. 144, cols. 1671–2.
165. Bowring to Parkes, 11 October 1856, Parl. Papers 1857, v. 12, pp. 64–5, para. 3.
166. Ibid., para. 4.
167. Bowring to Yeh, 14 November 1856, Parl. Papers 1857, v. 12, pp. 143–4.
168. Derby, 24 February 1857, Hansard, 3d series, v. 144, col. 1169.
169. Ibid., col. 1170.
170. Ibid., cols. 1195–1212.

Lord Lyndhurst pursued the matter further. What Bowring was effectively saying was, 'We know the Chinese have not been guilty of any violation of treaty, but we will not tell them so; we will insist upon an apology'.[171] Lyndhurst asked, 'Was there ever conduct more abominable, more flagrant, in which – I will not say more fraudulent, but what is equal to fraud in our country – more false pretence has been put forward by a public man in the service of the British government?'[172] Lord Carnarvon[173] 'could not understand by what sophistry Sir John Bowring reconciled these conflicting statements with his feelings as a gentleman, his position as the representative of the Sovereign, and, above all, with that national honour to which he so often appealed, but which he only insulted by that appeal'.[174] But no 'member of Her Majesty's Government who had yet spoken had for one moment dwelt upon, glanced, or hinted at' Bowring's behaviour in this respect.[175]

The debate went into the second night. Lord Methuen[176] regretted that Bowring had been criticized in such strong language, which must have tended to depreciate him in the eyes of the Chinese. He appealed to their lordships to support the British agents at that great distance from England, for if they did not, it was idle to expect that the country could be faithfully and effectually served by them.[177]

Lord St Leonards raised a different issue. He said that Commissioner Yeh had wished Bowring to treat the two matters of the *Arrow* and the entry into Canton City as separate, but that Bowring had refused to do so. 'If simple reparation for outrage in the *Arrow* case had been all we required, the admiral would doubtless have been long ago satisfied with what had been done', he said. This clearly showed that the war was commenced on grounds for which reparation had been obtained, and had been continued up to the present upon another pretext.[178]

The earl of Malmesbury made a new discovery. He found that Bowring had not informed Admiral Seymour of the expiry of the *Arrow*'s register. Together with Parkes, they were 'a triumvirate representing the English government, and only two of the triumvirate know of the flaw in the indictment'.[179] It was dishonourable enough to conceal that flaw from Yeh. To conceal it from the

171. Lyndhurst, 24 February 1857, Hansard, 3d series, v. 144, col. 1216.
172. Ibid., col. 1217.
173. He was Henry Howard Molyneux Herbert, fourth earl of Carnarvon (1831–90). He was to enter official life as under-secretary for the colonies, when, in February 1858, Derby became prime minister. *DNB*, v. 9, pp. 646–53.
174. Carnarvon, 26 February 1857, Hansard, 3d series, v. 144, col. 1316.
175. Ibid.
176. He was Frederick Henry Paul Methuen. See Hansard, 3d series, v.144, 'Rolls of the Spiritual and Temporal'. He is not listed in *DNB*.
177. Methuen, 26 February 1857, Hansard, 3d series, v. 144, col. 1322.
178. St Leonards, 26 February 1857, Hansard, 3d series, v. 144, col. 1333.
179. Malmesbury, 26 February 1857, Harsard, 3d series, v. 144, col. 1344.

admiral on the station, whose duty it became to extort reparation for the alleged insult to the British flag, was positively dangerous.[180]

The earl of Ellenborough[181] said that he could not comprehend why the foreign secretary, having spotted that contradiction, 'should not have instantly brought them under the notice of his Royal Mistress, and advised the Queen to direct him to tell Dr Bowring that Her Majesty could not permit any man to remain in her service who could state the thing he believed not to be true'.[182]

The earl of Granville made a rare and last-ditch attempt to defend Bowring: 'Sir John Bowring may have had a temporary doubt as to the right of the *Arrow* to protection, and there may appear a slight contradiction in the words he used, but he felt and knew that he had a good and valid ground for demanding reparation for the insult which had been offered'.[183] He asserted that Bowring was justified in assuming that the *Arrow* was a British vessel because he had no alternative.[184] That was Granville's public defence.

In private, Granville wrote on 10 March 1857 to his friend and political ally Lord Stratford de Redcliffe,[185] the British ambassador at Constantinople: 'You will probably think the opposition right in their estimate of the Doctor's proceedings at Canton'. Canning replied on 4 May 1857, 'I thought your speech very good indeed. I should not like to have had to make it. The subject would not have been *simpatico*'. He thought that Bowring was wrong about the lorcha and right about the entrance to Canton, but that Bowring's presumption in swelling the small case to the great on his own hook was indefensible. He also considered that 'there was nothing to do but uphold him – or rather the war and that makes the awkwardness of the question'.[186]

It seems that their lordships on both sides of the House agreed (publicly or in private) that the origins of the *Arrow* War lay partly in Bowring's actions, which were not beyond reproach by the standards of accountability in responsible government.

VI. The Canton City question in the eyes of their lordships

With regard to Bowring's use of the *Arrow* incident to make the unrelated demand for admission into Canton City, Lord Derby had harsh words to say.

180. Ibid., col. 1345.
181. He was Edward Law, earl of Ellenborough (1790–1871), formerly governor-general of India (1841–4), who was, for his services there, created earl of Ellenborough and Viscount Southan. In 1858, he was to take office with Derby as president of the board of control, for the fourth time. *DNB*, v. 11, pp. 662–8.
182. Ellenborough, 26 February 1857, Hansard, 3d series, v. 144, col. 1362.
183. Granville, 26 February 1857, Hansard, 3d series, v. 144, cols. 1372–3.
184. Ibid., col. 1371.
185. He was Stratford Canning, first viscount.
186. Quoted in Edmond George, *Life of Granville George Leveson Gower, Second Earl Granville* (London, Longmans, 1905), v. 2, p. 245.

On the basis of Bowring's official despatches, Derby thought the man possessed with a monomania. 'I believe he dreams of the entrance into Canton', he said. 'I believe he thinks of it the first thing in the morning, the last thing at night, and in the middle of the night if he happen to awake'. He continued, 'I do not believe he would consider any sacrifice too great, any interruption to commerce to be deplored, any bloodshed almost to be regretted, when put in the scale with the immense advantage to be derived from the fact that Sir John Bowring had obtained an official reception in the *yamun* in Canton'.[187] He found Bowring's demand particularly objectionable because of its contradiction to the strictest previous injunctions from England. Each time Bowring had argued against such injunctions: 'Dr Bowring says that he shall, of course, defer to his Lordship's instructions; he then enters into an argument of two pages to show that he had better not defer to those instructions'.[188] Bowring's demand to enter Canton City seemed quite unnecessary because there was no material advantage to be gained. Furthermore, enforcing such a demand meant that the British had to 'keep a force ready at hand to take satisfaction for the very first insult or act of violence that may take place'.[189] Derby observed that from the moment this unrelated demand was made, the case of the lorcha *Arrow* and the alleged insult to the flag were forgotten. Worse, Bowring misled the admiral to insist upon that unrelated demand as a sine qua non, which, if not yielded to, would render necessary more extensive operations.[190]

Lord Clarendon decided to defend Bowring only on one specific issue – the contravention of instructions: 'I defy any one to make out a schedule which shall include all cases in which the rule ought to be departed from'.[191] Such was the extent to which Clarendon would go towards defending a subordinate who had flouted his own instructions!

Lord Lyndhurst thought the papers clearly showed that from the first moment at which Bowring was appointed plenipotentiary in 1854, his ambition was to procure what his predecessors had failed to – namely, entry to Canton.[192] He recalled Palmerston's earlier view that to obtain entrance to the city by force of arms would render the result useless. He doubted that any sane man could have disregarded such advice and driven his country into a war for such a purpose.[193] The lord chancellor, however eloquent on other points, could find no suitable grounds to defend Bowring. He allowed the opposition a walk-over.[194]

187. Derby, 24 February 1857, Hansard, 3d series, v. 144, col. 1177. It is remarkable that Derby was able to come to such a conclusion by reading only Bowring's official dispatches, which are not quite as illuminating as Bowring's private letters.
188. Ibid., col. 1177.
189. Ibid., col. 1173.
190. Ibid., col. 1188.
191. Clarendon, 24 February 1857, Hansard, 3d series, v. 144, col. 1212.
192. Lyndhurst, 24 February 1857, Hansard, 3d series, v. 144, col. 1219.
193. Ibid., cols. 1219–20.
194. See the lord chancellor, 24 February 1857, Hansard, 3d series, v. 144, cols. 1220–5.

Earl Grey kept up the pressure. 'When Sir John Bowring applied for an interview with Commissioner Yeh, the Commissioner was ready to meet him,' he noted. Yeh had nominated Howqua's Renxin Mansion for that purpose. But 'Sir John's dignity would not allow him to go anywhere but to the official residence of the Commissioner. Therefore, there is no object to be gained by enforcing a right of entrance into the City'.[195]

The duke of Argyll[196] conceded that Bowring 'might have attached an exaggerated importance to our entrance into Canton'. But after the rupture had occurred, it was only natural that he should have been anxious to secure the settlement of a long-pending question which might occasion future disputes. It would certainly have been unjustifiable to pick a quarrel in order to obtain entry. But the 'papers contained no indication of any such intention'.[197]

Lord St Leonards considered Bowring's behaviour entirely unworthy of the representative of a civilized country, even when dealing with what he called 'a semi-barbarous' one.[198]

Lord Malmesbury believed that but 'for the handle it afforded for further proceedings to carry out the monomania of Sir John Bowring we should not have heard of this case of the *Arrow*. Much less reparation was at first required than was afterwards demanded, and which if taken, the affair of the *Arrow* would have been settled'.[199] In this case, 'the very perplexed question of the *Arrow* would have been fully satisfied' by the seizure of a junk, or at all events by the destruction of the barrier forts.[200] 'There was no degradation in the case of the Americans, in their view of the matter, after they had silenced the fort that had fired upon them'.[201]

The earl of Ellenborough thought that if Bowring had been genuine in his desire to meet Yeh, he should have accepted the latter's invitation to an interview at Howqua's mansion. Howqua was the leading merchant in Canton; his mansion was 'surely not an inappropriate place for the calm discussion of matters relating to trade'.[202] Instead, Bowring insisted on marching into the city 'with lighted matches and loaded guns for a public reception in Yeh's yamen'.[203]

---

195. Grey, 24 February 1857, Hansard, 3d series, v. 144, col. 1235.
196. He was the postmaster-general in Palmerston's cabinet. See Duke of Argyll, *George Douglas, Eighth Duke of Argyll, KG. K.T. (1823–1900): Autobiography and Memoirs*, ed. dowager duchess of Argyll, 2 vs. (London, John Murray, 1906).
197. Argyll, 24 February 1857, Hansard, 3d series, v. 144, col. 1241.
198. St Leonard, 26 February 1857, Hansard, 3d series, v. 144, col. 1331.
199. Malmesbury, 26 February 1857, Hansard, 3d series, v. 144, col. 1343.
200. Ibid., cols. 1343–4.
201. Ibid., col. 1344.
202. Ellenborough, 26 February 1857, Hansard, 3d series, v. 144, col. 1361.
203. Ibid.

VII. In sum

Bowring had been a member of the British Parliament for many years before he took up his appointment in Hong Kong. He was thoroughly familiar with parliamentary debates and procedures. He knew that his decisions and actions would be under scrutiny. Nonetheless he behaved in such a way as to incur the parliamentary denunciations just quoted.[204]

He probably deserved the blame. As a diplomat he was a disaster, due principally to his obsession with entering Canton City. We are intrigued that the Foreign Office did not pay sufficient attention to Addington's warning about him. Perhaps Palmerston overruled his permanent under-secretary of state.

Richard Cobden suspected that there must have been an understanding between Bowring and Palmerston that a more aggressive policy might be followed if a suitable opportunity arose:

> I perceive a great change in the tone of the correspondence between him and other Ministers with whom he had to deal. When Lord Clarendon came into office, there seems to be some slackening of the rein, leading to the inference that the check previously held over our representative was withdrawn, and that we were 'drifting' into a war with China, as we had into the late war, from the want of a firm hand on the part of persons in authority. Recollecting the instructions of Earl Grey, and looking into the correspondence which has taken place, I cannot help surmising that something must have taken place to lead our Plenipotentiary to suppose, that if we got into conflict with the Chinese on the question of entering Canton, it would not be unfavourably regarded at home.[205]

Equally baffling is the cause of Bowring's obsession, which will be explored further in the next chapter.

---

204. He was severely criticized not only in the House of Lords, but also in the House of Commons, as we see in Chapters 8–9.
205. Cobden, 26 February 1857, Hansard, 3d series, v. 144, cols. 1416–17.

5
Commissioner Yeh:
A 'monster'?

I. Introduction

We have seen how determined Sir John Bowring was to be received by Commissioner Yeh inside Canton, and how equally determined Yeh was to deny him that pleasure. In this chapter, we shall explore the reasons.

During the hostilities, Chinese soldiers did not discriminate between British civilians and British servicemen. They also ambushed individual British soldiers. On 5 December 1856, a marine and a seaman strayed from the Macao Fort, contrary to orders, to purchase vegetables. The marine was killed. The seaman jumped into the river and drowned.[1] The largest-scale attack on civilians happened on 30 December. The postal steamer *Thistle*, on her way from Canton to Hong Kong, was taken over by Chinese soldiers disguised as passengers. Eleven Europeans, including the Spanish vice-consul at Whampoa, were killed.[2]

In the age of imperialism, empire builders thought there was nothing wrong with shelling densely populated Canton at ten-minute intervals for days on end, or even deliberately setting fire to hundreds of packed civilian houses, causing numerous deaths. But the moment some Caucasian civilians were killed and a couple of British soldiers ambushed, there was a trerrific outcry. The death of the marine was depicted by Harry Parkes as a barbarous assassination[3] and by Admiral Seymour as murder.[4] The attack on the *Thistle* was described by the admiral as 'a most horrible massacre'[5] and by Bowring as a 'treacherous surprise'.[6] Condemnations by members of the British

---

1. Parkes to Bowring, 6 December 1856, Parl. Papers 1857, v. 12, pp. 185–6; Seymour to Admiralty, 14 December 1856, Parl. Papers 1857, v. 12, pp. 195–7, para. 7.
2. Bowring to Clarendon, 31 December 1856, Parl. Papers 1857, v. 12, p. 305; Seymour to Admiralty, 14 December 1856, Parl. Papers 1857, v. 12, pp. 195–7, para. 1.
3. Parkes to Bowring, 6 December 1856, Parl. Papers 1857, v. 12, pp. 185–6, para. 1.
4. Seymour to Admiralty, 14 December 1856, Parl. Papers 1857, v. 12, pp. 195–7, para. 7.
5. Seymour to Admiralty, 14 January 1857, Parl. Papers 1857, v. 12, pp. 315–17, para. 1.
6. Bowring to Clarendon, 31 December 1856, Parl. Papers 1857, v. 12, p. 305.

109

Parliament will be examined later. In sum, many Britons regarded Yeh as a monster.[7]

The question is, did Yeh personally order such attacks? Parkes did not think so. He attributed the attacks to Yeh's financial rewards for British heads generally.[8] His Chinese counterpart agreed, regretting that the attackers did not discriminate between Britons and non-Britons, or between military and nonmilitary personnel. This Chinese official also lamented that the attackers made no distinction between naval steamers and postal steamers.[9] Apparently Yeh did not foresee these consequences when he offered financial rewards for the heads of the 'English barbarians'.[10] Nor did he seem to have anticipated that the British reaction to the attack on the lone marine and seaman would be to burn down the entire village where the assaults took place, with the aim of 'proving to them how incommensurate are the rewards of the Imperial Commissioner with the consequences that such acts involve'.[11]

How well informed was Yeh of British strength, including military strength, and British intentions? It is clear that he was aware of British inventions such as railways and steamships. 'From railways we began to talk of steam boats, His Excellency asking many questions concerning them, who invented them, how we came to think of them, how long ago they were invented, how much it cost to make them?', recorded Alabaster in his diary.[12] Yeh was certainly aware of British military prowess through China's defeat in the Opium War, describing British shells as 'hellish'.[13] We had a glimpse, in the last chapter, of his initially conciliatory attitude until the British bombardment of Canton hardened his public stance. Here, a closer examination of that conciliatory attitude is in order. This is made all the more necessary by the view, taken by many Chinese who have written influential treatises, that both the origins and the responsibility of the *Arrow* War lay in the manner in which he handled the initial incident.[14] Indeed, he has been regarded as a monster not only by the British, but by his own compatriots as well.

---

7. See, e.g., the London newspaper *Morning Post*, 17 March 1857.
8. Parkes to Bowring, 6 December 1856, Parl. Papers 1857, v. 12, pp. 185–6, para. 3. As mentioned, Yeh resorted to unconventional tactics such as offering financial rewards for the heads of Britons, hopelessly outmatched as he was by the firepower of the Royal Navy. See Yeh's public proclamation, 28 October 1856, Parl. Papers 1857, v. 12, p. 94.
9. Hua Tingjie, 'Chufan shimo', in *Er ya*, v. 1, p. 169. Hua Tingjie was the magistrate of Nanhai, whose deputy, strictly speaking, was the official regarded by the Chinese authorities as equal in rank to the British consul. He wrote a most valuable eyewitness account of the *Arrow* War.
10. Yeh's public proclamation, 28 October 1856, Parl. Papers 1857, v. 12, p. 94.
11. Parkes to Bowring, 6 December 1856, Parl. Papers 1857, v. 12, pp. 185–6, para. 3.
12. Alabaster's diary, 12 January 1858. Alabaster was the interpreter who accompanied Yeh to his exile in India after his capture by the British in January 1858.
13. Ibid., 14 January 1858.
14. See Qixianhe shang diaosou, 'Yingjili Guangdong recheng shimo' (An account of the British entry into the city of Canton), in *Er ya*, v. 1, p. 219; Li Fengling, 'Yangwu xuji' (A supplementary account of foreign affairs), in ibid., p. 222; Xie Fucheng, 'Shu Hanyang Yexiang

II. Yeh's handling of the *Arrow* incident

Yeh's reply to Parkes's initial complaint about the *Arrow* incident is remarkable for its absence of any reference to the alleged insult to the British flag, an issue Parkes had specifically raised.[15] Although the Chinese did not have a national ensign at this time, for centuries they had had military flags, which were sacrosanct. As the governor-general of Guangdong and Guangxi, Yeh was the supreme commander of the armed forces of these two provinces. And having led these troops into battle against various formidable rebel groups in the previous few years,[16] Yeh would have had firsthand knowledge of the symbolic importance of military flags. Under the circumstances, is it possible that Yeh considered an insult to the British ensign by his own seasoned officers[17] so unlikely that he dismissed the allegation altogether? Parkes had made in the same letter two other allegations which to Yeh were equally unlikely. They were, again, that the *Arrow*'s Union Jack was flying when the boat was at anchor[18] and that the Chinese officers arrested the sailors despite the *Arrow*'s captain being on board to prevent them from doing so. Yeh knew from standard practice and years of service at Canton that neither would be remotely possible.

But Parkes was determined to humiliate Yeh's officers publicly in order to settle a personal account.[19] Such determination made life quite impossible for Yeh. With great difficulty he had just survived a general insurrection which had swept the entire province of Guangdong, including a prolonged siege of Canton itself. The rebels whom he had driven away from Canton threatened a counterattack at any moment.[20] The morale of his beleaguered armed forces, including those with harbour duties whom he used to fight the rebels on the water, was at best fragile. A public humiliation of Captain Liang Guoding and his men, as demanded by Parkes, causing the armed forces to lose face,

---

Guangzhou zhibian (Grand Secretary Yeh and the Guangdong episode), in ibid., p. 234; Xiao Yuan, 'Yueke tan Xianfeng qinian guochi' (The Cantonese recalling the national shame of 1857), in ibid., p. 236; Jiang Mengyin, *Di'erci yapian zhanzheng*, pp. 41–9; and Huang, 'Viceroy Yeh', pp. 93–4.

15. Parkes to Yeh, 8 October 1856, Parl. Papers 1857, v. 12, pp. 56–7, para. 3
16. See my *Yeh Ming-ch'en*, chapters 5–6.
17. One must remember that what have been conveniently referred to all along as water-police officers were in fact servicemen of the military establishment Green Standard performing the duties of marine police. See Chapter 2 for more details.
18. Yeh knew this to be normally impossible. 'It is an established regulation with the lorchas of your honourable nation, that when they come to anchor they lower their colours, and do not rehoist them until they again get under weigh. We have clear proof that when this lorcha was boarded her colours were not flying; how then could they have been hauled down?' (Yeh to Parkes, 24 October 1856, Parl. Papers 1857, v. 12, p. 89, para. 7). See Chapter 2 for more details.
19. See Chapters 2–3.
20. See my *Yeh Ming-ch'en*, chapters 5–6.

The personalities of imperialism

could shatter the morale of his soldiers and ruin his already precarious administration.

Furthermore, such humiliation was no ordinary loss of face, but an abasement of the nation's armed forces in front of and as demanded by another nation. It would be a national disgrace. Thus, however much Yeh had wished to avoid trouble by yielding to Parkes's demands, it is inconceivable that he could afford, or would have wanted, to pay such a price.

But Parkes was determined to force the issue as a pretext for war and proceeded to manipulate Bowring into authorizing an additional demand – an apology for the alleged insult to the flag.[21] To this additional demand Yeh replied that his officers had assured him that there had been no such affront.[22] Nonetheless Yeh half-apologetically gave this assurance: 'Hereafter, Chinese officers will on no account without reason seize and take into custody the people belonging to foreign lorchas; but when Chinese subjects build for themselves vessels, foreigners should not sell registers to them, it will occasion confusion between native and foreign ships, and render it difficult to distinguish between them'.[23]

Parkes was not to be deterred from taking military action by this, which he chose to regard as not a 'reliable assurance' and convinced Commodore Elliot of the same. Elliot immediately prepared for action as threatened.[24] Yeh, to avoid further trouble, accordingly ordered 'every one of the war-junks, which during the last few days have been at anchor before the city, [to leave] the neighbourhood'. In the end Elliot and Parkes spotted a junk moored at the custom-house.[25]

They seized it.

Apparently following Yeh's instructions, the crew did not offer any resistance. But considerable excitement was occasioned, 'and not a little uproar, among the Chinese fleet [of armed civilian vessels anchored opposite], which must have been heard in [Yeh's] residence, distant in a direct line not more than 200 yards'.[26]

Yeh pretended he was deaf.

An infuriated Parkes regretted Yeh's disregard 'of reason, justice, and the obligations of the Treaty'.[27] Yeh remained deaf.[28] A week later, on 21 October,

---

21. The pertinent documents include Parkes to Bowring, Desp. 153, 10 October 1856, FO288/213; Desp. 155, 11 October 1856, FO288/213; Bowring to Parkes, Desp. 127, 11 October 1856, FO288/213; Parkes to Bowring, Desp. 156, 12 October 1856, FO288/213.
22. Yeh to Parkes, 14 October 1856, Parl. Papers 1857, v. 12, pp. 68–9, para. 4.
23. Ibid., para. 5.
24. Parkes to Bowring, 14 October 1856, Parl. Papers 1857, v. 12, p. 67, paras. 2–3.
25. Ibid., para. 3.
26. Parkes to Bowring, 15 October 1856, Parl. Papers 1857, v. 12, pp. 70–1, para. 2.
27. Parkes to Yeh, 15 October 1856, Parl. Papers 1857, v. 12, p. 71, para. 3.
28. Parkes to Yeh, 21 October 1856, Parl. Papers 1857, v. 12, p. 81, para. 4.

Parkes wrote to Yeh at 6 P.M., 'By retaining the men you have seized in your custody, [you] signify your approval of this violation of the Treaty'.[29]

Yeh sprang into action.

He offered to return ten of the twelve sailors, keeping the two pirate suspects.[30] Parkes replied early next morning, 'Twelve men having been carried away, the same twelve men must be returned, and in the manner previously demanded; that is, they should be taken by Chinese officers to their vessel and given over to me there. If but one of their number be missing, I cannot undertake to receive them'.[31] Promptly the same morning Yeh forwarded all twelve sailors, but not in the manner required by Parkes.[32] Obviously Yeh was determined to protect his military officers from a public humiliation. He also stood firm on the question of China's jurisdiction over her own nationals and demanded that the two pirate suspects be returned to him at once.[33] Clearly he had intended the gesture to be a face-saving exercise for Parkes.

Parkes refused to reciprocate.

He declined to receive the twelve men and made no allusion to them in his reply to Yeh.[34] Instead, he lost no time in writing to Admiral Seymour, 'I have no alternative but to place the matter in the hands of your Excellency'. As if to force the hand of the admiral, he added, 'As my letter to the Imperial Commissioner was circulated among the British and Foreign community last evening, they are already apprized [sic] of the resort to force which this violation of treaty rights on the part of the Imperial Commissioner may at once occasion'.[35] The next day, 23 October, at 4 P.M. and with great satisfaction, Parkes announced to Yeh the arrival at Canton of the admiral, whose forces had just captured and dismantled the four barrier forts and the Macao Fort, and who 'will proceed with the destruction of all the defences and public buildings of this City and Government vessels in the river unless you at once comply with every demand that has been made'.[36]

Yeh had a relapse of voluntary deafness.

The next day, the Royal Navy attacked and captured the forts in the immediate vicinity of the city: the Bird's-Nest Fort in the Macao Passage, the Red Fort opposite the factories, and the two Shameen forts. Very little opposition was encountered,[37] as Yeh had ordered his soldiers not to resist.[38] He was

29. Ibid., paras. 3 and 5.
30. Yeh to Parkes, 21 October 1856, Parl. Papers 1857, v. 12, p. 82, para. 7.
31. Parkes to Yeh, 22 October 1856, Parl. Papers 1857, v. 12, p. 83, para. 5.
32. Parkes to Seymour, 22 October 1856, Parl. Papers 1857, v. 12, pp. 85–6, para. 6.
33. Ibid.
34. Yeh to Parkes, 24 October 1856, Parl. Papers 1857, v. 12, p. 89, para. 7.
35. Parkes to Seymour, 22 October 1856, Parl. Papers 1857, v. 12, pp. 85–6, para. 9.
36. Parkes to Yeh, 23 October 1856 at 4 P.M., Parl. Papers 1857, v. 12, pp. 88–9, para. 5.
37. Parkes to Bowring, 24 October 1856, Parl. Papers 1857, v. 12, p. 68, para. 1.
38. Hua Tingjie, 'Chufan shimo', in *Er ya*, v. 1, p. 165.

still hoping to avoid an armed confrontation. At the end of the day, he wrote to Parkes at 7 P.M., maintaining that the British flag had not been insulted.[39] On behalf of the admiral, Parkes dismissed Yeh's reply as a repetition of previous statements which had become 'entirely out of place', and hinted that Her Majesty's officers should be received by Yeh inside the walled city of Canton.[40]

Yeh refused to oblige.

Four days later, British forces breached the city wall and went to Yeh's official residence, a visit accompanied by scandalous scenes of vandalism. 'Following the British forces an idle and curious throng began to pillage the residence and to obtain whatever spoils lay to hand'.[41] This throng consisted mainly of Britons. Their chief accomplices were Americans, who 'ransacked with great haste [Yeh's] rooms and harem'.[42] Such damage to Yeh's personal property and standing could have been avoided if only he had agreed to receive the British. He did not. With this, it is time to look at the Canton City question in some detail.

III. The Canton City question: The early phase

The Canton City question is important enough historically to have merited a doctoral thesis covering the period 1842–9 alone.[43] The present section, and the following two, aim to emend and enrich that story with citations from the private papers of the key figures involved, including Yeh, Davis, Parkes, Bowring, Palmerston, and Clarendon, as well as company archives such as those of Jardine Matheson and Co. and the official and private Chinese papers which have since come to light. The focus is to determine the degree to which this question contributed to the *Arrow* War.

As mentioned in Chapter 4, Sir John Davis forced his way into Canton in 1847 to demand entry into the walled city. This action was sudden and unexpected. Even the British community living in the factory area in Canton was taken by surprise. David Jardine wrote: 'Between 1 and 2 o'clock of the night I was roused out of bed by Mr Macgregor [British consul at Canton] who called to communicate the news of the fleet of steamers having arrived at Whampoa – having on their passage disabled the guns (about 500) of the forts at the Bogue'.[44] But it was not until two days later that Jardine discovered the

39. Yeh to Parkes, 24 October 1856, Parl. Papers 1857, v. 12, p. 89, para. 7.
40. Parkes to Yeh, 25 October 1856, Parl. Papers 1857, v. 12, p. 90, paras. 2–3.
41. Costin, *Great Britain and China*, p. 211.
42. Quai d'Orsay, Chine 19, no. 31, De Courcy to Walewski, 10 November 1856, quoted in Costin, *Great Britain and China*, p. 211.
43. John J. Nolde, '"The Canton City Question", 1842–1849: A Preliminary Investigation into Chinese Antiforeignism and Its Effect upon China's Diplomatic Relations with the West.' Ph.D. dissertation, Cornell University, 1956.
44. David Jardine to Donald Matheson, 3 April 1847, Matheson Archives, B2/16, p. 1395.

main objective of the mission: 'entry to the City'.[45] At that time, Yeh was only the provincial treasurer. His superior, Commissioner Qiying, had to bear the full brunt of this affront, and was, observed Jardine, 'most awkwardly situated, he has no objections to their going in, but his views on this head are opposed to all the other officials and people'.[46] The people showed their opposition by making 'one or two attempts at riot' and Qiying had to despatch his soldiers to disperse them.[47] Fruitless negotiations went on for several days, until Davis ordered the British forces to prepare to attack the city on the morning of 6 April 1847. Only then, and at the last minute, did Qiying give in. He promised the British, in writing,[48] admission into the walled city two years hence, on 6 April 1849. This promise, commented Jardine, 'will I think have the effect of causing his recall and probably disgrace, opposed as he is by all the other authorities and literati here'.[49]

Indeed, Qiying was recalled the next year.

Why did the British want, and the Cantonese deny them, entry into the walled city? The English version of the Treaty of Nanking had permitted British subjects to reside at the 'cities and towns of Canton, Amoy, Foo-chow-foo, Ningpo and Shanghai'.[50] The Chinese version of the same treaty allowed them to reside at the *gangkou* (port) of those cities.[51] The question is, what real benefits would the British gain, and the Cantonese lose, by throwing open the city gates? One historian has stated that the British merchants at Canton were 'convinced that the disappointing trade returns at Canton after 1844 were the result of British official reluctance to force their way into the City'.[52] This statement requires evaluation.

Canton bought and resold foreign goods to other parts of China, not just to the Cantonese citizens in the walled city behind the port. In any case, would it have made so much difference if the British merchants took their goods to sell in the narrow and congested streets of the walled city instead of letting the Chinese merchants resell them there? In that author's source, the original words were: 'An active correspondence between the newly formed British Chamber of Commerce at Canton and the Manchester Chamber of Commerce convinced the latter that the restricted trade was due to official tolerance

---

45. David Jardine to Donald Matheson, 5 April 1847, Matheson Archives, B2/16, p. 1397.
46. Ibid.
47. David Jardine to Donald Matheson, 4 April 1847, Matheson Archives, B2/16, p. 1396.
48. See Bonham to Palmerston, 23 April 1849, Parl. Papers 1857, v. 12, pp. 241–7, para. 17. The English text of this written agreement may be found in ibid., p. 283.
49. David Jardine to Donald Matheson, 12 April 1847, Matheson Archives, B2/16, p. 1402.
50. Art. 2 of the Treaty of Nanking (1842), in Parl. Papers 1857, v. 12, p. 269.
51. Chu Dexin et al. (comps.), *Zhongwai jiuyuezhang huiyao* (A collection of old treaties) (Harbin, Heilongjiang renmin chubanshe, 1991), v. 1, p. 31.
52. Frederick Wakeman, Jr., *Strangers at the Gate: Social Disorder in South China, 1839–1861* (Berkeley and Los Angeles, University of California Press, 1966), p. 71.

of the hostile attitude of native authorities at Canton'.[53] So it was the hostility as symbolized by the denial of entry, not the denial itself, that was regarded as an issue by the British merchants at Canton. Even this view is not entirely accurate. As we have seen, a leading merchant, David Jardine, remarked that at least Qiying was not opposed to the British entering the city. But 'all the other officials and the people' were.[54] Why?

Among the papers of Sir John Davis there is a document which encapsulates the problem. This, an official reply from the governor of Guangdong to Davis, suggests that two years previously, in 1845, Davis had already demanded entry.[55] Similar documents in the Public Record Office in London make it possible to reconstruct the sequence of events since the Opium War. It seems that soon after the exchange of the Treaty of Nanking on 26 June 1843, Sir Henry Pottinger asked Qiying about entry to the walled city of Canton. Qiying replied that the Cantonese were violently opposed to such an idea.[56] Pottinger decided not to press the point. In March 1845, however, the British vice-consul and his two colleagues were robbed by some Cantonese. Davis, who had succeeded Pottinger, attributed the robbery to the contempt of the Cantonese for the Britons as a result of their successful denial of British access to the city.[57] While Cantonese hostility towards the British certainly existed,[58] Davis's use of an ordinary robbery to emphasize that hostility seems far-fetched. His demand thereupon to enter the city shows the extent to which he was prepared to go in order to gain entry. Promptly Qiying had the robbers arrested.[59] In response, Davis changed tactics. He argued that it was most unreasonable that foreigners should still be refused entry into the city while they were not so denied in the other treaty ports.[60] Qiying replied that all the Cantonese gentry had warned against opening the city gates to foreigners.[61] Davis reported this correspondence to London, and told Qiying so.[62] Qiying kept quiet.

Davis waited. Eight months later Qiying notified Davis that the last instalment of the indemnity for the Opium War was ready for collection.[63] According to the peace treaty, the Chusan group of islands, occupied by the British

53. Nathan A. Pelcovits, *Old China Hands and the Foreign Office* (New York, American Institute of Pacific Relations, 1948), p. 14.
54. David Jardine to Donald Matheson, 5 April 1847, Matheson Archives, B2/16, p. 1397.
55. Huang Entong to Davis, 31 December 1845, Davis Papers. I am grateful to Miss Lind, the descendant of Sir John, for permission to use this and other papers in the Davis collection.
56. Qiying to Pottinger, 9 July 1843, enclosed in Joint Declaration by Pottinger and Qiying re Exchange of Treaty, 26 June 1843, FO682/1976/92. The enclosure was probably left there mistakenly by Pottinger's Chinese secretary, as it postdated the joint declaration itself.
57. Davis to Qiying, 22 March 1845, FO682/1978/11.
58. See next chapter.
59. Qiying and Huang Entong to Davis, 29 March 1845, FO682/1978/14.
60. Davis to Qiying, 8 April 1845, FO682/1978/17.
61. Qiying and Huang Entong to Davis, 18 April 1845, FO682/1978/20.
62. Davis to Qiying, 24 April 1845, FO682/1978/22.
63. Qiying to Davis, 15 December 1845, FO682/1978/60.

since the war, should be returned to China once 'money payments, and the arrangements for opening the ports to British merchants' were completed.[64] Davis ignored Qiying's notification, but told Qiying instead that he had been instructed by London to keep the Chusan Islands until entry into Canton city had been achieved. The argument was that Canton was not opened to the same degree as other treaty ports.[65] A surprised Qiying countered that entry into Canton city had not been provided for in the treaty (which was true enough according to the Chinese version), that Davis could not demand it on the basis of instructions from London, and that a treaty would be meaningless if its terms might be altered according to one's instructions.[66] Governor Huang Entong joined the debate by asking why Davis persisted in demanding admission into the city, which had no connection whatever with the explicit British desire to trade with China.[67]

Other Britons could not wait. On 28 November, and again on 15 and 16 December 1845, groups of Britons brandishing pistols tried to force their way into the city. Qiying asked Davis to restrain his compatriots.[68] Davis, in turn, asked Qiying to issue a proclamation exhorting the Cantonese to be reasonable about the entry question. Qiying obliged. But no sooner were copies of the proclamation posted than they were publicly torn to pieces. The prefect of Canton was attacked and his yamen ransacked and burned down because of a rumour that he had British guests there.[69] A terrified Qiying and Governor Huang jointly issued a public apology, pretending that they had only wanted to test the water and that they had never really intended to let the barbarians enter the city.[70] A thoroughly humiliated imperial commissioner confessed to the emperor, should he continue to please the British at the expense of the Cantonese, that 'I honestly fear that we shall be cutting off our own limbs'; yet he had fears for another foreign war if the British should be too antagonized.[71]

'Could the circle be squared?' a distinguished historian has asked.[72]

Yeh found himself caught in this same trap when the promised two-year deadline began to approach in April 1849. By that time, Qiying had been recalled to Beijing. Xu Guangjin had replaced him as imperial commissioner, and Yeh had been appointed governor. Davis had been succeeded by Sir George Bonham. Thus, the responsibilities for Qiying's promise fell on the

64. Art. 12, Treaty of Nanking, in Parl. Papers 1857, v. 12, p. 271.
65. Davis to Qiying, 20 December 1845, FO682/1978/64.
66. Qiying to Davis, 21 December 1845, FO682/1978/65.
67. Huang Entong to Davis, 31 December 1845, Davis Papers.
68. Qiying to Davis, 21 December 1845, FO682/1978/65.
69. Qiying to Davis, 18 January 1846, FO682/1978/66.
70. Qiying's proclamation as translated by the British, enclosed in MacGregor to Davis, Desp. 13, 23 January 1846, FO228/61.
71. Qiying to Emperor, 28 May 1846, *YWSM (DG), juan* 75, folio 37b.
72. Wakeman, *Strangers at the Gate*, p. 80.

shoulders of a new generation of negotiators. The negotiations ended this time in a complete victory for the Chinese, as the next section shows.

IV. The Canton City question: The diplomatic coup of 1849

This victory was achieved by what John J. Nolde has called a 'false edict', transmitted to Bonham in Commissioner Xu's despatch of 1 April 1849.[73] In it, the emperor denied the British entry into the city of Canton, as a result of which Bonham agreed to let the issue remain in abeyance. Before Nolde, Huang Yen-yü had discovered that an earlier edict, dated 11 March 1849, in fact had permitted the British such entry.[74] This contradiction led Nolde to investigate and conclude first that the edict transmitted to Bonham was a false one and second that it was entirely the work of Commissioner Xu.[75]

Nolde's work was greeted with disbelief in China. Historians there know all too well that at stake in such a case would have been not only Xu's life and property, but those of all people related to him by blood or marriage for nine generations.[76] Thus, there was no lack of sceptics who sought to prove Nolde wrong. The first attempt was made by an archivist of the Palace Museum in Beijing. But despite a thorough search for many years, he could not find any edict remotely similar to the one Xu had transmitted to Bonham.[77] A research fellow of the Chinese Academy of Social Sciences then widened the net not only to search for the edict in question, but to scrutinize the court's registers of incoming memorials, outgoing edicts, and transfers of documents between different departments in the central government, with a view to finding references to the actual document in case it had been lost. He detected no trace of it either.[78] Both scholars had to concede that Nolde's conclusions were most probably correct.

The problem was that Nolde's conclusions, though plausible, were not watertight; they were based to a large extent on a comparison of the wording of the pertinent papers, the most crucial of which is not in the Chinese language – the text of the edict he unearthed exists in translation only.[79] But

73. John J. Nolde, 'The False Edict of 1849', *Journal of Asian Studies*, 20, no. 3 (1960), pp. 229–315.
74. Imperial edict, 11 March 1849, *IWSM* (DG), *juan* 79, folios 39b–41a, quoted in Huang, 'Viceroy Yeh', p. 95.
75. Nolde, 'False Edict', pp. 229 and 312.
76. The Chinese term for this kind of punishment is *zhujiuzu*.
77. Li Yongqing, 'Guanyu Daoguang ershijiu nian de "weizhao" kaoxi' (An investigation of the 'False Edict' of 1849), *Lishi Dangan* (Historical Archives), no. 2 (1992), pp. 100–6, reprinted in (K3) *Zhongguo Jindaishi* (Modern Chinese History), no. 6 (1992), pp. 79–85.
78. Mao Haijian, 'Guanyu Guangzhou fan rucheng douzhen de jige wenti' (Some problems related to the Canton City question), *Jindaishi yanjiu* (Modern Historical Studies), no. 6 (1992), pp. 43–70.
79. This appears to have been translated by the U.S. editor S. W. Williams of the *Chinese Repository*, in which the document was published.

then a second translation, in which the wording was different but the meaning similar, turned up in the British records.[80] And now the Canton Archive has yielded the original Chinese text of this critical document, as transcribed in a communication from Xu to Bonham.[81]

What does one make of it?

Apart from some embellishments to sweeten the pill, the key sentences in this transcribed text of the purported edict appear to have been taken word for word from what Xu had informed the emperor he was going to tell the British.[82] But because the text was most probably concocted, it is not surprising that the original edict cannot be found in the Canton Archive, or a copy of it in the Palace Museum, or references to it in the register of edicts and in related documents. Thus, Nolde's first conclusion about the edict being false is confirmed.

His second conclusion is more problematic. It is inconceivable that a conspiracy of this scale and importance could have been undertaken solely by one man. But Nolde had searched all the published Chinese primary sources and found nothing that would enable him to ask more questions.[83] However, there are other interesting documents in the unique Canton Archive. It appears that apart from Commissioner Xu, Governor Yeh also memorialized the throne. In this memorial, Yeh strongly opposed the idea of letting the British enter the city, arguing that the British demand was an attempt to subvert the government of Canton by setting the Cantonese against their own officials.[84] It appears that Yeh's report was received in Beijing on 14 April 1849 at the same time as Xu's, because an imperial edict issued on that day acknowledged receipt of both. This edict quoted, inter alia, Yeh's argument word for word: 'Foreign threat is of course worrying, but domestic rebellion is even more unnerving'. It also paraphrased Yeh's conclusion and transformed it into a new directive: 'The basis for pacifying the barbarians is to settle the people'.[85] It retracted a previous order to admit the British into 'the city for one look around'.[86] This previous order had been made on the basis of Xu's earlier

---

80. Xu to Bonham, 1 April 1849, Parl. Papers 1857, v. 12, p. 237. This was translated by the German missionary Charles Gutzlaff, who was employed as the Chinese secretary to Sir George Bonham.
81. I have since catalogued it and given it the reference FO682/1982/17, Xu to Bonham, 1 April 1849.
82. Xu Guangjin to Emperor (received in Beijing on 14 April 1849), *YWSM* (DG), *juan* 79, folios 44a–b.
83. Nolde, 'False Edict', p. 312, n. 88. The sources he has searched include the *YWSM*, *Da Qing lichao Shilu*, and *Donghua xulu*.
84. Yeh to Emperor, n.d. (received in Beijing on 14 April 1849), FO931/810. The old reference was FO682/112/3/19. See next note.
85. Imperial edict to Xu, Yeh, et al., 14 April 1849, FO931/787. The old reference was FO682/325/5.
86. Imperial edict, 11 March 1849, *YWSM* (DG), *juan* 79, folios 39b–41a.

report on his meetings with Bonham on 17 and 18 February.[87] In this report, Xu had begged for specific instructions.[88] Nolde comments that Xu 'was at his wits' end'.[89] Now it seems that it was Yeh who suggested a course of action acceptable to both Xu and the emperor, and thereby changed both their minds. Nolde's conclusion may have to be amended accordingly.

Frederic Wakeman Jr. and then James Polachek have suggested that Xu and Yeh decided to resist the British because in the course of 1848 Xu had been receiving reports through merchant channels that 'the current business depression in England and the increase in Anglo-French tension' would make the British unwilling to risk another war with China.[90] But if most of Xu's 'intelligence reports found their way to Peking'[91] and failed to convince the emperor that he might test British resolve anew, Xu and Yeh would have even less reason to do so, especially in view of the fact that the emperor had ordered them to admit the British into the city for a look around. Thus, the conclusions of both Wakeman and Polachek may likewise need to be modified.

The importance of this historical revision lies in the fact that Yeh's argument became enshrined in an imperial edict. Even more important, his argument turned defeat into victory. It is inconceivable that henceforth he could, or would want to, backpedal from that position. And as we have seen from the preceding three chapters, he did not.

One question remains. Why did Yeh decide to voice opposition, and such strong opposition, at this juncture? It seems that after the emperor had decided on 11 March 1849 to let the British into the city for a 'once and for all' look around, he was greatly worried about serious riots in Canton. On the same day, therefore, he issued a second edict. To Governor Yeh and the military leaders at Canton he sent a stern warning: keep the peace or face severe punishments.[92] Yeh knew only too well that he could not keep the peace, as there were bound to be riots. But suppose the British were resisted and they forced their way into the city, resulting in battles between them and the Cantonese – Yeh and the others would still be held responsible. But if the British were successfully resisted, there would be no riots. Yeh decided to resist. Thus, it seems that the imperial edict threatening severe punishments actually forced Yeh to take that decision, and thereby made him intransigent thereafter because his career and even his life were at stake.

87. Imperial edict to Xu, Yeh, et al., 14 April 1849, FO931/787.
88. Xu to Emperor (received in Beijing on 14 April 1849), *YWSM* (DG), *juan* 79, folios 36b–38b, quoted in Nolde, 'False Edict', pp. 308–9.
89. Nolde, 'False Edict', p. 308.
90. See Wakeman, *Strangers at the Gate*, p. 103; Polachek, *Inner Opium War*, pp. 252–3.
91. Polachek, *Inner Opium War*, p. 358, n. 29, referring to various memorials to the throne as contained in *YWSM* (DG), *juan* 79, folios 15a–16b, 17b–19a, 23a–24a, and especially 31a–32b.
92. Imperial edict to Governor Yeh, Tartar General Mu, Deputy Tartar General Wu, Commander-in-Chief of the marine forces Hong, and Commander-in-Chief of the land forces Xiang, 11 March 1849, FO931/781. The old reference was FO682/325/4/4.

Yet another reason for Yeh's subsequent stubbornness was one of his own actions. He and Xu had the latter's despatch of 1 April 1849, in which the false edict was transcribed, 'printed and published entire at Canton'.[93] Their intention is clear and in line with Yeh's argument; they wanted the support of the Cantonese in a united effort to resist the British demand. But by so doing, Yeh had burned his bridges in so far as the Cantonese were concerned. Henceforth, how dare he act in contradiction to an imperial order so publicly circulated?

Finally, his intransigence was consolidated by the very high rewards he received. The emperor made him a baron (*nanjue*). Senior officials wrote flattering poems to congratulate him. The Cantonese erected grand arches to commemorate him.[94] Thereafter, how could he possibly let the British into the city?

V. The Canton City question: The Trojan horse

The elation of the Cantonese caused considerable pain to the consul at Canton, Dr John (later Sir John) Bowring. Bowring officially took up this appointment on 13 April 1849,[95] but had in fact arrived there on 28 March.[96] So he was at Canton to hear the encouraging rumours circulating on that day about Commissioner Xu having just received an imperial edict admitting the British into the city.[97] This was quickly followed by news of the second (false) edict as received by Bonham on 1 April 1849.[98] Later, Bowring was to witness the wild celebrations of the Cantonese. These celebrations were unlikely to please any Englishman; they were positively painful to Bowring, who was already fifty-seven years old,[99] having been a member of Parliament from 1833 to 1837 and again from 1841 to 1849. He was not a brash young man prepared to be seasoned in the trials and trepidations of Canton. On the contrary, he was a fine senior scholar with a deserved international reputation and was particularly sensitive to affronts. In addition, he was a newcomer to the East, having just arrived from England with no previous experience at Canton.[100] Besides, he resented being saddled with a relatively low position in the consular service,

---

93. Bonham to Palmerston, 23 April 1849, Parl. Papers 1857, v. 12, pp. 241–7, para. 9.
94. See my *Yeh Ming-ch'en*, p. 160.
95. See Fairbank, *Trade and Diplomacy*, p. 474.
96. Bowring left Hong Kong for Canton on 27 March 1849. See Bowring to Palmerston, 27 March 1849, Broadlands MSS, GC/BO/83 (quoted here by permission of the trustees of the Broadlands Archives).
97. Bonham to Palmerston, 30 March 1849, Parl. Papers 1857, v. 12, pp. 231–4. In this despatch, Bonham referred to 'a private letter from Acting Consul Elmslie of the 28th' to this effect.
98. Xu Guangjin to Bonham, 1 April 1849, FO682/1982/17.
99. Coates, *China Consuls*, p. 498.
100. Bowring, *Autobiographical Recollections*, p. 216.

although he had gratefully accepted it from Lord Palmerston after failing dismally in his business investments.[101] Furthermore, he was full of self-importance. Before leaving England, for example, he asked Lord Palmerston if he might have an interview with the Queen so that he could impress the Chinese. Palmerston replied 'that there was a general rule, through which he could not break, that no persons under the rank of Ministers Plenipotentiary should have special audiences'.[102] To crown all, he was confident that he would succeed where Bonham was just about to fail. Even when he was leaving Hong Kong to take up his position in Canton, he predicted 'happy consequences from the power of intercourse with the mandarins'.[103] He expected Commissioner Xu to come to the consulate to pay his respects.[104]

Bonham's expectations were more moderate. Upon receiving Xu's despatch of 1 April 1849 in which the false edict was transcribed, Bonham made a last attempt. He proposed to pay Xu a visit of ceremony at his official residence within the walls of Canton because an excellent opportunity had just presented itself: 'A new Consul has arrived from England, and I shall have much pleasure in presenting him, and at the same time paying my respects to your Excellency'.[105] Xu agreed to meet both of them, not in his official residence, but in Howqua's Renxin Mansion just outside the walled city.[106] A dejected Bonham replied that 'the question rests where it was, and must remain in abeyance'. Cancelling his proposed trip to Canton, he added, 'The new Consul will be happy to have an interview with your Excellency at the place you propose'.[107] An exultant Xu declined to receive the consul in the absence of the plenipotentiary. Instead, he offered to 'order some officers to meet him'.[108]

Xu's decision, like the conspiracy to forge the second edict, would have been undertaken in consultation with Yeh. Whom did they finally ask to receive the consul? This question heralds an episode that is not considered significant enough for its pertinent documents to be included in the Parliamentary Papers, but that is extremely important in the present context because it devastated Bowring. These documents, in the Chinese language, were transcribed at the

101. After his election for Bolton in 1841, Bowring embarked all his fortune in ironworks in Glamorganshire. In 1847, a period of severe depression set in, and Bowring was in financial ruin. Bartle, 'Political Career of Sir John Bowring', pp. 402–16.
102. Bowring, *Autobiographical Recollections*, p. 288.
103. Bowring to Palmerston, 27 March 1849, Broadlands MSS, GC/BO/83.
104. Bowring to Palmerston, 12 May 1849, Broadlands MSS, GC/BO/84.
105. Bonham to Xu, 4 April 1849, Parl. Papers 1857, v. 12, pp. 237–8. The Chinese translation may be found in FO682/1982/18, Bonham to Xu, but the date of this document is 2 April 1849.
106. Xu to Bonham, 6 April 1849, FO682/1982/19. The English translation of this document may be found in Parl. Papers 1857, v. 12, p. 239.
107. Bonham to Xu, 9 April 1849, Parl. Papers 1857, v. 12, p. 240.
108. Xu to Bonham, 14 April 1849, in ibid. For the Chinese original, see Xu to Bonham, 14 April 1849, FO682/1982/21.

time into an entry book and have been thus preserved in the Public Record Office in London.

Before Xu and Yeh could decide whom to ask to do the honours, Bowring requested, through Bonham, that the officers hold ranks as high as Bowring's own. The grain intendant, a prefect in the civil hierarchy, and a colonel in the military were among the suggested candidates.[109] Three days later, Bowring again made a request through Bonham. He said that he was different from all other British consuls because he had been appointed by Her Majesty the queen herself. When his predecessor, A. W. Elmslie was appointed acting consul, he was received by the provincial treasurer. Therefore, he himself must be received by an even more senior official.[110]

Bowring had confused all the ranks in the Chinese hierarchy. The provincial treasurer had a rank of (2b) in a hierarchy of nine. The next senior official would have been Governor Yeh himself (2a). Bowring's earlier request, again, included the grain intendant (4a) and a prefect (5a).[111]

The final choice by Xu and Yeh would have been regarded by Bowring as nothing but an insult. They sent the magistrates of Nanhai and Panyu, whose rank was (6b), below anything that Bowring had asked for. Their rationale seems to have been that Bowring as consul was reponsible for British diplomacy at Canton, while the two magistrates were jointly responsible for the administration of the same provincial capital and as such were the two most senior magistrates in the entire province, generally referred to as *liang shouxian*. The venue was still Howqua's Renxin Mansion, where a banquet was prepared. The despatch conveying this invitation to dinner ended with the words: 'Thus it cannot be said that I, the Great Minister, am not perfectly hospitable'.[112]

Bowring turned down the invitation, and turned to Palmerston, complaining of 'the humiliating helplessness in which a Consul is placed'.[113] He expressed his 'sore sorrow' at finding himself engaged in a controversy about his own dignity.[114] He warned the Chinese of the 'perils of the retrograde policy'.[115] They refused to be warned. Instead, they printed the imperial edict elevating Xu and Yeh to be members of the aristocracy, and distributed copies throughout Canton and its vicinity.[116] Bowring could not take it any more. He pleaded with Palmerston to let him visit the other ports in China, or at least to give him leave of absence because 'some change is found absolutely necessary for the preservation of health'.[117]

109. Bonham to Xu, 20 April 1849, FO677/26.   110. Bonham to Xu, 23 April 1849, FO677/26.
111. See my *Yeh Ming-ch'en*, fig. 1, 'The official hierarchy of the province of Kwangtung', on p. 41.
112. Xu to Bonham, 30 April 1849, FO682/1982/22.
113. Bowring to Palmerston, 12 May 1849, Broadlands MSS, GC/BO/84.
114. Bowring to Palmerston, 23 May 1849, Broadlands MSS, GC/BO/85.
115. Bowring to Palmerston, 11 June 1849, Broadlands MSS, GC/BO/86.
116. Copy of a printed imperial edict dated 7 May 1849, enclosed in ibid.
117. Bowring to Palmerston, 19 June 1849, Broadlands MSS, GC/BO/86.

The personalities of imperialism

But he was forced to stay and, more painfully, to witness the wild celebrations of the Cantonese. Eight years later, in 1856, he was still looking back on this episode of his life with great emotion: 'The Emperor wrote that he had "wept tears of joy" at the success of the Imperial Commissioner in *"quietly keeping the English barbarians out of the city"*. Several hundred promotions took place. Six triumphal arches were raised by imperial decree in honour of the wisdom and the valour by which the schemes of the barbarians had been frustrated'.[118] To Parkes, therefore, he issued the following instructions when he thought the *Arrow* incident had at last given him the excuse for settling this account: 'I think this occasion should be taken to destroy one or more of the granite monuments, which record the success of Seu's [Xu's] policy in keeping us out of the city. A more emphatic lesson than this could hardly be given'.[119]

The drama was acted out in Beijing, too, and not just in 1849. The effects of the subsequent saga on both Bowring and Yeh were no less profound than any other. On 1 December 1850, the new emperor[120] meted out severe punishments to the former imperial commissioner, Qiying, and his patron, Grand Councillor Muzhanga. Explicitly using the 1849 victory as evidence, the emperor accused Qiying of having suppressed the Cantonese in order to please the foreigners at the expense of China's national interests. Referring implicitly to Qiying's public appeal to the Cantonese to let the British enter their walled city in January 1846, as well as the equally public destruction of Qiying's proclamations and the prefect's yamen,[121] the emperor accused Qiying of having nearly caused a rebellion. Qiying was dismissed as one of the four grand secretaries of state (rank 1a), and relegated to the waiting-list for appointment to be an assistant department director, (rank 5b). Muzhanga was also dismissed and with the severe injunction that he was never to be reappointed to any position under any circumstance.[122]

Would Yeh not tremble at the idea of letting the British into the city thereafter? Would Bowring not be all the more determined to demolish this 'retrograde policy'[123] by crashing the gates of Canton?

118. Bowring to Clarendon, 14 November 1856, MSS Clar. Dep. C57 China (quoted here by kind permission of the present Lord Clarendon).
119. Bowring to Parkes, 21 October 1856, Parkes Papers.
120. The emperor referred to here is Xianfeng, who had succeeded Daoguang early in 1850.
121. See Section 3 of this chapter.
122. Imperial edict, 1 December 1851, *Da Qing lichao shilu* (hereafter cited as *Shilu*) (XF), *juan* 20, folios 28b–31a. In a spirited defence of Qiying, a Chinese historian has accused the emperor of having dismissed Qiying without specific charges. Apparently he was not aware of the pertinent events of 1846 and 1849, and thus failed to note the explicit and implicit charges. See Yao Tingfang, *Yapian zhanzheng yu Daoguang huangdi, Lin Zexu, Qishan, Qiying* (The Opium War and Emperor Daoguang, Lin Zexu, Qishan, and Qiying), 2 vs. (Taibei, Sanmin shuju, 1970), v. 2, pp. 375–6.
123. Bowring to Palmerston, 11 June 1849, Broadlands MSS GC/BO/86.

Bowring was all the more alarmed, in terms of British national interests, when he learned that this new emperor, greatly emboldened by the victory of 1849, intended to try to suppress the importation of opium and prohibit its smoking. Commissioner Xu 'has received imperial orders to stop the opium trade', Bowring told Lord Palmerston, 'and here he has a subject to grapple with far greater than the "barbarian question"'.[124] To Bowring's mind, Xu had likewise been so emboldened as to have become a 'reckless, resolute fellow', whose policy, if left unchecked, would 'lead to some catastrophes'.[125]

The rumour about a renewed attempt at opium suppression was not without foundation. On 1 April 1849, just a few hours before Xu transmitted the false edict to Bonham, he acknowledged the emperor's fear that Bonham could very well be using the occasion to force China to legalize the opium trade.[126] It is even possible that such a fear was originally instilled in the emperor by Xu and Yeh. Their object would have been to change his mind about letting the British into the city.[127] Once that object was achieved, it seems, they were unwilling to risk their careers by embarking on something which had failed before. But Bowring had no way of knowing this, and the subject was kept alive by a Draconian vice-regal proclamation, authorized by the emperor, absolutely prohibiting the use of opium. This proclamation was translated and published in the *North China Herald*, Shanghai.[128]

Who put this idea into the emperor's head? Bowring would probably think it was Xu. Some scholars might have thought it was Yeh, who, they said, was 'determined to avenge China's national disgrace'.[129] A search in the Chinese primary sources shows that in fact the intendant at Shanghai was responsible.[130] The emperor, in turn, asked the intendant's superior, the viceroy at Nanjing, to investigate and report.[131] The viceroy did not wish to risk his career either. Shrewdly he replied that he was in the process of mounting a vigorous campaign to apprehend lawbreakers, and would include thereby those who had broken the opium prohibition.[132] The emperor endorsed the reply as

124. Bowring to Palmerston, 23 May 1849, Broadlands MSS GC/BO/85. See also Bowring to Bonham, 19 May 1849, Parl. Papers 1857, Session 2, v. 43, p. 114.
125. Bowring to Palmerston, 12 May 1849, Broadlands MSS GC/BO/84.
126. Xu to Emperor, 1 April 1849, FO931/785 (old reference FO682/112.3.20).
127. Ibid.; a careful reading of this document certainly gives one this impression.
128. Proclamation by the Viceroy at Nanjing, 17 August 1850, in *North China Herald*, 7 September 1850. See Morse, *International Relations of the Chinese Empire*, v. 1, pp. 548–9.
129. Qixianhe shang diao-sou (pseud.), 'Yingjili Guangdong rucheng shimo', in *Er ya*, v. 1, p. 212; Xie Fucheng, 'Shu Hanyang Yexiang Guangzhou zhibian (Grand Secretary Yeh and the Guangdong episode), in *Er ya*, p. 228.
130. Guilin to Emperor (received in Beijing on 15 March 1850), *TWSM* (DG), *juan* 4, v. 1, pp. 126–9.
131. Emperor to Lu Jianying, 15 March 1850, *TWSM* (DG), *juan* 4, v. 1, pp. 129–30.
132. Lu Jianying to Emperor (received in Beijing on 21 April 1850), *TWSM* (DG), *juan* 4, v. 1, pp. 141–2.

The personalities of imperialism

'perused'.[133] But Bowring had no way of fathoming the internal politics of China. He continued to be haunted by the fear of an imminent campaign to suppress the opium trade – a campaign mounted by a government greatly emboldened by their supposed victory over the British with regard to the Canton City question.

And why was Bowring so worried about the suppression of opium? Because he was aware that 'three or four million of Indian revenue' depended on the trade.[134] As mentioned, Bowring had been a member of Parliament in 1833–7 and again in 1841–9, and in fact had served on a parliamentary commission inquiring into the United Kingdom's commercial relations with China in the 1840s.[135] As a member of Parliament, he would have had automatic access to the annual statistical returns tabled in Parliament each year. He probably paid a great deal of attention to these statistics when the Opium War raged in 1841–2. As a member of the parliamentary commission of inquiry, he would have studied those statistics more vigorously than usual. All along, therefore, Bowring had a fairly accurate perception of the importance of the opium trade.

Thus, a fresh and important element was introduced into Bowring's approach towards the Canton City question: British economic interests. The protection of these interests, in his view, depended upon crashing through the city gates of Canton. Herewith emerges a vital factor in our investigation into the origins of the *Arrow* War: the economics of imperialism, involving not only the United Kingdom and China, but also India. This will be examined in Part Six. For the present, it is important to mention that this 'opium scare' was quickly followed by the dismissal of Qiying and Muzhanga. The dismissal was interpreted as part and parcel of a China reasserting itself and sent shock waves through London. Six years later the matter was raised in the parliamentary debate about the *Arrow* War.[136]

To conclude, when Bonham desisted from entering the city, the Cantonese officials and people thought that threat was gone. Little did they realize that they had just created a Trojan horse in the person of Consul Bowring, who was parked just outside the city gates. Bowring felt thoroughly humiliated. His private humiliation and patriotic concern turned into an obsession, as we have seen in Chapter 4. One may appreciate Bowring's position. He himself put it to Lord Palmerston frankly: 'Truly if that question were to be estimated solely by the value of the right to pass the gates of Canton, the right, in itself, is valueless. But [Xu's] object is of higher aim and involves the gravest conse-

---

133. Emperor's endorsement on Lu Jianying's memorial which was received on 21 April 1850 (see previous note), *YWSM* (DG), *juan* 4, v. 1, p. 143.
134. Bowring to Clarendon, 4 October 1855, MSS Clar. Dep. C37 China.
135. See Bowring, *Autobiographical Recollections*.
136. See, e.g., Gladstone, 3 March 1857, Hansard, 3d series, v. 144, cols. 1792–3.

quences. He wants to defeat – to triumph over the foreigners'.[137] Given this logic, it is not surprising that Bowring blamed the intransigence of 'monster Yeh' for causing the bombardment of Canton.

VI. A real monster?

But we should find out whether Yeh really looked like a monster. After he had been captured by the British forces in January 1858 and was detained aboard HMS *Inflexible* in Hong Kong, an artist made a sketch of him. This sketch was reproduced in *The Times*'s war correspondent G. W. Cooke's book *China*,[138] and has been reprinted time and again in books dealing with the subject or the period. According to this sketch, Yeh was a real monster. Or was he made out to be one? Some British journalists went on board and filed this report:

> Many of our readers have no doubt seen a front face and profile purporting to be the likeness of the front face and profile of Commissioner Yeh. Fuseli [a British artist] used to eat raw beef steaks and raw onions when he was desirous of conjuring up any of his hideous fancies. The artist who made the above sketches must have been dieting himself in the same way and painted from a disordered stomach. We accidentally had a good view of the real man, and saw nothing in him of the truculent ruffian depicted by the artist.[139]

What did the real Yeh look like?

> He is a big-headed, fat-faced, intelligent-looking Chinese, much better looking than Keying [Qiying] and not so bulky as Whang [Huang Entong], the tall Chinese who was here with Keying in 1845. He was dressed in a loose faded blue silk robe, garnished with two large patches of snuff stains on the breast, and had on a small skull cap . . . Some other gentlemen who happened to be on board deemed it proper to take off their hats to him, on which he half rose from his seat and courteously returned the salute, taking off his cap.

The reporters continued, 'All the officers of the ship seem, after true English fashion, to have taken a fancy to their prisoner, and respect him for the cool, dignified manner in which he bears his fall and imprisonment; and he had created the impression among them that he is an able, intelligent man'.[140]

137. Bowring to Palmerston, 27 March 1949, Broadlands MSS GC/BO/83/1.
138. W. G. Cooke *China: Being 'The Times' Special Correspondent from China in the Years 1857–8, with Corrections and Additions* (London, G. Routledge, 1858).
139. *Hong Kong Register* (newspaper clipping), 16 February 1858, Ryl. Eng. MSS 1230/84.
140. Ibid.

6
Rule Britannia and *vox populi, vox Dei*

I. Introduction

We have seen how determined Bowring was to force the gates of Canton, and why Yeh was equally determined to deny him satisfaction despite the rapid escalation of hostilities. Yeh's determination was based on the opposition displayed by the Cantonese to Britons entering their city. In this chapter, I attempt to explain this opposition and to establish whether it formed part of the origins of the *Arrow* War. After all, the British government claimed it did and for that purpose had all pertinent correspondence assembled, printed, and distributed to the members of Parliament for debate.[1]

John Nolde has made a special study of the Cantonese people of this time, including their behaviour and attitudes.[2] He concludes that their opposition was due to xenophobia. He adopts the definition of xenophobia, offered by the *Oxford Dictionary*, as a 'morbid dread or dislike of foreigners'.[3] Furthermore, he makes a distinction between the 'popular xenophobia' exhibited by the masses and 'official xenophobia' as a government policy. These manifestations will be examined in turn.

II. Popular xenophobia or protonationalism?

Nolde thinks that long before the Opium War 'a spirit of bitter anti-foreign feeling had lurked in the hearts of most Cantonese and that for a European to live among them was to live dangerously'.[4]

Nolde cites as evidence the views of authors like H. B. Morse, but does not

---

1. Parl. Papers 1857, v. 12, pp. 325–560, containing a blue book of 236 pages entitled 'Correspondence Respecting Insults in China', covering the period 20 December 1842 to 8 December 1856. The great majority of the incidents happened at Canton between 1842 and 1849.
2. Nolde, 'Xenophobia at Canton'.
3. Ibid., p. 1, col. 2.
4. Ibid., p. 2, col. 2. Likewise, Frederic Wakeman Jr. calls the Cantonese attitude towards foreigners 'virulent xenophobia'. See his *Strangers at the Gate*, p. 73.

show how they came to their conclusions. He quotes three contemporary accounts of Cantonese misconduct, but does not give the circumstances. Thus, it is impossible to comment on either these views or these accounts. He himself lists eighteen antiforeign incidents in the 150 years prior to the Opium War. The first began 'when a Chinese was killed' by some drunken sailors; the second 'when a group of British seamen attacked the entourage of a Chinese official'; the next four were 'acts of a judicial nature taken against foreigners by the Chinese authorities', such as the execution of a U.S. seaman who had killed a Chinese woman; the remaining twelve were 'rarely more than scuffles between small groups, [as] often as not caused by the ill-considered acts of the foreigners themselves'.[5] In the end Nolde feels duty-bound to qualify his view by saying that although 'xenophobia' was present, it was not widespread.[6]

The turning point came in 1841 during the Opium War. It involved a military engagement between the British forces and the villagers who had formed themselves into militia units around an area called Sanyuanli, just north of Canton. In the years to follow, the incident became something of a national legend. John King Fairbank and Teng Ssu-yü interpreted it as 'the first stirrings of modern Chinese nationalism'.[7] They have conceptualized it as 'protonationalism' to explain the Cantonese opposition towards the British entering Canton City.[8] The basis of this idea was a manifesto issued by the villagers of Sanyuanli in which they denounced the British in fiery terms.[9]

It seems that the passion of the villagers was aroused after the British forces occupied the forts to the north of Canton, holding the city to ransom. Before that ransom was paid, some British officers roamed about in the vicinity of Sanyuanli and opened a few tombs to see how the Chinese embalmed their dead. Others followed suit in search of treasure.[10] The Cantonese were among the most fervent ancestor worshippers in the world, and this desecration of

5. Nolde, 'Xenophobia at Canton', p. 2, col. 1, to p. 3, col. 2.
6. Ibid., p. 3, col. 2.
7. J. K. Fairbank and S. Y. Teng, *China's Response to the West* (Cambridge, Mass., Harvard University Press, 1954), p. 35.
8. Ibid.
9. Ibid., pp. 35–6, including a translation of that proclamation.
10. *Guangzhou fuzhi* (Local gazetteer of the prefecture of Guangzhou), juan 81, folio 39a. This Chinese account is collaborated by British sources. See, e.g., J. Elliot Bingham, *Narrative of the Expedition to China* (London, Colburn, 1842), v. 1, pp. 231–2; and D. McPherson, *Two Years in China: Narrative of the Chinese Expedition from Its Formation in April 1840 till April 1842* (London, Saunders and Otley 1842), p. 148. In December 1979 and again in December 1980 I visited Sanyuanli Museum, where pertinent documents had been judiciously collected and preserved, where maps and models showing exactly where the engagements had taken place were exhibited, and where the weapons used by the militiamen were displayed. I also visited the temple, which the militia had used as its headquarters, and Niulangang, where a famous military engagement took place. I wish to thank the History Department of Zhongshan (Sun Yatsen) University in Canton for arranging the fieldwork for me.

their ancestral tombs caused enormous fury. Their rage was soon augmented when British soldiers raped some Chinese women around Sanyuanli.[11] On 29 May 1841, about seventy-five hundred villagers engaged the British forces. A sudden thunderstorm caught a detachment of Sepoys and their British officers out in the paddy-fields, anchoring them in the mud and drenching their muskets. The villagers immediately set upon them, killing one and wounding some fifteen others.[12]

Might the Sanyuanli spirit be described as protonationalism? Perhaps not, because its focus was the protection of women and ancestral tombs, and its concern did not extend beyond the immediate families and villages.

Nolde prefers to call it 'xenophobia'.[13] Here, he has a case stronger than his previous one regarding the 150 years before the Opium War. The Sanyuanli villagers' dread and dislike of the British soldiers were genuine. But Sanyuanli did not feature again physically in any way in Anglo-Chinese relations after 1841. Why should feelings there affect the course of events at Canton? Nolde has not explained.

The Sanyuanli spirit is relevant in the following ways.

First, that spirit spread like wildfire to all other villages in the Canton area and to the city itself. It seems to have compensated for the citizens' loss of face when their city lay in the shadow of British guns and was subsequently ransomed by their officials. It reinforced the citizens' feeling of defiance towards the British. The British had always been forbidden to enter Canton City. Now the citizens became absolutely determined to continue their practice of exclusion. In the countryside, the Sanyuanli spirit created a paranoia about the foreign devils bent on entering their villages to rape their women or loot their ancestral graves. Bowring observed that the peasants and country people showed much greater alarm when they saw him than did the citizens of Canton – the women and children invariably scampered away screaming and hid themselves.[14] This fear meant that no foreigners would be safe from attacks, provoked or otherwise, should they venture into any village, and not necessarily just those villages in the Sanyuanli area. Naturally, the British merchants resented this defiance and hostility. But as Sir John Davis said, 'Killing some hundreds or thousands would hardly tend to reconcile the survivors to us.'[15] Thus, the standoff continued. The blue book listing the 'insults in China' after 1842 confirms this point.[16] 'Insults' in these villages inevitably dragged the Canton authorities into diplomatic wrangles. Many Britons preferred to blame these 'insults' on the closed city gates

11. Initially, the British denied this. But some eight years later, Sir John Davis tacitly admitted it. See Davis to Palmerston, Desp. 23, 8 February 1848, FO17/140.
12. See Wakeman, *Strangers at the Gate*, pp. 17–19.
13. Nolde, 'Xenophobia at Canton', p. 4, col. 1.
14. Bowring to Palmerston, 12 May 1849, Broadlands MSS, GC/BO/84.
15. Davis to Palmerston, Desp. 23, 8 February 1848, FO17/140.
16. Parl. Papers 1857, v. 12, pp. 325–560.

of Canton rather than the cause of the Sanyuanli spirit. The voluminous correspondence relating to the Canton City question bears this out.[17] One exception was Sir Henry Pottinger, as we shall see later.

Second, the Sanyuanli militiamen of 1841 were dispersed, not by the British forces, but by the Canton authorities, who subsequently paid the British a ransom of six million Spanish silver dollars for sparing the city. In the Canton Archive there is a document authorizing the prefect of Canton to negotiate the terms of that ransom.[18] It was the same prefect who hurried to Sanyuanli to dislodge the militia leaders, who were members of the local gentry. He threatened these leaders with severe punishments should their followers cause any incident. The village gentry quietly slipped away, leaving an extremely unhappy crowd to disperse grudgingly.[19] This temporary victory of the Canton authorities would have serious repercussions. One of the emperor's watchdogs, Censor Cao Lütai, subsequently toured the Canton area and talked to as many people as he could. He found that the general feeling prevalent among the people was of intense resentment against the Canton authorities. They seemed to think that the Sanyuanli militiamen, had they not been dispersed by their own officials, could have exterminated all the British forces and thereby prevented the payment of that hefty ransom. The ransom was paid without firing a single shot of resistance, which was a further source of resentment. The censor concluded that the Sanyuanli incident was the origin of Cantonese hostility towards their own officials.[20]

Third, each time the Cantonese gentry felt threatened by a British demand to enter their city, as in 1849 and 1856, they would, in addition to hiring urban workers as mercenaries, summon their fellow gentry in the surrounding villages to lead their militiamen into the city for its defence. There, the villagers vowed to defend the city as if they were defending their homes. To the citizens and villagers alike, the ancient walls had come to symbolize Cantonese independence and self-respect, which had been sadly undermined by their own officials' capitulation to the British demand for ransom. Their hostility towards the foreigners' push to enter their city was entirely defensive and found expression only when provoked. The Cantonese may have had too high an estimation of the military capabilities of their spears and arrows and too low an opinion of the British breechloaders, Gatling guns, Maxims, new Brunswicks and light field artillery.[21] But their independence was what they firmly believed in.

Fourth, such a belief was unduly reinforced by politically motivated glorifi-

17. Ibid., pp. 1–283.
18. FO682/912, Copy of authority given by the imperial commissioners to the prefect of Guangzhoufu, Yu Baoshun, to conclude terms of agreement for ransom of Canton City, 27 May 1841.
19. Wakeman, *Strangers at the Gate*, p. 19.
20. Cao Litai to Emperor, 10 March 1846, *YWSM* (DG), *juan* 75, folios 13a–14b.
21. That sort of view was not restricted to the Cantonese of the nineteenth century. See, e.g., Mou

cation of the Sanyuanli incident by scholar-officials. On the basis of the original rustic manifesto by the Sanyuanli militia chiefs warning the 'vengeful' British not to return, at least three urban scholars manufactured reproductions. These later documents reflected not so much the concerns of the village defenders, but the preoccupation of the self-appointed armchair strategists who were unhappy with the way the Manchu general, Ishan, had conducted the Opium War. The aim was to spread the Sanyuanli spirit widely among the literati. The literature multiplied, including moving poems that were to circulate throughout China via scholarly networks and popular ballads that were distributed as far as Beijing. One scholar-official even alleged in private correspondence that the villagers had surrounded a thousand or more British troops, killing eighty or ninety of them, and wounding numerous others.[22] Laurels like these appear to have had the effect of inflating the self-confidence of the Cantonese gentry and militiamen beyond reality.

Thus, the gentry of the villages and of Canton City – the traditional leaders of the populace – assumed a decisive though unofficial role in determining the Canton City question. Since publication of my *Yeh Ming-ch'en*, it has been accepted that as demagogue-like as Commissioner Yeh might have been, there was really little room for him to manoeuvre when it came to dealing with this *vexata quæstio*.[23] He could defeat an overwhelming number of rebels besieging Canton, while city after city in other parts of China were falling under similar circumstances. But he could not allow the British into his city. To do so would be to lose the only ally he had as he 'struggled to suppress Taiping-inspired secret society uprisings in the Pearl River delta'.[24] He was, as the saying goes, caught between a rock and a hard place.

III. Patriotism or sedition?

On 16 September 1841, three-and-a-half months after the Sanyuanli incident, the prefect of Canton went to supervise a civil service examination. As soon as he entered the examination hall, the candidates began to jeer, shouting, 'All of

---

Anshi, 'Cong Yapian zhansheng kan shengbai de jueding yinshu shi ren bushi wu qi (From the Opium War one can see that what decided victory and defeat was men and not weapons), *Renmin ribao* (People's Daily), 11 October 1965. For the European 'fire-power revolution' of this time, see D. R. Headrich, *The Tools of Empire: Technology and European Imperialism in the Nineteenth Century* (Oxford, Oxford University Press, 1981), chapter 2. I am pleased that finally, during a visit to the Chinese Academy of Social Sciences in November 1996, I came across Mao Haijian's book *Tianchao de bengkui* (The collapse of the celestial empire) (Beijing, Joint Publishing Co., 1995), in which the author made a realistic assessment of the relative military strength of the British and Chinese forces.

22. James Polachek has meticulously traced, identified, and assessed the literature that seems to have grown out of the original Sanyuanli manifesto. See his *Inner Opium War*, pp. 165–9.
23. Polachek, *Inner Opium War*, p. 6. See my Conclusion, this volume, for more analysis of this aspect of Qing foreign policy.
24. Ibid.

us have read the writing of the sages and know rites and proper decorum. We will not take an examination given by a traitor'.[25] They threw their inkstones at him, driving him out of the hall. The prefect tendered his resignation on the grounds of ill health.[26]

By May 1844, exactly three years after the Sanyuanli incident, the British consul at Canton observed: 'The authorities stand in awe of the people, instead of the people standing in awe of the authorities'.[27] As mentioned in the preceding chapter, the moment Commissioner Qiying announced on 13 January 1846 that he would let the British enter the city, his proclamation to that effect was torn to pieces by an angry crowd. The prefect of Canton[28] was attacked and his yamen ransacked and burned down because of a rumour that he had British guests there.[29] The attitude of the mob on this occasion is important: 'The officials dispense with the *dao* of the Qing to welcome foreign devils. They consider us, the people, as their fish and meat'. Referring to the prefect, they shouted, 'If he is going to serve the barbarians, he cannot again be an official of the Great Qing'.[30]

There is no doubt that the authorities regarded them as seditious, but they could not say so to the patriotic Cantonese. Instead, they had to affect to commend them in order to avoid further disturbances. On this occasion, Commissioner Qiying and Governor Huang Entong jointly issued an abject apology for their earlier proclamation.[31] They continued, 'If the people are really all averse to the English entering the City, how should we be willing to act quite contrary to their feelings, and in a devious spirit, comply with the prayers of the English? Do not cherish feelings of doubt and suspicion'.[32] What were they going to do with the prefect of Canton? He seemed to be enjoying remarkably good health, so they resorted to recommending to the emperor that he be suspended.[33] After having second thoughts, they felt that they had to justify the suspension, so they hastily despatched a second memorial the same day. They explained that had the prefect been allowed to continue in his position, the hostility of the Cantonese towards the authorities would be aggravated to the point of possible rebellion.[34] The emperor reacted to this

25. Translated by Wakeman, *Strangers at the Gate*, p. 73.
26. Cao Lütai to Emperor, 10 March 1846, *YWSM* (DG), *juan* 75, folios 13a–14b.
27. Lay to Pottinger, Desp. 8, 1 May 1844, FO228/40.
28. A new man now occupied this position; he was Liu Xun.
29. Qiying and Huang Entong to Davis, 18 January 1846, FO682/1979/4a.
30. Translated by Wakeman, *Strangers at the Gate*, p. 77.
31. Joint proclamation by Qiying and Huang Entong as translated by the British authorities, enclosed in Desp. 13, 23 January 1846, FO228/61.
32. Ibid., translated by Wakeman, *Strangers at the Gate*, p. 78.
33. Qiying and Huang Entong to Emperor (received in Beijing on 26 February 1846), *YWSM* (DG), *juan* 75, folios 9a–10b. This was the first memorial of this day.
34. Qiying and Huang Entong to Emperor (received in Beijing on 26 February 1846), *YWSM* (DG), *juan* 75, folios 11a–12b. This was the second memorial of this day.

challenge by the Cantonese to his authority by approving the suspension.[35] *Vox populi, vox Dei.*[36]

In the light of this extraordinary turn of events, the view that 'until 1850, at least, it was Beijing that made the critical decision on foreign and domestic policy, and little can be learnt by focusing upon events in the distant southeast'[37] should be reconsidered.

In April 1847, as noted in the preceding chapter, it was only after general orders had been issued to the British armed forces for an attack on the city that Commissioner Qiying agreed to let the British enter – not immediately (how dare he?), but in two years' time.

Then in 1849, as noted, Qiying's successor, Commissioner Xu, as well as Governor Yeh, had to risk decapitation by resisting a genuine imperial edict and concocting a false one in order to placate the Cantonese, hoping the British would believe their lie. What is relevant here is that Xu used, as his justification for resisting orders and for forging an imperial edict, the Cantonese hostility to foreigners entering the city, tracing such hostility to the Sanyuanli incident. He continued: 'The moment the entry question is raised, popular anger soars to the point of wanting to eat [the Britons'] flesh and sleep on their skin. Persuasion is useless. Nearly a hundred thousand militiamen have already gathered in Canton for its protection'.[38]

All the evidence seems to show that the hostility was restricted to the prevention of foreigners entering the city of Canton or surrounding villages. If the hostility was so restricted, can it be called xenophobia? Perhaps not, unless it can be proved that the general disposition of the Cantonese, before and particularly after the Opium War, was one of 'morbid dread or dislike of foreigners'[39] and not restricted to particular issues. This question will be explored further in the next section.

IV. Popular xenophobia? *Civis Romanus sum*

Let us begin with the observations of China's antagonists. Captain Charles Elliot,[40] who had made war on the Cantonese in 1840, believed that before the war, 'there was no part of the world where the foreigner felt his life and

35. Imperial edict, 26 February 1846, *YWSM* (DG), *juan* 75, folio 12b.
36. Ironically, Bowring used this expression a lot in his private correspondence.
37. Polachek, *Inner Opium War*, p. 9.
38. Xu to Emperor (received in Beijing on 14 April 1849), *YWSM* (DG), *juan* 79, folios 43a–44b.
39. This is the definition given by the *Oxford Dictionary* of the word 'xenophobia'.
40. Charles Elliot (1801–75) entered the navy in 1815. From 1830 to 1833 he was protector of slaves in Guiana. In 1834, when commissioners were appointed to superintend affairs of trade in China, he went as their secretary and in June 1836 became chief superintendent and plenipotentiary. In January 1840 active hostilities began with China virtually under his direction. He was to become chargé d'affaires in Texas 1842–6, and of St Helena 1863–9. He became rear-admiral in 1855, vice-admiral in 1862, and admiral in 1865. See Clagette Blake, *Charles Elliot, R. N.: A Servant of Britain Overseas* (London, Cleaver-Hume, 1960).

property to be more secure than at Canton'.[41] His successor, Sir Henry Pottinger, remarked that up to the Sanyuanli incident of May 1841, there had been 'no general popular feelings of ill-will or antipathy towards the British nation on the side of the people', who had been as civil and as well disposed as he had invariably found them in the other parts of China since he left Nanjing.[42] An independent observer may also be quoted. An American who had lived in Canton for twenty years, from 1825 to 1844, remarked that before the war, 'should a foreigner get into a disturbance in the street, it was generally safe to say that it was through his own fault'. He echoed Elliot's view: 'In no part of the world could the authorities have exercised a more vigilant care over the personal safety of strangers who of their own free will came to live in the midst of a population whose customs and prejudices were so opposed to everything foreign'.[43]

These observations confirm the analysis earlier in this chapter, which questioned Nolde's view that before 1840 'a spirit of bitter anti-foreign feeling had lurked in the hearts of most Cantonese and that for a European to live among them was to live dangerously'.[44] The view of another author may also be assessed here. H. B. Morse wrote in great detail about the life of foreigners in Canton before the Opium War.[45] He concluded by drawing up a list of complaints by foreign merchants. In this list the hostility of the common people was conspicuously absent. It is inconceivable, therefore, why he should then go on to assert that after the war, the Cantonese '*remained* implacably hostile'.[46]

Even after the war, the Cantonese were not indiscriminately hostile. Let us again turn to the observations of China's antagonists. Rear-Admiral Sir Thomas Cochrane[47] took a six-hour walk in the suburbs of Canton in 1846 and concluded that the inhabitants were a peaceable people, unless needled to the breaking point by devil-may-care British merchants. He observed that U.S., French, Dutch, and other foreign nationals seemed to be able to live in peace and harmony with the Cantonese. He saw no reason why Britons could not do the same.[48]

41. *Digest of Despatches*, p. 70, quoted by J. Nolde, 'Xenophobia in Canton', p. 3
42. Pottinger to British merchants, 16 December 1842, enclosed in Pottinger to Aberdeen, Desp. 71, 20 December 1842, FO17/59.
43. William C. Hunter, *The Fan Kwae at Canton before Treaty Days, 1825–1844* (London, Kegan Paul, 1882), pp. 26–7.
44. Nolde, 'Xenophobia at Canton', p. 2, col. 2.
45. Morse, *International Relations of the Chinese Empire*, v. 1, pp. 86–7.
46. Ibid., p. 368. Emphasis added.
47. Sir Thomas John Cochrane (1789–1872) initially served in the West Indies station of the Royal Navy before becoming the governor of Newfoundland (1825–34), M.P. for Ipswich (1839–41), rear-admiral and second in command in China (1842–5), and commander-in-chief (1845–7). In due course of seniority he became vice-admiral in 1850, admiral in 1856, and admiral of the fleet in 1865. *DNB*, v. 4, p. 631.
48. Cochrane to Admiralty, 21 January 1847, enclosing two letters to Sir John Davis in Hong

The personalities of imperialism

Three years later, Bowring, the new British consul at Canton, also went on fact-finding expeditions. Jostling among the immense crowds in the streets outside the walled city, he concluded that his own forbearance and self-control, his attention to children, his avoidance of anything looking like a menace or an insult had invariably created a friendly and often cordial feeling. He remarked that the Chinese were characteristically gentle and polite. Even when men, women, and children crowded round him and his companions, they showed 'great courtesy on the part of the well-bred – and even the countless multitudes of the labouring population made way for us'.[49]

During the Dragon Boat festival, he went with two English ladies to see the boat race. 'When they observed that our boat stopped to look at the procession, two of the boats turned back and passed and repassed several times to give the ladies an opportunity of a thorough examination. Loud shouts and redoubled exertion accompanied their civility'.[50] Even more important was Bowring's realization that the term *fangui*, normally translated as 'barbarian or foreign devil, do not necessarily convey an offensive meaning, as I have frequently heard it said by beggars in their humblest supplications, and in cases where the party so called was an object of respect and gratitude for essential services rendered'.[51] These observations, particularly those by Bowring, seriously question the view that the Cantonese hostility towards the British was 'virulent xenophobia'.[52]

The 'xenophobia' interpretation is based on the clashes between the Cantonese and the British after the Opium War, involving deaths and serious destruction of property on both sides.[53] There were twenty-four such incidents between December 1842 and the spring of 1849. Five were particularly serious and have been studied in detail by both Nolde and Wakeman. The first grave incident was caused by a lascar stabbing a Chinese fruit vendor in Canton on 7 December 1842. The second started on 16 June 1844 when the Americans, playing skittles in the garden of the factory area, first beat some Cantonese spectators with sticks and canes, then fired into the mob, killing one Cantonese. The third erupted on 8 July 1846, when Charles Compton, a British merchant, kicked down a fruit stall that was in his way, tied up the owner, and gave him a severe beating. A hostile crowd gathered. The foreign merchants took it upon themselves to disperse the crowd and shot dead three of them. The fourth happened on 15 December 1847, when six Englishmen decided to investigate a village called Huangzhuqi outside Canton. When a crowd of villagers

Kong, 20 November and 3 December 1846, Adm. 1/5575, quoted by Graham, *China Station*, p. 241.
49. Bowring to Palmerston, 12 May 1849, Broadlands MSS, GC/BO84.
50. Bowring to Palmerston, 7 July 1849, Broadlands MSS, GC/BO87.
51. Idid.
52. As argued in Wakeman, *Strangers at the Gate*, p. 73.
53. See Nolde, 'Xenophobia at Canton'; Wakeman, *Strangers at the Gate*, chapters 1–8.

Rule Britannia and vox populi, vox Dei

gathered, some Englishmen lost their nerve and opened fire, killing two of them. None of the Englishmen left the village alive. The fifth, in February 1849, was when Sir George Bonham demanded entry into Canton City. About a hundred thousand Cantonese took up arms, which were laid down only after Bonham posted a notice forbidding foreigners to enter the city.[54]

All five incidents show that the Cantonese did not take the initiative to riot or to take up arms; they were goaded into such actions. Thus, 'xenophobia' is not an appropriate interpretation of these incidents. Furthermore, the scholar who first proposed such an interpretation, Nolde, appears to have had difficulty explaining the peace and quiet, and even the feeling of amity, that prevailed between the incidents. I say this because he simply omitted to do so.

In the context of my analysis, perhaps attention should be focused on the instigators of these incidents rather than on the respondents. Let us again start from the beginning. On 29 August 1842, the Treaty of Nanking was signed. On 2 December, the British representative, Sir Henry Pottinger, arrived back in Hong Kong from Nanjing, where he had signed the peace treaty.[55] On 7 December, serious violence broke out at Canton. What caused the violence? Apparently, some foreign merchants and their wives 'had walked about the outskirts of the city, and had even crossed the river to Honan – an exposure which is at total variance with ideas of decorum and propriety amongst the better orders of Chinese'. Others 'had publicly talked of selecting spots for their future country residences in the neighbourhood of Canton, and had avowedly crossed the river to Honan for that purpose, which are all indiscretions calculated to give offence and cause ill will'.[56] In short, the British merchants returned to Canton after the war, determined to show that they were the victors. *Civis Romanus sum*.[57]

Even the lascars were infected; 170 of them went ashore without their officers on the morning of 7 December 1842, picked a quarrel with some Chinese fruit vendors, and stabbed one of them. By the end of the day, the English, Dutch, and Greek buildings in the foreign factories were burned down.[58] *Vox populi, vox Dei*.

54. Nolde, 'Xenophobia in Canton'; Wakeman, *Strangers at the Gate*, chapters 2–9.
55. Pottinger to Qi Gong, 13 December 1842, enclosed in Pottinger to Aberdeen, Desp. 71, 20 December 1842, FO17/59.
56. Pottinger to Aberdeen, Desp. 71, 20 December 1842, FO17/59.
57. Palmerston once said, 'As the Roman, in days of old, held himself free from indignity when he could say *Civis Romanus sum*, so also a British subject, in whatever land he may be, shall feel confident that the watchful eye and the strong arm of England will protect him against injustice and wrong.' Hansard, 3d series, v. 62, cols. 380–444, Lord Palmerston's speech, 25 June 1850. This is quoted in *Brewer's Dictionary of Phrase and Fable* (London, Cassell, 1963), p. 207. The British merchants at Canton, however, abused the privileges they enjoyed under that watchful eye.
58. Sir Hugh Gough to Lord Stanley, 13 December 1842, encl. 3, in Pottinger to Aberdeen, Desp. 71, 20 December 1842, FO17/59.

The personalities of imperialism

The British merchants at Canton jointly wrote to Pottinger alleging that the attack on the foreign factories was premeditated and organized. They accused the Cantonese authorities of being unable or unwilling to protect them. They requested that 'their Excellencies the naval and military Commanders-in-chief may be moved to place such a force for their defence in Canton as may seem expedient'. Otherwise, they would have to leave, and all the businesses would fall into the hands of the Americans, to whom the Chinese were not hostile.[59]

Pottinger replied that the Chinese attack was provoked and not premeditated and that if British merchants would not restrain their lascars, they had to face the consequences. As for the Cantonese mob, he remarked that such a mob did not exist until the Sanyuanli incident of May 1841 and that the change to exasperation and excitement 'had been brought about by ourselves'. He passionately appealed to his compatriots to 'soothe the very excitement' instead of aggravating it and to go on 'as in past times, quietly and unobtrusively' with their mercantile pursuits. He had sufficient reason to believe that the Cantonese authorities were not unwilling but were *unable* to control the mob. Mobs, whether they were in China or 'in England and other of the most civilized nations of Europe', were invariably unmanageable. He turned down their request for 'troops and ships-of-war' on the grounds that such military presence 'would inevitably lead to further ill-will, heart-burning, and violence, and its only result must be disappointment, and in all likelihood, a renewal of hostilities between the Governments of England and China'.[60]

But the British merchants would not listen. They insisted that their behaviour had been 'peaceable and unobtrusive'.[61] Fortunately, Pottinger had the support of the foreign secretary. His action was approved by Lord Aberdeen, who added, 'Her Majesty's Government cannot hold themselves responsible either for the protection or indemnification of parties who, by their own misconduct ... shall render themselves obnoxious to the Chinese Government or people'.[62] It is indeed a pity that Bowring did not take this principle to heart in the case of the *Arrow*.

Pottinger's successor, Sir John Davis, was less fortunate. Davis had merely approved a fine of $200 imposed by the British consul on Charles Compton, whose aggressive action had led to the death of three Chinese.[63] He had complained only, 'I am not the first, who has been compelled to remark that it

---

59. British merchants to Pottinger, 13 December 1842, encl. 4, in Pottinger to Aberdeen, Desp. 71, 20 December 1842, FO17/59.
60. Pottinger to British merchants, 16 December 1842, encl. 5, in Pottinger to Aberdeen, Desp. 71, 20 December 1842, FO17/59.
61. British merchants to Pottinger, 23 December 1842, enclosed in Pottinger to Aberdeen, Desp. 73, 23 December 1842, FO17/59.
62. Aberdeen to Pottinger, Draft 46, 1 April 1843, FO17/64.
63. Davis to Palmerston, Desp 119, 26 September 1846, FO17/114.

is more difficult to deal with our own countrymen at Canton than with the Chinese government'.[64] But the new foreign secretary, Lord Palmerston, reacted angrily. He declared that even if the British merchants were the scum of the earth masquerading as the salt of it, wherever they were in danger 'thither a British ship of war ought to be'.[65] Consequently, Palmerston gave them what Aberdeen had refused, a steamer, to be posted to Whampoa,[66] a few miles downriver from Canton. But the British merchants were still not happy, because the steamer was out of sight of Canton. They had requested that it be moored right to the factory riverfront. Their aim was obvious; they had wanted an iron monster there puffing smoke to cow the Cantonese. When their government still refused to oblige, they hired their own steamer for that purpose. Even Palmerston was irritated by this truculent show of independence.[67]

Speaking outside the context of the British government's 'China policy', Palmerston was equal in his anger when denouncing Compton and others who 'amuse themselves by kicking over fruit-stalls and by making foot-balls of the Chinese'.[68] The same merchants had tried earlier to force their way into Canton City, brandishing pistols as they went.[69]

The entry crisis of 1849 was a watershed in Anglo-Chinese relations for the period 1842–56. When Commissioner Xu and Governor Yeh reversed Qiying's policy, they sided with the people and conspired to refuse British entry into the city. It worked. A grateful people presented honorific tablets inscribed, 'The People's Will is as strong as a walled City'.[70] A printed pamphlet explaining the reasons for the tablets stated, 'If Their Graces had not constantly commiserated with the secret troubles of the people, and roused them by encouragement, it would have been impossible for the public determination to become as strong and firm as a walled City'.[71] Thenceforth, they trusted their imperial commissioners, first Xu, and, from 1852 onwards, Yeh, to hold the fort. The effects of this development were dramatic. Suddenly the riots in Canton ceased. Short of any more incidents to analyse, Nolde had to cut short his study of Cantonese 'xenophobia', stopping at the year 1849.[72]

In a word, it was the British venturing into the villages, and their demand to

64. Davis to Palmerston, Desp. 158, 12 November 1846, FO17/115.
65. Palmerston to Davis, Draft 37, 10 December 1846, FO17/108.
66. Davis to Palmerston, Desp. 27, 12 February 1847, FO17/140.
67. Palmerston to Bonham, Draft 107, 31 October 1849, FO17/152.
68. Memorandum on an interview between Lord Palmerston and the China Deputation, 28 June 1847, FO17/135 (domestic various).
69. Qiying to Davis, 27 December 1845, FO682/1978/66.
70. *Chinese Repository*, May 1849, quoted in Morse, *International Relations*, v. 1, pp. 397–8. The presentation of the tablets would have been organized by the prominent members of the gentry, who, traditionally, were the community leaders.
71. Translated and enclosed in Bonham to Palmerston, Desp. 66, 18 May 1849, FO17/155.
72. Nolde, 'Canton City Question'. See also his article, 'Xenophobia in Canton'.

enter the city, that were the occasions for nearly all the incidents in the Canton area after the Opium War. Since the Cantonese by no means showed a 'morbid dread or dislike of foreigners' in general and since the cause of the incidents under discussion might well be described as British xenophobia, Nolde's interpretation of Cantonese hostility may no longer stand; the shoe is on the other foot.

Thus, no sooner had Bonham received the false edict than he had a government notice issued, directing 'that no British subject shall for the present attempt to enter the city'. He had this notice circulated in the Canton factory area and printed in the newspaper.[73] He was terrified that the hotheads among the British merchants might be so incensed by the imperial refusal to honour Qiying's undertaking as to attempt another forcible entry of the city.

The Taiping Rebellion erupted in Guangxi shortly afterwards. Disaffected elements in Guangdong had already started a series of sporadic revolts which drew Xu and Yeh away from Canton at various times. These revolts grew in number and intensity until the entire province was engulfed in a general insurrection in 1854, threatening Canton itself[74] and even the security of Hong Kong.[75] There was an ironic change in the attitude of the British merchants. Now they needed the Canton government to hold the rebels at bay to protect their trade, lives, and property. It would have been suicidal to undermine the authority of the Canton government by embarrassing it any further. Indeed they found it expedient 'to exercise all precaution and foresight, in order to entitle themselves to the favourable consideration of the [Chinese] Government, should damage or detriment be done to them'.[76] Seldom had British merchants in Canton been as well behaved as between 1849 and 1856.

The paradox is that during the same period, louder and louder noises might be heard from Bowring, as the next section shows. In Lord Palmerston, Bowring was to find strong backing finally in 1856. But already in 1849, Palmerston had thundered over the Cantonese celebrations, 'The British Government well knows that, if occasion required it, a British military force would be able to destroy the town of Canton, not leaving one single house standing, and could thus inflict the most signal chastisement upon the people of that City'.[77]

V. Official xenophobia? *Rule Britannia*

Apart from the 'insults' – or 'popular xenophobia' as some historians would call it – official xenophobia has also been held as part of the origins of the *Arrow*

---

73. 'No. 15 Government Notification', dated 2 April 1849, *Chinese Repository* 18 (1849), p. 211, quoted in Huang, 'Viceroy Yeh', p. 50, n. 29.
74. See my *Yeh Ming-ch'en*, chapters 5–6.
75. See Graham, *China Station*, p. 284.
76. Bowring to Clarendon, Desp. 21, 11 January 1855, FO17/226.
77. Palmerston to Bonham, Draft 68, 18 August 1849, FO17/152.

War. Thus, another blue book, entitled 'Correspondence Relative to Entrance into Canton, 1850-55', was distributed to members for debate over the *Arrow* War in the February-March 1857 session of the British Parliament.[78] The constant theme in the correspondence was that as an official policy the Canton government instigated, cultivated, and encouraged popular hostility towards foreigners.

Both the evidence and the analysis thereof thus far seem to suggest that this puts the cart before the horse. The Canton officials were the victims, not sponsors, of such hostility. In the preceding section, it was submitted that the so-called insults had been caused not so much by the alleged popular xenophobia, as by the bad behaviour of some British merchants, which in itself might be put down to British dislike of foreigners. In the same vein, it will be seen in the following pages that part of the origins of the *Arrow* War may be found, not in official xenophobia, which was almost nonexistent, but in the indiscretion of some British officials.

As mentioned in Chapter 5, personal humiliation in 1849 and patriotic concern over the opium revenue in India had made Bowring obsessed with forcing open the gates of Canton. He was convinced that if he were to be respected by the Chinese, and if China's opium prohibition were to remain a dead letter, the Cantonese authorities must not be allowed to enjoy their triumph over the city question for long. Thus, Bowring felt obliged to continue kicking the gates of Canton to warn the bigots inside not to become too adventurous. To these reasons were soon added his concern for the United Kingdom's trade with China and the humiliation of continuing to be frustrated by the Canton authorities in his relentless attempts to force the issue, until finally the *Arrow* incident gave him the opportunity to show not only the flag but the guns as well.

On 19 January 1852, the Foreign Office, now headed by Lord Granville, appointed Bowring acting superintendent of trade during Bonham's absence, but instructed him 'to avoid the irritating discussions' with the Canton authorities.[79] Obviously Granville was not prepared to jeopardize a lucrative trade by provoking another ugly disturbance in pursuit of a shadowy goal.

Bowring accepted the appointment, pledged himself to obey the instructions, and immediately proceeded to argue against them: 'The popularity at Court, and in the country, of Seu [Xu], the present Imperial Commissioner, is mainly attributable to the reputation he enjoys of having, more than any other man, successfully repelled the advances and counteracted the policy of foreigners.' Already, Xu had imposed an additional duty on tea exports at Canton and had to some extent reorganized the warehouse monopoly. The £9 million sterling of revenue which the China trade was contributing to the

78. Parl. Papers 1857, v. 12, pp. 1-55.
79. Granville to Bowring, Draft. 1, 19 January 1852, FO17/186.

British and Indian treasuries could not be adequately protected 'under the existing system of exclusion'. Bowring further argued that entry 'into the City of Canton may be effected without difficulty' and that 'no period more appropriate than the present could be found for peremptorily urging upon the Chinese authorities' the demand for such entry. He did so on the grounds that the current rebellions were bound to make them more conciliatory and that there had been no public agitation since 1849. Indeed the Cantonese had been friendly:

> I have been in the habit of taking my walks, in all directions, within a circuit of twenty to thirty miles (avoiding entrance within the city gates), frequently alone, visiting and holding intercourse with the people, and without the smallest anxiety on my part, or the slightest incivility or interruption on the part of the natives. In this manner I have been an unmolested spectator of their great military reviews, of their public executions, of their dramatic performances in the open air, of their religious, civil and social ceremonies.[80]

The more Bowring wrote, the more he was convinced by his own arguments; so should Lord Granville be, he thought. He concluded his despatch by mentioning, almost casually, that in announcing his temporary appointment to the Chinese commissioner, he had already requested 'an early reception'.[81] Bowring's letter was received in the Foreign Office on 14 June 1852. The reaction was predictable:

> Sir, I have received your despatch of the 19th of April, and I have to state to you in reply, that it is the intention of Her Majesty's Government that you should strictly adhere to the instructions given to you by Earl Granville, by which you were enjoined to avoid all irritating discussions with the Chinese authorities; and in conformity with the rule thus prescribed to you, you will abstain from mooting the question of the right of British subjects to enter into the City of Canton.[82]

Meanwhile, the Canton authorities had replied:

> We earnestly desire a personal interview with your Excellency, that we may have an opportunity for open and unreserved conversation with you. At present, however, we really have not the leisure to admit of it; one of us, the Commissioner [Xu], being just now occupied at Kaou-chow [Gaozhou] with the supreme direction of the forces there engaged; and the other, the Governor [Yeh], being actively employed at the provincial City, in attending to the supplies required by the troops, and the multifarious correspondence connected therewith. With your Excellency's permission, we should defer the matter until the hostilities shall have been reported as at an end, and the Commissioner shall have returned to Canton, when we will address your Excellency

---

80. All the quotations in this paragraph are from Bowring to Granville, Desp. 1, 19 April 1852, FO17/188.
81. Ibid.
82. Malmesbury to Bowring, Draft 18, 21 June 1852, FO17/186.

again, naming a time for the interview, which we mutually anticipate with so much delight.[83]

Recent research shows that this answer was not an attempt at avoiding the issue. Xu and Yeh were genuinely involved in suppressing serious rebellions,[84] which was acknowledged by Bowring himself.[85]

The Chinese response brought an about-face in Bowring, who told the Foreign Office that he had 'quite anticipated the answer', and then went on to suggest a 'demonstration' of force.[86] This caused one of the strictest injunctions from Whitehall: 'Her Majesty's Government would deprecate extremely a disturbance of the existing state of things, which would be more easily effected than allayed'.[87]

Bowring gave in, but not without lodging a strong protest:

> I venture most emphatically, to assure your Lordship that I never should have presumed to solicit the authority from Her Majesty's Government, for undertaking the settlement of the long-protracted question as to our right of access to that City, had I not been fully persuaded, after a very long residence in and knowledge of Canton, that the time was singularly favourable for effecting the object, and that I could have effected it without endangering the public peace and with great advantage to our social, political, and commercial relations with China.[88]

Indeed Bowring seems to have believed that his own charisma would succeed where lesser men had failed and that he could safely crash through the gates of Canton without resistance. He was halted by the Foreign Office injunction, but remained unconvinced.

A year later, on 13 February 1854, Bowring was appointed Her Majesty's minister plenipotentiary in the Far East upon Bonham's retirement. His special task was to negotiate a new treaty with the Chinese under the guise of treaty revision. As regards the city question, he was instructed to treat it with 'much caution'. He must not use 'menacing language' let alone 'force', lest 'we might place in peril the vast commercial interests which have already grown up in China, and which, with good and temperate management, will daily acquire greater extension'.[89] Bowring was quick to realize that these instructions were not as uncompromising as those he had received a year before. But of course Lord Palmerston was now prime minister, and Lord Clarendon, who shared Palmerston's views, was foreign secretary.

83. Xu and Yeh to Bowring, 25 April 1852, enclosed in Bowring to Granville, Desp. 12, 29 April 1852, FO17/188.
84. See my *Yeh Ming-ch'en*, chapter 5.
85. Bowring to Granville, Desp. 1, 19 April 1852, FO17/188.
86. Bowring to Granville, Desp. 12, 29 April 1852, FO17/188.
87. Malmesbury to Bowring, Draft 18, 21 July 1852, FO17/186.
88. Bowring to Malmesbury, Desp. 120, 8 September 1852, FO17/192.
89. Clarendon to Bowring, 13 February 1854, Parl. Papers 1857, v. 12, p. 15.

Bowring took great courage from these changes. He felt bold enough to reverse the priority of his instructions by putting the city question before treaty revision. In his first despatch to Commissioner Yeh announcing his new appointment, he foreshadowed a second despatch 'on the subject of [his own] reception'.[90] Yeh replied, 'It would gratify me exceedingly to meet Your Excellency, that we might demonstrate publicly our friendly sentiments; but having just now the management of military operations in various provinces my time is completely occupied. When I obtain a little leisure I will certainly select an auspicious day for meeting your Excellency'.[91] Recent research has shown that Yeh was indeed preoccupied with the Taiping and other rebellions at this time.[92]

On the same day that this reply was written and before he had received it, Bowring produced another despatch, listing his grievances and putting on top of the list nonadmission into Canton City. He added, 'Nothing would be more painful to me than irritating and unfriendly discussions, the consequences of which might be deplorable'.[93] Yeh argued, as may be expected, that the Cantonese were violently opposed to foreigners entering their city, and that Bowring's immediate predecessor had given up the demand because he, too, had recognized this. Then he mentioned that Bowring's despatch did not bear an official seal, presumably 'from inadvertence'.[94] In a separate despatch of the same day Yeh proposed to meet Bowring on 22 May in Renxin Mansion next to the foreign factory, the same place at which Xu had offered to meet Bonham in 1849.[95]

Here, Bowring had the opportunity to do two things: to meet Yeh on 22 May or to do something about the missing seal. He decided on the latter and sent his Chinese secretary, W. H. Medhurst,[96] to Canton in Her Majesty's war steamer *Barracouta* to affix his official seal to his previous despatch and to deliver in person his rejoinder to Yeh's latest despatches 'either into the hands of the Imperial Commissioner, or of such high mandarins as he may authorize to receive it'.[97]

Apparently Bowring was hoping that the presence of a barbarian interpreter

90. Bowring to Yeh, 17 April 1854, FO682/1987/13.
91. Yeh to Bowring, 25 April 1854, Parl. Papers 1857, v. 12, pp. 17–18. The Chinese text may be found in FO682/1987/14.
92. See my *Yeh Ming-ch'en*, chapter 6.
93. Bowring to Yeh, 25 April 1854, Parl. Papers 1857, v. 12, pp. 16–17.
94. Yeh to Bowring, 7 May 1854, Parl Papers 1857, v. 12, p. 20. The Chinese original is in FO682/1987/19.
95. Yeh to Bowring, 7 May 1854, Parl. Papers 1857, v. 12, p. 21, The Chinese original is in FO682/1987/20.
96. Originally a printer born in Batavia, W. H. Medhurst became a Congregationalist missionary to China and joined the British trade superintendency staff in 1840. Later he became consul before retiring at the age of 54. He was subsequently knighted. See Coates, *China Consuls*, p. 494.
97. Bowring to Yeh, 9 May 1854, Parl. Papers 1857, v. 12, pp. 20–1.

uttering Chinese and a warship puffing smoke would dwarf the mandarins. But this clumsy exercise meant that Yeh did not get the seal or the replies when he had expected them. Indeed, his deputy had been running between the yamen and the British consulate empty-handed. The imperial commissioner was quite insulted. 'After having yourself sought an interview, and induced me to fix a day for it, why subject me to this further delay? Such successive breaches of engagement augur ill for the easy conduct of business hereafter'.[98]

When Medhurst did arrive, Yeh again sent his usual deputy, the sub-magistrate of Nanhai, to meet him. However, Medhurst thought it was beneath him to be met by an official of that rank. Yeh then sent a full magistrate who had the additional title of a prefect, whom Medhurst still thought he could not receive without prejudice to his position as Bowring's delegate. Meanwhile the steamer had to leave Canton, and Medhurst left with it.[99]

Yeh exploded:

I have gone out of my way to condescend compliance with Mr Medhurst's desire ... More than ten days have elapsed without my receiving any rejoinder ... and as the day fixed by me is fast approaching, I beg you will at once inform me whether or not you will decide upon seeing me. As I am just now engaged in attending to the military arrangements connected with several provinces, my time is so fully taken up that I fear if the period fixed upon be allowed to pass by, I shall have less leisure than ever at my disposal. Pray accept my best wishes for your abundant prosperity.[100]

Bowring accepted the compliments but not the appointment: 'I am now making arrangements for my immediate departure with his Excellency the Admiral, and several of Her Britannic Majesty's ships of war'.[101]

Where was Bowring going? He had told Lord Clarendon previously that if Yeh agreed to see him inside the city, 'we shall have gained a very important point; should he refuse, we shall have another substantial grievance, which will justify my proceeding to the capital'.[102] So off he steamed to North China. Arriving at Shanghai, he complained about his treatment at Canton to the viceroy of Liang Jiang, stationed at Nanjing,[103] who replied, 'As your Excellency cherishes such a dislike of discourteous treatment, you must doubtless be a most courteous man yourself'.[104] Bowring must have wondered whether he would have done better at Canton. There Yeh at least agreed to talk to him. In

---

98. Yeh to Bowring, 17 May 1854, ibid., p. 24. The Chinese original is in FO682/1987/25.
99. Medhurst to Bowring, 18 May 1854, Parl. Papers 1857, v. 12, p. 23.
100. Yeh to Bowring, 17 May 1854, ibid., p. 24. The Chinese original is in FO682/1987/25.
101. Bowring to Yeh, 24 May 1854, Parl. Papers 1857, v. 12, p. 24.
102. Bowring to Clarendon, 25 April 1854, ibid., pp. 15–16.
103. Bowring to Yi-liang, 10 July 1854, ibid., p. 28.
104. Yi-liang to Bowring, 18 July 1854, ibid., pp. 28–9.

The personalities of imperialism

any case, the time for treaty revision was approaching and he was told to start at Canton. So back to Hong Kong he steamed.

There, he wrote to Yeh on 22 August 1854, saying that the Treaty of Nanking was due for revision in another week and he was therefore sending Medhurst to Canton for preliminary talks.[105] His instructions to Medhurst were that he should include a request for 'an official reception within the walls of Canton'.[106] Fortunately for Bowring's reputation, the talks broke down not because of the city question but because Yeh professed not to have the power to negotiate radical changes to the existing treaty.[107] Bowring steamed back to Shanghai in September, and from there further north to the Peiho, near Tientsin, in October.[108] There he was again referred back to Canton. He could not have stayed on to argue even if he had wanted to. The winter was beginning to set in. HMS *Rattler* was beginning to rattle in the wind.

Back in Hong Kong, Bowring received from Yeh a request for cooperation against what Yeh called bandits on the waters of Canton.[109] By this time, he had defeated the land rebels who had besieged Canton on three sides. Now he had to deal only with those on the south, who were originally river pirates. There had been precedents of British requests for Chinese cooperation to suppress piracy, which were invariably and unconditionally granted.[110] Yeh probably thought it was time for reciprocation. Yet Bowring read a great deal into it: 'Great must be the alarm and extreme the perplexities and perils, which have induced the present Mandarin to supplicate the aid of outer Nations'.[111] To Yeh he replied, 'As the circumstances appear so urgent I shall, accompanied by the Admiral and several ships of war, proceed to Canton on Wednesday next'. On 12 December 1854, the day after Bowring replied, Admiral Stirling steamed up the Canton River in Her Majesty's frigate *Winchester*, accompanied by the steamer *Styx*. The following day Bowring followed in the *Rattler*. Both men arrived at Canton on the same day, 14 December. Bowring described what followed:

Immediately on arrival, I announced our presence to the Viceroy, and he sent two Mandarins of the rank of District Magistrate to make courteous inquiry after my health.

105. Bowring to Yeh, 22 August 1854, enclosed in Bowring to Clarendon, Desp. 128, 5 September 1854, FO17/215.
106. Bowring to Medhurst, 22 August 1854, enclosed in Bowring to Clarendon, Desp. 128, 5 September 1854, FO17/215.
107. Yeh to Bowring, 1 September 1854, enclosed in Bowring to Clarendon, Desp. 128, 5 September 1854, FO17/215. Those radical changes included the opening of the entire interior of China, or at least the Yangtze River basin, where the famous Chinese tea and silk were produced in large quantities. See Clarendon to Bowring, Desp. 1, 13 February 1854, FO17/210.
108. Bowring to Clarendon, Desp. 173, 10 November 1854, FO17/217.
109. Yeh to Bowring, 7 October 1856, enclosed in Bowring to Clarendon, Desp. 230, 11 December 1854, FO17/218.
110. See my *Yeh Ming-ch'en*, chapter 6.
111. Bowring to Clarendon, Desp. 230, 11 December 1854, FO17/218.

I hoped that the extreme perplexities of the Chinese authorities, with the country around them in confusion and conflagration, and the City menaced daily by the rebel forces, would have induced the Mandarins to grant me an official and amicable interview, in order to discuss matters which interest them so deeply, but I am sorry to say, even the straits to which they are reduced and the dangers with which they are surrounded have so little abated their obstinate pride and unteachable ignorance, that they still turn a deaf ear to my well-meant proposals.[112]

What Bowring failed to realize was that if Yeh opened the gates of Canton, he would lose the support even of those inside the city. Besides, the worst for Canton – the seige – was over, and he could deal with the remnants on the river in his own good time. Not surprisingly Yeh declined the conditional aid from Bowring, who returned to Hong Kong with yet another bitter disappointment.

Six months later, Rutherford Alcock was appointed British consul at Canton. Bowring wrote to Yeh, 'If your Excellency should now be disposed to receive me, I should be glad to have an opportunity of personally introducing Mr Alcock ... Should your Excellency not consent to receive me officially, I shall be glad if you will allow Mr Alcock personally to present his credentials'.[113] Yeh reminded Bowring of his rejection of the earlier proposal to meet at Renxin Mansion, adding, 'As regards the arrival of the British Consul at Canton, there is no precedent for an interview with him. There never was a deputation to receive your Excellency for instance, during the many years that you were Consul here'.[114] Yeh was rubbing salt into Bowring's unhealed wounds.

Then on 8 October 1856 the *Arrow* incident occurred, the first diplomatic incident since 1849. As we saw in Chapter 4, Bowring readily seized the occasion for taking action. 'Out of these troubled waters', he told his son, 'I expect to extract some healing food'.[115] The Royal Navy bombarded Canton City, but the city gates remained firmly closed. Even after the British returned a year later with large reinforcements and French allies – even after the Anglo-French forces had actually entered the city from all directions and were everywhere searching for him – Yeh was still saying, 'Give them anything, money, anything, but not admission into the city!'[116] *Vox populi, vox Dei.*

Yeh's exclamation consolidates an interpretation of the conduct of Qing foreign policy first advocated some twenty years ago and now generally accepted among scholars, namely, that local politics rather than the supposedly

112. Bowring to Clarendon, 25 December 1854, FO17/218.
113. Bowring to Yeh, 11 June 1855, Parl. Papers 1857, v. 12, p. 38.
114. Yeh to Bowring, 9 July 1855, ibid., p. 9.
115. Bowring to Edgar Bowring, 16 October 1856, Ryl. Eng. MSS 1228/161.
116. Hua Tingjie, 'Chufan zhimo', in *Er ya*, v. 1, p. 184.

all-pervading Confucian conservatism might have played the greater role in distorting Chinese diplomacy.[117]

VI. In sum

It seems clear that we may not attribute the origin of the *Arrow* War to the so-called xenophobia of the Cantonese, because this did not exist. Certainly, British merchants complained of much hostility from the Cantonese people up to 1849, hostilities which Western historians have conceptualized as popular xenophobia. But such hostility was invariably the result of extreme provocation from daredevil British merchants such as Compton. Otherwise, all accounts suggest that the Cantonese people were normally friendly and helpful. If we have to regard the friction as an origin of the *Arrow* War, then we must look beyond that friction and pinpoint its source – the provocation which, in turn, may be traced to that feeling of 'European ascendancy'.[118] This provocative ascendancy was a cause of the *Arrow* War, but not its respondent.

And certainly Bowring complained of much hostility from Commissioner Yeh as early as 1849, hostility which Western historians have conceptualized as official xenophobia. But such hostility was invariably the result of unauthorized demands which Yeh could not meet, such as entry to the city. In this respect, an origin of the *Arrow* War may similarly be traced to the indiscretion of some British officials, but not to the response.

Indeed, if we were to use the same evidence presented in this chapter to ask the reverse question, namely, whether instead of the Cantonese people and officials, the British merchants and diplomats were xenophobic, many might answer in the affirmative. The position of the strangers from the other side of the globe is easily understandable. Living far away from home in what was to them a very trying climate[119] and feeling terribly isolated among a multitude of people whom they could not and would not understand, they could easily develop a siege mentality. It only needed Parkes and Bowring to blow it out of all proportion.

Let us look at the matter from a different angle. The Cantonese people and officials may have had good reason to keep their city gates closed to foreign merchants and diplomats. What they did not realize was that such action could be seen as an affront to the *Pax Britannica* if not to other nations such as the United States (which had not yet imposed the *Pax Americana* and was therefore

117. For that interpretation of Qing foreign policy, see Wong, *Yeh Ming-ch'en*. For the general recognition and acceptance of that interpretation, see Polachek, *Inner Opium War*, p. 4. For more analysis of the conduct of Qing foreign policy, see the Conclusion, this volume.
118. Davis to Palmerston, Desp. 10, 26 January 1847, FO17/123; and Palmerston to Davis, 11 March 1847, FO17/121.
119. The British consular reports are full of complaints about the heat and other exacting climatic conditions.

not quite so offended): witness *The Times*'s comment that Yeh's refusal to receive Her Majesty's representative inside the city signified the termination of friendly relations.[120]

This has prompted some historians to interpret the *Arrow* War as a war for diplomatic recognition.[121] However, we shall need to go beyond the gates of Canton to locate the origins of the *Arrow* War. Battering down those gates was only a means to an end. The end was to be a new treaty which would further British national economic interests. In this regard, Bowring was not entirely irrational when he put the Canton City question before treaty revision. He was convinced that until the spirit of Chinese defiance, epitomized in the closed gates of Canton, was broken, there was no hope of getting radically new and fundamental concessions. The same argument subsequently persuaded Lord Elgin in 1857 to subdue Canton first before doing anything else in China. It was perceived that achieving a settlement with China depended first and foremost on crashing the gates of Canton. In Bowring's own words, 'The insult is I cannot get entrance... convincing us that nothing but his [Yeh's] utter humiliation will enable us successfully to negotiate'.[122] Admiral Seymour agreed, 'Any attempt... [at] negotiation elsewhere would... confirm the Chinese in their belief of the impregnability of Canton, on which, as it is alleged, rests the whole system of their exclusiveness and arrogance towards strangers.'[123]

120. *The Times*, 2 January 1857.
121. Douglas Hurd, for example, wrote, 'The British and French, and to a lesser extent the American Governments, came slowly to the conclusion that it was not enough to defend the letter of the existing Treaties; they must be prepared to use force to get themselves recognised, in practice as well as theory, as the equals of the Government in Beijing' (*Arrow War*, p. 27).
122. Bowring to Edgar Bowring, 21 November 1856, Ryl. Eng. MSS 1228/163.
123. Seymour to Admiralty, 10 July 1857, Adm. 1/5583.

Part IV
The rhetoric of imperialism

In Part I of this book, we have seen the confusion of imperialism; and in Parts II and III, its pretexts and personalities. Here we shall investigate how they were publicly dealt with in Britain, first in the press and later in parliamentary debates. In the course of doing so, we hope to explore further the origins of the *Arrow* War.

We shall also evaluate, inter alia, a dominant interpretation of the *Arrow* War – that which is prevalent in the People's Republic of China today. I refer to the view that the *Arrow* War, like the Opium War before it, was a determined and almost unanimous attempt on the part of the British imperialists to 'conquer, enslave, plunder, and slaughter'[1] the Chinese people. Apparently, this interpretation stems from the writings of Karl Marx, who in turn formed that view on the basis of what he had read in the British press and heard during the parliamentary debates over the issue. At the time, Marx was a reporter for the *New York Daily Tribune*. He wrote fifteen articles on the *Arrow* War for that newspaper, which also featured a related piece by Friedrich Engels.[2] Since 1949, Marx's influence has been such that the entire academic world in the People's Republic of China has changed its traditional title for the conflict from 'Anglo-French Allied Forces' to the 'Second Opium War', apparently because Marx coined the latter title in his articles.

There is, of course, the question of how accurately Marx, a German Jew living in Manchester and London, really understood the nuances of events at Canton. Born in Germany in 1818 and expelled from both Germany and France because of the publication of his *Manifesto of the Communist Party* in 1848, he had lived in England only since 1849. Thus, although he listened to the debates in the British Parliament, it is doubtful how accurately he understood the nuances of British politics. There is the further problem of Chinese historians trying to view Victorian England through the eyes of Marx. Even when an historian in China bypasses Marx to read Hansard and *The Times*, as

1. See Wang Di, 'Minzu de zainan yu minzu de fazhan', p. 36.
2. See Makesi Engesi, *Makesi Engesi lun Zhongguo*. Again, the English originals of these articles have been collected in Marx, *Marx on China*.

The rhetoric of imperialism

Professor Jiang Mengyin has done,[3] there are still difficulties. The debates in the British press and in Parliament reflect the complexities of a kind of political dialogue which does not exist, and has never existed, in China. Professor Jiang has written the standard book in the Chinese language on the *Arrow* War. Nearly all subsequent Chinese works on the subject have been a combination of his scholarship and Marxist ideology.

It is important, therefore, to investigate what transpired in those debates and what Marx's fellow journalists were saying about that dispute. Thus, Chapter 7 will deal with the press debate, Chapter 8 with the debate in the House of Lords, and Chapter 9 with that in the House of Commons. The prime minister, Lord Palmerston,[4] lost the debate in the Commons, and called a general election,[5] the so-called 'Chinese Election', which returned him to office.[6] To various degrees these topics have been studied by at least five modern historians: Arthur Silver,[7] C. E. Jackson,[8] Angus Hawkins,[9] E. D. Steele,[10] and, more recently, Miles Taylor.[11] Their passion is British politics, while I am mainly concerned with the origins of the *Arrow* War.

3. See Jiang, *Di'erci yapian zhanzheng*.
4. For a specialist study of Palmerston in this particular period, see Steele, *Palmerston and Liberalism*.
5. The term 'general election' should be put in the context of its own time. The franchise in 1857 was very restricted. There was a property and a residence qualification that left the majority of males without a vote. The qualifications were lowered in 1867 and again in 1884. It was not until 1918 that all men over the age of twenty-one were granted the right to vote. Women got the right to vote in 1918, too, but at an age level higher than that of men – thirty years. Thus, when politicians and journalists of 1857 talked about appealing to the nation, the country, and the general public, they were using these terms in a context very different from the current one. For details, see Jenifer Hart, *Proportional Representation: Critics of the British Electoral System, 1820–1945* (Oxford, Clarendon Press, 1992); see also Francis Barrymore Smith, *The Making of the Second Reform Bill* (Cambridge University Press, 1966).
6. Like the question of franchise, one must not confuse today's concept of a general election, bestowing the power to rule, with the realities of the mid-Victoria era. At that time, ministries still regarded themselves as 'primarily charged with administrative responsibility, and not with the execution of a political programme endorsed by the electorate'. That was a legacy of royal control over the choice of a prime minister (see Sir David Lindsay Keir, *The Constitutional History of Modern Britain since 1485*, London, Adam & Charles Black, 1969, p. 407). The importance of the part played by the Queen in making ministries may be gleaned from the fact that minority governments held office 1846–7 (Russell's first ministry), 1858–9 (Derby's second ministry), 1866–8 (Derby's third ministry), and a coalition in 1852–5 (Aberdeen's ministry) (ibid.). Not until 1868 (Derby and Disraeli ministry) did a government immediately resign after an adverse general election, and as late as 1892 Lord Salisbury awaited a defeat in the Commons before resigning (ibid., p. 407, n. 4).
7. Arthur Silver, *Manchester Men and Indian Cotton, 1847–1872* (Manchester, Manchester University Press, 1966), pp. 82–4. His concern is mainly with the Manchester electorate.
8. See C. E. Jackson 'The British General Elections of 1857 and 1859', unpublished D.Phil. thesis, University of Oxford, 1980.
9. See Angus Hawkins, *Parliament, Party and the Art of Politics in Britain, 1855–59* (London, Macmillan in association with the London School of Economics, 1987), chapter 3.
10. See Steele, *Palmerston and Liberalism*, pp. 74–6.
11. See Miles Taylor, *The Decline of British Radicalism, 1847–1860* (Oxford, Clarendon Press, 1995), pp. 269–84.

7
Marx, *Punch*, and a political press:
The debate among the British newspapers

I. Peace or war: *The Times*

The general public in Britain first heard about the *Arrow* quarrel on Monday 29 December 1856 through a telegraphic despatch from Trieste.[1] On New Year's Day, the overland mail arrived. At once *The Times* published a second edition and printed a summary of a report from their correspondent in Hong Kong.[2] The next day, *The Times* reproduced the entire report detailing events up to 15 November 1856.[3] On 6 January 1857, the British government published in the *London Gazette* Admiral Sir Michael Seymour's despatch to the Admiralty, with enclosures, about the operations of the Royal Navy in the Canton River, the destruction of Chinese forts, and the bombardment of Canton.[4]

How did the British press react to the news of this undeclared war? *The Times* editorial of 2 January 1857, that is, the same day on which *The Times* printed in full the report from its own correspondent in the Far East, is noteworthy. The editor warned the nation that to tolerate Yeh's behaviour would be entirely to forfeit the position already acquired by the Opium War (1839-42) and to present Britons to the Chinese as a nation devoid of honour and self-respect. It argued that Yeh's refusal to receive Her Majesty's representative was in itself the termination of friendly relations and an advertisement that the Treaty of Nanking, as far as Canton was concerned, was virtually at an end. It proclaimed that without the protection of the treaty, British merchants at Canton, cut off from the rest of the world and placed on the soil of a half-civilized empire and a hostile people, would have no security for their lives or property. The editor condemned Yeh's conduct throughout as arrogant and insulting.[5]

1. *The Times*, 29 December 1856.
2. Ibid., 1 January 1857. The despatch was dated 29 November 1856.
3. Ibid., 2 January 1857. The despatch was also dated 29 November 1856.
4. *London Gazette*, 6 January 1857.
5. *The Times*, 2 January 1857, p. 6, col. 4.

153

This was exactly the sort of message that Parkes had wished to convey to the British government and the British public by telling untruths about the flag and distorting Yeh's intentions, as we have seen in Chapter 3.

After the government's publication of Admiral Seymour's report in the *London Gazette* on 6 January 1857, the editor of *The Times* stiffened his attitude further. The real issue was whether Britain ought to assert the rights which natural law and 'our own superiority in arms and civlization give us' to enforce free communication with Yeh inside Canton.[6] Here, the editor reflected fairly faithfully the attitude of the admiral, an attitude formed on the basis of the misinformation that Parkes and Bowring had given him, including concealment of the expiry of the *Arrow*'s register. The editor concluded: 'We are therefore actually at war with China'. In the interest 'of humanity and civilization we ought not to let the matter drop.' Hence China must pay ample indemnity: 'Our honour and interest urge us to place our relations with the Chinese Empire on a new footing'.[7] In other words, the editor thought that the quarrel should be used to demand a new treaty from China.

Now, was *The Times* controlled by the British government, as so many Chinese historians have alleged that it was? If it was, then the editor's words would have been as good as those of Lord Palmerston. To anybody who has any knowledge of the history of the British press, 'control' would be too strong a word to apply to *The Times* in any case. In fact, Palmerston and *The Times* had been at loggerheads for a very long time: witness the paper's violent editorial attacks on him. Palmerston himself complained that from the time he first went into the Foreign Office, for some reason or other which he could never discover, '*The Times* has been animated by undeviating hostility, personal and political, towards me'.[8] Apparently, *The Times* thought that Palmerston was not liberal enough and not curbing Russian expansion energetically enough.[9]

But by 1855, after John Delane[10] had become the editor, there was a reconciliation. Delane appears to have taken the first step in that direction, being conscious of the fact that prolonged separation from customary and necessary sources of news and inspiration would prove injurious to his paper.[11] That separation would become positively dangerous to its circulation once the new Stamp Act[12] permitted the emergence of the penny press.[13] Out of journalistic

6. *The Times*, 8 January 1857, p. 8, col. 2.   7. Ibid., col. 3.
8. Palmerston to the Queen, October 1855, quoted in *History of The Times, v. 2, 1841–1884: The Tradition Established* (London, Office of *The Times*, 1939), p. 236. For the animosity between Palmerston and that newspaper, see ibid., pp. 236–58.
9. See *History of The Times*, v. 2, pp. 236–7.
10. For a biography of him, see Arthur Irwin Dasent, *John Thaddeus Delane, Editor of The Times: His Life and Correspondence*, 2 vs. (London, Office of *The Times*, 1908).
11. See *History of The Times*, v. 2, p. 261.
12. For details, see C. D. Collet, *History of the Taxes on Knowledge: The Origin and Repeal*, 2 vs. (London, T. Fisher Unwin, 1899).
13. The market for this penny press appears to have been the rapidly swelling ranks of the artisans,

prudence, therefore, Delane thought he could give detached support to Palmerston for those sides of his policy upon which the country as a whole was agreed.[14] A meeting was arranged at the house of Sir William Molesworth in August 1855: 'Palmerston and Delane talked. The talks developed into an understanding. Delane came to recognize Palmerston as the Right Man in the Right Place'.[15]

Thereafter, the two men became increasingly close until Palmerston's death in 1865, with Palmerston taking the initiative to discuss details of national policy with the editor in personal interviews.[16] To keep Delane on side, Clarendon, the foreign secretary, once declared to the editor that 'whether they [telegrams] come by night or by day, I have ordered that they shall always go *first to The Times*'.[17] One must be careful to distinguish between newsworthy telegrams and official documents, however. As we shall see in Part Five, Clarendon received Bowring's despatch about the *Arrow* incident on 1 December 1856. But Delane had to wait until 29 December 1856 for the arrival of the telegraphic despatch from Trieste before he knew anything about the dispute.

When Palmerston's government was subsequently defeated on 3 March 1857 in the House of Commons over the *Arrow* quarrel, he held a cabinet meeting the next day, which resolved to dissolve Parliament, and then both he and Clarendon wrote to inform Delane of the decision. Palmerston began thus: 'It is due to you considering the handsome and powerful support which you have given to the Government, that you should have the earliest intimation of the course which we mean to pursue'.[18] In his letter, Clarendon remarked that 'the dishonest coalitions and the dishonest speeches of our public men are doing infinite mischief . . . and I shall be much surprised if your friend Yeh . . . does not turn the vote of last night to work against us in China'.[19] It is said that

who were thereby better informed and more intellectually independent than any previous generations of working men. This working-class elite had developed with the tremendous expansion of basic industries such as iron and steel, engineering, shipbuilding, railways, and building. They included shipwrights, engineers, puddlers, forgers and moulders, engine drivers, cabinet-makers and upholsterers, painters, carpenters, bricklayers, bakers, and butchers. They lived in cleaner cottages and on different streets from the labourers, as well as joining different Friendly Societies and frequenting different public houses. See F. B. Smith, *The Making of the Second Reform Bill* (Cambridge University Press, 1966), pp. 2–10.

14. See *History of The Times*, v. 2, p. 263.
15. Ibid., pp. 263–4.
16. Ibid., v. 2, p. 321.
17. Clarendon to Delane, 28 September 1857, Printing House Square Papers (hereafter cited as P. H. S. Papers), D. 8/52, quoted in *History of the Times*, v. 2, p. 322.
18. This letter (P. H. S. Papers, D. 8/7; Dasent, I, 249) is dated 4 February 1857, but was no doubt written on 4 March, the date of Clarendon's letter to Delane, which stated that the Cabinet had just met and that Palmerston 'promised me he would write to you'. See *History of the Times*, v. 2, p. 323.
19. Clarendon to Delane, 4 March 1857, P. H. S. Papers, D. 8/7; Dasent, I, 258, quoted in *History of the Times*, v. 2, p. 324.

Delane took Clarendon's hint and printed a warning that the new coalition would not gain confidence by 'throwing everything into confusion'.[20]

Therefore, it is fair to say that at the time of the *Arrow* War, *The Times* was close to the government and its editorials generally reflected their line of thinking. Now, the British government could decide on war or peace upon receipt of the news of the *Arrow* quarrel. If *The Times* should be crying out for war and for a new treaty, may we assume that the government had decided on the same? This question will be explored further in Part Five, when an attempt will be made to probe behind the scenes by scrutinizing government and other documents. But for our immediate concerns, one of which is to assess Marx's view, and thereby that of the modern Chinese, of *The Times*, we might say that it was not controlled by the government, though at times it reflected fairly accurately the government's line of thinking.

In terms of our search for the origins of the *Arrow* War, a knowledge of the close friendship between Delane and Palmerston is important. It helps explain the somewhat different attitudes of *The Times* on 2 and 8 January. The editorial of 2 January would have been written when Palmerston was resting at his Broadlands estate. That of 8 January would have been penned after Palmerston had returned to London and probably had a word with Delane. Thus, on 2 January, the editor had shown his editorial independence by stating that there were 'indeed matters in dispute, such as whether the lorcha out of which the men were taken was carrying British colours'.[21] On 8 January, however, he categorically alleged that the Union Jack had been hauled down. And as if to play down the effect of his earlier statement, he now dismissed the *Arrow* incident as immaterial. 'The immediate cause of hostilities was, as is generally the case in war, of small moment'.[22]

If we may not depend on the perceptiveness of the most influential British newspaper to offer us any clues to the origins of the war apart from the government's determination to wage it on the basis of the casus belli invented by Parkes, we shall have to look to other papers for further enlightenment. Next, therefore, let us look at the *Morning Post*.

II. The tirade against Yeh: The *Morning Post*

The *Morning Post*[23] alleged that Yeh's 'perverse discourtesy' and 'mulish pertinacity'[24] were the cause of the entire trouble. Were Great Britain to overlook

20. Quoted in ibid.
21. *The Times*, 2 January 1857, p. 6, col. 3.
22. Ibid., 8 January 1857, p. 8, col. 3. Editorials might not have always been written by the editor, but he would have read and approved them.
23. For a history of that newspaper, see Reginald Lucas, *Lord Glenesk and the Morning Post* (London, Alston Rivers, 1910). See later for an assessment of the position of the *Morning Post* at this time.
24. *Morning Post*, 2 January 1857.

the slightest infractions of treaty or international law on the part of a 'barbarous Eastern Power' or to disregard the most trivial slights or venial errors, long experience had taught 'our naval and military commanders that the wrongdoer would proceed from slight to insult, from insult to aggression, and from aggression to outrage'. The paper argued that the most humane and, in the end, the most pacific and least expensive manner of dealing with the Chinese was to chastise them in the most severe and exemplary fashion. The paper concluded that it was not sufficient in China to exhibit and demonstrate Britain's power. Britain must actually use it manfully against 'an insincere, distrustful, and arrogant people, before they can be brought to reason or to acknowledge they are in the wrong'.[25]

So this paper, without conducting any investigation or balancing the probabilities, simply jumped to the conclusion that the Chinese were in the wrong; and that if they should deny it, must be made to admit they were wrong. We have seen how Parkes exhibited this very attitude. In the age of British imperialism, such a view was commonplace.

Three days later, the *Morning Post* went further: 'As far as past years teach us anything on the subject there seems no way of reaching the heart of China but by the sword'. An attempt was made to rationalize this attitude: the East had to be bombarded periodically in the interests of commerce and civilization. Every bombardment, every new understanding would contribute something towards these goals. The vessel of war cleared the way for the vessels of commerce. The admiral preceded the merchant; the merchant introduced the missionary and the traveller. These, in turn, took with them the seeds of civil advancement, which, dropped by the wayside, would bear fruit in after years, and lay the foundation of new necessities, which would, in due course, call in the aid of steam and gas, the printing press and the telegraph, the school and the church, the railroad and the Athenaeum, and, 'why not? – the elective franchise and the House of Commons'.[26]

Here, the paper had just stated what it regarded as the yardstick for advanced civilization of the time – the elective franchise, which eventually developed into universal suffrage in the twentieth century. Ironically, that paper's hero, Lord Palmerston, was himself unwilling to widen the British electorate at this time.[27]

In any case, argued the *Morning Post*, there was no alternative to war: 'Right or wrong, we are in the quarrel, and there is nothing but to go on with it. It may have begun in misunderstanding, but now it has proceeded to a length that

25. Ibid., 2 January 1857.
26. Ibid., 5 January 1857.
27. See, e.g., Michael Bentley, *Politics without Democracy, Great Britain, 1815–1914: Perception and Preoccupation in British Government* (Oxford, Basil Blackwell in association with Fontana, 1984); and Taylor, *The Decline of British Radicalism*.

admits of only one termination'.[28] Great Britain could not accept the threat to her material interests posed by Yeh: 'To yield to a savage of this kind were to imperil all our interests, not only in the East, but in every part of the world'.[29]

The logic in this argument is clearly imperialistic. On the one hand, the paper conceded that the quarrel might have been caused by a misunderstanding. On the other, it regarded the misunderstanding as irrelevant because British gunboats had, regardless, gone too far for second thoughts to prevail. What was to be done? First, 'we must bombard and batter down Canton until reparation be made'. Second, 'we must adopt other and decisive measures to bring the war to a speedy termination'. Then the paper alleged that the 'last Chinese mail took out these instructions to our naval commander'.[30] How did the editor know? Was he privileged to some government information?

Checking the British Foreign Office records, I find that on 17 January 1857 the Admiralty had transmitted to Whitehall a further report by Seymour on his operations in the Canton River. Clarendon replied on 24 January that 'some additional measures' were necessary to 'open the eyes of the Chinese authorities', and therefore 'Her Majesty's Government are of opinion that . . . all the forts below Canton should be effectually destroyed'. In addition, 'Her Majesty's Government consider that the next step should be to detach a naval force to the Yang-tsu-Keang'. The objective was to 'intercept as far as possible the water communications to Beijing by the Grand Canal or other internal waters'.[31] Such a step would seriously disrupt supplies to the national capital.

These instructions fit the tone and details of the editorial in the *Morning Post*. It is quite probable, therefore, that some information of a general nature had been leaked to that newspaper. The secondary literature on the British press reveals that the *Morning Post* was often excessive in supporting Palmerston, to the point of compromising the person it sought to champion, as the following incident shows.

The *Morning Post* unknowingly seized upon a clerical error to keep up its tirade against Yeh. In a telegram that came via Paris, reference was made to the burning down of the *hongs* – the foreign factories on the riverside of Canton. Somewhere along the line the word '*hong*' was rendered as Hong Kong. This made a sensational story. The *Morning Post* proclaimed that the attack upon Hong Kong was indicative of the fixed determination on the part of the Chinese to push the quarrel to the furthest extreme. It asserted that under these circumstances there was no alternative for Bowring and Seymour but to go on until they had brought Yeh to terms by the destruction of his city.[32]

28. *Morning Post*, 31 January 1857.
29. Ibid., 3 February 1857.   30. Ibid.
31. Foreign Office to Admiralty (2d draft), 24 January 1857, FO17/279, pp. 220–3.
32. *Morning Post*, 31 January 1857.

This is another piece of quite remarkable logic. It was all right with the paper for the Royal Navy to batter down Canton, but the Chinese must not be allowed to touch Hong Kong – and the report about Hong Kong was false anyway. In sum, the *Morning Post* attributed the origin of the *Arrow* quarrel to Yeh, who must be punished speedily, or else British interests would be imperilled.

III. The eulogies for Yeh: The *Daily News* et al.

After an examination of available reports the *Morning Chronicle* was prepared to throw in a good word for Yeh, portraying him as a gentleman rather than the villain of the piece: 'A fair and candid examination of his acts will show that he acted with much dignity and forbearance, and a lofty sense of duty'. The editor denounced those newspapers which had depicted the conduct of Yeh as the height of barbarous insolence and obstinacy. It also did much soul searching: 'We are not saying that it may not be consistent with policy, or even with a very high morality in the abstract, thus to compel the opening up of relations with the barbarians'. But it certainly was unworthy of the dignity of a great nation pretending to lead civilization, to attain such an object through pretexts so miserable as those relied on in the present instance. The editor thought it was not the act of conquest or spoliation that was so hateful, so much as the attempt to varnish it with a kind of moral justification, which had no foundation in facts.[33]

Thus, on the basis of the case presented by Parkes, and without knowing he had in fact faked the casus belli, this paper regarded the pretexts as miserable. Its views probably reflected mid-Victorian values of justice and humanity, the political stance of the Peelites, who had dealings with that paper,[34] or both. In any case, these views were remarkably similar to those of William Gladstone,[35] who publicly attacked Palmerston in the House of Commons[36] and privately wrote that the censure vote on Palmerston did 'more honour to the H[ouse] of C[ommons] than any I ever remember'.[37] There were no contradictions between his public ambitions and private feelings on the issue.

---

33. *Morning Chronicle*, 8 January 1857.
34. See Stephen Koss, *The Rise and Fall of the Political Press in Britain, v. 1, The Nineteenth Century* (London, Hamish Hamilton, 1981), p. 111.
35. William Ewart Gladstone (1809–98) had been lord of the treasury (1834), under-secretary for the colonies (1835), vice-president (1841) and then president of the Board of Trade (1843), secretary for the colonies (1845), and chancellor of the Exchequer (1852–5). Four times he was to become prime minister between 1868 and 1893. See H. C. G. Matthew's two books, *Gladstone, 1809–1874* (Oxford, Clarendon Press, 1986), and *Gladstone, 1875–1898* (Oxford, Clarendon Press, 1995). See also *The Gladstone Diaries, v. 5, 1855–1860*, ed. M. R. D. Foot and H. C. G. Matthew, 14 vs. (Oxford, Clarendon Press, 1978).
36. See Chapter 9.   37. *The Gladstone Diaries*, v. 5, p. 202, Tuesday, 3 March 1857.

The Times's initial reaction was to regard Yeh's refusal to give audience to the representative of England as a termination of friendly relations.[38] Having considered the matter over the weekend, it now showed much understanding for Yeh. It thought that the seizure of the *Arrow*'s crew might or might not be a piece of premeditated insolence; but Yeh's official proclamations at once showed the sentiment uppermost in his mind: the British were manufacturing an excuse again to force the gates of Canton City. It felt that Yeh had at least offered redress in the matter of the *Arrow*, though absolutely refusing to open Canton City.[39]

The editor of *The Times* was one of the few observers, who, having digested the pertinent official correspondence and reports, was judicious enough to acknowledge that Yeh had half-apologized for the *Arrow* incident. It even sympathized with Yeh for the way Bowring had seized a flimsy excuse to start a war, wishing that Bowring and his advisers had taken care to have a better case for a quarrel than in this instance.[40] In view of Yeh's having made a half-apology, Parkes and Bowring should have been equally gracious and accepted his goodwill gesture.

The *Spectator*[41] agreed. British interference in China might not, in fact, end in furthering the progress of civilization because it had begun in such a way as 'to place us in a false position before the Chinese, in the eye of reason, and according to the letter of the public law'.[42]

The *Daily News* went even further. Indeed, it turned the extravagance of the *Morning Post* the other way around. The editor found himself reluctantly compelled to come to the conclusion that 'a more rash, overbearing, and tyrannical exercise of power has rarely been recorded than that upon which it now becomes our painful duty to comment'. He lamented that in order to avenge the irritated pride of a British consul and punish the folly of an Asiatic governor, 'we prostitute our strength' to the wicked work of carrying fire and sword, desolation and death 'into the peaceful homes of unoffending men, on whose shores we were originally intruders'.[43]

Whatever might have been the issue of the Canton bombardment, the editor of the *Daily News* maintained, 'The deed itself was a bad and a base one – a reckless and wanton waste of human life at the shrine of a false etiquette and mistaken policy'. He regretted the attempt of some London journals to prejudge the question of the *Arrow* by declamatory invective against the Chinese. He took the view that the British proceedings at Canton were characterized

38. *The Times*, Friday, 2 January 1857.
39. Ibid.
40. Ibid., 5 January 1857.
41. The *Spectator* was a weekly. It was introduced in 1828 and later became a platform for philosophic radicalism. See Koss, *Political Press*, v. 1, p. 48.
42. *Spectator*, 17 January 1857.
43. *Daily News*, 2 January 1857.

throughout by overbearing insolence and conscious bad faith.[44] He condemned the widening of the quarrel by the introduction of the additional and unrelated demand to enter Canton City. He thought it mean and paltry in the highest degree to evade a decision on the merits of the original quarrel by raising another.[45]

At the same time, the *Daily News* was full of admiration for the Chinese elite like Yeh. They were a people of high refinement and ancient cultivation, eminently instructed and singularly governed in all their relations by their own views of what was just and fitting. They had no feudalism, no landed aristocracy; but they were an empire 'when the ancestors of the Fitz-Battleaxes were a horde'. They knew no passport to high office but proven merit. They set aside the claims of family in favour of talent with a singleness of mind, which to an administrative reformer must have seemed the highest stretch of political virtue. They had discovered quite early on an appetite for universal competitive examination which went far beyond the zeal of Sir Charles Trevelyan and Sir Stafford Northcote.[46] The *Daily News*'s portrayal of Yeh as a cultured and fair person probably reflects its labour movement affiliation and explains its humanitarian and class-critical perspective. Tirade or eulogy aside, if we want to find out what some of the temperate British journalists thought was the real origin of the war, let us listen to Mr Punch.

IV. 'About the English of it': *Punch*

This was the title which *Punch* gave to a satire it wrote on the casus belli. It took a sober look at the voluminous official correspondence pertinent to the *Arrow* quarrel. Pretending that all the correspondence was originally in Chinese, it set about translating it into English. In so doing, the journal gave itself all the freedom in the world to condense the key items into a few lines and put them back into the mouths of the authors, sometimes as official despatches and at other times as private notes. Strung together, these imaginary letters told the story within the framework of that weekly's interpretation of the original despatches and what it thought the quarrel was all about.[47]

---

44. Ibid., 9 January 1857.
45. Ibid., 12 January 1857.
46. Ibid., 2 January 1857. The report of Sir Charles Trevelyan (1807–86) and Sir Stafford Northcote (1818–87), entitled *The Organisation of the Permanent Civil Service* (dated 20 March 1853, in Parl. Papers 1853, v. 28, p. 161), eventually led to the adoption of examinations for entry into the civil service in the United Kingdom. These examinations were based on knowledge of the Roman and Greek classics and mathematics, in the same way that the Chinese civil service examinations were based on knowledge of Confucian classics (see *DNB*, v. 19, pp. 1135–6; and, v. 14, pp. 639–44, respectively). See also Oliver MacDonagh, *Early Victorian Government, 1830–1870* (London, Weidenfeld & Nicolson, 1977).
47. *Punch*, 24 January 1857.

Punch recast Parkes's very first letter to Yeh about the *Arrow* incident as follows: 'Sir, – One of your war-boats has boarded an English lorcha, the *Arrow*, lying near the Dutch Folly, has carried off twelve of her Chinese crew, and hauled down the English flag'. The letter continued, 'I went to the war-boat, and explained to the Officer in command that I wouldn't stand it, and that he must send the men up to the British Consulate. The Officer refused, and told me to be hanged, and said if I didn't get out of that, he would make me'. It added:

Not wishing to be ducked, I left the boat, and now write to request that you will at once give order to Captain Leang-gwo-ting, to send the men back to the *Arrow*. *I may as well mention that I have written to our Plenipotentiary and our Commodore* [emphasis added]. You know neither will stand any nonsense, and if you don't send the men back at once, and with a proper apology, I won't be answerable for the consequences. So look out for squalls.

The sentence in italics shows that *Punch* had grasped the crux of the matter: Parkes was simply trying to bully Yeh into submission.

Parkes's communication to the commodore was recast thus:

My dear Elliot, Here is a chance for you. These fellows have seized some men aboard a lorcha flying English colours. I have written to desire Yeh to send them back. I haven't got his answer, but of course he won't. You know what a pig-headed brute he is, and besides, there is no doubt the lorcha's colonial registry was not renewed when it last expired. This will give him a legal ground for refusal, but of course I shall not condescend to discuss the point of law with him. I fully anticipate your thirty-two pounders will be required to reduce him to reason; so bring up *Sibylle* without delay, there's a good fellow.

Parkes's official despatch to Bowring was transformed into a private note:

I enclose Yeh's answer to my letter. As I expected, he offers no apology, but takes advantage of the legal quibble, as to the *Arrow*'s right to fly our colours; but he luckily misses the strong point that her registry was not renewed on the 27th of September last, as it ought to have been. The story of the pirate on board is new to me. It may or may not be true, but at all events we may fairly contend there is no reliance on the evidence of natives given under duress. I hope you will not see any objection to my having written to Elliot to bring up the *Sibylle*. I think the sooner we come to great guns the better. These Qhihis will discuss points with us for an eternity.

In other words, *Punch* saw through Parkes's ploy of forcing Bowring's hand by writing to call up the *Sibylle* without Bowring's previous authority. At least one historian has adopted the contention that 'there is no reliance on the evidence of natives given under duress'.[48] As we have seen in Chapter 2, it was

---

48. Costin, *Great Britain and China*, p. 207.

not the arrested crew of the *Arrow*, but the Chinese officers who said that the Union Jack was not flying at the time of the incident.

The postscript to the *Punch* version of Parkes's note reads: 'I forgot to mention that Yeh sent back nine of the men. Of course, I refused to receive them. His pretext for keeping back the others, that they are under legal examination, is ridiculous. What business has he to set up Chinese law against the demands of a British Consul?' In the eyes of *Punch*, Parkes regarded himself as superior to Chinese law.

Yeh's answer in *Punch* begins with the detection of pirate suspects employed as sailors on board the *Arrow*, leading to the detention of the entire crew for examination. It concluded:

I trust that this answer will satisfy you that the taking of the men is not intended as an insult to the British flag, but that they were seized on legal grounds, for a serious offence, in due form of Chinese law, and on board a Chinese vessel. I hope the promptness with which I have given this examination, will satisfy you that I have done nothing for which any apology is required, and still less for which I and the City need fear any of the consequences to which you refer.

Like *The Times*, *Punch* could see that Yeh was indeed conciliatory and half-apologized for a wrong which he denied had ever been committed. In *Punch*, Bowring replies to Parkes privately:

I'm afraid you have been in rather too great a hurry to punch Yeh's head; but as you have got me into the mess, I suppose I must see you through it. Why the mischief didn't you satisfy yourself before making any row in the case, that the *Arrow* had a right to fly the British flag? Then we should have been all right. But, as it is, it is as clear as that two and two make four, that she had no such right whatever; her registry, by virtue of which alone she hoists our colours, having expired on the 27th ult.

The reply continues: 'Luckily – as you say – Yeh doesn't take this point, so that we have a loophole left to creep out of. *De non existentibus et non apparentibus eadem est ratio*,[49] as Noy puts it in his maxims, – a work which I dare say you never read. By the bye, it would be just as well if you *would* read a little international law'. The note concludes:

But, really, if you get us into many rows of this kind, I cannot answer for bringing either you or myself creditably out of the scrape. The plain English of it is, that we haven't a legal leg to stand upon, so I have ordered up Seymour and the big guns . . . And as to consequences, I am afraid I must own to a little sympathy with [Yeh] in his disregard of them.

After this penetrating comment on Parkes's role in the *Arrow* incident, Parkes is made to react:

49. This may be liberally translated, 'Not to be seen is the same thing as not to exist'.

I feel the full force of your letter. We are in a hobble. It is a great comfort Yeh does not take the point of the expiration of registry. He still refuses all apology, but reiterates his assertion of this lorcha being a Chinese and not a British vessel. Though this is quite true, he does not put it on a legal ground, and I have therefore directed Elliot to seize an imperial junk.

Thereupon, Parkes writes to Yeh: 'If you don't apologize in twenty-four hours I'll batter your house about your ears. It's all nonsense arguing the point about the ownership of the lorcha and the law of the case. Apologise, or it will be the worse for you'. Parkes also writes to the admiral: 'Old Yeh sticks to his case. If you can take the Bogue forts it may convince him he's in the wrong'.

Yeh replies:

You tell me your Admiral has taken the Bogue forts. I know it – and I am sorry for it – but taking twenty forts will not make black white, nor force me to make an apology when I am conscious of having done no wrong. You English profess to reverence Heaven, to pray in your churches on Sundays, and to esteem justice. How do you reconcile all these with taking the Bogue forts in this case?

Here *Punch* inserted this italicized comment: '*The 26th, being Sunday, was observed as a day of rest. It is clear that Britons DO respect the Sunday, for all the COMMISSIONER YEH's offensive insinuations*'.

The next day, Rear-Admiral Sir Michael Seymour writes to Parkes, 'I am really ashamed to go on pitching into these helpless Chinamen in this style, especially while they are in the right and we in the wrong'. He continues:

But, if I must give them more powder and shot, can't you manage to find a decent excuse? Suppose you insisted on Yeh's receiving my call? If he can't, I shall have no objection to blow him and his Yamun into the middle of next week. Couldn't you put our right on the old Treaties of 1842–46?

Parkes obliges: 'You are our preserver. I shall at once insist on Yeh's receiving you. I am afraid the Treaties are rather stale to revive very effectively, but I will try it on'. Yeh replies: 'You insist on Yeh's receiving your Admiral. Yeh says nay'. A jubilant Parkes reports to Bowring: 'It's all right at last. I am sure you will be relieved to hear that Yeh refuses to receive Seymour. We have a clear right under the Treaties to insist on his doing so. The consequences of the refusal be on his own head'.

Here, Mr Punch seems to believe, wrongly of course, that the request for entry into Canton City originated with Seymour. He is not to blame, not having access to Parkes's private papers which clearly show that Bowring was the instigator.

Bowring is made to reply: 'I am delighted that you and Seymour have got on legal ground at last, though I wish we had insisted on the Treaties a little sooner. I am afraid we may be told at home that the Statute of Limitations applies to the case'. He added: 'But we have gone too far to recede. Tell

Seymour to blaze away, but to kill as few people as possible, and not to destroy more private property than is absolutely necessary. My heart bleeds for these infatuated Chinese'. He concludes:

> I can't understand Yeh's holding out against Seymour's guns, though I admit he had the best of it against your arguments. I know that under similar circumstances I should have thought twice before refusing an apology. In an ancient Spartan or a modern Swiss, Yeh's conduct might be called heroic. In a Chinaman it is culpably obstinate, and cannot be submitted to for a moment.

The episode ends with this comment from *Punch*: 'Yeh will know another time what it is to refuse to receive a British Admiral when he does him the honour to volunteer a call'.[50]

It is said that the English, more than any other nation, are good at laughing at themselves. Indeed, the whole point about this satire is that Mr Punch was in no doubt as to the culpability of Parkes and Bowring. Nor did he hesitate to say that these diplomats lacked a just cause for war. He was convinced that the violent measures taken in the name of avenging an alleged insult to the flag were not the best means to teach Yeh a lesson. He proposed, instead, to ship Yeh and a few other mandarins to England to make them learn some English law, study representative government, visit the public offices, and inspect the factories. The object was, of course, to make them aware of 'our astounding resources as a fighting nation' and subdue them 'by a profound consciousness of our superior morals and of our excelling virtue'.[51] This last, presumably, is sarcasm.

V. Marx on the *Arrow* quarrel: The *New York Daily Tribune*

In his capacity as a journalist, Karl Marx contributed to the press debate by writing eighteen articles, fifteen of which were published in the *New York Daily Tribune*, sometimes as leaders.[52] In the opening paragraph of his first article, published on 23 January 1857, he said that a careful study of the official correspondence between the British and Chinese authorities at Hong Kong and Canton must produce upon every impartial mind the conviction that the British were wrong in the whole proceeding. *The Times* had conceded that 'there are, indeed, matters in dispute, such as whether the lorcha ... was carrying British colours'. Marx felt that the doubt thus admitted was confirmed when one remembered that the provision of the Treaty of Nanking related only

---

50. *Punch*, 24 January 1857.
51. Ibid., 14 February 1857.
52. The three unpublished articles were written in 1860 and apparently remained unpublished. See Karl Marx, *Marx on China: Articles from the 'New York Daily Tribune', 1853–1860* (with an introduction and notes by Dona Torr) (London, Lawrence & Wishart, 1968), p. 98, note.

The rhetoric of imperialism

to British ships, 'while the lorcha, as it abundantly appears, was not in any just sense British'.[53]

Thereupon, Marx reproduced what he thought was Parkes's first letter to Yeh, which he described as being 'dated Oct. 21'. The date fitted the contents of that letter. But Parkes's very first letter to Yeh was in fact written on 8 October 1856.[54] Here, Marx appears to have relied for his information on the *London Gazette*, in which was published Seymour's report to the Admiralty, with enclosures. Marx proceeded to interpret Parkes's letter thus: 'The British Consul accuses the Chinese Governor-General of seizing the crew, of hauling down the British flag, of declining to offer any apology, and of retaining the men seized in his custody'. He sided with Yeh on the question of the *Arrow*'s nationality: '. . . rightly so, because she was built by a Chinese, and belonged to a Chinese, who had fraudulently obtained possession of a British register'.[55]

Marx supported Yeh's argument that 'the invariable rule' with British ships was to lower their ensign when they anchor, and to re-hoist it only when they 'again get under way'. The *Arrow* was at anchor when she was boarded. 'How then could a flag have been hauled down?' Marx agreed with *The Times* about Yeh's probably having offered an apology, contained in a letter which Parkes did not condescend to open.[56] He thought that the force of Yeh's dialectics disposed so effectually of the whole question that Seymour had no choice but to decline any further argument on the merits of the case of the lorcha *Arrow*.[57]

Marx concluded that there were two distinct acts in this diplomatic and military drama. The first was commencing the bombardment of Canton on the pretext of a breach of the Treaty of 1842 whereby Chinese suspects on British vessels had to be claimed through the British Consul;[58] the second, widening that bombardment on the excuse of Yeh's having clung stubbornly to the Convention of 1849 whereby Bonham had proclaimed the abandonment of the right to enter Canton.[59]

Marx also commented on the editorials of *The Times* and the *Daily News*.

The Times had remarked, 'By this outbreak of hostilities, existing treaties are annulled, and we are left free to shape our relation with the Chinese Empire as we please'.[60] Marx thought that this pronouncement would do no discredit

---

53. Ibid., p. 11.
54. For the full text of that letter, see Chapter 2.
55. Marx, *Marx on China*, p. 12.
56. Ibid., p. 13.
57. Ibid., p. 14, quoting Seymour.
58. Marx was wrong here. It was the Supplementary Treaty (1843) which contained such a provision, not the Treaty of Nanking (1842) itself.
59. Marx, *Marx on China*, p. 16.
60. Ibid. This quote may be found in the editorial of *The Times*, 2 January 1857, p. 6, col. 3.

even to General William Walker of Nicaragua, a U.S. filibusterer who had led a privately armed expedition to proclaim the independence of Lower California, and then declared himself President of Nicaragua in 1856. Thereupon the editor of the *New York Daily Tribune* commented that in China the British, 'with all their horror of *our* filibustering propensities', still retained 'in common with ourselves, not a little of the old plundering, buccaneering spirit' of their common ancestors.[61]

Marx approved the attitude of the *Daily News*. He quoted its editorial extensively, and concluded that the paper was 'humane and becoming.'[62] Had Chinese historians been able to read Mr Punch, they might prefer him to Karl Marx if only because Mr Punch entertainingly, happily, unreservedly, and therefore most effectively, punched big holes in the government representatives's pretensions.

Again, if Chinese historians had had easy access to the British press and Hansard, they might realize that some of Marx's crucial pronouncements on the *Arrow* War were not so original at all. Pivotal among these pronouncements was this: 'It is, perhaps, a question whether the civilized nations of the world will approve this mode of invading a peaceful country, without previous declaration of war, for an alleged infringement of the fanciful code of diplomatic etiquette'.[63] Marx's use of the term 'civilized nations' is interesting. Of course, even his critique of rapacious capitalism was always founded on the understanding that Western nations were civilized – capitalism functions only in civilizations. Nonetheless his terminology often baffles Chinese Marxist historians, who have always wondered why the Chinese, despite having the longest surviving civilization in the world, were not regarded as civilized.

VI. A political press

We have seen the passion aroused in the British press by the *Arrow* quarrel. Since we rely on the press quite extensively for information in this part of our study, an examination of the British press at this time is in order.

The repeal of the stamp duty in 1855, together with the abolition of the tax on advertisements two years earlier, created a new forum for national debate by offering newspapers a vastly enlarged readership. A parallel increase in literacy accelerated the process – the Department of Education was established in 1856 to provide administrative backbone to the Committee of the Privy Council on Education (created in 1839). The result was a doubling of

---

61. Ibid., p. 16, n. 1, quoting the *New York Daily Tribune*, 17 April 1857.
62. Ibid., p. 17.
63. Ibid.

the number of white-collar workers in the 1860s and again in the 1870s.[64] Improvements in printing and distribution methods also played a part, as did the introduction of the telegraph and of railways and the establishment of news agencies. All these in turn led to an enhanced potential for political influence. With scant pretence of objectivity, many editors and proprietors vied to reciprocate this welcome attention. Consequently, newspapers were used on an unprecedented scale by politicians to serve party or personal ambitions. Newspapers became intimately bound to political organizations or to factions and individuals within them, so that people spoke of the 'political press'.[65]

It was deemed mandatory for any political movement to have its own organ.[66] Through their newspapers, political leaders took soundings, made threats, dangled concessions, and redefined their positions. They could score points, then safely retreat from them. Without soiling their hands, they could stand aloof while their battles, ostensibly against rival journals, were fought for them.[67] It is now generally agreed that most of the metropolitan papers of the 1850s and 1860s were indebted in one way or another to political groups, with the exceptions of *The Times*, the *Daily Telegraph*, and the *Clerkenwell News* (later the *Daily Chronicle*).[68]

In this context, a few words about the political groupings in Britain at this time are in order. In brief, there were two major political parties, the Liberals (Whigs) and the Conservatives (Tories). The Liberals, led by Lord Palmerston, were in power; but had to put up with dissidents within the party like Lord John Russell, a former prime minister,[69] whose 'hostility to the government' seemed pretty well-known.[70] The Conservatives were formally split into two

---

64. James Bowen, 'Education, Ideology and the Ruling Class: Hellenism and English Public Schools in the Nineteenth Century', in G. W. Clarke (ed.), *Rediscovering Hellenism: The Hellenic Inheritance and the English Imagination* (Cambridge University Press, 1989), pp. 161–86: p. 171. However, universal education was not introduced until 1870 (England's Elementary Education Bill), and compulsory attendance not established until 1880.
65. Koss, *Political Press*, v. 1, pp. 1–3. The scale of its use by the politicians in the mid-nineteenth century was new, although the 'political press' itself went back to the eighteenth century.
66. Ibid., p. 9.
67. Ibid., p. 148.
68. Lucy Brown, *Victorian News and Newspapers* (Oxford, Clarendon Press, 1985), p. 61. The relative independence of *The Times* is well known. The *Daily Telegraph* was developed by the Levy-Lawson family as a straight commercial enterprise and was too successful to be in the market for subsidies (Brown, *Victorian News and Newspapers*, p. 61).
69. See Steele, *Palmerston and Liberalism*, pp. 74–6.
70. Aberdeen to Graham, 31 January 1857, Graham MSS Bundle 131, quoted in Hawkins, *Parliament*, p. 53. On the first day of the parliamentary session on 3 February 1867, Russell criticized the government's policy over Naples, whereupon Clarendon 'complained bitterly' of Russell's speech, accusing it of being 'by no means friendly in tone to the government'. See ibid., p. 54, quoting Greville's memoirs and Grey's diary.

factions in 1846.[71] One was led by Lord Derby[72] and included Disraeli[73] and Malmesbury.[74] The other, led by Sir Robert Peel[75] (until his death on 2 July 1850) and therefore called the Peelites,[76] included Gladstone, Aberdeen,[77] Graham, Herbert,[78] and Cardwell.[79] Then there was the Manchester Peace Party, which was a collection of Radicals led by Richard Cobden,[80] who upheld universal peace and free trade as their highest ideals. To add to the fluidity in Parliament, there were small knots like the Independent Irish Party, the Catholic Party, the Tenant Party, and fringe Liberals who were semi-detached. Thus, the period under review was one of incoherence in terms of parliamentary politics.[81]

As mentioned, *The Times* was not exactly Palmerston's tool, but since 1855 he had begun to build a rapport with its editor, John Delane. The *Morning Post* had already swung to Palmerston around 1850, from when the new owner, T. B. Crompton, appointed Peter Borthwick the editor.[82] Borthwick was sensitive to the general popularity of Palmerston's foreign policy, while Palmerston was

71. The Conservatives were split during Peel's ministry over the repeal of the Corn Laws in 1846. For details, see Travis L. Crosby, *Sir Robert Peel's Administration, 1841–1846* (Newton Abbot, David & Charles, 1976).
72. As mentioned, he had been prime minister in 1852 and was to become prime minister again in 1858 and 1866. See Jones, *Lord Derby*.
73. Again, Benjamin Disraeli (1804–81) was chancellor of the Exchequer in Derby's ministry in 1852, 1858, and 1866. In February 1868, he became prime minister. See Monypenny and Buckle, *The Life of Benjamin Disraeli*.
74. Again, he was James Howard Harris, third earl of Malmesbury (1807–89), formerly secretary of state for foreign affairs in Derby's first ministry in 1852. He again occupied that position in Derby's second ministry in 1858–9. He wrote *The Memoirs of an Ex-Minister: An Autobiography*.
75. The Rt. Hon. Sir Robert Peel (1788–1850), Baronet, became secretary of state for the Home Department in 1822 and prime minister in 1834–5 and 1841–6. See Crosby, *Sir Robert Peel's Administration, 1841–1846*.
76. For the development of the Peelites as a 'party', see J. B. Conacher, *The Peelites and the Party System, 1846–1852* (Newton Abbot, David & Charles, 1972).
77. He was prime minister in 1852–5. See J. B. Conacher, *The Aberdeen Coalition, 1852–1855: A Study in Mid-Nineteenth-Century Party Politics* (Cambridge University Press, 1968).
78. Sidney Herbert (1810–61) was the second son of George Augustus, eleventh earl of Pembroke and formerly secretary at war. In June 1859, he was to become secretary for war and, in, 1860, Baron Herbert of Lea. *DNB*, v. 9, pp. 663–5.
79. Edward Cardwell (1813–86) was formerly secretary to the treasury (1845–6) and president of the Board of Trade (1852–5). He was to become secretary for Ireland in 1859, secretary for the colonies in 1864, secretary for war in 1868, and Viscount Cardwell of Ellerbeck in 1874. *DNB*, v. 3, pp. 952–4.
80. Again, Richard Cobden (1804–65) was a champion of free trade. His famous pamphlets included *England, Ireland, and America*, and *Russia, by a Manchester Manufacturer*. He sat for Stockport (1884–7), the West Riding of Yorkshire (July 1847 to April 1857), and Rochdale (May 1859 till his death on 2 April 1865). See Edsall, *Richard Cobden: Independent Radical*; and Hinde, *Richard Cobden: A Victorian Outsider*.
81. See MacDonagh, *Early Victorian Government*.
82. Wilfrid Hindler, *The Morning Post, 1772–1937: Portrait of a Newspaper* (London, George Routledge, 1937), p. 178. See also Lucas, *Lord Glenesk and the Morning Post*.

quick to flatter both Peter Borthwick and his son Algernon.[83] The benefits were mutual. Supporting Palmerston, the *Morning Post* now achieved a larger circulation than any rival except *The Times*. Favouring the *Morning Post* with newsworthy information, Palmerston found in it a sure shield and defence against his enemies.[84] Thereafter, the *Morning Post* gave Palmerston unqualified support on most issues and sometimes even praised him, it is said, on briefs prepared by Palmerston himself.[85] During the Crimean War, Charles Greville[86] observed that Palmerston continued to put articles into the *Morning Post* that were 'full of arrogance and jactance' and calculated to raise obstacles to the peace. 'This is only what he did in '41, when he used to agree to certain things with his colleagues, and then put violent articles in the *Morning Chronicle*, totally at variance with the views and resolutions of the Cabinet'.[87] Seen in this light, the articles of the *Morning Post* on China, quoted earlier, could very well have been penned by Palmerston – they fitted perfectly the public speeches he was going to make during the parliamentary debate and the election.[88] There was an allegation that the paper was in Palmerston's pay.[89] That may be an exaggeration, but it is well known that Palmerston used it, and the *Globe*, to say the things that tact (if not modesty) forbade him from saying openly.[90]

As for the *Globe*,[91] reportedly it was Palmerston who had kept it going as a Whig paper,[92] contributing directly 'to its columns and to the pockets of its editors'.[93] In 1866, the year after Palmerston had died, the paper shifted to the Conservatives. Apparently the *Globe* could more easily reconcile itself to conservatism than to the leadership of Palmerston's immediate successor, Lord John Russell. Thereupon Russell relied informally on the *Daily News*.[94]

In fact, Russell had tried to buy the *Daily News* in 1855, but the purchase never came to fruition.[95] In the end, he had to 'make do with a casual and circuitous arrangement' with that paper.[96] It is said that the *Daily News* was

83. Hindler, *Morning Post*, p. 190.   84. Ibid., p. 191.
85. Ibid., p. 194.
86. Charles Cavendish Fulke Greville (1784–1865) was a clerk of the Privy Council and kept a journal from 1818 to 1860, from which historians have benefitted greatly. There is a short summary of his life in *Leaves from the Greville Diary*, arranged with introduction and notes by Philip Morrell (London, Eveleigh Nash & Grayson, 1929), pp. xi–xiii.
87. Quoted in Hindler, *Morning Post*, p. 197.
88. See Chapters 9–10.
89. Stanley to Aberdeen, 13 May 1855, Aberdeen Papers, BM MSS, Add. 43072/145, quoted in *History of The Times*, v. 2, p. 262, n. 3.
90. Koss, *Political Press*, v. 1, p. 148.
91. The *Globe* was an evening newspaper, founded in 1803 originally as a trade journal for booksellers. Slowly it awakened to political controversy and took the side of the Whigs. See ibid., p. 45.
92. Ibid., p. 123.
93. Ibid., p. 45.
94. Ibid., p. 148.
95. Ibid., pp. 116–17.
96. Ibid., p. 118.

'pious and pedagogic'[97] and that the *Telegraph* 'served the Liberalism of convention, the *Daily News* the Liberalism of conviction'.[98] We have seen the pious defence of the Chinese by the *Daily News*. That seems very much in line with the attack which Russell was about to launch in the House of Commons on Palmerston's China policy,[99] for which Russell was to pay dearly in the 'Chinese Election' of 1857.[100] However, the relationship between the *Daily News* and Russell was never very obvious or clear-cut, which has led to the suggestion that the paper was linked to a parliamentary party, although there are obscurities in such a story.[101]

In 1850, Disraeli and Lord Stanley (who succeeded his father to become the fourteenth earl of Derby in June 1851), tried unsuccessfully to buy *John Bull*.[102] When Derby became prime minister in 1852, he cautioned Disraeli, his chancellor of the Exchequer, about making such journalistic forays too public, lest they should be accused of using Secret Service money for that purpose. But they clearly needed their own organ, and a less blatant approach than buying a newspaper might be to start a new one. Thus, in May 1853, they founded a six-penny weekly, the *Press*. Disraeli wrote its very first leading article. But the financial burden was too great, and Disraeli soon found himself out of pocket.[103]

In 1858, the political distribution of all London newspapers looked like this: conservative, 17; liberal, 39; neutral/independent, 64; total, 120.[104] Meanwhile, the growth of the provincial press after 1855 greatly activated local politics. The trenchant opposition of the *Manchester Guardian*[105] to John Bright's[106] candidacy in the Chinese Election[107] of 1857 may be cited as a classic example of this kind.[108]

97. Ibid., p. 99.   98. Quoted in ibid.   99. See Chapter 9.
100. See Chapter 10.
101. Brown, *Victorian News and Newspapers*, p. 61.
102. Founded in 1820, it has been described as 'a strident voice of unreconstructed Toryism'. Koss, *Political Press*, v. 1, p. 48.
103. Alan J. Lee, *The Origins of the Popular Press in England, 1855–1914* (London, Croom Helm, 1976), pp. 146–7. See also *History of The Times*, v. 2, p. 264; and Monypenny and Buckle, *The Life of Benjamin Disraeli*, v. 3, chapter 14.
104. Lee, *Popular Press*, p. 291, table 29. The statistics for 1857 would have been much more pertinent to our needs, but alas they are not available.
105. The *Manchester Guardian* began as a weekly in 1821, went biweekly in 1836, and developed into a daily in 1855. One of its co-owners and joint editors was Jeremiah Garnett (Koss, *Political Press*, v. 1, p. 48). In 1959, the paper moved its headquarters to London and changed its name to the *Guardian*. See Alastair Hetherington, *Guardian Years* (London, Chatto & Windus, 1981), p. 1.
106. John Bright (1811–88) was a cotton spinner and manufacturer, being a partner in the firm of John Bright and Brothers, of Rochdale. He had sat for Manchester since July 1847. See William Roberston, *The Life and Times of the Right Honourable John Bright* (London, Cassell, 1884); and Keith Robins, *John Bright* (London, Routledge & Kegan Paul, 1979).
107. See Chapter 10.
108. Koss, *Political Press*, v. 1, p. 122.

The rhetoric of imperialism

The country press, to a considerable extent, followed the lead of *The Times*.[109] Palmerston appears to have exploited this leadership to its fullest extent during the Chinese Election, leading Cobden to comment that the prime minister had 'made greater use of that means of creating an artificial public opinion than any Minister since the time of Bolingbroke'.[110] The result was a landslide victory for Palmerston.[111]

Apart from the leadership shown to the provincial press by *The Times*, the Liberals had far more newspapers in the country than the Conservatives, the latter having traditionally looked upon the provincial press with suspicion and anxiety. Since the reduction in the stamp duty in 1836, there had been a spate of new papers, most of them Liberal, clamouring for the redistribution of seats in favour of the urban areas.[112] The political distribution of all English provincial newspapers in 1858 was like this: Conservative: 80; Liberal, 175; neutral/independent, 139; total, 394.[113]

The periphery could also invade the metropolis. For example, the *Morning Star*, which Richard Cobden and John Bright helped to launch in 1856, was conceived as a London outpost of Manchester radicalism.[114]

Generally speaking, we may observe that John Bright and Richard Cobden had close associations with the *Morning Star*, the Peelites with the *Morning Chronicle*, the Derbyites with the *Standard* and the *Morning Herald*, Disraeli with the *Press*, and Palmerston with the *Morning Post* and the *Globe*. The *Times* was initially hostile and then friendly towards Palmerston, but was not his 'servant', unlike the other two papers. These servants were not always reliable, unpredictably showing too much devotion or too little, and were often unable to judge which was appropriate until the damage was done.[115]

Finally, it is important to stress the increasing influence of the press in the 1850s, especially in relation to the Chinese Election, in what passed for 'mass' politics at the time. It seems that there had been no real precedent for the British newspaper jingoism[116] of 1857 (and the newspaper counter-rhetoric this evoked).

109. Cobden to Richard, 17 June 1856, quoted in ibid., p. 122.
110. Cobden to Richard, 7 March and 22 April 1856, quoted in ibid., p. 132. This is not to suggest that the *Manchester Guardian* closely followed *The Times*.
111. See Chapter 10.
112. Lee, *Popular Press*, p. 133.
113. Ibid., p. 290, table 28. Here again, the statistics for 1857 would have been much more pertinent to our needs, but alas they are not available either.
114. Koss, *Political Press*, v. 1, p. 139.
115. Ibid., p. 111.
116. Jingo was used as a nickname for those who supported the policy of Lord Beaconsfield in sending a British fleet into Turkish waters to resist the advance of Russia in 1878; hence, a blatant 'patriot' (*Shorter Oxford Dictionary*, v. 1, p. 1133).

VII. In Sum: No Watergate

We are dealing with a period that preceded the age of investigative journalism and with reporters who were British and had a different attitude towards the establishment from that of their modern U.S. counterparts. In our pursuit of the origins of the *Arrow* War, therefore, we may not expect shattering revelations such as Watergate.[117] Nonetheless, the great proliferation of newspapers at this time, and hence of expressions of views, enriches enormously our understanding of what the *Arrow* War meant to the British public. More important, we are not fed only with views sympathetic to or even steered by the government. The opinions of its political opponents may be heard just as clearly. In this sense, the debate in the press among those papers with strong party affiliations may be regarded as a prelude to the great pitched battles which were about to rage in both houses of Parliament. Furthermore, there were a great many neutral and independent newspapers, both in the metropolis and in the country, whose views were less coloured by political or patriotic passions, but which seldom filtered through to the rest of the world in the books written by diplomatic historians.

117. Watergate is one of the most well-known political scandals of modern history. In 1972, Richard Nixon, then president of the United States, was forced to resign because he was shown to have been involved in unlawfully bugging the headquarters of his political opponent in the runup to a federal election. See, e.g., Philip B. Kurland, *Watergate and the Constitution* (Chicago, University of Chicago Press, 1978).

8
The *Arrow* incident and international law:
The debate in the House of Lords

The House of Lords had some of the greatest legal minds in the world. The law lords therein constituted the highest legal authorities in the British Empire. It was not by coincidence, therefore, that Lord Derby, who moved a censure resolution against the government on account of the bombardment of Canton, began the China debate[1] on 24 February 1857 by appealing to their lordships 'to deal with the question in a purely judicial spirit'.[2]

It is fascinating to see their lordships thresh out the legal complexities of the case of the *Arrow*, and thence what some of them regarded as the origins of the war. That protracted debate may be boiled down to the following major issues: whether the British flag was flying; whether an insult was intended; whether the *Arrow* was entitled to fly the British flag; the expiry of the *Arrow*'s register; abuses of the colonial ordinance whereby the *Arrow*'s register had been granted; whether the actions of Parkes, Seymour, and Bowring were justified; whether Bowring had acted in the best interest of the nation; the Canton City question; the right to make war; whether it was a just war; whether the debate was motivated by justice and humanity or by party politics; and how important the China trade was.

One may put these various issues into three main categories: legal technicalities, issues of justice and humanity, and trading matters. Let us begin with the legal arguments, if only because some of them have already been introduced in previous chapters. In Chapter 2, for example, we have heard the views of their lordships on the question of whether the British flag was actually flying when it was allegedly hauled down. Here, we shall continue with the issue of whether an insult was intended thereby.

1. Angus Hawkins has a pungent paragraph on the debate in the House of Lords within the context of British politics. See his *Parliament*, p. 59.
2. Derby, 24 February 1857, Hansard, 3d series, v. 144, col. 1155.

I. Was an insult intended?

Lord Derby did not think so. The reason was that the Chinese had declared throughout that the *Arrow* was not a British vessel and that they had gone on board a Chinese ship and seized Chinese pirate suspects. Nonetheless, they promptly returned nine of the crew the following day 'and in the course of another day or two, on the urgent demands of the British authorities, the whole of the twelve men'.[3]

Lord Clarendon[4] disagreed. He said that 'there can be no doubt, whatever, that a deliberate insult was intended both to that British vessel and to the British flag'. First, the flag: he regarded the alleged hauling down of the flag as a deliberate attempt by the Chinese officers to show their animus, or else the animus of the instructions under which they had acted. Second, the vessel: he claimed that the Chinese had always considered a lorcha, Portuguese in its origin, to be a foreign vessel, in contradistinction to a junk, which was native Chinese. Boarding a foreign vessel without reference to the pertinent consul was therefore an insult to that vessel.[5]

Lord Lyndhurst[6] believed otherwise. On the basis of the papers presented to parliament for the debate, he judged that there was not the slightest foundation for imputing such an intention to the Chinese.[7] He also denied that, legally, the *Arrow* could possibly have been regarded as a British vessel.[8] If the *Arrow* was not a British vessel, her boarding by the Chinese officers was not an insult.

Here, Lyndhurst lived up to his reputation of having an extraordinarily sharp legal mind. On the basis of the English documents alone, he was able to see that animus could not possibly be attributed to Yeh, who, as governor-general, was too senior to have been the first person to receive the intelligence about pirates on board the *Arrow* and who certainly was not the person who had instructed the squad of Chinese marine police to board that vessel.

Earl Grey[9] developed Lyndhurst's argument about the nationality of the *Arrow*. He argued that even if the *Arrow* had been an undoubted British ship, the Chinese authorities, by the general law of nations, would have been perfectly

---

3. Ibid., col. 1183.
4. Again, he was George William Frederick, fourth earl of Clarendon (1800–70) and foreign secretary since 1853.
5. Clarendon, 24 February 1857, Hansard, 3d series, v. 144, col. 1200.
6. Again, Lord Lyndhust (1772–1863) had been three-time lord chancellor. He spoke rarely and only on great occasions and preferred 'to speak on public questions unfettered by the ties of party'. *DNB*, v. 4, pp. 1107–14.
7. Lyndhurst, 24 February 1857, Hansard, 3d series, v. 144, col. 1217.
8. For his reasons, see next section.
9. Again, he was the Third Earl Grey (1802–94), who was secretary of state for the colonies in 1846–52. See Ward, *Grey and the Australian Colonies*.

entitled to board her. He said, 'In our own waters we do not go to the French or American Consul in order to board a French or American ship'.[10] What limited that general law of nations was Article 17 of the Supplementary Treaty with China. This article stipulated that Chinese subjects accused of offences against the laws of China could not be taken out of British ships by the Chinese authorities without reference to the British consul. The question then became one of defining what was regarded as a British vessel when the treaty was made. By the law of England then in force, no ship could be British unless it was owned exclusively by a British subject or subjects.[11] Thus, Earl Grey contended that under any fair construction of the treaty, the *Arrow* was not a British ship.[12] If the *Arrow* was not a British ship, no insult was intended.

The earl of Carnarvon[13] looked at the question from a different angle. That the Chinese officers allowed the British flag to be hoisted 'again' showed that there certainly was no animus, but rather the reverse.[14]

Not being able to counter this argument, Lord Methuen[15] adopted a novel approach. He inferred, from the great promptitude with which Yeh returned the men, that Yeh must have believed the *Arrow* to be a British vessel. If so, it was pretty clear that his intention was to insult the British flag.[16] Here Lord Methuen ignored the fact that Yeh had repeatedly and officially denied in writing that the *Arrow* was a British ship. As we have seen, Yeh returned the sailors promptly only because Parkes had demanded it.

Lord St Leonards[17] repeated Carnarvon's reference to the episode in which the captain of the *Arrow* was allowed to 're-hoist' the British flag,[18] which made it doubtful if an insult to the flag was ever intended.[19] Even assuming that the flag had been insulted, 'After we had attacked the forts and destroyed them, we ought to have considered that the insult to our flag had been atoned for . . . But why bombard Canton?'[20] The U.S. flag had been fired upon, too. But after destroying some forts the Americans considered that they had exacted suffi-

10. Grey, 24 February 1857, Hansard, 3d series, v. 144, col. 1220.
11. Ibid., col. 1230.
12. Ibid., col. 1232.
13. Again, young Carnarvon (1831–90) was to enter official life as under-secretary for the colonies in 1858. In June 1866 he joined Derby's third ministry as colonial secretary. He opposed Derby's Reform Bill in 1867 and resigned. In 1874 he again became colonial secretary. *DNB*, v. 9, pp. 646–53.
14. Carnarvon, 26 February 1857, Hansard, 3d series, v. 144, col. 1317. Carnarvon said that it was the two Chinese sailors left on board the *Arrow* who hoisted the flag again. In fact, it was Captain Kennedy who did so. See Kennedy's deposition as outlined in Chapter 2.
15. He was Frederick Henry Paul Methuen. See Hansard, 3d series, v. 144, 'Rolls of the Spiritual and Temporal'. He is not listed in *DNB*.
16. Methuen, 26 February 1857, Hansard, 3d series, v. 144, col. 1321.
17. Lord St Leonards (1781–1875) was lord chancellor in Derby's first ministry in 1852; his judgements were very rarely reversed. *DNB*, v. 19, pp. 152–4.
18. St Leonards, 26 February 1857, Hansard, 3d series, v. 144, col. 1329.
19. Ibid., col. 1330.
20. Ibid., col. 1332.

cient reparation and retired.[21] St Leonards could have added, if he had known, that in fact the U.S. president subsequently criticized Commodore Armstrong's destruction of the forts[22] and might have censured him had he not retired promptly.

The earl of Ellenborough[23] added that the Chinese officers had restrained their servicemen who had used contumelious expressions towards the captain of the *Arrow*.[24] Thus, even if there had been an insult, which was doubtful, it could not have been intentional.

The almost complete lack of response to this point from the government seems to suggest that it, too, privately agreed that there had been no intention to insult the flag. Some government members felt duty-bound to speak up for the government. Their lukewarm defence of the alleged intention to insult may be seen as another indication of the general unease felt even in government circles.

II. Was the *Arrow* entitled to fly the British flag?

This question depends on the answer to another: Was the *Arrow* legally a British vessel? Lord Derby thought she was not. The history of the *Arrow*[25] showed that she was 'Chinese built, Chinese captured, Chinese sold, Chinese bought and manned, and Chinese owned'.[26] What metamorphosed her into a British vessel was the Hong Kong ordinance of 1854, which allowed British subjects in the colony to register their vessels with the Hong Kong government and obtain British protection.

Derby considered the ordinance itself to be invalid because it contravened the laws of England.[27] That invalidity might have been removed by an order of Her Majesty in council. But to date, no such order had been passed for the confirmation of the said ordinance[28] because the Board of Trade objected to it.[29] The colonial ordinance was, therefore, waste paper.[30]

21. Ibid., cols. 1332–3.
22. See Tong, *United States Diplomacy in China*, pp. 196–7.
23. As mentioned, Edward Law, earl of Ellenborough (1790–1871), was formerly governor-general of India (1841–4). In 1858, he was to take office as president of the Board of Control, for the fourth time (*DNB*, v. 11, pp. 662–8). See also *History of the Indian Administration of Lord Ellenborough, in his correspondence with the Duke of Wellington. To which is prefixed ... Lord Ellenborough's letters to the Queen during that period*, ed. Charles Abbot, Second Baron Colchester (London, Bentley, 1874).
24. Ellenborough, 26 February 1857, Hansard, 3d series, v. 144, col. 1360.
25. A detailed history of the *Arrow* may be found in an extract from the *China Mail* of 11 December 1856, included in Parl. Papers 1857, v. 12, pp. 134–5.
26. Derby, 24 February 1857, Hansard, 3d series, v. 144, col. 1160.
27. Ibid., cols. 1160–1.
28. Ibid., col. 1163.
29. Ibid., col. 1161.
30. For an exposition of British maritime laws of this period, see Sarah Palmer, *Politics, Shipping and the Repeal of the Navigation Laws* (Manchester, Manchester University Press, 1990).

Even if the ordinance had been valid, he said, the Chinese owner of the *Arrow* could not have been a British subject because, according to the attorney-general of Hong Kong, the Chinese population of sixty thousand there hardly contained ten who could legally be called British subjects. It had been deemed inadvisable to naturalize the local inhabitants, and the then recent settlement of the colony, only since 1841, had not yet produced any adult British subjects by birth.[31] If the owner of the *Arrow* was not a British subject, that owner was not entitled to a register. Furthermore, since the owner of the *Arrow* was a Chinese subject, the Hong Kong government could not legally grant him a register which absolved him from his natural allegiance, enabling him to scorn the Chinese officials who attempted to arrest him in his unlawful courses.[32]

Derby asked their lordships, as men of sense, as men of honour, as British legislators, whether they would sanction, upon the part of unauthorized officials in China, an act which they would stigmatize on the part of Her Majesty's lawful advisers, in the exercise of that prerogative which was vested in Her Majesty alone?[33] Finally, Lord Derby thought that the colonial ordinance materially altered the stipulations of the Supplementary Treaty of 1843, which the British governor of Hong Kong had no right to do.[34]

In reply, Lord Clarendon argued that the colonial ordinance would have contravened the Imperial Act if it had bestowed a British register. But since it had bestowed only a colonial register for trading merely between China and Hong Kong, there was no contravention.[35] He likened the Hong Kong register to those granted at Gibraltar, Malta, Malacca, Singapore, and Malabar.[36]

We can see that Clarendon's argument was becoming quite strained. Thereupon Lord Lyndhurst laid down a principle which he believed no one would henceforth contest successfully: 'You may give any rights or any privileges to a foreigner or to a foreign vessel as against yourselves, but you cannot grant to such a foreigner a single right or privilege as against a foreign state'.[37]

The duke of Argyll[38] agreed that this principle was incontestable. But he argued that it had no bearing on the question under review, because its operation had been suspended by the terms of the Supplementary Treaty. Many Chinese had worked for the British during the Opium War, and it was

---

31. Derby, 24 February 1857, Hansard, 3d series, v. 144, col. 1161.
32. Ibid., col. 1164.
33. Ibid., col. 1165.
34. Ibid., col. 1167.
35. Clarendon, 24 February 1857, Hansard, 3d series, v. 144, cols. 1197–8.
36. Ibid., cols. 1198–9.
37. Lyndhurst, 24 February 1857, Hansard, 3d series, v. 144, col. 1213.
38. He was the postmaster-general in Palmerston's cabinet. See Duke of Argyll, *George Douglas, Eighth Duke of Argyll*.

especially for the protection of these Chinese against their natural sovereign that the Supplemental Treaty had been made. In view of this, he argued that whether or not the *Arrow* was a British vessel had to be determined by the intentions of the treaty, and not by technical arguments upon an Act of Parliament of which the Chinese had never heard.[39]

It seems that there is a missing link in the duke's otherwise logical argument. The Supplementary Treaty might have deprived the Chinese authorities of their sovereign right to search British vessels in Chinese waters for offenders against Chinese law. It had not provided that a Chinese-owned vessel such as the *Arrow* could become a British vessel by paying a fee in Hong Kong, which was a separate matter altogether. Contrary to the duke's claim, therefore, Lord Lyndhurst's principle had not been suspended by the Supplementary Treaty in any way. But nobody contradicted Argyll at this point, because the debate was soon adjourned, 'an unusual thing in the Lords'.[40]

When the debate resumed on 26 February 1857, the earl of Carnarvon pursued the question whether the lorcha was an English or Chinese vessel. The character of a ship was determined by the nationality of the owner.[41] As the owner of the *Arrow* was not a British subject, it could not be a British vessel. Even in the unlikely event of the owner of the *Arrow* having been a naturalized British subject resident in Hong Kong, the Chinese legislature had not absolved him of his natural allegiance.[42]

Here, the earl of Carnarvon was too imaginative in assuming that Manchu China had a legislature similar to the houses of Parliament in the United Kingdom, although the absence of such a legislature by no means undermined the validity of Carnarvon's argument.

Indeed, to Carnarvon's contention Lord Methuen, who spoke after him, had no answer.[43] Thereupon Lord St Leonards kept up the pressure. He took Lord Clarendon to task over the issue of the colonial ordinance granting only a colonial register, not a British register: 'Was it, then, to be understood, after all the discussion that had taken place, that the register was not a British register? Was the *Arrow* an English ship without a British register?' Here Clarendon interjected, 'With a colonial register'. St Leonards continued: 'If it were colonial only it was mere waste paper; if it were British, let it stand or fall by the Imperial law. What right had the colonial authorities of Hong Kong to regulate proceedings in the river of Canton?'[44] He concluded that the *Arrow* was not a British ship within the meaning of the treaty.[45] Lord

---

39. Argyll, 24 February 1857, Hansard, 3d series, v. 144, col. 1241.
40. Greville diary, 17 February 1857, as reproduced in *Leaves from the Greville Diary*, p. 782.
41. Carnarvon, 26 February 1857, Hansard, 3d series, v. 144, col. 1311.
42. Ibid., cols. 1312–13.
43. See Methuen, 26 February 1857, Hansard, 3d series, v. 144, cols. 1321–2.
44. St Leonard, 26 February 1857, Hansard, 3d series, v. 144, col. 1327.
45. Ibid., col. 1329.

Wensleydale[46] preferred the word 'English' in the Imperial Act to be understood in a more lax sense, so that it would include the *Arrow* case.[47]

What the earl of Malmesbury[48] was going to say is significant in the context of the present study. He observed that the ablest lawyers in the land had argued at length on both sides of the question and were still firmly convinced that the opposite side was wrong. He asked, 'If the noble and learned Lords and the Peers of England are perplexed with the technicalities of the question, how much more must a semi-barbarous officer like the Chinese Commissioner and his countrymen be perplexed by the accusations made against them?'[49] Thereupon, he made an important contribution: 'The Ordinance was not known to, and not understood by the Chinese, and . . . it was in fact an *ex post facto* law riveted on to the treaty. How can such an instrument bind them unless both parties thoroughly understand it and agree to it?'[50]

The earl of Granville[51] disagreed, partially anyway. Going back to the correspondence of 1855, he found that after Yeh had seized and dismantled two lorchas convicted of smuggling, Bowring transmitted to Yeh a translation of the colonial ordinance. 'On the part of Yeh not the slightest symptom of objection is given to that communication – for all that appears it had his full acquiescence'.[52]

Here, his lordship had answered the charge that the colonial ordinance was not known to the Chinese. He might even have answered the charge that the Chinese had not agreed to it, if silence could be construed as consent in a case like this. But he had not answered the charge that the Chinese had not understood it. If Bowring had not made Commissioner Yeh understand it, legally Bowring had failed in performing his duty of care, and consequently Yeh could not be held legally responsible for something which had not been explained to him properly.

The earl of Albemarle[53] had a new idea: English or not, the *Arrow* could not

---

46. As mentioned in Chapter 2, he was James Parke (1782–1868), who had been sworn of the Privy Council, placed on the Judicial Committee in 1833, and raised to the peerage in 1856. *DNB*, v. 15, p. 226.
47. Wensleydale, 26 February 1857, Hansard, 3d series, v. 144, col. 1340.
48. Again, he was James Howard Harris, third earl of Malmesbury (1807–89). He was secretary of state for foreign affairs in 1852 and was to occupy that position again in 1858. In June 1866, he became lord privy seal. He wrote *The Memoirs of an Ex-Minister*.
49. Malmesbury, 26 February 1857, Hansard, 3d series, v. 144, col. 1342.
50. Ibid., col. 1346.
51. Again, he was Granville George Leveson-Gower, second earl of Granville (1815–91) and president of the Privy Council in Palmerston's cabinet. See Fitzmaurice, *Life of Granville George Leveson Gower*.
52. Granville, 26 February 1857, Hansard, 3d series, v. 144, col. 1369.
53. He was George Thomas Keppel, sixth earl of Albemarle (1799–1891), formerly one of the private secretaries to John Russell, then prime minister, in 1847. On the death in 1851 of his brother, the fifth earl, he succeeded to the title. He wrote a book entitled *Fifty Years of My Life*.

have been a Chinese vessel. All Chinese vessels were called junks, not lorchas. A junk was supposed to represent a huge marine animal – a regular monster; it had a large mouth, formidable teeth at the cutwater, two huge eyes to enable it to see with, and the high stern forming the monster's tail. Furthermore, the word 'lorcha' was a disyllable, and the Chinese language had not a disyllable in it; their words were all monosyllables, and that alone showed that the lorcha could not have been a Chinese vessel.[54] This was a novel argument. But Albemarle seems to have forgotten that Yeh had never argued on points of linguistic nicety, only of ownership.[55]

On this as on other issues, their lordships on both sides of the case could not agree. On balance, however, the government's arguments appear weak and contrived.

III. The expiry of the *Arrow*'s register

Even assuming that the colonial ordinance was in order, the register of the *Arrow* granted thereby was not. As already discussed, it had expired about two weeks before the *Arrow* incident occurred. The government tried to argue that since the *Arrow* was not in the waters of Hong Kong when its register expired, she was technically 'at sea'. Normally, a vessel 'at sea' was not called upon to renew its register until it reached its home port. But as Lord Derby pointed out, when Consul Parkes received the register of the *Arrow* on 3 October 1856, the consul was bound to notice that it had already expired and should have insisted on an application for a fresh register, which could have been made 'during any part of the time she was lying in the harbour of Canton, because Hong Kong was within twelve hours' distance by steam'.[56] Lord Clarendon ignored that argument, insisting that the *Arrow* was technically 'at sea' and was therefore still entitled to British protection.[57]

It was, of course, the captain of the *Arrow* who had initiated this argument, which was then transmitted by Parkes to Bowring,[58] after Bowring discovered that the *Arrow*'s register had already expired on 27 September 1856 and after Bowring had made it quite clear that from that day onwards the *Arrow* had not been entitled to protection.[59] Therefore, the captain's argument was only a belated and feeble attempt to defend his untenable position. It was this unin-

54. Albemarle, 26 February 1857, Hansard, 3d series, v. 144, col. 1353.
55. Albemarle's speech seems to be in character with his intellectual inclinations. It is said that he idled at Westminster School from the age of nine until nearly sixteen, whereupon the headmaster pronounced him unfit for any learned profession. An ensigncy was obtained for him in the old 3rd Battalion of 14th Foot Regiment. He worked his way up step by step until he finally attained the honorary rank of full general in 1874. *DNB*, v. 11, pp. 43–4.
56. Derby, 24 February 1857, Hansard, 3d series, v. 144, col. 1170.
57. Clarendon, 24 February 1857, Hansard, 3d series, v. 144, col. 1200.
58. See Parkes to Bowring, 12 October 1856, Parl. Papers 1857, v. 12, pp. 65–6, para. 3.
59. Bowring to Parkes, 11 October 1856, Parl. Papers 1857, v. 12, pp. 64–5, para. 3.

spiring argument which the government now struggled to defend in order to uphold the validity of the *Arrow*'s expired register.

Lord St Leonards proceeded to discredit completely the 'at sea' argument. Upon the face of the colonial ordinance, every vessel, without exception, must be absolutely re-registered at the end of the twelve months. The object was abundantly clear: to make vessels report themselves regularly at this interval. There was a further proviso that such a register should be deposited at the office of the colonial secretary of Hong Kong one week before the expiration of the year. Did not this prove it to be absolutely necessary that the registers should be renewed within the year? If the 'at sea' argument were allowed, a door would be opened to the very mischiefs against which the colonial ordinance had aimed to guard, and a vessel could very well keep the British flag flying for six or seven years and still claim British protection.[60] Bowring himself had explicitly stated that once the *Arrow*'s register had expired, she was no longer entitled to British protection.[61]

In response, Lord Wensleydale asked passionately, 'But was it to be supposed that these ships would lose their national character if their licences expired, in whatever part of the globe they might happen to be at the expiration of the prescribed period?'[62] Lord Wensleydale's passion shows how stretched the government had become. Of course these ships would *not* find themselves in any part of the globe other than that patch of water between Hong Kong and the five treaty ports in South China, all of which were within a few days' sail of the home port. The colonial ordinance did not give registers to ocean-going vessels, only to small craft engaged in the coastal trade with China.

Lord Wensleydale then went to the extent of saying that the architect of that ordinance, Bowring, 'had mistaken his case in supposing that the licence had expired; for it was clear it had not, as on the evidence it appeared that the captain of the lorcha at the moment of the seizure was intending to return to Hong Kong, and renew his licence, having previously deposited his licence in the registry at that place'.[63]

Here, Wensleydale seems to have become rather confused. Or else he was trying to confuse their lordships. First, the register had expired in every sense of the word, and nobody could have imagined otherwise. The mere intention to renew it did not actually revalidate it. Second, he probably meant that the *Arrow* was still entitled to British protection despite the expiry of its register. But if Sir John Bowring had ruled that the *Arrow* was no longer entitled to protec-

---

60. St Leonards, 26 February 1857, Hansard, 3d series, v. 144, col. 1330.
61. Ibid., col. 1331. For Bowring's statement, see Bowring to Parkes, 13 October 1856, Parl. Papers 1857, v. 12, p. 66.
62. Wensleydale, 26 February 1857, Hansard, 3d series, v. 144, col. 1341.
63. Ibid.

tion once its register had expired, who should have known the intention of the ordinance better than the architect himself? Third, the captain had deposited his register in the British Consulate at Canton, not at the registry in Hong Kong.

IV. British legal arguments and Chinese perceptions of the origins of the war: An assessment

The debate in the House of Lords on the legal technicalities of the *Arrow* incident was a manifestation of the rule of law. Confucius had rejected the notion of the rule of law, taking the view that to enact laws simply induces people to think of ways to break them. A superior way to govern the people, he maintained, is to lead by example. He thought that if the rulers were virtuous, then the people would follow suit; this is the concept of rule of virtue (*renzhi*).

Consequently most Chinese people, not just their historians, tend to take a moralistic view of events. After all, a major role of generations of official historians in China has been seen to be one of writing history in such a way as to extol moral behaviour, a role not dissimilar to that of most historians in the West until the Enlightenment.

Historians in China who read the House of Lords debates would be baffled in more ways than one, hindering their attempts to pinpoint the origins of the war. They would be amazed by the level, and perplexed by the adversarial nature, of the legal arguments, especially those which embarrassed the government. The Chinese concept of the rule of virtue has developed into a strong tradition of emphasizing harmony and humanity (*ren*),[64] which are sustained by certain principles governing interpersonal relationships. Such principles include respect for one's seniors and benevolence to one's juniors. The respect would often be extended to covering up the faults, however serious, of one's seniors; and the benevolence, to protecting vigorously one's juniors. The respect is essentially reverence for authority. Between two equals, one would expect one's friend to take one's side, or at least be helpful, in an argument with a third party, so that one does not lose face. This, in the context of nationalism associated with modern Chinese historiography, could lead to charges of national betrayal should any Chinese speak up, however justifiably, for the nation's foreign foes, past or present.

This kind of attitude perhaps accounts for Professor Jiang Mengyin's passing

64. Here we are talking about harmony and humanity. Towards those who had broken the law, or even suspects, traditional China had, when compared with Britain of this time, a very inhumane system of extracting confessions, methods which had ceased to be employed in Britain and Europe since about three hundred years earlier.

over the debate on the legal technicalities of the *Arrow* dispute. He may have found it incomprehensible that some of the distinguished peers should have spoken up for the Chinese with whom their own government forces were engaged in hostile action, and at whose hands some Britons had lost their lives. What he does not seem to have appreciated is that these peers might not have had any affection for China at all, but upholding justice was very dear to their hearts. They would attack their own government if, in their judgement, that government had acted unlawfully. The rule of law was as important to them as the rule of virtue to the Chinese people.[65]

Parliamentary rhetoric aside, no Briton would think that Lord Lyndhurst, a former lord chancellor in three ministries, and Lord Derby, a former prime minister who was to occupy that position again in 1858 and 1866, were unpatriotic simply because they attacked Palmerston's China policy. Indeed, Lord Lyndhurst has been portrayed as having subdued the bitterness of his political adversaries 'by the commanding powers and unmistakable patriotism by which every speech he made was distinguished'.[66] Derby has been described as having 'had a very strong sense of duty'. In 1855, during the darkest hours of the Crimean War, he declined the Queen's invitation to form a ministry because 'he probably thought that a government formed by Lord Palmerston and supported by the conservative opposition would be a stronger government than his own'.[67]

To a Chinese observer of the debate in the House of Lords, Lord Ellenborough, for example, would appear to be friendly to China. But it was the same Ellenborough who, the moment he arrived in India on 21 February 1842 as its governor-general, increased the force intended for China and refused, on grounds of policy, to allow the disasters in Afghanistan to curtail the program of operations already decided for China. The original design of the British government had been to operate by the Yangtse River, which was subsequently changed for a movement to the Peiho. Ellenborough, convinced by the information of Lord Colchester that China was most vulnerable along the Yangtse, on his own responsibility reverted to the original scheme, pressed forward the reinforcements from India, and by the summer of 1842, was able to report to the Cabinet on the successful conclusion of the Chinese war.[68]

In relation to the origins of the *Arrow* War, the judgements of the law lords who spoke either for or against the government are of immense interest to the

65. For some further thoughts, see my article 'The Rule of Law in Hong Kong: Past, Present and Prospects for the Future', *Australian Journal of International Affairs*, 46, no. 1 (May 1992), pp. 81–92.
66. *DNB*, v. 4, p. 1113.
67. *DNB*, v. 5, p. 1012.
68. See Sir Henry Marion Durand, *The First Afghan War and Its Causes*, 2 vs. (London, Longmans, Green, 1879).

historian. In the present case, the strength of the arguments against the credibility of the alleged insult to the flag, and the obvious weakness of those in its defence, fortify my contention that the flag was probably not flying and therefore could not have been hauled down, that no insult was ever intended, and that the expiry of the register had deprived the *Arrow* of British protection. Conversely, they also undermine the argument that the government had to wage the war in order to defend British national honour and pride. How can a legally dubious case be honourable and worthy of pride?[69]

In the present instance, their lordships were debating the legality of the *Arrow* affair, not friendship with China. A legal case, in its ideal form, should be devoid of emotions, friendly or hostile; so should history. But Chinese historians prefer to regale their readers by reproducing such pronouncements as Derby's portrayal of Bowring's monomania,[70] which is easily understood within the Confucian context of personal moralities and interpersonal relations. One cannot help feeling that China, and indeed any other nation which has been affected by British imperialism, may have much to gain by a more intimate knowledge of British history, and vice versa.[71]

V. Justice and humanity

As mentioned, Derby began his speech by appealing to their lordships to approach his motion in a purely judicial spirit, without reference to any considerations but those of equity, justice, and humanity, and to dismiss from their minds every consideration connected in the slightest degree with party ties or political predilections.[72] He concluded his speech by appealing to the spiritual lords of the House, especially and emphatically, as men of peace, as the servants of Him who came to bring 'peace on earth and good-will among men',[73] and as special guardians of religion and virtue.[74] He asked them to

69. To date, however, Chinese historians seem to have shown scant interest in the legal technicalities of the case. By attempting to gain some understanding of the British legal position over the *Arrow* incident, British views on patriotism, and the adversarial nature of the parliamentary tradition, Professor Jiang and his colleagues could have produced more convincing interpretations of the origins of the war.
70. See Jiang Mengyin, *Di'erci yapian zhanzheng*, p. 43, and all subsequent publications that have reproduced Professor Jiang's quotation.
71. If we were to take to its logical conclusion David Fieldhouse's concept of the close interrelationship between metropolis and periphery, British scholars might also gain a different perspective on their own history outside the British Isles. For Fieldhouse's concept, see his *The Colonial Empires: A Comparative Survey from the Eighteen Century* (London, Weidenfeld & Nicolson, 1965). Statements such as that John Russell 'protested against the arbitrary seizure of the *Arrow* in Chinese waters' (*DNB*, v. 17, p. 461) and that the 'Taiping insurrection shortly afterwards [1854] broke out' (*DNB*, v. 2, p. 986) could be avoided. Of course, it was not the *Arrow* but her crew that was seized, and the Taiping insurrection had broken out in 1851.
72. Derby, 24 February 1857, Hansard, 3d series, v. 144, col. 1155.
73. Ibid., col. 1192.
74. Ibid., col. 1193.

disown the representatives of a Christian nation who had proved themselves to be uncharitable, unforbearing, barbarous, and bloodthirsty. He asked them to vindicate the Christian character of the nation, to stand forward in defence of humanity and religion.

To the temporal peers he also appealed, 'humbly, earnestly', to declare by their vote that they would not sanction the usurpation by inferior authorities of the Crown's prerogative to declare war, the bombardment and the shelling of an undefended and commercial city, and the shedding of the blood of unwarlike and innocent people, without warrant of law or moral justification.[75]

With the exception of the reference to Christianity, party, and the vote, many Chinese would agree that the values extolled by Derby are identical to Confucian teachings. Why have their historians not gone into that speech in any detail?

In response to Derby, Clarendon asked their lordships to vote against a resolution which would fetter the discretion and tie the hands of Her Majesty's servants in China, 'which will cast disgrace upon our name and our flag, and will bring ruin upon our trade with that country'.[76]

Earl Grey renewed the appeal to the reverend bench: 'There is the fatal injury done to the religion which this country professes. Can we believe that the religion we profess can be recommended to an unbelieving people by such an example as this?'[77] By adopting Derby's resolution, he maintained, the House would relieve itself from any responsibility for the blood which had been shed.[78]

The earl of Carnarvon echoed some of Grey's sentiments, saying that the effect of the war was injurious to the cause of Christianity in China and that the reference to the observance of the Sunday was one of the most painful and least creditable in the whole papers.[79]

Lord Malmesbury developed this theme further, by looking at two points. First, he drew attention to the immense danger of entrusting to British agents in foreign states the right to wage war at their own discretion. That was a question of policy. Second, he pointed out the inhumanity of the acts which had been committed in the name of Great Britain. He insisted that even if the *Arrow* was proved to be British from stem to stern, what took place aboard would not justify the conduct of the British officials, and the calamities which followed from that conduct. He made an emotional appeal to their lordships: 'I feel that the honour of the country is at stake in this instance equally with its

75. Ibid., col. 1194. 76. Clarendon, 24 February 1857, Hansard, 3d series, v. 144, col. 1212.
77. Grey, 24 February 1857, Hansard, 3d series, v. 144, col. 1236.
78. Ibid., col. 1237.
79. Carnarvon, 26 February 1857, Hansard, 3d series, v. 144, col. 1320.

morality'. He feared that a foreigner like Count de Montalembert, who in a recent publication had extolled the virtues of the English, while at the same time passing very leniently over their faults, would point out, in some future page, with horror, and even with disgust, this aggression on the part of civilized England. Malmesbury could have been a Confucian scholar. He continued, 'No man honours party feeling, in its proper place, more than I do . . . but on a question of conscience and morality, we ought to fling mere party considerations to the winds . . . I feel shame for my country!'[80]

The earl of Ellenborough added that much had been done to injure the national character, for which the government had made themselves responsible; but for which he asked the House not to make itself responsible.[81] He concluded his speech with these words: 'I trust the House will, by its vote tonight, protect us from the further prosecution of a war which is at once a folly and a crime'.[82]

Lord Granville seized upon Ellenborough's speech, saying it was clearly an attack on the government.[83] He set about neutralizing the opposition's appeal to the bishops. He observed that this was not the first time the opposition, fearing that the reverend prelates were not going to vote as they wished, constituted themselves as lay readers for the occasion and delivered a sermon to the Episcopal bench.[84] He trusted that the spiritual lords would be undismayed by the lessons addressed to them for the purpose of obtaining votes. He believed, too, that the young lords had quite sufficient intelligence to judge for themselves.[85] The bishop of Oxford denied that it was a question of political partisanship. Rather, it was a case that 'rises into a higher and more serene atmosphere, one which has to do with national justice or national crime'.[86]

Historians in China have paid insufficient attention to this debate on the issues of justice and humanity and, by overlooking it, failed to appreciate the Victorian liberal conscience, which partly motivated some of the speeches. Consequently, they have tended to paint all Britons in the same colour – greedy imperialists bent on plundering and slaughtering the Chinese. The origins of the war were many and varied and cannot be lumped into one ideological basket.

On the other hand, to what extent was this debate related to party politics as well? This question will be explored in Chapter 12. But before we leave the

80. Malmesbury, 26 February 1857, Hansard, 3d series, v. 144, cols. 1351–2.
81. Ellenborough, 26 February 1857, Hansard, 3d series, v. 144, col. 1361.
82. Ibid. col. 1365.
83. Granville, 26 February 1857, Hansard, 3d series, v. 144, col. 1365.
84. Ibid., col. 1375.
85. Ibid., col. 1376.
86. Bishop of Oxford, 26 February 1857, Hansard, 3d series, v. 144, col. 1377.

House of Lords, let us examine the third dimension of the debate, that of Britain's commercial interests in China.

VI. The China trade

Derby's speech also referred to the trade with China. That trade was vast and had been continually and rapidly increasing. It was important to Britain and to those engaged in it. It had so increased that the single article of tea had advanced in ten years from 41,000,000 to 87,000,000 pounds annually; and the increase in the import of silk had been during the same period enormous. Derby lamented that this valuable trade had been put in danger by the government's agents in China.[87]

In response, Clarendon referred to the trade with China very briefly, and only at the end of his speech. Short of more logical arguments he simply asked the House to vote against a resolution which he maintained would bring ruin upon British trade with China.[88]

Lyndhurst regretted that at Canton trade had been suspended, the property of Britons imperilled, and the foreign factories burnt down. Blaming Bowring, he believed that these were the consequences of the mischievous policy of one of the most mischievous men he ever knew.[89] To this the lord chancellor,[90] who was next to speak, had no answer.[91]

Grey kept up the pressure. Forcing open the gates of Canton would only undermine the authority of the Chinese government and encourage further disorder, which in turn would jeopardize British trade. Thus, Britain might run the risk of being cut off from the almost 'exclusive supply of tea, an article which has become almost a necessity of life to our population, and one of the main items of support to the revenue'.[92] Grey knew about tea; his father, the second Earl Grey, had made a great name for himself by selling Chinese tea under the brand name of Earl Grey tea. Subsequently the earl of Albemarle supplied some figures. He said that tea contributed to the British revenue between £5 and £6 million and that the China trade added upwards of £3 million to the Indian revenue.[93] What was the item that augmented the Indian revenue? Albemarle did not say, but one's thoughts naturally turn to opium. Might the trade in tea and opium be related to the *Arrow* War?

This question must be put in the wider context of Britain's overall trade with

---

87. Derby, 24 February 1857, Hansard, 3d series, v. 144, col. 1156.
88. Clarendon, 24 February 1857, Hansard, 3d series, v. 144, col. 1212.
89. Lyndhurst, 24 February 1857, Hansard, 3d series, v. 144, col. 1220.
90. As mentioned in Chapter 2, he was Robert Monsey Rolfe (1790–1868), lord chancellor since December 1852. *DNB*, v. 17, pp. 158–61.
91. Lord chancellor, 24 February 1857, Hansard, 3d series, v. 144, cols. 1220–5.
92. Grey, 24 February 1857, Hansard, 3d series, v. 144, col. 1236.
93. Albemarle, 26 February 1857, Hansard, 3d series, v. 144, col. 1354.

China, the extension of which the government had sought to pursue under the guise of treaty revision in 1854, entrusting that task to Sir John Bowring.[94] Bowring, as we have seen, attributed his failure to the Cantonese spirit of resistance as manifested in the closed gates of Canton.[95] He was convinced that if only he could batter down the city gates, 'great glory – and great good – will be the result'.[96] The government members of Parliament, particularly Lord Palmerston and Lord Clarendon, were fully aware of Bowring's disposition, through not only the official despatches but also the extraordinarily numerous and lengthy private letters Bowring sent them.[97] The foreign secretary, Lord Clarendon, apparently approved all the steps taken by Bowring in relation to the *Arrow* quarrel.[98]

In a public debate, obviously Clarendon could not reveal Bowring's frustration in order to justify Bowring's means, although he publicly spoke of using the 'law of force' against China.[99] Even without Clarendon's announcing Bowring's commercial objectives, the earl of Ellenborough must have known something to accuse Bowring of having acted 'throughout with no motive whatever but that which is denounced – general covetousness and the desire of making money by the misfortunes of mankind'.[100] He was referring, of course, to the drug trade.

VII. An unavoidable subject: Opium

The *Arrow* quarrel was to rekindle the controversy over the opium trade. The earl of Shaftesbury had wanted to bring forward a motion on that issue, but that was quickly swept aside by the *Arrow* debate itself.[101] However, opium was such a key topic, so inextricably interwoven with Britain's relations with China that it simply could not be wished away. One might expect, therefore, that even during the debate on the *Arrow* dispute, various references were nonetheless made to the subject.

Lord Derby, who opened the debate, could not avoid pointing out that the colonial ordinance of Hong Kong greatly facilitated smuggling along the coast

---

94. For the full details of the government's intentions, see Bowring's letter of appointment from Clarendon, dated 13 February 1854, in FO17/210.
95. See Chapter 4. For more details about treaty revision, see Chapter 12.
96. Bowring to Parkes, 26 October 1856, Parkes Papers.
97. See Bowring's private letters to Palmerston, collected in Broadlands MSS, GC/BO series and also Bowring's private letters to Clarendon, collected in MSS Clar. Dep. C8, C19, C37, C57, and C85 series.
98. Clarendon to Bowring, 10 December 1856, Parl. Papers 1857, v. 12, pp. 69–70; and Clarendon to Bowring, 10 January 1857, Parl. Papers 1857, v. 12, p. 157.
99. Clarendon, 24 February 1857, Hansard, 3d series, v. 144, col. 1203. This has been quoted in Chapter 2 and its context given therein.
100. Ellenborough, 26 February 1857, Hansard, 3d series, v. 144, col. 1364.
101. Shaftesbury's motion will be examined in Chapter 13.

of China and that the most important item involved in this smuggling was opium.[102] But Lord Clarendon refused to be drawn into a debate on opium there and then.[103]

Earl Grey referred again to the same subject, suspecting that opium was smuggled by Chinese vessels bearing colonial registers, 'a fact which I hope will receive the serious consideration of the noble Lord (the earl of Shaftesbury) who has given notice of a Motion on the subject of the opium trade'.[104] The duke of Argyll, who answered for the government, kept quiet on the subject.[105]

The earl of Carnarvon raised the point again: 'In 1822-3, we entered into a solemn engagement with the Chinese to suppress the traffic in opium'. But as stated by the earl of Derby, 'this very colonial ordinance tended to facilitate that traffic'.[106] The next government speaker, Lord Methuen, likewise declined to say anything of this.[107]

The earl of Albemarle once more referred to it: 'Our trade with China amounted, including the trade with India, to £15,000,000 of imports, and about the same amount of exports, . . . [contributing] upwards of £3,000,000 to the Indian revenue'.[108]

Lord Ellenborough was the first to put opium in the context of the United Kingdom's global trade. Having been governor-general of India and three times president of the Board of Control, he spoke with authority on the subject. He began by saying that the China trade 'is a great link in the chain of commerce with which we have surrounded the whole world'. The chain worked like this. The United Kingdom paid the United States for cotton, 'the staple of our greatest manufacture', by bills upon England. The Americans took some of those bills to Canton and swapped them for tea. The Chinese exchanged the bills for Indian opium. Some of the bills were remitted to England as profit; others were taken to India to buy additional commodities and to furnish the money remittance of private fortunes in India and the funds for carrying on the Indian government.[109]

Opium was discussed not only in terms of national economic interests. The bishop of Oxford warned the assembly: 'Do not for a moment believe that the Chinese are unobservant witnesses of these, your contradictions. It was but a few years ago that you were taunted by them – "How can we believe that

102. Derby, 24 February 1857, Hansard, 3d series, v. 144, col. 1167.
103. Clarendon, 24 February 1857, Hansard, 3d series, v. 144, cols. 1203ff; and Derby, 24 February 1857, Hansard, 3d series, v. 144, cols. 1155ff.
104. Grey, 24 February 1857, Hansard, 3d series, v. 144, col. 1232.
105. See Argyll, 24 February 1857, Hansard, 3d series, v. 144, cols. 1238-43.
106. Carnarvon, 26 February 1857, Hansard, 3d series, v. 144, col. 1319.
107. See Methuen, 26 February 1857, Hansard, 3d series, v. 144, cols. 1321-2.
108. Albemarle, 26 February 1857, Hansard, 3d series, v. 144, col. 1354.
109. Ellenborough, 26 February 1857, Hansard, 3d series, v. 144, col. 1363.

you wish to introduce Christianity when you are the great importers of opium?"'.[110]

How exactly was opium related to the *Arrow* War? Their lordships did not say. We shall explore the subject further in subsequent chapters.

VIII. In sum

The search by historians in China for the origins of the *Arrow* War appears to have been hampered by at least four factors in so far as their use of Hansard is concerned.

First, the Confucian concept of *renzhi* seems to have fostered a dismissive attitude towards legal arguments in the British Parliamentary debates. Consequently, their attempts to prove that the flag had not been insulted rarely go beyond educated assertions, although their avowals appear more credible than those made by Clarendon, if only because Clarendon's sound so unconvincing.

Second, Marxist ideology unwittingly restricts their scope of search for the origins of the war. Marx labelled the war the Second Opium War, declaring that it had much to do with opium. If Marx had judged so already, it had to be true, or at least taken for granted – so some historians in China have been inclined to think or want to appear to think. Consequently, nobody in China seems to have taken any steps to explore the relationship between opium and the *Arrow* War. It has simply been assumed that it was a second opium war.

Third, Marx had made sweeping statements about the origin of the war being an imperialist attempt to plunder and slaughter the Chinese. That in turn has not only limited but at times aborted Chinese attempts to gain a deeper understanding of the issues involved. For example, many of the parliamentary attacks on Parkes, Bowring, and the bombardment of Canton have been interpreted as confessions of guilt and, thereby, admissions that Britain was in the wrong.[111] Beyond that, there does not seem much point in exploring further. Such a moralistic and simplistic approach is historically diminishing.

Fourth, modern nationalism appears to have made it extremely difficult, if not impossible, to accept that there was something called the 'Victorian liberal conscience', whose pronouncements could offer penetrating insights into the origins of the war. In the end, simplistic generalizations about the origins of the *Arrow* War do not really help either the interpersonal or the international harmony which Confucius valued so much.

In terms of our continuing search for the war's origins, our study of the House of Lords debate has been rewarded by at least three clues: the impor-

---

110. Bishop of Oxford, 26 February 1857, Hansard, 3d series, v. 144, col. 1384.
111. See Jiang Mengyin, *Di'erci yapian zhanzheng*, pp. 70–80, and all subsequent publications that have reproduced Professor Jiang's arguments.

tance of tea to the British revenue, of opium to the Indian revenue, and of the China trade to Britain's global trade. The way in which these might have constituted origins of that war, however, will have to be explored further in subsequent chapters.

9
Triumph of the liberal conscience:
The debate in the House of Commons

This chapter covers some of the salient points raised during the four-day debate in the House of Commons[1] – from Thursday, 26 February, to Tuesday, 3 March 1857 (with a weekend break midway).[2] Since some of the issues had been debated in the House of Lords, and hence covered in previous chapters,[3] their treatment will not be repeated here, unless there were novelties in the Commons debate.

I. What were the motives behind the pretext for war?

Richard Cobden opened the debate by asking, 'Why did the Government allow us to drift into a quarrel in which our cause is bad, if for years sufficient grounds have existed for interference?' He wondered why the government had to wait till their representatives had stumbled into a quarrel, and commenced a war for which, in the opinion of the best lawyers, there were no legal grounds.[4]

This question of the timing of the quarrel is of serious interest: why

---

1. Miles Taylor has a perceptive analysis, within the context of British politics, on the debate in the House of Commons. See his *The Decline of British Radicalism*, pp. 271–3. For the House of Commons in this period, see William White, *The Inner Life of the House of Commons* (London, T. F. Unwin, 1898). Of course, not everybody could become a member of Parliament. See Helen Elizabeth Witmer, *The Property Qualification of Members of Parliament* (New York, Columbia University Press, 1943).
2. Chinese readers might like to know that the speeches made in the House of Commons, as in the House of Lords, did not follow any particular sequence or logical order. Condensing these speeches under particular headings in this and the previous chapter has given them a coherence and a simplicity which the debates themselves did not possess. The distortion is as plain as the advantages. The former might be forgiven on the grounds that our object is to trace the origins of the *Arrow* War, not to reconstruct a complete picture of the debates.
3. See Chapters 1–8.
4. Cobden, 26 February 1857, Hansard, 3rd series, v. 144, col. 1404. For the legal opinions on the matter, see later in this chapter.

not before, and on more grave matters? We shall explore this further in Chapter 11.

Cobden also wondered if China would have been treated in the same way had it been stronger: 'I ask you to consider this case precisely as if you were dealing with another Power. If you please, we will suppose that instead of being at Hong Kong dealing with Canton, we are at Washington dealing with Charleston', where an incident similar to the *Arrow* affair had occurred. In those circumstances, Cobden said, 'We had patience, we did not resort to force'.[5]

Relative military strength was certainly an important consideration; so were the interests involved. Britain had just taken on Russia, because the interests involved were considered significant enough to warrant war. The same should have applied in the case of China – but what were those interests?

Cobden severely criticized his long-standing friend, Sir John Bowring. He was particularly upset by Bowring's attitude towards the *Arrow*'s register. It will be remembered that Bowring instructed Parkes not to inform the Chinese authorities that it had already expired. Cobden professed that when he read this in *The Times* while in the country, he could not believe its fidelity, but sent to London for a copy of the *London Gazette*, in order that he might read the letter in the original. Alas, he had to conclude that it was 'the most flagitious public document that I ever saw.'[6]

Our concern is different: Why had Bowring gone to such an extent to pick a quarrel? We have learnt in the preceding chapters that treaty revision was a major consideration, and the interests involved will be quantified in Part Six. Cobden, however, was not yet done.

He observed that Bowring had acted contrary to instructions. There were letters from successive secretaries of state for foreign affairs: Malmesbury, Granville, Grey, all of whom had given peremptory directions that on no account should aggressive measures be resorted to without recourse to England.[7]

On this point the secretary of state for the colonies, Henry Labouchere,[8] tried to mount a defence. He maintained that instructions might be modified and that in new circumstances new plans might be made.[9] He also claimed that

5. Ibid., col. 1395.   6. Ibid., col. 1396.
7. Ibid., cols. 1416–17.
8. Henry Labouchere (1798–1869) was formerly a lord of the admiralty, under-secretary of war, and president of the Board of Trade. In November 1855 he was appointed secretary of state for the colonies. He was to be created Baron Taunton of Taunton in the county of Somerset in 1859 (*DNB*, v. 11, pp. 367–9). He lived in Portland Place, as did his brother, who was a banker and philanthropist; and he used to reply to callers who had confused him with his brother by saying that the '*good* Mr Labouchere lives at No.16'. See Algar Labouchere Thorold, *The Life of Henry Labouchere* (London, Constable, 1913), a book about his nephew, who was also called Henry.
9. Labouchere, 26 February 1857, Hansard, 3d series, v. 144, col. 1430.

the character of the local Chinese government was such that it was impossible to apply to them those maxims which were proper and usual between civilized nations. He would agree most cordially that there was no reason why, because a nation was 'semi-barbarous', Britain should act towards it with violence and with a disposition to make 'might the rule of right'. On the contrary, Britain was bound by every consideration of religion and policy to be more than ordinarily forbearing with such nations. But, he argued, it was on the other hand more necessary to make a display of force sooner, in dealing with nations which understood no other argument than force, than it would be in dealing with 'Christian and civilised communities'.[10]

Here, Labouchere dressed up Clarendon's 'law of force'[11] by trying to give moral justification to British proceedings.

He went on to administer a second coat of varnish: 'My hope is, that the dispute will not spread into a general war with the empire of China'. He expected that the conflict would result in Britain's commercial relations being placed on a far more satisfactory footing than before, which would ultimately benefit the Chinese themselves. He trusted in God the time might come, when the Chinese would enjoy the blessings of civilization and be emancipated from 'the tyrannical and cruel Government which, like its Commissioner at Canton, seems only to exist for the misery and degradation of the human race'.[12]

Chinese diplomatic historians who take offence at this rhetoric might like to confer with their political historians, who have denounced the tyranny of the Manchu regime in even stronger terms than these.[13] Marx and Engels used similar language in their writings on China at this time.[14] This is not to endorse the British misapprehension that China lacked a civilization, however.

Bearing these facets in mind, let us proceed to examine the third coat of varnish, which was applied by the high sheriff for Cardigan, Mr Lloyd

---

10. Ibid., col. 1431.
11. Clarendon, 24 February 1857, Hansard, 3d series, v. 144, col. 1203.
12. Labouchere, 26 February 1857, Hansard, 3d series, v. 144, col. 1433.
13. A similar need for such consultation might be found in some areas of Taiping studies. Up to the late 1970s, for example, Taiping specialists in China had held two foreign contemporaries of the Taipings in great esteem. They had done so for no other reason than some leaders of the Taiping Rebellion having praised them as true friends, as it turned out, by mistake. I discovered that the two foreigners were, in fact, Captain Charles Elliot and Admiral Sir Gordon Bremer, who engaged the Chinese during the Opium War. (See my Chinese paper presented to the First International Conference on the Taiping Rebellion, held in Nanjing in 1979. This was later published as an article, entitled 'Taiping jun chuqi shi beishang hai she dongjin de wenti chutan' [Why did the Taipings go north at the beginning of their rebellion when they should have gone east?], *Taiping tianguo shi yicun*, v. 1 [Beijing, Zhonghua shuju, 1981], pp. 258–80.) If the Taiping specialists had consulted the diplomatic historians, together they might have worked out the true character of the two Britons and thereby avoided the embarrassment of praising and condemning them at the same time.
14. See their articles collected in *Marx on China*.

Davies.[15] He said that the practical point was not whether Bowring was right or wrong, but whether an enquiry now would serve any useful purpose. The recent attack on Canton, he conceded, 'was nothing short of a massacre'. But there was no use crying over spilt milk. The war had to be won first. Then the British government might properly and dispassionately inquire whether their representatives in China had acted with precipitancy and had jeopardized lives and property which they ought to have protected.[16]

This is deluxe varnish, so crystal-clear that anybody can see through it. We all know that victors in the battlefield are rarely merciful towards the defeated. And an inquiry after a victory is unheard of. All this goes to show that the government must have been in a pretty awkward position, being obliged to employ such rhetoric to justify Bowring's objectionable measures. Thus, we are all the more curious about the forces that had propelled Bowring to such actions.

II. 'We have been insulted'

On the very morning of the day on which Lord Derby was to call attention in the House of Lords to the *Arrow* quarrel in China, a blue book entitled 'Correspondence Respecting Insults in China' was presented, in the name of the Queen, to both houses of Parliament. Richard Cobden saw through the trick immediately. Many honourable members – plain, simple-minded country gentlemen, he said, who did not have so voracious an appetite for blue books as he had, would say, 'Mercy on us! Here is a book of 225 pages, all about the insult we have suffered in China'. A logical conclusion to draw would be that war was justified and it was time to wage it.

Cobden judiciously read the tome, and what did he find? – garbled extracts from correspondence extending from the year 1842 to the year 1856. What did these extracts relate to? – a few street riots; a few village rows; an Englishman straying out of bounds to shoot was hooted back by the peasants; an Englishman went out shooting, shot a boy, and blinded him. That sort of 'insult.'[17]

Cobden thought that it was an insult to the House to have brought down a blue book of that calibre in order to make up a case against China.

Worse still, the blue book deliberately omitted the correspondence which showed that provocations by British merchants were invariably the cause of the 'insults'. He quoted one such omitted letter, from Sir John Davis, dated 15

---

15. John Lloyd Davies (1801–60) became high sheriff for Cardigan in 1845. A Conservative, he was opposed to the Maynooth Grant. He was first returned for the Cardigan district in February 1855 and sat until he retired in 1857. *BMP*, v. 1, p. 103.
16. Davies, 26 February 1857, Hansard, 3d series, v. 144, col. 1448.
17. Cobden, 26 February 1857, Hansard, 3d series, v. 144, col. 1405.

February 1847: '. . . not that I have any expectation of the occurrence of acts of violence and disorder, if our own people will only behave with common abstinence'. Sir John Davis added that a letter from Major-General D'Aguila, then at Canton, would corroborate all that Rear-Admiral Sir Thomas Cochrane, Davis himself, and the British consul had had occasion to report on this subject.[18] Davis concluded, 'I believe a great deal – I may say everything depends upon ourselves, and that a kind manner and a bearing free from offence is the best security against all approach to violence and insult'. Cobden went on to read other extracts of similar letters which had been excluded from the blue book.[19]

Cobden was proud of the mercantile interests which he represented. But even he conceded that British merchants displayed a haughty and inflexible demeanour in their intercourse with other nationals.[20] He also doubted if it was always for their benefit, as merchants, that they should be able to summon to their aid an overwhelming force to compel the local authorities to yield to their demands of whatever kind.[21] '*Civis Romanus sum* is not a very attractive motto to put over the door of our counting houses abroad', he concluded.[22] What Cobden does not seem to have realized was that, behind the scenes, even the prime minister, Lord Palmerston,[23] was irritated by the truculence of the British merchants at Canton.[24]

In public, the government had to put on a brave face. However, for them to resort to tactics such as misleading the House by the alleged insults makes one feel all the more intrigued by the real origins of the war. They must have known that such a ploy could easily backfire; and it did, when Cobden pointed out that these so-called insults, if they had been insults at all, had been provoked by the British merchants to begin with, and really had nothing to do with the *Arrow* quarrel.

William Gladstone went further. The government had selected all the pertinent correspondence with the obvious intention of fanning up patriotic feelings against China. He said, 'I really do not believe that there is much room for discussion founded upon that cabbalistic phrase *Insults in China*'. He recalled

18. Ibid., col. 1406.
19. Ibid., col. 1407.
20. Ibid., col. 1410.
21. Ibid., col. 1409.
22. Ibid., col. 1410.
23. He was Henry John Temple, Third Viscount Palmerston, G.C.B., K.G. (1784–1865). He had been secretary at war (1809–28) and secretary of state for foreign affairs (1830–4, 1835–41, 1846–51). He became prime minister in March 1855, a position he was to hold till March 1858, and again June 1859–65. He sat for Tiverton from June 1835 until his death on 18 October 1865. See Lloyd C. Sanders, *Life of Viscount Palmerston* (London, W. H. Allen, 1888); Kingsley Martin, *The Triumph of Palmerston: A Study of Public Opinion in England before the Crimean War*, revised edition (London, Hutchinson, 1963); Jasper Ridley, *Palmerston* (London, Constable, 1970); and Steele, *Palmerston and Liberalism*.
24. See Chapter 6, quoting Palmerston to Bonham Draft 107, 31 October 1849, FO17/152.

that the secretary of state for the Home Department had clarified that the title of that book, which undoubtedly was delusive, had naturally its origins in the nature of things, 'although the book does not consist of a string of insults inflicted upon the British by the Chinese'. On the contrary, it gives the firm impression that the Chinese had treated the English community with 'kindness and justice'.[25]

If that blue book had failed to enflame patriotic feelings inside Parliament, it succeeded magnificently outside, as we shall see in the next chapter.

III. 'Let the punishment fit the crime'

This pronouncement by Gladstone[26] highlights another aspect of the debate. The opposition members constantly argued that, even if Chinese culpability were to be admitted, the punishment inflicted on them was out of all proportion to the wrong they had allegedly done. Among them was the rector of the University of Glasgow, Bulwer Lytton.[27] Granting for a moment the right of the *Arrow* to be considered an English vessel, he asked, 'Was the act of the Chinese so inexcusable – was it so outrageous, so insulting to the dignity of this country as to warrant the terrible revenge we had inflicted?'[28] He reiterated, 'Observe, this is not merely a question of who was right and who was wrong, but whether the Chinese were so outrageously in the wrong as to justify the terrible punishment we have inflicted'. He upheld that Englishmen were not the Dracos of legislation; no insult was punishable by death even in Britain. 'Are we mild philosophers in our domestic legislation,' he asked, 'and ruthless exterminators in the enforcement of every questionable point of international law?'[29]

A barrister and future judge, Robert Phillimore,[30] took the same line. Assuming that the British authorities were right in everything which they had done with respect to this vessel, he wondered how the case of Bowring would thereby benefit. 'Let the House look at the hideous disproportion between the offence and the chastisement!' He continued, 'If the point of law was so doubtful that the most eminent lawyers of England differed in opinion as to its

---

25. Gladstone, 3 March 1857, Hansard, 3rd series, v. 144, col. 1793.
26. Ibid.
27. Edward George Bulwer Lytton (1805–70) sat for St Ives (1831), Lincoln (1832–41), and Hertfordshire from July 1852 until created Baron Lytton in July 1866. He was elected rector of the University of Glasgow in 1856 and was to become secretary of state for the colonies from June 1858 to June 1859. *BMP*, v. 1, p. 248.
28. Lytton, 26 February 1857, Hansard, 3rd series, v. 144, col. 1438.
29. Ibid., col. 1439.
30. Robert Joseph Phillimore (?–1885) was the author of *Two Letters to Ashburton on International Law* and *Letter to Mr Gladstone*, both respecting ships, as well as other legal works. Later he was to become dean of the Court of Arches (1867–75), a judge (1867), a baronet (1881), and a member of several royal commissions. *BMP*, v. 1, pp. 310–11.

construction, in God's name, and in the name of our common humanity, why was Canton bombarded?'[31]

The argument of a future lord chancellor, Roundell Palmer,[32] was most interesting: Yeh's protest that the flag was not flying might have been accepted as a virtual apology for the allegation that it had been hauled down. It was not reasonable to ask a man to apologize for an offence which he denied having committed. In any case, the seizure of a junk at Canton was sufficient to save Bowring's face.[33]

These statements reflect the Victorian liberal conscience and a strong devotion to the rule of law. They rendered the position of the government exceedingly awkward. And the harder the government tried to defend that position, the more tantalized we are in our pursuit of the origins of the war.

A barrister, Thomas Chambers,[34] said, 'It was impossible to say that the lorcha was the cause of what had happened. Nobody ever contended that it was'. Well, if the *Arrow* incident was not the cause of the war, what was? Something fundamental? The answer he went on to supply, however, is disappointing. The incident was, 'no doubt, the occasion of hostilities', he said, 'as the last drop put into a cup of water made it run over; but the storm had been collecting ever since the treaty was made – ever since 1842'.[35]

The young Robert Cecil[36] could not agree: 'Now, was that a fair defence? What would they say to a jury who would, on an indictment for arson, find a man guilty because he had previously committed a murder?'[37]

Consequently, some government members shifted their ground again. They contended that the quarrel had been enlarged because the time was ripe to do so. This goaded a former secretary at war, Sidney Herbert,[38] to counter that the so-called auspicious moment must have referred to the conclusion of the Crimean War in March 1856. He speculated that Bowring would have heard about this in the beginning of July and would have expected the Royal Navy to be thenceforth free to assist him with his grand schemes in China. 'In 1856

---

31. Phillimore, 26 February 1857, Hansard, 3rd series, v. 144, col. 1597.
32. Roundell Palmer (1812–95) was to become solicitor-general (1861–3), attorney-general (1863–6), lord chancellor (1872–4 and 1880–5), first baron of Selbourne (1872), and an earl (1883). *BMP*, v. 1, p. 300.
33. Palmer, 3 March 1857, Hansard, 3d series, v. 144, col. 1726.
34. Thomas Chambers (1814–91) was to become a Queen's counsel in 1861. He sat for Hertford from July 1852 till July 1857, when he was unsuccessful. In July 1865 he was to be elected for Marylebone and sat until he retired in 1885. He was knighted. *BMP*, v. 1 p. 72.
35. Chamber, 3 March 1857, Hansard, 3d series, v. 144, col. 1780.
36. He was the Rt. Hon. Cranborne, Viscount (1830–1903), who sat for Stamford from August 1853 until he succeeded as third marquis of Salisbury in April 1868. He was to become secretary of state for foreign affairs (1878–80) and prime minister (June 1885–February 1886 and June 1886–1902). See Robert Taylor, *Salisbury* (London, Allen Lane, 1975).
37. Cecil, 27 February 1857, Hansard, 3d series, v. 144, col. 1540.
38. For a biography of Herbert, see Arthur Hamilton Gordon, First Baron Stanmore, *Sidney Herbert, Lord Herbert of Lea: A Memoir*, 2 vs. (London, John Murray, 1906).

he had the largest fleet in the Canton River which had been there for years', said Herbert, who proceeded to give details of the various ships in Chinese waters at the time of the *Arrow* incident. He continued, 'Having got this great assistance, it occurred to Sir John Bowring, to use his own expression, "that the circumstances are auspicious for requiring the fulfilment of treaty obligations as regards the City of Canton"'.[39]

Thus, the opposition members seem to have implied, and the government members did not attempt to deny, that the *Arrow* quarrel was merely a sideshow. What, then, was the real cause of the war?

IV. Jingoism

Jingoism began with the vice-president of the Board of Trade, Robert Lowe.[40] He simply assumed that the flag of the *Arrow* had been torn down. It was perhaps not very philosophical that a flag, which was nothing more than a bit of painted linen, should represent the national honour and dignity, he said. And he dared say the association of ideas rested on no profound metaphysical principle; if it were torn down by the Chinese and a little soiled in the encounter, it probably could be washed or replaced by a new one. Then in a melodramatic way, he chanted, 'Yet this very flag brave men had held to their breast and glued there with their best heart's blood rather than surrender it on the field of battle even to a gallant enemy'. The same flag, at which he alleged the opposition members sneered, 'brave and honourable men had nailed to the mast, and had preferred to go down with it to the depths of the ocean rather than endure the ignominy of hauling it down in the face of the enemy'. He declared that 'these emblems of power, dignity, and honour' were themselves a power and an influence over the human mind, and in proportion as Britons regarded and respected them would they be regarded and respected by others.[41]

The jingoism extended to high praise for Lord Palmerston. Referring to the Crimean War, a future magistrate, Nicholas Kendall,[42] believed that ninetenths of the English people had not forgotten that to the noble lord at the head

39. Herbert, 2 March 1857, Hansard, 3d series, v. 144, col. 1671.
40. The Rt. Hon. Robert Lowe (1811–92) was educated at Oxford and Lincoln's Inn. In 1842 he went to Sydney, Australia, and in 1843 sat in the Legislative Council for New South Wales. He returned to England in 1850 and became a leader-writer for the *The Times*. From August 1855 to March 1858, he held the post of vice-president of the Board of Trade and paymastergeneral. He was to become chancellor of the Exchequer in 1868. In 1880, he was raised to the House of Lords as Viscount Sherbrooke of Sherbrooke, in Warlingham, Surrey. See James Winter, *Robert Lowe* (Toronto, Toronto University Press, 1976).
41. Lowe, 3 March 1857, Hansard, 3d series, v. 144, cols. 1843–4.
42. Nicholas Kendall (1800–78) went to Trinity College, Oxford, and became a special deputy warden of the Stannaries in 1852. First returned for Cornwall East in July 1852, he sat until he retired in 1868. A Conservative, he was opposed to the existing constituencies being swamped by the too sudden lowering of the franchise. He was to become police magistrate of Gibraltar (1868–75). *BMP*, v. 1, p. 218.

of Her Majesty's government was due Britain's release from those difficulties – 'aye, and that, too, under a pressure which no one but the noble Lord would have withstood. Well then, we are at war with the Chinese; and I put it to you, who is the most likely man to get us out of it?'[43]

Mr Bernal Osborne, secretary of the Admiralty,[44] agreed. Palmerston had remained at his post in times of difficulty when the war waxed hot and success was doubtful. He remained at the helm when he was 'deserted by a body of Gentlemen[45] for whom individually I entertain the greatest personal respect, but whose public course, I think, has been neither prudent nor patriotic'. But Palmerston weathered the storm, brought the vessel of state into smoother waters, 'and now you seek to throw him overboard, the man who never forgot a friend, and who has no enemies but those of his country and his country's honour'. Osborne asked rhetorically, 'Is this a proper course – is this the gratitude which the country owes to the noble Lord?'[46]

Palmerston's appeals to patriotism were even more moving. He contended that Cobden's statement about Great Britain having one policy for the strong and another for the weak was tantamount to saying that Britons were cowards. He listened, he said, with great pain to the tenor and tone of the speech by Cobden. Because, to him, there pervaded the whole of it an anti-English feeling, an abnegation of all those ties which bound men to their country and to their fellow-countrymen, which he would 'hardly have expected from the lips of any member of the House. Everything that was English was wrong, and everything that was hostile to England was right', he said.[47]

Palmerston tried to stir up further patriotic feelings by abusing Yeh. He described Yeh as an 'inhuman monster' who was one of the most savage barbarians that ever disgraced a nation and who had been guilty of every crime which could disgrace and debase human nature. If Cobden's motion had been agreed to, Yeh would in future be able to do what he liked and to claim that the cowardly Englishmen were afraid of him: 'I have driven away all the barbarians that were here. They tell me that England is a great Power

---

43. Kendall, 3 March 1857, Hansard, 3d series, v. 144, col. 1743.
44. Ralph Bernal Osborne (1808–82) had been secretary of the Admiralty since 1852 and continued in that position until 1858. Disraeli characterized his oratory as 'a wild shriek of liberty'. See P. H. Bagenal, *The Life of Ralph Bernal Osborne, MP* (London, Bentley, 1884).
45. Here, Osborne was referring to what had happened in February 1855, when Palmerston formed his first ministry. By that time, the Crimean War had broken out. The Queen had originally sent for Derby, and then John Russell, but neither succeeded in forming a ministry. So the Queen sent for Palmerston. Already seventy years old, Palmerston accepted the challenge and formed a government which included Gladstone, Graham, and Sidney Herbert. The trio resigned within three weeks, on Palmerston's reluctant consent to the appointment of Roebuck's committee of inquiry into the management of the Crimean War. See *Gladstone Diaries*, v. 5, pp. 25–9, 18–21 February 1855.
46. Osborne, 3 March 1857, Hansard, 3d series, v. 144, col. 1759.
47. Palmerston, 3 March 1857, Hansard, 3d series, v. 144, col. 1812.

and has a great navy and army; but Englishmen are afraid of me', mimicked Palmerston. Then he touched a raw nerve, alleging that henceforth Yeh would allow British property to be plundered by whoever chose to take it.[48]

Palmerston continued to play on the feelings of his audience: 'We have been told that in the course of a few months 70,000 heads – Chinese heads – have been struck off by the axe of the executioner of the barbarous Yeh'. He continued, 'We have further been told that the remains of 5,000 or 6,000 people were left reeking in the place of public execution'. Worse still, the authorities 'had not even taken the trouble of removing those mutilated remains from the view of the new victims coming to execution'.[49]

Palmerston also attempted to create indignation against the opposition by suggesting that he was the victim of a political conspiracy, which was bound to be detrimental to the country: 'There have been combinations recently entered into among men who had for a long course of time been kept apart by the strongest differences of opinion'. He alleged these conspirators had concluded a secret agreement that could not see the light of day, because it was aimed at turning out the ministers whose positions they wanted to occupy.[50]

Disraeli pointed out how Palmerston had in fact strayed from the debate.[51] He rejected Palmerston's charge that there was a political conspiracy against him: 'I really think the time has come when both sides of the House should cease indulging in these platitudes'.[52] He accused Palmerston of trying to cover 'a weak and shambling case by saying – what? – that he is the victim of a conspiracy'.[53] He believed that Palmerston should not try to complain to the country that he was such a victim 'the instant that the blundering of his Cabinet is detected, and every man accustomed to influence the opinion of the House unites in condemning it'.[54]

Cobden, for his part, denied that he was anti-English, insisting that his only motive of conduct in the House was to promote the just interests of his country, believing them to be in harmony with the interests of the whole world. He refused to take back what he had said about his old friend Bowring: 'I repeat those words, and I am sorry that a sense of duty compels me to do so'.[55] He rejected Palmerston's charge of conspiracy, stating distinctly that he had consulted absolutely no one in the House except Thomas Milner-Gibson with

48. Ibid., col. 1830.
49. Ibid., col. 1822.
50. Ibid., cols. 1831–2.
51. Disraeli, 3 March 1857, Hansard, 3d series, v. 144, col. 1834.
52. Ibid., col. 1838.
53. Ibid., col. 1839.
54. Ibid., col. 1840.
55. Cobden, 3 March 1857, Hansard, 3d series, v. 144, col. 1841.

regard to the terms of his motion. He vowed that neither directly nor indirectly was any intimation given of his motion to any other member. 'I challenge contradiction of that assertion from any and every quarter',[56] he exclaimed, adding that he had no political ambitions: 'I shall not take office in consequence of any change of ministry, nor do I hope or expect that the division on my Motion will lead to that change of Ministry of which the noble Lord has so much dread.'[57]

Cobden was wrong in his predictions, as we shall see later.

V. The defence of Bowring

The lord advocate[58] defended Bowring in a way which was not found in the House of Lords. He pointed out that Bowring's statement about the expiry of the *Arrow*'s register could mean one of two things. One was that Bowring had not scrupled to deceive the Chinese to effect his ends. The other was that since the Chinese had no knowledge of the expiration of the ship's papers, they could not legitimately use the fact as an argument and therefore their intention had been to insult the British flag.[59]

Labouchere also tried to defend Bowring. But he managed to do so only in very general terms, by asserting that China's relations with foreign nations had been so unsatisfactory of late that a temporary disruption to trade was a worthwhile price to pay in order to teach the Chinese a lesson.[60] He endorsed Bowring's use of the *Arrow* incident as a pretext to make the entirely unrelated demand of entering the city of Canton, even arguing that such a move could only be 'conducive of an amicable settlement of the differences'.[61]

But it was Palmerston's defence of Bowring that proved most effective, because it had a powerful emotional appeal. He reproached Cobden for his disloyalty to his old friend Bowring: 'My notion of a friend of twenty years' standing is to view his faults with indulgence, to make excuse, if excuse can be made, for any error he has committed; and that he should never be the man to expose the first false step, which it may be his opinion he has taken'.[62] He added:

I have always understood that the way in which friends ought to deal with each other is that indicated by the poet.

---

56. Ibid., cols. 1843 4.
57. Ibid., col. 1844.
58. As mentioned, he was the Rt. Hon. James Moncrieff (1811 74), who sat for Leith district (1851 9) and Edinburgh (1859 68) until he was appointed lord of sessions as Lord Moncrieff in 1869. He was created a baronet in 1871 and made Baron Moncrieff in 1874. *BMP*, v. 1, pp. 273 4.
59. Lord advocate, 27 February 1857, Hansard, 3d series, v. 144, col. 1517.
60. Labouchere, 26 February 1857, Hansard, 3d series, v. 144, col. 1424.
61. Ibid., col. 1429.
62. Palmerston, 3 March 1857, Hansard, 3d series, v. 144, col. 1810.

The rhetoric of imperialism

> Be to their faults a little blind,
> Be to their virtues very kind,
> And fix a padlock on the mind.[63]

Palmerston then taunted Cobden for not having acted according to those principles.[64]

This appeal to personal loyalty is characteristic of Palmerston, who had consistently protected his subordinates in a similar fashion.[65] In this sense, Palmerston was perhaps even more Confucian than the contemporary Chinese mandarins who, in a private capacity, might be benevolent towards their juniors, but in their official roles, often dealt with their subordinates rather harshly.[66]

Miles Taylor has interpreted Palmerston's motives for this defence of Bowring as a tactical device to discredit Cobden by implying that Cobden was engaged in personal innuendo, thus turning Bowring's radical pedigree, a potential liability, into a positive asset.[67] We would prefer that Palmerston had elaborated upon Bowring's purpose for his extraordinary action, if that purpose were defensible in public; in fact, this is precisely what he soon did, as the next section shows.

VI. Technicalities and generalities

Gladstone protested that Cobden had been accused of technicalities: 'If you show that there is no ground for these proceedings you are accused of entangling yourself in technicalities, and if you speak of the general rules of amity and peace which should bind nations, you are accused of flying off into generalities'. Thus, alternating between technicalities and generalities, 'the defence of what is indefensible is carried on'.[68] Gladstone reminded the House how this case of the technicalities stood: 'If you fail in your proof of the technicalities you fail altogether'. But if the British government succeeded in their proof of the technicalities they had not yet succeeded in the main issue, but merely laid the first step of a long process.[69] Following this preamble, Gladstone gave an example: 'If you are about to hang a man, and, although

63. Ibid., col. 1829.
64. Ibid.
65. In 1848, for example, he protected even the person who, without his authority, made public his rather dictatorial letter to the queen of Spain, which caused a diplomatic row. See Lloyd C. Sanders, *Life of Viscount Palmerston* (London, W. H. Allen, 1888).
66. Such harshness was partly due to the statutes. For example, a local district official whose seat of government was overrun by the rebels, for example, could face capital punishment. See my *Yeh Ming-ch'en*, chapter 6.
67. Taylor, *The Decline of British Radicalism*, p. 273.
68. Gladstone, 3 March 1857, Hansard, 3d series, v. 144, col. 1794.
69. Ibid.

you find a technical flaw in the proceedings, yet persist in hanging him, is that a technical offence only?' Or, was it not also an offence against the first principle of justice, tending to undermine the essential safeguards of society?[70] With this example, he returned to the case in point. The government had put together with most elaborate skill a parcel of pleas to impart a British character to that which was Chinese, 'and if you fail in your argument you have not an inch of ground to stand upon. But if you succeed in your argument, what follows?' Not that Britain would be justified in going to war, for to do that the British government had to show not only that there had been some denial of a right which Britain was entitled to claim, but also that the magnitude of the injury inflicted was sufficient to justify a recourse to arms. Unless this case was proved, he thought the government might as well never have begun their process of reasoning.[71]

Referring to the illegal activities of the *Arrow*, Gladstone blamed the government for having obtained Hong Kong under one pretence and used it for other ends. They had exacted Hong Kong from China for the purpose of careening and refitting their vessels. Instead, they had relocated some 60,000 Chinese within it, and from these migrants were found the means of sustaining and organizing a fleet of coasters whose business it was to enlarge that smuggling traffic which Britain was bound by treaty to put down.[72]

Gladstone showed sympathetic condescension for the Chinese soldiers who had killed the occasional blue-jacket and for the person who tried to poison the inhabitants of Hong Kong. 'They resort to those miserable and detestable contrivances for the destruction of their enemies which their weakness teaches them.'[73]

Obviously the term 'guerrilla warfare' had not gained much currency in the vocabulary of Gladstone's time, despite the success of the Spanish guerrillas against Napoleon Bonaparte. But within the context of Victorian politics, Gladstone's was a powerful speech. An eyewitness noted that Gladstone 'delivered for nearly two hours an oration which enthralled the House, and which for argument, dignity, eloquence, and effect is unsurpassed by any of his former achievements'.[74]

Palmerston seems to have had considerable difficulty responding to Gladstone's case. One reporter observed, 'Lord Palmerston rose, pale, anxious, unnerved, evidently shaken by the consciousness of the effect which Mr Gladstone's speech had produced upon the House'.[75] One must remember,

70. Ibid.
71. Ibid., cols. 1794–5.
72. Ibid., col. 1801.
73. Ibid., col. 1803.
74. John Morley, *The Life of William Ewart Gladstone* (London, Edward Lloyd, 1908), v. 1, p. 419.
75. *Saturday Review*, 7 March 1857. This was founded by John D. Cook in November 1855 as 'a weekly review without news but with reviews of all the stirring subjects'. Quoted in Koss,

however, that Palmerston was now seventy-three years old and was suffering from a bad cold.[76]

He made no serious attempt to meet Gladstone's arguments. Rather, he directed an emotional appeal to ordinary Englishmen by concentrating on the *Arrow*'s flag: 'I say that it is immaterial to the question whether by the technicalities of the law you can or cannot show that at the moment she had not a right to be protected'. The animus of an insult, the animus of violation of the treaty was in the Chinese, he asserted, and therefore Britain had a right to demand not only an apology for the wrong that was done, but an assurance that it should not be repeated.[77]

The moment that the national flag and national honour were involved, Palmerston said, reprisals alone would not be enough. If demands were refused in the first instance and no accommodation was arrived at, further and increased demands had to be put forward as hostilities went on. 'Yeh cannot complain if he has subjected himself to additional demands',[78] he proclaimed. These additional demands were necessary 'for the purpose of our promoting our present interest'.[79] He elaborated on this: Bowring had aimed at expanding the market for British manufactures from 'a narrow strip of land not extending very widely from the coast' to the entire Chinese population estimated at 350,000,000, 'a third of the whole human race'.[80]

To Earl Grey, Palmerston's whole performance was 'in the lowest tone of mere party speaking and bad jokes, full of misrepresentation, and an appeal to all the worst feelings and prejudices of his hearers'.[81] Charles Greville thought Palmerston's speech was 'very dull in the first part and very bow-wow in the second; not very judicious, on the whole bad, and it certainly failed to decide any doubtful votes in his favour'.[82] More sensational was his pronouncement about the poisoning of British residents in Hong Kong, about which some fresh information had reached him on the eve of this last night of the debate.[83]

Political Press, v. 1, p. 88. For a history of this journal, see M. M. Bevington, *The Saturday Review, 1855–1868* (New York, Columbia University Studies in English and Contemporary Literature, 1941).
76. Greville diary, 3 March 1857, Greville MSS 41122, cited in Greville, *Memoirs*, v. 8, p. 97; and, in turn, quoted in Hawkins, *Parliament*, p. 61. In fact, earlier, in January, Palmerston had had such a sharp bout with the gout in one foot that he had to use crutches for some days. See Palmerston to Sulivan, 20 January 1857, in *The Letters of the Third Viscount Palmerston to Laurence and Elizabeth Sulivan, 1804–1863*, ed. Kenneth Bourne, Royal Historical Society, Camden fourth series, v. 23, p. 313, no. 361.
77. Palmerston, 3 March 1857, Hansard, 3d series, v. 144, col. 1814.
78. Ibid., col. 1825.
79. Ibid., col. 1826.
80. Ibid., cols. 1827–9.
81. Grey diary, 28 February 1857, Grey MSS C3/19, quoted in Hawkins, *Parliament*, p. 61.
82. Greville diary, 3 March 1857, Greville MSS 41122, cited in Greville, *Memoirs*, v. 8, p. 97; and, in turn, quoted in Hawkins, *Parliament*, p. 61.
83. Palmerston to Clarendon, 1 March 1857, MSS Clar. Dep. C69, folio 155.

However, Palmerston's defence gave material justification to the military measures that had been taken, and this proved to be a very clever tactic to divert attention from Gladstone's closely argued case. With this justification by market forces, the historian draws closer to the pivotal origins of the war.

VII. The China trade

Cobden made one important point: ' Since 1842 we have not added to our exports to China at all, at least as far as our manufactures are concerned. We have increased our consumption of tea; but that is all.'[84] This prompted the former chief justice of Bombay, Sir Erskine Perry,[85] to say 'The sole principle of policy which ought to govern our intercourse with China was that which had reference to the mutual benefit of trade'.[86]

These observations were, in reality, complaints about what might be perceived nowadays as an imbalance in the bilateral trade with China and manifestations of a certain degree of anxiety to do something about it. How far did the British government share such a concern, and to what extent did it constitute an origin of the war? The House did not pursue the subject far enough to provide us an answer. But the clue is there for us to ask further questions.

The lord advocate added, 'With interests so grave at stake it would be better, and even more just, even if a false move had been made, to proceed rather than to go back'.[87] This was a familiar chant. Others had made a similar plea. But what were these grave interests? Why did he and others like him beat around the bush? Lord John Russell[88] seems to have known what they were driving at and decided to be deliberately difficult. He defied the government to say that they had a justifiable cause of war with China, or any right to claim the revision of Britain's treaties with that empire, upon two such 'contemptible pleas' as the alleged insult to the flag and the Chinese refusal to admit Britons into Canton City.[89] Charles Greville commented that Russell's speech was the great event

---

84. Cobden, 26 February 1857, Hansard, 3d series, v. 144, col. 1412.
85. Again, Sir Erskine Perry (1807–58) was educated at Trinity College, Cambridge, was called to the bar at the Inner Temple in 1834, became a judge of the Supreme Court at Bombay in 1841, and chief justice there in September 1847. He resigned in 1852. He was first elected for Devonport in May 1854 and sat until appointed a member of the Council of India in 1858. *BMP*, v. 1, p. 308.
86. Perry, 26 February 1857, Hansard, 3d series, v. 144, col. 1460. Sir Erskine Perry was to vote for Cobden's motion, and thereby incurred great hostility in his own constituency – see Chapter 10, this volume.
87. The lord advocate, 27 February 1857, Hansard, 3d series, v. 144, col. 1517.
88. For a biography of Russell, see Spencer Walpole, *The Life of Lord John Russell*, 2 vs. (London, Longmans, 1889).
89. Russell, 26 February 1857, Hansard, 3d series, v. 144, cols. 1472–3.

of the night, being one of his very best efforts and extremely successful with the House.[90]

Palmerston took up Russell's challenge. He said that the Treaty of Nanking had given Britons unbounded expectations of trading with a third of the whole human race. However, 'We have been greatly disappointed'.[91] Consequently an appeal was made to the Chinese for treaty revision. Unfortunately, that had been rejected. Otherwise there would be an immense augmentation of European commerce with China. He asked, '[What] are we to do in this state of things?'[92]

The message is now very clear. As Disraeli said in his response to Palmerston's speech, the government was attempting 'by force to increase our commercial relations with the East',[93] using the *Arrow* quarrel and the Canton City question as the springboard. It seems that many members of the house knew exactly what was going on; they were just reluctant to say so. Thus, although Cobden had opened the debate with references to the China trade and Palmerston and Disraeli concluded the debate by referring to the same, in between, very few members spoke about it. They preferred to labour on any subject other than what had already been condemned as 'general covetousness' by Lord Ellenborough in the House of Lords.

In our efforts to trace the origins of the *Arrow* War, we should be grateful that Palmerston called a spade a spade. It is intriguing that he should have accepted Russell's challenge. Why could he not simply have ignored him, as he had ignored Gladstone's argument from the rule of law? Apparently he could not or would not. He had been summarily dismissed as the secretary of state for foreign affairs when Russell was prime minister, on 19 December 1851. Russell's excuse was flimsy. In private conversation with the French ambassador, Count Walewski, Palmerston had indicated his approval of Louis Napoleon's *coup d'état* of 2 December 1851. The pretext was made worse by the fact that Russell himself had expressed a similar opinion to the same person at about the same time. Shortly after his dismissal, Palmerston brought down Russell's government by moving an amendment to the militia bill. When Palmerston himself became prime minister in February 1855, Russell declined any offer of office, but then agreed to be secretary of state for the colonies upon the resignation of Sidney Herbert. Promptly Palmerston sent this acutely unhappy colonial secretary to the peace negotiations in Vienna, leaving him to bear the stigma of that unpopular peace. By July of the same year, Russell felt obliged to resign.[94] Thereafter he remained out of office, devoting himself to

90. Greville diary, 17 February 1857, in *Leaves from the Greville Diary*, pp. 781–2.
91. Palmerston, 3 March 1857, Hansard, 3d series, v. 144, col. 1827.
92. Ibid., col. 1828.
93. Disraeli, 3 March 1857, Hansard, 3 series, v. 144, col. 1836.
94. Bentley, *Politics without Democracy*, pp. 159–60.

literature and travels on the Continent, whence he had just returned in time to join the *Arrow* quarrel in Parliament.[95]

Before the debate, he was seriously 'talked to',[96] and Lord Minto advised him to give Palmerston cordial though independent support.[97] But Russell had other thoughts: 'We have heard much of late – a great deal too much, I think – of the prestige of England. We used to hear of the character, of the reputation, of the honour of England'.[98] His plea for Britain to admit an injustice, once committed, was consistent with the advice he had given Palmerston in 1849, when the latter was his foreign secretary.[99] Then there was his personal agenda. His attack on a Liberal government under Palmerston has been perceived by some of his contemporaries and at least one modern scholar as 'calculated to impress everyone who heard it with the feeling that his object was to turn the government out' and to 'seduce the supporters of Lord Palmerston'.[100]

Thus, Russell's Victorian liberal conscience, coupled with old wounds[101] and new ambitions, seem to have prompted him to challenge the firebrand to break the silence. Unfortunately, 'the increased bitterness of his tone'[102] became all too obvious to everybody, and he was to pay dearly for it afterwards.[103]

Russell's background partly explains his apparent privileged access to such information as the government's determination to obtain treaty revision from China, and his ability to challenge Palmerston to make a public admission of it. One gets the impression that what Palmerston had revealed was merely the tip of the iceberg. It will be fascinating to find out what exactly happened behind the scenes. This will be attempted in Part Five, wherein the political alignments and realignments consequent on the *Arrow* dispute in Parliament will be explored.

VIII. The opium trade

As is to be expected, opium received even less mention than the China trade. The former chief justice of Bombay, Sir Erskine Perry, quite deliberately

95. Prest, *John Russell*, p. 378.
96. W. W. Clarke to Parkes, 6 December 1856, Russell Papers, Public Record Office, P.R.O. 12G, quoted in ibid., p. 379.
97. Minto's memo, 27 December 1856, Minto Papers, quoted in ibid.
98. Spencer Walpole, *The Life of Lord John Russell*, 2 vs. (London, Longmans, 1889), v. 2, p. 286.
99. Prest, *John Russell*, p. 379.
100. Elliot to Minto, 27 February 1857, Minto Ms. 11754, folio 424; and Dunfermline to Panmure, 27 February 1857, Dalhousie Ms. GD45/14/631; both quoted in Hawkins, *Parliament*, p. 60.
101. His 'hostility to the government seems pretty well known', observed Sir James Graham. Aberdeen to Graham, 31 January 1857, Graham MSS Bundle 131, quoted in Hawkins, *Parliament*, p. 53.
102. H. C. F. Bell, *Palmerston*, 2 vs. (London, 1936), v. 2, p. 168. Charles Greville also observed that Russell was 'exceedingly bitter and displayed without stint or reason his hostile *animus*'. Greville diary, 27 February 1857, in *Leaves from the Greville Diary*, p. 783.
103. See next chapter.

ventured on to that subject, although he had been advised previously that all members 'ought to shut their eyes to this, as having nothing to do with the immediate question before the House'. He maintained that it had all to do with the question. For it had produced those deep feelings of hostility to the English merchants and the English government on the part of the Chinese, as well as a reciprocal feeling of animosity on the part of the English. He said he had been informed that almost every one of the British merchants in China was engaged in the illicit traffic in opium, that 30 million dollars'[104] worth of opium were annually sold by British merchants in this illicit trade, at least three-fifths of which was sold at this very port of Canton.[105]

Samuel Gregson accused Perry of having scandalized the English merchants at Canton. Gregson asserted categorically that none of the British merchants he represented 'had anything whatever to do with that traffic'. Short of anything more novel to add, he tried to dispose of the matter swiftly by saying, 'That, however, had nothing to do with the question before the House'.[106]

I wonder if Gregson really expected anybody to believe his sweeping statement! He was obviously irritated by the subject of opium and wanted to get rid of it as quickly as possible. He himself was intimately connected with the illicit trade, having been the head of the firm of Gregson and Company, East India and China Agents, Austin Friars. At the time of the debate, he was a director of the London Assurance Corporation which offered policies to those trading with China, including those involved in opium smuggling. He was also a director of the East and West India Dock Company.[107] In addition, he was the chairman of the East India and China Association in London, on whose behalf he had just written to lobby the government to widen its demands on China.[108] His letter was included in the Parliamentary Papers tabled for the occasion.[109] It was, of course, the prominent members of that same association in London, especially William Jardine of the most substantial opium agency in China, Jardine Matheson and Company, who had masterminded British strategy and the terms of peace in the Opium War.[110]

More discreet than Gregson was the cofounder of Jardine Matheson and Company, James Matheson. He was by this time back in England, had been

104. The dollars referred to here were Spanish silver dollars, each being worth approximately five shillings (see Parl. Papers 1840, v. 37, pp. 247–88). Therefore, 30 million dollars was worth approximately £7.5 million.
105. Perry, 26 February 1857, Hansard, 3d series, v. 144, cols. 1461–2.
106. Gregson, 26 February 1857, Hansard, 3d series, v. 144, col. 1463.
107. *BMP*, v. 1, p. 167.
108. Gregson to Clarendon, 6 January 1858, Baring Papers HC6.1.20, in the company archives of Baring Brothers. The original of the same document may be found FO17/279. For more details, see Chapter 12.
109. See Parl. Papers 1857, v. 12.
110. For a more detailed analysis of that episode, see Chapter 13.

210

knighted, sat for Ross and Cromarty, and was present at the debate. But he decided not to speak. Nor did he subsequently vote. His kinsman and business associate, Alexander Matheson, M. P. for Inverness, also kept his own counsel, but later voted with the Noes.[111]

Before that vote was taken, Sidney Herbert pursued the subject further: 'We know that this trade is necessary to Indian finance'. Thereupon, a banker, Mr Kinnaird[112] interjected, 'Hear, hear!' Herbert continued, 'My hon. friend [Mr Kinnaird], I know, thinks this trade exceedingly abominable'.[113] John Roebuck[114] agreed. He thought that the government of China regarded themselves as the conservators of public morality and in that character considered the use of opium immoral. 'They see an outside people very shrewd, and possessed of great powers, doing all they can to introduce into their country by smuggling what they call this most deleterious drug'.[115]

A fearless Palmerston, in his concluding speech, made this frank statement: 'At present the nature of our commerce with the Chinese is such that we can pay for our purchases only partly in goods, the rest we must pay in opium and in silver'.[116]

IX. The penal dissolution

Cobden had professed that he did not expect the division over his motion to lead to a change of ministry.[117] His motion was carried by 16 votes – 263 for the motion, 247 against.[118] This division, in the view of Gladstone, did 'more honour to the H[ouse] of C[ommons] than any I ever remember'.[119]

Cobden was also wrong in forecasting Palmerston's reaction to the adverse vote. In fact, even before Cobden made his predictions and before Gladstone had occasion to rejoice, Palmerston had determined both to interpret

111. Beeching, *The Chinese Opium Wars*, p. 229.
112. The Hon. Arthur Fitzgerald Kinnaird (1814–87) was the third son of the Eighth Kinnaird. He was educated at Eton and was attached to the British Embassy at St Petersburgh in 1835. Later he became private secretary to the earl of Durham and a partner in the firm of Ramson, Bouverie & Co., Bankers. He sat for Perth from 1837 to 1839 and again from 1852 until he succeeded his brother as the tenth baron in January 1878. *BMP*, v. 1, p. 222.
113. Herbert, 2 March 1857, Hansard, 3d series, v. 144, col. 1677.
114. John Arthur Roebuck (1801–79) was called to the bar in 1831. A disciple of Bentham and a friend of John Stuart Mill, he professed advanced political opinions, which he resolved to uphold in the House of Commons. In 1849, he was returned for Sheffield unopposed in May, and with that constituency he was closely identified until death. He was to be made a privy councillor in 1878 by the Tory government. *DNB*, v. 17, pp. 95–7.
115. Roebuck, 3 March 1857, Hansard, 3d series, v. 144, col. 1786.
116. Palmerston, 3 March 1857, Hansard, 3d series, v. 144, col. 1828.
117. Cobden, 3 March 1857, Hansard, 3d series, v. 144, col. 1844.
118. Hansard, 3d series, v. 144, cols. 1846–50.
119. Tuesday, 3 March 1857, *Gladstone Diaries*, v. 5, p. 202.

The rhetoric of imperialism

Cobden's motion as a vote of censure and to dissolve Parliament,[120] although the actual decision to do so was not formally taken until the Cabinet met on 5 March 1857.[121]

Later that day, Lord Granville in the Lords, and Lord Palmerston in the Commons, announced the intention of the government to dissolve Parliament in consequence of their defeat over the *Arrow* question.[122]

Lord John Russell was quite alarmed, describing the dissolution as 'penal', being inflicted on the House for having voted according to its conscience,[123] while the duke of Argyll smugly portrayed it as 'thoroughly deserved'.[124] Russell knew his seat in the City of London had been endangered by his attack on Palmerston. His fears proved correct in the so-called Chinese Election which followed. But why did even some of Palmerston's own party vote against him?

X. 'As if I had been in a jury-box'

Sir Francis Thornhill Baring,[125] a former chancellor of the Exchequer and first lord of the Admiralty who had been returned by the Liberals for thirty years,[126] was among those who voted against Palmerston. He explained, 'I had no choice left, and deliberately, and as if I had been in a jury-box, I gave my vote that the papers laid upon the table failed to establish satisfactory grounds for the violent measures resorted to at Canton on the late affair of the *Arrow*'. He agreed that he would be told that, however true these words might be, the motion was still practically a censure on the government, and it would be his duty to vote against it. 'I have been a party man all my life, and am not willing to underrate party considerations', he said. In many cases, he perfectly understood that, weighing the evils or advantages of two alternatives, it might be entirely justifiable to prefer the retaining of a good government in office rather than the carrying of any particular motion, however good. 'But there must be some limit to these party feelings', he declared. 'I cannot rate war and all its horrors as a light matter'. For the shedding of blood, even of enemies, he believed all were responsible to a higher tribunal: 'we have no right to go to war

120. Taylor, *Decline of British Radicalism*, p. 274, n. 50.
121. Hawkins, *Parliament*, pp. 61–2.
122. Malmesbury, *Memoirs of an Ex-Minister*, v. 2, p. 53.
123. *Punch*, 14 March 1857.
124. Argyll, *Autobiography and Memoirs*, v. 2, p. 70.
125. The Rt. Hon. Sir Francis Thornhill Baring (1796–1866), baronet, was educated at Eton and at Christ Church, Oxford, where he obtained a double first class in 1817. He was called to the bar at Lincoln's Inn in 1823, was a lord of the Treasury (1830–4), chancellor of the Exchequer (1839–41), and first lord of the Admiralty (1849–52). He sat for Portsmouth from 1826 until he retired in 1865. He was created Baron Northbrook in January 1866. *BMP*, v. 1, p. 21.
126. *The Times*, 11 March 1857.

without a justifiable cause, and I do not reckon as a justifiable cause the desire to keep my friends in office'.[127]

Who put Baring in a jury-box? Baring himself did; or more precisely, his liberal conscience did.

John Roebuck independently elaborated this aspect of English life. Previously, he had moved a resolution congratulating Palmerston in the Don Pacifico debate in 1851.[128] But now over the Chinese quarrel, he spoke against him. If one assumed that the Chinese had been wrong in boarding the *Arrow*, he said, then great luminaries of the law in Britain were wrong too, because the Chinese had been considered right by some of the greatest lawyers in England. He wished that members of the House would exchange their positions with the Chinese and suppose that these transactions took place in the city of Liverpool and the Mersey. He found that Englishmen, and Westerners generally, had one rule of morality for the West and another for the East. This double standard, he observed, had been put forward boldly in the House of Commons on the present occasion. He felt that if the British flag had been tarnished at all, it had not been tarnished by the Cantonese allegedly pulling it down, but by its flying over the heads of men who had been engaged in hurling shot and shell among defenceless people in order to get into their city. He knew what the feelings of Londoners would be if their city had been so bombarded under similar pretences. If Britain had been under despotism it might be said that the people were not to blame, the fault was with their rulers. But the liberal institutions of Britain enabled the people to blame their governors, and if they did not do so they would have taken upon themselves the responsibility of the acts of their governors. In this respect, he thought that the attorney-general spoke as if he had a retaining fee and a brief.[129]

Some Liberal back-benchers agreed with Baring, Roebuck, and others, but there was little they could do as Palmerston was 'very popular – people troubling themselves very little about the justice or injustice of the [China] war and angry at the supposed coalition'.[130]

Jasper Ridley has observed that the only members of note who spoke out in support of the government in the House of Commons were a number of junior ministers.[131] Does the silence of the majority of the senior ministers suggest that

---

127. Baring was quoted verbatim by John Russell in 'John Russell's Address to the Electors of London', *Globe*, Thursday, 12 March 1857, p. 2, col. 6.
128. See Ridley, *Palmerston*, p. 466.
129. Roebuck, 3 March 1857, Hansard, 3d series, v. 144, cols. 1783–5.
130. Hawkins, *Parliament*, p. 63, quoting Bruce to his wife, 8 March 1857, in H. A. Bruce, *Letters of Rt. Hon. H. A. Bruce, G. C. B., Lord Aberdare of Duffryn*, 2 vs. (Oxford, privately printed, 1902), v. 1, p. 150.
131. Ridley, *Palmerston*, p. 466. The only two senior ministers who spoke were Clarendon and Labouchere. But of course both were the 'government'. Clarendon was the chief defendant,

basically they shared the same sense of justice, but could not and would not speak against their own ministry? We shall find out more in subsequent chapters.

XI. In sum

By listening patiently to the honourable members debate, we have been rewarded in several ways. First and foremost, the prime minister stated publicly that the government had wanted to expand British commercial interests in China by asking the Chinese authorities to revise the Treaty of Nanking. That peaceful means having failed, the government declared they had decided retrospectively to support Bowring's quarrel with Commissioner Yeh so that coercive measures might now be employed towards that goal. In a crude form, herein lies the link between ministerial thinking and economic realities. Our next step should be to attempt to see if there is concrete evidence to substantiate the words of the prime minister, because he did not supply it to the House.

Second, the prime minister conceded that among the commercial interests which the government had wanted to promote in China was opium, which was important to the Indian revenue and to British trade. Seen in the light of these dimensions to the war, the *Arrow* incident itself has become, to some extent, incidental to the British scheme of things. Its relevance would seem to depend on the way in which it continued to be used as a pretext for war.

Third, the violent exploitation of this incidental factor upset quite a lot of Britons at home, including many among Palmerston's own ranks. They objected to the unnecessary bloodshed and the apparent illegality of the British case. They voted against Palmerston according to their conscience. Such a conscience vote was possible because at this time members of Parliament were gentlemen of means. They were not paid for being members, and therefore enjoyed a great deal of freedom of action. These aspects of English life – the rule of law and the Victorian liberal conscience – have been completely overlooked by historians in China. For a long time any Chinese who took such values seriously would be regarded as bourgeois. Consequently, any Chinese historian who espoused such values would be regarded as bourgeois, a label which has caused untold misery to many intellectuals in the past. Given inhibitions of this kind, the lack of understanding of Victorian England is not surprising.

What is surprising is that the Victorian liberal conscience seems to have been forgotten by the Western world at large. Perhaps this is the result of close to a

being the foreign secretary and as the *Arrow* quarrel was within his jurisdiction. Labouchere was the secondary defendant, being the colonial secretary and as the *Arrow* dispute hinged on the colonial register and colonial governor of Hong Kong.

century, since the Great War,[132] of modern party politics, especially the rule by caucus whereby members of Parliament could be expelled from the party should they refuse to toe the party line. Thatcherism[133] in the 1980s may also have played a part.

But at the time of the *Arrow* War, steadfast adhesion to the rule of law and the liberal conscience rose above even patriotism. For example, Edward Cardwell (1813–86) voted against Palmerston's policy over the *Arrow* incident, thus risking, and losing, his seat for the city of Oxford. Yet he has been described as 'thoroughly patriotic and public-spirited'.[134] Sidney Herbert spoke and voted against the same policy. Yet, John Roebuck had described Herbert's performance as secretary at war at the beginning of the Crimean War thus: 'No man could have been more intent upon the honour of his country and on performing the duties of his office'. Subsequently he was to die prematurely in his capacity as the secretary for war, having 'sacrificed his health for unremitting devotion to duty'.[135]

Oddly enough, these English values have been overlooked even by some patriotic British diplomatic historians,[136] economic historians,[137] and imperial historians[138] all too eager to defend their past. Only British political historians, treating the *Arrow* quarrel entirely within the context of domestic politics, appear to have touched upon them.

In a representative government such as the Westminster system, official policies theoretically reflect the interests of the electors. We shall proceed, therefore, to examine the behaviour of the constituents in the next chapter. The aim is to find out the sort of pressure, if any, sectional interests might have brought to bear on their parliamentary representatives and thence on government policies with respect to the *Arrow* War. Already, the *Morning Post* had observed, 'It is a singular and satisfactory fact that every British merchant who addressed the House on the Chinese question, or who has the slightest personal or commercial knowledge of China, or the Chinese people, has spoken strongly in favour of the Government'.[139]

132. See George Dangerfield, *The Strange Death of Liberal England* (New York, Carpicorn, 1961).
133. See Dennis Kavanagh, *Thatcherism and British Politics: The End of Consensus?* (Oxford, Oxford University Press, 1987); and Robert Skidelsky (ed.), *Thatcherism* (London, Chatto & Windus, 1988).
134. *DNB*, v. 3, pp. 952–4.
135. *DNB*, v. 9, pp. 663–5.
136. See, e.g., Costin, *Great Britain and China*.
137. See, e.g., A. J. Sargent, *Anglo-Chinese Commerce and Diplomacy* (Oxford, Clarendon Press, 1907).
138. See, e.g., Platt, *Finance, Trade, and Politics*.
139. *Morning Post*, 4 March 1857.

10
'Johnny' is on his knees:
The 'Chinese Election'

I. George Cruikshank wields his pen

'Twas honest English, 'Ayes' and 'Noes'
That won a vote in former day,*
Till Peace-at-any-price arose,
And, sympathising with our foes,
Obtain'd it – Quaker-like – for Yeh[1]

Palmerston's defeat over Cobden's motion goaded a Dr W. Gourley to write immediately to the Foreign Office: 'I hope the Ministry have *not resigned*, but whether they have or not I am determined to do what I can', he declared, 'to dispel the delusion under which a very large portion of the public are at present labouring through the speech of Mr Cobden and others'.

Apparently he had access to some sketches of the horrible and barbarous punishments the Chinese officials inflicted upon their own people. He would send these sketches to his friend, George Cruikshank, 'the first artist in Europe' – indeed a great draughtsman – with a request that he would put all else aside and reproduce the sketches in his own peculiar style 'to be hung up in every picture shop of any note in the metropolis'.

He was confident that these reproduced sketches would do more to enlist the sympathy of the public in favour of the ministry than all the speeches that could be delivered in or out of Parliament. What made him so sure? George Cruikshank's[2] 'matchless delineation of the horrors of drunken-ness have done

---

* As mentioned in the text introducing Part Four, various authors on British politics have written or commented on the general election of 1857, sometimes called the 'Chinese Election'. Our concern here is more with the Chinese aspect of the event.
1. Referring to the adverse vote in the House of Commons, someone known only as 'S. L.' wrote this poem, entitled 'Yea–Nay Voting', for the *Globe*, 7 March 1857, p. 3, col. 6.
2. For a biography of George Cruikshank, see Michael Wynn Jones, *George Cruikshank: His Life and London* (London, Macmillan, 1978). For reproductions of his works, see John Wardroper, *The Caricatures of George Cruikshank* (London, Gordon Fraser, 1977); and Richard A. Vogler, *Graphic Works of George Cruikshank: 279 Illustrations, Including 8 in Full Colour* (New York, Dover, 1979). Unfortunately, none of the sketches mentioned by Dr Gourley appears to have been included in these publications.

more for the cause of Temperance in this country and in America', he claimed, 'than all the lectures that have ever been delivered upon that subject'.[3]

Clarendon was pleased. 'Should be thanked', he minuted, 'no doubt his scheme will be useful in dispelling the delusions which have been created respecting humanity of the Chinese'.[4] A reply was drafted on 11 March.[5] Gourley was excited by 'the approbation of Lord Clarendon'.[6]

On 24 March 1857, Dr Gourley again wrote. The 'modern Hogarth, Mr George Cruikshank, is now busily engaged in sketching some of the Chinese legal *barbarities*': disjointing, chipping to pieces, tearing the body asunder by pullies, skinning alive, etc. 'Really the whole civilised world ought to combine together to check these horrible atrocities and endeavour to teach these wretches the common principles of humanity', wrote Dr Gourley.[7] Clarendon again minuted, 'Ack[nowledge] with thanks'.[8]

Gourley's measures, and Clarendon's endorsement of them, may have been parochially expedient; but they were internationally perilous in the long run. Amid jingoistic chants of an election, Cruikshank's sketches could be misunderstood by their spectators. Such press descriptions of the Chinese as 'a barbaric and intractable race',[9] 'a race of treacherous barbarians',[10] could be read as complementing the drawings. Cruikshank himself might not have intended his drawings to be understood that way; he himself had been appalled in 1818 by the hanging of two women in Ludgate Hill for passing forged £1 notes,[11] but that was not sufficient to indict the British as 'a barbaric and intractable race'. It would have been more accurate to say that the Chinese rulers were beastly towards those of their own subjects whom they regarded as offenders.[12]

3. Gourley to Foreign Office, Regent's Park, 5 March 1857, FO17/280, pp. 39–40. FO17/280 is a bound volume of papers labeled 'domestic various' which, unlike the official despatches, had no despatch numbers. To assist in the identification of individual documents, therefore, page references in the bound volume are given.
4. Clarendon's minutes, dated 6 March 1857, on Gourley to Foreign Office, Regent's Park, 5 March 1857, FO17/280, pp. 39–40.
5. Foreign Office to Gourley, 11 March 1857, FO17/280, p. 105.
6. Gourley to Foreign Office, 12 March 1857, FO17/280, p. 128.
7. Gourley to Hammond, 24 March 1857, FO17/280, p. 226.
8. Clarendon's minute, dated 25 March 1857, FO17/280, p. 226. A letter of appreciation was drafted the next day; see Foreign Office to Gourley, 26 March 1857, FO17/280, p. 238.
9. See, e.g., *Globe*, Friday, 6 March 1857, p. 2, col. 3: 'Look on the Picture and Then on That'.
10. *The Times*, 16 March 1857.
11. John Laurence, *A History of Capital Punishment* (New York, Citadel, 1963), p. 13. See also V. A. C. Gatrell, *The Hanging Tree: Execution and the English People, 1770–1868* (Oxford, Oxford University Press, 1994); and Leon Radzinowicz, *History of the English Criminal Law and Its Administration from 1750*, v. 1, *The Movement for Reform* (London, Stevens, 1948).
12. Chinese diplomatic historians may legitimately object to Cruikshank's sketches for possibly obscuring the true origins of the *Arrow* War. But their specialists on Sun Yatsen will testify that Sun was to make similar denunciations of the barbarity of Manchu legal proceedings forty years later (see his 'Judicial Reform in China', *East Asia*, 1, no. 1 [July 1897], pp. 3–13). The

II. Company men close ranks

News of the government's defeat in the House of Commons on 3 March 1857 was received with 'universal regret and dissatisfaction. Scarcely on any political point within modern experience has the feeling of the commercial community been expressed with such general unanimity.'[13]

The directors of the Manchester Chamber of Commerce and Manufactures promptly held a meeting on the morning of 5 March 1857 and adopted the following resolution: 'That a memorial to the Earl of Clarendon be prepared to pray for increased protection to the persons and property of British residents in China, which this Board fears will be imperilled by the proceedings in the House of Commons on the 3rd instant'. The subcommittee, to which the preparation of this memorial was referred, considered that the urgency of the case was such that in order to avoid the least delay, 'a mere recital of the resolution' should be communicated at once to Lord Clarendon 'without the formality of a memorial'.[14]

The resolution carried with it overtones of near hysteria. Nobody could seriously believe that the Chinese would hear about the adverse vote overnight and immediately set about exterminating all Britons within their reach. The mail to Hong Kong by steamship took about two months. In addition, all the reports indicated that the Royal Navy had been bombarding Canton, not the Chinese junks showering Hong Kong with stink pots. The directors were experienced mature men, who would take a lot to be shaken. What caused this commotion?

This question will be examined in the last section of this chapter. Being concerned in this section with the preliminaries of the election, we observe here that Clarendon showed every sympathy and compassion in the instant reply he offered, assuring the chamber that 'measures have already been and will continue to be taken to afford the increased protection' solicited.[15] The tone was of reassuring a child.

The course adopted by the Liverpool merchants was more considered. On Thursday 5 March, an address to Palmerston from 'the merchants and in-

---

    irony of history is such that Sun, in making those denunciations, was probably inspired by the concern expressed by the British public for his safety and well-being during his detention inside the Chinese Legation in London (see my *Origins of an Heroic Image*). This concern would, very likely, have been a result of the general viewing of Cruikshank's sketches, which in turn may be taken as an indication of the success of Dr Gourley's electioneering efforts on behalf of Palmerston's government.

13. *The Times*, Thursday, 5 March 1857, p. 7, col. 3, 'Money-Markets and City Intelligence'.
14. Bazley to Clarendon, 5 March 1857, FO17/280, p. 37. Thomas Bazley was the president of the said chamber. For more details about the activities of that chamber, see Arthur Redford, *Manchester Merchants and Foreign Trade*, v. 2, *1850–1939* (Manchester, Manchester University Press, 1956).
15. Foreign Office to Bazley, 6 March 1857, FO17/280, p. 62.

habitants generally of Liverpool is now being extensively signed in the Exchange'.[16] The next day, a deputation consisting of Alexander Sleigh, Thomas Baines, and Alfred Higgins, and introduced by members for their borough, waited upon Palmerston at his residence in London, Cambridge House. They presented the address signed by more than eleven hundred leading bankers, merchants, shipowners, and brokers of Liverpool, expressing their warm approbation of the conduct of Palmerston's government over the *Arrow* quarrel.

In presenting the address, the leader of the deputation said that it had been 'signed by men of every shade of political character, and with an enthusiasm quite unprecedented'. The address also condemned the 'incongruous and factious coalition in Parliament which has made the present unfortunate state of matters in China the pretext for displacing your government'. Palmerston was said to be 'much pleased with this mark of confidence'.[17]

In the City of London, a petition soliciting Palmerston to allow himself to be nominated for the City at the approaching election, was set on foot on 5 March 1857. In a short time it received several hundred signatures. Reportedly, the 'sentiment of honest indignation which prevails at the conduct of the coalition has seldom been equalled; and on all sides are heard the strongest expressions of confidence in Lord Palmerston.'[18]

The initiative was in fact taken by the underwriters and subscribers at Lloyds, whose total number was about 1,500, but whose average daily attendance was around 500. Of the latter, 375 put down their signatures at the Baltic Coffee-house; and an additional 100 applied to sign after the address had been withdrawn. It was said that this demonstration was 'entitled to be regarded as one of the most important that could have been made at the present juncture'.[19]

It is well known that Lloyds was the largest insurance institution in the world. Their interest in the political debate indirectly but materially corroborates Ellenborough's story that the China trade was a vital link in Britain's global commercial chain.[20]

In the afternoon of the same day, the signed address was presented to Palmerston at the Treasury, by Richard Thornton, the oldest member of that establishment. A similar petition from members of the Stock Exchange was handed in at the same time. But Palmerston declined the honour.[21]

Meanwhile, a court of common council was held on 5 March 1857 in the City of London for the despatch of public business. Deputy Rathbone said that

16. *Globe*, 6 March 1857, p. 2, col. 4, 'Liverpool, Thursday'.
17. Ibid., col. 3, 'The Liverpool Address to Lord Palmerston'.
18. Ibid., col. 4, 'Public Opinion for Lord Palmerston: The City'.
19. *Globe*, 7 March 1857, p. 3, col. 5, 'Public Opinion for Lord Palmerston: The City'.
20. See Chapter 8.
21. *Globe*, 7 March 1857, p. 3, col. 5, 'Lord Palmerston and the Stock Exchange', quoting the *Shipping Gazette* of 6 March 1857.

The rhetoric of imperialism

the Corporation of London must adopt measures 'to support Her Majesty's ministers in the course they had pursued. (Hear, hear)'. The clerk of the court proclaimed that custom stood in the way of discussion. Deputy Dakin insisted that if ever a crisis could justify departure from the corporation's general custom of not coming forward in support of ministers, 'that crisis had arrived. (Hear hear)'. Thereupon the lord mayor compromised by intimating that he would be willing to receive a proposition in the usual form from the members of the court. In the course of the day it was decided that court would shortly be held whereby resolutions on the subject might be brought forward.[22]

This extraordinary general meeting was held in the Guildhall on 9 March 1857 in conformity with the following notice: 'In consequence of a requisition numerously signed to express the opinion of this Court upon the consequences likely to arise to the commerce of the country from the decision of the House of Commons on Tuesday night last, and to take such steps as they may think necessary'. There was a large attendance. The lord mayor took the chair at 2 o'clock. Mr Besley moved a resolution regretting the vote in the House of Commons and expressing thanks to Palmerston and the other ministers for the course they had taken, 'which justly entitles them to the confidence of the country'. An amendment was defeated, and the original motion 'was carried with loud cheers'.[23]

Also on 9 March 1857, the *Globe* reported that the principal London firms connected with the China trade had gathered together to sign and present an address to Palmerston. The importance of these firms would be 'appreciated by all who are conversant with the standing of the mercantile houses of London', said the *Globe*. At the head of the list was Matheson and Co.; followed by Gregson and Co.; Crawford, Colvin, and Co.; and Palmer, McKillop, Dent, and Co.[24]

Among them, Matheson and Co. was the London office of the famous Jardine Matheson and Co. of Hong Kong. The head of Gregson and Co., Samuel Gregson, had tried to cut short any debate over opium in the House of Commons.[25] Robert Wigram Crawford, a senior partner of Crawford, Colvin, and Co., had by now joined a vigorous move to oust Lord John Russell from his seat in the City of London.[26] Lancelot Dent, of Palmer, McKillop, Dent,

22. *Globe*, 6 March 1857, p. 2, col. 4, 'Court of Common Council'.
23. Ibid., 10 March 1857, p. 1, col. 6, 'Meeting of the Common Council'.
24. The other firms were J. Thomson, T. Bonar, and Co.; Finlay, Hodgson, and Co.; Robert Benson and Co.; Morris, Prevost, and Co.; Sanderson, Frys, Fox, and Co.; Arbuthnot, Latham, and Co.; T. A. Bibb and Co.; Gledstanes and Co.; W. A. Lyall and Co.; Maitland, Ewing, and Co.; Harvey, Brand, and Co.; Daniel, Dickinson, and Co.; Mackay and Read; Frith, Sands, and Co.; Dallas and Coles; and Anderson Brothers and Co. See the *Globe*, 9 March 1857, p. 4, col. 2, 'Public Opinion for Lord Palmerston: The City'.
25. See Chapter 9.
26. Robert Wigram Crawford (1813–89) was not only a partner in the firm of Crawford, Colvin, and Co., East India Merchants and Agents; he was also a director of the Bank of England, of

and Co., was the man whose arrest Commissioner Lin had ordered on the grounds that Dent been involved in extensive opium-smuggling operations right up to the time of the Opium War.[27]

These firms, twenty in total, offered their cordial thanks for the firmness which Palmerston had displayed 'upholding the honour of Great Britain, and in a determination to protect the lives and property of British subjects, peaceably engaged in commercial intercourse with China'. They were confident that Palmerston would not be deterred by the Commons' adverse vote from continuing to maintain a 'firm and dignified attitude' until the China trade was 'placed on a permanent footing of security and peace'.[28]

How might the opium trade in China be placed on such a footing? – by making the Chinese government legalize it.

At Bristol, it was said that the greatest anger existed among Derby's supporters, who felt that he had sacrificed the dignity of a party leader by his coalition 'with an anti-English section of the house'. Many leading men apparently did not scruple to say that their confidence in the Derby opposition had been so shaken that they would hesitate in giving support to a Tory candidate.[29] In the course of the day, Saturday, 7 March 1857, the feeling of the inhabitants of Bristol found expression in the subjoined address to Palmerston, which was handed out at the commercial rooms. The address expressed surprise and regret that a ministry, so remarkable for the security it had obtained for mercantile intercourse with foreign nations, should have been defeated in a vote respecting the *Arrow* dispute, a vote which it claimed had 'gained no sympathy in the hearts of the British people'. The petitioners concluded by thanking Palmerston for resorting to an appeal to the people, convinced that the result of that appeal would not confirm the decision of the House of Commons.

Apparently, the originator of the address was a sugar refiner,[30] sugar, of course, being a usual accompaniment in Britain to the drinking of China tea.

Subsequently on Thursday, 12 March, a deputation led by the sugar refiner and accompanied by the local M.P. had an interview with Palmerston to present the address 'thanking his Lordship that, instead of yielding the reins of government into other hands, he has resorted to the constitutional alternative of appealing to the people'.[31] In Newcastle-upon-Tyne, it was reported that

which he had been deputy governor; chairman of the East Indian Railway; commissioner of lieutenancy for London; and an East India proprietor. He had sat for Harwich before (*BMP*, v. 1, p. 94). Now he targeted the City of London and was to become one of the four so-called commercial candidates nominated in an attempt to exclude Lord John Russell from the contest. See later in this chapter.

27. See Chang, *Commissioner Lin*, p. 150.
28. *Globe*, 9 March 1857, p. 4, col. 2, 'Public Opinion for Lord Palmerston: The City'.
29. Ibid., 6 March 1857, p. 2, cols. 4–5, 'Bristol'.
30. Ibid., 9 March 1857, p. 4, col. 2, 'Bristol'.
31. Ibid., 14 March 1857, p. 2, col. 3, 'A Cabinet Council . . .'.

'the great proportion of the manufacturing and maritime classes in this great district sympathise with Lord Palmerston in the present crisis'.[32]

'Like many of the wars in which England has engaged, this is a merchants' war', observed the *Manchester Guardian*, 'and the deputations from mercantile bodies and trading towns which besiege Palmerston's doors show how keenly it touches those who rise so eagerly in his defence'.[33] Thus, day by day the *Globe* printed accounts of addresses presented to Palmerston by merchants in London, Liverpool, and Bristol.[34] In pursuit of commercial interests, the merchants were direct and straightforward, and had no time for the sophistry, or falseness, that pervaded most of what was said in Parliament.

We observe, in addition, that Palmerston appears to have favoured the *Globe* with all these addresses.[35] More than other cities and towns, Manchester overreacted to the adverse vote in the House of Commons in several ways. An attempt to explain this near hysteria will be made at the end of this chapter. Suffice here to say that the reason was related to the complex causation of the *Arrow* War.

On 10 March 1857, it was reported that Lord Elgin[36] was to be sent to China as plenipotentiary to settle the *Arrow* dispute.[37] A modern scholar has suggested that Palmerston might have staged the appointment of Elgin because of its belatedness[38] – two months after the publication of Seymour's despatch in the *London Gazette*. However, in view of the merchant princes' urging Palmerston to take immediate steps to protect British lives and property in China on the grounds that the adverse vote had greatly endangered them, we cannot help feeling that the appointment was probably related to pressure from this quarter. As for its belatedness, we must remember that the Commons vote was not taken until 3 March 1857, and the Cabinet had to meet to decide on a list of candidates, approach them one after another in the case of refusals, and wait for the acceptance of an offer.[39] The appointment of Elgin within a week of the

32. Ibid., 6 March 1857, p. 2, col. 4, 'Newcastle-on-Tyne'.
33. *Manchester Guardian*, 11 March 1857.
34. See *Globe*, 5–9 March 1857.
35. For the close relationship between Palmerston and the *Globe*, see Chapter 7.
36. Again, James Bruce (1811–63), eighth earl of Elgin and twelfth earl of Kincardine, was formerly governor of Jamaica (1842–6) and governor-general of Canada (1846–54). After his mission to China, he, in the spring of 1859, accepted Palmerston's offer of postmaster-general. In 1861, he was appointed governor-general of India, where he died in 1863. See Walrond (ed.), *Letters and Journals of James, Eighth Earl of Elgin*.
37. *Globe*, 14 March 1857, p. 2, cols. 1–2.
38. See Taylor, *Decline of British Radicalism*, p. 274, quoting George Hadfield's speech at Sheffield (*The Times*, 25 March 1857, p. 8); Richard Cobden's speech at Huddersfield (ibid., 28 March 1857, p. 8); and the editorial of the *Weekly Dispatch*, 15 March 1857, p. 7.
39. Initially, three candidates were considered at a Cabinet meeting: Sir Bartle Frere, the duke of Newcastle, and Lord Elgin. Newcastle was chosen, but he declined. Then Lord Elgin was offered the commission, and he accepted it. See Argyll, *Autobiography and Memoirs*, v. 2, pp. 77–8.

adverse vote was in fact exceedingly speedy. This move may have been due to the sudden need for electioneering and the pressures from the commercial classes for immediate action.

III. A cat among the pigeons

> Confederate crew, your appeal to the nation,
> Your failures and blunders, your recommendation,
> Will teach you that England of honour so jealous,
> Loves not coalitions composed of such fellows.[40]

Palmerston's dissolution of Parliament was 'penal' indeed. Events were to prove that seldom was a victory in debate more dearly purchased. In fact, to many of the 'conquering heroes', it was to be considerably more harassing than a defeat.[41] On 11 March 1857, for example, *The Times* reported that the member for Aylesbury, Mr Henry Layard,[42] intended to give up contesting the borough after he had found that 'all but unanimous dissatisfaction expressed at his vote against Lord Palmerston'.[43] The member for Devonport, Sir Erskine Perry, decided to soldier on and addressed a large meeting of his constituents. At the end of his speech, a vote of no confidence was proposed, causing a 'scene of great confusion'.[44] At Oxford City, a placard was issued, calling upon the voters to withdraw their support from its M. P., Edward Cardwell, because 'a gentleman of thoroughly independent English principles would be brought forward in opposition'.[45] Meanwhile, the voters resolved that Cardwell should be invited to attend a public meeting to explain his reasons for having voted against Lord Palmerston's government.[46] Cardwell learned Perry's lesson and decided to issue a written statement first in order to test the water.[47] At

---

40. *Punch*, 14 March 1857, p. 103.
41. Ibid., 28 March 1857.
42. The Rt. Hon. Austen Henry Layard (1817–94) was well known as the excavator of ancient Nineveh, many finds from which were deposited at the British Museum. He received the honorary degree of D.C.L. at Oxford in 1848. He was under-secretary of state for foreign affairs (in 1852 for a few weeks, and again from July 1861 to July 1866). He was elected lord rector of Aberdeen University in 1855 and 1856. He sat for Aylesbury from July 1852 to July 1857. He was to become ambassador to Madrid (1869–77) and to the Sultan of Turkey until 1880. His publications include *Nineveh and Its Remains*, 2 vs. (London, 1850), and *Discoveries in the Ruins of Nineveh and Babylon* (London, John Murray, 1853). For a biography of Layard, see Gordon Waterfield, *Layard of Nineveh* (London, John Murray, 1963); see also *BMP*, v. 1, p. 230.
43. *The Times*, 11 March 1857.
44. Ibid.
45. *Globe*, Friday 6 March 1857, p. 2, col. 4, 'Oxford'.
46. *The Times*, 11 March 1857.
47. *Globe*, 14 March 1857, p. 4, col. 3, 'Oxford'. His statement read: 'The speech from the throne invited our attention to transactions of a lamentable kind, which had recently taken place in China; and papers on that subject were submitted to us for our decision. If the government had then announced the intention, which has since been made known, of sending out a superior authority to China, the motion which was actually made would have been quite

Portsmouth, Sir Francis Thornhill Baring found that he had 'given serious offence to some of his oldest supporters by voting for Mr Cobden's motion'.[48] At Tynemouth, William Lindsay[49] was asked to give a public explanation of his parliamentary conduct.[50]

In the City of London, Lord John Russell was told by all his friends that he had no chance whatever of reelection, and it was therefore useless to try.[51] Mr de Jersey attempted to defend Russell at a special general meeting of the city's Common Council by saying that Russell was 'the same man he ever was', and was immediately met with the interjection: 'He had always been a humbug. (Laughter)'.[52]

Consequently, some of the election addresses of the opposition members were noticeably apologetic in tone, as the candidates nervously tried to frame excuses for the stand they had taken in Parliament. For example, Sir Francis Thornhill Baring said that although he voted against the government, he did so only because he could not approve of the conduct of Bowring and that he saw 'no reason why difference on one point should interfere with the general support I have hitherto given to Lord Palmerston's Administration'.[53] At Tynemouth, an intimidated Lindsay said that he would have voted with the government on that occasion if Lord Palmerston had promised to do what he had now done – to send out a competent person as a commissioner, with authority to act in the matter.[54] It was observed that the 'oldest and the boldest of them hardly dare as yet to glory in their triumph; and instead of being proud of it, the most of them would fain shirk the subject altogether'.[55] All suffered from Palmerston's allegation of a coalition.

Yet the member for Lanarkshire in Scotland, Baillie Cochrane,[56] was forth-

unnecessary: and I, at least, should not have voted for it. No such intention was expressed, and Parliament was obliged either to approve or to condemn extreme severities, resorted to by the plenipotentiary in China, in a manner wholly unauthorised by the spirit of his instructions from the home government'.

48. *The Times*, 11 March 1857.
49. William Shaw Lindsay (1816–77) founded the well-known shipping house of Messrs W. S. Lindsay and Co., Austin Friars, London. He authored various letters and pamphlets on maritime affairs and published in 1842 a book entitled *Our Navigation and Mercantile Marine Laws*. He sat for Tynemouth from March 1854 to March 1859, when he was elected for Sunderland. *BMP*, v. 1, p. 239.
50. *The Times*, 13 March 1857.
51. Argyll, *Autobiography and Memoirs*, v. 2, pp. 74–5.
52. *Globe*, 10 March 1857, p. 1, col. 6, 'Meeting of the Common Council'.
53. *The Times*, 13 March 1857.
54. Ibid.
55. *Punch*, 28 March 1857, p. 121.
56. Alexander Dundas Wishart Ross Baillie-Cochrane (d. 1890), was the elder son of Admiral Sir Thomas John Cochrane, K.C.B., who had served in the Far East and one of whose letters was quoted by Cobden in the Commons debate. He sat for Bridgport (1841–6 and 1847–52) and for Lanark (January to April 1857). He was to sit for Honiton (1859–68). He was appointed captain of the First Lanark Rifle Volunteers in 1860 and created Baron Lamington on 3 May 1880. *BMP*, v. 1, p. 83.

right: 'I humbly and conscientiously feel that it was a vote demanded by every principle of justice and humanity; and while I refrain from reflecting on the conduct of others, I rejoice that a British House of Commons has vindicated our national character for mercy and truth'.[57] Richard Cobden, too, stuck to his conscience, as we shall see later.

Punch gauged fairly accurately the feeling of the nation when it produced the following short satires. One was under the title 'Prophecy': 'Is Lord Palmerston wrong in supporting his subordinates at Canton? Cobden says "Yeh." The Country will say "Nay" '.[58] The second was entitled 'Turner's Collection': 'The division on the China debate might be characterised as "Turner's Collection", considering the number of gentlemen who turned their coats on that occasion'.[59] The third was entitled 'English Heads at a Chinese Price': 'Yeh offers £5 for the head of an Englishman. Had he listened to some of his supporters in Parliament, he would surely have reduced the market price of the article'.[60] Perhaps the most penetrating was this one: 'A tiresome debate – The Chinese controversy has been altogether a Bo(w)ring discussion'.[61]

Mr Punch clearly perceived that the country really had no time for such debates as those in Parliament. What people wanted was sensation, and Palmerston was going to give them plenty of that.

On Saturday, 21 March 1857, Parliament was prorogued at 1:30 P.M.,[62] heralding a feverish election campaign:

> Bills great and small, on each dead wall,
>   With hustings pledges – old in story
> The long purse shakes, the voter wakes,
>   And the green candidate's in his glory.
> Go, members, go – set the loose shiners flying;
> Go, members; exit session, dying, dying, dying.
> Oh, hark oh, hear there's gin and beer,
>   In boroughs, counties, freely flowing;
> Oh, sweet and far, from tap and bar,
>   Each his own trumpet's blandly blowing.
> Go – let us hear the country's voice replying –
> Go, members – wind up, session, dying, dying, dying.[63]

The opposition members were dubbed by some newspapers the 'Chinese Coalition'. It had become the 'Chinese Election'.

57. *The Times*, 12 March 1857.   58. *Punch*, 14 March 1857, p. 107.
59. Ibid.
60. Ibid., p. 108.
61. Ibid.
62. *Globe*, 21 March 1857, p. 2, col. 2, 'Prorogation of Parliament on this Day'.
63. *Punch*, 21 March 1857, p. 119. This poem appears to have been written to the tune 'Air of the Bugle-Song' in *The Princess: A Medley*, by Alfred, Lord Tennyson. See *The Poetical Works of Alfred, Lord Tennyson* (London, Ward, Lock, 1908), pp. 140–99: p. 163, cols. 1–2.

IV. The wicked must be punished

As mentioned in Chapter 9, an attempt was made to poison the foreign community in Hong Kong by secreting arsenic into the bread of a baker's shop, news of which reached London during the debate in the House of Commons.[64] Palmerston's supporters tried to capitalize on the incident to whip up an almighty sensation. On the last day of the China debate, when Palmerston lashed out on the poisoning, the *Morning Post* echoed as follows: 'Have not the perpetrators of these monstrous iniquities placed themselves outside the pale of all laws? Ought they not to be dealt with as noxious animals, – as wild beasts in human shape, without one single redeeming virtue?'[65] Who was behind this poisoning? – 'Monster Yeh'. It described him as the most truculent miscreant who had butchered seventy thousand of his own countrymen and who subsequently stimulated, 'by a large reward, the murder of our countrymen'. Thereupon the *Morning Post* penned this battle cry: 'Talk of international law with sanguinary savages such as these! There is but one law for such demons in human shape, and that is a law of severe, summary and inexorable justice'.[66]

Here is British xenophobia in full cry. According to the *Morning Post*, it was all right for the Royal Navy to bombard densely populated Canton, but the Chinese would have to be demons in human shape if they retaliated. In Chapter 6, I have argued that the siege mentality of British diplomats and merchants at Canton might have encouraged xenophobia. The rhetoric of the *Morning Post* suggests that British xenopobia might have had deepers roots than that.[67]

In the wake of the bread poisoning, announcing the details of the expedition to be sent to China was certain to increase the excitement and lift the militant passion of the electors to Palmerston's advantage. So it was revealed that the force to be assembled at Hong Kong would consist of two brigades of infantry, composed of the 5th Fusiliers, already on their passage from Mauritius; the 59th Regiment, already at Hong Kong; the 23rd Fusiliers, the 82nd, 90th, and 93rd Regiments, which would proceed as soon as the shipping arrangements

---

64. Palmerston to Clarendon, 1 March 1857, MSS Clar. Dep., C69, folio 155.
65. *Morning Post*, 3 March 1857.
66. Ibid.
67. Indeed, while discussing early-twentieth-century comparative anatomy, William Adams notes that it was not until the 1930s – a generation after the reports he discusses – 'that notions of racial superiority and inferiority came seriously to be questioned'. See his *Nubia: Corridor to Africa* (London, Allen Lane, 1977), p. 92. Here, Adams is speaking of European notions, including those of Englishman Sir Grafton Elliot Smith. For some casual and unguarded expressions that may be interpreted as British xenophobia, see the diary of James Lees-Milne, *Prophesying Peace* (London, Chatto & Windus, 1977). See also V. G. Kiernan, *The Lords of Human Kind: European Attitudes towards the Outside World in the Imperial Age* (London, Weidenfeld & Nicolson, 1969).

were completed. This force would be further reinforced by four companies of artillery from Woolwich, 1,000 marines and 100 men of the Royal Engineers, while in the shape of auxiliary corps, it would be accompanied by one battalion of the military train and 200 men of the medical staff corps. The commander-in-chief would be Major-General Ashburnham, while other senior commanders would include Major-General Sir Robert Garrett, Major-General Straubenzee, Adjutant-General Pakenham, and Quartermaster-General Wetherall.[68]

The *Morning Post* fanned the fire vigorously, capitalizing still further on the Hong Kong poisoning incident: 'The hideous villainy, the unparalleled treachery, of these monsters of China, on whom the seraphic Gladstone and the un-English Cobden bestowed their unnatural and mischievous sympathy, had defeated itself by its very excess of iniquity'. Why? 'The poisoner had put such an immense amount of arsenic into the dough, that the deadly dose acted as an emetic, and was discharged from the human stomachs'. Then the *Morning Post* attempted to make the blood of its readers boil: 'But who shall tell the vomitings, the rigours, the excessive prostration of strength, the nausea, the spittings of blood, occasioned to hundreds of our countrymen, twelve thousand miles removed from their homes and all the comforts of European medical treatment?'[69]

Another faithful supporter of Palmerston, the *Globe*, was to prove that it was quite capable of fabricating documentation, like Commissioner Xu in 1849. To heighten the sensation, it invented a supposed statement by Allum, the baker of the poisonous bread: 'I have acted agreeably to the order of the Viceroy which was brought to me by a satellite of the Mandarins. They told me that the English having declared war on my country, it was my duty to assist in their destruction; that the soldiers used fire and sword to fight them, and that I was to use poison; that it was natural to do everything to injure an enemy; and that, moreover, if I disobeyed his orders, my family at Canton would be thrown into prison, and all my property confiscated'.[70]

Soon, the *Globe* was caught out. Disraeli's weekly organ, the *Press*, was to report that Allum had been acquitted. One of the incriminating pieces of evidence against Allum had been that he left Hong Kong for Macao on the morning of the poisoning. But he contended that he did so with the intention of finding a safer place for his wife and children. With him and his family was indeed some of the poisonous bread for their own use. Upon hearing of the suspicion against him, Allum immediately returned to Hong Kong to make a

68. *Globe*, 14 March 1857, p. 2, col. 3, 'The China Expedition'.
69. *Morning Post*, 17 March 1857.
70. *Globe*, 24 March 1857. Allom has been identified as Zhang Peilin. See Choi Chi-cheung, 'Cheung Ah-lum: A Biographical Note', *Journal of the Hong Kong Branch of the Royal Asiatic Society*, v. 24 (1984), pp. 282–7.

voluntary statement to the authorities. In a subsequent court hearing, he was found not guilty.[71] But before that happened, he and his fellow suspects, forty-two in all, were confined for twenty days in a cell fifteen feet square, with no closet, no bedding, and no change of clothing. To crown all, the attorney-general, Chisholm Anstey, showed animus against the defendant at the trial,[72] which Britons at home, always legal-minded, found most objectionable.

However, the truth came out too late to be of any political significance. By the time the *Press* printed the story on 11 April 1857, the election was over. The sensation created by the *Globe*'s beat-up had served its useful purpose. Later, *The Times*'s special correspondent followed up the story from Hong Kong. He reported that an action was again brought against Allum, this time for selling unwholesome bread. Once again, the attorney-general showed animus against the defendant. He rested his case upon the common-law obligation of a baker to sell only bread fit for human consumption. The presence of arsenic was fully proved. The jury returned a guilty verdict. Allum was fined 1,010 dollars.[73] If the behaviour of the attorney-general reflected the intense hatred of the Britons in Hong Kong, we may glean from this the degree of sensation produced in Britain during the election.[74]

From Palmerston's electioneering point of view, the editorials of the *Morning Post* and the *Globe* would have been perfect complements to the drawings of George Cruikshank. The latter depict the cruelty of the Chinese towards their own people, whereas the former portray their alleged persecution of foreigners. Leaders of the opposition were also targeted. Even before the dissolution of Parliament, the *Morning Post* had this to say of Lord Derby, who had defended Yeh and the Chinese: 'Yeh, his plaintiff, is his client and idol even though the insolent Mandarin has set thirty – nay one hundred – pieces of good sycee silver on the head of every Englishman; and Bowring, the defendant, is his aversion'.[75]

The speech of the member for Woodstock, the marquis of Blandford,[76] who sought reelection, was much cooler and more considered: 'The recent events in China, while they call for our heartfelt commiseration in consequence of the

71. *Press*, 11 April 1857.
72. Ibid.
73. Cooke, *China*, p. 55.
74. After Palmerston was reelected, his government felt duty-bound to print another blue book for the edification of its members, entitled *Copies of, or extracts from, any papers connected with the confinement of Chinese prisoners at Hong Kong, and with the trial of a baker and others on the charge of poisoning* (Parl. Papers 1857, Session 2, v. 43, pp. 169–206) to put the record straight.
75. *Morning Post*, 28 February 1857.
76. J. W. Blandford (1822–83), second marquis of Blandford, was first elected for Woodstock in April 1844, a borough which he represented with short breaks until he succeeded as the seventh duke of Marlborough in July 1857. He was to become lord president of the Council in 1868. *BMP*, v. 1, p. 38.

miseries entailed by loss of life and destruction of property, owe their origin to an aggressive act on the part of the Chinese authorities'.[77]

But the newspapers and parliamentary hopefuls soon ran out of things to say about Yeh. Thus, the *Morning Post* began criticizing the Chinese people: 'The Romish missionaries describe the Chinese as unclean, sordid, and wallowing in the most sensual vices without stint or shame'. It continued, 'These reports, written more than a century ago, are verified to the letter by Protestant, Baptist, and Nonconformist English authorities in our own day, and also by American missionaries'.[78] Later it added, 'The Chinese . . . were cruel, sceptical, and avaricious, desperately intent on gain, prone to material enjoyments, perfect materialists in action, and always keenly looking to their temporal interests'.[79] Obviously the editor of the *Morning Post* had never read Confucius or Lao Zi. Was that newspaper talking about the Chinese people or the empire builders of Britain?

The *Morning Post* went on to tell British women – this in the age of the kitchen skivvy and the match-girl – how lucky they were compared with the womenfolk in China: 'Then, as now, Chinese women were kept in servitude and slavery, considered inferior and degraded beings, and forced to do all the drudgery and heavy work of the household'. In short, life for a woman in China was worse than death. So unbearable was the condition of the sex in China, that suicides, said to be very common among the men, were ten times more common among the women. Small wonder, the paper claimed, that Chinese women were only too happy to rid themselves of an existence which it was a burden to bear. Besides, the mandarins like Yeh and others 'have ever been indifferent to the fate of the women, whom they regard as the very brutes of the earth'.[80] Such editorials strangely overlooked perhaps the worst crime against Chinese women – foot-binding.

Lord Palmerston would never run out of things to say about Yeh. As we shall see in the next section, what he said was unmatched by any of the journalists, however gifted they might be in the craft of agitation.

V. The firebrand flares up

> The Coalition its banner unfurls.
> Come hither: the talking is done.
> Not by gloss of Dizzy and Gladstone's pearls
> Of speech will the battle be won.

---

77. *The Times*, 12 March 1857.
78. *Morning Post*, 28 February 1857.
79. Ibid., 3 March 1857.
80. Ibid.

Come out, old rough-rider, defying purls,
And astonish them every one.[81]

Although the firebrand[82] had declined the merchants' request to stand for the City of London, he accepted an invitation to address a dinner at Mansion House on Friday 20 March 1857, the day before Parliament was prorogued. It was hosted by the lord mayor of London and attended by, inter alia, the *corps diplomatique*, the entire Cabinet, and other members of both houses of Parliament. When he and Lady Palmerston arrived, they were greeted with 'enthusiastic applause'.

Despite the presence of foreign diplomats, Palmerston played on the patriotic feelings of his English audience for the purpose of electioneering. He immediately captured their attention by saying, 'We felt that great wrong had been inflicted upon this country'. In what way? – 'Our fellow-countrymen in a distant part of the globe had been exposed to every sort of insult, outrage, and atrocity (loud cheers)'. He said he had received numerous expressions of support from all parts of the kingdom, addresses from men of all ranks and of all shades of politics – from Whigs, Tories, and Radicals – declaring it right that 'when the interests of the country are at stake party differences should be forgotten, and the whole people should rally together to vindicate the honour of the empire (cheers)'. He knew, and he believed every Briton knew, that 'such will be the result of the appeal we are about to make'. He ridiculed the opposition for having aspired to power by making 'the humiliation and degradation of their country a stepping-stone to office (cheers)'.[83]

Palmerston asked, 'If those who voted against us had risen to power, what ought they to have done as the logical and inevitable consequence of their vote?' He provided a rousing answer: they would have apologized to the Chinese barbarians for the wrongs which the government was supposed to have done, rebuilt the forts which 'our gallant soldiers had destroyed', and 'sent from Woolwich new cannon in lieu of those which our brave seamen had rendered unserviceable'.

More stirring stuff was to follow: they would have paid the rewards which had been given for the 'heads of our merchants, and the cost of the arsenic which had been used in poisoning our fellow subjects at Hongkong (cheers)'. Palmerston professed he could not really envy the feelings of those who could witness with calmness the heads of respectable British merchants on the walls of Canton, or the murders and assassinations and poisonings perpetrated on his fellow-countrymen abroad, and who, instead of feeling their

81. *Punch*, 14 March 1857, p. 104. Dizzy was Disraeli's nickname; see Hesketh Pearson, *Dizzy: The Life and Nature of Benjamin Disraeli, Earl of Beaconsfield* (London, Methuen, 1951). 'Old rough-rider' obviously refers to Palmerston.
82. Firebrand was one of the nicknames given to Lord Palmerston by his contemporaries.
83. *The Times*, 21 March 1857, p. 9, cols. 3–6.

blood boil with indignation at such proceedings, 'would have us make an abject submission to the barbarians by whom these atrocities were committed (cheers)'.[84]

Palmerston was making up a lot of stories here. No British merchant, however seriously he had broken the law, ever had had his head hung up on the walls of Canton. Nobody ever asked him to submit to the Chinese. And no 'atrocities' such as poisoning were ever committed until the Royal Navy had bombarded Canton.

On 23 March 1857, Palmerston issued a written address to his constituents at Tiverton. It was printed in *The Times* and reprinted in the evening newspapers such as the *Globe*.[85] Thousands of copies of this address were also distributed all over Britain. It is said that for the first time in British political history the prime minister made a personal appeal to the whole nation as well as to the electors in his own constituency.[86] The most catching,[87] and therefore the best known, was the first sentence in this paragraph: 'An insolent barbarian, wielding authority at Canton, had violated the British flag, broken the engagements of treaties, offered rewards for the heads of British subjects in that part of China, and planned their destruction by murder, assassinations, and poisons'.[88] When Charles Greville read it the next day, he was moved to write in his diary that he was inexpressibly disgusted at the enormous and shameful lying with which the country was misled.[89]

On 26 March 1857 Palmerston went to his own constituency, the borough of Tiverton, for the nomination proceedings the following day. There was a great crowd waiting to receive him at the railway station, and it welcomed him warmly, following him, cheering, to his hotel. Later, when he addressed the electors, there was loud and prolonged cheering. He repeated his boast about having received addresses from a great number of large commercial and other towns, which did honour to the national feeling of the country. He praised the opposition for having behaved, during the whole of the war with Russia, in accordance with the feelings and the spirit of the country; then he condemned them for refusing to support the government over the outbreak in China, accusing them of splitting the House of Commons in the hope of gaining office.[90]

Amidst loud and prolonged cheers, he added that the insolent barbarian Yeh 'unites in his person all the obstinacy, all the cruelty, and all the perfidy that ever were collected in one single man. (Cheers and laughter)'. He asserted

84. Ibid.
85. Ibid., 24 March 1857, col. 1. See also *Globe*, 24 March 1857, p. 2, col. 6
86. Jasper Ridley, *Lord Palmerston* (London, Constable, 1970), p. 468.
87. Ibid.
88. *The Times*, 24 March 1857, p. 9, col. 1. See also *Globe*, 24 March 1857, p. 2, col. 6.
89. Greville diary, 24 March 1857, in *Leaves from the Greville Diary*, p. 785.
90. *The Times*, 28 March 1857, p. 6, cols. 3–6: col. 4.

that Yeh began, after long-continued insult and violation of treaty engagements, by an outrageous attack upon the British flag. 'It was the duty of our officers on the spot to resent that attack, to require apology for the past, and assurance of abstinence for the future (cheers)'. Britons had heard a great deal of technical argument about registers, colonial ordinances, and imperial laws; but the question was to him a broad and simple one, he said. Here was a vessel with the British flag flying, he asserted, with a British register and a British subject in command; and the only pretence was that 'one old man was the father of a son who in some other part of China was believed to be a pirate. (Great laughter and cheers)'.[91] Three cheers were then given for Lord and Lady Palmerston, and three cheers for the Queen.[92]

But there were other reactions. Charles Greville observed that Palmerston's address to Tiverton, following his speech at the Mansion House, excited great indignation, both being 'full of deception and falsehood'. He recorded that John Russell was 'particularly incensed, and said these two productions were unworthy of a gentleman, and so they were'.[93] With hindsight, one can see that Russell and Palmerston represented simply different styles of Victorian politics. It is said, for example, that the cold and distant Russell 'won temporary popularity among the radicals by promising them more than it was in his power to give', while Palmerston 'promised them little or nothing but national security and progress by his own methods, a hearty handshake and a risqué joke'.[94] But when Palmerston jovially attributed Commissioner Lin's anti-opium activies in 1840 to the machinations of the alleged locally grown 'poppy interest' in China,[95] for instance, it ceased to be funny and became really risky.[96] Robert Gavin has conceptualized similar utterances as reflecting Palmerston's world-view. I shall assess this view in Chapter 18, within the context of a wider picture.

VI. Mind your language

It was Lord Malmesbury, not Lord John Russell, who responded publicly to the firebrand's electioneering addresses. He penned a fourteen-page letter to *The Times*, which opened pungently: 'My Lord, I am one of those who thought it their duty to vote against your government upon the China question, and

---

91. Ibid.
92. Ibid., col. 6.
93. Greville diary, 28 March 1857, in *Leaves from the Greville Diary*, p. 785.
94. Gavin, 'Palmerston's Policy towards East and West Africa, 1830–1865', p. 7.
95. Palmerston, 9 April 1840, Hansard, 3d series, v. 53, col. 940.
96. There was no indigenous poppy interest to speak of in China until the British had forced the Chinese authorities to legalize opium as a result of their victory in the *Arrow* War. Thereafter, the Chinese began to cultivate the poppy openly and on a large scale. Palmerston's statement was therefore groundless and misleading on a grand scale.

who have, in consequence, been exposed to your public invectives and misrepresentations on the subject'. He said he was compelled to answer the prime minister through the press, as he could not do so in Parliament which had just been prorogued. 'Vituperation might be legitimate as electioneering claptrap', he wrote, 'but was it decent to use the table at the Mansion House as a hustings?' He found Palmerston's language particularly objectionable: 'This is the language of the Prime Minister of England at the banquet of the first magistrate of her capital, surrounded by foreign ambassadors, and all the talent, rank and wealth of his party'.

Second, he pointed out that Palmerston had misled the public in his widely distributed election address, wherein the prime minister had implied that Yeh's outrages preceded British seizures of ships, shelling of forts, and bombarding of Canton and were therefore the provocations to 'our aggression'. The reverse was true, he said; with the exception of the supposed violation of the British flag on the *Arrow*, all the others were subsequent to and in retaliation for 'our operations conducted without any declaration of war'.

Third, Malmesbury was particularly offended by Palmerston's accusation that he and others had endeavoured to make the humiliation and degradation of Britain the stepping-stone to power. He reminded him that even Lords John Russell and Derby had supported his government unreservedly during every phase of the Crimean War.

Malmesbury's concluding paragraph merits a lot of thought in relation to our search for the origins of the *Arrow* War: 'The country having been committed, my humble vote will support a war which has now become necessary to English interests and honour, but which at first might have been avoided, without a sacrifice of either'.[97]

Palmerston's reply was short and biting as ever:

My dear Lord Malmesbury,
I have received this Evening your letter of this day. I have neither Time nor Inclination to renew the China debate. I have used a Right to express publicly my opinion of the Conduct of public Men on an occasion of no small public Importance, and I have nothing to retract or to qualify.
Yours faithfully,
Palmerston.[98]

Malmesbury wrote afterwards that his protest had 'considerable success' and that he received many compliments, among others from Lords Clarendon and Grey, which he thought were worth having.[99] Clearly Palmerston was relying not on facts but on British nationalism. Small wonder that the *Daily News* took

97. *The Times*, 26 March 1857, p. 9, col. 6.
98. Quoted in Ridley, *Lord Palmerston*, p. 469.
99. Malmesbury, *Memoirs*, v. 2, p. 65.

great exception to Palmerston's abuses levelled at Yeh and the Chinese. It stated that Yeh and his alleged atrocities – those 70,000 decapitated rebels who figured in the statistics of electioneering Palmerstonians; the insults to the British flag; the poisoning of British subjects at Hong Kong; the heads of British merchants grinning on spikes above the ramparts of Canton – were all admirable topics for those panderers to the weaknesses of the British people who meant to make their way to Parliament through the excited ignorance of a misinformed public.[100]

The *Daily News* thought that the story of the 70,000 decapitations was in all probability purely mythical.[101] It concluded that all the evidence showed that no insult to the British flag was ever intended by Yeh. It asserted that no British subject had in fact been poisoned or assassinated. In any case, no attempt was made to poison and no reward offered to assassinate, until Her Majesty's plenipotentiary had aroused by violence the worst passions of a semibarbarous race, violence which even the government admitted to be a matter of regret, violence which every dispassionate Englishman regarded as a matter of national scandal and reproach.[102]

The *Manchester Guardian* also objected to the language employed by the Palmerstonians in adoring their hero. It thought that the animated and dramatic picture of the creator of fleets and armies – the champion of the honour and name of England attacked by a pack of wicked conspirators, and bravely defending himself against sordid factions – was highly suitable for general circulation. Such a picture hardly lost its effect even when reflection 'reminds you that the vote of censure was as honest and honourable a vote as the House ever gave, and was carried against a Liberal Minister by Liberal voices'. In fact, the real portrait should be 'the familiar "old stager" – the pleasant, shifty Epicurean', who created no army, never vanquished Russia, and was chiefly famous for having made inflammatory speeches, written offensive despatches, appropriated the credit of other men's work, and 'stuck like an oyster to his place'.[103]

The *Manchester Guardian* continued its demystification of Palmerston: 'Nobody mistakes him for a great statesman, nobody thinks him in earnest; every educated person knows what worthless stuff his popularity is made of, and those who swell the cry the loudest are the most ready to laugh at it in the free intercourse of society'.[104] This passage makes us feel all the more tantalized by

100. *Daily News*, 25 March 1857.
101. The *Daily News* went overboard here. For some estimates of the number of decapitations based on documentary evidence, see my *Yeh Ming-ch'en*, chapter 6.
102. *Daily News*, 25 March 1857.
103. *Manchester Guardian*, 11 March 1857.
104. Ibid., 18 March 1857.

the object of its attack, namely, the charismatic Palmerston, whose machinations will be dealt with in the next section.

On the other hand, Mr Punch complained about the 'most unfitting bellicosity of language' displayed by Richard Cobden and members of his Peace Society. He considered that the vehemence, with which they had been 'giving it' to all who dared differ from them on the merits of the China question, made him tremble for the safety of his ears should the country decide for carrying on the war with increased vigour.[105]

In Yeh's China, such dissident voices were inconceivable. Yeh could comfort himself with the knowledge – if he ever got to know of it – that he had defenders in distant England. In his homeland, he heard nothing but abuse once he had fallen from grace. All his compatriots, from the emperor[106] down to the paddler,[107] blamed him, and him alone, for the *Arrow* War.

VII. Long live Palmerston

A great deal of the government's electioneering appears to have hinged on Palmerston's role in the Crimean War. The election address by Robert Lowe of Kidderminster is typical of the Palmerstonian fervour. He described Palmerston as a statesman who, 'deserted by many of his colleagues, carried us triumphantly through the late Russian war, whose firmness secured us an honourable peace, and whose vigilance prevented our losing by artifice what we had acquired by arms'. He said that the opposition, 'having failed to drive this country into capitulation with Russia, are now seeking to humble her in the dust before the barbarous insolence of the Viceroy of Canton'.[108]

The member for Ashburton, who was also a tea dealer,[109] told his constituents, 'Recollect, Lord Palmerston got us out of our difficulties in the war, and if you return me you will return one who will support the foreign and domestic policy of Lord Palmerston'.[110] The member for Evesham, Mr Holland,[111] said that support for his reelection meant the people of Evesham would 'support the Minister who took the helm when no one else could handle it; who

---

105. *Punch*, 4 April 1857, p. 134.
106. Imperial edict, 27 January 1858, *YWSM* (XF), no. 683, in *juan* 17, v. 2, p. 623.
107. Xiao Yuan, 'Yueke tan xianfeng qinian guochi', in *Er ya*, v. 1, pp. 236 51: p. 236.
108. *The Times*, 12 March 1857.
109. He was George Moffatt (d. 1878), a partner in the house of Moffat and Co., wholesale tea-dealers, London and Liverpool. He sat for Dartmouth (1845 52), for Ashburton (1852 9), for Honiton (1860 5), and for Southampton (1865 8). *BMP*, v. 1, p. 273.
110. *The Times*, 13 March 1857.
111. Edward Holland (d. 1875) was a liberal who was in favour of a considerable extension of the franchise. He was first returned for Evesham in July 1855, for which he sat until he retired in 1868. *BMP*, v. 1, p. 196.

steered us through a disastrous struggle to a successful issue'.[112] A candidate for Yorkshire (North Riding), said, 'If I had been in Parliament, I should have certainly supported the Minister who has so successfully carried us through unexampled difficulties'.[113]

The newspapers which supported the government fanned the fires further. *The Times* said, 'Lord Palmerston, whatever his faults of omission or commission may be, proved himself a true man when all was uncertain and dark around him'.[114] The *Morning Post* was even louder in its lauding of Palmerston, 'whose British heart rose within him when he heard of Chinese misdeeds'. It felt that a man with a cold heart, a slavish spirit, a metaphysical understanding, and a clouded casuistical perception as to right or wrong, might have acted otherwise; but the disposition of Palmerston was ardent, dauntless, and thoroughly British, and Palmerston had deemed it proper, in vindication of the national flag, and for the assertion of national rights, to obtain redress. All the special pleading in the world, doubled up with casuistical 'Jesuit' logic, said the paper, would not induce the people of England to think that 'Viscount Palmerston's decision on the question was not bold, was not British, was not spirited, was not wise'.[115] It is remarkable how often and how quickly the issue was reduced to qualities of race and nation.

Punch published a parody of a poem in nine stanzas by Tennyson, of which the first and the last stanzas of the satiric version are reproduced here:

> Come unto the country, Pam,
> Now their triple shaft has flown
> Come unto the country, Pam,
> You're the man, and you alone
> So honest men think at home and abroad,
> And the Coalition's blown.
>
> It is coming, and many a seat
> Is aquake with anxious dread
> Old Pam they intended to beat,
> But he'll lick them instead.
> Old Pam they intended to beat;
> But England indignant will tread
> Cobden, Dizzy, and Gladstone under her feet,
> And set Pam at the Ministry's head.[116]

---

112. *The Times*, 13 March 1857.
113. Ibid.
114. Ibid., 14 March 1847.
115. *Morning Post*, 25 March 1857.
116. *Punch*, 14 March 1857, p. 104. The original poem may be found in *Maud*, by Alfred, Lord Tennyson and collected in *The Poetical Works of Alfred, Lord Tennyson*, pp. 244 66: no. 22, on p. 258, col. 1, to p. 259, col. 2.

This and similar laurels caused even some of the popular press to think that the 'Palmerstonian Mania' had gone too far. *Reynolds's Newspaper*[117] wrote: 'Anything more unreasoning, stupid, brutish than the clamour which is now abroad in favour of this arch-charlatan it would be impossible to discover within the compass of the countless volumes in which are recorded the frenzies, the madnesses, and the hallucinations of the human race'. The paper exclaimed: 'What a truly melancholy exhibition! The foremost nation of all the Old World rushing, and screaming, and swearing, and shouting in mad hysterical hallelujahs, the praises of a man whose principal characteristic was an unconquerable disposition to jest at national calamities, and whose greatest recommendation was a species of boasts'.

The newspaper went on to characterize Palmerston's ministry: 'A foreigner has said of our soldiers, that they were lions led by asses'. It marvelled that a country containing the greatest amount of genius of every description should have entrusted its destiny to the keeping of one 'stupendous quack, with his underlings, mental imbeciles, noble dunces, West-end dandies, fashionable fibrils, and antiquated frivolities'.[118]

The *Nonconformist*[119] thought that *Reynolds's Newspaper* had overreacted. It considered that the current 'popular delusion' about Palmerston was perhaps not entirely unjustified. After all, said the paper, he had been a vigorous and moderately successful war minister who boldly took office when other men shrank from the responsibility. From Russia he obtained a peace generally admitted to be honourable to all parties. He showed courage, sagacity, and address in his conduct of affairs during that eventful period and the country was grateful to him. Thus, Palmerston was worthy of esteem and regard, said the paper; but to show the gratitude of the country by making his name a substitute for political principles, and his continuance in office the end and purpose of a general election, was to evince much the same incoherency as did those silly constituencies who, because a man had done something famous, however ignorant or careless of politics he might be, forthwith sent him to the House of Commons.[120]

Charles Greville also lamented the 'egregious folly of the country' at Palmerston's being made such an idol in this ridiculous way.[121] But although

117. It was a radical weekly journal launched by G. W. M. Reynolds in 1849. See Koss, *Political Press*, v. 1, p. 89.
118. *Reynolds's Newspaper*, 22 March 1857. It is said that Disraeli had done well for having resisted in 1850 the approaches by G. W. M. Reynolds for a liaison with the paper which was 'marked by an unsettled Radicalism that did not stop short of republicanism.' Koss, *Political Press*, v. 1, p. 89.
119. The founder and editor of the *Nonconformist* was Edward Miall, who had voted against Palmerston in the House of Commons and who was to lose his seat for Rochdale in the coming election. See A. Miall, *The Life of Edward Miall* (London, Macmillan, 1884).
120. *Nonconformist*, 25 March 1857.
121. Greville diary, 24 March 1857, in *Leaves from the Greville Diary*, p. 785.

The rhetoric of imperialism

the British electorate was to remove the firebrand from office less than a year after the 1857 election, at the time of that election, there was, as Lord Shaftesbury observed, 'no measure, no principle, no cry . . . but simply, were you, or were you not . . . for Palmerston'.[122]

VIII. Down with the 'Chinese Coalition'

The story is incomplete without quoting some more of the press denigrations of the opposition leaders, by way of highlighting the 'Palmerstonian Mania'. Of Richard Cobden, *Punch* had this to say:

> Richard Cobden has a knack,
> Talk away, Yeh-o, boys
> Of hauling down the Union Jack,
> Assailed by any foe, boys.
> Come Pope, come Czar, come Savage – why
> I know not, still his best he'll try
> To make old England's colours lie
> In degradation low, boys.[123]

With regard to Lord Aberdeen,[124] the *Morning Post* supposed that no man of fairness, sense, or spirit could say otherwise than that it would be ungrateful and unjust to change a premier of spirit, energy, and vigour, thoroughly British to the heart's core, for a half-hearted, half-resolved, metaphysical minister, wanting political pluck and manhood, 'like Lord Aberdeen'.[125] As for Sir James Graham or Mr Gladstone, the *Morning Post* said that 'though the one is able as a debater and administrator, and the other as a dialectician and casuist, yet they are both so indirect and tortuous in all their ways, that the national gorge rises at the very thought of them'. There remained Lord Derby, 'whose failure is too recent to allow him to hope for a new lease of power'.[126]

With respect to the so-called Chinese Coalition, *The Times* thought that the country would never forget that in the hour of trial, when the destiny of the empire was imperilled, their courage failed them – they trembled in the presence of danger. Therefore, the paper judged that the advent to office of Lord Derby and the coalitionists would be a national calamity.[127] As we shall see in Chapter 12, this comment by the editor of *The Times* was apparently prompted by Lord Clarendon.

122. Quoted in Woodward, *The Age of Reform*, p. 162.
123. *Punch*, 14 March 1857, p. 101. The tune was that of 'British Sailors Have a Knack', probably a sea shanty.
124. He was a former prime minister. See J. B. Conacher, *The Aberdeen Coalition, 1852–1855: A Study in Mid-Nineteenth-Century Party Politics* (Cambridge University Press, 1968).
125. *Morning Post*, 25 March 1857.
126. Ibid.
127. *The Times*, 14 March 1847.

Punch added: 'Disraeli whines over the death of Party. However, he can congratulate himself upon one party being still in existence. For, since Russell, Roebuck, and Gladstone have joined him on the China question, he may indeed be proud of being at the head of a Small Tea Party'.[128] With regard to Cobden's party, Mr Punch claimed that a splendid banner was being worked at Manchester, by order of the Peace Society, that Mr Cobden and his party might go to the country under it. Its material was said to be superior calico, printed with the device of a willow pattern and the motto of "Cant On"'.Then there was a 'Nickname for Gladstone's Coalition – "The Oxford Sausage"'.[129] And this coalition was not going to last:

> Coalition hot;
>   Coalition cold;
> Coalition gone to pot,
>   'Ere a month is told.[130]

Predictably, the powerful parliamentary speeches by the so-called coalition were used against them in the electioneering campaign:

> When Derby last on place began
>   To cast a longing eye,
> He entertained three serving men
>   And all of them were – sly.
>
> The first he was a Jesuit,
>   The second a Charlatan,
> The third he was a Peacemonger,
>   And all for the Derby ran.
>
> The Jesuit he loved splitting hairs,
>   The Charlatan an apt rap;[131]
> But the Peacemonger loved downright cant,
>   Adroitly mixed with clap-trap.

128. *Punch*, 14 March 1857, p. 110. For Roebuck, see R. E. Leader, *Life and Letters of John Arthur Roebuck, PC, QC, MP with Chapters of Autobiography* (London, Edward Arnold 1897). The reference to a Small Tea Party is doubtless an allusion to the Boston Tea Party, in which a group in disguise boarded British vessels in Boston Harbour to throw overboard the chests of tea with which the ships were loaded. *Punch* was probably suggesting thereby that these men were anti-imperialist and subversive.
129. *Punch*, 14 March 1857, p. 110.
130. Ibid., 21 March 1857, p. 112. This seems to be based on the nursery rhyme: 'Pease Porridge Hot'; see Iona Opie and Peter Opie (eds.), *The Oxford Book of Nursery Rhymes* (Oxford, Clarendon Press, 1951), No. 400, on p. 345.
131. A rap was a counterfeit coin, worth about half a farthing, which passed for half a penny in Ireland in the eighteenth century owing to the scarcity of genuine money (*Shorter Oxford Dictionary*, v. 2, p. 1746); hence the expression 'not worth a rap'. But here, 'rap' is used in the modern sense of 'discussion', to go with 'cant' and 'clap-trap'.

The rhetoric of imperialism

> The Jesuit's splitting his hairs in vain,
>   In vain does the Charlatan rail,
> And the Peacemonger hates to be joked on the point,
>   But – his cant's uncommonly stale.[132]

Then came this rousing question: 'On the re-election of any of the Chinese members, will they be required to take the usual form of oath, or like their brethren at Canton, will they merely break a saucer?'[133] And this comment: if the emperor of China would like to decorate the 'Chinese members' with peacock's feathers, the British public would gladly supply the tar.[134]

Some opposition newspapers feared that such vicious attacks on the integrity of those who opposed jingoism would endanger the seats of the most independent and conscientious members of the House and threaten the country with a parliament pledged to support the 'turbulent and aggressive foreign policy' of the prime minister. 'It remains, indeed, to be seen whether the present excitement will not wear itself out before the time for the actual election arrives, and be succeeded by a reaction in favour of moderation and justice', wrote the *Manchester Guardian*. This newspaper found that the cries of the 'vindication of the honour of our flag' and the necessity of 'upholding our representatives at a distance' carried a great deal of weight with the constituencies.[135]

The *Morning Star* regretted that the brazen imposture of Palmerstonianism threatened to paralyse the honest judgement of Englishmen.[136] It hoped that the public would soon begin to see the trap set for them. It felt that, understandably, Lord Palmerston's game was to hurry on the elections before the people awoke out of their temporary infatuation.[137] Such a view sounds very much like one coming from Richard Cobden, and it could well have been, as the paper was 'a sounding-board for the two politicians whose names were most closely identified with it'[138] – Cobden and Bright.[139]

But the Palmerstonian bandwagon continued to gather momentum – and the principal targets of its rhetoric were the 'stars' of the *Arrow* show – Russell, Gladtone, and Cobden himself.

IX. 'Johnny' is on his knees

As mentioned in Chapter 9, Lord John Russell[140] challenged the government to say they had a justifiable cause of war with China, 'or any right to claim the

---

132. *Punch*, 28 March 1857, p. 121.
133. Ibid., 21 March 1857, p. 119.
134. Ibid., 28 March 1857, p. 122,
135. *Manchester Guardian*, 18 March 1857.
136. *Morning Star*, 20 March 1857.
137. Ibid., 28 March 1857.
138. Koss, *Political Press*, v. 1, p. 110.
139. Bright was overseas at this time, and that leaves Cobden. See later in this chapter.
140. When the Crimean crisis loomed large and the Queen sent for Lord John Russell,

revision of our treaties' with her.[141] Palmerston accepted the challenge and did make such a statement. Russell found out in no time that he had made himself very unpopular in his constituency, the City of London. Not only the merchant princes in the City, but those as far afield as Bristol confessed they were 'grieved and astonished' to learn of Russell's behaviour in Parliament.[142]

On 10 March 1857, the City of London Liberal Registration Association held a general meeting at the London Tavern to consider the question of nominations for the coming election. Considerable interest was aroused; and reporters from all the daily newspapers arrived, only to be barred at the door. What did the association have to hide from the public eye? The subsequent resolution spoke for itself: only businessmen might be nominated for the coming general election, so that the interests of the City might be more truly represented. The target was obvious: Russell was neither a businessmen nor had he represented the interests of the City when he tackled Palmerston recently in the House of Commons. A carefully prepared digest of the proceedings was subsequently released. In it, 'Russell's retirement from the contest' was announced, as it turned out, without Russell's prior knowledge. The announcement was received with 'a cold and most significant silence'.[143]

The City magnates were not exactly consistent. Had they not just invited Palmerston to stand? But Palmerston stood up for their interests, they might well have argued, although he was not a businessmen. Clearly, the key question was not so much that the candidates had to be businessmen, but that they must promote, at least defend, the commercial interests of the City. According to the duke of Argyll, Russell was told by all his City friends that he did not stand a chance of reelection. Apparently this was impressed on him so universally, by those who knew the constituency best, that he decided to give up.[144]

But obviously it was difficult for a former prime minister, who still had a promising future career, to abandon such an important seat. The next day Russell tried to retrieve the situation by addressing his electors in writing: 'On looking carefully over the papers relating to this subject, I found that in the miserable affair of the *Arrow*, reprisals had been resorted to, and reparation offered'. What aggravated the issue was Bowring's sudden grafting of the

>   Palmerston magnanimously consented to serve again under 'Johnny', but Russell failed to form a ministry.
> 141. Russell, 26 February 1857, Hansard, 3d series, v. 144, cols. 1472–3. It will be remembered that John Russell was a Whig, a former Liberal prime minister.
> 142. *Globe*, 7 March 1857, p. 3, col. 5, 'Bristol', quoting the *Bristol Gazette*, 6 March 1857.
> 143. *The Times*, 11 March 1857, p. 12, cols. 3–6, 'Election Intelligence'; col. 3, 'City of London Registration Association'. See also the *Globe*, 11 March 1857, p. 1, col. 4, 'Election Intelligence: City of London Registration Association'.
> 144. Argyll, *Autobiography and Memoirs*, v. 2, pp. 74–5. According to John Prest, Russell merely gave his supporters the impression that he would not stand, and they invited Raikes Currie to take his place (see Prest, *Russell*, p. 379). If so, he was creating a lot of confusion, and not a little difficulty for himself, as we shall see later.

Canton City question onto the *Arrow* dispute. If only the government had announced earlier their intention of despatching a senior person to Hong Kong, 'with instructions to defend the lives and properties of British subjects, and to restore as soon as possible a state of peace', he would have voted with them. He said he was at a loss to perceive why a course advisable on 10 March 1857 should not have been taken on 10 January. Or, if Bowring was worthy of entire approval in January, why he should be virtually superseded now, when his policy and his conduct remained the same.[145]

We can see that, already, Russell had shifted his position from one of taunting the government for their pursuit of naked interests to one of protecting British property and lives overseas.

But his nonrepentance appears to have angered his electors further, and the *Globe* argued against him in a long editorial, saying basically that he did not care about the honour and interests of his country.[146] One almost suspects that Palmerston had a hand in this editorial.[147]

On the afternoon of 13 March 1857, a meeting was held in the Guildhall to consider 'the decision recently come to by the House of Commons relative to the affairs of Canton, and to express its high confidence in Her Majesty's government', pursuant to a requisition from 800 merchants, bankers, traders, and electors of the City of London. Mr Raikes Currie, M. P.,[148] moved that in view of the House of Commons' censure for Palmerston's China policy, the meeting express the conviction that no other course was fairly open to a British statesman or was compatible with safety to the property and lives of 'our fellow-countrymen in that quarter, and with the honour and dignity of the nation'. An amendment was defeated. The original resolution was affirmed by an overwhelming majority, amidst enthusiastic cheering. One of the candidates for the City, R. W. Crawford, then moved that a committee be appointed to draw up an address embodying the resolution to be presented by a deputation to wait upon Lord Palmerston. His motion was adopted unanimously.[149]

It goes without saying that Russell was conspicuously absent from the proceedings in what had been his constituency for sixteen years. The *Globe* commented, 'The voice of the City of London made itself unmistakably heard yesterday in open meeting, and heard in unison with that of all the other

145. Russell, 'Lord John Russell's Address to the Electors of London', *Globe*, Thursday, 12 March 1857, p. 2, col. 6.
146. *Globe*, 12 March 1856, p. 2, cols. 1–2.
147. See Chapter 7 for the close relationship between Palmerston and the *Globe*.
148. Raikes Currie (1801–81) was a banker in London, a Bank of East India proprietor, and a director of the Sun Fire Office. He had been sitting for Northampton since July 1837 (*BMP*, v. 1, p. 98); but now he appears to have set his sights on the City of London.
149. *Globe*, 14 March 1856, p. 1, cols. 5–6, 'Great Meeting in the City of London'.

popular and commercial communities which have already addressed the Prime Minister in the language of confidence and support'.[150]

Russell found it increasingly difficult to sit at home. At the last minute, he changed his mind and spoke on the hustings.[151] What may have encouraged him was the knowledge that Clarendon had put in a good word for him with the City magnates, to Palmerston's disapprobation.[152] Clarendon did not wish to see a former prime minister 'very sore and sour' being relegated to a family borough.[153] Russell also received the assistance of the chief government whip, W. G. Hayter,[154] 'who did everything in his power to help'.[155]

With influential support from such quarters, Russell again tried his luck on 19 March, addressing a crowded meeting at the London Tavern. He began by saying that if a gentleman were disposed to part with his butler, his coachman, or his gamekeeper; or if a merchant were disposed to part with an old servant, a warehouseman, a clerk, or even a porter, he would say to him, 'John (loud laughter) . . .'.[156] The laughter was occasioned by the familiar Russell family way of pronouncing 'John' as 'Jahn'. The storm of laughter ended in tumultuous cheering.[157]

Russell continued with his metaphor: 'John, I think your faculties are somewhat decayed; you are growing old; you have made several mistakes, and I think of putting a young man from Northampton in your place. (Laughter and cheers)'.[158] The Northampton man was Raikes Currie,[159] who, as we have seen, moved a resolution at a public meeting in the Guildhall in support of Palmerston.

Russell went on, 'I think a gentleman would behave in that way to his servant, and thereby give John an opportunity of answering that he thought his faculties were not so much decayed, and that he was able to go on, at all events,

---

150. Ibid., p. 2, col. 2, editorial.
151. Argyll, *Autobiography and Memoirs*, v. 2, pp. 74–5.
152. Palmerston to Clarendon, 24 March 1857, MSS Clar. Dep. C69, quoted in Steele, *Palmerston and Liberalism*, p. 74.
153. Clarendon to Wodehouse, 19 March 1857, BL Add. MSS 46692, quoted in ibid., p. 74.
154. Sir William Goodenough Hayter (1792–1878) became a Queen's counsel in 1839, and was successively judge-advocate-general, financial secretary to the Treasury, and parliamentary and patronage secretary, the latter post which he held until March 1858. He was described as an admirable 'whip'. *DNB*, v. 9, p. 307.
155. Hayter to Russell, 25 March 1857, PRO, 30/22/13C, quoted in Steele, *Palmerston and Liberalism*, p. 74.
156. *The Times*, 20 March 1857, p. 7, cols. 4–6, 'Lord J. Russell in the City': col. 4.
157. Argyll, *Autobiography and Memoirs*, v. 2, p. 75.
158. *The Times*, 20 March 1857, p. 7, cols. 4–6, 'Lord J. Russell in the City': col. 4
159. He had sat for Northampton for more than twenty years. At the general meeting of the City of London Liberal Registration Association, held on 10 March 1857 and at which he was present, he was formally invited to stand as the fourth member. See the *Globe*, 11 March 1857, p. 1, col. 4.

some five or six years longer (cheers)'. In so far as the *Arrow* quarrel was concerned, he insisted that upon reading all the papers, Bowring was not justified in the 'measures of violence he had taken (hisses)', and therefore that it was not consistent with the 'character, the reputation, and the honour of the British nation to approve of those proceedings. (Hear hear)'.[160]

Russell professed that he could answer for himself and thought that he could answer for some forty-eight gentlemen who, sitting on the Liberal side of the House, came to the same conclusion, and gave the same vote as Sir Francis Baring, that none of them had any concert or combination with any other party.[161] Here, he was discreetly denying the charge, levelled by Palmerston, that he was part of the so-called Chinese Coalition. He went further, 'My decided opinion is that Lord Palmerston's Government ought to be supported. (Hear hear)'.[162]

Thereupon, Mr Bennoch moved that the meeting had heard with satisfaction the manly determination of Lord John Russell to appeal to the electors of the City of London, and thereby pledged their utmost support. Speaking to his motion, Bennoch condemned the decision of the Registration Association as improper, unwise, and indiscreet, as seeming to say, 'Commercial men only ought to represent the City of London; we are commercial men; and we must represent the City'. His motion was seconded and put to a vote. At first there were about twenty hands held up against it, but upon the negative being put a second time the number was reduced to half-a-dozen. The chairman then declared the resolution to have been carried *nemine contradicente.*[163]

The duke of Argyll praised Russell's performance, saying that Russell called his constituency his master, and pleaded that an old servant ought not to be dismissed without being given an opportunity to explain himself. He put it down as 'a specimen of the great qualities of courage which were inherent in the man'.[164]

The *Globe* made an about-turn. It now declared that it should view with regret any mischance which should exclude Russell from the House of Commons for a single day or inflict upon him the mortification even of a cold return. It regarded Russell as occupying a position before the country which rendered him 'independent of the passing question of the day'.[165] If Palmerston had been contributing directly to the columns of the *Globe* 'and to the pockets of its editors',[166] we may assume that Russell now had the blessing of the prime minister.

160. *The Times*, 20 March 1857, p. 7, cols. 4–6, 'Lord J. Russell in the City': col. 4.
161. Ibid., col. 4.
162. Ibid., col. 5.
163. Ibid., col. 6. Liberally translated from Latin, *nemine contradicente* means 'no one contradicting'.
164. Argyll, *Autobiography and Memoirs*, v. 2, pp. 74–5.
165. *Globe*, 20 March 1857, p. 2, col. 1, editorial.
166. Koss, *Political Press*, v. 1, p. 45.

Argyll thought that Russell had won over his electors by his 'Jahn' performance.[167] The very fact of the *Globe*'s volte-face indicates that the battle was far from over. Russell had to fight the four 'Liberal and Commercial' candidates, as they were called (Rothschild, Duke, Crawford, and Currie). Indeed, *The Times* commented that his principal hope of success was based on the probability that the electors who had any cause for dissatisfaction with any one of the four commercial candidates would eliminate the least popular name from their ticket.[168] With the resources of the City of London Liberal Registration Association at their disposal, canvassing by the commercial candidates was reported to be more systematic and better organized than that of Russell, who depended entirely on the efforts of a corps of volunteers.

The Times observed that subsequent attempts to dislodge Russell on 25 March had failed, but gave no details.[169] Apparently the City of London Liberal Registration Association had held a meeting in yet another attempt to discredit Russell. But Baron Rothschild[170] broke ranks; whereupon the chairman (unidentified) asked whether or not the baron wanted to act in concert with the other three candidates. Rothschild gave a noncommittal answer, amidst cheers, laughter, and some confusion. A resolution in support of the four commercial candidates was put to a show of hands, and lost; thereupon, the motion in favour of Russell was submitted to the vote and was carried amid loud cheers and by a large majority.[171]

In this fluid situation, Russell had to work harder still for his seat. He dramatically modified his tone towards Palmerston: 'I quite allow that Lord Palmerston is a man who is fit to preside over the councils of this empire. (Loud cheers and faint hisses)'. The cheers were probably for Palmerston, and the hisses for Russell's about-turn. Russell was not deterred from his praise of Palmerston: 'I think he deserves the support of the House of Commons and of the nation (cheers)'. There followed a few dignified words of self-defence: 'But I cannot admit that if the House of Commons come to a vote adverse to the Government they ... are to be stigmatised as desiring to make the degradation and humiliation of their country a steppingstone to power. (Cheers)'. He insisted that the House of Commons should be independent, and ought to vote upon the merit of every question. They might make mistakes, but they must not be 'browbeaten as they have been by any Minister. (Cheers)'.[172]

---

167. Argyll, *Autobiography and Memoirs*, v. 2, pp. 74–5.
168. *The Times*, 25 March 1857, p. 8, col. 3.
169. Ibid.
170. For a history of the Rothschild family, see Derek Wilson, *Rothschild: A Story of Wealth and Power* (London, Deutsch, 1988).
171. *Globe*, 26 March 1857, p. 1, col. 5.
172. *The Times*, 28 March 1857, p. 5, col. 3.

The rhetoric of imperialism

Russell was back in the running, although the merchant princes had earlier 'turned their princely backs' on him.[173] The casualty in this exercise seems to have been Raikes Currie. Dazzled by the prospect of replacing Russell in the 'Imperial City of London, which was justly entitled to lead and guide the country',[174] he had abandoned his safe seat at Northampton. His motion in support of Palmerston, embodying a thinly veiled attack on Russell, had been carried with acclamation at a public meeting in the Guildhall only four days previously.[175] Now that Russell had launched a successful comeback, Currie had to make his speech amidst so many cheers and expressions of disapprobation that he was unable to obtain a hearing from the audience. In the end, he turned to the reporters on his left and addressed his speech to them. When a show of hands was called, three-quarters were for Russell and one-quarter for Currie.[176]

A poll was then demanded on behalf of Currie, whereupon the Crier of the Court read out a list of the polling places and announced that the poll would be taken the day after (i.e., 28 March 1857), between 8 A.M. and 4 P.M. The subsequent poll put Russell third among the four candidates elected.[177]

It is said that thereafter Russell was careful not to neglect the opinion of his constituency.[178] In terms of the origins of the *Arrow* War, did pressure from the commercial interests play a similar role in the causation of the war? We shall explore this issue in Part Five. As for Lord John Russell, when he came to write his memoirs, of the *Arrow* War debate and the Chinese Election he had not a single word to say.[179]

---

173. Steel, *Palmerston and Liberalism*, p. 75, quoting D. MacCarthy and A. Russell, *Lady John Russell: A Memoir* (London, 1926), p. 170: Lord John Russell to Lady Melgund, 1 April 1857; and PRO, 30/22/13C, Russell to Elliot, 4 April 1857.
174. *The Times*, 28 March 1857, p. 5, col. 2, to p. 6, col. 2, 'The Elections: Nominations': p. 5, col. 4.
175. *Globe*, 14 March 1856, p. 1, cols. 5–6, 'Great Meeting in the City of London'.
176. *The Times*, 28 March 1857, p. 5, col. 2, to p. 6, col. 2, 'The Elections: Nominations': p. 5, col. 4. As for the other three candidates, for Baron Rothschild about half the hands of the assemblage were held up, for Sir J. Duke about the same, while Mr Crawford had not quite so many.
177. Prest, *Russell*, p. 379.
178. Taylor, *The Decline of British Radicalism*, p. 283, quoting M. B. Baer, 'The Politics of London, 1852–1868: Parties, Voters, and Representation', 2 vs. Unpublished D.Phil. thesis, University of Iowa, 1976, v. 1, pp. 163–9.
179. There is a complete blank about the Chinese Election in Earl Russell, *Recollections and Suggestions, 1813–1873*, 2d ed. (London, Longmans, Green, 1875). Therein, we find a quantum leap from chapter 6, which deals with the ministry of Lord Aberdeen and the origins of the Crimean War, to chapter 7, which deals with British foreign policy from 1859 to the death of Lord Palmerston. The words 'China' and '*Arrow*' do not exist in the Index either. There are entries in the Index for the general elections of 1807, 1841, 1868, and 1874, but not that of 1857.

X. The raging 'Jesuit'

Gladstone[180] offered himself for reelection as member for the University of Oxford. He was unopposed, yet for a man who was anxious to make his views known, he had to operate under a great handicap. He was not allowed to make speeches, only to leave his card at the Common Rooms of the Colleges. This imposition of silence was a severe restriction to a man who, for volubility of utterance, memory, and calculating powers, hardly had an equal. 'He is denied the auxiliaries of brass bands and strong ale, of processions and banners, and all the vulgar resources on which common men rely, and has not even their chances for displaying his unsurpassed fecundity of political expression'.[181]

But according to the duke of Argyll, Gladstone did something quite novel. He made a speech 'in every town – every village – every cottage – everywhere where he had room to stand'.[182] He wondered 'what chance could there be of such a man as Gladstone being just or temperate when he was raging about the country, addressing mobs entirely ignorant of the subject?'[183]

Gladstone's diaries reveal that on Monday, 23 March 1857, he went back to his property at Hawarden, near Chester. From there, he went electioneering at Chester, Rhyl, Flint, Buckley, Mold, Holywell, Mostyn, Bistre, Hope, and Liverpool, all within a day's return journey from his home.[184] We may observe that Gladstone's peregrinations about Flintshire foreshadowed his Midlothian campaign (1878–80).[185] In this sense, Argyll's observation about Gladstone's behaviour being an innovation of the Chinese Election is noteworthy.

In fact, Gladstone was canvassing for his brother-in-law, Sir Stephen Glynne.[186] On Saturday, 4 April, he went off at nine to the nomination at Flint, where he 'nearly split his chest' in speaking against some thirty roarers.[187] The hustings were erected at the back of the shire hall. Several thousand persons assembled to witness the proceedings, which lasted nearly three hours and

---

180. In press satire, Gladstone was often referred to as the 'Jesuit', apparently for two reasons: first, he was a 'high church' Anglican and very ostentatiously religious; and second, for his 'jesuitical' reasoning, so-called after the kind of specious argumentation for which the Jesuit Order was famous. The Jesuits being Catholics, this nickname was apparently chosen for its appeal to the entrenched antipapist feeling in England.
181. *The Times*, 12 March 1847.
182. Argyll, *Autobiography and Memoirs*, v. 2, p. 75.
183. Ibid., v. 2, p. 76.
184. *Gladstone's Diaries*, v. 5, pp. 208–13: Monday, 23 March, to Monday, 6 April 1857.
185. See Matthew, *Gladstone, 1875–1898*, chapter 2.
186. *The Times* (6 April 1857, p. 7, col. 4) said that Glynne had represented the county of Flintshire in two parliaments, from 1837 to 1847. In fact, Sir Stephen Richard Glynne (1807–74), baronet, had sat for Flintshire in the parliaments of 1831, 1832, 1835, and 1837, was not returned in 1841, but succeeded on petition; thereupon he sat until 1847 (*BMP*, v. 1, p. 158). Now, in 1857, he wanted to sit for Flintshire again and apparently asked Gladstone to help.
187. *Gladstone Diaries*, v. 5, p. 212.

were of 'the most uproarious character'. The sitting member, Mostyn,[188] was the first to speak. He taunted Gladstone by asserting that the electors would tell Gladstone 'his eloquence was deceptive, his promises illusory and that all his fair speeches would be in vain. (Cheers)'. Mostyn himself relied on jingoism: 'What patriot would have denied his support to Lord Palmerston in carrying to a successful and honourable termination a great war?' Thereupon a voice from the crowd shrieked: 'Gladstone did'.[189] Glynne spoke next and carefully avoided any reference to the *Arrow* quarrel.[190] Gladstone then tried to speak in support of Glynne, but constantly there were: 'Violent interruption', 'Groans and hisses', 'Great laughter and cheers', and 'Violent commotion', although he referred to 'the war in China' only once and only with those words.[191] The endless uproar was reported to be a determined attempt by a portion of the mob to prevent his being heard.[192]

When the votes were counted on Tuesday, 7 April 1857, Gladstone's gallant efforts to help his brother-in-law had all failed.[193] He wrote, 'We digested as well as we could the defeat of yesterday which cut us deeply rather as a scandal & offence of the county than as a personal or family disappointment'.[194] On 9 April, Gladstone went back to London, but 'the affairs of Tuesday' remained 'bad to feed or sleep upon'.[195]

XI. The 'peacemonger' takes refuge in Huddersfield

> And, Cobden, if you dare contest the West Riding,
> Oh won't you just get, as the boys say, a hiding
> Unless that same Riding, whose saddle you sit in,
> Indeed, is a province of Russia, not Britain.[196]

Cobden saw that the signs were ominous. He decided to abandon his Yorkshire seat of West Riding, whereupon the sitting member for Huddersfield, Lord Goderich, was put forward by the Liberal Party as a candidate.[197] Thinking that he might have a chance at Huddersfield, Cobden went there to campaign

---

188. The Hon. Thomas E. Mostyn Lloyd-Mostyn (1830–61) went to Eton and Christ Church, Oxford. A Liberal in favour of a large extension of the ballot, he was first elected for Flintshire in 1854, when his father, who had wrested the seat from Glynne in 1847, succeeded to a peerage. *BMP*, v. 1, p. 279.
189. *The Times*, Monday, 6 April 1857, p. 7, col. 4, 'Flintshire', Mostyn's speech.
190. Ibid., 'Flintshire', Glynne's speech.
191. Ibid., cols. 4–5, 'Flintshire', Gladstone's speech.
192. Ibid., col. 4, 'Flintshire'.
193. Morley, *Gladstone*, v. 1, p. 421.
194. *The Gladstone Diaries*, v. 5, p. 213, Wednesday, 8 April 1857.
195. Ibid., p. 214, Thursday, 9 April 1857.
196. *Punch*, 14 March 1857, p. 103.
197. *The Times*, 13 March 1857.

instead.[198] Swapping battlefields, however, did not mean changing the battle cry. As he told Sir James Graham, 'Were I in your position, I would fight the battle on the Chinese question, and make the people thoroughly understand it'.[199]

On 21 March he addressed a crowded gathering in the local theatre at Huddersfield. He began by referring at great length to the affairs in China and alluded minutely to all the circumstances connected with the *Arrow*. He reminded the meeting that his motion had had the support of every man of intellect, including Lord Goderich (who had just left Huddersfield to campaign for Cobden's old seat of the West Riding), Lord John Russell, Sir Francis Baring, and 'every man in the House who was not in the government but who had been in office', except Mr Ellice,[200] who, in his subsequent election address, 'condemned his own vote' for Palmerston.[201]

The reception of the audience was rapturous, with so much thumbing in the air but particularly stamping on the floor that one of the overcrowded side galleries gave way. Confusion ensued and, a rush being made towards the exits and the stage, great fear was entertained that many people might be trampled underfoot. Cobden wisely decided not to continue his speech, and the assembly separated as quietly as they could under the circumstances.[202]

Cobden persevered next day in the gymnasium-hall, in which a meeting was convened by circular. There was a 'most crowded attendance of electors at the appointed time', and on presenting himself, Cobden was received with 'immense cheering'. He began by recapitulating his arguments on the Chinese question, and then went on to elucidate his political views. In the end a motion was passed declaring him a fit and proper person to represent the borough. The result was received with rounds of applause.[203]

Thereafter, Cobden conducted an active canvass, holding two or three meetings each day in Huddersfield and the villages within the borough. On 24 March, he addressed a gathering of between 3,000 and 4,000 at the Queen's Hotel. As usual, he began with the *Arrow* question. Referring to the appointment of Lord Elgin, he expressed a very strong suspicion that there had been 'a trick on the part of the government' to exploit the *Arrow* affair so as to achieve 'a minority and get a dissolution', because, Cobden believed,

198. Morley, *Cobden*, p. 655.
199. Quoted in Parker, *Life and Letters of Sir James Graham, Second Baronet of Netherby, 1792–1861*, v. 2, p. 303.
200. Edward Ellice the younger (1810–80) went to Eton and Trinity College, Cambridge. At the by-election of 1837 he was elected member for Huddersfield. When Parliament was dissolved he was returned for St Andrews burgs and represented the constituency for forty-two years, on every occasion maintaining the principles of free trade. *DNB*, v. 6, pp. 665–6.
201. *The Times*, 21 March 1857, p. 8, col. 2.
202. Ibid., col. 3.
203. Ibid., 23 March 1857, p. 9, col. 4.

The rhetoric of imperialism

Palmerston did not have a domestic policy with which to appeal to the country.[204] On the question of national prestige, he proclaimed that all the world in arms could not disgrace the British flag, 'if it had right and justice on its side. (Cheers)'.

When the ballots were counted, Cobden polled only 590 votes, against 823 for his opponent.[205] It would seem that the thousands of people who swarmed to hear him in Huddersfield came only for the beer.[206]

XII. A parliament of 'nobodies'

At Manchester, Cobden's close associate, John Bright,[207] was at the bottom of the poll. Another of his colleagues, Thomas Milner-Gibson, also lost his seat in that city. 'Nothing had been seen like it since the disappearance of the Peace Whigs in 1812, when Brougham, Romilly, Tierney, Lamb, and Horner all lost their seats'.[208] Argyll rejoiced that 'our foes were scattered like chaff before the wind, and the peace party and the Manchester party were wiped out of the House of Commons'.[209] Even Prince Albert was moved to describe it as 'an instance in our Parliamentary history without parallel'.[210]

The Chinese Election was thus in many ways unprecedented.

It became a self-fulfilling prophecy to say that the 'most independent and conscientious members of the House'[211] might lose their seats. It was estimated that no less than one-sixth of the most conspicuous men in the former House of Commons were thrust out.[212] Thereupon *Punch* commented, 'From the

204. Ibid., 25 March 1857, p. 8, cols. 2–3.
205. Morley, *Cobden*, p. 657.
206. Obviously, the majority was not enfranchised. It has been estimated that the electorate at this time was only about 1,430,000 (see Smith, *Second Reform Bill* , p. 2) in a population of 28,427,000 (Parl. Papers 1861, v. 58, p. 627). There was a large population of artisans who were quite separate from the improvident, 'irredeemably dangerous and depraved' masses, and who read the penny press which opened to them a new world of political information; but they were not entitled to vote. This is perhaps why the proliberal crowds that swarmed to hear Cobden did not materialize in the polling booths. Subsequently the Second Reform Bill, when passed in 1867, increased the electorate to 2,470,000 (Smith, *Second Reform Bill*, p. 2), with rather different implications for imperial policy. It was 'the crucial Act in that process by which Britain, alone among large European nations, peacefully adjusted her institutions to meet the emergence of a powerful working class' (ibid., p. 3).
207. As mentioned, John Bright (1811–88) was a cotton spinner and manufacturer in Rochdale. He had sat for Manchester since July 1847. See Roberston, *John Bright*, and Robins, *John Bright*.
208. Morley, *Cobden*, p. 657.
209. Argyll, *Autobiography and Memoirs*, v. 2, p. 74
210. Queen Victoria, *The Letters of Queen Victoria: A Selection from Her Majesty's Correspondence between the Years 1837 and 1861*, ed. Arthur Christopher Benson and Viscount Esher, 3 vs. (London, John Murray, 1908), p. 300: 4 September 1858.
211. *Manchester Guardian*, 18 March 1857.
212. Morley, *Gladstone*, v. 1, p. 421.

number of nobodies that are returned to Parliament, we are afraid that the next Session may already be characterised, in the Palmerstonian phrase, as "[a] fortuitous concurrence of atoms"'. So small were some of the atoms, observed Mr Punch, that he feared the Queen would have to open Parliament with a microscope.[213]

These 'nobodies' were 'a new breed of radical politician, adventurers and job-hunters'.[214] They have been described as unprincipled, 'whose notion of the national interest was as short as their pockets were deep'.[215] The return of members with Bank of England or East India Company backgrounds, among them Wigram Crawford, raised fears that the 'worship of Mammon' had seized the London electorate.[216] This is interesting to our pursuit of the origins of the *Arrow* War: To what extent did this mercantile faction influence Whitehall?

Before we come to that question, however, mention should be made of some survivors. At Sheffield, John Roebuck continued his attack on Palmerston's China policy, describing the *Arrow* quarrel as the pretext for England's renown being cast into the dust, degraded, and made dishonourable. He was reelected.[217]

At Carlisle, Sir James Graham withstood the popular cry for war. 'I voted against war with China eighteen years ago', he said, 'I voted against it yesterday, I would do so again to-morrow ... Englishmen ought to fight their equals, not to trample on their inferiors'.[218] Graham was returned at the head of the poll.[219]

In South Wiltshire, Sidney Herbert continued his parliamentary theme: 'When we got into difficulties with China, our agents did not act with that spirit of plain dealing which ought to characterise all our transactions with foreign nations'. In his opinion that was 'thoroughly repugnant to all principles of fair dealing and a disgrace to British diplomacy'.[220] He was returned.

At Buckinghamshire, Disraeli declared that the plea for dissolution was only a pretext because, since the dissolution, Palmerston had announced that his agent in China would be superseded, 'thus acknowledging the justness of the

---

213. *Punch*, 11 April 1857, p. 148.
214. Taylor, *Decline of British Radicalism*, p. 280.
215. Ibid., p. 282.
216. Ibid., p. 280, quoting the *Examiner*, 4 April 1857, p. 208; and the speech of William Wilkinson at Lambeth, in *The Times*, 1 April 1857, p. 5.
217. Hawkins, *Parliament*, p. 74.
218. Quoted in Charles Parker, *Life and Letter of Sir James Graham*, v. 2, p. 305. For a fairly full reproduction of his speech, see the *Globe*, 28 March 1857, p. 4, col. 4.
219. Reportedly, one of his audience said: 'I never recollect witnessing so complete a triumph over adverse and suspicious feelings in so brief a space of time'. See Parker, *Life and Letter of Sir James Graham*, v. 2, p. 305.
220. See his speech in the *Globe*, 20 March 1857, p. 1, col. 4.

vote of the House of Commons'.[221] He was returned unopposed – 'a bloodless victory, but not less a triumph', he said.[222]

XIII. Election postmortem

A dominant interpretation of Palmerston's victory has been, for a long time, his personal popularity, particularly his recent triumph in the Crimean War.[223] To some extent, the findings in this chapter reinforce that interpretation.

Conversely, why did the opposition poll so badly?

A dissolution of Parliament, or 'an appeal to the country', observed *The Times*, was not merely 'an appeal from a small to a large body of men, but from a class to the nation – from a special to the general public, from sophisticated to natural opinion'.[224] By 1857, the Parliament was already four years old. It was said that a parliament of that age could have lost a good deal of its rapport with the public mind. The opposition all thought that they were doing what would be immensely popular. 'They firmly expected that the country would be with them in their denunciations of the Canton bombardment and their technical triumph about the expired register', said *The Times*. 'If Mr Disraeli, for instance, had not considered the question a suitable one for the great pitched battle of the Session, he would certainly have waited'. They read the blue book and 'thought their triumph certain'.[225]

Did Disraeli really think in the way alleged by *The Times*? We shall find out when we probe behind the scenes in the next part of this book. Even if he did not, he would have been overruled by his chief, Lord Derby, in which case we need simply replace the name Disraeli with Derby and *The Times*'s case remains the same.

But they had scarcely gained the parliamentary victory when they found they were lost men. The country rose with a cry of indignation. 'It is scarcely possible to find any one who does not condemn in the strongest terms the conduct of the Coalition', commented *The Times*. Merchants, tradesmen, squires, clergyman, farmers, all joined in declaiming against the late vote. Thus, all opposition members were 'forced to go to their constituencies with apologies and expressions of penitence, because they had no conception that in attacking the Minister who had restored the country to its place in Europe they had touched the ark of England's national feeling'.[226]

Recent scholarship, particularly thematic studies such as those on Victorian

221. Disraeli's address to his constituents, in the *Globe*, 19 March 1857, p. 1, col. 5.
222. Quoted in Buckle, *Benjamin Disraeli*, v. 4, p. 75.
223. This interpretation dominates the biographies of Palmerston and some of his contemporaries, especially those in the *DNB*.
224. *The Times*, 16 March 1857.
225. Ibid.
226. Ibid.

politics, radicalism, and liberalism, have provided perspectives different from the overwhelming emphasis on Palmerston's personal popularity. Next to the *Arrow* quarrel, for example, the question as to whether candidates had local constituency connections has been spotted as the most commonly mentioned issue in the election addresses.[227] This has effectively undermined the thesis that the 1857 election was a 'plebiscite' dominated by Palmerston alone,[228] and has subsequently been conceptualized as a contest between attention to local issues (which the electors wanted) and parliamentary independence (upon which the candidates insisted).[229]

Among the examples cited to support this concept was the dumping of Lord John Russell as a candidate for the City of London on the grounds that the constituency wanted to be represented by men connected with the City and not 'statesmen' who would be prevented from devoting time to their constituents.[230] In the context of the present analysis, we are bound to observe that the major interest of the City constituents was in all descriptions of business connected with the China and India trade; and Russell had committed the unforgivable act of challenging Palmerston, successfully, to admit in the House of Commons that the government had sought to extend the China trade by rather ungentlemanly means. In a strange way, therefore, this new interpretation of British political behaviour reinforces the significance of the *Arrow* quarrel in the so-called Chinese Election.

Russell's subsequent reelection excluded only the weakest of the four 'commercial candidates', Raikes Currie. Wigram Crawford got in, and as a senior partner in a firm that had substantial business interests in China and as a deputy governor of the Bank of England, he would be a powerful ally to Samuel Gregson, the chairman of the East India and China Association of London and proprietor of Gregson and Co.

With this, we find ourselves entering the latest debate on imperialism – gentlemanly capitalism.[231] One argument in that theory is that the gentlemanly capitalists in the City, by virtue of their proximity to Whitehall, exercised much

227. Jackson, 'The British General Elections of 1857 and 1859', p. 149; see also Hawkins, *Parliament*, p. 65.
228. See A. J. P. Taylor, 'Palmerston', in his *Essays in English History* (London, Hamilton, 1976); and Gavin, 'Palmerston's Policy towards East and West Africa, 1830–1865', p. 9. Before them, G. E. Buckle said the same thing (see *The Life of Benjamin Disraeli*, v. 4, p. 74).
229. See Taylor, *Decline of British Radicalism*, pp. 275–8. This included independence from blind loyalty to party. Thus, Miles Taylor has observed that throughout the election campaign Palmerston 'emphasised the importance of party loyalty to stable government and denigrated parliamentary independence as faction and self-aggrandisement'. In this sense, the idea of the Liberal Party as a broad church, 'built around the twin altars of Whiggery and radicalism, was shattered by the results of the 1857 election' (ibid., p. 280) – another landmark of the Chinese Election.
230. Taylor, *Decline of British Radicalism*, p. 277, quoting the *Daily News* (11 March 1857, p. 5; 14 March 1857, p. 3; 18 March 1857, pp. 5–6), and *The Times* (18 March 1857, p. 5).
231. See Cain and Hopkins, *British Imperialism*.

influence on Britain's imperial policy. The initial rejection of Lord John Russell by his City electorate, the intervention of the foreign secretary, and the consequent reinstatement of this future prime minister all indicate the close relationship between the City and the Foreign Office, and thereby lend support to the theory. To what extent, then, did these gentlemanly capitalists actually influence the specific policies of the Foreign Office, especially policies towards the *Arrow* War? The evidence so far indicates that they fervently *supported* the aggressive policy already decided upon by the government; there is no suggestion that they helped formulate such a policy. If this is indeed the case, the 'gentlemanly capitalism' interpretation of British imperialism at this time is severely qualified. Later, we shall explore this facet further.

In a related vein, the Lancashire merchants threw out that group of outstanding men who, as the Manchester school, had made Manchester a power in the nation. At Manchester itself, the merchants repudiated their most able spokesmen, John Bright[232] and Thomas Milner-Gibson.[233] Such an action has been described as suicidal, committed at a time when the cotton trade needed all the political influence it could muster to persuade the British East India Company to listen to its needs. Cobden, Bright, and Milner-Gibson were political personalities to be reckoned with and commanded the attention of the government and the country. Their removal has been described as a 'devastating political storm', attributed partly to the electors having been swayed by the government's jingoism. Other explanations include the School's pacifism during the Crimean War and its support for franchise reform.[234] 'Manchester had cut off its nose to spite its face', concluded one historian.[235] 'The great towns of Lancashire prefer any mediocrities to Bright and Cobden', observed a contemporary.[236]

We noted earlier that the Manchester merchants appear to have become rather hysterical as a result of the adverse vote in the House of Commons.[237] Manchester was, of course, the centre of the Lancashire cotton industry; and Lancashire the home of the most important cotton industry in the world.[238] The concerns of the Manchester merchants were not just those of manufacturers keen to expand the China market, but also those of exporters of

232. George Macaulay Trevelyan, *The Life of John Bright* (London, Constable, 1913).
233. Milner-Gibson was particularly well known for his oratory. Like Lord Palmerston, he combined great powers of argument with a happy use of ironic humour. When Palmerston regained office in 1859, he appointed Milner-Gibson as president of the Board of Trade, with Cabinet rank. *DNB*, v. 7, pp. 1164-5.
234. Arthur Silver, *Manchester Men and Indian Cotton, 1847-1872* (Manchester, Manchester University Press, 1966), p. 82.
235. Ibid., p. 84.
236. Greville diary, 4 April 1857, in *Leaves from the Greville Diary*, p. 787.
237. See Bazley to Clarendon, 5 March 1857, FO17/280, p. 37.
238. Arthur Redford, *Manchester Merchants and Foreign Trade, v. 2, 1850-1939* (Manchester, Manchester University Press, 1956), p. xx.

goods to India, where the interruption of the opium trade could cause serious problems since their Indian customers depended on that illicit trade for their funds.[239]

Some statistics may indicate the importance to Lancashire of the China and India markets combined. In 1860, for example, 43 per cent of the total value of British cottons exported was taken by four markets: 20.7 per cent by India, 8.7 per cent by the United States, 6.8 per cent by Turkey, and 6.5 per cent by China.[240] The Manchester merchants would have had every reason to become hysterical if something like 27.2 per cent[241] of their export market were in jeopardy. They wanted the government to push on with the *Arrow* War and to conduct it vigorously. Anybody who stood in the way must be swept aside.

This makes the ousting of Bright all the more striking, for two reasons.

First, the mass meeting held on 29 January 1857, initially called to hear Bright's offer of resignation on the grounds of ill health, had ended as a great demonstration of his 'firm hold on the constituency'.[242] If his pacifism and radical views had been the key factors for his rejection two months later, these grievances would have revealed themselves at that meeting. Businessmen, generally hard-headed, would not have been lightly swayed by jingoism. They would have been more easily excited by the prospects of gain, or tipped off balance by threats of bankruptcy. And the *Manchester Guardian* was by no means jingoistic, but its editorials were extraordinarily hostile to Bright during the election.[243]

Second, Bright was not even in Westminster to vote against Palmerston. Nor was he at Manchester to defend his seat. He was in Italy recovering from a nervous breakdown brought on by the strains of the Crimean War.[244] But Cobden's gallant efforts to canvass on Bright's behalf at Manchester, and Cobden's continued and vehement insistence that 'Lord Palmerston, the despotic ruler of this country', must be checked,[245] was not what the Manchester electors wanted to hear. On the contrary, they insisted that Palmerston be unleashed to wage the *Arrow* War wholeheartedly. Cobden's speeches in Manchester appear to have made the electors identify Bright with Cobden, and thereby put Bright at the bottom of the poll.

239. Chang, *Commissioner Lin*, pp. 192–3, quoting Parl. Papers 'Memorials Addressed to Her Majesty's Government by British Merchants Interested in the Trade with China', 1840.
240. D. A. Farnie, *The English Cotton Industry and the World Market, 1815–1896* (Oxford, Clarendon Press, 1979), p. 138.
241. That is, the markets of India and China combined.
242. Silver, *Manchester Man and Indian Cotton*, p. 83.
243. Ibid., p. 84, n. 2.
244. Ibid., p. 83.
245. See his speech at Manchester, printed verbatim in *Globe*, 20 March 1857, p. 1, cols. 3–4. A short summary of his speech may be found in *The Times*, 19 March 1857, p. 9, col. 3.

When the Manchester electors woke up to their own folly, everybody was in shock – including the victors, 'who had been hastily mobilised only after the dissolution'.[246] The *Manchester Guardian* has been described as 'very shame-faced'.[247] If the magnitude of hysteria is an indication of the extent of material interests involved, can we not go further than the general percentages on cotton alone, mentioned above, and quantify all the pertinent interests? What role did economic realities play in the causation of the *Arrow* War?

With this, we find ourselves entering another controversy: the imperialism of free trade,[248] regarded by some as an origin of the *Arrow* War.[249] The cardinal principle of the Manchester school was free trade, and the period 1846–60 has been regarded as the climax of free trade.[250] Why, then, did the champions of free trade oppose the war? Conversely, by rejecting the leading members of that school because of their opposition to that war, were the merchants now declaring that they were abandoning free trade, or were they demanding something more important than free trade with China?

There are other questions, some having been raised as early as the time of the election, by Sir James Graham, Richard Cobden, and others. The first was: Why did Palmerston choose to interpret Cobden's very mild motion as one of censure? On this question 'hinges the appeal to the country, and the dissolution which is intended', said Graham.[251]

Second, and again according to Graham, the whole issue could have been defused if the government had only said to Bowring that they regretted extremely the course which had been adopted, and which had led to such an effusion of blood; that they had no doubt their officers had acted in difficult circumstances to the best of their judgement; that they regretted the past; and that steps should be taken immediately to improve relations with China, and to take precaution to prevent the recurrence of such evils in the future.[252] But Palmerston would not do that. Why?

Third, Cobden, Russell, Baring, Cardwell,[253] Herbert,[254] Lindsay,[255] and others all said that if the government had announced before the debate their intention of sending out somebody to supersede Bowring, the Chinese question would not have been heard of in the Commons. This led Cobden and others

246. Silver, *Manchester Man and Indian Cotton*, p. 83.
247. Ibid., p. 84, n. 2, commenting on its leader of 30 March 1857.
248. See Gallagher and Robinson, 'Imperialism of Free Trade'.
249. See ibid.; and Platt, *Finance, Trade, and Politics*, p. 265.
250. Redford, *Manchester Merchants and Foreign Trade*, v. 2, chapter 1, which bears the title 'The Climax of Free Trade, 1846–1860'.
251. *Globe*, 19 March 1857, p. 1, col. 6, 'Sir James Graham'.
252. Sir James Graham's election speech, in the *Globe*, 19 March 1857, p. 1, col. 6
253. See his election address in ibid., 14 March 1857, p. 4, col. 3.
254. Ibid., 20 March 1857, p. 1, col. 4.
255. *The Times*, 13 March 1857.

to accuse Palmerston of having contrived his own defeat in the debates.[256] In the absence of a satisfactory explanation, a modern scholar seems to accept Cobden's conspiracy theory.[257] However, doubts have been raised earlier in this chapter, in view of the merchant princes' besieging Palmerston's door from 5 March onwards. These and other issues will be explored in the remaining chapters.

256. See Cobden's speech at Huddersfield in ibid., 28 March 1857, p. 8.
257. See Taylor, *Decline of British Radicalism*, p. 274, quoting three sources: George Hadfield's speech at Sheffield (*The Times*, 25 March 1857, p. 8), Richard Cobden's speech at Huddersfield (ibid., 28 March 1857, p. 8), and the editorial of the *Weekly Dispatch*, 15 March 1857, p. 7.

Part V
The mechanics of imperialism

In Part IV, we got tantalizingly close to the pivotal origins of the *Arrow* War, principally through the imprecise public statements made during the debates in Parliament. Now in Part V, we hope to follow those clues and do something which the British public at the time, including Marx, could not have done. We shall probe behind the scenes, to find out some details of Cabinet meetings; private correspondence among the political leaders; secret negotiations among the British, French, U.S., and Russian governments; and the like. To do so, we shall have to start our story in each of this part's three chapters from the moment London received news about the quarrel in China, or even before. The time scale will be the same, the focus different. Thus, Chapter 11 will deal with the diplomacy of imperialism, Chapter 12 the politics of imperialism, and Chapter 13 the lobbies of imperialism.

A telling example of Marx's ignorance of what was actually going on may be found in the fact that the general public in Britain did not get to hear about the *Arrow* quarrel until Monday 29 December 1856. On this day *The Times* printed a telegraphic despatch from Trieste, in which were outlined events from the *Arrow* incident of 8 October to the capture of the Bogue forts on 12–13 November.[1] But Whitehall had already received on 1 December Bowring's despatch about all this[2] and had been keeping quiet all the time. Why?

The answer is that the secret search for French and U.S. allies for an envisaged military operation against China had begun well before Whitehall heard anything about the *Arrow* incident. In fact, it had begun as early as 24 September 1856, before the *Arrow* incident occurred, as we shall see.

---

1. *The Times*, 29 December 1856. By 1856, the telegraphic links had been established to Italy and as far as the Black Sea; but those to India were not available until 1869. See Brown, *Victorian News and Newspapers*, p. 227.
2. See Chapter 11.

11
Behind the scenes:
The diplomacy of imperialism

I. Business as usual

Palmerston's cabinet learnt about the *Arrow* quarrel much earlier than the British public, by almost a month. On 1 December 1856, the Foreign Office received bundles of Bowring's despatches, with enclosures. Analysed hereunder are those despatches related to the affairs at Canton.

The first[1] was dated 13 October 1856, with seventeen enclosures, all of which were about the *Arrow* incident and its immediate aftermath. Lord Clarendon got round to reading these documents four days after their arrival, on 5 December. He minuted: 'Ask the lord advocate[2] if the treaty had been infracted'.[3] The document was referred to the lord advocate the next day.[4]

The second was dated 14 October, in which Bowring forwarded Parkes's despatch on the rebellions in South China, and on which Clarendon simply pencilled 'C'.[5] As mentioned before, Parkes's intention in writing this sort of despatch, which was a mere regurgitation of stale news, seems to have been to assure Bowring that he might safely use coercive measures against China.[6] By forwarding the same despatch to London, Bowring was giving Whitehall the same message.

In the third, dated 15 October 1856, Bowring reported that Yeh had refused

1. Bowring to Clarendon, Desp. 326, 13 October 1856, FO17/251.
2. He was James Moncreiff. As we have seen in Chapter 9, he was to defend vigorously the government's position in the House of Commons.
3. Clarendon's exact words were: 'L. A. as to infraction of Treaty, D5/56 C'. See Clarendon's minute, dated 5 December 1856, on Bowring to Clarendon, Desp. 326, 13 October 1856, FO17/251.
4. Clarendon's minute: 'Queen's Adv., Dec 6', on Bowring to Clarendon, Desp. 326, 13 October 1856, FO17/251.
5. Clarendon's minute on Bowring's Desp. 334 of 14 October 1856, FO17/251.
6. See Chapter 3.

261

to redress the alleged insult to the British flag. Clarendon again referred it to the lord advocate.[7] This was done on 6 December.[8]

From none of these Whitehall proceedings may we hear any battle cries, or smell any gunpowder, notwithstanding Parkes's blatant suggestion that force might safely be used against China. It was all business as usual. The lord advocate was duly consulted on the points of law, and on 10 December Clarendon approved Bowring's proceedings.

On 16 December, Bowring's despatch of 16 October reached London. In it Bowring reported the seizure of a large war junk. Clarendon read it immediately and minuted: 'Approve proceedings, D16/56 C'.[9] On 1 January 1857, Bowring's despatch of 20 October arrived at Whitehall. Therein Bowring reported that he had written to the U.S. minister in China, Dr Parker, on the question of treaty revision and expressed a belief that the minister would be bound to fail in his solo approach towards the Chinese authorities for treaty revision. Clarendon got round to reading it on 4 January 1857 and approved Bowring's report.[10] Let us examine the matter of treaty revision, about which we have heard so much in previous chapters.

II. Treaty revision

In February 1854, when Clarendon appointed Bowring British minister plenipotentiary in China, he instructed him to revise the Treaty of Nanking. The four conditions highest in priority were, to:

1. obtain access generally to the whole interior of China;
2. obtain free navigation of the Yangtze River;
3. effect the legalisation of the opium trade;
4. provide against the imposition of transit duties on foreign goods.[11]

These and other conditions were not so much a request for revising the existing terms of the Treaty of Nanking as a demand for a completely new treaty.

Bowring was not a career diplomat, and one is inclined to interpret his promotion as being related to his experience in negotiating commercial treaties. Palmerston said as much subsequently, stating that Bowring had been

---

7. Clarendon's exact words were: 'L. A. with the other despatch, D5/56 C'. See Clarendon's minute, dated 5 December 1856, on Bowring to Clarendon, Desp. 326, 13 October 1856, in FO17/251.
8. Clarendon's minute: 'Queen's Adv., Dec 6', on Bowring to Clarendon, Desp. 326, 13 October 1856, in FO17/251.
9. Clarendon's 16 December 1857 minute on Bowring's Desp. 337 of 16 October 1856, FO17/251.
10. Clarendon's 4 January 1857 minute on Bowring's Desp. 341 of 20 October 1856, FO17/251.
11. Clarendon to Bowring, Desp. 2, 13 February 1854, FO17/210.

The diplomacy of imperialism

associated with Clarendon in 'commercial negotiations with Paris'.[12] He added that Clarendon had consulted him before making the appointment, as somebody who had 'more knowledge of' Bowring. And Palmerston himself had agreed on the same grounds: Bowring had 'distinguished himself by his eminent knowledge of commercial matters'.[13]

Why was it necessary to request a new treaty under the guise of treaty revision?

No sooner had the Treaty of Nanking been signed than the British merchants expressed great dissatisfaction with it. To begin with, opium had not been legalized despite victory in the Opium War. Thus, the property and persons of British merchants, the great majority of whom were engaged in the opium trade at this time, continued to be at risk in China. Second, commercial expansion had not met their high expectations. When the five treaty ports were opened, British merchants had anticipated the sale of manufactured goods to increase sharply, if not five-fold – they now had five ports instead of only one through which to trade. They flooded the market with items quite irrelevant to Chinese needs, such as pianos and cutlery. Manchester also made a 'great blind effort' at exporting worsted and cotton manufactures, and was likewise disappointed.[14] All this culminated in the great slump of British trade in China in 1848,[15] which was heralded by the London crisis the year before. Thereupon some Britons believed that there was little prospect of the sale of British manufactures improving dramatically because China was self-sufficient, as Assistant Magistrate Mitchell of Hong Kong argued in 1852. But Mitchell's report was shelved by the governor of Hong Kong, Sir George Bonham, and did not come to light until 1858, when Lord Elgin enclosed it in one of his despatches.[16]

Instead, Consul Alcock's views gained ascendancy. He argued that China might be self-sufficient, but that British goods could still invade the vast inland trade, particularly in the rich Yangtze River valley and along the Grand Canal.[17] Bonham was so impressed with Alcock's report that he forwarded it to

12. Palmerston, 3 March 1857, Hansard, 3d series, v. 144, col. 1810. Clarendon was associated with Bowring in his capacity as the president of the board of trade in 1846–7. See E. L. Woodward, *The Age of Reform, 1815–1870* (Oxford, Clarendon Press, 1954), pp. 638.
13. Ibid.
14. See George Wingrove Cooke's article in the *Economist*, 4 September 1858. It was an eminent firm at Sheffield that sent out a large consignment of knives and forks and 'declared themselves prepared to supply all China with cutlery'. The pianos were from London. In the end they were sold 'at prices which scarcely realised their freight'.
15. Report on the decline of trade at Canton (1848), FO682/137/1/42 (Canton Archive). This document is now reclassified as FO931/482.
16. Elgin to Foreign Office, 31 March 1858, FO17/287, quoted in Pelcovits, *Old China Hands*, p. 15. A Foreign Office minute reads: 'I think your Lordship would be interested by the inclosure. It appears it was not sent home by Sir G. Bonham'.
17. Alcock to Bonham, 13 February 1850, enclosed in Bonham to Palmerston, Desp. 46, 15 April 1850, FO17/166.

263

Lord Palmerston, who was then foreign secretary. Palmerston duly instructed Bonham to approach Beijing to make alterations to the treaty, which would, inter alia, give British subjects free access to the interior for trade, secured by a system of passes.[18] But Bonham's attempts to communicate with Beijing for this purpose failed. Palmerston thundered: 'I clearly see that the time is fast coming when we shall be obliged to strike another blow in China'.[19] But there were other considerations: Would the country sanction a war on the basis of a demand to change an existing treaty? Palmerston held back.

Since direct requests had been turned down and a war might be difficult to arrange, Palmerston began to look for some legal grounds to make China grant further concessions. This was found in the so-called treaty revision.

The Treaty of Nanking (1842) did not provide for the revision of any of its clauses at any time. In the Sino-American Treaty of Wangxia (1844), however, there was a clause to this effect.[20] The clause began by stipulating that once the treaty had been signed, both parties should abide by it and must not lightly make any changes. But in view of the fact that conditions at the five ports varied, 'experience may show that inconsiderable modifications are requisite in those parts which relate to commerce and navigation', in which case both parties should get together again in twelve years' time to discuss such minor changes. The clause ended with a warning that Britain and other countries must not use this clause to make unreasonable demands at will.

Nonetheless, Palmerston decided to use this Sino-American clause to claim the right to make substantial revisions to the Treaty of Nanking under the most-favoured-nation principle as contained in the Sino-British Supplementary Treaty of the Bogue (1843).[21] This claim was in itself dubious. If China and the United States had subsequently agreed to make minor changes to their treaties, Britain could of course share the privileges arising out of these modifications. Whether or not it could claim the *right* itself to revise its own treaty, however, was a question for the law officers. These officers, when eventually consulted by Lord Clarendon in April 1857, denied that Britain could claim such a right.[22]

18. Palmerston to Bowring, Draft 73, 3 September 1850, FO17/164.
19. Palmerston's minutes on 'Mr Bonham's 65, 67, 72', following an application for consular positions at Ningpo and Foochow, and signed 'P. 29-9-50', FO17/173 (domestic various). This has been quoted by both Costin (*Great Britain and China*, p. 150) and Fairbank (*Trade and Diplomacy*, p. 380). On the basis of Palmerston's minute, Fairbank entitled a section of his book 'Palmerston's Thoughts of War' (ibid., p. 379).
20. See Article 34 of the Treaty of Wangxia, signed on 3 July 1844. A similar clause may be found in Art. 35 of the Sino-French Treaty of Whampoa, signed on 24 October 1844. The texts of these and other treaties in the Chinese and foreign languages were printed side by side in *Treaties, Conventions, etc., between China and Foreign States* (Shanghai: Published at the Statistical Department of the Inspectorate General of Customs, 1908).
21. See Article 8 of this treaty, signed on 8 October 1843.
22. Clarendon to Elgin, Draft 7 (secret and confidential), 20 April 1857, FO17/274. See later for more details.

But before they were consulted, Palmerston and then Clarendon, as successive foreign secretaries, soldiered on with demands for treaty revision. By 1854, twelve years had elapsed since the signing of the Treaty of Nanking, and Clarendon instructed Bowring to approach the Chinese government formally with a view to revising the treaty.[23] Upon a close examination of the treaties and of the correspondence between his predecessors with successive Chinese imperial commissioners, Bowring found that he could not claim the right to revise the Treaty of Nanking.[24] Nonetheless he went ahead as instructed because, as he himself told Lord Clarendon, 'Now at all events I *have* an end and an object, *to open China*'.[25]

To Bowring's inquiry as to whether he had been authorized by the Chinese emperor to revise the treaty, Yeh replied that he had been instructed to observe the treaty to the letter and not to change it in any substantial manner. He added, 'The power of the Sovereign in this country is absolute, that of the minister altogether limited'.[26]

Thereupon, Bowring steamed to the Peiho in HMS *Rattler*. He was joined by Peter Parker, the U.S. minister, but his French counterpart declined to participate on the grounds that he had no man-of-war at his disposal – he sent an attaché.[27] They were met by a high-ranking Chinese official near Tianjin. Bowring presented eighteen points for a new treaty. The emperor[28] decreed that it was too early for the Americans and the French even to think of treaty revision. As for the English, their treaty contained no provision for revision. 'What do you mean by a treaty', he asked, 'if you do not intend to keep it?' He added, 'Even if we work on a most-favoured-nation principle, what are the English asking for? For something which neither the Americans nor the French have received?'[29] This reply came close to the advice Lord Clarendon eventually received from his law officers.

By 1856, twelve years had lapsed since the signing of the Sino-American treaty, which contained a provision for treaty revision. Bowring wrote to Yeh requesting treaty revision on the same stale grounds.[30] In his reply, dated 30 June 1856, Yeh reiterated his master's stinging response.[31] Bowring

23. Clarendon to Bowring, Desp. 2, 13 February 1854, FO17/210.
24. Bowring to Clarendon, 27 April 1854, MSS Clar. Dep. C19 China.
25. Bowring to Clarendon, 5 September 1854, MSS Clan Dep. C19 China.
26. Yeh to Bowring, 1 September 1856, FO682/198/54 (originally Canton Archive). The English version was enclosed in Bowring's Desp. 128 of 1854, in FO17/215.
27. G. F. Bartle, 'Sir John Bowring and the Chinese and Siamese Commercial Treaties', *Bulletin of the John Rylands Library of Manchester*, 44, no. 2 (March 1962), pp. 295–6.
28. As mentioned, he was Emperor Xianfeng, who reigned from 1851 to 1861.
29. Imperial edict, 23 October 1854, *Shilu* (XF), *juan* 144, folios 3–4.
30. Bowring to Yeh, 16 May 1856, FO230/74. This is a copy of the Chinese original of Bowring's despatch.
31. Yeh to Bowring, 30 June 1856, FO682/1898/10. The English translation of this document was enclosed in Bowring to Clarendon, Desp. 202, 3 July 1856, FO17/248.

exploded: 'Nothing can be more contemptuous than the manner in which – after a silence of 45 days – my communication has been met'.[32] His report reached London on 30 August 1856.[33] Palmerston was furious. A long and considered despatch to the British ambassador in Paris, Lord Cowley, was completed on 24 September 1856,[34] initiating a new phase in international relations.

III. Seeking French allies: Trade and treaty revision

Enclosed in the despatch to Lord Cowley was a copy of Yeh's reply of 30 June 1856, declining treaty revision. The despatch began gravely, 'The state of affairs in China, as represented by Her Majesty's Plenipotentiary, has now become so critical that it appears to Her Majesty's Government desirable that the Powers whose interests are at stake should lose no time in deciding upon the course which should be pursued by them'. Yeh's refusal to 'recognise the obligation to concur in a revision of the treaty' was denounced as 'most strikingly' arrogant.

The ambassador was instructed to approach the French government formally and urgently with a view to organizing a joint naval expedition to proceed to the Peiho River, and as far up that river as might be practicable, to announce to the Chinese emperor that the powers wanted their treaties revised and 'the vast resources of that Empire opened up to the industrial enterprise of foreign nations'. And the emperor of China had 'better consult the interests of his Empire by deferring to the wishes of the Treaty-Powers', rather than turning a deaf ear to their representations.

The French government was to be informed that Britain was about to send to the China seas vessels of light draft, 'partly to be available for conveying Her Majesty's Plenipotentiary with a respectable display of force over the bar and up the waters of the Peiho'. If the French agreed to participate, then the U.S. minister in London would be similarly approached, while the French government might also think fit to make a simultaneous approach to the U.S. minister in Paris.[35]

The French government deliberated the matter for about a month. On 22 October, the French foreign minister, Count Walewski, wrote to the French ambassador in London, Count Persigny, saying that the French government welcomed the British initiative and would be pleased to contribute materially towards a tripartite enterprise. In case the Chinese emperor should refuse to yield to a show of force, Admiral Hamelin had been asked to instruct

32. Bowring to Clarendon, Desp. 202, 3 July 1856, FO17/248.
33. See Foreign Office endorsement on Bowring to Clarendon, Desp. 202, 3 July 1856, FO17/248.
34. Clarendon to Cowley, Desp. 1099, 24 September 1856, FO17/261, p. 75.
35. Ibid.

Captain Pigeard to collect nautical information necessary for a hostile operation.[36]

Why did the French respond so favourably and energetically, although belatedly? News had just reached Paris of the execution of a French missionary, M. Père Chapdelaine, in the interior of China.[37] In the envisaged tripartite advance towards Beijing, the French government wanted their minister to demand, above all else, reparations, including the dismissal of the Chinese magistrate who had sentenced the missionary to death, the announcement of that dismissal in the *Beijing Gazette* as a warning to all Chinese officials, and a monetary indemnity. Count Walewski asked Lord Cowley about possible British reaction to this French position. Subsequently Cowley showed him a letter from Clarendon, which fully admitted the necessity of satisfying the French demand. Then Walewski sent out some ambiguous signals. On the one hand, he emphasized that offensive military operations against China had not yet received definite approval from the French government and that possibly the French government would not go as far as occupying the island of Chusan in order to cow the Chinese emperor. On the other, he thought it a good idea to order the immediate departure of French ships to China.[38] His message seems to have been this: the French government was prepared to act, but the British government must give first priority to the French demand for redress. He asked Persigny to feel free to pass his note to Clarendon for the information of the British Cabinet.[39]

The British Cabinet discussed the matter, and gave permission to the French officer named by Walewski, Captain Pigeard, to communicate with the British Board of Admiralty, in order that he might obtain the same full information as a British admiral would have possessed should coercion become necessary. This is a remarkable concession, given Anglo-French naval rivalry at this time.[40] But the Cabinet also realized that the material benefits of a war would accrue almost entirely to Britain, as France had little trade with China. As

---

36. Walewski to Persigny, 22 October 1856, FO17/261, p. 76.
37. According to Alabaster's diary of 4 April 1858, Yeh had this to say about Chapdelaine: 'The people of the place he was at suspected him of being a rebel or least of having had intercourse with them and seizing him, carried him before the tribunal of the district magistrate to whom he professed himself to be a Canton man and there was proof of his complicity with the rebels and as from his speech, dress, appearance and assertions they believed him to be a Cantonese, they put him to death as such neither knowing his nation nor his creed which latter has never been called in question and he reiterated again and again that if he had known him to be a Frenchman he would have sent him back as he had always done in other cases'. Alabaster was the interpreter assigned to accompany Yeh to his exile in India and kept a diary recording his conversations with Yeh. Alabaster's papers and diaries are now in the possession of Mr David St Marn Sheil who lives in Hong Kong. I am grateful to Mr David St Marn Sheil for kindly giving me access to the papers and diaries.
38. Walewski to Persigny, 22 October 1856, FO17/261, p. 76.
39. Ibid.
40. See C. I. Hamilton, *Anglo-French Naval Rivalry, 1840–1870* (Oxford, Clarendon Press, 1993).

regards Walewski's ambiguous signals, Clarendon agreed that it might be desirable to insist upon redress of the French grievance 'in the first instance', but it should be presented at the same time as 'the demand for immediate though subsequent revision of the treaties'. In other words, Clarendon wanted to give equal first to both the French demand for redress and the British demand for treaty revision.

In case coercion was thought necessary, 'Her Majesty's government are of opinion that a more direct and effectual pressure would be made by taking up a position in the Yang-tse-Kiang, than by occupying the island of Chusan'. The latter would involve a military occupation; while the former might be carried out by naval means alone. And by seizing the entrance to the Grand Canal in the Yangtse River, Beijing's artery to the central and southern parts of China would be cut off, 'a measure productive of the most serious annoyance and danger to the Chinese government'.

Gaining a foothold in the Yangtze River would have the additional advantage of obtaining access to the populous cities and districts watered by that river, as well as to the large cities in the neighbourhood of the seaboard of the provinces south of that river. 'It is impossible to over-estimate the advantages, in a commercial point of view, of even so limited an extension of intercourse with China'. All these points were conveyed to Cowley for the information of the French, on 31 October 1856.[41]

The French government spent the next month or so pondering the British proposition. They agreed that a combined operation in the Yangtze River would be more effective as a means of coercion than the occupation of Chusan. However, they felt that they could not proceed further in this respect until Captain Pigeard had completed his inquiries at the British Admiralty and reported his findings to Admiral Hamelin. They also agreed that the British and French demands should be presented simultaneously to the Chinese government, but insisted that the French demand should be the first of the two firsts. Their reasons may be summarized as follows. The Chinese government could feign willingness to consider treaty revision, thus making the demand for redress less pressing. Negotiations for treaty revision could go on indefinitely, further weakening the moral force of the demand for redress. By the time the treaties were eventually revised, the Chinese neglect of the demand for redress could leave France out there on a limb, thus breaking the concert of common action.

The French conclusion was this. The powers must agree that a fair redress had to be acquired before the details of treaty revision were approached. If Britain should consent to this modus operandi, then the next step would be to agree on the measures of coercion, which in turn would have to wait for the

41. Clarendon to Cowley, Desp. 1316, 31 October 1856, FO17/261, p. 76b.

completion of Captain Pigeard's research in the British Board of Admiralty. These points were made in a despatch to the French ambassador in London on 20 November 1856.[42]

The ambassador took these points to Clarendon. When the British government had not responded by 26 November 1856, he wrote formally to Clarendon, enclosing a copy of his instructions which he had already discussed with Clarendon verbally. He now indicated that the French government wished to reach a complete agreement as soon as possible because the issues to be decided were of secondary importance. He looked forward to the time when he might report promptly to his government the views of the British government.[43] His diplomatic note was received in Whitehall on 27 November.

Understandably, Clarendon still did not react. If the French should dread the prospect of the British eventually getting treaty revision while the French themselves should miss out on redress, equally the British Cabinet would worry about the French pulling out of the alliance once they had got their immediate redress. Would Britain then go on to declare war on her own, and on the sole excuse that China had refused to revise the treaty? If Palmerston had considered it unwise in 1851 to attack China on this ground alone, that consideration still held good in 1856.

On 1 December 1856, Bowring's report on the *Arrow* quarrel reached Whitehall. As we have seen, even before the British government knew anything about the *Arrow* trouble, they had been planning for war, and for that purpose actively cultivating allies for almost three months, ever since Bowring's earlier report on Yeh's final refusal to entertain treaty revision reached London on 30 August 1856.[44] Since Bowring's initial approach in 1854 to the Chinese authorities on the question of treaty revision had been met repeatedly with evasive answers, Palmerston must have feared for the worst and consequently must have been contemplating the use of force, making it all the more probable that in his interview with Parkes early in 1856, he suggested the bellicose young consul be on the lookout for a casus belli.[45]

Herein lies a partial answer to Sir James Graham's puzzlement, which was, no doubt, shared by many of his contemporaries.[46] Graham had wondered why the government did not, while showing sympathy for the difficult circumstances in which Bowring was operating, simply tell him to patch up the differences with the Chinese.[47] Yeh would have welcomed this initiative with

42. Walewski to Persigny, 20 November 1856, FO17/261, p. 77b.
43. Persigny to Clarendon, 26 November 1856, FO17/26, p. 77b.
44. Bowring to Clarendon, Desp. 202, 3 July 1856, FO17/248. The date of 30 August 1856 was endorsed on this document as the date of receipt in the Foreign Office.
45. As argued in Chapter 3.
46. See Chapter 10.
47. *Globe*, 19 March 1857, p. 1, col. 6, 'Sir James Graham'.

open arms, in view of his highly conciliatory responses to the despatches from Bowring, Seymour, and Parkes. The British government did not wish to reciprocate Yeh's goodwill; and even if it had so wished, it could no longer do so because, as early as 1 December 1856, it had gone quite far on the warpath with France. Back-pedalling was now out of the question.

Cobden's bafflement may also be resolved. He was intrigued that the government should have decided to use a pretext as flimsy as the *Arrow* incident to start a war with China, while earlier and more convincing excuses had been overlooked.[48] The truth is, the *Arrow* incident did not turn Palmerston's thoughts to war; China's refusal to revise the Treaty of Nanking had already done so.

This also explains why news of the alleged insult to the flag was received so calmly at Whitehall on 1 December 1856 – because the government already knew exactly what they were going to do. All this puts the question of treaty revision, that is, of economic interests, and the *Arrow* incident itself, in a very different light. Economic interests undoubtedly carried most weight. But may we still attribute the war to the alleged insult to the flag? This will partly depend on the role which the quarrel subsequently played in the calculations of the British Cabinet.

All these calculations are reflected in Clarendon's instructions to Elgin. Therein it was revealed that Britain had no legal grounds for demanding treaty revision with China. But the *Arrow* quarrel had now provided the argument for a complete overhaul of the existing treaty[49] so as to allow British commercial penetration of the interior of China, opium to be legalized, and so on. Thus, Britain's determination to further her economic interests was the fundamental cause of the war, and the *Arrow* quarrel merely the pretext. Given these realities, it appears that whatever the subsequent amount of parliamentary rhetoric, and however loud, the fundamental course of events was already set.

Clarendon did not respond to Persigny's diplomatic note for another five days. The *Arrow* quarrel was certainly a new factor and seems to have influenced the Cabinet's decision to accept the French precondition. If the French should pull out prematurely, Britain could now still declare war on the grounds of defending national honour in addition to furthering British economic interests. French allies were still highly desirable, even if only for the purpose of splitting the bill half and half.

On 5 December 1856, Clarendon replied to Persigny formally. He agreed 'to present to the Chinese government, at one and the same time, the demand for reparation for the murder of the French missionary, and for the revision of the treaties; but to insist upon the former demand being immediately complied

48. Cobden, 26 February 1857, Hansard, 3d series, v. 144, col. 1404.
49. Ibid.

with'. He asked that the French government communicate this agreement to the U.S. government.[50]

Walewski was delighted and immediately prepared draft instructions to the French minister in China. He began by saying that the original treaty with China was of a merely transitory nature, albeit carrying the advantage of preparing the way for possible relations of a more regular and satisfactory character. The minister was thereby instructed to join hands with his British and U.S. counterparts to revise their respective treaties with China. He was instructed to obtain permanent residence of the French minister at Beijing and the right for Frenchmen to penetrate into the interior of China, as well as to establish themselves wherever it might be useful.[51]

By this time the Americans had replied to Walewski's communication and added the following to the list of demands: the despatching to and residence in Paris, London, and Washington, of Chinese diplomatic representatives; universal freedom of thought for Chinese subjects; and reform of the courts of justice in China. Walewski regarded the U.S. conditions as secondary and felt that they might jeopardize his first two cardinal demands. The French minister was further instructed not to enter into any negotiations about treaty revision before the redress for the death of M. Chapdelaine was satisfied. Finally, he was to take counsel with the French commanders-in-chief of the three naval divisions, but not to restrict their military actions once hostility had started. Walewski enclosed a copy of these draft instructions in his despatch to Persigny on 11 December 1856.[52]

On 13 December, Persigny transmitted to Clarendon Walewski's despatch and the enclosed draft instructions. These, Clarendon returned on 16 December, adding that 'Her Majesty's government agree generally in those instructions, and will issue similar ones to Her Majesty's Plenipotentiary in China'. However, Clarendon felt uneasy about that part of the instructions which would appear to contemplate recourse being had at once to measures of coercion in the Yangtze River, simultaneously with the entrance of a portion of the allied squadrons, with the plenipotentiaries on board, into the Peiho River, and without waiting to ascertain whether the Chinese government would accede to the demands to be made. Clarendon was in favour of giving the Chinese government a chance to avert war by making timely concessions.[53]

Interestingly, the correspondence between the two governments mentioned in this section was printed for Foreign Office use on 31 December 1856 and marked 'confidential' in bold.[54] It was intended for the information of all

50. Clarendon to Persigny, 5 December 1856, FO17/261, p. 78b.
51. Walewski to Persigny, 11 December 1856, FO17/261, p. 78b.
52. Ibid.
53. Clarendon to Persigny, 11 December 1856, FO17/261, p. 80.   54. See ibid., p. 75.

Foreign Office and other officials concerned. The Foreign Office was obviously in high gear preparing for military action. Indeed, having done their homework on the diplomatic front, they now had to turn their attention to the domestic scene because, on 29 December, *The Times* had printed a telegraphic message from Trieste, announcing to the general public the 'Bombardment of Canton'.[55] However, the story behind the domestic scene must be postponed to the next chapter, so that we may complete our study of the diplomacy of imperialism.

IV. Seeking U.S. allies: Trade and freedom of opinion

To accommodate the French, the British agreed to regard as secondary the U.S. demand for universal freedom of opinion in China. All along, however, they had been keen that the Americans join a tripartite expedition against China.

Like the British and the French, the Americans wanted to have their treaty with China revised and had been preparing for that day, which was to be 3 July 1856. Thus, on 5 September 1855, President Pierce formally appointed Dr Peter Parker the U.S. minister to China.[56] Parker was instructed above all to obtain residence of the U.S. diplomatic representative at Beijing and 'unlimited extension of our trade, wherever, within the dominions of China, commerce may be found'.[57] He was advised that cooperation with Britain and France would make it less likely that the Chinese authorities would oppose his requests.[58]

Parker set out for China via London and Paris, seeking joint action for treaty revision. Parker suggested to Clarendon that the naval forces of the three powers should anchor at the mouth of Peiho while negotiating with the Chinese government.[59] Clarendon gladly promised to propose a 'triple alliance' to his government.[60] In Paris, Parker made the same recommendation to

---

55. This was the title of *The Times* article, 29 December 1856, p. 6, col. 6.
56. Marcy to Parker, No. 1, 5 September 1855, U.S. State Department, 77:38, pp. 117–19. William L. Marcy was the U.S. secretary of state. Dr Parker was a Yale graduate of medicine who had served as a missionary in China for some twenty years. For a comprehensive biography of Dr Parker, see Edward V. Gulick, *Peter Parker and the Opening of China* (Cambridge, Mass., Harvard University Press, 1973). Professor Tong Te-kong has also written a perceptive history of Sino-American relations of this period. See his *United States Diplomacy in China* .
57. Marcy to Parker, No. 2, 27 September 1855, U.S. State Department, 77:38, p. 122.
58. Marcy to Parker, No. 3, 5 October 1855, U.S. State Department, 77:38, p. 131.
59. Minutes of Parker's interview with the earl of Clarendon, Fenton's Hotel, St James Street, London, 26 October 1855, U.S. Congress, Senate Executive Documents, No. 22, 35th Congress, 2d Session, 'Peter Parker Correspondence', p. 620.
60. Ibid.

Count Walewski, who responded equally favourably.[61] In Hong Kong, however, Parker found that Bowring was not prepared to go as far as demanding unlimited trade and universal freedom of opinion.[62]

In June 1856, Parker prepared to go north. But Commodore James Armstrong had been diverted to Japan with his flagship, the *San Jacinto*, and was able to provide him with only a sloop of war, the *Levant*.[63] Bowring could not get Admiral Seymour to convey him to the north in the absence of authorization from London.[64] The French chargé, Count René de Courcy, said he was still awaiting instructions.[65] Alone, Parker went from Macao to Shanghai. Then the U.S. consul at Foochow alleged to Parker that Bowring was trying to sabotage his mission by spreading rumours that Parker had been recalled by Washington.[66] It seems that Bowring did not wish to be upstaged in the ensuing action. By November 1856, Parker was still at Shanghai, where he heard that the *San Jacinto* had been disabled by an accident.[67] He returned to Macao, with his envisaged triple alliance in tatters.[68]

Meanwhile, the *Arrow* quarrel had erupted in Canton the month before. One U.S. perspective on Seymour's bombardment of Canton is light hearted: 'The brave officer, having lost an eye by the explosion of a Russian torpedo in the Baltic during the Crimean War, could see only one way to negotiate'.[69] Parker disapproved of the British bombardment of Canton, and upon his arrival at Hong Kong, deliberately avoided meeting Bowring by going on to Macao via Whampoa.[70] Now Bowring appealed to Parker for a joint Anglo-American communication to be sent to Tianjin.[71] Parker replied that the U.S. government 'must remain *neutral* in the controversy *solely* initiated by her Britannic Majesty's government, and specially British in origin'. Furthermore, Parker objected to Seymour's 'abuse' of the phrase 'all foreign officials' while

61. Parker to Marcy, Paris, 8 November 1855, U.S. Congress, Senate Executive Documents, No. 22, 35th Congress, 2d Session, 'Peter Parker Correspondence', pp. 621–2.
62. Bowring to Clarendon, Desp. 11, 6 January 1856, FO17/244.
63. Tong, *United States Diplomacy in China*, p. 179.
64. Such instructions were on the way, but arrived too late in the year for the flagship to set off. See Graham, *The China Station*, p. 297.
65. Tong, *United States Diplomacy in China*, p. 179.
66. Jones to Parker, No. 19, Foochow, 27 August 1856, U.S. Senate Executive Documents, No. 22, 35th Congress, 2d Session, 'Peter Parker Correspondence', pp. 961–2, quoted in Tong, *United States Diplomacy in China*, p. 181.
67. Parker to Marcy, No. 28, Shanghai, 1 November 1856, quoted in Tong, *United States Diplomacy in China*, p. 101.
68. Tong, *United States Diplomacy in China*, p. 182.
69. W. A. P. Martin, *A Cycle of Cathay or China, South and North* (New York, Fleming H. Revell, 1897), p. 143.
70. Parker to Bowring, U.S. Steam Frigate *San Jacinto*, Whampoa, 17 November 1857, quoted in Tong, *United States Diplomacy in China*, p. 188.
71. Bowring to Parker, No. 263, 15 November 1856, quoted in Tong, *United States Diplomacy in China*, p. 189.

demanding entry into the City of Canton. He officially dissociated the U.S. government from that demand.[72]

Parker doubtless feared that British belligerence might endanger legitimate U.S. negotiations for treaty revision. Bowring was left in a desperate position. Then at 11 P.M. on 14 December 1856, a mysterious fire broke out in the foreign factory area at Canton, destroying U.S., French, and other foreign possessions worth millions of dollars, but not those of the British. Nobody knew how the fire could have started in a place which Seymour had safely separated from the rest of Canton by having all the adjoining Chinese houses cleared away, and which was heavily guarded by British servicemen. One interpretation is that the British deliberately lit that fire in the U.S. factory, which the Americans had evacuated on 15 November 1856 on the advice of Yeh, followed by the French five days later. The destruction of U.S. and French property shattered Yeh's diplomatic coup. Worse still, it drew into the controversy the representatives of these two nations, who were somehow led to believe that the fire had been lit by the Chinese, and who therefore sent their claims to Yeh. Parker even asked Bowring if the U.S. claim might be included in the British demand for indemnification. Bowring was only too pleased to oblige, and Parker's passion for a triple alliance was rekindled.[73]

By this time Parker had been fully informed by Washington of the negotiations between Clarendon and Walewski for a triple alliance. He prepared a lengthy submission to his government. The three powers should make their presence felt at Peiho, he said. If the Chinese authorities ignored that, then the United States should occupy Taiwan; England, Chusan; and France, Korea (at this time a Chinese vassal state). He asked Washington for a force 'not less efficient and imposing than the Japan expedition of 1853–54'.[74]

Parker's 'confidential' submission was announced to Washington by the French before his own despatch arrived.[75] Meanwhile, news of U.S. involvement in the *Arrow* conflict also reached the U.S. State Department. The secretary of state, William Marcy, ordered an inquiry into Keenan's abuse of the U.S. flag:[76] 'The President is called upon by a high sense of duty to manifest

---

72. Parker to Bowring, U.S. Steam Frigate *San Jacinto*, Whampoa, 17 November 1857, quoted in Tong, *United States Diplomacy in China*, p. 189.
73. See the analysis by Tong, *United States Diplomacy in China*, pp. 185–6 and 189–92.
74. Parker to Marcy, No. 36, 27 December 1856, U.S. Senate Executive Documents, No. 22, 35th Congress, 2d Session, 'Peter Parker Correspondence', pp. 1087–8.
75. Marcy to Parker, No. 10, 27 February 1857, quoted in Tong, *United States Diplomacy in China*, p. 196.
76. As mentioned in Chapter 2, James Keenan, the U.S. consul at Hong Kong, had a sailor from one of the U.S. ships of war carry the American flag while he and the sailor followed the bluejackets into Canton after the Royal Navy blasted a hole in the city wall.

The diplomacy of imperialism

his displeasure at such conduct'.[77] He also bemoaned Commodore James Armstrong's attack on the barrier forts. It was indiscreet to send a boat from the *San Jacinto* to 'sound the River in the vicinity of the Forts'. Such action 'provoked the fire upon the boat'. Therefore the president was 'inclined to regret that there had not been more caution on the part of our naval force in the beginning and more forbearance in the subsequent steps.'[78]

On 27 February 1857, Parker's 'confidential' submission reached Washington. Marcy was quite irritated. Adoption of the submission meant war with China, 'and the Executive branch of this government is not the war-making power'. Only Congress might declare war.[79] President Pierce and Secretary Marcy then set about convincing President-elect James Buchanan and Secretary-to-be Lewis Cass that war with China was not warranted. British lobbying continued, however. Her Majesty's minister at Washington, Lord Napier, took up the matter with Cass in several meetings from 14 March 1857 onwards. Napier told Cass everything about British intentions except the demand to legalize opium. But Buchanan and Cass seem to have shared Marcy's earlier view that the British government had 'objects beyond those contemplated by the United States and we ought not to be drawn along with it however anxious it may be for our cooperation'.[80] They formally rejected the British approach on 10 April 1857.[81]

Marcy was quite right about the British keeping back their intention to demand opium legalization. The French were not told about it either. Witness the printed instructions to Bowring dated 9 February 1857, a copy of which had to be sent to the French in reciprocation for a similar French gesture.[82] Subsequently, the instructions to Elgin, dated 20 April 1857, were put into two separate documents. The first, obviously meant for the eyes of the French, merely referred to redress for grievances and treaty revision, among other demands.[83] It was in the second, a copy of which was not sent to Paris, that Elgin was instructed to obtain the legalization of opium.[84] Such was the diplomacy of imperialism. And why did Britain want opium legalized in China? As we have seen, Palmerston referred obliquely to this issue during the House of Commons debate. We shall pursue the matter in Part Six.

77. Marcy to Parker, No. 9, 2 February 1857, U.S. National Archives, State Department Diplomatic Instructions, 77:38, p. 147.
78. Ibid.
79. Marcy to Parker, No. 10, 10 February 1857, U.S. National Archives, State Department Diplomatic Instructions, 77:38, p. 151.
80. Marcy to Parker, No. 9, 2 February 1857, U.S. National Archives, State Department Diplomatic Instructions, 77:38, p. 145.
81. See Tyler Dennett, *Americans in Eastern Asia* (New York, Macmillan, 1922), p. 302.
82. Clarendon to Bowring, Draft 33, 9 February 1857, FO17/261.
83. Clarendon to Elgin, Draft 5, 20 April 1857, FO17/274.
84. Clarendon to Elgin, Draft 7 (secret and confidential), 20 April 1857, FO17/274.

V. Seeking Russian allies: Trade and territorial expansion

On 15 January 1857, Clarendon transmitted to Bowring a copy of a despatch from the British ambassador in Paris, reporting a conversation which had taken place between Count Walewski and General Kisseleff on the subject of the possible participation of Russia in the expedition which France had been preparing to despatch to China.[85] On 31 January 1857, the British ambassador at St Peterburg, Lord Wodehouse, wrote privately to Edmund Hammond:[86] 'Here they are very jealous of our proceedings which amuses me. I ask them about the Amur when they talk about China'.[87] Apparently, the Russians wanted to have a finger in the pie. Would Palmerston let them do so? With this, we shall have to deal with a question concerning the role British strategic considerations may have played in the causation of the *Arrow* War.

Britain's war with Russia in the Crimea had just ended. Strategically, that war was fought to halt the southward push of the Russians towards Constantinople. Perceptions of a similar push towards India were still being used by British officers there to obtain more and more resources to annex ever-wider areas of the Indian subcontinent.[88] British officers in China tried to use the same argument there in an attempt to stir their government to action. How realistic was their perception of the threat? How much weight was attached to their arguments? In short, to what extent might one attribute the British perception of a Russian threat to British interests in China as an origin of the *Arrow* War?

During the Crimean War, the British Admiralty received intelligence that Russia had a small squadron operating within striking distance of northern China. The perceived Russian intention was to extend a line of communication southwards through Manchuria. This opened up a frightening prospect for the British because, of all the powers, Russia alone was able to operate directly from home territory against China without outside intervention.[89] Admiralty intelligence indicated that by the beginning of 1855, Russia had established some 30,000 men in and around their forts on the north bank of the Amur River. British naval supremacy would be threatened and British trade extinguished.[90] '[I]f China be not electrified & organised by British energy &

---

85. Clarendon to Bowring, Draft 15, 15 January 1857, FO17/261, p. 33.
86. For a comprehensive biography of him, see M. A. Anderson, 'Edmund Hammond: Permanent Under-Secretary of State for Foreign Affairs, 1854–73'. Unpublished Ph.D. thesis, University of London, 1956.
87. Clarendon to Bowring, Draft 15, 15 January 1857, Hammond Papers, FO391/3.
88. M. E. Yapp has written a fascinating and convincing study on this subject. See his *Strategies of British India: Britain, Iran and Afghanistan* (Oxford, Clarendon Press, 1980).
89. Graham, *China Station*, p. 288.
90. Ibid., p. 289.

The diplomacy of imperialism

management; or brought under the influence which a more extended Commerce will give us, she will soon fall within the Dominion of Russia', wrote Admiral Stirling in his memoir for the Admiralty[91] – prophetic words, considering subsequent Russian influence in China in the first half of the twentieth century.

But the best efforts by the Royal Navy to trace the phantom enemy returned little but stale rumours. By midsummer 1855, it was clear that 'British interests in the China seas had nothing to fear from the Russians'.[92] This has led Gerald Graham to interpret Stirling's memoir as reflecting a desire to 'play the same paternal role in shaping Chinese destinies, as the British army had played in India.' The Foreign Office mandarins must have thought the same; and consequently, Stirling's memorandum 'vanished into the dusty pigeon-hole of Admiralty archives'.[93]

Bowring had also tried to exploit the perceived Russian threat some nine months before the *Arrow* incident by arguing that Russia was using her listening-post in Beijing, the Ecclesiastical Mission, to scheme against British interests.[94] But as we have seen in Chapter 1, Bowring's plea was completely ignored by Whitehall.

Bowring changed his tactics. On 29 September 1856, that is, ten days before the *Arrow* incident, he reported to Clarendon that a French missionary at Shanghai had written to his superior at Hong Kong alleging that the Russians had bought 800 *arpents* of land in Chusan with the intention of building a town.[95] On 3 October 1856, Bowring transmitted a report from the British consul at Shanghai, confirming the French report. It further claimed that the land was to be used for building a naval station for the pending arrival of a large Russian fleet to be deployed in the northern Pacific. Chusan was seen as an ideal spot for that purpose, being 'the key to the seaboard, and hence the interior, of the central provinces of China'.[96] At once Bowring wrote to Yeh.[97] Yeh replied that no permission had been given to the Russians 'to appropriate to their use Chusan or any other of those islands'.[98]

91. Admiral Stirling's 'Memoir on the Maritime Policy of England in the Eastern Seas', written from the *Winchester*, Hong Kong, enclosed in Stirling to Wood (Admiralty), Hong Kong, 15 November 1855, Adm. 1/5660, quoted in Graham, *China Station*, p. 290.
92. Ibid., p. 292.
93. Ibid., p. 290.
94. Bowring to Clarendon, Desp. 11, 5 January 1856, FO17/244.
95. Bowring to Clarendon, Desp. 311, 29 September 1856, FO17/250.
96. Robertson to Bowring, 20 September 1856, enclosed in Bowring to Clarendon, Desp. 318, 3 October 1856, FO17/251. Herein, Robertson referred to 800 *mou* (in pinyin it should be *mu*, a Chinese measurement) of land.
97. Bowring to Yeh, 3 October 1856, enclosed in Bowring to Clarendon, Desp. 325, 11 October 1856, FO17/251.
98. Yeh to Bowring, 10 October 1856, enclosed in Bowring to Clarendon, Desp. 325, 11 October 1856, FO17/251.

To intensify the lobbying, Bowring wrote to his predecessor, Sir John Davis, who had supervised British evacuation from Chusan in 1846 and therefore had a special interest in the matter. Davis took up the matter with Clarendon. In the course of this lobbying, what had been the rumoured purchase of 800 *arpents* of land now became the occupation of the entire Chusan group of islands. 'This is rendered quite probable by the known character of the Russian government, and the present weakness of the Tartar'. Davis emphasized that the envisaged occupation was 'in direct opposition to Article III of the convention signed (at Lord Aberdeen's suggestion) between Keying [Qiying] and myself on 4 April 1846 and ratified by Her Majesty and the Emperor of China'. He concluded: 'This emergency seems to call for active interference'.[99]

Clarendon minuted, 'Ack[nowledge] with thanks, the art[icle] in the treaty has been b[rough]t to the attention of the Imp[eria]l Com[missione]r who denies that any cession of territory in Chusan has been made to Russia'. He added, 'Bowring should be told to watch them. D6/56 C'.[100] On second thoughts, he consulted Palmerston, who reacted to Yeh's reply thus: 'This denies that cession of Chusan or any other island but does not deny the cession of land in Chusan'.[101] Clearly Palmerston was concerned. But the date of his minute was 22 December 1856, eight days after the British government had already reached a complete agreement with the French government jointly to take hostile action against China.[102]

Thus, Bowring's perceived Russian threat does not seem to have entered into the consideration of the British government when it was decided to wage the *Arrow* War. Treaty revision was the vital factor.

Palmerston had no intention whatever of letting Russia join the Anglo-French expedition against China. Nor would he run the risk of allowing the Russians, in the heat of the China quarrel, to set foot on Chusan. Accordingly, British military strategy was modified. Although on 31 October 1856 Clarendon had told Lord Cowley, and through him the French government, that occupation of Chusan was not a good idea,[103] and the French had agreed,[104] subsequently Clarendon instructed Elgin to include the occupation of Chusan as one of his options.[105]

Meanwhile, the Russians continued to send out feelers. On 29 January 1857,

99. Davis to Clarendon, 6 December 1856, FO17/259, pp. 172–4.
100. Clarendon's 6 December 1856 minutes on Davis to Clarendon, 6 December 1856, FO17/259, pp. 172–4.
101. Palmerston's 22 December 1856 minutes on Bowring to Clarendon, Desp. 325, 11 October 1856, FO17/243, p. 270.
102. Clarendon to Persigny, 16 December 1856, FO17/261, p. 80.
103. Clarendon to Cowley, 31 October 1856, FO17/261, p. 77.
104. Walewski to Persigny, 20 November 1856, FO17/261, p. 77.
105. Clarendon to Elgin, Draft 4, 20 April 1857, FO17/274, p. 9.

The diplomacy of imperialism

Bowring's report of the friendly visit to Hong Kong by the Russian frigate *Aurora* reached London.[106] Clarendon approved 'the friendly communication' which Bowring had entered into with the commander of that vessel,[107] but he alerted the Admiralty to this visit.[108]

On 10 March 1857, Clarendon received a letter from a Major G. Vallancey, which he immediately minuted: 'Circulate', whereby Palmerston read it as well.[109] Vallancey seemed to know China intimately. He argued, as he said he had done with Palmerston before, that 'sooner or later China will be brought under the influence of an European Power, and that Power will be, either England or Russia; consequently the sooner we forestall Russia the better for our country'. Why? 'The opening of China to us' would be 'a mine of inestimable value' with regard to British commerce. Vallancey concluded, 'I have as strong an opinion of the necessity of an energetic and decided action in China, as I hold should be the case on the frontiers of Afghanistan of which I have already made you acquainted'.[110] The Afghan Wars, of course, had been fought to halt Russian advance southwards toward India.

Intriguingly, Clarendon then wrote privately in April to Lord Wodehouse at St Petersburg requesting him to ask 'the Russians to co-operate with us in China'.[111] This change of policy might have been related to the recent but final U.S. rejection of the British invitation to form a triple alliance with Britain and France.[112] Wodehouse thought there was no harm in asking, although on the whole he did not think it very probable that they would agree: 'The Russians will pretend to be friendly and will intrigue against us in every way'.[113]

In the end, the Russians said they were going to send their own mission to China separately.[114] But their response to the informal soundings of Wodehouse for cooperation is interesting. They told him that they were 'disposed to act with us in China as far as is consistent with the peaceful relations between Russia and China'. Wodehouse commented: 'We shall not get much

106. See the Foreign Office endorsement on Bowring to Clarendon, 28 November 1856, FO17/253, p. 310.
107. Clarendon to Bowring Draft 38, 10 February 1857, FO17/261, p. 89.
108. Foreign Office to Admiralty, 6 February 1857, FO17/279, p. 317.
109. Clarendon's 10 March 1857 minutes on Vallancey to Clarendon, 9 March 1857, FO17/280, pp. 95-7.
110. Vallancey to Clarendon, 9 March 1857, FO17/280.
111. Wodehouse to Hammond (private), St Petersburg, 25 April 1857, Hammond Papers, FO391/3.
112. The rejection was tendered on 10 April 1857. See Tyler Dennett, *Americans in Eastern Asia* (New York, Macmillan, 1922), p. 302.
113. Wodehouse to Hammond (private), St Petersburg, 25 April 1857, Hammond Papers, FO391/3.
114. Clarendon to Elgin, Draft 17, 20 April 1857, enclosing Desps. 126, 135, 164, and 167 from the British minister at St Petersburg on the subject of a proposed Russian mission to China and the treaty concluded between Russia and Japan, FO17/274, p. 45.

practical assistance from Putiatin [the Russian plenipotentiary] but if the Chinese see him in friendly communication with Elgin, the moral effect may be useful'.[115]

He had forgotten his own earlier warning about the capability of the Russians to intrigue. Putiatin sailed to Hong Kong and joined the Anglo-French allies. Like the U.S. envoy, Putiatin remained nonbelligerent, a neutral observer of the hostilities. Yet he presented demands for a treaty like the belligerents. Moreover, unknown to the allies, Putiatin added a supplementary note, claiming the left bank of the Amur River and the right bank of the Ussuri as boundaries and artfully implying the backing of the European powers for his demand. By some ruse, his note reached the Chinese authorities in the same envelope as the U.S. one. During the subsequent negotiations at Tianjin in 1858, Putiatin managed to keep his demands for the Amur and maritime territories entirely secret from the other three envoys. The Chinese authorities unwittingly helped Putiatin's scheme by dealing separately with the powers in the hope of pitting one against another.[116]

To cut a long story short, the British, who shoulder the blame for starting and waging the *Arrow* War, received, in terms of territory, the Kowloon peninsula (47 sq. km). The Russians, without firing a shot, obtained a piece of land as large as France.[117]

VI. More questions

Why was the British government so anxious to find allies? Could not the most powerful empire in the world handle China alone? With these questions, we need to look at the resources at their disposal.

They had just fought the Crimean War at great cost. When the chancellor of the exchequer in Palmerston's first ministry, Sir George Cornewall Lewis, brought forward his first budget on 20 April 1855, he forecast a deficit of £23 million. Consequently, Lewis had to raise £16 million by a new loan, £3 million by Exchequer bills, and the remaining £4 million by increasing the

115. Wodehouse to Hammond (private), St Petersburg, 16 May 1857, Hammond Papers, FO391/3.
116. See Rosemary K. I Quested, *The Expansion of Russia in East Asia, 1857–60* (Kuala Lumpur, University of Malaya Press, 1968), pp. 96–9; Joseph Fletcher, 'Sino-Russian Relations, 1800–62', *Cambridge History of China, v.* 10, *Late Ch'ing 1800–1911, Part* 1 (Cambridge University Press, 1978), pp. 318–50. See also Yu Shengwu et al., *Sha-E qin Hua shi* (A history of Russian aggression against China), 3 vs. (Beijing, Renmin chubanshe, 1976–80), v. 3, chapter 3; and Zhao Zhongfu, *Qingji Zhong-E dongsansheng jiewu jiaoshe* (Sino-Russian negotiations over the Manchurian border issue, 1858–1911) (Taibei, Institute of Modern History, Academia Sinica, 1970), pp. 58–62.
117. Quested, *The Expansion of Russia in East Asia, 1857–60*, pp. 96–9. For the Chinese primary sources on this episode, see *Qingdai Zhong-E guanxi dangan shiliao xuanbian* (Selected sources on China–Russia relations during the Qing period, 3d series [1851–62]), compiled by the Ming-Qing section of the Palace Museum, 3 vs. (Beijing, Zhonghua shuju, 1979).

income tax from 14 pence to 16 pence in the pound and by raising the duties on sugar, tea, coffee, and spirits. By this budget national revenue by taxation was raised to £68,639,000, a sum 'largely in excess of any that had ever before been so levied'.[118] Even then, continual war expenses compelled Lewis, before that parliamentary session closed, to apply for power to issue £7 million of Exchequer bills instead of £3 million. He introduced his second budget on 19 May 1856, estimating the whole cost of the Crimean War at £77,588,711.[119] As no new taxes were to be levied, Lewis, to meet a deficiency of over £8 million, was once more compelled to find the money by means of a further loan.[120]

By the time he was preparing his third budget, the Crimean War had ended, but the *Arrow* quarrel had started. Long before Parliament was opened on 3 February 1857, the British government had begun rushing troops to China from India.[121] Thus, by March, exactly one year after the Crimean War had ended, there were still about 8,500 more men employed in the Royal Navy than before that war.[122] Hence, the duke of Argyll was perhaps not entirely fair in criticizing his cabinet colleagues responsible for the army and navy for submitting estimates based on war-time expenditures. He regarded it as 'a signal case of blindness'.[123] The secretary for war, Lord Panmure, might have proved himself wanting in sensitivity.[124] But is it not possible that the military chiefs were simply anticipating war expenditures in China?

On the other hand, the duke had concerns other than military. He was worried that the taxpayers would not put up with such high income tax once the Crimean War was over. Lewis told Clarendon that the hatred of income tax was bound to 'animate the people'.[125] 'Throughout January protest meetings were held up and down the country, criticizing both the retention and the inequitable nature of the income tax'.[126] In the end, Lewis asked the military

---

118. Sir Stafford Northcote, *Twenty Years of Financial Policy: A Summary of the Chief Financial Measures Passed between 1842 and 1861, with a Table of Budgets* (London, Saunders, Otley, 1862), p. 268.
119. Ibid., p. 295; Sydney Charles Buxton, *Finance and Politics: An Historical Study, 1783–1885* (London, John Murray, 1888) v. 1, p. 155.
120. Sir George Cornewall Lewis's budget speech, 1856, Hansard, 3d series, v. 142, cols. 329–55.
121. See Chapter 12.
122. Hamilton, *Anglo-French Naval Rivalry*, p. 155.
123. Argyll, *Autobiography and Memoirs*, v. 2, p. 72.
124. For the insensitivity of Panmure (1801–74), see *DNB*, v. 13, p. 85. On the other hand, the first lord of the Admiralty, Sir Charles Wood (1829–85), Baronet, was thoroughly sensible, having been secretary of the Treasury (1832 to November 1834), secretary to the Admiralty (1835–9), chancellor of the Exchequer (1846–52), and president of the Board of Control (1852–5). He was subsequently created First Viscount Halifax of Monk Bretton in 1866. *BMP*, v. 1, p. 416.
125. Cornewall Lewis to Clarendon, 9 January 1857, MSS Clar. Dep. C70, folio 139. See also Cornewall Lewis to Palmerston, 17 January 1857, Broadlands MSS, GC/LE, folio 92. Sir George Cornewall Lewis was the chancellor of the exchequer.
126. Taylor, *Decline of British Radicalism*, p. 270.

chiefs to revise their estimates, which were subsequently lowered from £24 million pounds sterling to £21 million.[127] That enabled him to reduce the income tax from 16 pence to 7 pence in the pound and make some small reductions in the tea, coffee, and sugar duties.[128]

The Crimean War had been fought with French allies. Now, with the conflict in China following hot on the heels of that in the Crimea, the British authorities were understandably anxious to secure allies additional to the French, to the extent of sounding out the Russians with whom they had just done battle. It has been said that in diplomacy there are no permanent friends or foes, only permanent interests. In this context, one cannot help but question the British interests involved in waging the *Arrow* War. This question will be dealt with in Part Six.

It is noteworthy that President Pierce refused to join the Anglo-French military expedition in the absence of congressional approval. Thus, the British descendants in the United States insisted on respecting the constitutional power of Congress to make war. Did Palmerston have the same regard for Parliament? Did he have the consent of Parliament to wage the *Arrow* War? Or were the interests involved so great that the rule of law was disregrded? Such may indeed be the exigencies of imperialist politics, as we shall see.

127. Argyll, *Autobiography and Memoirs*, v. 2, pp. 72–3.
128. Sir George Cornewall Lewis's budget speech, 13 February 1857, Hansard, 3d series, v. 144, cols. 629–64. He seems to have designed his budget to please only the voters. Before the Reform Bill of 1865, the voters were well-off Britons, among whom many paid income tax. The majority of the British adult population of working age were neither entitled to vote nor required to pay income tax. All had to pay indirect taxes, such as duties on tea, coffee, and sugar. Thus, the budget gave the well-to-do a reduction of over 50 per cent in income tax, while the poor gained only small reductions in the indirect taxes they had to pay.

12
Behind the scenes:
The politics of imperialism

As with the preceding chapter, we shall begin our analysis from the moment London received news of the quarrel in China, or even before.

I. Commercial interests

As mentioned, on Monday, 29 December 1856, Britons first learned about the *Arrow* incident and the bombardment of Canton through a telegraphic message from Trieste.[1] The attitude of *The Times* to 'all this slaughter and desolation must be one of regret that anything should have occurred to render so strenuous an appeal to armed force necessary'. Everybody was left to guess what the cause was. Genuinely feeling uneasy about the bloodshed, the paper expressed the hope that 'enough has been done to render anything more of the same kind superfluous.' Unbeknownst to the public, the British government was envisaging that much more of the same kind might be necessary in the immediate future.

The paper continued, 'In a town so thickly inhabited, containing more than a million and a half of inhabitants, the effect of a bombardment must have been dreadful, and the loss of life enormous'. Thereupon the Victorian liberal conscience spoke out loudly and clearly, 'We hear only, however, the loss of property by fire'.[2]

But there was another dimension to the quarrel. The telegraphic message ended with this: 'Commerce was at a standstill'.[3] This caused terrific excitement. *The Times* complained that the telegraphic news, 'without caring whose feelings it may shock, whose sympathies it may wound, or whose nerves it may shake, blurts out its message with blunt, unmannerly brevity, leaving us to swallow it as well as we may'.[4] News of the stoppage of trade immediately

1. *The Times*, 29 December 1856, p. 6, col. 6.
2. Ibid., 30 December 1856, p. 6, col. 3: editorial.
3. Ibid., 29 December 1856, p. 6, col. 6.
4. Ibid., 30 December 1856, p. 6, col. 3: editorial.

raised the price of tea which 'is a matter of importance to every family in this country'. Indeed, the news had instantly caused near consternation in the tea markets of the United Kingdom, 'and in the early part of the day several thousand chests were purchased, in some instances on Liverpool accounts . . . Some effect was also produced on the price of silk, which experienced an advance of 6d. per lb.'. *The Times* continued, 'The stoppage of trade at this moment is peculiarly unfortunate. The failure of silk in Southern Europe rendered the Chinese export especially valuable'.[5] What was to be done? Obviously China had to be made to lift the stoppage of trade.

It was a case of liberal conscience versus commercial interests.

On 2 January 1857, *The Times* came down heavily in favour of commercial interests, and thereby changed its tune completely. 'We have no reason to suppose at present that enough has been done to bring the Chinese authorities to reason'.[6] So the paper was preparing its readers for more bloodshed. How did it defend this envisaged further bloodshed? Not by a claim to avenge an insult to the flag or to a British ship, because it was disputable whether the *Arrow* 'was carrying the British colours, and whether the Consul was entirely justified in the steps that he took'. But, 'By this outbreak of hostilities, existing treaties are annulled, and we are left free to shape our future relations with the Chinese empire as we please'. As if that point had not been made strongly enough, the editor repeated himself in the next paragraph: 'The treaty lately existing between us is destroyed by the recent outbreak of hostilities'. Consequently, 'We have a new treaty to make'.[7] One almost suspects that Palmerston had had a word with the editor, John Delane,[8] before this editorial was written.[9] With the most influential newspaper unreservedly in support of treaty revision so early in the piece, the government had scored their first victory in a frantic campaign to persuade the British public that another war with China was necessary.

Some of Palmerston's cabinet colleagues were not so easily convinced. They, too, had to square their liberal conscience with ecoonomic interests. 'Sir Charles Wood, Earl Granville, and Sir George Cornewall Lewis all wrote to Lord Clarendon'.[10] Particularly noteworthy are the views of Lewis, because of his general reputation as a sober-minded politician who enjoyed the confidence of moderate men of all parties. Granville described him as 'cold-blooded

5. Ibid., col. 4.
6. Ibid., 2 January 1857, p. 6, col. 3: editorial.
7. Ibid.
8. For a biography of him, see Arthur Irwin Dasent, *John Thaddeus Delane, Editor of The Times: His Life and Correspondence*, 2 vs. (London, Office of *The Times*, 1908).
9. For the close relationship between Palmerston and Delane, see *History of the Times*, v. 2, pp. 321ff.
10. Taylor, *Decline of British Radicalism*, p. 269. As mentioned before, Sir Charles Wood, Baronet, was the first lord of the Admiralty; Earl Granville was lord president of the Council; and Sir George Cornewall Lewis, Baronet, was chancellor of the Exchequer.

as a fish, totally devoid of sensibility or nervousness, of an imperturbable temper, calm and resolute, ... and exceedingly popular in the House of Commons, from ... the credit given him for honour, sincerity, plain-dealing and good intentions'.[11] Lewis and his two cabinet colleagues expressed doubts about the wisdom of Bowring's actions, and called for an early meeting of the Cabinet. Clarendon agreed, and 'the Cabinet met at the end of the first full week of the new year',[12] the Monday of which was 5 January 1857. But before the Cabinet met, the government published in the *London Gazette* of Tuesday, 6 January, the despatches received from Admiral Seymour concerning naval operations at Canton.[13]

The effect of the publication on the business community in London was immediate. The chairman of the East India and China Association in London, Samuel Gregson, M.P., wrote to Lord Clarendon. 'In fact a new treaty will now be required', he emphasized, in which 'it will be necessary to revise the tariff ad valorem rates for the assessment of duties, and it would be desirable to obtain permission to trade at any other, in addition to the five ports'. Besides, it would be a great advantage 'to have the navigation of the large rivers'. Canton City must be entered so as to demolish Chinese resistance to British penetration into China. Many members of the Association had been resident in China, and 'would at any time be ready to give local information derived from their own experience'. When a new treaty was being drawn up, 'we hope we may be allowed, as on the former occasion, to submit such further suggestions as may occur to us for the maintenance and extension of our commerce with China'. The petition ended with some impressive figures to show that 'our trade with China has become one of the greatest National importance':

The import of tea in 1842:	42,000,000 lbs;
That in 1856:	87,000,000 lbs;
The import of silk in 1842:	3,000 bales;
That in 1856:	56,000 bales.[14]

Here was another source of strong support for the government's envisaged war with China.[15]

11. Greville diary, 8 February 1857, Greville MSS 41122, cited in Greville, *Memoirs*, v. 8, p. 86, and in turn, cited in Hawkins, *Parliament*, p. 55.
12. Taylor, *Decline of British Radicalism*, p. 269, using as his source of information Clarendon to Lewis, 6 January 1857, MSS Clar. Dep. C533.
13. Draft Foreign Office circular to H.M. Representatives abroad, 7 January 1857, FO17/261.
14. Gregson to Clarendon, 6 January 1858, FO17/279. A copy of the same document may be found in the company archives of Baring Brothers, Baring Papers HC6.1.20.
15. The influential members of that association included William Jardine and James Matheson, cofounders of the most important opium agency in China. William Jardine almost single-handedly masterminded British strategy for the Opium War, and his suggestions for the terms of a peace treaty were closely followed by Lord Palmerston, who was then foreign

Clarendon minuted, 'Acknowledge with thanks and try to assure them that their letter shall receive from H.M. Government all the attention which the great importance of the subject demands'. He added that he would have much satisfaction in receiving from them any suggestion or advice with respect to the new treaty which it was desirable to negotiate with China.[16]

Some of Clarendon's cabinet colleagues were not similarly enthused. One almost suspects that the publication of Seymour's despatches prior to the pending cabinet meeting was designed to influence the liberal conscience therein. Besides, one suspects that it is perhaps not pure coincidence that on 8 January, *The Times* demanded that Britain should 'enforce the right of civilised nations to free commerce and communications with every part of this vast territory'. It further argued that there was no use in 'treating with such a power as if it belonged to the enlightened communities of Europe'.[17] A week later, Clarendon still found himself having to write to placate Cornewall Lewis. However, he could only repeat what *The Times* had already suggested, namely, Lewis must not assume that the Chinese were motivated by the same sort of principles as 'ourselves'. In the face of barbarism, he implied, moderation made little sense.[18]

On 17 January 1857, the Admiralty transmitted to Clarendon a further report from Seymour of operations on the Canton River. It seems that another cabinet meeting resulted in a long document, dated 24 January 1857, containing instructions to the Admiralty as to what to do next. The preamble said that Seymour's extra pressure did not seem to have produced any effect on Yeh. Additional measures were therefore necessary to open his eyes. 'With this view Her Majesty's Government are of opinion' that all the forts up to Canton, that were not desirable to hold, should be destroyed to make it quite clear 'to the Chinese that it is to our forbearance alone, and not to any want of power on our part', that the preservation of the lives and property of the Cantonese was owing. 'It is impossible for Her Majesty's Government to form an opinion' whether Yeh's conduct was a direct result of Beijing's policy. But if Bowring and Seymour should think it was, then to enforce the demands made by the admiral at Canton, as well as that for treaty revision, 'Her Majesty's Government consider that the next step should be to detach a naval force to the

---

secretary. See Chang, *Commissioner Lin*. Now the Foreign Office did not seem to be as decidedly influenced by the commercial interests as before. In fact it resisted some of their more aggressive suggestions. For details, see Chapter 13, this volume.

16. Clarendon's minutes on Gregson to Clarendon, 6 January 1858, FO17/279. The official reply may be found in ibid., Foreign Office to Gregson, Draft, 8 January 1858, while the original, signed by E. Hammond, is in the company archives of Baring Brothers, Baring Papers HC6.1.20.
17. *The Times*, 8 January 1857,
18. Clarendon to Lewis, 15 January 1857, MSS Clar. Dep. C533; and Lewis to Clarendon, 15 January [1857], MSS Clar. Dep. C70, folios 163-4; both quoted in Taylor, *Decline of British Radicalism*, p. 269.

Yang-tzu-keang'. Furthermore, the government had reason to believe that the French government was 'prepared to associate themselves with them in any measures calculated to bring the present state of things to a satisfactory conclusion', and that the U.S. government might do the same. Therefore, Seymour should readily accept cooperation which might be offered to him on the part of the naval forces of France and the United States, and should 'act with them with the utmost cordiality'.[19]

On the same day, 24 January 1857, Clarendon requested the India Board to send to Hong Kong a native regiment from the Madras Presidency,[20] in view of the Bombay Presidency's expressed inability to comply with a requisition from Bowring for a second European regiment.[21] On 26 January, the India Board agreed to despatch immediately one regiment of native infantry from Madras.[22]

On 29 January, the chairman of the East India and China Association in Liverpool wrote to Lord Clarendon. He presumed that the recent hostilities at Canton 'will render it compulsory on Her Majesty's advisers to require from the Chinese government new treaty stipulations'. These should include free entry into Canton and other cities; permanent residence of a British ambassador at Beijing; an ad valorem duty of 5 per cent on all imports and exports; the opening to foreign trade of any port on the coast of China, or on the banks of any navigable river at any time British merchants should think fit; and free access to all the ports and rivers of China.[23]

On behalf of Clarendon, Hammond happily acknowledged receipt of the petition, thanking the Association for its suggestions, which 'will be borne in mind.'[24] Of course the government gladly heard what they wanted to hear. A certain C. D. Bruce also wrote to Hammond, on 30 January 1857, transmitting an extract from a friend's letter from Shanghai: 'I think the Cantonese will see the City burned rather than give way. It is *not* the Governor who opposes, it is emphatically the *public*. It is well our Government should know this, for I think Admiral Seymour deceives himself'.[25] Obviously the writer at Shanghai knew the real situation at Canton. Hammond's reaction was, 'Don't take the trouble of acknowledging this'.[26]

19. Foreign Office to Admiralty, 2d Draft, 24 January 1857, FO17/279, pp. 220–3.
20. Foreign Office to India Board, Draft, 24 January 1857, FO17/279, p. 230. Madras was renamed Chinai in 1996 (*South China Morning Post*, 23 November 1996, p. 9). I shall continue to call it Madras since all the records in this period refer to it as such.
21. India Board to Foreign Office, 23 January 1857, FO17/279, pp. 213–15.
22. India Board to Foreign Office, 26 January 1857, FO17/279, p. 233.
23. Turner to Clarendon, 29 January 1857, FO17/279, p. 247. This document was later printed in Parl. Papers 1857, v. 12, pp. 201–2. Charles Turner was the chairman of the East India and China Association of Liverpool.
24. Hammond to Turner, 31 January 1857, FO17/279, p. 287.
25. Bruce to Hammond, 30 January 1857, FO17/279, p. 286.
26. Hammond's minutes on Bruce to Hammond, 30 January 1857, FO17/279, p. 286.

But that writer was not the only one who wanted to vent his feelings. On 2 February 1857, a document was printed with the title 'Memorial of the Inhabitants of Manchester to the Queen on the Massacre at Canton'. It read:

May it please your Majesty,

We, the undersigned, inhabitants of Manchester, in public meeting assembled, beg leave to convey to your Majesty the feelings of shame and indignation with which we have learnt the news of the destruction, by your Majesty's forces, of innocent life at Canton.

We believe from the published evidence, that the hostile acts committed by Admiral Seymour, with the concurrence of Sir John Bowring and Mr Consul Parkes, cannot be justified on the plea of necessity, and are worthy of the gravest and heaviest censure.

In the person of your Majesty only is invested the prerogative of declaring war and making peace, to be by your Majesty exercised according to law, which prerogative has been usurped by the slave servants of your Majesty.

We, therefore, most humbly and earnestly implore your Majesty to recall immediately Admiral Seymour, Sir John Bowring, and Mr Consul Parkes, and to order a searching inquiry into their conduct, to the end that justice may be done, and the British nation may be freed from the charge of participating in such acts.

And your petitioners will ever pray.
   Signed on behalf of the meeting
                                          J. E. Nelson, Chairman.[27]

The petition was enclosed in a letter to Clarendon from John Buxton, who signed himself as the chairman of the Free Trade, Home and Foreign Affairs Association of Manchester.[28] Clarendon minuted, 'Ack[nowledge] rec[eipt]', but without the usual 'thanks'. Hammond minuted, 'Ack[nowledge]d'.[29]

On 3 February 1857, the Queen opened Parliament. The government had to confront several issues. The first was income tax.[30] Another was electoral reform. Foreign problems included the Persian question, which Lord Grey said he would make his great '*cheval de bataille*',[31] trouble with Naples, and of course the China quarrel. However, the Queen's speech 'told us nothing',[32] which has been interpreted as reflecting the government's anxiety over all these issues coming at once.[33]

Lord Derby entertained high hopes of dislodging Palmerston's cabinet with

---

27. Petition to the Queen, 2 February 1857, FO17/279, p. 327.
28. Buxton to Clarendon, 6 February 1857, FO17/279, p. 325. His letterhead revealed that he was the chairman of the said association.
29. Clarendon's 11 February 1857 minutes on Buxton to Clarendon, 6 February 1857, FO17/279, p. 325. Hammond's minutes were dated 13 February 1857.
30. To some extent this question was examined in Chapter 11.
31. See Graham MSS Bundle 131, Aberdeen to Graham, quoted in Hawkins, *Parliament*, p. 53.
32. Malmesbury, *Memoirs*, v. 2, p. 58.
33. Hawkins, *Parliament*, p. 53.

the question of income tax.[34] But the chancellor of the Exchequer was ready for him. Cornewall Lewis proposed a reduction of the income tax from 16 to 7 pence in the pound, and dramatically preempted opposition attack.[35] Thereupon Derby began to perceive the China quarrel as a more effective weapon with which to tackle Palmerston, saying that he '*must* bring forward the case of China, in some shape or another'.[36] Disraeli agreed that Bowring's proceedings were indefensible, but advised caution. He feared that if Palmerston were driven to the country, his popularity earned during the recent Crimean War was bound to return him at the polls. But Disraeli was overruled by Derby. Thereupon Derby intimated to his reluctant party that he was prepared to cooperate with Gladstone or anyone else who would endeavour to defeat the government.[37]

Gladstone responded positively, and on 4 February at 3 P.M., he 'called on Lord Derby and remained with him above three hours'. He reciprocated Derby's sentiments by saying that he was 'content to act [against Palmerston] without enquiring who was to follow'.[38]

On the other hand, support for the government from the business community was snowballing. The Manchester Commercial Association wrote to Clarendon on 5 February 1857, expressing views very similar to those already voiced by the East India and China Associations of both London and Liverpool. In addition, the Manchester Commercial Association suggested that Shanghai should be put under British rule and declared a free port.[39]

On 9 February, Clarendon responded, in yet another long document, to the Admiralty's transmission of Seymour's third report. He expressed his satisfaction that Seymour had destroyed the French Folly Fort and the Blenheim forts. These, together with the U.S. destruction of the barrier forts, had accomplished the objective contained in his instructions of 24 January, namely the laying waste of all forts on the Canton River which it might not be desirable to hold. Thereupon, Clarendon directed that a blockade of the Peiho should be added to the earlier plan of taking up positions in the Yangtze, thus cutting off all access by water to the capital and, thereby, supplies from the southern

34. Grey diary, 4 February 1857, Grey MSS C3/19, quoted in ibid., p. 55.
35. Ibid., p. 56.
36. Derby to Disraeli, 11 February 1857, Hughenden MSS B/XX/S/146; and Grey diary, 11 February 1857, Grey MSS C3/19; both quoted in Hawkins, *Parliament*, pp. 56 and 58.
37. Buckle, *Disraeli*, v. 4, p. 72. Consequently, Disraeli was at first reluctant to speak up in the House of Commons and, when asked to do so by Malmesbury, replied 'very sulkily, even pretending not to understand what I meant by asking him if he intended to speak. "Speak! upon what?"' (Malmesbury, *Memoirs*, v 2, p. 62). In the end, however, Disraeli yielded to the persuasions of his friends and did not let his disapproval of the party tactics affect his oratory (Buckle, *Disraeli*, v. 4, p. 72).
38. *Gladstone Diaries*, v. 5, p. 193.
39. Fleming to Clarendon, 5 February 1857, FO17/279, pp. 303-4. Hugh Fleming was the secretary of that association.

provinces. Further, 'the instructions which Your Lordships will give to Sir Michael Seymour in conformity with what I have now stated will be equally applicable to joint as to separate operations'.[40]

Here, the Cabinet seems to have decided that in view of the escalation of the *Arrow* quarrel, Britain should go ahead and wage a general war with China even if the expected French, and the envisaged U.S., cooperation were not forthcoming.

On 16 February, Derby gave notice in the House of Lords that as soon as the papers relating to China were tabled, he would move a specific motion accordingly.[41] Lord Lyndhurst, more from a sense of justice than party affiliation,[42] was also reported to be 'in high force, with the Blue books before him, getting up the China case'.[43] In the House of Commons, Richard Cobden was preparing to do the same as part of his world peace mission.

At last there emerged public opposition to naked self-interest. It was opposition not entirely of a political nature either, as clearly was the case with Lord Lyndhurst and Richard Cobden. This resistance was due, apparently, to the liberal conscience.

Now that parliamentary focus had shifted to events in China, the foreign secretary suddenly found himself the target of public attention. He had to defend an almost indefensible case; and he could not expect warm support from his conscience-stricken cabinet colleagues. Charles Greville saw Clarendon on the morning of 17 February and found him 'low, worn, and out of sorts'. Clarendon told Greville he 'wished to Heaven he could be delivered from office; everything went wrong, the labour, anxiety, and responsibility were overwhelming'. Then Clarendon said something intriguing: '[A]nd the difficult state of our relations with France was more than could be endured'. He could not depend on the French government and never knew from one day to another what the consequences of their conduct might be.[44]

It will be remembered from the preceding chapter that Clarendon, after a great deal of effort, had persuaded the French government to join in a military expedition to cow the Chinese. The French were very aware that, because they had relatively little trade with China, the material benefits of the expedition would accrue almost exclusively to the British. Besides, Anglo-French relations since the end of the Crimean War had rapidly lost their warmth. Whitehall blamed the French emperor for seeking a rapprochement with the tzar indecently quickly, so that by this time the Admiralty was actually taking care to

40. Foreign Office to Admiralty, 9 February 1857, FO17/279, pp. 333–43.
41. Hawkins, *Parliament*, p. 59.
42. *DNB*, v. 4, pp. 1107–14.
43. Greville diary, 17 February 1857, Greville MSS 41122, quoted in Hawkins, *Parliament*, p. 56.
44. Greville diary, 17 February 1857, as reproduced in *Leaves from the Greville Diary*, pp. 781–2.

ensure that the Royal Navy in the Black Sea was capable of 'meeting both the French and Russian squadrons there'.[45]

Not surprisingly, the French now seemed to be amusing themselves by keeping Clarendon on tenterhooks. One day, Clarendon might confidently enclose a copy of a despatch from the British ambassador at Paris containing the substance of the instructions with which Walewski had furnished the French representative in China, M. de Bourboulon.[46] Three days later, Clarendon would have to write to Bowring again, stating that Walewski 'concurred' in the propriety of delaying furnishing Bowring with instructions respecting the demand to be made by the treaty powers for the revision of the existing treaties.[47]

More seems to have been going on than meets the eye. Clarendon would be in some difficulty if Walewski suddenly pulled out, leaving the British to fight the war alone and to foot the entire bill. In that case, even the 'cold-blooded' chancellor of the Exchequer might become heated. It was probably as an attempt to cope with the uncertainty of French intentions that, as we observed earlier in this chapter, the Cabinet seems to have prepared for all contingencies by informing Seymour that his instructions were 'equally applicable to joint as to separate operations'.[48]

Palmerston informed his colleagues at a cabinet meeting that an attack on the government was being prepared on the grounds of Bowring's having violated the principles of international law. He added that 'the legal members of the House were shaking their heads very much about it'.[49] Thereupon he proposed an unprecedented measure, to call in the attorney-general to the meeting – unprecedented because the opinion of the law officers had always been given in writing and circulated in a paper to the Cabinet. The advantage of a personal appearance was, of course, that the opinion could be elucidated by questions and answers. The Cabinet agreed, and Richard Bethell[50] was summoned.[51]

Ever since the attorney-general was described in the House of Commons by John Roebuck as speaking as if he had a retaining fee and a brief,[52] we have been looking forward to hearing his legal opinion.

---

45. Hamilton, *Anglo-French Naval Rivalry*, p. 78.
46. Clarendon to Bowring, Draft 12, 10 January 1857, FO17/261, p. 25.
47. Clarendon to Bowring, Draft 14, 14 January 1857, FO17, 261, p. 31.
48. Foreign Office to Admiralty, 9 February 1857, FO17, 261, pp. 333–43.
49. Argyll, *Autobiography and Memoirs*, v. 2, p. 67.
50. Richard Bethell (1800–73) had been attorney-general since 1856. In 1857, his constituency was Aylesbury. He became lord chancellor in 1861 under the title of Baron Westbury of Westbury in the county of Wilts. *DNB*, v. 2, pp. 426–31.
51. Argyll, *Autobiography and Memoirs*, v. 2, p. 67.
52. Roebuck, 3 March 1857, Hansard, 3d series, v. 144, cols. 1783–5.

'Before he had spoken ten minutes, my attention had been, first thoroughly aroused, and then irresistibly attracted', recalled the duke of Argyll. Bethell gave 'a most careful and accurate statement of the facts of a complicated case – on an equally careful definition of the principles applicable to them, and on a clear indication of the conclusions to which he thought they pointed'. Concluding, he shook his head ominously and warned that 'a very serious case against us on the points of international law could be, and probably would be, made out in the House of Commons'.[53] It became clear to everybody at the cabinet meeting that 'were it not for his office, it would give him immense pleasure to take the part of leading counsel against us'.[54]

We recall that, in public, the law lords could not agree on the legality of the actions taken by Parkes and Bowring over the *Arrow* incident. Given the views of the attorney-general, we wonder if those of their lordships on the side of the government would have been similar if likewise offered in a 'secret and confidential' capacity.

II. The liberal conscience

Having heard the attorney-general's exposition of the case, Argyll was impressed with the man but less with the possible consequences of his argument. Argyll said he did not care to ask Bethell whether Bowring's conduct had or had not been somewhat more high-handed than necessary. He thought that common sense would compel support for Bowring. After all, Bowring had merely, 'after the manner of his master', sent British ships and British guns to blow some Chinese forts out of the water.[55] A disavowal of the plenipotentiary, 'when such serious action had been taken, would inflict a severe blow on all our officers who might succeed him, and throw into confusion the whole system on which our commerce rested in that part of the world'.[56]

This was a pragmatic view, the view which somebody in office was likely to take. That was why Argyll believed this commonsense view would be taken by the country and by the House of Commons.[57] He was not worried about the House of Lords. Nonetheless, the government had to counterbalance the liberal conscience. And what better weapon to do so than with the submissions of the commercial lobbies? The memorials from the East India and China Association of both London and Liverpool were therefore included in the blue book entitled 'Papers Relating to the Proceedings of Her Majesty's Naval Forces at Canton', which was tabled in Parliament.[58]

53. Argyll, *Autobiography and Memoirs*, v. 2, p. 68. A copy of Bethell's legal opinion of the *Arrow* incident is to be found in the British Foreign Office Confidential Prints, 686A (FO/L.O.R.)
54. Argyll, *Autobiography and Memoirs*, v. 2, p. 69.
55. Ibid., p. 66.
56. Ibid., p. 68.
57. Ibid., p. 69.   58. See Parl. Papers 1857, v. 12, pp. 201 3.

This strategy appears to have carried a lot of weight in the House of Lords, although at one stage, the government had to resort to a most unusual tactic. Lord Derby's speech emphasizing justice and humanity was noticeably moving to many listeners, especially representatives of the Church. The permanent under-secretary for foreign affairs, Edmund Hammond, there officially to help out his minister, scribbled this note for his master, 'A report judiciously circulated of the declining health of the Archbishop of Canterbury would probably neutralise the effect of Lord Derby's wordy peroration as regards the Bench of Bishops'. Hammond continued, 'and a similar report, contradicted on Friday, as to the contemplated appropriation of vacant Garters might not be without its effect on others'.[59]

The fact that this sort of tactic was thought necessary testifies to the anxiety of the government about the liberal conscience of the peers and bishops. As for Edmund Hammond, he was a known Palmerstonian. When Lord Malmesbury succeeded Lord Granville as foreign secretary in 1852, he asserted that 'the chief of the clerks, Mr Hammond, was a very strong partisan on the other side', that is, Palmerston.[60]

The sympathies of another permanent under-secretary of state, that for the colonies, Frederick Rogers, were different. To him the Chinese war seemed 'one of the greatest iniquities of our time'. He was half-alarmed lest he should be found responsible for it, by allowing to pass the colonial ordinance under which 'Sir John Bowring has made such a fool of himself'.[61]

The liberal conscience seems to have gained the upper hand in the House of Commons, wherein Palmerston was defeated over Cobden's China motion.

The defeat is all the more remarkable because the government appears to have taken every precaution against Cobden's motion, to the extent of apparently doctoring it. Cobden had realized that a simple motion of censure would play straight into Palmerston's hands, allowing him to divert a foreign policy issue by making it a question of party loyalty, as he had so successfully done before. So Cobden tried to overcome that difficulty by designing two resolutions. The first stated that the papers tabled in Parliament failed to establish the grounds for the bombardment of Canton. The second called for a select committee to be appointed to inquire into the state of commercial relations with China. The first might be accused of provoking a vote of censure, but the second was aimed at providing the Liberal opposition with a means of expressing their dissent without necessarily censuring the government.[62] However, the government trimmed the two resolutions down to one and turned that

59. Hammond's notes for Clarendon, 25 February 1857, FO17/279, pp. 445–6.
60. *DNB*, v. 8, p. 1125.
61. Quoted in Frank Welsh, *A History of Hong Kong* (London, HarperCollins, 1993), p. 206.
62. Cobden to Richard [15 February 1857], Cobden Papers, BL Add. MSS, 43,658, folio 266, quoted in Taylor, *Decline of British Radicalism*, pp. 271–2.

resolution into a vote of censure on the government's policy on China. If the resolutions were *deliberately* amended, 'the culprit may have been Moffatt who first informed Clarendon of Cobden's original motion two weeks earlier, suggesting that it did amount to a vote of censure'.[63]

Cobden professed that 'he was utterly at a loss to conceive how the mistake had arisen'. He thought that 'directions ought to be given the printer to use more care in dealing with the manuscripts that were put into his hands'. He observed that 'a pencil mark had been run through the figure "2", and the world "Resolutions" converted into the singular from the plural'.[64] Gleefully Palmerston said he thought it was incumbent upon Cobden to have looked at the votes and seen whether his notice was printed in the manner he had proposed to submit them to the House.[65]

In the end Cobden proceeded with only his first resolution,[66] wherein 'more temperate words, more well-weighed and carefully considered words in reference to transactions in my opinion so flagrant, could have been employed', said Sir James Graham. 'There is not in these words a single syllable of censure'.[67] But Palmerston wanted to portray the motion as one of censure, and thereby deployed his party loyalty arguments. The representation, by Disraeli, of Cobden's motion as a vote of no confidence in the government[68] was just what Palmerston wanted.

But Cobden successfully gave verbal expression to the very real uneasiness of the country, including that of members of Palmerston's own Liberal Party who subsequently were to vote against him. After two nights of debate in the House of Commons, Lord Malmesbury observed that Palmerston had become so nervous that he had 'a meeting this morning to threaten a dissolution in case he is not supported'.[69] In addition, 'private summons were sent by telegraph to every government vote that could be brought to the House, even those abroad'.[70]

This step could cut both ways, as the members so summoned might not sympathize with the government's China policy either. The government then adopted a last-minute 'carrot-and-stick' approach. The carrot took the form of 'cards for receptions, dinner invitations, and offers without end of service and attention'.[71] The stick was wielded at a Liberal meeting in Downing Street on Monday, 2 March, at which Palmerston spoke to the 'wavering members',

---

63. Taylor, *Decline of British Radicalism*, p. 272, n. 42.
64. Cobden, 26 February 1857, Hansard, 3d series, v. 144, col. 1484.
65. Palmerston, 26 February 1857, Hansard, 3d series, v. 144, col. 1485.
66. Cobden's motion, 26 February 1857, Hansard, 3d series, v. 144, col. 1485.
67. Sir James Graham's electioneering speech, in *Globe*, 19 March 1857, p. 1, col. 6.
68. Disraeli, 3 March 1857, Hansard, 3d series, v. 144, cols. 1834–40.
69. Malmesbury, *Memoirs*, v. 2, pp. 61–2.
70. Grey diary, 28 February 1857, Grey MSS C3/19, quoted in Hawkins, *Parliament*, p. 61.
71. *Daily News*, 2 March 1857.

The politics of imperialism

giving them a reason which they could quote 'for changing their intended course'.[72] He stressed the importance of loyalty to good government and the great danger of the Liberal government being turned out by the opposition.[73] The dissidents defended their continued opposition to the government's China policy on the basis of liberal principles. Subservience to the government on matters of principle would mean 'the destruction of the Liberal party'.[74]

Palmerston went into the fourth and final night of the debate on 3 March 1857 confident that he had turned Cobden's motion into one of censure. Liberal dissidents could not express their opposition without appearing to censure the government. If they voted independently, they would be seen to be joining the 'Chinese Coalition'. Besides, Palmerston received fresh information about the poisonings in Hong Kong.[75] This he used as compelling evidence of the barbarism of the Chinese and made the cornerstone of his defence of Bowring's actions.[76]

Nonetheless, Palmerston was defeated. This was an indication of the strength of the liberal conscience in the House of Commons, at least in so far as disapproving the means to an end was concerned. Bowring's actions were only a means to an end. The end was to overhaul Britain's treaty relations with China. Thus, when the government defended Bowring, it was obliged to defend his means as well. Why did the government members not speak up about the end? Because it was taboo. No minister would dare stand up and frankly say, 'I have acted in this matter for the extension of British power ...' He who did so 'would be frozen by the silence of a shocked assembly, and deserted as though stricken by the plague of social proscription'.[77] In this respect, the firebrand was an exception. He dared stand up to ask what, now that the peaceful approach for treaty revision had failed, was the government supposed to do next?[78] Disraeli had no answer except to accuse him of attempting 'by force to increase our commercial relations with the East'.[79] But that begged the question. Disraeli really had no answer. And of course, when he got into office in Derby's administration a year later, he continued with the war which Bowring had started, and indeed with the same end in mind.

The person most badly caught in the crossfire between the liberal conscience and naked interests was Gladstone. He vigorously attacked Palmerston and

72. T. Archer and A. H. Stirling, *Queen Victoria: Her Life and Reign*, 4 vs. (London, Gresham, 1901), v. 3, p. 227.
73. *Manchester Guardian*, 3 March 1857, p. 3.
74. Taylor, *Decline of British Radicalism*, p. 272, quoting the *Daily News*, 2 March 1857, p. 4. Dr Taylor interprets this view of the *Daily News* as having been voiced in anticipation of the Liberal Party meeting on that day.
75. Palmerston to Clarendon, 1 March 1857, MSS Clar. Dep. C69, folio 155.
76. Palmerston, 3 March 1857, Hansard, 3d series, v. 144, col. 1823.
77. *Morning Star*, 6 March 1857, editorial.
78. Palmerston, 3 March 1857, Hansard, 3d series, v. 144, col. 1828.
79. Disraeli, 3 March 1857, Hansard, 3d series, v. 144, col. 1836.

the war in February 1857. When Palmerston regained office in June 1859, Gladstone accepted the invitation to become chancellor of the Exchequer.[80] Apparently, Gladstone had sent word that he was prepared to join Palmerston's cabinet, on condition that he be given this post. He asked for it. Now he had to request Parliament to approve nearly £4 million to carry on the war in China. John Roebuck took him to task:

> It was my fate to sit on the benches opposite, just under the present Chancellor of the Exchequer, when he delivered a speech to this House ... He then, Sir, fulminated against the Administration of that day for undertaking a Chinese war. He pointed out how vain were the ends they sought; and how mischievous were the means they took to attain those ends. But now, places being changed, opinions change, and I find him supporting the very vote which on that occasion he described as a disgrace to the country ... I would ask him, and his colleagues who on that occasion went with him into the lobby, how it is that, on this occasion, black has become white and white has become black.[81]

Gladstone replied, 'Sir, I feel no difficulty whatever – (Much laughter)'. His defence was that that he was merely performing his 'public duty'.[82]

Gladstone was caught in more ways than one. During the debate in the House of Commons in February 1857, he had spoken against Palmerston's waging of the Persian War without the previous sanction of Parliament by disguising it as one of the 'Indian wars'. Such a measure 'is utterly at variance with the established practice of the country, dangerous to the Constitution, and absolutely requiring the intervention of this House'.[83] The truth is Palmerston never obtained parliamentary consent for the *Arrow* War either. Now that Gladstone had joined Palmerston's cabinet and requested more money to finance the *Arrow* War, Earl Grey took him to task: 'There is in the present Government a very distinguished person who only three years ago laid down, in very clear terms, what is the correct rule to follow on this subject'.[84] That rule was firmly based on 'precedents, showing how in former times great Ministers have acted', Earl Grey continued. During the dispute with Spain in 1790, for example, Pitt personally brought down a message from the Crown, which read: 'His Majesty recommends it to his faithful Commons, on whose zeal and public spirit he has the most perfect reliance, to enable him' to prepare for war. In 1826, a similar message was brought down by Canning himself to both houses of Parliament.[85] Now, Earl Grey referred to Gladstone's speech, not

---

80. Argyll, *Autobiography and Memoirs*, v. 2, p. 137. For the hostility of *The Times* towards Gladstone's appointment, see *The History of The Times*, v. 2, p. 330. For an analysis of Gladstone's joining Palmerston, see Hawkins, *Parliament*, pp. 261–2.
81. Roebuck, 13 July 1860, Hansard, 3d series, v. 159, col. 1897.
82. Gladstone, 13 July 1860, Hansard, 3d series, v. 159, col. 1898.
83. Gladstone, 3 February 1857, Hansard, 3d series, v. 144, col. 145.
84. Grey, 24 January 1860, Hansard, 3d series, v. 156, cols. 23–4.
85. Ibid., cols. 19–20.

expecting him to respond but intending it as support for his amendment to the Queen's speech.[86] The amendment was rejected.[87]

Earl Grey had made a similar point on 9 March 1857, shortly after the announcement was made that a plenipotentiary would be sent to settle the *Arrow* dispute. 'Almost for the first time in our history', he said, 'we were engaged in a war which had not been formally made known to their Lordships by a Message from the Crown' and which Parliament had not been called upon to consider up to the moment when a large force was being despatched from Britain.[88]

But was that not the beauty of Palmerston's dissolution of Parliament? Grey also complained that the announcement was tardy and 'had the appearance of having been extorted from the Government'.[89] Was that not also within Palmerston's calculations? Palmerston's manipulation of the *Arrow* issue was masterly.

III. Party politics

Lady Clarendon noted with incredulous surprise that Gladstone 'who voted in the last division with the Derby ministry should not only be asked to join but allowed to *choose his office*'.[90] What was the relationship between party politics and imperialism in general, and the *Arrow* War in particular?

Party affiliations and party discipline were not as strong as they are today. We have seen briefly in Chapter 7 the various political parties in Britain at this time. Commenting on the fluidity of the party situation, John Russell said in 1855, 'The House of Commons is as unstable as water'.[91]

The *Arrow* quarrel was to make some radical changes to the political scene in Britain. Initially, it enabled many disparate elements to form an anti-Palmerstonian alliance: Derby, Gladstone, Russell, Cardwell, Cobden, in what Palmerston called 'a fortuitous concourse of atoms'. As the debate raged in

---

86. The amendment was to insert, 'After the words "Stipulations of the Treaty of Tien-tsin", "but humbly to express to Her Majesty our Regret that when the Preparations for the intended Expedition were commenced, Her Majesty's Servants did not advise Her Majesty to communicate to Parliament without Delay the Measures which had been decided upon, in order that Parliament might have an Opportunity of forming a Judgment on their Propriety, and that its previous Sanction might be obtained for the Expense they might occasion'. Grey, 24 January 1860, Hansard, 3d series, v. 156, col. 27.
87. Amendment, 24 January 1860, Hansard, 3d series, v. 156, col. 73.
88. Grey, 9 March 1857, Hansard, 3d series, v. 144, col. 2042.
89. Ibid., col. 2039.
90. Lady Clarendon's diary, 14 June 1859, quoted in Hawkins, *Parliament*, p. 262 (emphasis added).
91. Russell to Minto, 22 July 1855, Minto MSS 11775, folio 102, quoted in Hawkins, *Parliament*, p. 53. For the political parties of this time, see Gary W. Cox, *The Efficient Secret: The Cabinet and the Development of Political Parties in Victorian England* (Cambridge University Press, 1987). See also Peter Mandler, *Aristocratic Government in the Age of Reform: Whigs and Liberals, 1830–1852* (Oxford, Clarendon Press, 1990).

The mechanics of imperialism

Parliament, it became clear that the China question not only created new alliances but split old ones. It drove a wedge, for example, between the Radicals, that is, between pacifist Little Englanders like Cobden, and jingoists like Robert Lowe and Osborne, as we have seen in Chapter 9. It led Cobden to launch a violent attack on Lowe, stigmatizing him as a 'Parliamentary failure'.[92]

The subsequent Chinese Election created some permanent landmarks in British politics. The pacifists were routed. Cobden, Bright, Milner-Gibson, Layard, and Miall[93] all lost their seats. The 'expulsion' of these men 'from parliament was, in itself, worth a dissolution', said Clarendon.[94] The Peelites, too, were 'broken' and 'smashed as a party',[95] if they ever were a party rather than a faction after Peel's death. It paved the way for Gladstone to join Palmerston's ministry in 1859, the alternative being to continue 'losing the best years of [his] life'.[96]

So Palmerston's penal dissolution had worked wonders for him. The *Arrow* quarrel provided the excuse for which he had been looking to dissolve Parliament. Clarendon revealed that Palmerston 'would have been quite ready to dissolve last year, but there was no good excuse for it'.[97] The defeat over Cobden's motion provided both the excuse and a favourable issue with which to exploit Palmerstonian popularity, running so high since the recent conclusion of the Crimean War, beyond Westminster and Clubland. The coalition 'has unintentionally rendered a great service to the Government' which, Palmerston told the Queen, 'is more likely to gain strength by a general election brought about as the approaching election will be, than if... the dissolution had taken place without any particular event out of which a distinction between opposing parties could have been drawn'.[98]

'Moreover, the cabinet's determination to dissolve parliament as soon as possible would prevent others raising alternative issues with which to complicate a simple electoral sanction of "Palmerstonian" axioms'.[99] Unwittingly,

---

92. Cobden launched that attack on Wednesday 18 March 1857 at Manchester, where he was canvassing in support of the sitting members Milner-Gibson and Bright. See *Globe*, 20 March 1857, p. 1, cols. 3–4: col. 4.
93. Again, Edward Miall (1809–81) was for some years an Independent minister, but quit to establish in 1841 the *Nonconformist* newspaper, of which he was the sole proprietor and editor. By the standards of his time, he was a Liberal of 'extreme' opinions, being in favour of manhood suffrage. He sat for Rochdale from July 1852 to April 1857, when he lost his seat. See Miall, *Edward Miall*.
94. Clarendon to Cornewall Lewis, 28 March 1857, MSS Clar. Dep. C533.
95. Granville to Canning, 8 April 1857, Granville MSS PRO 30/29/21/2.
96. Gladstone to Heathcote, 16 June 1859, Gladstone MSS 44209, folio 38, quoted in Hawkins, *Parliament*, p. 261. See also Bentley, *Politics without Democracy*, p. 161.
97. Clarendon to Howard, 7 March 1857, MSS Clar. Dep. C137, folio 339.
98. Quoted in Steele, *Palmerston and Liberalism*, p. 73.
99. Hawkins, *Parliament*, p. 62, analysing Delane MSS 8/9, Clarendon to Delane, 4 March 1857. J. T. Delane was the editor of *The Times*.

The politics of imperialism

Lord Shaftesbury raised on 5 March 1857, the day after the *Arrow* debate finished in the House of Commons, the question of the opium trade,[100] and asked that the papers pertinent to opium be tabled.[101] *Punch* portrayed superbly the awkwardness this created for the government. It concocted a covering note from the president of the Privy Council, enclosing a letter purporting to be from the attorney-general and another from the solicitor-general. Of these two letters, Richard Bethell was alleged to have ended his with 'Lord Shaftesbury had better shut up shop' and Stuart Wortley with 'I am afraid Shaftesbury, though a worthy man, is a bit of a fidgety milksop'.[102]

We shall see how Hammond dealt with that crisis, in Chapter 13.[103] It suffices here to say that by the time the pertinent papers were printed, on 9 April 1857,[104] the election was over.

Another reason for the dissolution was the belief that there was really no other political leader at the time in a position to form a government, because the opposition was no more than a combination of 'all the scrabs and debris of parties which had resulted from many fractures'.[105] To look at it another way: 'We cannot wonder that the three parties represented by Mr Disraeli, Mr Gladstone, and Mr Cobden should be found united against the Ministry, for the Ministry was called into existence by the shortcomings, blunders, and weaknesses of all three'.[106]

In fact Gladstone had previously joined Palmerston's first cabinet in 1855. At that time, he was appointed chancellor of the Exchequer. But he soon resigned[107] and had felt very isolated since. 'For thirteen years, the middle space of my life, I have been cast out of party connections: severed from my old party and loath irrevocably to join a new one'.[108] Why did Palmerston offer him a position? Gladstone's 'power of speaking' was what Palmerston wanted for the government, and he 'dreads it in opposition'.[109]

Herbert, too, was to join Palmerston's cabinet in 1859 and was appointed to head the War Department![110] Lord John Russell was by now upon his own insistence appointed foreign secretary! Cardwell was given the secretaryship

---

100. Shaftesbury's notice of motion, 5 March 1957, Hansard, 3d series, v. 144, col. 1884.
101. Extract of Shaftesbury's motion of 20 March 1857, FO17/280, p. 253.
102. *Punch*, 28 March 1857, p. 129.
103. The most revealing primary source used therein was Smith to Hammond, 28 March 1857, FO17/280, p. 251.
104. Hammond's 9 April 1857 minutes on Smith to Hammond, 28 March 1857, FO17/280, p. 251.
105. Quoted in Steele, *Palmerston and Liberalism*, p. 70.
106. *The Times*, Thursday, 5 March 1858, p. 8, col. 3, editorial.
107. Woodward, *The Age of Reform*, pp. 639–40.
108. Gladstone to Heathcote, 16 June 1859, Gladstone MSS 44209, folio 38, quoted in Hawkins, *Parliament*, p. 261.
109. Clarendon to Duchess of Manchester (? 16 June 1859), quoted in Hawkins, *Parliament*, p. 262.
110. Wood diary, 14 June 1859, Hickleton MSS, A8/D, quoted in Hawkins, *Parliament*, p. 262. Like Gladstone, Herbert had been in Palmerston's first cabinet in 1855.

of Ireland.[111] All these former opponents of the *Arrow* War were now in Palmerston's cabinet to bring the war to a successful conclusion.

Thus, most of those who had attacked Bowring's initiation of the *Arrow* War had, by the end of the war in 1860, either continued with the war when they gained power, as did Derby and Disraeli in 1858–9, or joined Palmerston's cabinet to send money (as did Gladstone), troops (as did Herbert), or negotiators (as did Russell) to finish the war. There is no doubt that these men, who opposed the war in 1857, did so partly to embarrass the government by exploiting the liberal conscience of the time. This is not to say that they did not share such liberal views themselves when they denounced the means to the end. But in the final analysis, they supported the end of that war, which they would have defined as being in the national interest of Britain.

Let us look at the matter in another way. Since the resignation from Palmerston's cabinet in 1855 by Gladstone and other Peelites, apparently Lord Aberdeen had been urging them to join Palmerston's Liberal Party. After the Chinese Election of 1857, at which the greater part of the Peelites lost their seats, Aberdeen wrote to Gladstone arguing that 'there is no such thing as a distinctive Peelite party in existence'. His rationale was that after Lord Derby's overthrow by a junction with the Liberal Party and the formation of a government which recognized parliamentary reform as a fundamental issue, the whole relation of parties was changed, and 'I consider the amalgamation of Peel's friends with the Liberal Party to have practically taken place'.[112] It is said that Aberdeen's influence prevented Gladstone from throwing himself into the ranks of the Conservative Party.[113] The alternative was the Liberals.

Given the nature of British party politics of this time, Chinese historians need not become too excited either by the attacks on Commissioner Yeh or the praises of him. Just listen to the homily by *The Times*: 'If Parkes, Bowring, Seymour, Palmerston, Labouchere and their colleagues have beaten you with rods, Derby, Ellenborough, Russell, and Graham humbly hope that they may live to give you a taste of scorpions'.[114] As for Gladstone, *Punch* believed that he was merely playing chess.[115]

Such were the politics of imperialism in the eyes of a free press.

IV. Behind parliamentary rhetoric

Viewed in this light, the defeat of Palmerston by the adverse vote in the House of Commons gave him a much stronger hand. As one newspaper editor

---

111. Ibid.
112. Quoted in Sir Arthur Gordon, *The Earl of Aberdeen* (London, Sampson Low, Marston, 1894), pp. 296–7.
113. Gordon, *Aberdeen*, p. 298.
114. *The Times*, 28 February 1857.   115. *Punch*, 7 March 1857, p. 98.

pointed out at the time, 'That vote will have no influence on the course of events in China; will neither undo what has been done, nor stay the employment of force till force has bent the stubbornness of the Chinese to our Western will'. Thus, the editor felt that the House of Commons was in fact simply voting on the question of whether Lord Palmerston should continue in office or not, because it knew that its vote would have no practical effects in China. Had the situation been different, had the members known that their votes would affect the course of events which they were nominally discussing, there would always have been too much patriotism and good sense in the House to allow the great interests of the country to be made a mere stalking-horse for party. The result of all this was 'that we have not the honest opinion of the British Parliament upon the justice or expediency of our proceedings in China, but simply their decision that they do not object to a change of Ministry at home'.[116] Ultimately, therefore, Argyll was right about the 'common sense' of the House of Commons, too.

The kind of language used in Parliament must be seen in the same light. The editor of the *Manchester Guardian* summed up the extravagance of the parliamentary debates superbly: 'The just inference from all this is, that we, none of us, probably, think so badly of each other as it might sometimes be supposed from our language' The editor continued, 'The grand mistake that is sometimes made consists in taking at their full nominal value the expressions of censure or approbation which are expended on political contemporaries'.[117] The enormous amount of strong language, lavished out of some of the best-furnished stocks in the world on the front-line agents at Canton and others, was indeed mighty stuff. 'What indignant invective, what invocation to Heaven, what metaphorical cleansing of the hands of this unprecedented sin!' The editor exclaimed, ' If only one half of what has been said be true, we ought to undergo a national purification by fire and blood before we can be admitted into the human community again'.[118]

The mistake that the Chinese authority on the subject has made is to take all that indignant invective literally,[119] out of a misconception of the character of parliamentary government due to the absence of such a form of government in China.

The truth, according to the *Manchester Guardian*, was that few in the House really thought worse of others for having formed a different opinion about the quarrel with China. And their condemnation of Bowring should be seen in a similar light. Nobody doubted, for example, that his conduct conformed to government policy, although he might have erred through want of judgement

116. *Spectator*, 7 March 1857.
117. *Manchester Guardian*, 28 February 1857.
118. Ibid.
119. See Jiang, *Di'erci yapian zhangzheng*, pp. 71-3.

or temper. Despite the constantly expressed alarm and horror at the proceedings of one another, 'we are inwardly conscious that the general principles on which this country conducts its intercourse with weaker and distant nations are firmly established on a sound basis; and that it is only to a very limited extent in the power of any government to modify them in application'.[120]

What were these general principles to which everybody must conform, whosoever might be in power? – the commercial interests of the world's greatest trading nation. 'Like many of the wars in which England has engaged, this is a merchants' war,' observed the *Manchester Guardian*.[121] We have seen in Chapter 10 the kind of open lobbying by the merchant princes immediately after the dissolution of Parliament. We have seen some of the backstage lobbying in this chapter; and we shall see more in the next chapter, wherein we shall also ascertain the extent to which the government yielded to such pressure groups.

V. A political sacrifice

As mentioned in the preceding chapter, it was business as usual for the British government when news of the *Arrow* quarrel quietly reached Whitehall on 1 December 1856. It continued to be so for some considerable time thereafter. On 10 January 1857, four days after the government published Admiral Seymour's first despatch, Clarendon acknowledged receipt of the despatch which Bowring had begun writing on 23 October 1856 and completed on 15 November. Clarendon 'entirely' approved the course which Bowring and Seymour had taken and instructed Bowring 'to convey to Mr Parkes a similar approval of his conduct'.[122]

In a separate despatch of the same day, Clarendon enclosed a copy of the letter from the chairman of the East India and China Association of London containing observations relative to the revision of existing treaties with China, and a copy of the Foreign Office reply.[123] In a third despatch of that day, Clarendon enclosed a copy of a despatch from the British ambassador in Paris stating the substance of the instructions with which Count Walewski had just furnished the French plenipotentiary, M. de Bourboulon, on the latter's return to China.[124] On 26 January 1857, Clarendon sent Bowring a copy of the instructions which the Admiralty had addressed to Seymour, 'authorising the interruption in the Yang-tse-keang of the water-communication with Pekin . . . for a revision of the present treaties'.[125]

120. *Manchester Guardian*, 28 February 1857.   121. Ibid., 11 March 1857.
122. Clarendon to Bowring, Draft 10, 10 January 1857, FO17/261.
123. Clarendon to Bowring, Draft 11, 10 January 1857, FO17/261.
124. Clarendon to Bowring, Draft 12, 10 January 1857, FO17/261.
125. Clarendon to Bowring, Draft 17, 26 January 1857, FO17/261; see also Draft 33, 9 February 1857, FO17/261.

The politics of imperialism

The formal instructions to Bowring to use coercive measures to effect treaty revision were despatched on 9 February 1857. The preamble is interesting: 'The recent interruption of amicable relations with China, and the events connected with it, of themselves entitle Her Majesty's Government to insist upon such a revision'. It seems that by now Clarendon had consulted the law officers and realized that demanding treaty revision on the basis of the most favoured nation principle was no longer an option. But for the *Arrow* quarrel, therefore, Britain would have had no excuse for treaty revision.

Clarendon's draft despatch to Bowring was a printed document, enclosing the correspondence between the British and French governments, likewise printed, between September and December 1856. These documents had to be printed because Britain was actively contemplating war and a large number of people concerned would have to be informed and mobilized. Bowring was instructed in the spirit of that Anglo-French correspondence, which has been dealt with in the preceding chapter.

He was told to demand permanent residence of a British minister in Beijing, as well as the penetration of the interior of China, so that, inter alia, 'British merchants may purchase, either by themselves or by their agents at the place of production, the teas or other raw productions'. Such articles, once so purchased, must be exempted from any duties, 'if there are any, on their transport to the coast'. Bowring was told that Her Majesty's government agreed with the French position that the U.S. demands were secondary. Clarendon's long despatch ended on the note that the government relied on Bowring's intimate knowledge of local conditions, with which his 'long residence in China will have familiarised' him, to carry out his instructions effectively.[126]

Bowring might look forward to the realization of his dream of opening up China to British exploitation.

Supplementary instructions were to follow. On 10 February 1857, Clarendon transmitted to Bowring a copy of another letter from the chairman of the East India and China Association of London, petitioning the government to pressure the Chinese authorities into revoking the prohibition of Chinese emigration abroad, as the settlement at Singapore, for example, badly needed Chinese females.[127] In another despatch of the same day, Clarendon commanded Bowring to insert a stipulation in the new treaty that if any doubt or difference should arise as to the meaning of any article or stipulation, 'such doubt or difference shall be determined by reference to the English version'.[128]

---

126. Clarendon to Bowring, Draft 33, 9 February 1857, FO17/261.
127. Clarendon to Bowring, Draft 39, 10 February 1857, FO17/261. This demand was subsequently incorporated in the instructions to Elgin. See Clarendon to Elgin, Draft 5, 20 April 1857, FO17/274.
128. Clarendon to Bowring, Draft 40, 10 February 1857, FO17/261.

The mechanics of imperialism

In yet another despatch of the same day, Bowring was instructed, in view of the sudden imposition of internal duties on tea destined for exportation, to secure the right of British merchants to send their own agents to purchase Chinese produce at the places of production and to transport such produce to the treaty ports free of internal duties.[129]

On 4 March 1857, Clarendon transmitted to Bowring further petitions to secure a revocation of the Chinese prohibition on emigration, this time from the East India and China Association of Liverpool and from the Chamber of Commerce at Glasgow.[130]

Thus, despite the fierce attacks on Bowring in both houses of Parliament, beginning with Derby's speech in the House of Lords on 24 February 1857[131] and ending with cries for a division in the House of Commons on 3 March,[132] the government seems to have been determined to give Bowring free rein to continue putting pressure on the Chinese authorities. Bowring had been waiting almost a decade for this chance – to negotiate a new treaty with China.

But one of his sons, Edgar J. Bowring of the Board of Trade, had been alarmed on 6 January, when the government published Seymour's despatch in the *London Gazette*. He wrote to Edmund Hammond complaining that 'the unfortunate publication by the Admiralty of all the enclosures in Sir Michael Seymour's Despatch' only told 'half the story'. The other half was the unanimity in favour of what had been done among the mercantile community in London, Liverpool, and Hong Kong, 'much as the people there quarrel about everything else'.[133] What he did not realize was that the chairman of the East India and China Association of London had already submitted a thinly veiled suggestion to Clarendon to send 'a first class Representative and Plenipotentiary' to negotiate 'a new Treaty'.[134] However, the government did not seem to have paid much attention to the suggestion at the time.

The duke of Argyll said that, shortly before the dissolution, Palmerston raised in a cabinet meeting the question of sending out to China a new plenipotentiary.[135] The timing of this decision is important. Parliament was dissolved at 1.30 p.m. on 21 March 1857.[136] So the decision would have been made before that date, in fact before 10 March, when Clarendon informed Bowring that 'Her Majesty's Government have determined to send out con-

---

129. Clarendon to Bowring, Draft 44, 10 February 1857. The right mentioned therein was later changed to the right of British merchants or their agents. See Clarendon to Elgin, Draft 5, 20 April 1857, FO17/274.
130. Clarendon to Bowring, Draft 56, 4 March 1857, FO17/261.
131. Derby, 24 February 1857, Hansard, 3d series, v. 144, col. 1170.
132. Kinnaird, 3 March 1857, Hansard, 3d series, v. 144, col. 1846. Kinnaird was the last to speak, and 'of whose speech only a few sentences could be heard amid cries for a division'.
133. Edgar Bowring to Hammond, 14 January 1857, FO17/279, p. 178.
134. Gregson to Clarendon, 6 January 1858, FO17/279. See also Baring Papers, HC6.1.20.
135. Argyll, *Autobiography and Memoirs*, v. 2, p. 77.
136. *Globe*, 21 March 1857, p. 2, col. 2, 'Prorogation of Parliament on this Day'.

siderable military re-inforcements and a Plenipotentiary'.[137] But, as we have seen, until 4 March 1857 Clarendon was still despatching instructions to Bowring concerning the demands to be included in the envisaged new treaty, fully expecting Bowring to undertake the necessary negotiations.[138] Thus, the decision seems to have been taken some time between 4 and 10 March.

In Chapter 10, it has been suggested that the appointment of Elgin (reported in the press on 10 March 1857) might not be indicative of Palmerston's having contrived his own defeat in the House of Commons.[139] Rather, it might have been related to the pressure from the merchant princes, who began besieging Palmerston's doors from 5 March onwards. The findings in this chapter[140] tend to reinforce the latter theory. The uproar of the merchant princes on account of the adverse vote in the House of Commons on 3 March, their boardroom meetings, public gatherings, mass petitions, and deputations to Palmerston, coupled with the fierce attacks on Bowring in both houses of Parliament earlier, appear to have changed the mind of even the prime minister. Now he decided to supersede Bowring.

This episode, besides that of Russell's grovelling to the City magnates in order to keep his seat,[141] seems to reinforce the theory of gentlemanly capitalism. But to what extent did these 'gentlemanly' capitalists actually influence specific imperial policies, especially those toward China? This question will be examined in the next chapter.

Bowring was told that whoever the plenipotentiary might be, Her Majesty's government relied upon his patriotism and sense of public duty cheerfully to afford all the assistance in his power to that person.[142] While the election was still raging on, another despatch, dated 25 March 1857, informed Bowring that Lord Elgin had been appointed plenipotentiary and that arrangements had been made for the immediate despatch of a force of different arms to Singapore, where it was expected they would arrive about the same time with Lord Elgin.[143] These actions may be interpreted as a sign of confidence that Palmerston would win the coming election and therefore would be in a position to pursue the business of war.[144] In any case, it reflects as his belief that the

137. Clarendon to Bowring, Draft 72, 10 March 1858, FO17/261.
138. Clarendon to Bowring, Draft 56, 4 March 1857, FO17/261.
139. For the conspiracy theory, see Taylor, *Decline of British Radicalism*, p. 274, quoting George Hadfield's speech at Sheffield (*The Times*, 25 March 1857, p. 8); Richard Cobden's speech at Huddersfield (ibid., 28 March 1857, p. 8); and the editorial of the *Weekly Dispatch*, 15 March 1857, p. 7.
140. See, in particular, Section I.
141. See Chapter 10.
142. Clarendon to Bowring, Draft 72, 10 March 1858, FO17/261.
143. Clarendon to Bowring, Draft 88, 25 March 1858, FO17/261.
144. Indeed, the Cabinet was very confident at the beginning of the election, believing that Palmerston was 'dictator for the moment' and 'set on a bed of roses.' See Hawkins, *Parliament*, p. 65, quoting Brougham MSS 28122, Bedford to Brougham, n.d. (? March 1857).

next government would have, in the words of the duke of Argyll, the 'common sense' to continue with the war, if he were to be unexpectedly defeated at the polls.

What was the Cabinet to do with Bowring? According to Argyll, 'We could not safely continue that official in the same position'.[145] The Cabinet felt that he had to be restrained before and even after Elgin's arrival. Thus, in the despatch of 10 March 1857, Bowring was told, 'Your functions will be in abeyance in all matters connected with the recent outbreak at Canton, and military and naval operations and negotiations for peace and the revision of treaties'.[146] This point was repeated on 25 March 1857: 'Your Plenipotentiary powers for negotiating with the Chinese government will, as I have already informed you, be in abeyance during the Earl of Elgin's presence in China'.[147] These instructions were again repeated on 21 April and made more specific: 'Your own residence during Lord Elgin's mission will be within the colony of Hong Kong'. As regards Bowring's communications with the Chinese authorities, his 'functions will as I have already informed you be in abeyance'.[148]

To keep up the facade of the government's unreserved support for their agents abroad, Palmerston declared that the appointment of Elgin was 'intended as no disparagement to Sir John Bowring'.[149] Lord Elgin was being sent out 'without superseding Sir John Bowring, who will continue as he is, trusted and confided in by the English Government'. Once Elgin had achieved his mission, 'he will return and leave Sir John Bowring in exactly the same position in which he is now'.[150] As Bowring ought to know, such promises were worth no more than the now-defunct Treaty of Nanking.

VI. *Argumentum baculinum*

Palmerston had some warm words to say about Elgin: 'We have chosen a man of high rank and great experience, who distinguished himself by his government of Canada. (Cheers)'. He had successfully negotiated a treaty with the United States. He was a man of great ability and conciliatory dispositions, with a full knowledge of the intentions of the government at home. He would be backed by 'an overwhelming naval force, double that which Sir William Parker

---

145. Argyll, *Autobiography and Memoirs*, v. 2, p. 77.
146. Clarendon to Bowring, Draft 72, 10 March 1858, FO17/261.
147. Clarendon to Bowring, Draft 88, 25 March 1858, FO17/261.
148. Clarendon to Bowring, Draft 106, 21 April 1858, FO17/261.
149. Palmerston's speech at Tiverton, as printed in *The Times*, Monday, 30 March 1857, p. 6, cols. 4-6: col. 5.
150. Ibid., col. 6. Palmerston expected that Elgin would have accomplished his mission within a year. It took him three years. Meanwhile, Bowring completed his second term at Hong Kong and returned to England in 1859. Thus, Bowring never resumed the same position which he had held in 1857.

had in the late China war – and backed also by a large military force. (Cheers)'.[151] At last Palmerston was able to wield the stick which he had been threatening to use since 1851 – *argumentum baculinum*.[152]

Thus, the dissolution had eased rather than exacerbated Palmerston's problems. Now he had a free hand in his China policy. On the other hand, parliamentary attacks on Bowring appear to have obliged the government to adopt a more cautious approach towards China. As we have seen, the government at last heeded Addington's warning about Bowring's 'superfluity of sail',[153] and accordingly took steps to restrain him. As we also saw, the legality of the demand for treaty revision was to be examined by the law officers of the Crown, whose verdict was: 'Her Majesty's Government are not entitled to claim a revision of the British Treaties'. Consequently, Elgin was instructed *not* to rest his demand for treaty revision on Article 8 of the supplementary Sino-British treaty. Rather, he was to argue that the *Arrow* quarrel entitled 'Her Majesty's Government to insist upon such a revision of existing engagements as may put their relations with the Chinese Empire on a more satisfactory footing than at present'.[154]

A minute on this draft instruction reads: 'Seen by Lord Palmerston'.[155]

Also seen by Palmerston were other draft despatches to Elgin on this day, 20 April 1857. One concerned the appointment of Frederick Bruce, Elgin's brother, as his public secretary, 'with Dormant Full Powers' to take over the mission should Elgin become incapacitated in any way.[156] The other directed Bowring to attach Parkes to Elgin's mission.[157]

Altogether, seventeen despatches were drafted for the benefit of Elgin on 20 April. Apart from those already mentioned, the rest dealt with subjects that included the Queen's letter to the Chinese emperor; the Queen's granting Elgin 'Full Power' as embodied in the Great Seal; letters to the Admiralty and to the War Department; correspondence with British ministers in France, the United States, and Russia; despatches instructing Bowring to offer archival, consular, and legislatorial assistance; military assistance from the government

---

151. Ibid., col. 5.
152. This was part of Palmerston's minutes on 'Mr Bonham's 65, 67, 72', FO17/173 (domestic various). Liberally translated, the expression may be taken to mean 'teaching by caning'. This sort of language was not reserved only for the Chinese. Palmerston's constant activity and disposition to tender advice or mediation in Europe itself had procured him the reputation of a universal meddler, and the blunt vigour of some of his despatches and diplomatic instructions conveyed a pugnacious impression which led to the nickname of firebrand. See Sanders, *Life of Viscount Palmerston*.
153. Addington to Clarendon, 26 August 1854, MSS Clar. Dep. C8 China.
154. Clarendon to Elgin, Draft 7 (secret and confidential), 20 April 1857, FO17/274.
155. Foreign Office minute on Clarendon to Elgin, Draft 7 (secret and confidential), 20 April 1857, FO17/274.
156. Foreign Office minutes on Clarendon to Elgin, Draft 8, 20 April 1857, FO17/274.
157. Foreign Office minutes on Clarendon to Elgin, Draft 14, 20 April 1857, FO17/274.

of India, and naval assistance at Ceylon and Singapore; and negotiating a treaty with Japan.[158]

Two of these seventeen drafts, Nos. 4 and 5, were in printed form.[159] They were long documents and constituted the official instructions as to how Elgin should go about his business in China and what demands to make. Like the instructions to Bowring on 9 January 1857, they were printed because a large number of departments and people had to be informed.

Draft No. 4 instructed Elgin to leave by the mail steamer scheduled for 26 April. He was informed that a force of infantry and artillery, consisting of about 1,500 men, had already been despatched from England to Singapore, there to await further orders. At Hong Kong he would find, in addition to the force previously stationed there, the 5th Regiment of about 750 men from Mauritius and a detachment of about 350 Indian troops from Singapore. Part of an Indian regiment had also been sent to Hong Kong from Madras, and a second detachment may have been sent from Singapore. The naval commander would continue to be Rear-Admiral Seymour, and the army commander Major-General Ashburnham. On his way through Paris, Elgin was to communicate directly with the French government. The demands he was to make on the Chinese government were:

1. Reparations of injuries to British and French subjects.
2. Complete execution of the stipulations of the existing treaties.
3. Compensation to British subjects for losses during the *Arrow* quarrel.
4. Diplomatic representation at Beijing.
5. Treaty revision.

Draft No. 5 spelt out the details for treaty revision, including:

1. Opening all ports along the China coast and banks of rivers to foreign trade.
2. Permission for British merchants to purchase the produce of China at the place of its production, with no duties payable on such articles in their passage to the coastal ports for embarkation.
3. Legalization of the opium trade.
4. British cooperation in the suppression of piracy.
5. Free travel and protection of missionaries in the interior of China.
6. Revocation of the prohibition against emigration of Chinese subjects.
7. Full confirmation of the right of extraterritoriality.
8. Confirmation of the most favoured nation principle.
9. Resolution of all doubts by reference to the English text of the (revised) treaty.

One striking feature is that, all the time, Palmerston denied that Britain was 'at war with China', insisting that it was merely a local quarrel with Commis-

158. Clarendon to Elgin, Drafts 1–17, 20 April 1857, FO17/274.
159. They were subsequently included for publication in 1859 in a blue book entitled 'Correspondence Relative to the Earl of Elgin's Special Missions to China and Japan, 1857–1859'.

sioner Yeh of Canton.[160] Yet Elgin was instructed to undertake one or more of the following operations:

1. Blockade of the Peiho (near Beijing).
2. Occupation of the entrance of the Grand Canal in the Yangtze River.
3. Occupation of the Island of Chusan.
4. Blockade of Chapoo and/or any other ports of China.
5. Interruption of the passage of the Grand Canal where it crosses the Yellow River.
6. Landing above Canton and the interruption of its supplies.
7. Establishment of a British force in the upper part of Canton.

Thus, military operations were to stretch from Canton to the proximity of Beijing. Palmerston would not describe these proceedings as war because war had not been sanctioned by Parliament. As we have seen, the preceding Parliament had censured the government's military actions in the Canton River, a censure which the new parliament never overturned.

As early as 6 April 1857, the Foreign Office had written to the Admiralty requesting it 'to direct that accommodation may be provided for the Earl of Elgin and suite on board the steamer which conveys the Indian and China mail of the 26th of April from Suez to Singapore'.[161] As Elgin was instructed to make considerable demands on China by means of coercive measures, where did the ideas for these demands come from?

160. Palmerston's speech at Tiverton, as printed in *The Times*, Monday, 30 March 1857, p. 6, cols. 4–6: col. 5.
161. Foreign Office to Admiralty, 6 April 1857, FO17/280, p. 317.

13
In the wings:
The lobbies of imperialism

I. Commercial expansion

The very first demand which Elgin was instructed to make, namely, 'the opening of all ports along the China coast and the banks of rivers to foreign trade', was related to the submissions of the various business associations in Britain. As we have seen, official publication of Admiral Seymour's first despatch concerning military operations in the Canton River prompted some very influential commercial and industrial associations to lobby the government to demand further concessions from China. They included the East India and China Association in London,[1] the East India and China Association in Liverpool,[2] the Chamber of Commerce and Manufactures in Glasgow,[3] the Manchester Commercial Association,[4] and the Chamber of Commerce and Manufactures of Manchester.[5] Individuals who wrote included a certain E. Cousins[6] and a James Vavasseur.[7]

Their submissions were touched upon in the preceding chapter only in so far as the government tried to use them as signs of support for its policy towards China, to the extent of having the memorials of the East India and China Associations in London and Liverpool tabled in Parliament. In this chapter, the demands of the various pressure groups will be examined in detail.

---

1. Gregson to Clarendon, 6 January 1858, FO17/279. A copy of the same document may be found in the company archives of Baring Brothers, Baring Papers HC6.1.20.
2. Turner to Clarendon, 29 January 1857, FO17/279, p. 247. This document was later printed in Parl. Papers 1857, v. 12, pp. 201–2.
3. Kinnear to Clarendon, Glasgow, 14 February 1857, enclosing a memorial from the said Chamber, dated the same day, FO17/279, p. 383.
4. Fleming to Clarendon, 5 February 1857, FO17/279, pp. 303–4. See also Fleming to Clarendon, 7 March 1957, FO17/280, p. 74.
5. Bazley to Clarendon, 5 March 1857, FO17/280, p. 37. T. Bazley was the president of the said chamber.
6. Cousins to Clarendon, 26 February 1857, FO17/279; see also the reply in FO17/280, p. 19, Foreign Office to Cousins, Draft, 4 March 1857.
7. Vavasseur to Clarendon, Camberwell 24 February 1857, FO17/279, pp. 430–1.

310

Let us begin by recalling the commercial lobbies that came to the fore at the time of the Opium War. About 300 firms, mostly connected with the cotton industry, in Manchester, London, Leeds, Liverpool, Blackburn, and Bristol, petitioned Lord Palmerston, then foreign secretary, to intervene. Their concerns were related not only to their interests as manufacturers cut off from a market in China, but also to their interests as exporters of goods to India, where the interruption of the opium trade could cause them serious inconvenience because their Indian customers depended on the opium trade for their funds.[8]

More remarkably, William Jardine, who had an extensive opium empire in China and close business relationships with the City of London, saw Palmerston and literally masterminded the government's approach towards China and the Opium War, down to details such as the size of ships to be deployed[9] and the terms of the treaty to be proposed to China, leaving blank only the names of the islands to be occupied and the amount of the indemnity to be exacted from China.[10] That episode might be regarded as a classic example of gentlemanly capitalism.

In the *Arrow* War, neither the Jardines nor the Mathesons appear to have played a similarly active role. True, the chairman of the East India and China Association in London, to which they belonged, wrote to Clarendon immediately after publication of Seymour's first despatch. But there is no record of the chairman or any other member of that Association seeking to influence the Foreign Office except by letter. Times had changed. During the Opium War, Palmerston actively sought the views of the London agent of Jardine Matheson and Co., Mr John Abel Smith. This led one historian to comment that 'Palmerston depended almost exclusively on Smith for intelligence from Canton'.[11] But since the conclusion of peace, systematic official reporting from successive plenipotentiaries at Hong Kong and British consuls stationed at the five treaty ports had acquainted the Foreign Office with all they thought they needed to know about conditions in China.[12] The Foreign Office no longer needed to be told what to do with China.

8. Chang, *Commissioner Lin*, pp. 192–3, quoting Parl. Papers 'Memorials Addressed to Her Majesty's Government by British Merchants Interested in the Trade with China', 1840.
9. Jardine to Palmerston, 27 October 1839, FO17/35; see also Chang, *Commissioner Lin*, pp. 193–4.
10. Draft of articles of treaty to be proposed to China (prepared by William Jardine), enclosed in Palmerston to Captain Charles Elliot and Admiral George Elliot, Desp. 2, 10 February 1840, FO17/37, pp. 103–19.
11. Chang, *Commissioner Lin*, p. 193, quoting FO17/35 and 36, passim.
12. Ironically, the intelligence reports on the Taiping and other rebellions in China in this period have furnished Chinese historians with sources of information equal to any they can find in China. See Prescott Clarke and Jack S Gregory (eds.), *Western Reports on the Taiping: A Selection of Documents* (Canberra, Australian National University Press, 1982). Indeed, many of the documents collected in the famous *Taiping tianguo* (Sources on the Taiping Heavenly Kingdom, 8 vs. [Shanghai, Renmin chubanshe, 1952]) were copied from Chinese pamphlets deposited in

The East India and China Association in London, being close in proximity to Whitehall, noted the change. Their submission, therefore, did not go overboard. The submission by the same association in Liverpool, however, certainly annoyed someone who was unashamedly proud of the mercantile interests he represented,[13] Richard Cobden. That submission suggested that the British government insist on the right of opening to foreign trade any port on the coast of China or on the banks of any navigable river at any time they saw fit, and obtain for British ships of war the free navigation of and access to all the ports and rivers of China.[14]

'Let us, by way of illustration and bringing the matter home, suppose that this is a document which has come to us from Moscow, and that it is addressed, not to China, but to Turkey', said Cobden.[15] This was certainly a powerful analogy, in that Great Britain had just fought a bloody war with Russia in the Crimea. He asked, 'Can you imagine anything more stunning than the explosion which would take place at Liverpool if such a ukase as that were to come to us from Russia?'[16] What Cobden might not have realized was that, behind the scenes, the Foreign Office mandarins were also restraining the commercial lobbies, as the next section shows.

II. Territorial expansion

Various suggestions for territorial acquisition were made. They included Shanghai, Taiwan, the Chusan group of islands, and in one case the whole of China.

It was the Manchester Commercial Association which suggested that Shanghai should be put under British rule and declared a free port.[17] At this point, the government felt that the mercantile spirit had gone too far. 'I am to express to you his Lordship's thanks for your suggestions and to inform you that they will be duly attended to', replied Hammond politely but firmly, 'with the exception of the suggestion that Shanghai should be placed under British Rule, which cannot be entertained by Her Majesty's Government'.[18]

Refusing to be snubbed, the Association defended their proposition by

the British Museum and in the University Library at Cambridge. See also my article, 'The Taipings' Distant Allies: A Comparative Study of the Rebels at Shanghai and at Canton, and Their Interaction with the Treaty Powers, 1853–1855', in A. R. Davis (ed.), *Austrina* (Sydney, Oriental Society of Australia, 1982), pp. 334–50.

13. 'All my sympathies are with the mercantile classes, and my public life has been passed in enlarging the sphere of their honourable and beneficial employment', he said (Cobden, 26 February 1857, Hansard, 3d series, v. 144, col. 1407).
14. Ibid., col. 1410.
15. Ibid., cols. 1410–11.
16. Ibid., col. 1411.
17. Fleming to Clarendon, 5 February 1857, FO17/279, pp. 303–4.
18. Foreign Office to Fleming, Draft, 10 February 1857, Hansard, 3d series, v. 144, p. 351.

wishing that 'his Lordship should clearly understand' that 'they would disclaim any intention of advocating its forcible acquisition'; rather, the 'object might be achieved purely by negociation and upon terms perfectly satisfactory to the Chinese Government'.[19] How Shanghai might be put under British rule, without forcible acquisition and even to the satisfaction of the Manchu court at Beijing, was never explained.

Whitehall stood firm. 'With respect to your observations in regard to placing Shanghai "under British rule", I am to observe that the association has probably not borne in mind that Shanghai is one of the Five Ports assigned for Trade to Foreign Nations and that the possession of it by Great Britain would be a just cause of complaint on the part of other countries'.[20]

The Association had distinguished company in the person of Major G. Vallencey. He also suggested to Clarendon that British forces should take possession of the 'Town and harbour' of Shanghai, and hold them as 'Material Guarantee' while negotiating with Beijing. On second thoughts, he went further. In no case ought Shanghai be allowed to slip 'out of our hands when once in our possession, whatever treaty we may make, the cession of that Town and Harbour must be comprised with as one of the stipulations'.[21] Clarendon reminded Vallency that France together with the United States 'have by Treaty with China a right of freely trading with that City, and that they would not see with indifference the forcible occupation of it by Great Britain'.[22]

With respect to Taiwan, Colonel G. Fielding wrote on 9 March 1857: 'Before the end of our last war with China, I submitted to Lord Derby (then Secretary of State) a suggestion for our taking and keeping the Island of Formosa'. In the event, instructions had already been sent out which led to the treaty of peace. But as 'it is not impossible that our present disputes at Canton may lead to a war with China', Colonel Fielding took the liberty of enclosing a copy of a memorandum for his lordship's perusal. Some people preferred taking Chusan, which would be a good commercial port, but Colonel Fielding felt that its immediate proximity to the mainland appeared to him an objection and it was in any case too small for its produce to be of much value.[23]

In his memorandum, Colonel Fielding set out his reasons for 'taking possession of the Island of Formosa with a determination to keep it'. The document is remarkable for its detail. Fielding noted that Formosa was 'the granary of the great tea province of Fohkien [Fujian]', so that a British Formosa could force the emperor 'to give us tea in exchange for rice'. With industrious exploitation

19. Fleming to Clarendon, 7 March 1957, FO17/280, p. 74.
20. Foreign Office to Fleming, 12 March 1857, FO17/280, pp. 118–19.
21. Vallancey to Clarendon, 9 March 1857, FO17/280, pp. 95–7.
22. Clarendon's 10 March 1857 minutes (p. 124) on Vallancey to Clarendon, 9 March 1857, FO17/280, pp. 95–7. For the draft reply, see 12 March 1857, FO17/280, p. 122.
23. Fielding to Clarendon, Newnham Paddox, Rugby, 9 March 1857, with enclosure, FO17/280, pp. 99–101.

of the island, Fielding thought, 'We should soon have a little China of our own'.[24] Clarendon showed the letter and its enclosure to Palmerston and instructed that it be acknowledged with thanks, without committing the government one way or another.[25] The reply was drafted and sent on the same day.[26]

Who was this Colonel Fielding? He was George Fielding, but his signature was so hard to read that the Foreign Office mistook him for his younger brother Percy Fielding. Once the Foreign Office had mistaken George Fielding for his younger brother, Lieutenant-Colonel Percy Fielding of the Coldstream Guards, George immediately recommended his younger brother for service in China: 'His character as a good officer is very well known at the Horse Guards'.[27] As for Colonel the Honourable George Fielding himself, he had been 'employed 12 years in the Political Department in India and latterly as Resident at a Native Court'. He now lived at Rugby.[28]

The available records seem to show no sign of Whitehall either adopting his proposal or taking his brother. The former is important in the context not only of our pursuit of the origins of the *Arrow* War, but of our general interpretation of the nature of British imperialism at this time. To any Western government looking for territorial acquisition in China, Taiwan, as portrayed by Fielding, would have been exceedingly attractive in terms of its economic value, strategic importance, and viability as a colony. The refusal to take up Fielding's proposal is a strong indication that territory, for its own sake, was not what Whitehall was after. In the *Arrow* War, Britain was seeking principally the expansion of trade, not territory. If it should occupy Taiwan, and if its French allies and potential U.S. and Russian allies should similarly seize territory in China of equal size, China might be partitioned and Britain's dream of opening the whole of China to free trade would be shattered. In this regard, the theory of the imperialism of free trade holds a lot of water.

True, Britain subsequently did ask China to cede the southern tip of Kowloon peninsula in the Beijing Convention of 1860. But the consideration there was overwhelmingly the defence of the island of Hong Kong which had been ceded in 1842, and the integrity of Victoria harbour lying between the island and the peninsula.[29]

With respect to Chusan, it was *The Times* that appears to have been the first

---

24. Enclosure in ibid.
25. Clarendon's 11 March 1857 minutes (p. 98) on Fielding to Clarendon, Newnham Paddox, 9 March 1857, with enclosure, FO17/280, pp. 99–101.
26. Foreign Office to Fielding, 11 March 1857, FO17/280, p. 107.
27. Fielding to Clarendon, Rugby, 17 March 1857, FO17/280, p. 158.
28. Ibid.
29. See Justin Cahill, 'From Colonisation to Decolonisation: A study of Chinese and British Negotiating Positions with Regard to Hong Kong'. History IV honours thesis, University of Sydney, 1995.

to advocate its occupation. 'The British authorities should make up their minds as to what they intend to demand and what guarantees they intend to take', the editor wrote on 8 January 1857. 'The occupation of Chusan, and perhaps some point still nearer to the capital, a stipulation for the residence of an Ambassador at the Imperial Court, and free entrance for men of all nations into the country, are parts of the programme which naturally suggest themselves'.[30]

A certain R. Montgomery Martin had his own peculiar way of pushing for the occupation of Chusan, and even the whole of China. On 7 February 1857 he wrote to Clarendon insisting 'as an act of Justice, that my Reports on Hong Kong, on Chusan and on our Relations with China in 1844–5 may be included in the official papers to be laid before Parliament'.[31] Hammond identified the writer as a former Hong Kong 'Colonial Secretary or something of the kind but not under the F. O'.[32] Clarendon thought that as 'he was not connected with F. O., I cannot present his reports'.[33] Refusing to be ignored, Martin appears to have prevailed upon his local member of Parliament to move that his papers be tabled. Thus, on 13 February 1857, a resolution to that effect was passed in the House of Commons. Thereupon the colonial secretary, Henry Labouchere, wrote to Clarendon for those papers.[34]

On 2 March 1857, Clarendon transmitted the reports to Labouchere, but requested that a proof of the printed version be sent to him before it was presented to Parliament.[35] The proof was forwarded to Clarendon on 18 March with the comment that it should be presented, if possible, before the dissolution of Parliament.[36] On 20 March, the Foreign Office returned to the Colonial Office 'the Proof of those Papers in which Mr Labouchere will perceive certain Passages marked which Lord Clarendon suggests should be omitted'.[37]

I have traced the pertinent Parliamentary Papers and Martin's original manuscripts. Omitted in the printed version were five paragraphs in his report on Chusan,[38] and thirteen paragraphs in his minute on the British position in

---

30. *The Times*, 8 January 1857, p. 8, col. 3.
31. Martin to Clarendon, 7 February 1857, FO17/279, p. 330.
32. Hammond's minutes on Martin to Clarendon, 7 February 1857, FO17/279, p. 330. In fact, Martin had been the colonial treasurer in Hong Kong. See next two notes.
33. Clarendon's minutes on Martin to Clarendon, 7 February 1857, FO17/279, p. 330. Subsequently it took a resolution in the House of Commons for the government to table those papers. See Colonial Office to Foreign Office, 28 February 1857, and enclosure, House of Commons resolution, 13 February 1857, FO17/279, pp. 453–5.
34. Colonial Office to Foreign Office, 28 February 1857, enclosing a copy of the House of Commons resolution of 13 February 1857, FO17/279, pp. 453–5.
35. Foreign Office to Colonial Office, 2 March 1857, FO17/280, p. 1.
36. Colonial Office to Foreign Office, 18 March 1857, FO17/280, p. 178.
37. Foreign Office to Colonial Office, 20 March 1857, FO17/280, p. 200.
38. Compare the printed version in Parl. Papers 1857, v. 12, pp. 615–30, with the original manuscript of Martin's report on the island of Chusan, dated 30 August 1844 and enclosed in Davis to Aberdeen (separate), 28 October 1844, FO17/89, pp. 128–54.

China.[39] In so far as Chusan was concerned, the suppressed passages revealed that Martin had urged Whitehall to colonize Chusan, otherwise he was certain that France would. Stationed at Chusan, two regiments, a couple of frigates, and two steamers would be sufficient not only to keep the whole of China in check, but even to go on the offensive by occupying the mouth of the Grand Canal, 'and in one week dictate terms of peace without seeking reinforcements in India'. In the suppressed passages in his minute on the British position in China, Martin insisted that China was 'destined by Divine Providence to be the next great arena for the development of British civilisation' after India. If Britain did not occupy China, other nations would do so and thereby convert China 'into an engine injurious to our interests and productive of great and permanent national injury'. Here is the classic self-justification of imperialism – *we owe it to ourselves.*

Robert Fortune, a British adventurer who had travelled extensively in China and who had secretly made cuttings of Chinese tea plants to be grown in India, also urged the occupation of Chusan by hastily adding a last section to the book he was publishing at this time. He argued that British troops and the fleet might rendezvous in its commodious harbours and that Chusan was healthier than Hong Kong, a feature which would be of great importance to the service personnel.[40]

In the end, the British government took up the suggestion of *The Times* and of Robert Fortune, and instructed Elgin to regard the temporary occupation of Chusan as an option. However, the decision seems to have been more related to a perception of the Russian threat, as we have seen. In any case, the occupation was not envisaged to be permanent, only as a 'guarantee' as *The Times* said. Thus, Martin's dream, however fantastic, of colonizing Chusan, not to say the whole of China, remained a hallucination. As such, it is not difficult to see why Whitehall wanted to suppress some of his views. If published, a great deal of international suspicion about Britain's territorial ambitions in China would be aroused, which might result in a partition of China to the jeopardy of British commercial expansion throughout the whole of China.

III. Colonial expansion

By colonial expansion I do not mean territorial acquisition, but rather the expansion of the population in existing colonies by securing settlers from China.

On 9 February 1857, the chairman of the East India and China Association

---

39. Compare the printed version in Parl. Papers 1857, v. 12, pp. 630–7, with the original manuscript of Martin's report on the British position in China, dated 19 April 1845 and enclosed in Davis to Aberdeen (separate), 21 April 1845, FO17/99, pp. 99–133.
40. Robert Fortune, *A Residence among the Chinese* (London, John Murray, 1857), pp. 434–5.

The lobbies of imperialism

in London again wrote to Clarendon, requesting that in the negotiation of a new treaty, the propriety of legalizing the emigration of females should be urgently pressed upon the Chinese government. In support of his request he enclosed a memorandum by several highly respected members of the houses of business established in China and Singapore.[41] Hammond offered to transmit the papers to Bowring, but added that Clarendon felt doubtful, from the prejudices which existed in China against female emigration, that any attempt to promote the object in view would meet with success.[42]

On 14 February, the directors of the Chamber of Commerce and Manufactures of Glasgow wrote to Clarendon requesting the government to take advantage of the *Arrow* quarrel to put pressure on the Chinese government to lift the prohibition of Chinese female emigration. The memorial began with the fact that for some years past there had been considerable immigration of Chinese males into Singapore and British West Indian colonies, 'affording a very valuable supply of labour, especially to the West Indies'. There were 50,000 Chinese males in Singapore, for example, but no Chinese females. The only way to induce the Chinese males to become permanent settlers, 'which is very desirable', was to make it possible for them to bring their families.[43]

Hammond offered to transmit a copy of the memorial to Bowring, adding as before that the Chinese prejudice against such a move might be difficult to overcome.[44] Behind the scenes, however, Hammond wrote on 23 February to the India Board, enclosing a copy of the Chamber's memorial and his own reply to it. The India Board consulted the Court of Directors of the East India Company, which considered it 'most desirable, on every account, to promote the introduction of Chinese Females into Singapore'.[45] The members of the India Board told Hammond that they 'fully concur' in that opinion.[46] On 23 February, the East India and China Association in Liverpool also wrote to Clarendon on this subject.[47] The Foreign Office gave a pro forma reply.[48]

It is interesting to note that on 24 February, James Vavasseur wrote to Clarendon on the same subject with regard to Australia. 'At present great numbers of Chinamen find their way to Australia enticed by the gold; their industry and knowledge of useful arts make them desirable colonists'. If the Chinese could and would bring their wives, and if the colonial governments in Australia would, by granting portions of land or by other inducements, encour-

---

41. Gregson to Clarendon, 9 February 1857, and enclosures, FO17/279, pp. 345-9.
42. Foreign Office to Gregson, 10 February 1857, FO17/279, p. 344.
43. Kinnear to Clarendon, Glasgow, 14 February 1857, enclosing a memorial from the said chamber, dated the same day, FO17/279, p. 383.
44. Foreign Office to Kinnear, 20 February 1857, FO17/279, p. 404.
45. James C. Melvill to India Board, 12 March 1857, FO17/280, p. 144.
46. William Leach to Hammond, 14 March 1857, FO17/280, p. 142.
47. Turner to Clarendon, 23 February 1957, FO17/279, p. 420.
48. Foreign Office to Turner, 27 February 1857, FO17/279, p. 449.

317

age them to settle, they would soon become a 'valuable addition to the population of Australia, who would greatly help to develop the resources of the country'.[49] Hammond transmitted a copy of Vavasseur's letter to Labouchere, asking him if it would be desirable to take any steps with reference to the suggestion therein.[50]

On 12 March, the Manchester Commercial Association petitioned Clarendon on the same subject with respect to British settlements in the Straits of Malacca, Australia, and other colonies.[51] The Foreign Office offered its stock reply.[52]

On 19 March, Robert Ironson, secretary of the Liverpool Chamber of Commerce, sent a memorial to Clarendon on behalf of Council of the Chamber complaining about the inadequate supply of cotton wool, the only apparent remedy being to encourage the 'industrious labourers' of China to settle in the West Indies to grow cotton; but these labourers would not emigrate there unless their women were allowed to go with them. Consequently, the Chinese government must be made to relax their rules about female emigration.[53]

In a separate memorandum, the Liverpool Chamber of Commerce impressed upon the government that should 'the present disturbances in China result in a revision of the Treaty, the subject of Free Emigration from all ports of China is of vital importance to the British Settlements in the Straits of Malacca'.[54] Whitehall asked Robertson Ironson, the secretary of the said Chamber, to 'inform the Council that their representations will have Lord Clarendon's best attention but that His Lordship fears from enquiries already made that Chinese females object to emigration'.[55]

On 21 March, the West India Committee wrote to Clarendon on 'the desirability of obtaining permission, by any new treaty which may be concluded, for emigrants, both male and female, to embark on British ships for the British West India Colonies'. The limited experiments which had hitherto been made by the introduction of about 2,000 Chinese immigrants into Guiana, Trinidad, and Jamaica had proved that these people were excellent labourers. All parties who had resorted to China for emigrants had preferred males, because their object had been to obtain effective labourers. The British West India proprietors were doubly actuated by the same motive, but they were still more anxious to connect with the acquisition of labour, even at some expense, than with the benefit of colonization.[56] Whitehall replied that 'the

49. Vavasseur to Clarendon, Camberwell, 24 February 1857, FO17/279, pp. 430–1.
50. Foreign Office to Colonial Office, 4 March 1857, FO17/280, p. 21.
51. Fleming to Clarendon, 7 March 1957, FO17/280, p. 74.
52. Foreign Office to Fleming, 12 March 1857, FO17/280, pp. 118–19.
53. Memorandum to Clarendon (received 20 March 1857), FO17/280, p. 197.
54. Ironson to Clarendon, 19 March 1857, FO17/280, pp. 193–5.
55. Foreign Office to Ironson, 24 March 1857, FO17/280, p. 222.
56. Macgregor to Clarendon, 21 March 1857, FO17/280, pp. 218–19.

subject will have Lord Clarendon's best attention', and added the stock clause about Chinese females objecting to emigration.[57]

On 27 March, the Colonial Office replied to the Foreign Office. Mr Labouchere would be glad if all restrictions upon emigration from China, whether of males or females, were removed, but these obstacles existed, owing to the fundamental laws of the Chinese empire and the rooted habits of the people by which it was inhabited. Under the circumstances Labouchere did not feel that 'any British interest was involved in such a manner as would justify urging this point as one of the necessary conditions of peace with China.'[58] Clarendon minuted: 'Concur'.[59] A letter to that effect was subsequently sent to the Colonial Office.[60]

Despite Clarendon's concurrence with Labouchere on the subject, the Cabinet seems to have decided to adopt the view of the India Board, and Clarendon instructed Elgin to that effect. 'Her Majesty's Government have received from many quarters earnest representations as to the importance of obtaining from the Chinese Government a revocation of the prohibition now existing against the emigration of Chinese subjects', he told Elgin. The prohibition was a dead letter anyway. Although no Chinese law was actually violated by female emigration, it was thought worthwhile to try to obtain a formal recognition on the part of the Chinese emperor of the right of all classes of his subjects to leave the country should they wish to do so.[61]

IV. Missionary expansion

Missionary lobbying[62] began with a letter from a certain Edward Dillon to Edmund Hammond on 16 March 1857, enclosing an extract of the journal of Reverend Geoffrey Piercy, dated at Macao 12 November 1856. He maintained that the author, being one of the missionaries at Canton, 'could scarcely be supposed to speak approvingly of warlike measures which were not rendered imperative and inevitable by the most outrageous and continuous provocation on the part of the Chinese authorities.' In addition, he insisted that the missionary, being 'on the spot before hostilities broke out, and having remained at Canton up to a recent date', would be able to form a 'calm and conscientious opinion as to the entire affair'.[63]

57. Foreign Office to Macgregor, 26 March 1857, FO17/280, p. 236.
58. Colonial Office to Foreign Office, 27 March 1857, FO17/280, p. 249.
59. Clarendon's 27 March 1857 minutes on Colonial Office to Foreign Office, 27 March 1857, FO17/280, p. 249.
60. Foreign Office to Colonial Office, 2 April 1857, FO17/280, p. 303.
61. Clarendon to Elgin, Draft 5, 20 April 1857, FO17/274.
62. For some background information, see G. I. T. Machin, *Politics and the Churches in Great Britain, 1832–1868* (Oxford, Clarendon Press, 1967).
63. Dillon to Hammond, 16 March 1857, FO17/280, p. 149.

Clarendon minuted, 'Ack[nowledg]e with thanks'.[64] What had the Reverend Mr Piercy said in his letter?

> The English Government cannot go back; and though it is fearful to contemplate the immense loss of life which will result, yet it must place its honour, and the protection it guarantees to all under its flag, in an inviolable position. We, as Missionaries, weep over the miseries let loose on this people; but we cannot shut our eyes to the fact, that nothing but the strong arm of foreign power can soon open the field for the entrance of the Gospel. If 'pride goeth before destruction, and a haughty spirit before a fall', then it was inevitable that chastisement from some power would sooner or later result.[65]

On 19 March, Lord Chichester, president of the Church Missionary Society, wrote to Clarendon, enclosing a copy of a memorial which he had previously transmitted to Clarendon in 1855. In his letter, Chichester said that the prospect of a renewal of amicable relations with China presented a favourable opportunity for obtaining additional protection and liberty of action for the missionaries. He maintained that the missionaries of other Christian states were not restricted to residence in one of the five treaty ports.[66] Here, Chichester was wrong. Missionaries of every Christian state, like every foreigner, were restricted by treaty to the five ports. Those who went to live outside the ports did so in violation of the treaty provisions.

The memorial of 1855, which Chichester now transmitted once again to Clarendon, is interesting. It began by saying that, since 1844, the Church of England had employed missionaries to preach in China and that, in 1849, Dr George Smith, one of the Society's former missionaries, was appointed bishop of Victoria in Hong Kong. It then went on to say, discreetly, that the Society's work in China had not been made possible by the Anglo-Chinese Treaty of 1842. Rather, it was the French government that had demanded protection for missionaries, which was subsequently granted in the Franco-Chinese Treaty of 1843. Only because of this, British missionaries might claim similar protection via the most favoured nation treatment provided in the

---

64. Clarendon's minutes (n.d.) on Dillon to Hammond, 16 March 1857, FO17/280, p. 149. Accordingly, a letter was drafted on 18 March 1857.
65. Extract of a letter of the Rev. Geoffrey Piercy, Macao, 12 November 1856, enclosed in Dillon to Hammond, 16 March 1857, FO17/280, pp. 149–50.
66. Chichester to Clarendon, 18 March 1857, FO17/280, pp. 183–4. The writer simply signed himself 'Chichester'. When the Foreign Office replied, the addressee was referred to as 'Lord Chichester'. See Foreign Offic to Chichester, 23 March 1857, FO17/280, p. 220. He is thereby identified as Henry Thomas, earl of Chichester. See Hansard, 3d series, v. 144, 'Roll of the Lords Spiritual and Temporal'. He must not be confused with Ashhurst Turner, bishop of Chichester; see ibid. If the bishop had been the writer, he would have signed himself '+ Ashhurst, Cicestrensis'. I am grateful to my colleague Mr Tony Cahill, who informed me that bishops in the nineteenth century usually signed themselves with a cross, then their Christian name, followed by the name of their diocese in Latin (the Latin for Chichester is Cicestrensis), and to another colleague, Dr Lyn Olson, who found out the Latin for Chichester for me.

The lobbies of imperialism

Anglo-Chinese Supplementary Treaty of 1843. Now that the British and French governments were contemplating a revision of treaties, the memorialists 'urgently press on your Lordship's noting' the importance of securing for the missionaries the 'protection for life, and property, the privileges of residence', subject only to such qualifications or restrictions 'as may be deemed necessary to provide against any improper use or abuse of the privileges so secured to them'.[67]

The memorialists were a little slow to act. By the time they composed their memorial in 1855, the exact terms for treaty revision had been despatched to Bowring eleven months before. And those terms made no reference to missionary privileges in China.[68] Now in 1857, Whitehall promised that the 'matter shall have Lord Clarendon's best attention'.[69]

The Wesleyan Methodist Mission was even slower off the mark. On 24 March 1857, its secretary, Rev. E. Hoole, D. D., wrote to Clarendon. He made the same complaint that the existing treaties between Great Britain and China did not mention the missionaries and that 'any legal rights or privileges now enjoyed by British Missionaries in that Empire accrue to them in virtue of the Stipulations of the French Treaty'. Even then, missionaries might not legally travel beyond the five treaty ports, 'nor acquire nor occupy either any place of worship, or school, or a cemetery' . The Mission was 'strongly of opinion that such a state of things should not be permitted to continue for any longer period than may be absolutely inevitable'. The Mission hoped that Clarendon would see it 'due to the honour of Great Britain, to the great principles of liberty, and above all to the interests of Christianity' to instruct Elgin to obtain, for all missionaries from the Chinese authorities, the right of unrestricted travel throughout China, of renting or purchasing residences, and of erecting schools and places of worship.[70]

Clarendon minuted: 'Shall have my best attention'.[71] True to his word, Clarendon instructed Elgin to obtain, if possible, 'for members of all Christian communities, security for the free exercise of their religious worship, and protection for the life of missionaries and other peaceful travellers in the interior of the country'.[72]

This is unprecedented and must be one of the exceptional instances in which Whitehall actually agreed to take up the cause of the British missionaries.[73] The

67. Memorial of the Church Missionary Society to Clarendon, 5 January 1855, enclosed in Chichester to Clarendon, 19 March 1857, FO17/280, p. 183.
68. Clarendon to Bowring, Desp. 2, 13 February 1854, FO17/210.
69. Foreign Offic to Chichester, 23 March 1857, FO17/280, p. 220.
70. Hoole to Clarendon, 24 March 1857, FO17/280, p. 229.
71. Clarendon's 27 March 1857 minutes on Hoole to Clarendon, 24 March 1857, FO17/280, p. 229. A reply to that effect was drafted on 2 April 1857; see FO17/280, p. 301.
72. Clarendon to Elgin, Draft 5, 20 April 1857. FO17/274.
73. It was not to be repeated either. While the French and German governments continued to intervene on behalf of their missionaries in China, indeed used missionaries' incidents to

British government had a firm policy not to mix commercial interests with missionary zeal, partly for fear that the latter might jeopardize the former. Consequently British missionaries had been left to fend for themselves as best they could. In the *Arrow* War, the British government departed from its long-standing policy, for two possible reasons. One might be to placate, in particular, the spiritual lords who had opposed the war. The second might be related to the fact that the French allies were going to act wholeheartedly on behalf of their missionaries anyway, and Britain had agreed to support the French priority. There would be no extra effort involved in securing for British missionaries the same privileges for which the French were aiming.

Whatever the reason, British government support for missionary demands was yet another 'first' among the many 'firsts' occasioned by the *Arrow* War.

V. The anti-opium lobby: A motion withdrawn

Nobody seems to have written to the Foreign Office lobbying the government to make the Chinese authorities legalize the opium trade. This is not surprising. Those Britons most intimately connected with that traffic were in China and India. In Britain, instead, many appear to have written to the earl of Shaftesbury[74] calling upon him to exert pressure on the House of Lords to put an end to British involvement in the opium trade.[75]

The two-day debate in the House of Lords on Derby's *Arrow* motion ended on 26 February 1857. Shaftesbury, who had given notice of his intention to bring forward a motion on the opium trade, voted with the government to defeat Lord Derby's motion.[76] The four-day debate in the House of Commons ended on 4 March 1857, and Shaftesbury was quite put out by Palmerston's defeat.[77] The next day, Thursday, 5 March, Derby asked whether Shaftesbury still intended to make a substantive motion in order to take the sense of the

---

further their imperial interests there, Whitehall continued to remain aloof from missionary squabbles. For the position of the French government in this respect, see Chapter 11; for that of the German government, see John E. Schrecker, *Imperialism and Chinese Natonalism: Germany in Shangtung* (Cambridge, Mass., Harvard University Press, 1971).

74. He was Antony Ashley Cooper, seventh earl of Shaftesbury (1801–85). He was the personification of the philanthropic spirit of the nineteenth century, being intimately associated with the Climbing Boys Act, the Factory and Ten Hours Acts, Mines and Collieries Regulation Acts; the establishment of ragged schools, training ships, and refuges for boys and girls; the abolition of slavery; the protection of lunatics; and the promotion of the City Mission and the Bible Society. See Edwin Hodder, *Life and Work of the Seventh Earl of Shaftesbury*, 3 vs. (London, Cassel, 1886).
75. See Chapter 16.
76. List of Not Content, Hansard, 3d series, v. 144, col. 1386.
77. Shaftesbury was upset not only because he was Palmerston's stepson, but also because the prime minister had allowed him to exercise a great deal of influence over ecclesiastical appointments.

house upon it, and, if so, whether he would lay the words of the motion before the house.[78]

Shaftesbury replied that when he gave the notice it was certainly his intention to bring forward a substantive motion. Upon going deeper into the subject he was convinced that the whole system, from first to last, was altogether illegal and had not the sanction of law for any portion of its operation. Therefore, he had decided to put the matter into the hands of some learned counsels and obtain their opinion upon it. Then he would frame his motion in such a manner that the question should be brought forward legally and technically with a view to its being submitted to the judges of the realm. He had wanted to bring forward his motion on the previous Monday, 2 March 1857. But the learned counsels had not been able to give their opinion upon it, and therefore he postponed his motion until the following Monday.[79]

The learned counsels were unable to give an opinion the previous week probably because the legal minds on both sides of the house were occupied with debating the legality of the *Arrow* incident. Now he wished to bring forward his motion on Monday, 7 March. For that purpose, he would lay the motion upon the table the following day and would move on Monday that certain questions should be submitted to the judges of the realm.[80]

He explained that when he first gave notice of his intention to raise this subject in the house, he had wished to move an address to the Crown, praying that a commission of inquiry should be issued. Upon further deliberation, he had determined to move a resolution condemnatory of the traffic. But upon still further contemplation, he thought it best to ask their lordships to refer the matter for the opinion of the judges, which was what he had now decided to do.[81]

For this decision, he had already been accused by many in letters, in newspaper articles, and in private conversation of assisting the government by causing delay. He denied such charges, saying that, on the contrary, his motion would embarrass the government the most. His choice was influenced by the expected chances of success of each option, he said. If he took up his first option, he was certain to be told that commissions were very expensive, very long in their operation, and in any case the matter was so important that the Crown and Parliament might not be bound by the appointment of such a commission. If he adopted his second option, he was bound to be told, as he had been told before by the late Sir Robert Peel, that abstract resolutions were very inconvenient and meant little or nothing. As a result, he thought the

---

78. Notice of Motion, Question, Lord Derby's question, 5 March 1857, Hansard, 3d series, v. 144, col. 1884.
79. Shaftesbury's reply, 5 March 1857, Hansard, 3d series, v. 144, col. 1884.
80. Ibid.
81. Shaftesbury, 9 March 1857, Hansard, 3d series, v. 144, col. 2029.

third option of referring the question to the judges would be most likely to succeed.[82]

Thus, on 9 March 1857, Shaftesbury formally put forward his motion, declaring that he knew of nothing that had of late more occupied the public mind and more scandalized the public conscience than the immoral system of opium trade, which was one of the most flagitious instances of unscrupulousness in the pursuit of wealth that humankind had ever witnessed. So long as that trade existed it was impossible that peace, honour, and good order should prevail between British India and China. Its existence was most disgraceful to the national character of England. Opium and Christianity could not enter China together, he maintained. Opium had done more to discredit Christianity in China than anything else. No parliament had ever ventured to give a legislative sanction and positive enactment authorizing the monopoly and the trade in opium.[83]

Shaftesbury moved that the judges of the Crown be asked to rule, first, on the legality of the monopolistic production and sale of opium by the East India Company and, second, on the legality or otherwise of the Company's promoting that contraband trade in view of the mutual agreement in the Anglo-Chinese Supplementary Treaty to suppress smuggling.[84] He was confident that the judges would declare the traffic altogether unlawful; but should they announce such an abomination existed by act of Parliament, he should then, if life were spared him, in the next Parliament bring the whole subject to the attention of their lordships.[85]

Given the nature of the motion, it is not surprising that the lord chancellor was the first to speak after Shaftesbury. He spoke against the motion. He argued that the first part of the motion presumed that the Company, 'by their *employés*', had systematically gone on violating the law, illegally obtaining revenue to the extent of millions in the year. If that were so, every person so engaged was liable to be tried and punished. Therefore, it would be most inconvenient that their lordships should be called upon to prejudge the persons accused without giving them an opportunity of defending themselves. He suggested that Shaftesbury had better desist from his motion, because the judges were not going to sanction it anyway.

To sweeten the pill, he said that since Shaftesbury had brought the matter to the attention of the government, he was prepared to say that 'when they shall have ascertained clearly and distinctly what were the facts as to the manufacture of opium by the East India Company', they would have no objection to consulting the law officers of the Crown.

82. Ibid.
83. Ibid., cols. 2027–8.
84. Ibid., col. 2033.
85. Ibid.

As regards the second part of the motion, he thought that it depended on a construction of the treaty, which had nothing to do with whether the Company had acted legally or not. Hence, he hoped that Shaftesbury 'would not embarrass – not the government but rather their Lordships – by pressing his Motion'.[86]

Shaftesbury was persuaded and said he was ready to withdraw his motion upon an assurance that the whole subject should be submitted to the law officers of the Crown and that their opinions should be given after a full investigation of the facts.[87]

One can almost hear Earl Grey calling out to Shaftesbury not to take the pill, however sweetened. In his view, such a legal opinion 'would not be worth the paper on which it was written'. What could one expect government lawyers to say about a long-standing and lucrative government policy? The question involved was 'too high a one to be decided by mere technical law', he said. Instead, it ought to be considered by Her Majesty's government and by those whom they employed in China, 'upon higher principles of policy and equity, and as connected with the general state of our relations with China'. The question was, he suggested, did their lordships regard 'the system now being pursued as being consistent with real justice and equity towards the Chinese and with our own treaty obligations?'[88]

The earl of Albemarle spoke against the motion. Quoting John Crawfurd, Dr Oxley, and Sir Benjamin Brodie, he argued that opium was not pernicious, only its abuse was. He noted that the opium eater became passive, whereas drunkards turned violent.[89]

His lordship was confusing the issue here. It was opium smoking, and not opium eating, which was pernicious. Orally taking opium had been prescribed as a painkiller for hundreds of years in China as elsewhere. Opium smoking, introduced to China by the Dutch, was terribly addictive and deleterious.

From one dubious argument Albemarle proceeded to another. The growth of opium in India must not be prohibited in the same way that barley and oats, which produced 'the more crime-creating spirit called gin', must not be banned in England; nor vines that made wine in France, Italy, and Spain; nor sugar cane, the source of rum.[90] His final comment is important in the context of the present analysis. The Indian revenue had to be sacrificed if the views of Shaftesbury were adopted.[91]

Earl Granville confused the issue further by objecting to Earl Grey's dis-

---

86. Lord chancellor, 9 March 1857, Hansard, 3d series, v. 144, cols. 2033–6.
87. Shaftesbury, 9 March 1857, Hansard, 3d series, v. 144, cols. 2036–7.
88. Grey, 9 March 1857, Hansard, 3d series, v. 144, col. 2037.
89. Albemarle, 9 March 1857, Hansard, 3d series, v. 144, cols. 2043–4.
90. Ibid., col. 2045.
91. Ibid.

missive attitude towards the law officers of the Crown.[92] Grey denied Granville's charge, saying that opium was not just a question of technicalities, but one involving higher and superior considerations.[93] Thereupon Granville confused everyone further by regretting that Grey felt 'the British authorities in China were encouraging the opium trade'.[94] Grey defended himself by saying that some of the despatches recently published seemed to show that British officials now regarded the opium trade with a more favourable eye.[95] Granville took Grey's remark to mean an attack upon his term when he was colonial secretary.[96] For such diversions, Palmerston must have been pleased.

Shaftesbury pulled the discussion back to his motion by insisting that he had never said one word in favour of a prohibition on the growth of opium by the East India Company. What he had indicated was the necessity of disconnecting the government from the traffic in opium. Other people might grow it if they wished, and the government might impose duties either upon its growth or transit, but let not the governor-general be seen to deal in this article.[97]

The earl of Ellenborough said he now understood that Shaftesbury's objection was not to the sale, but to the monopoly, of opium, and that Shaftesbury particularly desired that an inquiry be made into the legality of the opium trade and had entirely thrown over the moral part of the question. Thereupon Ellenborough asked the lord chancellor what he meant by submitting the question of opium to the law officers of the Crown.[98]

The lord chancellor replied that he had asked Shaftesbury to withdraw his motion, upon a pledge to consult the law officers of the Crown as to the legality or illegality of the traffic, having regard to the facts and the acts of Parliament.[99] How would the law officers obtain the facts?[100] They were all there, in the paper laid on the table by Lord Shaftesbury, answered the duke of Argyll.[101]

Lord Derby was getting impatient. The 'government had come to a private understanding with the noble Earl to put certain questions to the law officers, and obtain their opinion on the questions so put'.[102] There was no such private understanding, said Granville, but if Shaftesbury was satisfied with the good faith of the government, he should withdraw his motion without further ado.[103]

92. Granville, 9 March 1857, Hansard, 3d series, v. 144, cols. 2046–7.
93. Grey, 9 March 1857, Hansard, 3d series, v. 144, col. 2047.
94. Ibid.
95. Ibid.
96. Granville, 9 March 1857, Hansard, 3d series, v. 144, col. 2047.
97. Shaftesbury, 9 March 1857, Hansard, 3d series, v. 144, col. 2049.
98. Ellenborough, 9 March 1857, Hansard, 3d series, v. 144, cols. 2049–50.
99. Lord chancellor, 9 March 1857, Hansard, 3d series, v. 144, col. 2050.
100. Ellenborough, 9 March 1857, Hansard, 3d series, v. 144, col. 2050.
101. Argyll, 9 March 1857, Hansard, 3d series, v. 144, col. 2050.
102. Derby, 9 March 1857, Hansard, 3d series, v. 144, col. 2050.
103. Granville, 9 March 1857, Hansard, 3d series, v. 144, col. 2050.

Shaftesbury withdrew his motion.[104] That was on 9 March 1857. Apparently having great faith in the answer from the Crown law officers, Shaftesbury moved, on 20 March, for the pertinent documents to be tabled in Parliament.[105] *Punch* considered that 'the idea of Lord Shaftesbury bothering about Opium at a time when the elections are coming on is too ridiculous'.[106] Edmund Hammond had a word with H. S. Smith of Parliament Office in the House of Lords. Smith searched the journals and found that there had been precedents, in August 1841 during the debates over the Opium War with China, 'in which Returns *ordered* in the Session immediately previous to the Dissolution, were delivered to the new Parliament, under the former orders'.[107] So Lord Shaftesbury had to be content with keeping quiet for the moment, and by the time the papers were printed, on 9 April,[108] the election was over. Just another dose of the politics of imperialism.

On 24 August 1857, the lord chancellor tabled a copy of the legal opinion, dated 5 August, as to the legality or otherwise of the East India Company's manufacture and sale of opium.[109] It contained no surprises. The lord chancellor had more or less foreshadowed the outcome on 9 March. Shaftesbury had been confident that the law officers would rule as illegal the Company's opium activities because he had argued that such activities were of a commercial nature. In that context, the Act of 1833 had decreed that 'the said Company shall ... discontinue and abstain from all commercial business' from 22 April 1834.[110] The lord chancellor had contended, however, that by innumerable decisions, supported by the practice of two or three centuries, it had been held that dealing with the produce of one's own land, no matter to what extent, was not trading in the eyes of the law. If the Company, in order to make the most of its land, grew opium upon it and sold the opium, this was not necessarily violating the statute of 1833. Besides, if opium were produced 'for the purposes of the said Government', then it would be immaterial whether this manufacture was exercised by way of monopoly or not. There, he implied, the criterion would be whether monopoly was adopted as the best mode of raising revenue.[111]

Lord St Leonards did not object to the reception of the paper, but considered it unusual to refer to the law officers of the Crown for their opinion.[112]

104. Shaftesbury, 9 March 1857, Hansard, 3d series, v. 144, col. 2050.
105. Extract of Shaftesbury's motion of 20 March 1857, FO17/280, p. 253.
106. *Punch*, 28 March 1857, p. 129, purporting to be a letter from the solicitor-general, Stuart Wortley, written at Twisden Buildings, Temple.
107. Smith to Hammond, 28 March 1857, FO17/280, p. 251.
108. Hammond's 9 April 1857 minutes on Smith to Hammond, 28 March 1857, FO17/280, p. 251.
109. Lord chancellor, 24 August 1857, Hansard, 3d series, v. 147, col. 2003.
110. Shaftesbury, 9 March 1857, Hansard, 3d series, v. 144, col. 2031.
111. Lord chancellor, 9 March 1857, Hansard, 3d series, v. 144, cols. 2035–6.
112. St Leonards, 24 August 1857, Hansard, 3d series, v. 147, col. 2003.

Lord Campbell[113] concurred in thinking it a novelty. It was not respectful to the judges, who were their lordships' constitutional advisers, he said, that they should be passed over; and he did not approve of it. The lord chancellor believed that by 'common consent' it had been thought inconvenient to consult the judges, and therefore all parties agreed in asking the government to seek the opinion of their law advisers. The government had now done what they had undertaken to do. Their lordships were not bound to be guided by it or to give it more attention than they thought it deserved.[114] Nobody made a stir. Shaftesbury did not speak a word.

One cannot help smelling a rat among the government ranks, as did Mr Punch, who had anticipated the answer from the Crown law officers as follows:

1. The acknowledged duty of a Government is to take care that no hindrance is interposed to the people's obtaining the necessaries of life.
2. Opium has become a necessary of life to a Chinaman.
3. A Government failing in its duty ceases to be a Government.
4. A Chinese Government enacting laws against Opium is therefore no longer a Government.
5. If there is no Government there can be no Government laws against smuggling in Opium.
6. The Indian merchant who supplies the Chinese opium-smoker with his favourite stimulant violates no law.[115]

Even *Punch*, it seems, was anxious to dissociate Englishmen from the opium traffic, portraying it as transacted between Indians and Chinese. In face of such reticence, we shall have to look elsewhere for the connection between opium and the *Arrow* War.

VI. Questions unanswered

At this point, it is revealing to compare the instructions issued to Bowring in February 1854[116] with those to Elgin in April 1857[117] by putting them side by side as in Table 13.1. This table shows that in a milder and less specific form, Bowring had been instructed to obtain from China more or less the same fundamental concessions that Elgin was now told to acquire. And despite all the rhetoric about the alleged insult to the British flag, Elgin was not instructed to exact the pertinent reparations, only compensations to British subjects for

113. Campbell, John (1779–1861) was lord chief justice and was to become lord chancellor in 1859, on the advice, it is said, of Lord Lyndhurst. *DNB*, v. 3, pp. 831–8.
114. Lord chancellor, 24 August 1857, Hansard, 3d series, v. 147, col. 2003.
115. *Punch*, 28 March 1857, p. 129, purporting to be a letter from the attorney-general, Richard Bethell.
116. Clarendon to Bowring, Draft 2, 13 February 1854, FO17/210.
117. Clarendon to Elgin, Draft 5, 20 April 1857, FO17/261.

Table 13.1. *A comparison of instructions for treaty revision*

Bowring, 1854	Elgin, 1857
1. Access generally to the whole interior of China	1. Opening of all ports along the China coast to foreign trade
2. Free navigation of the Yangtze River	2. Opening of all ports along the banks of all rivers to foreign trade
3. Legalization of the opium trade	3. Legalization of the opium trade
4. Provision against the imposition of transit duties on foreign goods	4. Permission for British merchants to purchase the produce of China at the place of production, with no duties payable on such articles on their passage to the coastal ports for embarkation
5. Suppression of piracy on the China coast	5. British cooperation in the suppression of piracy
6. Regulation of the emigration of Chinese labourers	6. Revocation of the prohibition against emigration of Chinese subjects
7. Permanent residence at Beijing of a representative of the Crown (if that were not possible, then:)	7. Permanent residence at Beijing of a representative of the Crown
8. Habitual correspondence between H.M. representative and the Chinese chief authority at Beijing	(covered by 7)
9. Ready personal intercourse between H.M. representative and the governor of the province in which he might be residing	(covered by 7)
10. Resolution of all doubts by reference to the English text of treaty	10. Resolution of all doubts by reference to the English text of treaty
	11. Free travel and protection of missionaries in interior of China
	12. Confirmation of most favoured nation principle
	13. Full confirmation of the right of extraterritoriality
	14. Reparations for injuries to British subjects
	15. Compensation to British subjects for losses consequent on the *Arrow* quarrel

losses consequent on the quarrel (such as losses incurred when the British factory at Canton was burnt down) and even these were put at the bottom of the list. We should also note that this demand was quite separate from the *Arrow* incident itself, because the owner of the *Arrow*, not being a British subject, would not be entitled to such compensations. All this is further evidence that Britain would have waged a war with China at this time without the *Arrow* incident, and possibly without the lobby groups. As we have seen in this chapter, the British Foreign Office was no longer dependent on old China hands for intelligence or advice, as at the time of the Opium War. Thus, the present chapter extends the arguments advanced by Nathan Pelcovits,[118] of Foreign Office independence in the post–*Arrow* War period, backwards until at least the crucial years of 1856–7, when war was being secretly prepared.[119] If we were to consider Palmerston's annoyance with the intransigence of the British merchants at Canton in the 1840s,[120] we might conceivably extend that period further backwards in time for about a decade.

In terms of the theory of gentlemanly capitalism, the supreme influence exercised by the merchant princes on the Foreign Office during Opium War had declined, by the time of the *Arrow* War, to a relationship of interdependence and mutual benefit, with some healthy checks and balances on each other. With regard to the origins of the *Arrow* War, it was the Foreign Office that took the initiative for treaty revision, without any prompting from the gentlemanly capitalists. In addition, political expedience seems to have governed the timing of the publication of the kind of official document most conducive to a favourable reaction from the industrial, commercial, and financial communities. I am referring to the publication of Seymour's despatch in the *London Gazette* on 6 January 1857, which prompted the lobbying.[121] In this sense, it was the government using the merchant princes, rather than the latter influencing the former.[122]

118. See Pelcovits, *Old China Hands and the Foreign Office*. Pelcovits deals with the role of British merchants in Anglo-Chinese relations for the half-century between the Treaty of Tientsin and the Treaty of Portsmouth. Beyond that period, E. W. Edwards has some very interesting things to say in his *British Diplomacy and Finance in China, 1895–1914* (Oxford, Clarendon Press, 1987).
119. See Chapter 11.
120. See Chapter 6.
121. For details, see Chapter 12.
122. Unwittingly, the action of the government created an idol for the merchants. Upon his return to England in 1859, Seymour was presented by the China merchants with a handsome service of plate. *DNB*, v. 17, p. 1265.

Part VI
The economics of imperialism

In Part IV of this book we saw that Cobden[1] and Perry[2] expressed concern over the imbalance of trade with China. Earls Grey[3] and Albemarle[4] drew attention to the duties on tea being a significant source of revenue to Britain. Herbert,[5] Kinnaird,[6] and Ellenborough[7] spoke of the importance of the sale of Indian opium to China in terms of its contribution to the Indian revenue and to the United Kingdom's global trade. The prime minister defended the opium trade by saying that it helped to balance the trade deficit with China. In view of China's rejection of the British appeal for treaty revision, he wondered what else Britain could do to expand British trade and legalize opium in China.[8] Thereupon Disraeli spelled out what was in Palmerston's mind: to use the *Arrow* dispute as the casus belli by which to expand Britain's interests in China, where negotiations had failed.[9] Part V substantiated with documentary evidence the view that these spontaneous and brief references point to what were in fact the government's real intentions and concerns.

Part VI quantifies and analyses the basis for these concerns, especially those over Britain's commercial relations with China, in four chapters addressing the Anglo-Chinese trade up to the time of the *Arrow* War (and in some cases for a few years beyond), China's maritime trade, the problem of India, and finally the balance sheet.

The primary information for these chapters is from the British Parliamentary Papers containing the annual statistical returns prepared by the various government departments and tabled in Parliament each year. During the parliamentary debates on the *Arrow* quarrel, the importance of the Britain–

1. Cobden, 26 February 1857, Hansard, 3d series, v. 144, col. 1412.
2. Sir Erskine Perry, 26 February 1857, Hansard, 3d series, v. 144, col. 1460.
3. Grey, 24 February 1857, Hansard, 3d series, v. 144, col. 1236.
4. Albemarle, 26 February 1857, Hansard, 3d series, v. 144, col. 1354.
5. Herbert, 2 March 1857, Hansard, 3d series, v. 144, col. 1677.
6. Kinnaird's exclamation, 2 March 1857, Hansard, 3d series, v. 144, col. 1677.
7. Ellenborough, 26 February 1857, Hansard, 3d series, v. 144, col. 1363.
8. Palmerston, 3 March 1857, Hansard, 3d series, v. 144, col. 1828.
9. Disraeli, 3 March 1857, Hansard, 3d series, v. 144, col. 1836.

India–China trade was emphasized repeatedly and the pertinent statistics quoted liberally, witnessing the degree to which their lordships and the honourable members had relied on these statistics for their perceptions.[10] The key player at the front line, Bowring, had also been a member of Parliament for many years and had sat on committees inquiring into the state of the China trade.[11] He would have obtained his perceptions from the same statistics.

I am not suggesting that these members of Parliament had mastered the entire range of statistical detail presented in the following tables. I merely wish to quantify the general but crucial perceptions of the importance of pertinent British interests, which were pivotal in terms of the government's decision to wage a full-scale war on China on the basis of the *Arrow* quarrel.

Throughout these tables, the official value and the real value of commodities have been transcribed from the British Parliamentary Papers without attempting to make the two sets of values compatible. Official value, applied to imports, is the value given to the goods 'according to Rates fixed so long back as the year 1694', and hence reflects a value lower than the real worth.[12] Computed real value, also applied to imports, is calculated on the basis of the prices of the articles in bond, including all the charges of freight and lading, but exclusive of the duties.[13]

From 1854 onwards, British statisticians abandoned the official value and began using computed real value. Ideally, I should convert the official value of imports for the years before 1854 to computed real value so as to make them comparable with those after 1854,[14] and also to make them comparable with the declared value of exports which are likewise real value. But, what often mattered with political decision-making was not so much reality as perception. The 'values' available to us now are what were available to the members of Parliament who made war and peace. Only professional economists and statisticians would want to see the real value, and I doubt many of their lordships and the honourable members fell into that category. I propose, therefore, to cast pre-1854 values in terms of perceptions rather than reality.

The problem does not exist for the three years immediately before the parliamentary debates in February and March of 1857 on the *Arrow* War because, as mentioned, both imports and exports in the United Kingdom were expressed in real values from 1854 onwards. Furthermore, I have often rounded off all numbers to the nearest two or three decimal points of £1 million to make them more readable, as total accuracy is not really required for my argument.

10. See Chapters 7 and 8.   11. See Chapter 3.
12. Parl. Papers 1854–55, v. 51 (Pt. 2, 1854), pp. a2–a3. See next two footnotes.
13. Parl. Papers 1854–5, v. 51 (Pt. 1, 1854), pp. a2–a3.
14. This is exactly what was done by the late Ralph Davis in *The Industrial Revolution and British Overseas Trade* (Leicester, Leicester University Press, 1978).

14
Anglo-Chinese trade:
The Chinese should buy more

Anglo-Chinese trade in this period has never been systematically quantified; nearly all discussion of the origins of the *Arrow* War has revolved around the personalities. References to trade have always been very general.[1] This chapter fills that gap by collecting the annual statistics prepared by the Board of Trade in London and putting them into tables covering several decades. Such tables generally go back to when the statistics on certain topics were first made available and sometimes extend for a few years beyond the *Arrow* War in order to reveal the long-term trends. The reader is reminded that we are dealing with perceptions rather than reality. Hence, the 'official value' and the later 'computed real value', as well as the 'declared value', are all transcribed from the Parliamentary Papers without converting the official value to real value to make it comparable with the rest.

I. Export of British manufactures to China

Let us begin with the export of British manufactures to China. This was, of course, an overriding consideration for British policy makers. The two major items of manufacture exported to China and Hong Kong were cottons and woollens. The value – and here I use the original figures as found in the Parliamentary Papers rather than those I have truncated in Table 14.1 – of cottons exported to China and Hong Kong rose from £67,303 in 1827 to £2,090,158 in 1858. This was an increase of £2,022,855, or thirty-one-fold. That of woollens fell from £461,472 to £390,713, a decrease of £70,759, or 15 per cent. That of all the other articles rose from £81,860 to £359,576, an increase of £277,716, more than fourfold. The aggregate rose from £610,637 to £2,876,447, an increase of £2,265,810, or almost fivefold.[2] These figures appear even more impressive if presented in graphs, as Figure 14.1 shows.

1. See the works cited in Chapter 1.
2. See Parl. Papers 1859, Session 2, v. 23, p. 315.

333

Table 14.1. *U.K. exports to China (and Hong Kong), 1827–58 (£ million sterling, declared real value)*

Year	Cotton manufactures and cotton yarn 1	Woollen manufactures and worsteds 2	All other articles 3	Aggregate 4
1827	0.07	0.46	0.08	0.61
1828	0.09	0.62	0.07	0.78
1829	0.07	0.49	0.06	0.62
1830	0.06	0.47	0.03	0.56
1831	0.11	0.40	0.04	0.55
1832	0.05	0.47	0.02	0.54
1833	0.07	0.53	0.03	0.63
1834	0.22	0.58	0.04	0.84
1835	0.46	0.53	0.09	1.08
1836	0.58	0.66	0.08	1.32
1837	0.38	0.25	0.05	0.68
1838	0.74	0.41	0.05	1.20
1839	0.46	0.34	0.05	0.85
1840	0.33	0.16	0.03	0.52
1841	0.58	0.21	0.07	0.86
1842	0.72	0.15	0.11	0.98
1843	0.87	0.42	0.17	1.46
1844	1.58	0.57	0.16	2.31
1845	1.74	0.54	0.12	2.40
1846	1.25	0.44	0.11	1.80
1847	1.01	0.39	0.10	1.50
1848	0.95	0.38	0.11	1.44
1849	1.00	0.37	0.16	1.53
1850	1.02	0.40	0.15	1.57
1851	1.60	0.37	0.19	2.16
1852	1.91	0.43	0.16	2.50
1853	1.41	0.20	0.14	1.75
1854	0.64	0.16	0.20	1.00
1855	0.88	0.13	0.26	1.27
1856	1.54	0.27	0.40	2.21
1857	1.73	0.29	0.43	2.45
1858	2.09	0.39	0.36	2.88

Source: Parl. Papers 1859, Session 2, v. 23, p. 315.

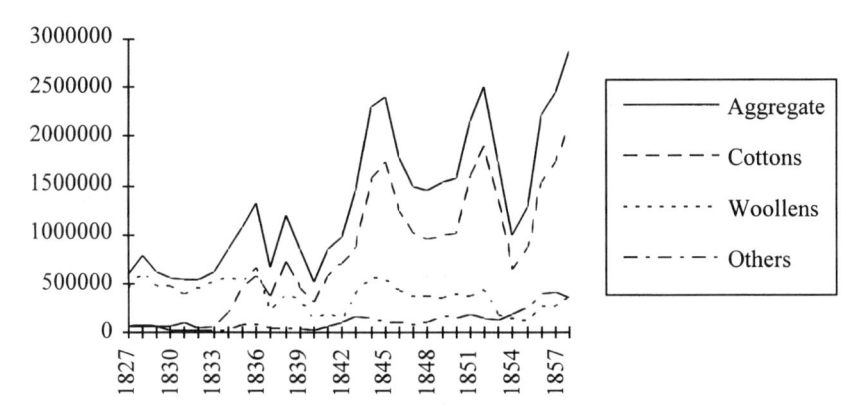

Figure 14.1. The declared value of U.K. exports to China (and Hong Kong), 1827–58 (£ million sterling; based on Table 14.1)

II. The apparent British trade imbalance with China

But the British policy makers were not impressed. The main dissatisfaction lay in the trade imbalance. Table 14.2 offers some idea of the United Kingdom's trade imbalance with China for this period. Given that the values in columns 2 and 3 are not compatible until 1854, I shall begin my analysis then. (Note that in all tables, column 1 is the first to the right of the left-hand column showing date or country.) Even at that time, the part of my table from the year 1854 onwards shows the trade imbalance but does not measure it. To measure the commodity trade gap, we would need exports at the prices paid by the Chinese at Chinese ports (including freight, insurance, etc.) minus imports at prices charged in Chinese ports to the British merchants. But at present, such comprehensive data is not available, and is in any case not required for my argument.

In 1854, that is, two years before the *Arrow* incident, the trade imbalance was well over £8 million sterling, as the value of British exports to China was 91 per cent of that of the imports from China. There was only one conclusion which the British policy makers could have drawn: China should buy more from the United Kingdom. It was in this year, 1854, that the British foreign secretary, Lord Clarendon, instructed the British representative in the Far East, Sir John Bowring, to revise the Treaty of Nanking in order 'to obtain access generally to the whole interior of the Chinese Empire'.[3] These instructions amounted to a demand for a new treaty and have been generally interpreted as indicative of a powerful impulse to increase exports to China. But as mentioned, Yeh transmitted his complete and final rejection of these British requests in his

3. Clarendon to Bowring, Desp. 2, 13 February 1854, FO17/210.

Table 14.2. *The United Kingdom's trade deficit with China, 1827–58 (£ million sterling)*

Year	Imports (aggregate official value) 1	Exports (aggregate declared value) 2	Trade deficit 3	Imports expressed as a percentage of exports (col. 1 ÷ col. 2) 4
1827	4.10	0.61	3.49	672
1828	3.48	0.79	2.69	441
1829	3.23	0.63	2.60	513
1830	3.23	0.57	2.66	567
1831	3.21	0.55	2.66	584
1832	3.21	0.55	2.66	584
1833	3.27	0.63	2.64	519
1834	3.51	0.85	2.66	413
1835	4.56	1.07	3.49	426
1836	5.42	1.33	4.09	408
1837	4.53	0.68	3.85	666
1838	4.31	1.20	3.11	359
1839	3.98	0.85	3.13	467
1840	2.39	0.52	1.87	456
1841	2.96	0.86	2.10	344
1842	3.96	0.97	2.99	408
1843	4.63	1.46	3.17	317
1844	5.57	2.31	3.26	241
1845	5.82	2.39	3.43	244
1846	6.64	1.79	4.85	370
1847	6.70	1.50	5.20	447
1848	5.82	1.45	4.37	402
1849	6.17	1.54	4.63	401
1850	5.85	1.57	4.28	371
1851	7.97	2.16	5.81	369
1852	7.71	2.5	5.21	308
1853	8.26	1.75	6.51	472
	Computed	Declared		
1854	9.13	1.00	8.13	913
1855	8.75	1.28	7.47	684
1856	9.42	2.21	7.21	426
1857	11.45	2.45	9.00	467
1858	7.04	2.88	4.16	244
Average	—	—	—	454

Source: Parl. Papers 1859, Session 2, v. 23, p. 319, for col. 1. Ibid., p. 315, for col. 2. Cols. 3–4 are my calculations.

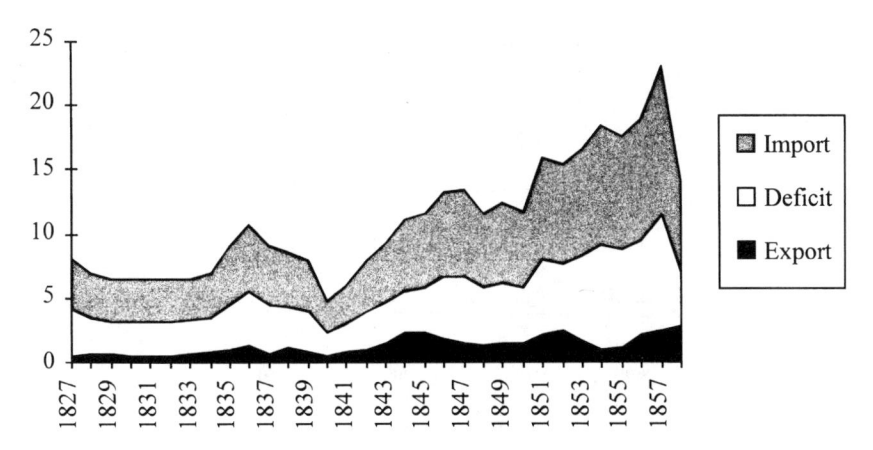

Figure 14.2. The United Kingdom's trade imbalance with China, 1827–58 (£ million sterling; based on Table, 14.2)

despatch dated 30 June 1856,[4] about three months before the *Arrow* incident occurred. Thus, we saw in Part Five that the thoughts of the British policy makers had already turned to war well before the arrival of the news about the *Arrow* incident, which then conveniently provided the casus belli for a full-scale war. Again, the point may be made even more pungently by means of a graph, which is provided in Figure 14.2.

III. British imports from China

An alternative to making the Chinese buy more British products was to reduce imports from China. But there were some unusual circumstances at the time of the *Arrow* War which made the British government just as determined to increase imports from China as they were to augment exports. Imports from China, especially tea and silk, played a significant role in the British economy. Tea enabled the British government to collect a significant amount of revenue by way of import duty, and Chinese raw silk was required by the British manufacturing industry. All in all, China was an important supplier of commodities to the 'workshop of the world'.

Table 14.3 shows the official value, and from 1854 onwards the computed real value, of the total imports from China for about thirty years up to the time

4. Yeh to Bowring, 30 June 1856, FO682/1989/9; and Chunglun to Bowring, 8 November 1854, FO682/1987/66. See also Yeh's initial reaction, in which he said that he had been instructed to observe the treaty to the letter and not to change it in any substantial manner (Yeh to Bowring, 1 September 1854, FO682/1987/54).

Table 14.3. *U.K. imports from China, 1828–58*
(£ million sterling)

Year	Tea 1	Silk 2	Other articles 3	Aggregate 4
Official value				
1828	3.268	0.078	0.135	3.481
1829	3.054	0.044	0.128	3.226
1830	3.190	0.007	0.035	3.232
1831	3.165	0.003	0.039	3.207
1832	3.171	0.010	0.026	3.207
1833	3.206	0.008	0.053	3.267
1834	3.203	0.214	0.090	3.507
1835	4.205	0.272	0.058	4.535
1836	4.852	0.474	0.097	5.423
1837	3.650	0.703	0.180	4.533
1838	3.900	0.279	0.131	4.310
1839	3.719	0.130	0.129	3.978
1840	2.258	0.091	0.040	2.389
1841	2.764	0.102	0.099	2.965
1842	3.741	0.066	0.149	3.956
1843	4.278	0.110	0.243	4.631
1844	5.175	0.141	0.249	5.565
1845	5.071	0.437	0.313	5.821
1846	5.453	0.678	0.511	6.642
1847	5.536	0.748	0.419	6.703
1848	4.735	0.862	0.222	5.819
1849	5.310	0.696	0.165	6.171
1850	4.937	0.700	0.212	5.849
1851	6.949	0.842	0.181	7.972
1852	6.530	0.945	0.238	7.713
1853	6.864	1.211	0.180	8.255
Computed real value				
1854	5.380	3.583	0.162	9.125
1855	5.120	3.433	0.195	8.748
1856	5.123	4.106	0.192	9.421
1857	4.310	6.911	0.228	11.449
1858	5.036	1.837	0.170	7.043

Source: Parl. Papers 1859, Session 2, v. 23, p. 319.

of the *Arrow* War. In 1828, which opens the table, the official value was around £3.48 million. If, at the time, an abjectly poor family in London could survive on three pence (3d.) a day⁵ (or £4.5 a year), £3.48 million was certainly a lot of money.⁶ The value of this trade increased steadily to around £11.45 million in real value in 1857, when the *Arrow* War began in earnest. The latter figure was made up of over £4.31 million worth of tea, £6.91 million worth of silk, and about £0.23 million worth of other goods.

IV. China's place in the United Kingdom's imports globally

The Board of Trade has kept valuable records since the eighteenth century.⁷ The large expansion of the United Kingdom's international trade, especially in the early 1850s, prompted even greater sophistication in statistical work. In March 1855, Parliament was presented with new sets of annual statements of the trade and navigation of the United Kingdom with foreign countries and with British possessions, for the year 1853.⁸ Some of these statements contained statistics dating back to 1849. Thus, we are able to compare and analyse the pertinent statistics for the ten years or so up to the time of the *Arrow* War. Of the sixty-two foreign countries and regions (excluding British possessions)⁹ from which the United Kingdom had imported goods in 1849, China was fourth. It occupied the same position in 1850, rising to third place in 1851, to second place in 1852, and then stayed in fourth place up to the time of the *Arrow* War. Even after the port of Canton was closed to foreign trade for the whole of 1857, and after the southern coast of China was adversely affected by Anglo–Chinese hostilities in 1858, China still occupied the fourth position (see Table 14.4).

Table 14.5 offers a different perspective. Here, it will be seen that the value of the United Kingdom's imports from China constituted an annual average of 8.26 per cent of the United Kingdom's global imports (excluding those from the British possessions, which will be dealt with in Table 14.6)¹⁰ from 1849 to 1857. In 1858, the *Arrow* War reduced this value to 5.62 per cent and hence the average for the entire ten-year period to 7.95 per cent. Considering that the

---

5. See Charles Booth (ed.), *Labour and Life of the People in London*, 8 vs. (London, Williams & Norgate, 1891–1902), especially, v. 2, pp. 293–304 and 335–49.
6. In the imperial scale, 12d. made 1s; 20s. made £1. Thus, £3.48 million was equivalent to 835.2 million pence, theoretically supporting 278.4 million abjectly poor families a day, or 773,333 such families a year.
7. See Davis, *The Industrial Revolution and British Overseas Trade*.
8. Parl. Papers 1854–5, v. 51 (Pt. 1, 1853), pp. a1–a3.
9. For accounting purposes, British statisticians made a distinction between, foreign countries and British possessions. The trade with the British possessions will be dealt with later in this chapter.
10. British statisticians distinguished between foreign countries and British possessions.

Table 14.4. *The top four countries (excluding the British possessions) from which the United Kingdom bought its imports, 1849–58 (£ million sterling)*

Year	United States 1	France 2	Russia or Prussia 3	China 4	China's place 5
Official value					
1849	26.56	8.18	R: 6.90	6.17	4
1850	20.67	8.45	R: 6.61	5.85	4
1851	23.62	8.08	R: 6.23	7.97	3
1852	9.18	6.59	R: 6.40	7.71	2
1853	27.46	8.62	R: 8.92	8.26	4
Computed real value					
1854	29.80	10.45	P: 9.06	9.13	3
1855	25.74	9.15	P:10.24	8.75	4
1856	36.05	10.39	R:11.56	9.42	4
1857	33.65	11.97	R:13.45	11.45	4
1858	34.26	13.27	R:11.94	7.07	4

Note: R = Russia; P = Prussia. The statistics show that Prussia replaced Russia in 1854 and 1855, the years of the Crimean War. Presumably Britain continued to import goods from Russia (furs and so on) but they were rerouted via Prussia.
Source: Parl. Papers 1854–5, v. 51 (Pt. 1, 1853), pp. 2–3, for the years 1849–53; 1859, Session 2, v. 28, p. 4, for 1854–8.

United Kingdom was then the greatest trading power in the world, this per centage was not small by any standard.

Let us do something which the British statisticians did not do, namely, add the United Kingdom's imports from foreign countries to those from the British possessions to find the total value of the United Kingdom's global imports and see where the value of imports from China stood in this context. Table 14.6 is the result. It shows that the value of imports from China constituted an annual average of 5.83 per cent of the value of the United Kingdom's global imports. This average would have been higher had there not been a sudden and sharp rise of imports from the British possessions in 1855; presumably they were supplies for the Crimean War.

This is presented visually in Figure 14.3.

The picture is not complete without a comparison of the value of the United Kingdom's imports from China with that from the British possessions. Table 14.7 shows such a comparison with the major colonies for the four years up to the time of the *Arrow* War. Here it will be seen that the value of the imports from China exceeded that from any British colony except the 'British East

Table 14.5. *China's percentage of the United Kingdom's global imports (excluding the British possessions), 1849–58 (£ million sterling)*

Year	United Kingdom's imports from China 1	United Kingdom's imports globally (excluding British possessions) 2	China's percentage of the United Kingdom's global imports (col. 1 ÷ col. 2) 3
1849	6.17	81.53	7.57
1850	5.85	74.58	7.84
1851	7.97	81.99	9.92
1852	7.71	82.56	9.34
1853	8.26	94.16	8.77
1854	9.13	118.24	7.12
1855	8.75	109.96	7.95
1856	9.42	129.52	7.27
1857	11.45	141.66	8.08
1858	7.07	125.97	5.62
Average	—	—	7.95

Source: Parl. Papers 1854–5, v. 51, pp. 2–3, for the years 1849–53; 1859, Session 2, v. 28, p. 4, for 1854–8. The calculations of percentages are mine.

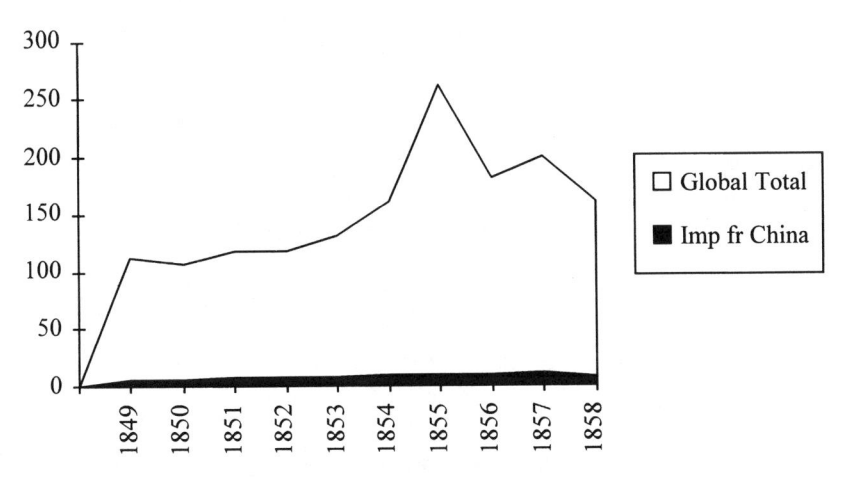

Figure 14.3. The place of China in the United Kingdom's global imports, 1849–58 (£ million sterling; based on Table 14.6)

The economics of imperialism

Table 14.6. *The place of China in the United Kingdom's global imports, 1849–58 (£ million sterling)*

Year	U.K. imports from British possessions 1	U.K. imports from foreign countries 2	Global total of U.K. imports 3	U.K. imports from China 4	China's percentage of the United Kingdom's global imports (col. 4 ÷ col. 3) 5
1849	24.35	81.53	105.88	6.17	5.83
1850	25.89	74.58	100.47	5.85	5.82
1851	28.49	81.99	110.48	7.97	7.22
1852	26.77	82.56	109.33	7.71	7.06
1853	28.94	94.16	123.10	8.26	6.70
1854	34.15	118.24	152.39	9.13	5.99
1855	143.54	109.96	253.50	8.75	3.45
1856	43.03	129.52	172.55	9.42	5.46
1857	46.18	141.66	187.84	11.45	6.10
1858	28.61	125.97	154.58	7.07	4.58
Average	—	—	—	—	5.83

Source: For the value of U.K. imports from foreign states (including China), see Parl. Papers 1854–5, v. 51, pp. 2–3, for the years 1849–53; and 1859, Session 2, v. 28, p. 4, for 1854–8. For the value of U.K. imports from the British possessions, see Parl. Papers 1854–5, v. 51, p. 5, for 1849–53; and 1857–8, v. 54, p. 5, for 1854–8.

Table 14.7. *A comparison of the United Kingdom's imports from China and from British possessions, 1854–7 (£ million sterling)*

Country	1854	1855	1856	1857
Br. E. Indies	10.67	12.67	17.26	18.65
China	9.13	8.75	9.42	11.45
Br. N. America	7.19	4.69	6.85	6.34
Australia	4.26	4.47	5.64	5.77
Br. W. Indies	3.98	3.98	4.57	5.22
Br. S. Africa	0.69	0.95	1.5	1.79
New Zealand	0.04	0.03	0.1	0.16

Source: Parl. Papers 1857–8, v. 54, pp. 4–5.

Indies' (British India). In 1857, for example, the computed real value of imports into the United Kingdom from China was 1.8 times that from British North America, twice that from Australia, 2.2 times that from the British West Indies, 6.4 times that from British possessions in South Africa, and 72.2 times that from New Zealand.

V. British import duty on Chinese tea

In this day and age, much importance is attached to increasing exports in order to achieve a favourable balance of payments. Thus, it may seem strange that we should be paying so much attention to the importance of China as a source of imports to the United Kingdom in the nineteenth century. But in those days, imports from China (and tea consumed in the United Kingdom in the mid-nineteenth century was almost entirely Chinese, as we shall see) did deserve such attention because, as mentioned, one of these, tea, enabled the British government to raise a significant amount of revenue by way of import duty. Up to 1784, such a duty ranged from 75.9 per cent to 127.5 per cent ad valorem. By the Commutation Act of 1784 it was reduced to 12.5 per cent. But some twenty years later it was again increased to 100 per cent,[11] apparently in order to find more money to fight Napoleon. The duty was not reduced, however, after the Napoleonic Wars.

This 100 per cent duty contrasted sharply with the export duty in China itself of 10 per cent.[12] Export duties are now almost nonexistent as most countries wish to encourage exports to achieve a favourable trade balance. Even in the nineteenth century, the British were sufficiently sophisticated in their economic thinking not to tax their own exports. In addition, they made the Chinese agree in the Treaty of Nanking to tax British imports at 5 per cent only. By the same treaty, the British restricted Chinese taxes also to 5 per cent on all Chinese exports. The exception was tea, which remained at 10 per cent because 'China had a natural monopoly' in tea.[13]

In China, taxes on imports and exports were an important source of revenue for the government. But dearer Chinese exports meant higher prices for the British consumer, which is why the British had restricted Chinese taxes on them also. In terms of revenue, then, the British government benefited more from Chinese tea than did the Chinese government itself. In real terms, by 1842 the import duty on tea in the United Kingdom was collected at a minimum rate of one shilling five pence per pound. This was more than 11.33 times the export duty on tea in China, which was only about one and a half pence per pound.[14]

11. Greenberg, *British Trade and the Opening of China*, p. 52.
12. Morse, *International Relations of the Chinese Empire*, v. 1, p. 534.
13. Ibid.   14. Ibid., pp. 308 and 534.

Table 14.8. *Tea duty and average tea consumption in the United Kingdom, 1801–60*

Year	Average rate of duty per pound paid by the consumer (pence) 1	Average price per pound in bond (pence) 2	Average price per pound inclusive of duty (pence) 3	Population of the United Kingdom (millions) 4	Average individual consumption (ounces) 5
1801	14.50	36.000	50.500	15.828	24
1802	15.50	37.500	53.000	15.966	25
1803	18.50	34.750	53.250	16.171	25
1804	28.25	36.000	64.250	16.407	22
1805	33.00	37.000	70.000	16.677	23
1806	37.25	39.000	76.250	16.917	21
1807	35.50	40.000	75.500	17.154	22
1808	37.25	39.500	76.750	17.385	23
1809	41.00	41.000	82.000	17.602	19
1810	35.75	40.000	75.750	17.841	22
1811	40.00	40.000	80.000	18.011	20
1812	37.25	39.750	77.000	18.270	21
1813	35.50	40.500	76.000	18.522	24
1814	39.00	41.750	80.750	18.832	21
1815	37.50	38.000	75.500	19.118	22
1816	35.50	35.750	71.250	19.463	19
1817	33.50	36.250	69.750	19.772	21
1818	35.00	37.000	72.000	20.076	21
1819	35.00	33.750	68.750	20.398	20
1820	33.00	33.250	66.250	20.705	20
1821	33.50	34.250	67.750	20.985	20
1822	34.25	34.000	68.250	21.320	21
1823	34.00	34.000	68.000	21.672	20
1824	33.50	34.000	67.500	21.991	20
1825	33.00	33.500	66.500	22.304	21
1826	31.00	30.250	61.250	22.605	21
1827	29.75	29.000	58.750	22.893	21
1828	28.25	28.250	56.500	23.200	20
1829	27.00	26.750	53.750	23.535	20
1830	27.00	27.250	54.250	23.834	20
1831	26.75	27.000	53.750	24.083	20
1832	26.75	26.250	53.000	24.343	21
1833	26.00	26.000	52.000	24.561	21
1834	24.75	25.250	50.000	24.820	23
1835	25.25	23.000	48.250	25.104	23
1836	22.75	19.000	41.750	25.390	31

Table 14.8. (cont.)

Year	Average rate of duty per pound paid by the consumer (pence) 1	Average price per pound in bond (pence) 2	Average price per pound inclusive of duty (pence) 3	Population of the United Kingdom (millions) 4	Average individual consumption (ounces) 5
1837	25.00	17.750	42.750	25.676	19
1838	25.00	19.500	44.500	25.895	20
1839	25.00	20.500	45.500	26.201	21
1840	25.75	31.250	57.000	26.519	19
1841	26.25	25.500	51.750	26.780	22
1842	26.25	24.250	50.500	27.006	22
1843	26.25	16.250	42.500	27.283	24
1844	26.25	14.750	41.000	27.577	24
1845	26.25	13.750	40.000	27.875	25
1846	26.25	13.000	39.250	28.189	27
1847	26.25	13.000	39.250	28.093	26
1848	26.25	12.250	38.500	27.855	28
1849	26.25	13.000	39.250	27.632	29
1850	26.25	15.250	41.500	27.423	30
1851	26.25	14.500	40.750	27.529	31
1852	26.25	12.250	38.500	27.570	32
1853	23.25	15.250	38.500	27.663	34
1854	18.50	15.500	34.000	27.788	36
1855	20.00	15.000	35.000	27.899	36
1856	21.00	14.750	35.750	28.154	36
1857	17.60	17.400	35.000	28.427	39
1858	17.00	16.625	33.625	28.654	41
1859	17.00	18.625	35.625	28.890	42
1860	17.00	18.750	35.750	29.150	42

Note: For easy reading and comparison, the figures originally recorded in shillings and pence in cols. 1–3 have been converted to pence. Similarly, the pounds and ounces in col. 5 have been converted to ounces. The population figures in col. 4 have not been truncated – the original figures seem to have been estimates, the last three digits of which invariably appeared in the form of '000'. The same parliamentary paper also gives the total annual tea consumption and the duty derived therefrom, but the figures differ from those in the Parliamentary Papers tabled annually, on which I also depend for other statistics. To be consistent, therefore, I have decided to use the figures in the annual reports for the annual tea consumption and duty therefrom – see the note in Table 14.9.

Source: Parl. Papers 1861, v. 58, p. 627.

Table 14.9. *Tea imported into the United Kingdom, entered for home consumption and the duty derived therefrom, 1835–58*

Year	Tea: Imported (millions of pounds) 1	Tea: Home consumption (duty payable) (millions of pounds) 2	Tea gross duty (£ million sterling) 3	U.K. total gross customs (on all goods including tea) (£ million sterling) 4	Tea duty as percentage of total U.K. customs duties (col. 3 ÷ col. 4) 5
1835	44.36	36.61	3.84	22.88	16.77
1836	46.89	49.84	4.73	23.67	19.98
1837	36.97	31.87	3.32	22.69	14.63
1838	40.41	32.37	3.36	22.97	14.65
1839	38.07	35.14	3.66	23.28	15.72
1840	28.02	32.26	3.47	23.47	14.80
1841	30.27	36.68	3.98	23.61	16.85
1842	40.71	37.39	4.09	22.60	18.10
1843	46.61	40.30	4.41	22.64	19.47
1844	52.80	41.37	4.52	24.02	18.84
1845	51.06	44.20	4.83	21.84	22.13
1846	54.77	46.73	5.11	22.50	22.72
1847	55.63	46.32	5.07	21.70	23.35
1948	47.77	48.74	5.33	22.66	23.52
1849	53.46	50.02	5.47	22.35	24.48
1850	50.51	51.18	5.60	22.06	25.37
1851	71.47	53.97	5.90	22.26	26.52
1852	66.36	54.72	5.99	22.19	26.98
1853	70.74	58.86	5.69	22.74	25.01
1854	85.79	61.97	5.13	22.25	23.05
1855	83.12	63.45	5.80	23.48	24.72
1856	86.20	63.30	4.81	23.96	20.06
1857	64.49	69.16	5.46	23.60	23.14
1858	75.43	73.22	5.27	24.09	21.89
Average	—	—	—	—	20.95

Sources: Parl. Papers 1837, v. 50, pp. 545–8, for the years 1835–6; 1839, v. 46, pp. 1–4, for 1837; 1840, v. 44, pp. 1–4, for 1838–9; 1842, v. 34, pp. 409–12, for 1840–1; 1843, v. 52, pp. 1–5, for 1842; 1845, v. 46, pp. 1–5, for 1843–4; 1847, v. 59, pp. 1–6, for 1845–6; 1847–8, v. 58, pp. 1–6, for 1847; 1850, v. 52, pp. 1–8, for 1848–9; 1851, v. 53, pp. 1–8, for 1850; 1852, v. 51, pp. 1–8, for 1851; 1854, v. 65, pp. 9 and 22, for 1852; ibid. and 1854, v. 39, pp. 10–12, for 1853; 1854–5, v. 50, p. 10, and 1854–5, v. 30, pp. 10 and 23, for 1854; 1856, v. 55, p. 10, and 1856, v. 38, pp. 10 and 23, for 1855; 1859, v. 25, p. 8, and 1857, Session 2, v. 25, pp. 10 and 24, for 1856; 1859, v. 25, p. 8, and 1857–8, v. 33, pp. 10 and 22, for 1857; 1859, v. 25, p. 8, and 1859, v. 15, pp. 4 and 23, for 1858.

Table 14.8 shows the average rate of duty, price per pound, and individual consumption of tea from the beginning of the nineteenth century to the end of the *Arrow* War. In that period, the population of the United Kingdom more or less doubled, as did the average individual consumption of tea.

Table 14.9 shows the amount of tea imported into the United Kingdom for about a quarter-century up to the time of the *Arrow* War, and the annual gross receipts from duties on tea. These receipts ranged from £3.8 million in 1835 to a height of £5.8 million in 1855, the year before the war broke out.

VI. The importance of tea duty compared with the United Kingdom's other sources of revenue

One way of assessing the importance of the tea duty is to measure it against some points of reference. The United Kingdom was at this time the greatest trading nation in the world, and its total customs duty was a very important source of national revenue. The statistics for that revenue have been supplied in Table 14.9, column 4. How important a component was the tea duty? The answer is provided in Table 14.9, column 5. For the period under review, tea duty made up an average of 20.95 per cent of the United Kingdom's entire customs revenue.

Let us put the revenue from tea duty in a wider context, say the United Kingdom's 'gross public income' from the end of the Opium War (1842) to the end of the *Arrow* War (1860). Table 14.10 provides such a context. Tea duty is subsumed under 'Customs',[15] but also added separately to show its position in the total picture. It will be seen that duties were by far the most important source of revenue, of which, as mentioned, tea duty made up more than a fifth. The picture will become even clearer if Table 14.10 is expressed in terms of per centages of the total gross income of the U.K. from the end of the Opium War to the end of the *Arrow* War. This is shown in Table 14.11.

Tea duty sits comfortably on a par with some of the independently listed items of British revenue, say, the combined 'land and assessed taxes'. The Parliamentary Papers show that for some years up to and including 1841, 'taxes' were shown as one item. After 1842, this item was subdivided into 'land and assessed taxes' and 'income and property taxes'. More details emerged

---

15. If we compare the total customs revenue listed in col. 4 of Table 14.9 with that listed in col. 2 of Table 14.10, it will be seen that the figures are not exactly the same. This can be explained. The statistics for Table 14.9 are based on annual reports, which do not include arrears. On the other hand, the statistics for Table 14.10 were apparently prepared retrospectively, and therefore included the arrears collected afterwards. Thus, tacking onto Table 14.10 the column on tea duty from Table 14.9 (which did not have the benefit of additional amounts collected retrospectively) puts tea duty at a disadvantage for the sake of comparison.

Table 14.10. *Tea duty added to a table of the United Kingdom's total gross income, 1842–60 (£ million sterling)*

Year	Total gross income 1	Customs 2	Excise tax 3	Stamp duty 4	Land and assessed taxes 5	Property and income tax 6	Post Office 7	Tea duty 8
1842	52.2	23.5	14.8	7.3	4.7	—	1.4	4.1
1843	51.1	22.6	13.6	7.2	4.5	0.6	1.6	4.4
1844	56.7	22.6	14.0	7.1	4.4	5.3	1.6	4.5
1845	58.2	24.1	14.4	7.3	4.4	5.3	1.7	4.8
1846	57.5	21.8	14.6	7.9	4.4	5.2	1.9	5.1
1847	58.2	22.2	15.0	7.7	4.5	5.5	2.0	5.1
1848	56.1	21.7	13.9	7.7	4.6	5.6	2.1	5.3
1849	57.8	22.6	15.2	6.8	4.5	5.5	2.2	5.5
1850	57.1	22.3	15.0	7.0	4.5	5.6	2.2	5.6
1851	57.1	22.0	15.3	6.7	4.6	5.5	2.3	5.9
1852	56.3	22.2	15.4	6.5	3.8	5.4	2.4	6.0
1853	57.3	22.1	15.7	6.9	3.6	5.7	2.4	5.7
1854	58.5	22.5	16.3	7.1	3.3	5.7	2.5	5.1
1855	62.4	21.6	16.9	7.1	3.2	10.6	2.4	5.8
1856	69.7	23.2	17.5	7.1	3.1	15.1	2.8	4.8
1857	72.2	23.5	18.3	7.4	3.1	16.1	2.9	5.5
1858	66.9	23.1	17.8	7.4	3.2	11.6	2.9	5.3
1859	64.3	24.1	17.9	8.0	3.2	6.7	3.2	5.4
1860	70.1	24.5	20.4	8.0	3.2	9.6	3.3	5.4
Average	—	—	—	—	—	—	—	5.2

Source: Most of the table is from *Abstract of British Historical Statistics*, compiled by B. R. Mitchell, with the collaboration of Phyllis Deane (Cambridge University Press, 1962), p. 393. The column on tea duty has been adapted from Table 14.9, col. 3, plus Parl. Papers 1860, v. 39, pp. 23–4 for the year 1859; and Parl. Papers 1861, v. 34, p. 22 for the year 1860.

later. Land taxes included 'tax on lands and tenements, and duties on offices and pensions'.[16] Assessed taxes included taxes on 'inhabited houses, servants, carriages, horses for riding, other horses and mules, dogs, horse dealers, hair powder, armorial bearings and game duty'.[17] Thus, land and assessed taxes were a comprehensive scheme of domestic taxes in the United Kingdom with which to compare the revenue from the duty on tea.

After the Opium War ended in 1842, trade began to return to normal. By using the original raw figures, instead of rounding them off to the nearest two

16. Parl. Papers 1859, Session 2, v. 15, p. 28.
17. Ibid.

Table 14.11. *Tea duty as a percentage of the United Kingdom's total gross revenue, 1842–60*

Year	Total gross income 1	Customs 2	Excise tax 3	Stamp duty 4	Land and assessed taxes 5	Property and income tax 6	Post Office 7	Tea duty 8
1842	100	45.02	28.35	13.98	9.00	—	2.68	7.84
1843	100	44.23	26.61	14.09	8.81	1.15	3.13	8.63
1844	100	39.86	24.69	12.52	7.76	10.40	2.82	7.98
1845	100	41.41	24.74	12.54	7.56	9.35	2.92	8.31
1846	100	37.91	25.39	13.74	7.65	8.93	3.30	8.88
1847	100	38.14	25.77	13.23	7.73	9.57	3.44	8.71
1848	100	38.68	24.78	13.73	8.20	9.62	3.74	9.50
1849	100	39.10	26.30	11.76	7.79	9.80	3.81	9.47
1850	100	39.05	26.27	12.26	7.88	9.69	3.85	9.80
1851	100	38.53	26.80	11.73	8.06	9.63	4.03	10.34
1852	100	39.43	27.35	11.55	6.75	9.46	4.26	9.06
1853	100	38.57	27.40	12.04	6.28	10.10	4.19	9.92
1854	100	38.46	27.86	12.14	5.64	9.95	4.27	8.77
1855	100	34.62	27.08	11.38	5.13	17.00	3.85	9.30
1856	100	33.29	25.11	10.19	4.45	24.20	4.02	6.89
1857	100	32.55	25.35	10.25	4.29	23.10	4.02	7.57
1858	100	34.53	26.61	11.06	4.78	16.10	4.33	7.88
1859	100	37.48	27.84	12.44	4.98	10.00	4.98	8.41
1860	100	34.95	29.10	11.41	4.56	14.90	4.71	7.74
Average	—	—	—	—	—	—	—	8.68

Source: Adapted from Table 14.10.

decimal points of £1 million, Table 14.12 shows that, in this year, revenue from tea duty was 91.09 per cent of that from the land and assessed taxes. This rose to 103.8 per cent the next year, and continued to rise steadily thereafter till it reached a height of 184.82 per cent in the year 1855, a year before the *Arrow* incident. It declined somewhat during the war, to 154.04 per cent in 1856; it rose to 173.06 per cent in 1857;[18] but declined again to 166.59 per cent in 1858.[19] It stabilized at 166.81 per cent in 1859, and climbed to 172.17 per cent in 1860, when the war ended. The average for the entire period was 135.75 per cent.

18. When hostilities were at a stalemate until December.
19. When the fighting spread to North China.

Table 14.12. *A comparison of the gross tea duty with the gross land and assessed taxes of the United Kingdom, 1842–60 (£ sterling)*

Year	Taxes (gross): Land and assessed 1	Tea (gross) duty 2	Tea duty expressed as a percentage of land and assessed taxes (col. 2 ÷ col. 1) 3
1842	4,489,806	4,089,671	91.09
1843	4,389,406	4,524,613	103.08
1844	4,433,462	4,834,007	109.03
1845	4,446,205	5,111,009	114.95
1846	4,479,944	5,066,860	113.10
1847	4,599,044	5,330,537	115.91
1848	4,513,452	5,471,641	121.23
1849	4,527,580	5,597,707	123.64
1850	4,540,308	5,902,433	130.00
1851	3,796,052	5,985,484	157.68
1852	3,565,077	5,686,193	159.50
1853	3,335,268	5,127,680	153.74
1854	3,229,642	5,127,680	158.77
1855	3,140,465	5,804,205	184.82
1856	3,119,410	4,805,088	154.04
1857	3,156,055	5,461,731	173.06
1858	3,165,437	5,273,316	166.59
1859	3,241,996	5,407,845	166.81
1860	3,149,385	5,422,209	172.17
Average	—	—	135.75

Sources: Col. 2 is copied from Table 14.9, while figures in the same column for 1859–60 are copied from Parl. Papers 1860, v. 39, pp. 23–4, and Parl. Papers 1861, v. 34, p. 22, respectively. References for the figures in col. 1 are Parl. Papers: 1843, v. 30, p. 8; 1844, v. 32, p. 8; 1845, v. 28, p. 8; 1846, v. 25, p. 8; 1847, v. 34, p. 8; 1847–8, v. 39, p. 8; 1849, v. 30, p. 8; 1850, v. 33, p. 8; 1851, v. 31, p. 8; 1852, v. 28, p. 10; 1852–3, v. 57, p. 10; 1854, v. 39, p. 10; 1854–5, v. 30, p. 10; 1856, v. 38, p. 10; 1857, Session 2, v. 25, p. 10; 1857–8, v. 33, p. 10; 1859, Session 2, v. 15, p. 10; 1860, v. 39, Part 1, p. 10; 1861, v. 34, p. 10.

VII. Tea duty could almost sustain the Royal Navy

Another way of assessing the relative significance of the revenue from tea duty is to compare it with the expenditure of the Royal Navy for the same quarter of a century or so up to the *Arrow* War. It will be seen from Table 14.13 that the period began with the tea duty paying the equivalent of 93.66 per cent of the

Table 14.13. *Comparison of the gross annual tea duty with the annual expenditure of the Royal Navy, 1835–57 (£ million sterling)*

Year	Tea: Annual gross duty 1	Royal Navy: Annual expenditure 2	Tea duty expressed as a percentage of the Royal Navy's expenditure (col. 1 ÷ col. 2) 3
1835	3.84	4.10	93.66
1836	4.73	4.21	112.40
1837	3.32	4.75	69.89
1838	3.36	4.52	74.34
1839	3.66	5.49	66.67
1840	3.47	5.60	61.96
1841	3.98	6.49	61.33
1842	4.09	6.64	61.60
1843	4.41	6.61	66.72
1844	4.52	5.86	77.13
1845	4.83	6.81	70.93
1846	5.11	7.80	65.51
1847	5.07	8.01	63.30
1848	5.33	7.92	67.30
1849	5.60	6.44	86.96
1850	5.90	5.85	100.90
1851	5.99	6.62	90.48
1852	5.69	6.64	85.69
1853	5.13	14.49	35.40
1854	5.80	19.65	29.52
1855	4.81	13.46	35.74
1856	5.46	10.59	51.56
1857	5.27	9.22	57.16
Average	—	—	68.96

Sources: Col. 1 is copied from Table 14.9. Sources for Col. 2 are Parl. Papers: 1830–1 v. 5, p. 19; 1831–2, v. 26, p. 19; 1833, v. 23, p. 19; 1834, v. 41, p. 14; 1835, v. 37, p. 14; 1836, v. 37, p. 14; 1837; v. 39, p. 14; 1837–8, v. 36, p. 14; 1839, v. 30, p. 14; 1840, v. 29, p. 14; 1841, v. 13, p. 14; 1842, v. 26, p. 14; 1843, v. 30, p. 14; 1844, v. 32, p. 14; 1845, v. 28, p. 14; 1846, v. 25, p. 14; 1847, v. 34, p. 14; 1847–8, v. 39, p. 14; 1849, v. 30, p. 14; 1850, v. 33, p. 14; 1851, v. 31, p. 14; 1852, v. 28, p. 16; 1852–3, v. 57, p. 16; 1854, v. 39, p. 16; 1854–5, v. 30, p. 14; 1856, v. 38, p. 14; 1857, Session 2, v. 25, p. 15; 1857–8, v. 33, p. 15; 1859, v. 14, p. 16; 1860, v. 39, p. 15; 1861, v. 34, p. 15.

Royal Navy's annual expenditure, in 1835. The next year, the figure rose to 112.4 per cent. A year later, the revenue from the tea duty declined sharply, but then steadily recovered until it again surpassed the Royal Navy's expenditure in 1850 (100.9 per cent). This was achieved despite dramatic increases in the Royal Navy's annual expenditure – between 1835 and 1847 it almost doubled.

Table 14.13 also shows that, in 1853, the Royal Navy's annual expenditure rocketed to more than twice that of previous years. A close reading of the sources reveals that, before 1854, the title of the entry was simply 'Navy'. From 1854 onwards, the title was 'Navy Services, including Transports and Packets'. Transports and packets were needed in 1854 because Britain was preparing for war with Russia. The Royal Navy's expenditure soared from the peacetime budget of the previous year of £6,640,595 to £14,490,105 (an increase of 118.20 per cent).[20] Still, in 1854 the revenue from tea duty amounted to the equivalent of 35.40 per cent of the Royal Navy's expenditure. The next year expenditure rose even higher than that of 1854: an increase of 135.61 per cent.[21] Still, tea duty amounted to the equivalent of 29.52 per cent of that augmented expenditure.

War with Russia was followed by war with Persia,[22] which was followed by war with China.[23] Such were the dynamics of imperialism.

This dynamism was made possible by shrewd economic thinking and skilful management, as reflected in the 100 per cent import duty on Chinese tea. This was good easy money, contributing to Britain's consolidated revenue, which sustained a policy of expansion and protected the United Kingdom's global interests. By contrast, the Manchu government, while levying a 10 per cent export duty on Chinese tea, used all that revenue to fight the Taipings. Such, too, was the strangeness of Chinese politics that even when Commissioner Yeh had stopped all foreign trade at Canton after the outbreak of the *Arrow* War, tea continued to be sold at the other four treaty ports and thus defeated his strategy to use the embargo to bring the British to the negotiating table.[24] Small wonder that he complained in one of his poems:

> A general must make shift as best he can;
> His countrymen look on, and mock his fate.[25]

Thus, Chinese tea continued to contribute towards the British coffers, financing the war against China: the equivalent of 35.70 per cent of the expenses of the Royal Navy in 1856 when the *Arrow* War began; 51.57 per cent in 1857, the year Canton was captured around Christmas; and 57.22 per cent

20. Parl. Papers 1854–5, v. 30, p. 14. That of the army rose from £6,763,488 to £8,380,882 (an increase of 123.91 per cent), and that of ordnance from £2,661,590 to £5,450,719 (an increase of 204.79 per cent).
21. Parl. Papers 1856, v. 38, p. 14. The Royal Navy's annual expenditure was £19,654,585, which was 295.98 per cent of the 1853 expenditure of £6,640,595.
22. Parl. Papers 1857–8, v. 33, p. 128.
23. Ibid.
24. See Wong, *Yeh Ming-ch'en*, chapters 9–10.
25. See ibid., p. 194. The translation is mine.

Table 14.14. *Gross public expenditure of the United Kingdom, 1835–60, with the revenue from tea duty added for comparison (£ million sterling)*

Year	Total gross expenditure 1	Total debt charges 2	Works and buildings 3	Salaries etc. of public depts. 4	Law and justice 5	Education, art, and science 6	Colonial, consular, and foreign 7	Army and ordnance 8	Navy 9	Cost of collection: Telegraphs and telephones 10	Tea duty 11
1835	48.9	28.5	0.22	0.51	0.72	0.11	0.48	7.6	4.5	0.7	3.8
1836	65.2	28.6	0.24	0.53	0.77	0.08	0.48	7.6	4.1	0.7	4.7
1837	54.0	29.4	0.25	0.60	0.93	0.19	0.20	7.9	4.2	0.7	3.3
1838	51.1	29.6	0.30	0.76	1.03	0.18	0.58	8.0	4.8	0.7	3.4
1839	51.7	29.4	0.24	0.72	1.42	0.20	0.48	8.2	4.4	0.8	3.7
1840	53.4	29.6	0.25	0.68	1.32	0.17	0.36	8.5	5.3	0.9	3.5
1841	53.2	29.5	0.25	0.75	1.29	0.27	0.30	8.5	5.4	1.1	4.0
1842	54.3	29.7	0.24	0.69	1.51	0.29	0.38	8.2	6.2	1.2	4.1
1843	55.1	29.6	0.28	0.78	1.54	0.27	0.35	8.2	6.2	1.4	4.4
1844	55.4	29.4	0.26	0.74	1.66	0.25	0.42	7.9	6.2	1.4	4.5
1845	54.8	30.6	0.32	0.72	1.73	0.25	0.36	8.1	5.4	1.4	4.8
1846	53.7	28.6	0.38	0.75	1.42	0.29	0.29	8.9	6.3	1.7	5.1
1847	55.4	28.3	0.39	0.80	1.57	0.33	0.49	9.1	7.3	1.7	5.1
1848	59.1	28.4	0.61	0.91	1.96	0.30	0.40	10.5	7.5	1.7	5.3

Table 14.14. (cont.)

Year	Total gross expenditure 1	Total debt charges 2	Works and buildings 3	Salaries etc. of public depts. 4	Law and justice 5	Education, art, and science 6	Colonial, consular, and foreign 7	Army and ordnance 8	Navy 9	Cost of collection: Telegraphs and telephones 10	Tea duty 11
1849	59.0	28.7	0.51	0.99	2.22	0.36	0.50	9.7	7.3	2.0	5.5
1850	55.5	28.5	0.48	0.94	2.28	0.37	0.41	8.9	6.2	2.1	5.6
1851	54.7	28.3	0.50	1.01	2.26	0.45	0.40	9.0	5.7	2.2	5.9
1852	54.0	28.2	0.50	1.01	2.20	0.46	0.46	8.7	5.0	2.1	6.0
1853	55.3	28.1	0.68	1.04	1.97	0.48	0.36	9.5	5.8	2.2	5.7
1854	55.8	28.1	0.78	1.06	2.22	0.56	0.34	9.4	7.8	2.7	5.1
1855	69.1	28.0	0.74	1.42	2.39	0.66	0.34	13.3	14	1.9	5.8
1856	93.1	28.2	0.77	1.32	3.04	0.83	0.34	27.8	19	2.4	4.8
1857	76.1	28.8	1.06	1.21	2.71	0.91	0.33	20.8	13	2.4	5.5
1858	68.2	28.7	0.85	1.43	3.07	1.06	0.39	12.9	9.6	2.7	5.3
1859	64.8	28.7	0.77	1.42	3.29	1.15	0.35	12.5	8.2	2.9	5.4
1860	69.6	28.7	0.68	1.47	3.44	1.27	0.42	14.1	11	2.9	5.4
Average	59.25	28.9	0.48	0.93	1.92	0.45	0.39	10.5	7.3	1.72	4.83

Sources: Adapted from *Abstract of British Historical Statistics*, p. 397. The 'tacked on' column, tea duty, has been adapted from Table 14.9, col. 3, and Table 14.12.

in 1858, when Beijing was humbled to sign the Treaty of Tientsin. Few Chinese officials could see beyond China's borders.[26]

The story is not complete without putting the annual expenditure of the Royal Navy in the wider context of the total annual expenditure of the United Kingdom; Table 14.14 does so. It will be seen from this table that the greatest item of expenditure was the payment of interest on the public debt. Next came that for the army and ordnance. The Royal Navy was in third place. As shown, the revenue from the tea duty was sufficient to meet a fair part of the Royal Navy's annual expenditure. It could certainly pay for the salaries of the entire civil establishment many times over; or for those of the colonial, consular, and foreign establishments; or for education, art, and science.

VIII. China: the major supplier of tea

Since the revenue from tea duty had a significant place in the United Kingdom's treasury, we should try to pinpoint, as close to the exact figures as possible, what proportion of the tea consumed in the British Isles was actually Chinese.

The first pertinent statistics appeared in 1853, but those of 1854 are analysed here because, again, a new system of accounting was introduced that year. The 'computed real value' replaced the old 'official value'; in addition, the average prices of imports were given in 1854 for the first time.[27] According to the 1854 statistics, tea was imported into the United Kingdom from 'Hanse Towns, China, USA, British East Indies and Other Parts' (see Table 14.15).

These places are worth considering one by one. The Hanse Towns were a mercantile league of North German towns where no tea was ever grown. China is the place where tea originated about 2700 B.C.; it reached Europe about 1610 A.D., whence the Dutch introduced it to the New World around 1650. Indeed, it was 342 chests of Chinese tea that were thrown into Boston harbour in 1773.[28] About two decades after the *Arrow* War, in the 1880s, tea was successfully cultivated in North Carolina and Texas, but abandoned because of the high labour costs involved. Thus, the tea imported into the United Kingdom from the United States, as indicated in Table 14.15, would have come from China originally, as both colonial America and the United Kingdom were buying tea heavily in China and sometimes reexporting to other countries depending on market demands. The Tea Act (1773) was one famous

---

26. I am not suggesting that Commissioner Yeh did. There is no evidence to show that he knew the significance of tea to the British government in terms of import duty. But he realized the importance of the China trade to the British merchants, hence his decision to stop trade as a weapon to bring the British diplomats to the negotiating table.
27. Parl. Papers 1859, v. 28, p. 20.
28. See the satire about Disraeli being at the head of a 'Small Tea Party' in *Punch*, 14 March 1857, p. 110.

Table 14.15. *Places from which tea was imported into the United Kingdom, 1854*

Source	In British vessels (pounds) 1	In foreign vessels (pounds) 2	Total imported (pounds) 3	Total gross duty received (£ sterling) 4
China	61,308,669	21,992,881	83,301,550	4,667,307
Br. E. Indies	530,613	97	530,710	32,995
Hanse Towns	49,358	4,666	54,024	15,142
United States	9,678	1,796,717	1,806,395	58,266
Other parts	98,507	846	99,353	8,189
Total	61,996,825	23,795,207	85,792,032	4,781,899

Note: In this table, the gross tea duty received in 1854 is not the same as that presented in Table 14.9 because of the different sources used. Short of a better explanation, I have to put it down as a statistical discrepancy in the order of 5 per cent, which is acceptable.
Source: Parl. Papers 1854–5, v. 51, p. 74.

example of the British authorities' attempt to reexport to America the Chinese tea which had hitherto been supplied by Dutch smugglers.[29] As for India, no tea was grown there until its colonial masters decided to experiment with its cultivation. Robert Fortune was sent to China to study tea plants and to make cuttings. By 1839, the governor-general of India was able to express 'fair hopes' of establishing a profitable tea culture there.[30] Fifteen years later, as Table 14.15 shows, the United Kingdom was able to import 530,710 pounds of tea from India.[31] Thus, it seems that all the tea in Table 14.15 could have originated from only two places, China and India.

This observation is supported by another source of information. Despite the various immediate places from which the United Kingdom imported tea, only two kinds were listed in the 'average prices fixed for the computed real value of the principal articles imported'. They were China and British East India

29. For a specialist study of the relationship between tea and the United States, see Peter D. G. Thomas, *Tea Party to Independence: The Third Phase of the American Revolution, 1773–1776* (Oxford, Clarendon Press, 1991). For an authoritative work on tea and its history, see William Harrison Ukers, *All about Tea*, 2 vs. (New York, Tea and Coffee Trade Journal, 1935). See also J. M. Scott, *The Great Tea Enterprise* (New York, Dutton, 1965).
30. Parl. Papers 1840, v. 37, p. 291.
31. The plantation-style large-scale production of tea in India and Ceylon eventually displaced the Chinese dominance in the tea markets before the end of the nineteenth century. See Robert Gardella, *Harvesting Mountains: Fujian and China Tea Trade, 1757–1937* (Berkeley and Los Angeles, University of California Press, 1994). For subsequent Chinese attempts to recapture the tea markets, see Dan Etherington and Keith Forster, *Green Gold: The Political Economy of China's Post-1949 Tea Industry* (Hong Kong, Oxford University Press, 1993).

(Assam).[32] As India was only beginning to produce tea, it is perhaps safe to assume that the tea imported from all the other places originated in China. In terms of quantity, therefore, Indian tea made up only 0.62 per cent of the total imported into the United Kingdom in 1854[33] and constituted the same percentage of the total tea duty.[34]

Another facet of the Chinese tea trade was the amount of British shipping engaged in it. Table 14.15 enables us to calculate that the tea carried in English vessels from the Hanse Towns was 91.36 per cent of all the tea reexported to the United Kingdom from that league; 73.60 per cent of all the tea that came directly from China; 0.54 per cent in the case of the United States (which is to be expected); 99.98 per cent in the case of India; and 99.15 per cent in the case of the rest of the world.

Yet another facet is the reexporting of tea from the United Kingdom to other parts of the world. Table 14.15 shows that 85,792,032 pounds of tea was imported into the United Kingdom in 1854. Of this, only 61,970,341 pounds (or 72.23 per cent of the total) was taken out of bond to be sold domestically.[35] Thus, 23,821,691 pounds (or 27.77 per cent) remained in bond or was reexported. Table 14.16 shows where some of this tea went: to most other European countries and their colonies, as well as British colonies such as Australia, Canada, and the West Indies, employing more British shipping and thus generating more revenue on the way. The United States is conspicuous by its absence, which is not surprising. The British attempt in 1773 to force on America 17 million pounds of Chinese tea stored in England[36] was apparently never forgotten.

Shipping was, of course, only one of the many services related to the tea trade. Insurance, brokerage, packaging, handling, inspection, financing, accounting, auditing, and other services also generated employment and income.

In sum, Chinese tea was lucrative to British merchants and significant to the British government. But why was the government able to levy a hefty 100 per cent import duty on tea, and why were the British merchants able to make such profits on it? The answer is simple: tea had become a daily necessity in the United Kingdom. Before its introduction, the common drinks of beer, gin, and whisky often led to quarrelsome behaviour. Tea not only quenched the thirst but acted as a mild stimulant. With milk and sugar added, tea also supple-

---

32. Parl. Papers 1859, Session 2, v. 23, p. 20.
33. This is obtained by dividing the 53,071 pounds of Indian tea by the 85,792,032 pounds of tea imported (see Table 14.15, col. 3).
34. This is obtained by dividing the £32,995 of duty raised on Indian tea by the total of £4,781,899 raised on tea imported (see Table 14.15, col. 4).
35. Parl. Papers 1854–5, v. 51, p. 74.
36. See Thomas, *Tea Party to Independence*.

Table 14.16. *Tea reexported from the United Kingdom, 1855*

Destination	Quantities (pounds)	Computed real value (£ sterling)
Prussia	5,247,554	329,339
Hanse Towns	2,793,136	175,298
Holland	1,252,557	78,611
Br. N. America	1,063,962	66,774
Denmark	814,708	51,131
Channel Islands	351,147	22,038
Turkey	334,013	20,963
Other countries	333,705	20,945
Portugal etc.[a]	315,203	19,783
Hanover	304,924	19,137
Gibraltar	277,178	17,396
Malta	130,771	8,207
Australia	95,648	6,004
Sweden	92,982	5,836
Belgium	83,814	5,260
Spain etc.[a]	74,517	4,676
Br. W. Indies	60,688	3,808
Total	13,626,507	855,206

[a] The etc. probably means the colonies of Portugal and Spain, respectively.
Source: Parl. Papers 1856, v. 56, p. 172.

mented the poor diet of the factory workers who provided the labour for the British Industrial Revolution. A sugar promotion of the time proclaimed, 'Sugar works for you with each bite you eat – for your body is an energy factory with sugar as its fuel'.[37] So tea was the vehicle whereby human energy was supplied to the British factories. Not only the labourers, but the middle and upper classes of British society all developed the habit of drinking morning tea and afternoon tea.[38] Thus, no sooner had the news of the *Arrow* quarrel reached London, for example, than *The Times* reacted thus: 'Anything which

37. Quoted from a sugar firm pamphlet used by Yudkin, *Pure, White and Deadly*, p. 30.
38. There is an interesting connection between the consumption of tea and the consumption of sugar in Britain. Around 1750, for example, the consumption of sugar per capita was about four or five pounds a year. After tea drinking became widespread in Britain, the consumption of sugar per capita increased fivefold to about twenty-five pounds a year by about 1850. See Yudkin, *Pure, White and Deadly*, p. 42. For a history of the tea trade in Britain, see Denys Forrest, *Tea for the British: The Social and Economic History of a Famous Trade* (London, Chatto & Windus, 1973). For a history of the tea clippers that shipped tea from China to Britain in the period under review, see David R. MacGregor, *The Tea Clippers: An Account of the China Tea Trade and of Some of the British Sailing Ships Engaged in It from 1849 to 1869*, 2d ed. (London, Conway Maritime Press, 1972).

tends to raise the price of tea is a matter of importance to every family in this country'.[39]

The supply of tea from China could be improved. Before the Opium War, trade was restricted to Canton, in the Pearl River delta in south China. Tea was produced in large quantities in the Yangtze River basin in central China and had to be carried on backs across mountain ranges which divided the two river systems before being sent on to Canton.[40] The Treaty of Nanking opened four more ports,[41] of which the most important was Shanghai, at the mouth of the Yangtze River. Tea could travel easily downstream to Shanghai to be exported. Consequently, the United Kingdom's next target was to open the entire Yangtze basin so as to give more direct, easier, and cheaper access to the tea-growing areas.

The achievement of that target had been made all the more urgent since 1853. In that year, a new mercantile tax known as the *likin* was instituted in Yangzhou in the lower reaches of the Yangtze River. It was a form of transit dues levied by local militia bureaux on goods passing through the trade routes. The purpose was to raise money to fight the Taipings, who had captured Nanjing further upstream along the Yangtze that year. This new tax was quickly adopted throughout the provinces in the Yangtze and Pearl river systems.[42] *The Times* exclaimed:

> It has become a matter of first-rate importance to this country that we should get free transit through China ... The Emperor and his corrupt officials can tax us by means of our necessities. Putting aside all question of advantage to be gained by the import trade, the tea question is imperative. There is at present no limit to the power of the Chinese to tax our industrious classes.[43]

A modern economist may argue that there were limits – as prices went up, Britons would drink less tea. While this is true enough, it was not what the British government wanted to see. If Britons drank less tea, the government would receive less tea duty. The best solution would be to try to keep the price of tea down so that it was still affordable despite a 100 per cent import duty in the United Kingdom. *The Times* concluded: 'Nothing but a power to go up to the tea countries and carry away the tea in our own ships will be of the smallest advantage'.[44]

The strategy was to persuade the Chinese authorities to 'revise' the Treaty of Nanking accordingly. As we saw, the Foreign Office instructed Sir John

39. *The Times*, 30 December 1856.
40. See my article 'Taipingjun chuqi'.
41. They were Shanghai, Ningpo (Ningbo), Foochow (Fuzhou), and Amoy (Xiamen).
42. See Luo Yudong, *Zhongguo lijin shi* (A history of *likin*) (Shanghai, Commercial Press, 1936); and Edward Beal, *The Origins of Likin, 1853–1864* (Cambridge, Mass., Harvard East Asian Research Center, 1958).
43. *The Times*, 31 July 1858.   44. Ibid.

Bowring 'to obtain free navigation of the Yangtze Kiang and access to the cities on its banks up to Nanking inclusive ... [and] to provide against the imposition of internal or transit duty on goods imported from foreign Countries, or purchased for exportation to foreign Countries'.[45] Generally, this instruction has been interpreted as an indication of a powerful impulse to increase exports to China. While this is certainly true, one must not overlook the strong desire to obtain tea at the lowest possible price by gaining access to the places of production. But the British design was frustrated by the Chinese – Commissioner Yeh rejected Bowring's plea for treaty revision on 30 June 1856.[46] So Parkes and Bowring seized upon the *Arrow* incident as an excuse to use coercion, as did their superiors in the British government.

Thus, one of the origins of the *Arrow* War ultimately lay in an indigenous product of China – tea. The financial benefits that tea brought to the United Kingdom, in terms of both trade and duties, produced higher expectations of even greater benefits if more direct, cheaper access were granted peacefully; but it was not. Eventually, when the experimental tea planting in India proved a great success, the United Kingdom could obtain all its tea from that colony. But in 1856, Britain was not certain that the Indian experiment would succeed. Even if it did, India could not soon be expected to replace China as the main supplier of tea to the United Kingdom.

IX. Imports of Chinese silk

Silk was another commodity which originated in China, in about 2640 B.C. Sericulture was jealously guarded for some three thousand years but eventually spread to Japan, India, and Iran. A silk industry was established in Byzantium in the sixth century A.D., after two Persian monks returned from China with silkworm eggs and seeds of the mulberry tree concealed in hollow staves. In the eighth century, the Arabs acquired sericulture, and in the twelfth the Italians introduced it to Europe.[47] The origins of the British silk weaving industry began in East London with the arrival of the Huguenots, who were fleeing from religious persecution in France, particularly after the revocation of the Edict of Nantes in 1685. Under the influence of these silk weavers the industry flourished for much of the eighteenth century. In the 1820s, about 25,000 were employed in the industry in Bethnal Green and Spitalfields in East London.[48] Thereafter, machinery replaced hand-weaving, and the United Kingdom con-

---

45. Clarendon to Bowring, Desp. 2, 13 February 1854, FO17/210.
46. Yeh to Bowring, 30 June 1856, FO682/1989/9.
47. For a specialist reference to Chinese silk, see Maryta M. Laumann, *The Secret of Excellence in Ancient Chinese Silks: Factors Contributing to the Extraordinary Development of Textile Design and Technology Achieved in Ancient China* (colophon with Chinese book title: 'Zhong guo gu dai pin deng feng zao ji zhi ao mi') (Taipei, Southern Materials Centre, 1984).
48. See A. K. Sabin, *The Silk Weavers of Spitalfields and Bethnal Green* (London, 1931).

Table 14.17. *U.K. imports of raw silk worldwide, 1857*

Source	In British vessels (pounds) 1	In foreign vessels (pounds) 2	Total (pounds) 3	Computed real value (£ sterling) 4
China	6,404,439	260,093	6,664,532	6,568,910
Egypt[a]	4,485,811		4,485,811	5,271,647
France	345,365	300	345,665	618,991
Turkey	216,305		216,305	191,721
Br. E. Indies	192,604		192,604	189,798
Malta	38,352		38,352	72,512
Holland	35,026	47,004	82,030	151,026
United States	9,499	4,065	13,564	12,193
Other parts	8,253	224	8,477	14,337
Russia	8,141		8,141	15,767
Belgium	7,802	1,180	8,262	13,965
Two Sicilies	6,840		6,840	10,775
Siam	3,392		3,392	4,706
Hanse Towns	813	3,143	3,956	7,491
Total	11,755,802	316,009	12,077,931	13,143,839

[a] For the most part in transit from India etc. The 'etc.' is interesting. In a late reference, the 'etc.' included China. See Parl. Papers 1866, v. 68, p. 79.
Source: Parl. Papers 1857–8, v. 54, p. 89.

tinued to buy raw silk for its manufacturing industry. As Table 14.3 shows, it bought £6,910,630 worth of silk from China in 1857, even though the *Arrow* War had started in earnest.

Raw silk had been exempted from import duty since 1845,[49] so unlike tea, the question of revenue from such a duty did not arise. But like tea, raw silk also generated employment and profits through related industries such as packaging, insurance, and freight from China. Furthermore, it produced income through manufacturing in the United Kingdom – the biggest item being ladies' undergarments (slips, stockings, etc.)[50] – through export of the manufactured silks, and again through the service industries that carried the goods to those markets. It generated tax revenue for the government, then, even without a duty.

First, let us look at the British service industry that shipped the raw silk from China. A Chinese service industry did not exist at this time. As is evident in Table 14.17, about 96 per cent of the Chinese raw silk shipped to the United

49. Parl. Papers 1854–5, v. 51 (1853), p. 64.
50. Hence, the British expression 'keep one's wife in silks'; and of course barristers still wear 'silks'.

The economics of imperialism

Kingdom was carried in British vessels. While the variables in the shipment of tea were so numerous[51] as to make it almost impossible even to estimate roughly the charges made by the service industry, we can attempt to get some idea of this for raw silk. The Jardine Matheson records indicate that in 1855, for example,[52] the asking price for a bale of raw silk in China was $340 (Spanish dollars). Joseph Jardine said that was far too expensive; but he was prepared to pay $320 per bale and on that basis to purchase 500 bales.[53] Let us assume that a compromise of $330 per bale was reached. When converted, this would become £82 10s. per bale.[54] Also let us assume that a bale of raw silk weighed approximately ninety pounds.[55] Thus, the cost of raw silk in China would be roughly 18s. per pound. Again let us assume that the raw silk bought in China in the latter half of 1855 would be sold in the United Kingdom in 1856. We find that the cost of Chinese raw silk in the United Kingdom in 1856 was 19s. 7d. per pound.[56] The difference between the cost in the U.K. and that in China would indicate roughly the amount of money paid to the service industry per pound of raw silk, which in this case would be 1s. 7d. Hence, for 5,048,997 pounds of Chinese raw silk, £399,712 went to the service industry and as profits to the dealers.

Where did Chinese silk stand in the United Kingdom's silk imports globally? Table 14.17 gives such a picture for 1857. In this year, the United Kingdom imported a total of 12,077,931 pounds of raw silk worldwide. Chinese raw silk constituted about 53 per cent of this total. Of the total, 11,761,922 pounds were carried in British vessels, or 97 per cent. The total cost (including freight) was £13,143,839.[57] Hence, the average cost per pound of raw silk in Britain was about £1.09 (or £1 1s. 9d.). Of this, 490,079 pounds were manufactured into pure silk goods and ribbons for export the following year. The total declared

---

51. To begin with, there were quite a few varieties of tea, each with its own price. Second, it is impossible to know how much of each variety was imported into the United Kingdom. We know only the total annual quantity of tea imported and its total real value. We do not know its total value when it left China.
52. The year 1855 has been chosen as an example partly because it was close to the time of the *Arrow* War. But more important, however, the price of silk found its way into the company correspondence of Jardine Matheson and Co. as a result of a sudden rise in the cost of silk in China due to rebellions there. See next note.
53. Matheson Papers, B4/5-16, p. 952, Joseph Jardine to David Jardine, Canton, 7 July 1855.
54. A Spanish dollar was worth about five shillings (Parl. Papers 1840, v. 37, pp. 276-7).
55. According to Morse, China exported 56,211 bales of silk from Shanghai in 1855. Most of it went to Britain, whose weaving industry turned the raw silk into manufactures. No figure was given for the silk exported from Canton in the same year. (*International Relations of the Chinese Empire*, v. 1, p. 366). This is not surprising as Canton was at this time engulfed in a general insurrection, with the rebels besieging the city. (Wong, *Yeh Ming-ch'en*, chapter 6). According to the Parliamentary Papers, the United Kingdom imported from China 5,048,997 pounds of silk in 1855 (Parl. Papers 1859, Session 2, v. 23, p. 319). If we divide this by 56,211 bales, we get roughly 90 pounds per bale.
56. Parl. Papers 1859, v. 28, p. 19.
57. Parl. Papers 1857-8, v. 54, p. 89.

Table 14.18. *U.K. exports of silk stuffs and ribbons, 1858*

Destination	In British vessels (pounds) 1	In foreign vessels (pounds) 2	Total (pounds) 3	Declared real value (£ sterling) 4
United States	127,025	5,923	132,948	133,902
Australia	90,949	9,863	100,812	159,781
Egypt	44,273	—	44,273	54,339
Br. N. America	28,413	—	28,413	37,853
Hamburg	20,156	1,052	21,208	25,773
St Thomas	15,499	1,835	17,334	19,697
Br. W. Indies	13,779	55	13,834	19,849
France	13,275	—	13,275	19,497
South Africa	10,122	—	10,131	13,628
Portugal etc.	7,641	20	7,661	10,345
Brazil	7,505	918	8,423	8,705
Buenos Aires	6,994	—	6,994	6,183
Br. E. Indies	5,587	3	5,590	7,151
Peru	5,040	—	5,040	5,714
Holland	4,956	652	5,608	6,081
Turkey	4,550	—	4,550	4,628
Mexico	4,127	273	4,400	4,412
Gibraltar	4,044	—	4,044	4,030
Uruguay	3,896	1,116	5,012	4,290
Sardinia	3,682	—	3,682	3,747
Chile	3,524	985	4,509	5,569
W. Africa	3,501	120	3,621	3,630
Belgium	3,213	773	3,986	4,672
Channel Is.	2,678	—	2,678	3,885
New Granada	2,605	215	2,820	3,267
Tuscany	2,483	—	2,483	2,184
Mauritius	1,960	50	2,010	2,818
Spain etc.	998	7,311	8,309	8,352
Cuba	—	4,140	4,140	5,009
Other countries	—	—	12,291	13,587
Total	442,475	35,304	490,079	602,578

Note: The total figures in cols. 1 and 2 are the totals of only the available figures (i.e., excluding the not available entries). In addition, the original source gives the total in column 1 as 442,484, which is 9 pounds more than the actual figure of 442,475.

Source: Parl. Papers 1859, session 2, v. 28, p. 200.

value was £602,578. The average value per pound of this finished product was about £1.23 (or £1 4s. 7d.). The value thus added to the average cost of raw silk in the United Kingdom was £0.14 (or 2s. 10d.) per pound. But the value added to the cost of Chinese raw silk in the United Kingdom would be greater, 5s. per pound.

These manufactures were sold worldwide, as Table 14.18 shows. More than 90 per cent of these exports were transported in British ships. Of the same quantities of raw silk imported, the United Kingdom reexported 2,314,519 pounds, mainly to continental Europe and the Americas.[58] This would have produced still more profits and given the British shipping and service industries more business on the way. If greater and more direct access to one of the major silk-producing areas of China, namely, the Yangtze basin, was granted, it was hoped that supply therefrom would be augmented and the cost lowered.

X. In sum

Not only then did the British policy makers have a powerful impulse to increase exports to China in order to redress the trade imbalance, which is understandable; but they also had a perhaps no less powerful desire to increase imports from China, which is not often appreciated. In these twin objectives lay some of the mysterious origins of the *Arrow* War.

58. Parl. Papers 1859, Session 2, v. 28, p. 199.

15
China's maritime trade:
The Chinese could buy more

I. Introduction

Chapter 14 showed that the British policy makers considered that the Chinese *should* have bought more manufactures from the United Kingdom in order to redress the imbalance in bilateral trade. This chapter demonstrates that they also thought the Chinese *could* have bought more.

Values will continue to be cast in perceptions likely to have been formed by the British policy makers on the basis of the statistics presented in the papers which were tabled in Parliament each year. In this regard, the statistics I present are one step further removed from reality than those in the last chapter. In the absence of similar statistics in China, I have to use the value *declared in the United Kingdom* as the value of British imports into China. In other words, the value of freight, insurance, trading profits, and the like, which were earned by the British who provided these services, are not included in the British imports into China. Similarly, I have to use the already problematic official value calculated in the United Kingdom as the value of Chinese exports to the United Kingdom. In other words, the value of freight, insurance, trading profits, and so forth, which were likewise earned by the British because they provided these services, are not included either. Thus, there is a double distortion in the figures I use. But these were the figures employed by the British policy makers to form their perceptions. Any attempt at adjusting such figures would distort their meaning at the time. As perceptions, not reality, were what really mattered in terms of the British decision to wage the *Arrow* War, I shall continue to cast the values accordingly.

By examining China's maritime trade through the Parliamentary Papers,[1] I shall attempt to reassess some aspects of the 'imperialism of free trade' controversy.[2] I also aim to verify the validity of the famous 'triangular trade' observation[3] in order to explore further the origins of the *Arrow* War.

1. The overland trade, mainly along the Russian border, is not the concern of this book.
2. See Gallagher and Robinson, 'Imperialism of Free Trade'.
3. Alexander Michie was the first to mention this triangular trade. See his *Englishman in China*,

365

The economics of imperialism

From the London perspective, it was mentioned in Chapter 14 that the importation of Chinese goods was many times the exportation of U.K. manufactures and produce to China. Perceptually, the imbalance reached an alarming 913 per cent when imports were expressed as a percentage of exports in 1854, two years before the *Arrow* War. In this same year, Clarendon instructed Bowring to revise the Treaty of Nanking to open the interior of China to British merchants.

II. Re-exports of foreign and colonial manufactures to China direct from the United Kingdom

From the Chinese perspective, U.K. manufactures and produce were not the only commodities imported direct from the United Kingdom; foreign and colonial manufactures and produce were also reexported from the United Kingdom to China. If these two sources of 'British' goods were combined, the picture becomes somewhat different, as Table 15.1 shows. But the difference is not great. The perceptually hefty import–export imbalance for the British in 1854 comes down only a little from 913 per cent to 886 per cent. The perceptual average for the period also comes down only slightly, from 454 per cent to 428 per cent.

The reality would have been quite different. Let us again use the year 1854 as an example. According to Table 15.1, the United Kingdom had a perceptual trade deficit of £8.10 million.[4] Because the United Kingdom provided the shipping both ways, while China did not, let us assume, therefore, that freight, insurance, and profits accrued entirely to the British, amounting to (after expenses), say, the generally accepted 20 per cent of the value of the commodities shipped. Thus, in 1854 British merchants earned 20 per cent in commodities exported to China, raising the £1.03 million declared value of British goods imported into China to the real value of £1.24 million.[5] They earned a similar 20 per cent of the value of the Chinese goods transported to the United Kingdom, reducing the £9.13 million official value of Chinese goods imported to the real value of £7.60 million.[6] The commodity trade gap was in fact about £6.06 million and not the perceived £8.10 million. But the perceived imbalance as conveyed by the Parliamentary Papers in 1857 was £8.10 million.

---

v. 1, p. 196. David Owen referred to it without further comment; see his *British Opium Policy*, p. 207. Michael Greenberg pursued this systematically in *British Trade and the Opening of China* by using the Jardine Matheson Archives as a case study.

4. This figure is arrived at by subtracting col. 1 (£1.03 million) from col. 2 (£9.13 million).
5. This is a rounded-off figure obtained by dividing £1.03 million by 100 and multiplying that by 120.
6. This figure is obtained by dividing £9.13 million by 120 and multiplying that by 100.

Table 15.1. *Value of imports from and exports to the United Kingdom, 1827–58 (£ million sterling)*

Year	Imported direct from the United Kingdom (Declared value; as declared in the United Kingdom) 1	Exported direct to the United Kingdom (Official value; as declared in the United Kingdom) 2	Exports expressed as a percentage of imports (col. 2 ÷ col. 1) 3
1827	0.63	4.10	651
1828	0.85	3.48	409
1829	0.69	3.23	468
1830	0.60	3.23	538
1831	0.61	3.21	526
1832	0.57	3.21	563
1833	0.65	3.27	503
1834	0.87	3.51	403
1835	1.15	4.56	397
1836	1.55	5.42	350
1837	0.81	4.53	559
1838	1.32	4.31	327
1839	0.89	3.98	447
1840	0.54	2.39	443
1841	0.91	2.96	325
1842	1.03	3.96	384
1843	1.75	4.63	265
1844	2.39	5.57	233
1845	2.51	5.82	232
1846	1.93	6.64	344
1847	1.60	6.70	419
1848	1.54	5.82	378
1849	1.59	6.17	388
1850	1.62	5.85	361
1851	2.23	7.97	357
1852	2.56	7.71	301
1853	1.81	8.26	456
	Declared value computed real value		
1854	1.03	9.13	863
1855	1.30	8.75	673
1856	2.29	9.42	411
1857	2.51	11.45	456
1858	2.97	7.04	237
Average	—	—	428

Note: Goods of United Kingdom, foreign, and colonial origin are included.
Source: Compiled from the statistics in Parl. Papers 1859, Session 2, v. 23, pp. 314–17.

Table 15.2. *Value of China's imports from, and exports to, the United Kingdom and India conjointly, 1827–58 (£ million sterling)*

Year	Imports (Declared value) 1	Exports (Official value) 2	Exports as a percentage of imports (col. 2 ÷ col. 1) 3
1827	3.13	4.78	153
1828	3.70	4.24	115
1829	2.90	3.95	136
1830	3.02	4.05	134
1831	3.01	4.02	133
1832	3.73	3.69	99
1833	3.25	3.72	115
1834	4.40	4.05	92
1835	3.94	5.08	129
1836	5.75	5.96	104
1837	6.12	5.06	83
1838	5.50	4.75	86
1839	5.11	4.44	87
1840	1.53	2.59	169
1841	3.04	3.59	118
1842	3.85	4.52	117
1843	5.85	5.20	89
1844	8.03	6.20	77
1845	7.95	6.63	83
1846	8.30	7.38	89
1847	6.74	7.37	109
1848	5.69	6.83	120
1849	8.06	7.00	87
1850	7.98	6.66	83
1851	8.51	8.96	105
1852	11.03	8.64	78
1853	9.37	9.12	97
1854	7.71	9.94	129
1855	7.72	9.66	125
1856	8.81	10.21	116
1857	10.02	12.05	120
1858	12.24	7.96	65
Average	—	—	108

Source: Compiled from the statistics in Parl. Papers 1859, Session 2, v. 23, pp. 320–3.

III. China also bought British Indian products

The two categories of products shipped directly from the United Kingdom were not the only commodities which the Chinese purchased from British merchants, however; they also bought large quantities of Indian products from the British. If these three categories of what appeared to them as British goods[7] were combined, the picture would be remarkably different, as Table 15.2 shows. Here, the import–export imbalance for the British in 1854 comes crashing down to 129 per cent, and the average for the period down to 108 per cent.

IV. Total 'British' exports to China

British merchants sold to the Chinese products that originated not only in the United Kingdom and British India, but in other British colonies and the rest of the world. The British East India Company has provided some statistics in this regard; until 1834, the company had a monopoly on trade with China.[8] Its statistics on its exports to China, therefore, may be regarded as total British exports to China. For the purpose of this study, it would be ideal if similar statistics were also available for the years leading up to the *Arrow* War. Alas, this is impossible because, as mentioned, the company's monopoly with China was abolished in 1834. Consequently, statistics showing the total value of exports to China by British merchants from sources all over the world and not routed via the United Kingdom, such as those provided by the company, were no longer available after 1834. It is not entirely satisfactory to use the statistics of two decades previously for a study of the *Arrow* War. But short of better indicators, this may suffice, as long as we are aware of the limitations under which we are working.

Table 15.3 shows a full list of commodities imported into China in the last year of the company's monopoly. It seems certain that the following items (listed in Spanish silver dollars) would not have originated in either the United Kingdom or India at this time: $216,000 worth of shark fins, $13,230 worth of bird's nests, $142,000 worth of betel nuts, $412,000 worth of rice, and $190,000 worth of pepper. From all accounts, these would have come from Southeast Asia. There is no suggestion that the Chinese gave up their shark's fin soup or their bird's nest soup, or stopped importing rice and pepper, after the company's monopoly was abolished in 1834. Thus, we may assume that these commodities continued to be exported to China by private British merchants after the company had disappeared from the scene.[9]

---

7. In modern terminology, these were British commodities, produced offshore.
8. The act terminating the monopoly was passed in 1833 and took effect in China in 1834.
9. The company wound up its business in China in 1834.

Table 15.3. *Quantity and value of goods imported into Canton by the East India Company and private traders in the financial year 1833–4*

	East India Co.		Private traders	
Product	Quantity	Value (Spanish dollars)	Quantity	Value (Spanish dollars)
Cotton (peculs)	116,246	1,842,333	326,393	4,884,407
Opium (chests)	nil	nil	17,613.50	11,618,716
Tin (peculs)	nil	nil	5,762	92,192
Iron (peculs)	20,203	32,324	9,735	26,285
Lead (peculs)	15,454	66,539	3,893	15,572
Steel (peculs)	nil	nil	1,486	7,058
Pepper (peculs)	nil	nil	23,122	190,757
Spices (peculs)	nil	nil	629	16,846
Rattans (peculs)	nil	nil	13,052	139,156
Betel nut (peculs)	nil	nil	57,025	142,562
Putchuck (peculs)	nil	nil	2,105	26,417
Sharks' fins (peculs)	nil	nil	6,820	216,132
Sandalwood (peculs)	nil	nil	3,680	41,400
Black and red wood	141	75	2,634	7,902
Saltpetre (peculs)	nil	nil	6,044	54,396
Ivory (peculs)	nil	nil	84	6,216
Pearls, cornelians etc.	nil	nil	—	312,767
Glassware etc.	nil	nil	—	12,508
Broadcloth (pieces)	17,640	87,321	9,574	268,072
Long ells etc. (pieces)	124,400	881,166	10,239	108,468
Camlets (pieces)	4,960	84,320	571	13,418
Cotton goods (pieces)	30,000	175,000	—	298,197
Cotton yarn (peculs)	1,800	91,800	1,344	53,760
Skins and furs (numbers)	nil	nil	18,069	17,306
Olibanum (peculs)	nil	nil	4,444	17,776
Smalts (peculs)	nil	nil	325	25,025
Cochineal (peculs)	nil	nil	42	14,280
Birds' nests (peculs)	nil	nil	630	13,230
Rice (peculs)	nil	nil	158,822	412,937
Clocks and watches	nil	nil	—	50,713
Sundry articles	nil	nil	—	92,169
Dollars	nil	nil	—	20,500
Total	—	4,046,769	—	19,119,140

Note: A Spanish dollar was worth approximately 5s. (see Table 15.11 for reference). A pecul (sometimes spelt 'picul') was a Chinese unit of weight equal to about 133.3 pounds (see R. K. Newman, 'Opium Smoking in Late Imperical China', *Modern Asian Studies*, 29, 4 [1995], p. 771, n. 15). 'Long ells' are a form a British textiles. 'Putchuck' (or putchuk) is the root of the plant *Aplotaxis auriculata* (Aucklandia Costus of Falconer), a native of Kashmir, exported to China and other Eastern countries, and used as a medicine and for making the Chinese joss sticks.
Source: Parl. Papers 1840, v. 37, p. 260.

V. British trade surplus with China

The picture is incomplete without looking at the list of commodities exported from China by the company (Table 15.4). Again, the data is from the last year of its monopoly. Comparing this table with Table 15.3, it will be seen that the company did not have a trade deficit with the Chinese at all; it had a surplus. In 1833-4, the company exported about 20 million Spanish dollars' worth of goods from China, but imported about 23 million worth, netting 3 million Spanish dollars.

Table 15.4. *Quantity and value of goods exported from Canton by the East India Company and private traders, in the financial year 1833-4*

	East India Co.		Private traders	
Product	Quantity	Value (Spanish dollars)	Quantity	Value (Spanish dollars)
Tea (peculs)	230,815	7,911,666	29,031	1,044,586
Raw silk (peculs)	nil	nil	9,920	3,097,167
Nankeens (pieces)	nil	nil	30,600	22,644
Sugar and candy (peculs)	nil	nil	28,439	264,140
Cassia (peculs)	nil	nil	17,607	145,258
Drugs (value only)	nil	nil	nil	36,757
Silk piece goods	nil	nil	nil	332,844
Tortoise shell	nil	nil	nil	7,822
Pearls and beads	nil	nil	nil	26,291
Chinaware	nil	nil	nil	13,525
Writing paper etc.	nil	nil	nil	106,543
S. American copper (peculs)	nil	nil	10,907	218,140
Cotton yarn (peculs)	nil	nil	201	8,442
Camphor (peculs)	nil	nil	2,430	53,460
Cochineal (peculs)	nil	nil	202	44,036
Vermilion (boxes)	nil	nil	3,576	121,584
Mother-of-pearl shells (peculs)	nil	nil	2,049	34,321
Rhubarb (peculs)	nil	nil	434	25,172
Alum (peculs)	nil	nil	10,213	20,426
Canes (value)	nil	nil	nil	14,389
Mats (nos.)	nil	nil	28,691	13,055
Cotton goods (peculs)	nil	nil	1,250	7,500
Brass leaf or foil (boxes)	nil	nil	81	3,726
Sundries (value)	nil	272	nil	115,694
Bullion (value)	nil	385,849	nil	6,576,585
Total	—	8,297,787	—	12,354,107

Soruce: Parl. Papers 1840, v. 37, p. 274.

The economics of imperialism

Table 15.5. *Value of the British East India Company's exports from, and imports to, Canton, 1820–34 (millions of Spanish dollars)*

Year	Imports[a] 1	Exports[b] 2	Imbalance in favour of the East India Company 3	China's exports expressed as a percentage of imports (col. 2 ÷ col. 1) 4
1820–1	17.75	14.08	3.67	79.32
1821–2	14.34	14.02	0.31	97.77
1822–3	15.30	12.53	2.77	81.90
1823–4	17.33	15.30	2.03	88.29
1824–5	16.00	13.76	2.23	86.00
1825–6	21.43	16.87	4.56	78.72
1826–7	21.80	18.26	3.54	83.76
1827–8	19.91	18.41	1.50	92.47
1828–9	21.57	18.90	2.67	87.62
1829–30	22.93	20.77	2.16	90.58
1830–1	21.95	19.91	2.04	90.71
1831–2	20.54	17.20	3.34	83.74
1832–3	22.30	17.71	4.59	79.42
1833–4	23.17	20.65	2.51	89.12
Average	—	—	—	86.39

[a] Including cost, insurance, and freight (commonly known as CIF).
[b] Including freight on board (commonly known as FOB).
Source: Parl. Papers 1840, v. 37, pp. 247–88.

This surplus may be regarded as a trade surplus in the bilateral trade between British and Chinese merchants, because of the East India Company's monopoly on that trade at the time.[10] In this sense, it becomes critical to examine the pattern of trade over time; Table 15.5 does so over fourteen years, until the company's monopoly ended. (The period would have been extended if the relevant data had been available.) Even so, the fourteen years show that the statistics of 1834 were fairly typical. The company had a consistent and substantial trade surplus for the entire period, ranging from $3.67 million in 1820–1, to $4.59 million in 1833–4, the year before the monopoly ended. The import–export imbalance for the company, or the export–import imbalance for China, averaged 86.39 per cent.

The difference is really one of perspective. Because policy makers in the United Kingdom could see only *their own* manufactures and produce going to China, and not the other goods which the British East India Company sold to China and which had their origins in places outside the United Kingdom, they

10. The bilateral trade included goods of indigenous origins and reexports.

Table 15.6. *The United Kindom's and China's perspectives, 1826–34*

	U.K. perspective		China's perspective	
Year	Trade deficit with China (£ million sterling)	Imports from China, expressed as a percentage of exports to China	Trade deficit with the East India Company (millions of Spanish dollars)	Exports to, expressed as a percentage of imports from, the East India Company
1826–7	3.49	671	3.54	83.76
1827–8	2.70	443	1.50	92.47
1828–9	2.60	514	2.67	87.62
1829–30	2.67	572	2.16	90.58
1830–1	2.66	586	2.04	90.71
1831–2	2.67	588	3.34	83.74
1832–3	2.63	518	4.59	79.42
1833–4	2.66	415	2.51	89.12
Average	2.76	538.38	2.79	87.18

Sources: Col. 1 is compiled from statistics in Parl. Papers 1859, Session 2, v. 23, p. 315, and 1840, v. 37, pp. 247–88; col. 3 is from Parl. Papers 1859, Session 2, v. 23, p. 319. Cols. 2 and 4 are my calculations.

thought British merchants were buying from China many times more than they were selling. A modern economist can appreciate that China was buying far more from the company than China was selling to the company. These different perspectives are made obvious in Table 15.6, which shows that in the last seven years[11] of the company's monopoly, the United Kingdom had an average annual deficit of about £2.76 million in its *bilateral* trade with China. On the other hand the Chinese had an average annual trade deficit of about £4.59 million with the company.

If the Chinese had told the British that China was already running a serious trade deficit with Britain and therefore could not be expected to buy more, the British would probably have understood (although they might not have listened). But the Chinese did not have statisticians of the same standard as the British. For centuries, foreign trade was conceived and used as a gesture of benevolence towards China's tributary states.[12] Given this background, it is not surprising that not one statistical document in the Canton Archive rivals the sophistication of its British counterparts. None of the despatches from the

11. Again, the time span would have been extended further each way if the statistics were available.
12. See J. K. Fairbank, 'Tributary Trade and China's Relations with the West', *Far Eastern Quarterly*, 1, no. 2 (1942), pp. 129–49.

successive imperial commissioners for foreign affairs at Canton to successive British plenipotentiaries at Hong Kong made any reference to the trade imbalance.

And the British were unable or unwilling to see China's trade deficit despite the availability of statistics.

IV. Quantifying the drain of silver from China

However, the Chinese government was acutely aware of the declining amount of silver bullion circulating in China. This decline is partly quantified in Tables 15.3 and 15.4. The last item in Table 15.4 shows that the British East India Company, in the financial year 1833–4, pulled out of China $385,849 worth of silver bullion, while private British traders shipped out of China $6,576,585 worth, making a total of $6,962,434. The last item in Table 15.3 shows that the company imported into China $20,500 worth of silver dollars. The difference constituted a net outflow of silver bullion from China of $6,941,934. Of course, other factors contributed to the silver shortage in China. One of them was hoarding; the moment there was a short supply, people began to hoard the precious metal.[13] But the Chinese government invariably blamed the outflow of silver only on the importation of Indian opium,[14] over which the company had monopolistic control.[15] This charge is partly substantiated by the second entry in Table 15.3, which shows that $11,618,716 worth of opium was imported into China in 1833–4 by private British traders; while the total value of the two major exports (tea and silk) in the same year (Table 15.4, entries 1 and 2) amounted to only $4,141,753. Since the company could not use all the surplus silver, it resorted to smuggling the precious metal out of China against a Chinese prohibition.[16] Thus, a Western writer in 1833 remarked that 'perhaps nothing could contribute more readily to the final reduction of the Chinese ... than this steady, non-ceasing impoverishment of the country by the abstraction of the circulating medium'.[17]

V. Bills of exchange from China

Smuggling was not a very gentlemanly business for 'the honourable company'. Hence, some of the surplus silver was also used to buy bills of exchange to be drawn upon India and London, as Table 15.7 indicates.

13. See Frank H. H. King, *Money and Monetary Policy in China, 1845–1895* (Cambridge, Mass., Harvard University Press, 1965), chapters 6–7.
14. For many of memorials on the subject, see *TWSM* (TK), *juan* 2, pp. 4ff, as referred to by Chang, *Commissioner Lin*, p. 245, n. 106.
15. See Chapter 16.
16. Herbert John Wood, 'Prologue to War: Anglo-Chinese Conflict, 1800–1834'. Ph.D dissertation, University of Wisconsin, 1938, pp. 181–2.
17. *Chinese Courier*, 6 April 1833.

Table 15.7. *Bills drawn upon India and London by the Company's Select Committee at Canton, 1820–35*

Year	India: Total amount received at Canton and payable in India (Millions of Spanish dollars) 1	London: Total amount received at Canton (Millions of Spanish dollars) 2	London: Total amount payable in England (£ million sterling) 3
1820–1	1.99	0.33	0.08
1821–2	1.81	1.17	0.28
1822–3	2.81	0.29	0.07
1823–4	2.55	0.39	0.09
1824–5	3.27	0.64	0.15
1825–6	1.16	0.24	0.05
1826–7	0.75	2.88	0.62
1827–8	1.77	0.53	0.11
1828–9	2.73	0.64	0.13
1829–30	0.82	0.56	0.12
1830–1	3.38	0.56	0.11
1831–2	5.20	0.32	0.07
1832–3	3.19	0.76	0.17
1833–4	3.17	nil	nil
1834–5	1.31	nil	nil
Total	35.91	9.31	2.05

Note: Amounts are rounded off.
Source: Parl. Papers 1840, v. 37, pp. 276–7.

Like the silver shipped out of China, the bills drawn upon India were partly remitted as profits and partly used to buy the next season's opium and other Indian produce for China. Those drawn upon London were remitted as profits, used both to buy more British manufactures for the China market and to pay for those exported to India. Thus, opium – producing the surplus silver which was partly shipped out of China to India and the United Kingdom and partly transformed into bills of exchange payable there – was an important medium in the 'triangular trade' among China, the United Kingdom, and India. Hence, when opium was being suppressed in China in 1839, the Manchester merchants complained to Lord Palmerston that the disappearance of this 'medium of return for our exports to India ... is causing us to suffer most serious inconvenience ... and may eventually entail very severe losses upon us'.[18]

18. Manchester merchants to Lord Palmerston, 30 September 1839, Parl. Papers 1840, v. 36, pp. 639–40.

VIII. Verifying the triangular trade perception

Writing in 1900, Alexander Michie observed that India was the creditor of China because of opium. China was the creditor of England because of tea and silk. England was, in turn, the creditor of India, not least because of the requirement to remit to England part of the India revenue and dividends on East India Company stock.[19] However, Michie was unable to quantify this triangular trade. Here we shall seek to verify it.

Writing in 1934, the distinguished historian David Owen referred to the triangular trade, but did no more than make this astute remark: 'If the drug had been suddenly withdrawn from the market, India would have had trouble making her remittances to England, and London tea tables might have been innocent of tea'.[20]

Working on the Matheson Papers at the University of Cambridge, Michael Greenberg was the first to substantiate this allegedly one-directional flow of goods from India to China, from China to the United Kingdom, and from the United Kingdom to India; but he was unable to quantify it. This is understandable. The trade handled by one agency alone, Jardine Matheson and Co., however important, was only part of the picture. In fact, the necessary figures may be obtained from the Board of Trade and East India House, on the basis of which Table 15.8 is compiled.

In the absence of these statistics, another distinguished historian, Tan Chung, concluded his own study of the phenomenon by making this observation: 'At last we see the equilibrium in the trade under review, namely: Indian opium for the Chinese, Chinese tea for the Britons, and British Raj for the Indians!'[21] Table 15.8 makes it clear that the United Kingdom sent more than just administrators to India. Here, as before, the values are not comparable until 1854, when all of them were expressed in 'real value', whether declared or computed. But in terms of perceptions, for about thirty years from 1827 to the time of the *Arrow* War, the United Kingdom annually exported, on average, about £7 million worth of goods to India. Furthermore, it exported each year on average about £1.37 million more to India than China was exporting to the United Kingdom, and about £2.1 million more than India was exporting to China, in what conventional wisdom has regarded as a one-directional triangular trade.

Trade is never a one-way flow of traffic. What Michie, Owen, Greenberg,

---

19. Michie, *Englishman in China*, v. 1, p. 196.
20. Owen, *British Opium Policy*, p. 207.
21. Tan Chung, 'The Britain–China–India Trade Triangle (1771–1840)', *Indian Economic and Social History Review*, 11, no. 4 (December 1974), pp. 411–31. Originally, Raja was a title given in India to a king or prince. Here Professor Tan used the term 'British Raj' to mean British colonial masters.

Table 15.8. *Triangular exports: From India to China, China to the United Kingdom, and the United Kingdom to India, 1827–58 (£ million sterling)*

Year	Indian exports to China (Declared value) 1	Chinese exports to the United Kingdom (Official value) 2	U.K. exports to India (Declared value) 3
1827	2.52	4.10	4.27
1828	2.91	3.48	3.96
1829	2.27	3.23	3.52
1830	2.45	3.23	3.74
1831	2.46	3.21	3.19
1832	3.18	3.21	3.32
1833	2.62	3.27	3.21
1834	3.56	3.51	2.96
1835	2.87	4.56	3.69
1836	4.43	5.42	4.74
1837	5.44	4.53	3.94
1838	4.30	4.31	4.17
1839	4.26	3.98	5.32
1840	1.01	2.39	7.12
1841	2.18	2.96	6.44
1842	2.88	3.96	5.68
1843	4.40	4.63	7.16
1844	5.72	5.57	8.62
1845	5.55	5.82	7.32
1846	6.51	6.64	7.17
1847	5.23	6.70	6.23
1848	4.24	5.82	5.86
1849	6.53	6.17	7.87
1850	6.40	5.85	8.80
1851	6.35	7.97	8.47
1852	8.52	7.71	7.89
1853	7.62	8.26	8.72
	Declared value	Computed real value	Declared value
1854	6.70	9.13	10.57
1855	6.44	8.75	11.37
1856	6.59	9.42	12.33
1857	7.57	11.45	13.66
1858	9.37	7.04	18.94
Average	4.78	5.51	6.88

Source: Compiled from statistics in Parl. Papers 1859, Session 2, v. 23, pp. 314–23.

and Tan have not considered was this triangular trade in reverse. Until this is done, one of the origins of the *Arrow* War remains obscured. Table 15.9 shows such a trade in reverse. If column 2 in Table 15.9 is compared with column 3 in Table 15.8, it becomes obvious that, each year on average, India was importing from the United Kingdom almost five times what China was. Inevitably, British policy makers would have to ask why this was so, and why China, which was larger and more populous than India, was buying fewer British products.

This question reinforces the issue raised in Chapter 14. There, the evidence suggests that British policy makers would have considered that the Chinese *should* purchase more U.K. products. Here, it appears that they would conclude that the Chinese *could* have bought more. But the Chinese did not. The logical argument would be to open up all of China for British products. Herein lay an important origin of the *Arrow* War.

Again, the values were not comparable until 1854. Hence, we are speaking in terms of perceptions rather than reality, perceptions which the British policy makers likely formed on the basis of annual statistics presented to Parliament. The subsequent parliamentary debates on the *Arrow* War, in which some of these statistics were quoted liberally, clearly witness the degree to which the members relied on these figures for their perceptions.[22]

The one critical medium in this triangular trade was opium. Looking beyond the triangular trade, we find something even more spectacular: the place which opium occupied in the United Kingdom's global trade, from the purchase of U.S. cotton for the Lancashire mills to the remittances of India to the United Kingdom.[23]

Because of the damage that opium was doing in China, the Manchu Court sent Commissioner Lin to Canton to suppress it, which led to the Opium War (1839–42).[24] Nevertheless some informed Britons pointed out that Indian opium adversely affected China's ability to purchase British products, and that therefore the drug should be banned. The British authorities knew only too well that opium revenue was important to the financial health of India.[25] To them, the ideal solution was to open up more of the Chinese market to British products while at least maintaining existing opium sales. This appears to have been part of the British policy makers' rationale when they asked the Chinese to revise the Treaty of Nanking.

22. See Chapters 8 and 9.
23. See Chapter 10, especially Lord Ellenborough's speech (Ellenborough, 26 February 1857, Hansard, 3d series, v. 144, col. 1363).
24. For a standard reference on the Opium War, see Chang, *Commissioner Lin*.
25. See Chapter 16.

Table 15.9. *Triangular imports: India from China, China from United Kingdom, and United Kingdom from India, 1827–58 (£ million sterling)*

Year	Indian imports from China (U.K. official value) 1	Chinese imports from United Kingdom (U.K. declared value) 2	U.K. imports from India (U.K. official value) 3
1827	0.69	0.63	3.65
1828	0.76	0.85	4.77
1829	0.73	0.69	4.52
1830	0.82	0.60	4.32
1831	0.81	0.61	4.61
1832	0.48	0.57	4.95
1833	0.45	0.65	4.55
1834	0.54	0.87	5.08
1835	0.52	1.15	4.99
1836	0.54	1.55	7.03
1837	0.53	0.81	7.08
1838	0.44	1.32	6.14
1839	0.46	0.89	6.94
1840	0.20	0.54	8.08
1841	0.63	0.91	10.48
1842	0.57	1.03	9.59
1843	0.57	1.75	9.08
1844	0.64	2.39	10.78
1845	0.80	2.51	11.12
1846	0.73	1.93	9.63
1847	0.67	1.60	11.61
1848	1.01	1.54	11.19
1849	0.83	1.59	12.42
1850	0.81	1.62	14.16
1851	0.99	2.23	14.97
1852	0.92	2.56	13.65
1853	0.87	1.81	16.83
	Computed real value	Computed real value	Computed real value
1854	0.81	1.03	12.97
1855	0.92	1.30	14.76
1856	0.79	2.29	19.37
1857	0.60	2.51	21.09
1858	0.92	2.97	17.41
Average	0.69	1.42	9.93

Source: Compiled from statistics in Parl. Papers 1859, Session 2, v. 23, pp. 314–23.

IX. Evaluating 'free-trade imperialism'

Some British historians have argued that this further opening of China was not just for the benefit of Britons alone. Britons championed free trade, and any other nation would be able to share the trading privileges acquired by them. This was one of the cornerstones of the Gallagher–Robinson theory of the 'imperialism of free trade'.[26] Even Christopher Platt, who had reservations about[27] and objections to[28] this theory, nonetheless agreed that 'Her Majesty's Government [had] no desire to obtain any exclusive advantages for British trade in China, but [were] desirous to share with all other nations any benefits which they [might] acquire in the first instance specifically for British commerce'.[29] To these historians, the origins of the *Arrow* War lay in the ideology of free trade, which is thought to have heavily influenced British policy makers.

While acknowledging the genuineness of British passion for free trade in this period, one must not lose sight of the United Kingdom's position vis-à-vis other Western nations trading in China. An examination of this is practicable only for the period of the British East India Company's monopoly on trade with China, because, as mentioned, the company kept records of all the goods sold to China that had their origins not only in the United Kingdom and India, but in the rest of the world. Furthermore, the company's statistics were complete, accurate, and reliable.

After the abolition of the company's monopoly in 1834, the British authorities had to obtain such information either from the Chinese customs-houses at the various ports or from private British merchants.[30] The former information was unreliable and the latter was incomplete. Further, it was reported in 1853 that the forwarding of manifests to the custom-house at Canton had been discontinued. At Xiamen (Amoy), scarcely half of the imports were reported, and the custom-house accounts of exports were little more than nominal.[31]

26. See Gallagher and Robinson, 'Imperialism of Free Trade'.
27. D. C. M. Platt, 'The Imperialism of Free Trade: Some Reservations', *Economic History Review*, 21 (1968), pp. 296–306.
28. D. C. M. Platt, "Further Objections to an 'Imperialism of Free Trade, 1830–1860'", *Economic History Review*, 26 (1973), pp. 77–91.
29. Platt, *Finance, Trade, and Politics*, p. 265, quoting Sargent, *Anglo-Chinese Commerce and Diplomacy*, p. 109. Sargent does specify his source. In fact, it is a quotation from Lord Clarendon's instructions to Lord Elgin, who, shortly after the *Arrow* War had started, was appointed high commissioner and plenipotentiary 'for the settlement of various important matters between Her Majesty and the Emperor of China'. Clarendon to Elgin, Desps. 1 and 2, both on 20 April 1857, collected in *Correspondence Relative to the Earl of Elgin's Special Missions to China and Japan, 1857–59*, (Reprinted by the Chinese Materials Centre, San Francisco, 1975), pp. 1–6.
30. Bonham to Clarendon, Desp. 84, 9 August 1853, FO17/204, para. 3.
31. Ibid., para. 7.

Table 15.10. *Value of Canton's exports, 1820–34 (millions of Spanish dollars)*

Year	To U.K. merchants 1	To U.S. merchants 2	To Dutch merchants 3
1820–1	14.08	4.09	—
1821–2	14.02	7.06	—
1822–3	12.53	7.52	—
1823–4	15.30	5.68	—
1824–5	13.76	8.50	—
1825–6	16.87	8.75	—
1826–7	18.26	4.36	—
1827–8	18.41	6.14	—
1828–9	18.90	4.55	—
1829–30	20.77	4.11	0.39
1830–1	19.91	4.26	0.42
1831–2	17.20	5.86	0.63
1832–3	17.71	8.23	—
1833–4	20.65	—	—

Note: It is unclear why the statistics for the Dutch were available only for the years 1829–32.
Source: Compiled from statistics in Parl. Papers 1840, v. 37, pp. 247–88.

Table 15.11. *Value of Canton's imports, 1820–34 (millions of Spanish dollars)*

Year	British	United States	Dutch
1820–1	17.75	4.04	—
1821–2	14.34	8.20	—
1822–3	15.30	8.34	—
1823–4	17.33	6.31	—
1824–5	16.00	8.96	—
1825–6	21.43	7.76	—
1826–7	21.80	4.24	—
1827–8	19.91	6.00	—
1828–9	21.57	4.03	—
1829–30	22.93	4.31	0.35
1830–1	21.95	4.22	0.21
1831–2	20.54	5.53	0.46
1832–3	22.30	8.36	—
1833–4	23.17	—	—

Source: Compiled from statistics in Parl. Papers 1840, v. 37, pp. 247–88.

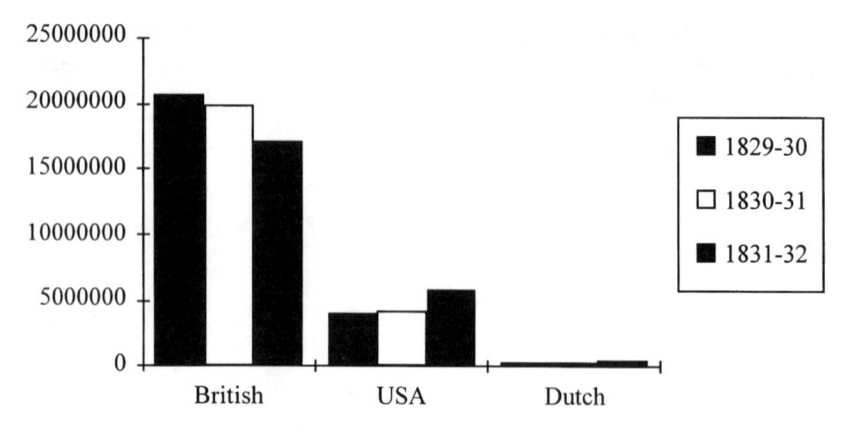

Figure 15.1. Value of Canton's exports, 1829–32 (millions of Spanish dollars; based on Table 15.10)

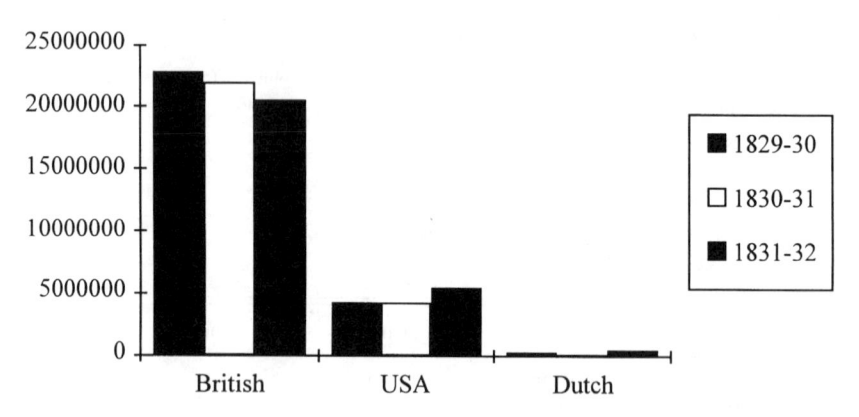

Figure 15.2. Value of Canton's imports, 1829–32 (millions of Spanish dollars; based on Table 15.11)

However, all the available evidence suggests that the dominant British position at the time of the company remained unchanged even several decades after the *Arrow* War.[32] Short of a better alternative, we are obliged to use the least unsatisfactory of these sources, that of the company's satistics, if we were ever to gain any indication of the extent of that dominance. Table 15.10 lists China's three major maritime export markets. Table 15.11 lists China's three major maritime sources of imports. In both cases, the United Kingdom had the lion's share, despite variations from year to year. In 1829–30, for example, the

32. See later in this chapter.

Table 15.12. *Value of Canton's import and export trade combined, 1820–34 (millions of Spanish dollars)*

Year	British 1	United States 2	Dutch 3	Spanish (estimates) 4
1820–1	31.83	8.12	—	1.50
1821–2	28.36	15.26	—	1.50
1822–3	27.83	15.86	—	0.70
1823–4	32.62	11.99	—	0.70
1824–5	29.76	17.46	—	0.70
1825–6	38.29	16.51	—	0.60
1826–7	40.06	8.61	—	0.67
1827–8	38.31	12.15	—	0.50
1828–9	40.47	8.58	—	0.50
1829–30	43.70	8.42	0.74	0.50
1830–1	41.86	8.49	0.63	—
1831–2	37.74	11.39	1.09	—
1832–3	40.01	16.59	—	—
1833–4	43.82	—	—	—

Source: Compiled from statistics in Parl. Papers 1840, v. 37, pp. 247–88.

value of British imports from China was about 5.06 times that of its closest rival, the Americans and about 52.9 times that of its second closest rival, the Dutch. In the same year, the value of British exports into China was 5.3 times that of the Americans and 65.2 times that of the Dutch. The picture looks even more impressive if the figures from 1829 to 1832 are visually quantified, as in Figures 15.1 and 15.2.

If imports and exports were combined to show the total volume of bilateral trade, then Spain might be included in the comparison as China's fourth largest maritime trading partner.[33] Table 15.12 shows such a comparison, which is complete only for the year 1829–30. Then, the British share was 5.2 times that of the Americans, 59.1 times that of the Dutch, and 87.4 times that of the Spaniards. Visually, the picture for the year 1829–30 is shown in Figure 15.3.

Thus, the United Kingdom was doing at least five times better than its closest competitor, and almost sixty times better than the second closest.

I have gone to some length to establish one critical point: that the British absolutely dominated China's maritime trade. This point is crucial when we

---

33. Separate figures for Spanish imports into and exports from China are unavailable and, hence, cannot be included in Tables 15.10 and 15.11.

The economics of imperialism

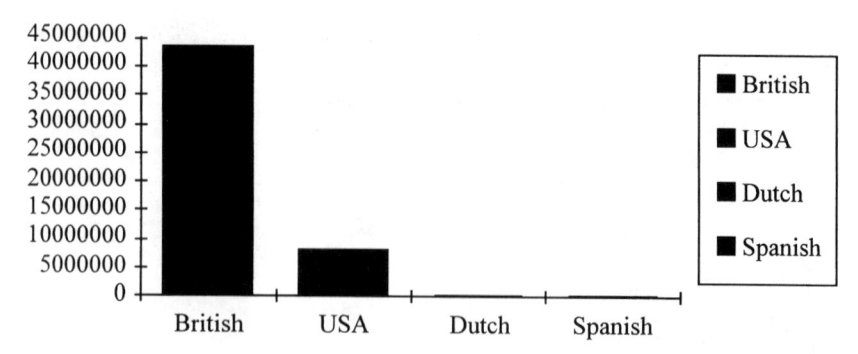

Figure 15.3. Value of Canton's import and export trade combined, 1829–30 (millions of Spanish dollars; based on Table 15.12)

assess the validity of the theory of the imperialism of free trade, not in general terms,[34] but as the main explanation of the origins of the *Arrow* War. If the United Kingdom was in a predominant trading position in China, its policy makers would have absolutely no reservations about advocating free trade, whatever the degree of their passion for such an ideology. Indeed, it was to their advantage to advocate free trade, because they could then dominate the entire China market. Had they been protectionist in China, then all their rivals would have followed suit, and China would have been divided into spheres of foreign influence, as it was about four decades later,[35] to the detriment of British trade there.[36]

There is no doubt about the sincerity of the believers in free trade as an

34. I am not suggesting that there is general agreement among historians about the meaning of the 'imperialism of free trade', either. Much controversy has arisen since Gallagher and Robinson introduced the debate in 1953. Authors who have subsequently written on the subject include those in William Roger Louis (ed.), *Imperialism: The Robinson–Gallagher Controversy* (New York, New Viewpoints, 1976); as well as Martin Lynn, 'The "Imperialism of Free Trade" and the Case of West Africa, c. 1830–c. 1870', *Journal of Imperial and Commonwealth History*, 15, no. 1 (October 1986), pp. 23–40; and Colin Newbury, 'The Semantics of International Influence: Informal Empires Reconsidered', in Michael Twaddle (ed.), *Imperialism, the State and the Third World* (London, British Academic Press, 1992), pp. 23–66.
35. It was Germany who led the way in such a division, partly because it could not yet compete with British products in the Chinese market. In vain did British diplomats try to keep an 'open door', so to speak, in China. Consequently, the British government declared South China and the Yangtze River basin within the British sphere of influence. See John Shrecker, *Imperialism and Chinese Nationalism: Germany in Shantung* (Cambridge, Mass., Harvard University Press, 1971).
36. The point about Britain being in favour of free trade because it was the dominant trading power is not new. See Tony Smith, *The Pattern of Imperialism: The United States, Great Britain, and the Late Industrializing World since 1815* (Cambridge University Press, 1981). What is new here is the argument against the use to which free trade has been put as the main explanation of the origins of the *Arrow* War.

ideology in nineteenth-century Britain. But very often, policy makers and administrators had things other than ideology to consider. This point is made amply clear by the British authorities' management of the opium monopoly in Bengal, as we shall see. They persistently and successfully resisted all attempts to free the cultivation, manufacture, and sale of opium from the monopolistic control of the East India Company. A public inquiry in 1830–2 failed to dislodge them.[37] Even a subsequent royal commission in the 1890s turned out to be a whitewash.[38]

I venture to suggest that a distinction should be made between those who were totally committed to free trade, such as members of the Manchester group including Richard Cobden, John Bright, and Milner-Gibson, and politicians such as Palmerston, Clarendon, and even Gladstone, who could be flexible enough to permit a monopoly if it made fiscal sense.[39] Even the Manchester merchants accepted this fiscal argument. In his budget of 1853, for example, Gladstone swept away many protective duties, but absolutely refused to remove the duties on French wines, which fetched £3 million sterling a year. The Manchester merchants tacitly recognized the importance of this revenue, and have been praised for having 'rightly acted on the principle that inconsistency in a good cause is sometimes justifiable'.[40]

The quotation from Lord Clarendon by Platt, already mentioned, in which Clarendon professed free-trade principles when instructing Lord Elgin to make war on China, is insufficient evidence to suggest that the origins of the *Arrow* War lay exclusively in a total commitment to the ideology of free trade.

Even before those instructions were drafted, a lobby group had written, 'In fact a new Treaty will now be required and we are quite willing to concur in the same liberality which was voluntarily accorded on the former occasion, by allowing to all other Powers all the advantages which we may obtain for our own Country'.[41] Clarendon had nothing to lose by expressing a similar sentiment in a public document such as his letter of instructions to Elgin at the time of war with China. Such an expression cannot be taken as conclusive evidence that free-trade ideology determined British policies towards war or peace with China.

37. See Chapter 16 and also my article 'Monopoly in India and Equal Opportunities in China: An Examination of an Apparent Paradox', *South Asia: Journal of South Asian Studies*, 5, no. 2 (December 1982), pp. 81–95.
38. Virginia Berridge and Griffith Edwards, *Opium and the People: Opiate Use in Nineteenth-Century England* (New Haven, Conn., Yale University Press, 1987), pp. 185–8.
39. See Chapters 9, 12, and 16.
40. Redford, *Manchester Merchants and Foreign Trade*, v. 2, p. 6. The author regards the period 1846–60 as 'the climax of free trade' and has used that as the title of his first chapter.
41. East India and China Association to the Earl of Clarendon, London 6 January 1857, Baring Papers, HC 6.1.20 The 'former occasion' referred to was the Opium War (1839–42).

16
The problem of India:
The Chinese should and could buy more

It has been noted that British policy makers thought that the Chinese should (Chapter 14) and could (Chapter 15) buy more British manufactures. This chapter shows that their perceptions of the pertinent statistics led them to believe that the Chinese could do so while at least maintaining the existing level of the purchase of opium from India. It attempts to evaluate further aspects of free-trade imperialism and other pertinent theories, exploring still further the origins of the *Arrow* War.

I. A debt-ridden India

It is often said that India was a tremendous asset to the British Empire. In fact, for the period under review India was a heavy liability.

One problem was that India, administered by the British East India Company,[1] had a net revenue which often fell short of expenses. For example, the company was in the red for four out of the seven years immediately before the *Arrow* War began in earnest (see Table 16.1, column 2). Even during the three years when the company had a surplus (see Table 16.1, column 1), it was far less than the annual deficit in the other years. Normally, loans are raised only when revenues are insufficient to meet expenditures. But Table 16.1, column 3, shows that whether the company was in the black or the red, it continued to borrow money both in England and in India. Why?

The answer is that these loans were related to the extension of British rule over more and more of the Indian subcontinent. As the company continued to extend its rule in India, it kept augmenting its debt year after year. This debt had a modest beginning of about £15.6 million sterling in 1800–1. Despite regular redemptions, it steadily surged to about £67.5 million sterling in the

1. For a classic work on the history of the British East India Company, see Cyril Henry Philips, *East India Company, 1784–1834* (Bombay, Oxford University Press, 1961). For a more recent work, see John Keay, *The Honourable Company: A History of the English East India Company* (New York, Macmillan, 1994).

Table 16.1. *The annual balance sheet in India, 1851–8 (£ sterling)*

Year	Surplus of net income from revenue over expenditure 1	Deficiency of net income from revenue compared with expenditure 2	Income: receipts from loans in India and in England 3
1851–2	733,775	—	796,674
1852–3	632,372	—	1,127,871
1853–4	—	1,962,904	25,672,234
1854–5	—	1,620,407	2,192,258
1855–6	—	820,003	2,656,042
1856–7	82,143	—	2,473,213
1857–8	—	7,864,221	14,945,517

Source: Parl. Papers 1859, Session 2, v. 23, pp. 28–9. The format of this table is adopted from that in the Parliamentary Papers.

Table 16.2. *Indian debt, 1801–58 (£ million sterling)*

Year	Debt: Contracted during each year 1	Debt: At the end of each year 2	Interest: Paid each year 3	Bengal opium: Net receipts each year 4
1800–1	3.74	15.61	1.43	—
1801–2	2.79	17.33	1.56	—
1802–3	3.84	19.25	1.52	—
1803–4	3.34	21.75	1.84	—
1804–5	4.69	25.12	1.90	—
1805–6	5.31	28.57	2.29	—
1806–7	5.87	31.09	2.41	—
1807–8	7.84	34.30	2.49	—
1808–9	2.92	34.47	2.47	—
1809–10	2.76	30.82	2.44	—
1810–1	17.70	27.45	1.77	—
1811–2	4.60	30.35	1.84	—
1812–3	1.22	29.63	1.93	—
1813–4	1.19	29.36	2.01	—
1814–5	1.63	30.00	1.92	1.02
1815–6	0.39	29.97	1.92	0.94
1816–7	0.72	30.67	1.96	0.82
1817–8	0.57	31.24	1.98	0.78
1818–9	1.62	32.76	2.02	0.74
1819–20	2.61	35.26	1.88	0.70
1820–1	0.28	34.64	2.17	1.26

Table 16.2. (*cont.*)

Year	Debt: Contracted during each year 1	Debt: At the end of each year 2	Interest: Paid each year 3	Bengal opium: Net receipts each year 4
1821–2	0.01	33.22	2.05	0.94
1822–3	0.17	31.18	1.92	1.35
1823–4	11.19	28.52	1.61	0.74
1824–5	1.98	29.19	1.63	0.74
1825–6	7.13	34.36	1.90	0.38
1826–7	2.88	36.06	2.05	1.20
1827–8	5.11	40.49	2.29	1.39
1828–9	1.46	40.24	2.28	1.43
1829–30	0.83	40.84	2.27	1.29
1830–1	1.34	42.05	2.31	1.18
1831–2	4.86	41.21	1.97	1.15
1832–3	2.56	41.40	1.95	1.21
1833–4	2.73	41.35	1.85	1.07
1834–5	3.39	39.77	1.80	0.73
1835–6	2.25	35.34	1.51	1.40
1836–7	1.19	35.96	1.56	1.53
1837–8	1.46	35.79	1.57	1.59
1838–9	0.59	33.98	1.50	0.95
1839–40	0.64	34.48	1.60	0.34
1840–1	1.54	35.92	1.66	0.87
1841–2	2.78	38.40	1.80	1.02
1842–3	2.55	40.48	1.91	1.58
1843–4	1.66	41.88	1.96	2.02
1844–5	1.68	43.50	2.01	2.18
1845–6	0.39	43.89	2.03	2.80
1846–7	3.00	46.88	2.18	2.89
1847–8	2.23	48.76	2.28	1.66
1848–9	1.33	51.05	2.39	2.85
1849–50	2.90	53.93	2.56	3.53
1850–1	1.23	55.10	2.59	2.75
1851–2	0.80	55.11	2.55	3.14
1852–3	1.13	56.21	2.60	3.73
1853–4	25.67	53.66	2.21	3.15
1854–5	2.19	55.51	2.19	3.40
1855–6	2.56	57.74	2.33	3.71
1856–7	2.47	59.44	2.40	3.62
1857–8	12.16	67.50	2.36	5.92

Sources: For cols. 1–3, see Parl. Papers 1859, Session 2, v. 23, pp. 78–9. For col. 4, years 1800–52, see Parl. Papers 1854–5, v. 40, pp. 325–39. For col. 4, years 1852–8, see Parl. Papers 1856, v. 45, pp. 16 and 28; 1857, Session 2, v. 29, pp. 73 and 79; 1857–8, v. 42, pp. 87 and 93; 1859, Session 2, v. 23, pp. 112 and 116; 1860, v. 49, pp. 148 and 152; and 1861, v. 43, pp. 32 and 36.

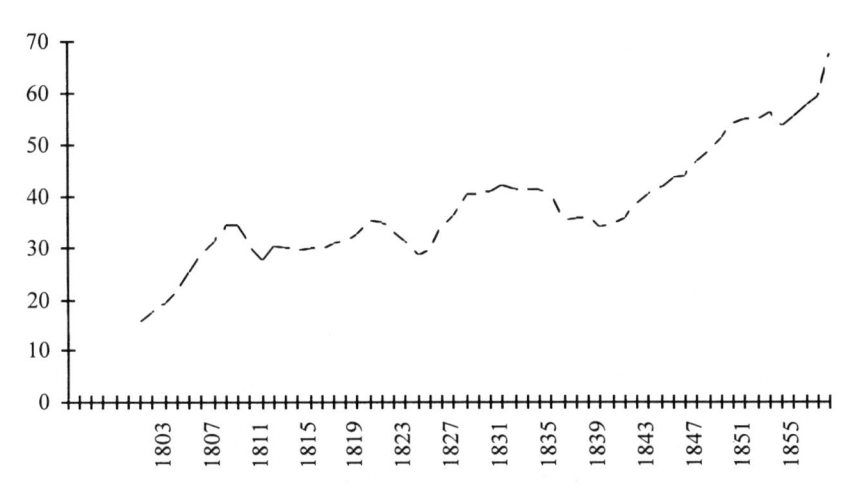

Figure 16.1. Indian debt, 1801–58 (£ million sterling; based on column 1, Table 16.2)

Arrow War year of 1857–8 (see Table 16.2, column 2). This was a quadruple increase.

Concomitant to the extension of British rule in India were indigenous rebellions; these also made India a liability. In the financial year 1857–8, for example, the annual deficit jumped to nearly £8 million sterling, and the annual loans soared to nearly £15 million sterling (see the last entry in Table 16.1), because extra money was needed to put down the Indian Mutiny and Civil Rebellion. Indeed, one of the consequences of the mutiny was the end of company rule in British India; the British government took over the reins. Visually, the remarkable increases in the Indian debt are presented in Figure 16.1.

Fortunately for the company, interest rates fell steadily over the same period, from a high of 12 per cent in 1800–1801 to a low of 3.75 per cent in 1857–8.[2] But for these falls and other favourable factors,[3] British India could have become insolvent if the company was forever bent on expansion, as it appeared to be. Indeed, the company had been insolvent before, in 1772, and had to be rescued by the British government.[4] Thereafter, Parliament kept a close watch over the debt for India, and ordered regular reports on the basis of which Table 16.2 has been compiled. Nonetheless, the debt continued to grow.

2. Parl. Papers 1859, Session 2, v. 23, pp. 78–9.
3. These other factors include the discovery of a new source of revenue, opium, which will be dealt with presently.
4. Beeching, *Chinese Opium Wars*, p. 23.

II. Opium revenue serviced the growing India debt

India's debt was permitted to grow because of the discovery of a major source of new revenue since about the turn of the nineteenth century – opium (see Table 16.2, column 4), which was produced in large quantities in Bengal. Significant revenue was also derived from levying charges after the establishment of the Malwa Opium Agency in 1823,[5] on the so-called Malwa opium, which was grown in the independent princely states of central India but passed through British territory at Bombay,[6] whence it was exported to China.

It is revealing to compare this fast-growing new revenue from opium with the interest on the Indian debt, especially after the Opium War in China. Before that war, the net revenue from opium varied from about one-third to one-half – and even the equivalent of – the interest on the India debt. After that war, the net opium revenue increased to more than two and a half times the interest paid (see Table 16.2, column 4). In other words, opium serviced the cost of imperial expansion in India.

III. Opium revenue in Bengal

Opium cultivation in India was 'negligible in size before British rule and mostly confined to Patna and its neighbourhood'. After British rule began, it increased by leaps and bounds, from about four thousand chests[7] in 1789 to about fifty thousand chests shortly after the *Arrow* War.[8]

One may play down the importance of opium by arguing that British rule on the Indian subcontinent had been extended even before it had the benefit of extra receipts from opium. A logical extension of this counterargument is that

---

5. India Office, Bengal Board of Revenue, Miscellaneous Proceedings (Opium), 27 June 1823, R. 102, v. 35, no. 3, paras. 34 and 40, quoted by Bakhala, 'Indian Opium', chapter 3, n. 36. Revenue from this source began to feature on a regular basis in 1830 (Parl. Papers 1865, v. 40, pp. 85–7). Some revenue in this score was listed in Parl. Papers 1822, v. 17, p. 560, but apparently not as part of a centrally planned long–term policy.
6. This was renamed Mumbai in 1996 (*South China Morning Post*, 23 November 1996, p. 9). I shall continue to call it Bombay as all the records in this period refer to it as such.
7. A chest of opium in India weighed 140 pounds. Opium dries out with time, and a chest leaving India at 140 pounds was usually reduced to the Chinese weight of one pecul (133.3 pounds) by the time it reached China. See R. K. Newman, 'Opium Smoking in Late Imperial China', *Modern Asian Studies*, 29, no. 4 (1995), p. 771, n. 15, quoting A. C. Trevor, Collector of Customs, Bombay, 10 October 1879, India, Separate Revenue, January 1882, no. 169.
8. B. Chaudhuri, 'Regional Economy (1757–1857): East India', in Dharma Kumar (ed.), *The Cambridge Economic History of India*, v. 2, c. 1757–c.1970 (Cambridge University Press, 1983), pp. 312 and 315. Indeed, the possibility of developing opium as an alternative to silver as a means of financing the China trade came after the acquisition of Bengal and its adjacent province of Bihar, which the British developed into the two main opium-growing areas in India. See K. N. Chaudhuri, 'Foreign Trade and Balance of Payments (1857–1947)', in ibid., p. 847.

Table 16.3. *Bengal salt, 1851–60 (£ million sterling)*

Year	Gross revenue 1	Cost of production 2	Percentage of cost of production over gross revenue (col. 2 ÷ col. 1) 3
1851–2	0.90	—	—
1852–3	1.19	—	—
1853–4	1.27	0.16	12.60
1854–5	1.35	0.17	12.59
1855–6	1.01	0.20	19.80
1856–7	0.99	0.24	24.24
1857–8	1.02	0.22	21.57
1858–9	1.19	0.25	21.01
1859–60	1.31	0.22	16.79
Average	1.14	0.21	18.37

Sources: Parl. Papers 1856, v. 45, p. 16, for the years 1851–3; a rupee is converted to £ at 2s. per rupee; Parl. Papers 1857, Session 2, v. 29, p. 73, for 1853–6; 1857–8, v. 42, p. 87, for 1856–7; 1859, Session 2, v. 23, p. 112, for 1857–8; 1860, v. 49, p. 221, for 1858–9; and 1861, v. 43, p. 107, for 1859–60.

British expansion there was not dependent on the opium revenue. Here again, the company had been insolvent before,[9] when opium revenue was not yet significant. One also has to remember that without this extra revenue, British India probably would not have been able to go beyond its existing level of borrowing, and hence its expansion would have been curbed. As it was, this extra income was a fairly steady source of revenue between 1815 and 1838. It was interrupted by the Opium War (1839–42), but then doubled and tripled after the war (see Table 16.2, column 4). By analogy, Paul Kennedy thinks that the bid by the Habsburg family for hegemony in Europe failed because its debt servicing consumed about two-thirds of its revenue.[10] In terms of British expansion in India, debt servicing was not a problem because Bengal opium covered it.

Was opium expensive to produce? The cost of some products could be so high as to make them unworthy of the effort. In Bengal, the production of both opium and salt were government monopolies.[11] Hence, there is a common

9. This happened in 1772; see Beeching, *Chinese Opium Wars*, p. 23.
10. Paul Kennedy, *The Rise and Fall of the Great Powers* (New York, Random House, 1987), chapter 2.
11. The only other commodity in which the government had a monopoly was saltpetre. See B. Chaudhuri, 'Regional Economy', p. 288.

Table 16.4. *Bengal opium, 1851–60 (£ million sterling)*

Year	Gross revenue 1	Cost of production 2	Percentage of cost of production over gross revenue (col. 2 ÷ col. 1) 3
1851–2	0.90	—	—
1852–3	1.19	—	—
1853–4	1.27	0.16	12.60
1854–5	1.35	0.17	12.59
1855–6	1.01	0.20	19.80
1856–7	0.99	0.24	24.24
1857–8	1.02	0.22	21.57
1858–9	1.19	0.25	21.01
1859–60	1.31	0.22	16.79
Average	1.14	0.21	18.37

Note: The term 'Bengal opium' is a generic one. It applied to the produce of the Ganges basin, particularly in the areas of Bihar and, later, Benares.
Sources: Parl. Papers 1856, v. 45, p. 16, for the years 1851–3; a rupee is converted to £ at 2s. per rupee; Parl. Papers 1857, Session 2, v. 29, p. 73, for 1853–6; 1857–8, v. 42, p. 87, for 1856–7; 1859, Session 2, v. 23, p. 112, for 1857–8; 1860, v. 49, p. 221, for 1858–9; and 1861, v. 43, p. 107, for 1859–60.

basis on which to compare the two. The conclusion is astounding. A comparison of Table 16.3 and Table 16.4 shows that during the period under review, in relative terms it cost about the same to produce net revenue from opium as from salt. Indeed, for the years of 1857–60, it was cheaper to produce net revenue from opium than from salt. The reasons are not hard to find. Apart from variables like prices – which will be dealt with shortly – one reason would be that once the opium industry was established, it became cheaper to produce the drug. In addition, it was a low-risk and high-yield investment; its illegality meant high prices in China.

Productivity was high because the most fertile land in colonial Bengal was chosen to grow the poppy.[12] Also, labour in India was generally cheap. The

12. Hugh Starks's evidence, 14 February 1832, Parl. Papers 1831–2, v. 11, Question (henceforth Q) 266. L. Kennedy's evidence, 25 February 1832, ibid., Q719, Q720, and Q760. Sir George Staunton's speech in Parliament, Hansard, 3d series, v. 53, col. 743. Because only the most fertile land was used to grow opium, the land under poppy rarely exceeded 2–3 per cent of the total cultivated area in the opium-growing regions even at the peak of cultivation. See J. F. Richards, 'The Indian Empire and Peasant Production of Opium in the Nineteenth Century', *Modern Asian Studies*, 15, no. 1 (1981), p. 61. In 1797, the land under cultivation in Bengal was about 25,000 acres. This was increased to 79,488 acres in 1828 and to 176,745 acres in 1838

The problem of India

labour for poppy cultivation was provided by the peasants (called *ryots*) to whom interest-free advance payments were made as an inducement to contract to cultivate the poppy.[13] A *ryot* who had signed such a contract and did not sow poppy was required to pay a penalty three times the initial advance.[14] Furthermore, a *ryot* was required by contract to deliver the entire produce at a fixed rate.[15] This rate was calculated to leave him 'only the cost of production'.[16] Nonetheless the *ryots* willingly entered into contracts year after year because one of the true advantages of poppy cultivation lay not in attractive cash profits but in security and protection from price vicissitudes which affected other cash crops not under state monopoly.[17]

Quality was guaranteed because only peasants from castes with traditional skills and a past record of successful cultivation were given the task.[18] As opium was a government monopoly, any merchant who dared deal in opium, or any cultivator who held back part of his produce, was subject to

(ibid., p. 65). After the Opium War (1839–42), this was increased again, at intervals, with annual averages for three five-year periods as follows: 275,523 acres (1848–53), 499,775 acres (1868–73), and 472,394 acres (1888–93) (ibid., pp. 67–8).

13. These advances were made in instalments and timed to meet the demand for rental instalments from occupancy tenants, who would thereby avoid paying the 12–30 per cent interest rates of village moneylenders. See Richards, 'Peasant Production of Opium', p. 79. See also Bakhala, 'Indian Opium', pp. 100–105.
14. Richards, 'Peasant Production of Opium', p. 64, quoting Rajeshwari Rrasad, *Some Aspects of British Revenue Policy in India, 1773–1833* (New Delhi, n.p., 1970), pp. 148–50.
15. L. Kennedy's evidence, 25 February 1832, in Parl. Papers, 1831–2, v. 11, Q767. The *ryots* found the advances attractive initially for two reasons. First, they were interest-free. Second, the advances were offered at a time when the *ryots* needed them most, that is, when the payment of the rent instalments became due – 'a coincidence not incidental, but deliberately planned by the government (B. Chaudhuri, 'Regional Economy', p. 327). It must be added that advances to the Indian peasants were quite common, and not just to those peasants cultivating opium. Advances were also made to those cultivating cotton, for example.
16. Hugh Starks's evidence, 14 February 1832, Parl. Papers, 1831–2, v. 11, Q255. This rate was fixed in advance. Up to 1822, it was Rs. 2 a *seer*. From 1823, it was Rs. 3 a *seer*. And in 1832, it was increased to Rs 3.5 a *seer*. There were eighty *seers* to a chest of opium. See Morse, *The International Relations of the Chinese Empire*, v. 1, p. 176. Seen in this light, Hugh Starks seems to have slightly overstated his case, because the rates were increased from time to time. There were also ancillary products such as oil squeezed from the poppy seed, seed cakes to feed cattle, thatching with poppy stalks, processed petals and stalk, and seed, all of which added a little to the peasants' income. Despite all this, it is nonetheless clear that the state monopoly did keep the price of crude opium finely on the economic edge. Peasant dissatisfaction and inflation prompted the Opium Department to raise the rates ultimately to Rs. 6 per *seer* in 1895. See Richards, 'Peasant Production of Opium', pp. 78–9.
17. This willingness evaporated when the company became too greedy and twice cut the rates in the period 1855–9. In protest, many opium cultivators changed to growing cotton, indigo, or sugar cane. See Benoy Chowdhury, *Growth of Commercial Agriculture in Bengal* (Calcutta, M. K. Maitre, 1964), pp. 36–40.
18. Richards, 'Peasant Production of Opium', p. 67. Apparently, Kachhis and Koiris were the two peasant castes most closely associated with the cultivation of opium (ibid., p. 73).

The economics of imperialism

criminal prosecution.[19] And opium was transported at all times under armed guard.[20]

The result of all this was that the net profit, by 1832, from the opium exported was at least 'fourteen times the prime cost',[21] reflecting 'the single-minded determination of an autocratic state to sustain and improve the profits of this lucrative enterprise' – a conclusion arrived at independently by an author who has conducted research on sources often different from my own.[22]

IV. Opium revenue in Bombay

By contrast, in colonial Bombay the East India Company derived revenue from selling passes to the opium merchants who transported Malwa opium from the still-independent states in central India for export from Bombay.[23] The fees for these passes were fixed from time to time.[24] The only expense in collecting such revenue was the administrative cost. In Bombay, too, the company was not involved in the actual production of salt in any significant amount, only in collecting its excise duty. Here, we have almost the same basis for comparing the expenses incurred in collecting both the salt and opium revenues. Tables 16.5 and 16.6 show that in Bombay, for the period under review and in relative terms, the opium revenue was at least ten times cheaper to collect than that from salt. Indeed it was so cheap that I have had to abandon my usual practice of rounding off figures at two decimal points and round them off at three (see Table 16.6).

19. Ram Chand Pandit's memorandum, as quoted in George Watt, *A Dictionary of the Economic Products of India*, 6 vs. (Delhi, Cosmos, 1889–96), v. 6, pt. 1, p. 39.
20. Richards, 'Peasant Production of Opium', p. 78, quoting Rivett–Carnac, 'Note on the Supply of Opium', which appeared as Appendix V of Parl. Papers 1894, v. 61, Royal Commission on Opium, *Report*.
21. James Mill's evidence, 28 June 1832, in Parl. Papers, 1831–2, v. 11, Q3037. He was the father of John Stuart Mill. Apparently, sugar and cotton were cultivated in India by the same method of making advances to the *ryots*. 'Merchants, both Company and private, Indian and English, offered advances to encourage cultivation and secure supply of commodities of shipment downstream to Calcutta'. But of course the profit margin of neither sugar nor cotton could ever hope to approach that of opium. See Tom G. Kessinger, 'Regional Economy (1757–1857): North India', in Kumar (ed.), *The Cambridge Economic History of India*, v. 2, pp. 261 and 267. See also B. Chaudhuri, 'Agrarian Relations: East India', in ibid., p. 146.
22. Richards, 'Peasant Production of Opium', p. 67.
23. Initially, the company tried to prevent Malwa opium from competing with Bengal opium in the China market by forbidding its passage through Bombay. This simply drove the traffic through Daman and Diu. The company changed its tactics and allowed unimpeded passage of Malwa opium through Bombay by charging fees on the export. See Richards, 'Peasant Production of Opium', p. 65. Owen, *British Opium Policy*, p. 101. See next note and also later in this chapter for more details.
24. This system was instituted in 1823. See India Office, Bengal Board of Revenue, Miscellaneous Proceedings (Opium), 27 June 1823, R. 102, v. 35, no. 3, paras. 34 and 40, quoted by Bakhala, 'Indian Opium', chapter 3, n. 36. See also Parl. Papers 1856, v. 40, p. 86; and India Office Bengal Separate Consultations, 13 July 1830, quoted in Owen, *British Opium Policy*, p. 101, n. 58.

Table 16.5. *Bombay salt revenue, 1851–60 (£ million sterling)*

Year	Receipt from salt (excise duty) 1	Charges 2	Net revenue (col. 1 − col. 2) 3	Charges expressed as a percentage of receipt (col. 2 ÷ col. 1) 4
1851–2	—	—	—	—
1852–3	—	—	—	—
1853–4	0.22	0.02	0.20	9.09
1854–5	0.23	0.03	0.20	13.04
1855–6	0.26	0.03	0.23	11.54
1856–7	0.24	0.03	0.21	12.50
1857–8	0.27	0.03	0.24	11.11
1858–9	0.25	0.03	0.22	12.00
1859–60	0.35	0.03	0.32	8.57
Average	0.26	0.03	0.23	11.12

Sources: Parl. Papers 1856, v. 45, pp. 28–9, for the years 1851–3; 1857, v. 29, p. 79, for 1853–6; 1857–8, v. 42. p. 93, for 1856–7; 1859, v. 23, p. 87, for 1857–8; 1860, v. 49, p. 255, for 1858–9; and 1861, v. 43, p. 111, for 1859–60.

Table 16.6. *Bombay opium revenue, 1851–60 (£ million sterling)*

Year	Receipt: Sale of opium passes 1	Charges 2	Net revenue (col. 1 − col. 2) 3	Charges expressed as a perentage of receipt (col. 2 ÷ col. 1) 4
1851–2	—	—	—	—
1852–3	—	—	—	—
1853–4	—	0.004	—	—
1854–5	—	0.006	—	—
1855–6	0.943	0.005	0.938	0.530
1856–7	1.084	0.006	1.078	0.554
1857–8	1.616	0.006	1.610	0.371
1858–9	1.444	0.006	1.438	0.416
1859–60	1.536	0.006	1.530	0.391
Average	1.325	0.006	1.319	0.452

Sources: Parl. Papers 1856, v. 45, pp. 28–9, for the years 1851–3; 1857, v. 29, p. 79, for 1853–6; 1857–8, v. 42. p. 93, for 1856–7; 1859, v. 23, p. 87, for 1857–8; 1860, v. 49, p. 255, for 1858–9; and 1861, v. 43, p. 111, for 1859–60.

The economics of imperialism

To look at the question in another way – say, horizontally instead of vertically – let us take the financial year 1858–9 in Bombay as an example. The expenses, expressed as a percentage of the gross revenue collected, for the post office were 90.02 per cent; for salt, 11.83 per cent; for land revenue and so forth, 10.52 per cent; for customs, 4.79 per cent; for stamp duties, 3.91 per cent; and for opium (even including the costs involved in buying and retailing £31,007 worth of the drug), only 1.84 per cent, lowest of all.[25]

V. The place of opium in India's revenues

Thus, the opium revenue was very good news to the British authorities. In Bengal, opium was remarkably cheap to produce, and in Bombay tax on opium was astonishingly cheap to collect.. Although the opium poppy was not grown in any amount worth mentioning in other parts of British India at this stage, the revenue from Bengal and Bombay constituted the second largest source of revenue in the whole of British India, as Table 16.7 shows. In this table, the five years closest to the *Arrow* War period have been chosen as examples. The table shows the twenty major sources of revenue in India. By 1857–8, opium revenue exceeded the third and fourth largest revenues, those for salt and customs, by more than three times. That it had become so much cheaper than either of them to collect – indeed cheaper than any other revenue – made the opium revenue the most valuable of all revenues. This cheapness was directly relative to the high prices which opium was able to fetch in the export market. In short, opium was a good cash crop with high turnover – very good news for debt-laden British India.

To pinpoint the place of the opium revenue in the total picture of Indian revenue, and hence its role in British expansion in India, we need larger runs of data than in Table 16.7. Let us select, therefore, the total gross opium revenue and the total gross Indian revenue to compile Table 16.8. This should give us some idea of the relationship between the two items over a longer period of time. According to the Parliamentary Papers, although statistics for the opium revenue in Bengal were available as early as 1797–8,[26] those in Bombay were not listed until 1821–2.[27] Thus, we begin with the latter date.[28]

25. Parl. Papers 1860, v. 49, p. 152. The figures have been rounded off at the second digit after the decimal.
26. See Parl. Papers 1801, v. 7, p. 6.
27. See Parl. Papers 1822, v. 17, p. 560.
28. Compiling col. 2 was fairly straightforward; the value was already expressed in pounds sterling. I simply had to add up the triennial revenues from all the British possessions in India at the time to create a gross total Indian revenue. Col. 1 is a little more complicated. The value prior to 1853–4 was expressed in rupees, so I had to convert the rupees into sterling according

[footnote 28 continued on p. 399]

Table 16.7. *Twenty major revenues of India, 1853–8 (£ million sterling)*

Source	1853–4	1854–5	1855–6	1856–7	1857–8
Land	14.849	15.066	15.935	16.604	15.317
Opium	4.479	4.416	4.871	4.690	6.864
Salt	2.575	2.707	2.486	2.518	2.131
Customs	1.283	1.437	1.975	1.962	2.149
Abkarry	0.720	0.737	0.797	0.859	0.794
Tributes etc.	0.623	0.507	0.499	0.504	0.544
Stamp duties	0.497	0.508	0.518	0.583	0.456
Sayer	0.268	0.309	0.344	0.383	0.268
Post Office	0.191	0.189	0.220	0.166	0.389
Judicial	0.134	0.159	0.179	0.192	0.299
Marine	0.114	0.127	0.164	0.161	0.178
Moturpha	0.106	0.103	0.102	0.102	0.108
Mint receipts	0.096	0.074	0.185	0.246	0.364
Interest	0.064	0.093	0.086	0.061	0.063
Misc. (Rev. Dept.)	0.057	0.068	0.099	0.152	0.228
Excise	0.031	0.035	0.042	0.043	0.05
Small farms	0.026	0.027	0.022	0.012	—
Sale of presents	0.005	0.008	0.009	0.018	—
Electric telegraph	—	0.004	0.016	0.022	—
Toll and ferry	—	—	0.069	0.062	—
Total	26.118	26.574	28.618	29.34	30.202

Sources: Parl. Papers 1857, Session 2, v. 29, pp. 70–1, for the years 1853–6; 1857–8, v. 42, pp. 84–5, for 1856–7; and 1859, 2. v. 23, p. 176, for 1857–8.

Table 16.8. *The place of opium in India's total gross revenue, 1821–58 (£ million sterling)*

Year	Opium revenue 1	India's total gross revenue 2	Opium revenue expressed as a percentage of gross Indian revenue (col. 1 ÷ col. 2) 3
1821–2	1.46	21.80	6.70
1822–3	2.52	23.17	10.88
1823–4	1.36	21.28	6.39
1824–5	1.52	20.75	7.33
1825–6	0.94	21.13	4.45
1826–7	1.72	23.38	7.36
1827–8	2.05	22.86	8.97
1828–9	1.93	22.74	8.49
1829–30	1.53	21.70	7.05
1830–1	1.34	22.02	6.09

Table 16.8. (cont.)

Year	Opium revenue 1	India's total gross revenue 2	Opium revenue expressed as a percentage of gross Indian revenue (col. 1 ÷ col. 2) 3
1831–2	1.44	18.32	7.86
1832–3	1.29	18.48	6.98
1833–4	1.49	17.67	8.43
1834–5	1.27	26.86	4.73
1835–6	1.88	20.15	9.33
1836–7	2.15	21	10.24
1837–8	2.28	20.86	10.93
1838–9	1.64	21.16	7.75
1839–40	0.78	20.12	3.88
1840–1	1.43	20.85	6.86
1841–2	1.60	21.84	7.33
1842–3	2.09	22.62	9.24
1843–4	2.64	23.59	11.19
1844–5	2.85	23.67	12.04
1845–6	3.58	24.27	14.75
1846–7	3.68	26.08	14.11
1847–8	2.74	24.91	11.00
1848–9	3.91	25.4	15.39
1849–50	4.50	27.52	16.35
1850–1	3.80	27.63	13.75
1851–2	4.26	27.83	15.31
1852–3	5.09	28.61	17.79
1853–4	4.48	28.28	15.84
1854–5	4.69	29.13	16.10
1855–6	4.87	30.82	15.80
1856–7	4.69	33.30	14.08
1857–8	6.86	31.71	21.63
Average	2.66	23.88	10.61

Note: If we compare the figures for the years 1853–8 in col. 2 with those in the last row in Table 16.7, we shall find that the former are larger than the latter. The explanation lies in the fact that the former represents the total gross revenue of India, while the latter is the sum of only twenty major revenues of India.

Sources: For col. 1, see Parl. Papers 1825, v. 24, pp. 6 and 14, for the years 1821–3; 1828, v. 23, pp. 6 and 14, for 1823–6; 1831, v. 19, pp. 30 and 38, for 1826–8; 1834, v. 44, pp. 4 and 12, for 1828–32; 1837–8, v. 41, pp. 4 and 16, for 1832–5; 1840, v. 37, pp. 180 and 190, for 1835–8; 1843, v. 25, pp. 50 and 60, for 1838–41; 1846, v. 31, pp. 14 and 24, for 1841–4; 1849, v. 39, pp. 12 and 22, for 1844–7; 1852, v. 36, pp. 16 and 28, for 1847–50; 1854–5, v. 40, pp. 16 and 28, for 1850–3; 1856, v. 45, pp. 16 and 28, for 1853–5; 1857–8, v. 42, pp. 87 and 93, for 1855–6; 1859, Session 2, v. 23, pp. 112 and 116, for 1857–8. In the above Parliamentary Papers, the first page reference is about Bengal, and the second about Bombay. For col. 2, see Parl. Papers 1859, Session 2, v. 23, pp. 78–9.

The problem of India

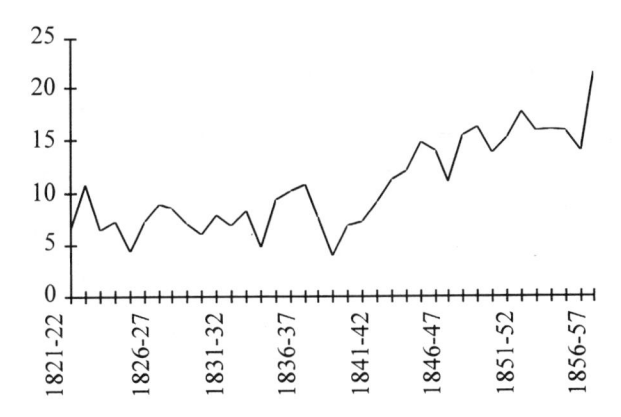

Figure 16.2. Gross opium revenue expressed as a percentage of gross Indian revenue, 1821–8 (based on column 3 of Table 16.8)

Table 16.8 shows that the opium revenue had a modest beginning, comprising merely 6.7 per cent of the total gross revenue of British India in 1821–2. This rose to 21.63 per cent in 1857–8.[29] This percentage rise from 1821 to 1858, as represented in column 3 of Table 16.8, is shown in Figure 16.2.

VI. Nearly all the opium went to China

In Bengal, the opium was auctioned at Calcutta to private traders who were then free to ship it to wherever they could find a market.[30] The currency used was the Indian rupee. (British statistians did not convert the rupee into sterling, so the tables in the rest of this chapter follow suit).

The bulk of auctioned opium went to China, as shown in the British statistics on which Table 16.9 has been compiled. These statistics were confirmed by the

to the exchange rate of 2s. to the rupee. (This rate was employed in Parl. Papers 1856, v. 45, p. 16.) Then I added up the triennial gross opium revenues in Bengal and Bombay. Finally, I rounded off the figures as before at two decimal points of £1 million to make them more readable.
29. This coincided with a decrease in land revenue because of the mutiny which erupted in 1857.
30. K. N. Chaudhuri, 'Foreign Trade and Balance of Payments (1857–1947)', in Kumar (ed.), *The Cambridge Economic History of India*, v. 2, p. 847. The practice of auctioning opium to private traders began in 1800, when the Emperor of China issued an edict prohibiting the importation of opium. The law-abiding East India Company thereupon ceased to sell opium at Canton and indeed prohibited carriage of the drug in any of its ships. 'Its good faith was so fully recognized that, through all the years which followed, its ships were never subjected to inspection or restraint because of opium.' To continue the trade, however, the Company auctioned Bengal opium in Calcutta and disclaimed any further responsibility for opium once it was sold by auction, leaving the private traders to smuggle the drug into China at their own risk. See Morse, *International Relations of the Chinese Empire*, v. 1, p. 176.

Table 16.9. *Bengal opium (Behar and Benares) exported to China and the straits settlements, 1829–64 (number of chests)*

Year	China 1	Singapore, Penang, etc. 2	Total 3	Gross revenue (Rs. millions) 4
1829–30	7,443	2.235	9,678	12.26
1830–1	5,590	1,526	7,116	10.90
1831–2	6,750	757	7,507	11.78
1832–3	7,540	1,845	9,385	11.93
1833–4	10,151	1,779	11,930	12.30
1834–5	9,480	1,570	11,050	10.86
1835–6	13,021	1,786	14,807	17.30
1836–7	10,493	2,241	12,734	18.34
1837–8	16,112	3,195	19,307	21.14
1838–9	14,499	3,722	18,221	14.60
1939–40	3,755	14,755	18,510	7.79
1840–1	5,817	11,593	17,410	11.36
1841–2	10,752	8,987	19,739	14.50
1842–3	11,867	4,651	16,518	17.16
1843–4	13,067	4,792	17,859	23.45
1844–5	14,709	4,083	18,792	24.39
1845–6	16,265	4,288	20,553	27.94
1846–7	20,668	4,322	24,990	31.25
1847–8	19,434	4,443	23,877	24.23
1848–9	27,870	4,417	32,287	28.38
1849–50	30,996	4,097	35,093	35.91
1850–1	28,892	4,010	32,902	31.55
1851–2	27,921	4,385	32,306	31.38
1852–3	31,433	4,745	36,178	40.20
1853–4	33,941	6,854	40,795	36.80
1854–5	43,952	7,469	51,421	36.95
1855–6	37,851	7,087	44,938	36.39
1856–7	36,459	5,982	42,441	38.19
1857–8	31,878	6,735	38,613	47.46
1858–9	33,858	827	34,685	51.75
1859–60	22,329	3,621	25.950	43.21
1860–1	15,688	3,621	19,309	35.72
1861–2	21,332	5,240	26,572	44.13
1862–3	25,846	6,815	32,661	46.41
1863–4	33,815	8,806	42,621	52.07

Source: Parl. Papers 1865, v. 40, pp. 92–4.

The problem of India

observations of U.S. merchants trading in China, one of whom wrote, 'It must be admitted, however, that China generally takes off the whole product of India'.[31] Even the small quantities of opium shipped from India to the straits settlements of Singapore, Penang, and so forth appear to have been destined for the Chinese market, smuggled there by Chinese junks.[32] Since most of the opium was sold in China, the sharp decline for the years 1839–42 might be explained by the fact that these were the years of the Opium War, following a vigorous campaign by Commissioner Lin to suppress the drug. The sharp rise in 1848 was probably due to the P&O beginning to carry opium cargo to China. The impact of steam on the opium trade was important. Early in the century, the east India Company held two public sales each year in Calcutta. Shortly after P&O carried its first opium cargo, the government decided to have sales monthly to achieve its policy of 'an annually increasing . . . supply'.[33] Let us graph column 1 of Table 16.9 to get an impression of the pattern of Bengal's opium exports to China (see Figure 16.3).

Here again, the sharp fall in this graph for the year 1839–40 can be explained; it was the time when Commissioner Lin vigorously suppressed opium in China. His seizure and burning of Indian opium, as we know, led to the Opium War.[34]

The second sharp decline in 1860–1 is more difficult to account for. That decline had in fact begun, albeit gently, in 1855–6. How much of it may be attributed to the general insurrection in the Canton area in 1855–6?[35] The decline continued with the outbreak of the *Arrow* War after 1856. May we blame it on the *Arrow* War?

The most dramatic fall happened in 1860, when the allied British and French forces fought their way into Beijing, ransacked the capital, and burned the Summer Palace. It seems unlikely that patriotic Chinese addicts[36] therefore boycotted British Indian opium in 1860. Moreover, there was almost no alternative to Indian opium. Turkish opium was considered very inferior, and little of it was sold in China;[37] so was Persian opium, which at this time made its way to western China overland through Bokhara – an obscure and tedious

31. A letter from a U.S. merchant to the U.S. minister to China, William Reed, dated 28 August 1858, Shanghai, and collected in *Correspondence Relative to the Earl of Elgin's Special Missions to China and Japan*, 1857–59, pp. 396–8: para. 25.
32. This is one of the discoveries made by Bakhala in his thesis – see his 'Indian Opium', pp. 74ff. Another discovery is the export of opium from Nepal by land to China via Lhasa.
33. Jardine Matheson Archive, reel 171, Calcutta, nos. 3254 and 3373, 2 and 27 July 1847. See also Harcourt, 'Black Gold', p. 11.
34. See, e.g., Chang, *Commissioner Lin*, chapters 5–6.
35. For details of the gravity of that general insurrection, see my *Yeh Ming-ch'en*, chapter 6.
36. Not all opium smokers are addicts; it all depends on the degree to which a smoker has become dependent on the drug. For a revisionist study on the opium smokers in China, see R. K. Newman, 'Opium Smoking in Late Imperial China', *Modern Asian Studies*, 29, no. 4 (1995), pp. 765–94.
37. Owen, *British Opium Policy*, pp. 68–9.

The economics of imperialism

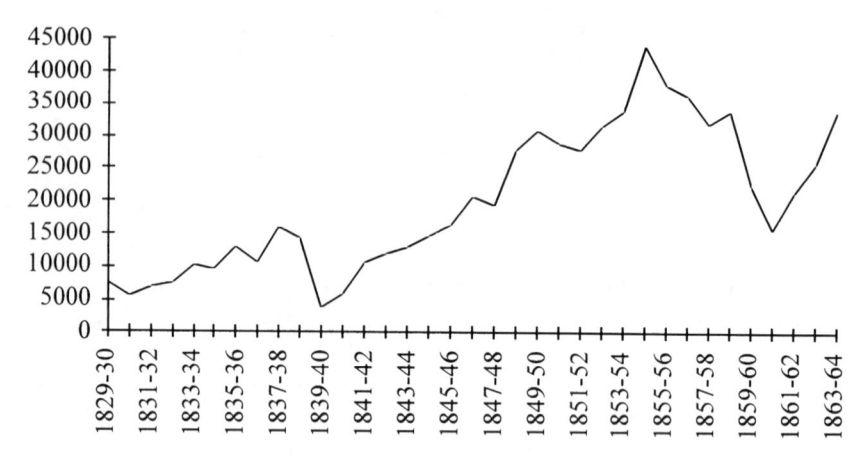

Figure 16.3. Bengal opium exported to China, 1829–64 (number of chests; based on column 1, Table 16.9)

route.[38] If we may not attribute the sharp fall in 1860–1 to the situation in China, probably we may not interpret the more gentle slide in 1855–60 in the same way.

I am more inclined to think, therefore, that these falls were related to supply in Bengal.

To verify this hypothesis, I have drawn up Figure 16.4 on the basis of column 1 (opium supply to China) and column 2 (opium supply to the straits settlements of Singapore, Penang, etc.) of Table 16.9. Therein, we find that the sharp fall in opium use in China during the Opium War was greeted by a sharp rise in the straits settlements.[39] On the other hand, the decline in China in the latter half of the 1850s corresponds to a similar decline in the straits settlement. I suggest that only a shortfall in supply would have this general effect.

This hypothesis is further confirmed by the pattern of the export of Malwa opium from Bombay to China, as shown in Table 16.10. In the year 1860–1, there was a dramatic rise in the supply of Malwa opium to China when, as mentioned, the supply of Bengal opium to China experienced a sharp decline. I suggest that the extra demand for Malwa opium was caused by the shortfall in Bengal opium.

This hypothesis may be further strengthened by graphing the supply of both Bengal and Malwa opium to China. We shall have to begin with 1848–9,

38. Ibid., p. 287.
39. It seems, therefore, that the British merchants might have a setback in their sales of opium to China during the Opium War; however, Indian opium reexported from the straits settlements by Chinese smugglers was not affected and, in fact, increased its sales in China.

The problem of India

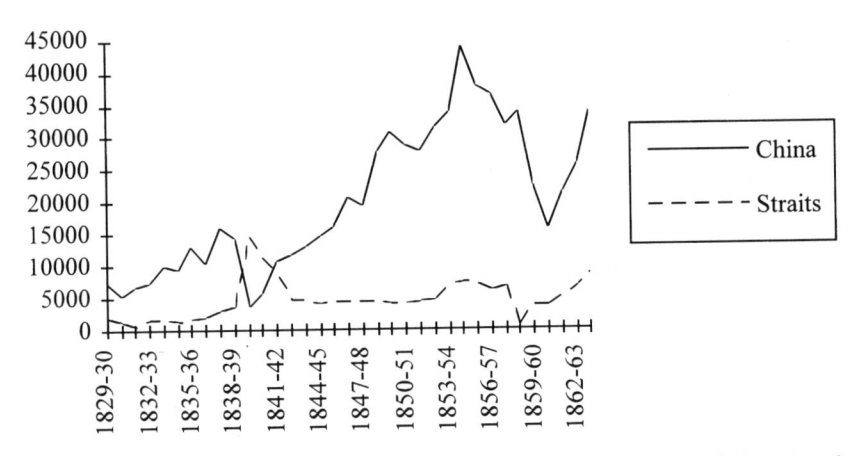

Figure 16.4. Bengal opium exported to China and the straits settlements, 1829–64 (number of chests; based on columns 1 and 2, Table 16.9)

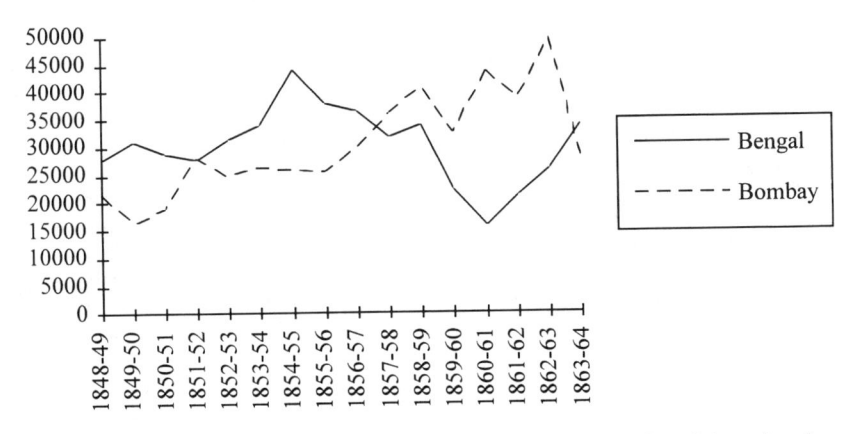

Figure 16.5. Bengal and Malwa opium exported to China, 1849–64 (number of chests; based on column 1, Table 16.9, and column 1, Table 16.10)

however, to obtain a continuous graph, because there are blanks in the duty for Malwa opium in some of the earlier years. It will be seen that for the period 1848–64, the falls in the supply of Bengal opium were always compensated by rises in the supply of Malwa opium (see Figure 16.5).

If we add up Bengal opium and Malwa opium and chart this total annual supply to China, we have a graph that leaves little room for dispute. Again, we shall have to begin with 1848–9 in order to obtain a continuous graph. We find in Figure 16.6 that the graph is fairly steady. It still has rises and falls, but

403

Table 16.10. *Malwa opium exported via Bombay to China, 1830–64*

Year	No. of chests exported to China 1	Rate of pass fees per chest (Rs.) 2	Amount of pass fees (Rs. millions) 3	Cost of collection (Rs. millions) 4
1830–1[a]	4,610.00	175	0.81	0.06
1831–2[a]	10,679.00	175	1.87	0.03
1832–3[a]	6,698.00	175	1.17	0.02
1833–4[a]	10,855.00	175	1.90	0.03
1834–5[a]	6,812.00	175	1.19	0.02
1835–6[b]	—	175 and 125	1.60	0.02
1836–7	20,882.50	125	2.43	0.06
1837–8	10,372.50	125	1.50	0.06
1838–9	17,353.0	125	2.68	0.05
1839–40[b]	—	125	0.08	0.05
1840–1	12,022.50	125	2.25	0.04
1841–2[a]	14,473.00	125	1.81	0.05
1842–3[a]	19,369.00	125	2.42	0.03
1843–4[a]	16,944.00	200	3.39	0.03
1844–5[a]	18,150.50	200	3.63	0.04
1845–6[b]	—	200 and 300	6.03	0.04
1846–7	17,389.75	300	6.01	0.04
1847–8[b]	—	300 and 400	3.72	0.04
1848–9	21,392.25	400	8.91	0.05
1849–50	16,513.00	400	7.32	0.04
1850–1	19.138.00	400	6.98	0.04
1851–2	28,168.50	400	11.30	0.04
1852–3	24,979.50	400	11.16	0.04
1853–4	26,113.50	400	9.60	0.04
1854–5	25,958.25	400	11.00	0.06
1855–6	25,576.00	400	10.06	0.06
1856–7	29,846.50	400	11.57	0.06
1857–8	36,125.50	400	16.16	0.06
1858–9	40,849.00	400	14.44	0.06
1859–60	32,534.00	400 and 500	15.36	0.06
1860–1	43,691.00	500 and 600	24.40	0.07
1861–2	38,680.00	600 and 700	24.44	0.07
1862–3	49,485.50	700 and 600	32.43	0.03
1863–4	28,210.50	600	14.84	0.04

Note: Any amount below 1 rupee is omitted from this table.

[a] No record exists for supplying the exact number of chests exported to China during the years so marked, and the figures in column 2 have therefore been approximately calculated from the figures in column 4 by the statisticians who originally complied this table.

[b] In the years so marked, approximations are impossible, two rates of duty having existed, while the actual number of chests is not recorded.

Source: Parl. Papers 1865, v. 49, p. 86.

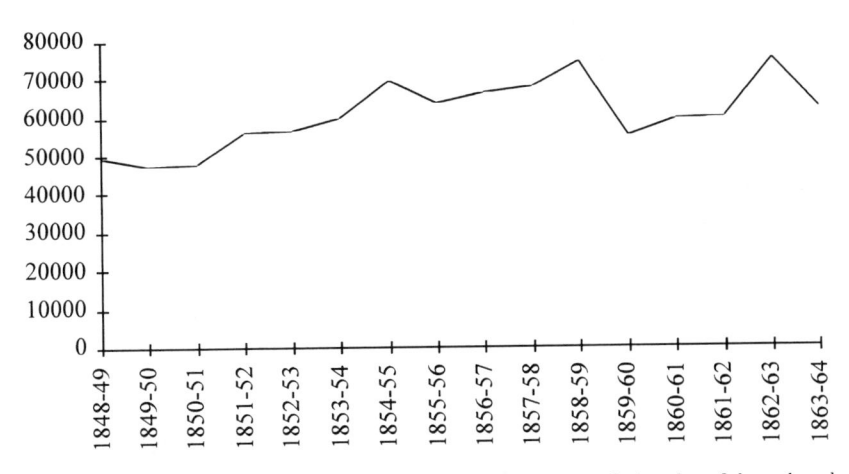

Figure 16.6. Total Bengal and Malwa opium exported to China, 1849–64 (number of chests; based on column 1, Table 16.9, and column 1, Table 16.10)

nothing as spectacular as those found in Figure 16.4. This suggests that the demand in China was fairly steady.

The resolution of one question raises another. If the shortfall in the supply of Bengal opium in China had been compensated by an increase in the supply of Malwa opium, why should opium still have fetched such a phenomenally high price in 1860–1 when auctioned at Calcutta? These high prices were, of course, directly related to the demand in China. The high prices in China, therefore, are reflected in Table 16.9. There, in 1860–1, the mere 15,688 chests of Bengal opium shipped to China (together with the 3,621 chests shipped to the straits settlements,[40] totalling 19,309 chests), had fetched about Rs. 35.72 million when auctioned at Calcutta.[41] The price was about Rs. 1849.91 per chest. However, in 1854–5, the 43,952 chests of Bengal opium shipped to China (together with the 7,469 chests shipped to the straits, totalling 51,421 chests), had fetched only about Rs. 36.95 million when auctioned at Calcutta.[42] The price then had been merely Rs. 718.58 per chest. Thus, the price in 1860–1 was more than 2.57 times that of 1854–5.

It seems that there was a similar rise in the price of Malwa opium. One indication of this is the escalation in the fees charged on Malwa opium passing through the British port of Bombay on its way to China. As column 2 in Table

40. Most of these, as noted earlier, would have been reexported to China.
41. That is, before they were shipped to China or to the straits settlements, whence most were then reexported to China. See the year 1860–1 in Table 16.9.
42. See the year 1854–5 in Table 16.9.

16.10 shows, the rate went up from Rs. 400 to Rs. 500 per chest in 1859–60, to Rs. 600 per chest in 1860–1, and to Rs. 700 per chest in 1861–2.

Again, it seems that these high prices were directly related to demand in China. The high prices of opium in China may be explained by the miserable state to which China had been reduced by domestic unrest and foreign war. The Taiping Rebellion began in 1851 and was not suppressed until 1864. About 20 million people perished;[43] the devastation was unbelievable.[44] The Red Turban Rebellion started in the Canton area in 1854, claiming still more lives and causing more misery.[45] The *Arrow* War erupted in 1856–7, ending with the devastation of Beijing in 1860. The despairing survivors may have sought refuge in opium regardless of its cost.

VII. Opium, tea, silk, and the United Kingdom's global trade balance

The money obtained by selling opium in China was used by the British merchants to buy tea and silk; and they had more cash than they could spend. The British superintendent of trade in the Far East, Charles Elliot, once made a most revealing remark. He testified that in 1836 Bengal opium fetched $18 million in China.[46] The number of chests of Bengal opium sold in China in that year was 10,151.[47] Thus, the sale price per chest was about $1,773, or £443.3.[48]

Elliot also made the interesting observation that the $18 million fetched by the sale of Bengal opium was about $1 million in excess of the combined value of the two staple exports of tea and silk. This testimony indicates the usefulness of searching for the pertinent statistics for that year and tracing similar statistics both backwards to when they first became available and forwards up to the *Arrow* War, a total of twenty years. The result is Table 16.11. Here, the values in column 1 are not compatible with those in columns 2, 3, and 4. But as mentioned before, the values are perceptions rather than reality. Therefore, compatibility is not an issue. It should also be noted that the British merchants

---

43. See Flavia Anderson, *The Rebel Emperor* (London, Victor Gollancz, 1958), p. 7.
44. See Yung Wing, *My Life in China and America* (New York, Holt, 1912; Arno reprint, 1978), chapter 12.
45. See my *Yeh Ming-ch'en*, chapter 6.
46. Elliot to Palmerston, 1 February 1837, Parl. Papers 1840, v. 36, p. 90, quoted in Costin, *Great Britain and China*, p. 50. Elliot referred to Indian opium; but he would have known only the value of Bengal opium, which in India was under the control of the British East India Company. He would have had no idea of the total value of Malwa opium smuggled to China by the Parsees. Strictly speaking, therefore, what he meant by Indian opium was only Bengal opium.
47. See Table 16.9, which is based on Parl. Papers 1865, v. 40, pp. 92–4.
48. This figure is obtained by converting $1,773 at the rate of 5s for $1 (see the rate used in Parl. Papers 1840, v. 37, pp. 247–88).

Table 16.11. *Value of Bengal opium and Chinese tea and silk, 1928–57 (£ million sterling)*

Year	Opium: Declared value (in India) 1	Tea: Official value (based on Chinese prices) 2	Silk: Official value (based on Chinese prices) 3	Total value of tea and silk (based on Chinese prices; col. 3 + col. 4) 4
1828	1.263	3.268	0.078	3.346
1829	1.393	3.054	0.044	3.098
1830	1.480	3.190	0.007	3.197
1831	2.326	3.165	0.003	3.168
1832	1.804	3.171	0.010	3.181
1833	2.272	3.206	0.008	3.214
1834	1.910	3.203	0.214	3.417
1835	2.866	4.205	0.272	4.477
1836	3.934	4.852	0.474	5.326
1837	2.904	3.650	0.703	4.353
1838	2.791	3.900	0.279	4.179
1839	0.191	3.719	0.130	3.849
1840	1.268	2.258	0.091	2.349
1841	1.939	2.764	0.102	2.866
1842	2.820	3.741	0.066	3.807
1843	4.230	4.278	0.110	4.388
1844	4.134	5.175	0.141	5.316
1845	5.542	5.071	0.437	5.508
1846	4.271	5.453	0.678	6.131
1847	3.508	5.536	0.748	6.284
1848	5.346	4.735	0.862	5.597
1849	5.544	5.310	0.696	6.006
1850	5.074	4.937	0.700	5.637
1851	6.082	6.949	0.842	7.791
1852	6.471	6.530	0.945	7.475
1853	5.802	6.864	1.211	8.075
Computed real value				
1854	5.685	5.380	3.583	8.963
1855	5.593	5.119	3.433	8.552
1856	6.506	5.123	4.106	9.229
1857	8.241	4.310	6.911	11.221

Sources: For the value of opium in India, see Parl. Papers 1859, Session 2, v. 23, pp. 322–3. For the value of tea and silk bought in China, see ibid., p. 319.

paid for the freight and other services en route to China, where they sold the opium to local Chinese smugglers.

According to this table, it seems that in 1836 the British merchants bought tea and silk to the total value of £5,326,139. Thus, the opium, while still in India, was worth £1,391,680 less than the combined value of tea and silk in China. Once the opium was shipped to China and sold to Chinese smugglers, the money fetched was sufficient not only to have made up this difference and to have paid for freight and other services, but to leave extra cash to the order of $1 million, or £250,000.[49] Using the same ratio for the other years, the extra cash would have been tripled in the years immediately preceding the *Arrow* War, because the amount of Bengal opium sold in China approximately tripled and because the British managed to keep the selling price fairly steady.[50] The main point here is that opium had always more than paid for the tea and silk purchased in China.

Assuming that the extra cash per annum for the years 1854–7 was $3 million, or £750,000, the amount fetched annually by selling Bengal opium to China would be £9.713, £9.302, £9.979, and £11.971 millions.[51] The significance of this to the United Kingdom's global balance of trade is made obvious in Table 16.12. Again, we have to begin with 1854 because the computed real value of imports into the United Kingdom was 'not ascertained' until that year.[52] And until then, Britons did not seem to realize that they had a phenomenal global trade deficit, which would have been made much worse if they did not have Bengal opium to sell to China.

The actual deficit was far worse than what these figures convey. Recall that the British merchant princes panicked when they heard about the disruption of trade in China, saying that their Indian buyers depended on opium sales to purchase British products.[53] Thus, the loss of these sales also meant the loss of substantial sales to India. A rough impression of this combined loss is conveyed in Table 16.13. It is curious that the figures in columns 1 and 2 are so close to each other.

The loss of U.K. exports to India would compound the problem of the United Kingdom's balance of trade in visible commodities. The deficit presumably was made good by invisible exports. It is in *this* area that the theory of gentlemanly capitalism comes into its own.

---

49. Converted at the round figure of 5s. for $1, $1 million dollars would be £250,000.
50. See Table 16.9, col. 1. For the ability of the British to keep the selling price fairly steady, see later in this chapter.
51. These figures are obtained by adding £0.5 to those in col. 4 of Table 16.11 for the years 1854–7.
52. See Parl. Papers 1856, v. 56, pp. 11–12.
53. Chang, *Commissioner Lin*, pp. 192–3, quoting Parl. Papers 'Memorials Addressed to Her Majesty's Government by British Merchants Interested in the Trade with China' (1840).

Table 16.12. *Opium and the United Kingdom's balance of trade, 1854–7 (computed real value in £ million sterling)*

Year	Total imports 1	Total exports 2	Deficit (col. 1 − col. 2) 3	Opium sales in China 4	Deficit (without opium sales in China; col. 3 + col. 4) 5
1854	152.389	115.821	36.568	9.713	46.281
1855	143.542	116.691	26.851	9.302	36.153
1856	172.544	139.220	33.324	9.979	43.303
1857	187.844	146.174	41.670	11.970	53.640

Sources: Figures for cols. 1–2 are from Parl. Papers 1857–8, v. 54, p. 11. Col. 4 is taken from Table 16.11, col. 4, adding £0.75 to each figure therein.

Table 16.13. *Opium and U.K. exports to India, 1854–7 (computed real value in £ million sterling)*

Year	Bengal opium sales in China 1	U.K. exports to India 2	Deficit (without opium money) 3	Assumed deficit (col. 2 + col. 3) 4
1854	9.173	9.128	46.281	55.409
1855	9.302	9.949	36.153	46.102
1856	9.979	10.546	43.303	53.849
1857	11.970	11.667	53.640	65.307

Source: Cols. 1 and 3 are taken from Table 16.12. Col. 2 is from Parl. Papers 1857–8, v. 54, p. 15.

Indeed, Bengal opium worked more wonders than those already described. As mentioned in Chapter 9, Lord Ellenborough was the first to put it in the context of Britain's global trade. Having been governor-general of India and three times president of the Board of Control of India, he spoke with authority on the subject. He said that the sale of Bengal opium to China was a great link in the chain of commerce with which Britain had surrounded the world. The chain worked like this. The United Kingdom paid the United States for cotton by bills upon England. The Americans took some of those bills to Canton and swapped them for tea. The Chinese exchanged the bills for Indian opium. Some of the bills were remitted to England as profit; others were taken to India to buy additional commodities, as well as to furnish the money remittance of

Table 16.14. *Bengal opium and U.S. cotton, 1854–7 (computed real value in £ million sterling)*

Year	Bengal opium sales in China 1	Purchase of U.S. raw cotton 2	Opium receipts expressed as a percentage of cotton purchases (col. 1 ÷ col. 2) 3
1854	9.713	20.175	48.144
1855	9.302	20.849	44.616
1856	9.979	26.448	37.731
1857	11.97	29.289	40.869

Sources: Col. 1 is taken from Table 16.14, col. 2. Col. 2 is from Parl. Papers 1857–8, v. 54, p. 13. Col. 3 is truncated to the nearest decimal.

private fortunes in India and the funds for carrying on the Indian government at home.[54]

How much of the Bengal opium returns in China went towards paying for U.S. cotton? Ellenborough did not specify. It might not have been a phenomenal amount because the bulk of it appears to have been used to purchase tea and silk. Nonetheless, a comparison of the amount of money expended on buying U.S. raw cotton with the money received by selling Bengal opium in China can be revealing. Table 16.14 shows that opium receipts could pay for about 38 to 48 per cent of the U.S. cotton that fuelled the British Industrial Revolution.

VIII. The role of Chinese silver bullion in the Indian economy

In the preceding section, we found that there was a surplus of about $2 million in silver bullion after Chinese tea and silk had been purchased with opium money. This surplus was attributable to the sale of opium only, as the value of other goods sold by British and Indian merchants to China was not counted herein. We also saw in the preceding chapter that in the year 1833–4, when the pertinent trade figures were complete and reliable under the East India Company monopoly, $6,941,934 worth of silver bullion was shipped out of China as a result of the company's trade surplus.[55] What happened to this silver?

54. Ellenborough, 26 February 1857, Hansard, 3d series, v. 144, col. 1363.
55. It will be remembered that this figure was arrived by comparing Table 11.3 with Table 11.4.

The problem of India

Part of this silver surplus was transported to British India, where it helped resolve the silver scarcity for minting.[56] There was increasing demand for this precious metal, as the Indian silver rupee had become the medium for the entire trading network of the Indian Ocean.[57] Some of this Chinese silver was also used to purchase British manufactures (especially in Bombay) and found its way to the United Kingdom.[58] Some was used by the British and Indian merchants to purchase spices and other goods in Southeast Asia for India and for reexport to the Middle East.[59]

Furthermore, this silver surplus does not include large fortunes made by the Parsees who smuggled Malwa opium into China, as Malwa opium was never under the control of the company. One of these, Jamshetji Jeejeebhoy (1783–1859), deposited a net profit of 30 million rupees in the Bank of Bombay.[60] This is not to count the commodities which the Parsees had already purchased in China and shipped back to India, including tea, silk goods, camphor, cinnamon, copper, brass, and Chinese gold.[61] All in all, the Indian and British merchants trading with China contributed greatly to the rise and prosperity of Bombay, for example.[62] One indication of this prosperity was the number of banks formed in rapid succession: the Presidency Bank of Bengal in 1836, the Presidency Bank of Bombay in 1840, the Bank of Western India in 1842 (renamed the Oriental Bank in 1845), and the Mercantile Bank of India, London and China in 1855.[63]

The conventional wisdom is that the United Kingdom was buying a lot of tea and silk from China, but that China was not buying anything equal in value; hence the United Kingdom was obliged to sell Indian opium to China to balance the books.[64] This was true enough, but only of the situation as seen in the United Kingdom. The present research shows that opium was not just helping to balance the United Kingdom's trade with China. It generated huge profits; it funded imperial expansion and maintenance in India; it provided the much needed silver to develop the trading network among the countries bordering on the Indian Ocean; it assisted the growth of Bombay and other Indian cities; it enabled the United Kingdom to obtain tea and raw silk from

---

56. Bakhala, 'Indian Opium', pp. 310ff and 333.
57. See W. H. Chaloner, 'Currency Problems of the British Empire', in Barrie M. Ratcliffe (ed.), *Great Britain and Her World, 1750–1914, Essays in Honour of W. O. Henderson* (Manchester, Manchester University Press, 1975).
58. Bakhala, 'Indian Opium', pp. 310 and 333.
59. Ibid., pp. 310 and 341.
60. Sunil Kumar Sen, *The House of Tata, 1839–1939* (Calcutta, Progressive, 1975), p. 8.
61. Ibid., p. 9.
62. See S. M. Edwardes, *The Rise of Bombay: A Retrospect* (Bombay, Times of India, 1902).
63. Sen, *House of Tata*, p. 12.
64. The tone was set by the most influential pioneer in the field, Hosea Ballou Morse, in his tome *The International Relations of the Chinese Empire*. See, in particular, v. 1, p. 540.

Table 16.15. *The triangular trade, 1854–7 (computed real value in £ million sterling)*

Year	U.K. exports to China 1	U.K. imports from China 2	U.K. exports to India 3	U.K. imports from India 4	Bengal opium sales in China 5	Chinese exports to India 6
1854	0.533	9.125	9.128	10.673	9.463	0.81
1855	0.889	8.747	9.949	12.669	9.052	0.92
1856	1.415	9.422	10.546	17.263	9.729	0.79
1857	1.729	11.449	11.667	18.650	11.721	0.62

Sources: Col. 1 is from Parl. Papers 1857–8, v. 54, p. 14; col. 2 from ibid., p. 12; col. 3 from ibid., p. 15; col. 4 from ibid., p. 13; col. 5 from Table 16.12, col. 4; col. 6 from Table 15.9, col. 1, which does not include the value of the goods the Parsees bought from China, because it is not available.

China for very little initial cost, and it was a great help in the United Kingdom's global balance of payments.

In addition, this China trade was a channel of remittance from India to London – the United Kingdom wanted Chinese tea, but not Indian opium. The Chinese tea so obtained, in turn, enabled the United Kingdom to levy a duty and hence to derive a revenue equivalent to a good part of the Royal Navy's annual budget (see Chapter 14). The Chinese raw silk so obtained kept some United Kingdom mills running and more ships sailing (see Chapter 10). Thus, there is obvious danger in restricting one's view to the scene in the United Kingdom alone because of the increasing complexities of international relations and trade. Greenberg noticed a flow of goods from India to China, and from China to the United Kingdom – the so-called triangular trade. His observation, however, has barely scratched the surface of what were significant economic interests to India and to the United Kingdom,[65] all of which depended to a large extent on one commodity – opium.

Let us quantify the computed real value of this triangular trade, as set out in Table 16.15. Unfortunately columns 5 and 6 are do not represent a complete picture of Indian exports to China, nor Chinese exports to India, because statistics for other aspects of the trade, such as the value of Malwa opium smuggled to China by the Parsees, do not exist. The figures for the value of goods which the Parsees bought from China may not be found either. If all such figures were available, the importance of opium would clearly be greater.

65. Tan Chung has developed Greenberg's observation. See his 'The British–China–India Trade Triangle, 1771–1840'.

IX. What if opium were suppressed in China?

As we saw, an attempt was made by China to suppress opium in 1839–40, but the Opium War put an end to it. However, the drug was not legalized by the Treaty of Nanking, which concluded the peace. However hard the British negotiators pushed the issue at the time, the Chinese authorities simply would not agree. Meanwhile, British policy makers realized that as long as opium was illegal in China, their position remained defenceless. They had to live with the fear that someday China could quite legitimately enforce its prohibition against the drug.

Even at the time of the Opium War, Lord Palmerston had directed Her Majesty's plenipotentiaries 'that if any British Subject shall introduce into China, Commodities which are prohibited by the Law of China, such commodities may be seized and confiscated by the Officers of the Chinese Government'.[66] To the Chinese emperor he conceded that the government of China had every right to seize and confiscate 'all the opium which they could find within the Chinese territory, and which had been brought into that territory in violation of the Law'. Thus, Chinese enforcement of the prohibition against opium was not what the British government was officially complaining about in 1840. In any case it could not in terms of the rule of law. Thus, it tried to argue that the Chinese government had 'determined to seize peaceable British Merchants, instead of seizing the contraband opium'.[67]

Pursuant to the rule of law, therefore, the British authorities, subsequent to the Opium War, persisted in their efforts to persuade the Chinese authorities to legalize opium.[68] Then they tried to persuade them to revise the Treaty of Nanking to this effect.[69] When both attempts failed, they resorted to war to make the Chinese change the law.

All this explains why London readily used the *Arrow* incident as a casus belli for a war which Whitehall had been plotting with the French. Lord Elgin was given the onerous task of demanding the legalization of the opium trade.[70] A deeply sensitive man, Elgin found it repugnant to impose on a defeated government so deleterious a change in its law. Thus, the Treaty of Tientsin was signed on 26 June 1858 without opium being legalized. Elgin elaborated on his position about four months later:

66. Lord Palmerston to the Plenipotentiaries (Admiral G. Elliot and Captain C. Elliot) Appointed to treat with the Chinese Government, Foreign Office, 20 February 1840, reprinted in full in Morse, *International Relations of the Chinese Empire*, v. 1, pp. 526–30: Appendix B, p. 629.
67. Lord Palmerston to the Minister of the Emperor of China, Foreign Office, 20 February 1840, reprinted in full in ibid., pp. 621–6: Appendix A, p. 623.
68. See the pertinent entries in my *Anglo-Chinese Relation*.
69. Lord Clarendon quite specifically instructed Bowring 'To effect the legalization of the Opium Trade'. Clarendon to Bowring, Desp. 2, 13 February 1854, FO17/210.
70. Clarendon to Elgin, 20 April 1858, in *Earl of Elgin's Special Missions to China and Japan, 1857–59*, pp. 4–6: para. 11.

The economics of imperialism

When I resolved not to press this matter upon the attention of the Chinese Commissioners at Tientsin, I did so not because I questioned the advantages which would accrue from the legalization of the traffic, but because I could not reconcile it to my sense of right to urge the Imperial [Chinese] Government to abandon its traditional policy in this respect, under the kind of pressure which we were bringing to bear upon it at Tientsin.[71]

The failure to legalize opium caused much dismay among the British opium smugglers in China. Articles 48 and 49 of the Treaty of Tientsin occasioned further unease. Article 48 read: 'If any British merchant vessel be concerned in Smuggling, the goods, whatever their value or nature, shall be subject to confiscation by the Chinese authorities, and the ship may be prohibited from trading further, and sent away as soon as her accounts shall have been adjusted and paid'. Article 49 read: 'All penalties enforced, or confiscations made, under this Treaty, shall belong and be appropriated to the public service of the Government of China'.[72] This was the letter of the law and reflected not only Elgin's sense of justice, but also the apparent Chinese government's determination to ban opium despite a second humiliating defeat by the British.

Even the U.S. merchants began lobbying their own minister in China to do something about it. As mentioned, Bengal opium was auctioned at Calcutta; anybody could buy opium there and ship it to wherever they liked. The Americans were next to the British in the amount of opium bought at auction and shipped to China. Of some 32,000 chests of Bengal opium imported illegally into Shanghai in 1857, for example, more than 6,300 belonged to the Americans.[73] In desperation, one U.S. merchant thought of an ingenious way to rectify the situation. Article 26 of the Treaty of Tientsin stipulated that the 'tariff shall be revised'. If the Chinese could be persuaded to revise the tariff in such a way as to include opium among the taxable imports, then opium would have been legalized de facto. He lobbied his minister, William Reed, to this effect,[74] and Reed was persuaded. In turn, Reed lobbied Elgin, appealing to his lordship's 'high sense of duty', urging him to 'induce or compel an adjustment of the pernicious difficulty' and assuring him that 'in such an attempt I shall cordially unite'.[75] Then came this powerful argument: 'I may be permitted to

71. Elgin to Reed, Shanghai, 10 October 1858, in *Earl of Elgin's Special Missions*, pp. 398-9, para. 2. William Reed was the U.S. minister to China.
72. See Treaty of Tientsin, reproduced in Michael Hurst (ed.), *Key Treaties for the Great Powers, 1814-1914* (Newton Abbot, David & Charles, 1972), p. 357.
73. Reed to Elgin, Shanghai, 13 September 1858, in *Earl of Elgin's Special Missions*, pp. 393-6: para. 12.
74. Letter from a U.S. merchant to William Reed, dated 28 August 1858, Shanghai, and in *Earl of Elgin's Special Missions*, pp. 396-8.
75. Reed to Elgin, Shanghai, 13 September 1858, in *Earl of Elgin's Special Missions*, pp. 393-6: para. 20. To strengthen his case, Reed enclosed a copy of the U.S. merchant's letter. See ibid., pp. 396-8.

The problem of India

suggest that perhaps no more propitious moment for so decisive and philanthropic a measure could be found than now, when the privileges of the East India Company, and what may be termed its active responsibilities, including the receipt and administration of the opium revenue, are about to be transferred to the Crown'.[76] Reed appears to have given Elgin just that additional push and support needed to carry out his instructions fully,[77] and so the responsibility for Bengal opium's breaking the law of China was soon to be transferred from the company to the British government.

It also seems that Reed's information about the behaviour of the Chinese officials at Shanghai had an additional effect on Elgin. These officials had begun breaking their own law by levying, sub rosa, a duty of twenty-four taels per chest on the contraband opium. Thereupon Reed deliberately professed that he was not clear how much of this illicit revenue went into the official local treasury, and how much into private pockets, because no published return was ever made.[78] In fact, what happened appears to have been that the governor-general of Liang Jiang, He Guiqing, deliberately contravened intructions from Beijing in order to get revenue to fight the Taipings.[79] Elgin's reaction was predictable: 'I shall not fail to instruct the gentlemen who are acting for me . . . to call the attention of the officers of the Chinese Government . . . to the considerations so ably stated in your letter'.[80] Whatever the reason, the impact on Elgin was the same. For the second conference on the tariff and trade rules, to be held on 13 October 1858 pursuant to Article 26 of the Treaty of Tientsin, Elgin instructed his deputies to broach the subject of opium legalization. The Chinese representatives made no objections. Thereupon opium was legalized by implication.[81]

Thus, one of the important origins of the *Arrow* War lay in Indian opium, upon which depended significant economic benefits to both India and the United Kingdom. In view of this analysis, the claim by Morse that 'the opium trade was not the cause which led the British government to engage in the first

76. Reed to Elgin, Shanghai, 13 September 1858, in *Earl of Elgin's Special Missions*, pp. 393–6: para. 21.
77. Morse, *International Relations of the Chinese Empire*, v. 1, pp. 553–4.
78. Reed to Elgin, Shanghai, 13 September 1858, *Earl of Elgin's Special Missions*, pp. 393–6, para. 13.
79. For the different priorities between the Emperor and regional leaders, such as He Guiqing, who had to confront the Taipings, see Guo Weimin, 'He Guiqing yu Xianfengti de duiwei zhengce zhi zheng jiqi yingxiang' (The disagreement between He Guiqing and Emperor Xiangeng on foreign policy). *Jindaishi yanjiu* (Modern Historical Studies), no. 6 (1993), pp. 77–89.
80. Elgin to Reed, Shanghai, 19 October 1858, in *Earl of Elgin's Special Missions*, pp. 398–9: para. 3.
81. Report on the Revision of Tariff etc., enclosed in Elgin to Malmesbury, Shanghai, 22 October 1858, and in *Earl of Elgins Special Missions*, pp. 400–403. Lord Malmesbury was now the foreign secretary, replacing Lord Clarendon.

war, ending with the Treaty of Nanking, nor did it contribute to the second war, ending with the Treaty of Tientsin',[82] cannot be sustained.

X. Further assessment of 'free-trade imperialism'

Other historians have interpreted both the Opium and the *Arrow* wars purely as a result of British determination to make China accept free trade, as if opium had very little to do with the conflicts.[83] 'The economic force behind the free traders was too great to be restricted or contained', wrote one scholar.[84] 'Opium did not even figure in the Treaty of Nanking',[85] wrote another. That opium did not feature in the Treaty of Nanking does not mean that opium had nothing to do with the Opium War. In addition, free trade might indeed have loomed very large in the minds of its believers. But as mentioned, policy makers often had considerations other than the passion of the time.[86] One of these, again, was the significance of opium to the Indian revenue, to the United Kingdom's revenue (by way of tea duty), and as an important medium in global trade.

If free trade had been the overriding principle of the British policy makers, then one of the very first things they would have done was open the opium industry of Bengal to free enterprise. But they did not. Indeed, when the British first acquired control of Bengal, they had every freedom in dealing with the opium question. As early as 1773, the governor of Bengal, Warren Hastings, had put three choices to the Bengal Council: first, monopoly by contract, which involved granting an exclusive concession to an individual or group to grow and market opium; second, monopoly by agency, that is, the East India Company would take into its own hands the entire production, manufacture, and sale of opium; third, free trade with every restriction removed, meaning there would be free entry into production by peasants and the trade laid open to all merchants indiscriminately. Despite his constant professions of free-trade principles, Hastings recommended monopoly by contract. His argument was that free trade would benefit ordinary commerce, but that opium was no ordinary commodity but rather 'a pernicious article of luxury, which ought not to be permitted but for purposes of foreign commerce only'.[87] In the end,

---

82. Morse, *International Relations of the Chinese Empire*, v. 1, p. 539.
83. See, e.g., Chang, *Commissioner Lin*; and Fairbank, *Trade and Diplomacy*.
84. Chang, *Commissioner Lin*, p. 15.
85. Platt, *Finance, Trade, and Politics*, p. 265, quoting Sargent, *Anglo-Chinese Commerce and Diplomacy*, p. 87.
86. With regard to the passion for free trade, see Bernard Semmel, *The Rise of Free Trade Imperialism: Classical Political Economy, the Empire of Free Trade and Imperialism, 1750–1850* (Cambridge University Press, 1970).
87. Letter from the president [Warren Hastings], Proceedings of President and Council, 15 October 1773, *Ninth Report from the Select Committee*, 1783 (henceforth cited as *Ninth Report*, 1783), App. 59A, quoted in Owen, *British Opium Policy*, pp. 22–3. Owen seems to be quite influenced

monopoly by contract was adopted.[88] The crux of Hastings's subsequent defence was the profits which monopoly by contract had brought to the company's treasury.[89] Thus, pragmatic economic interests, not abstract principles of free trade, were the deciding factor in this issue at the time.

It was the same pragmatism which, in 1797, led the company to go one step further towards absolute control. In that year, the company itself assumed a monopoly on Bengal opium.[90]

XI. Control of the opium market in China

Monopolistic control of opium was later extended from its source in Bengal to the market in China. The importance of controlling the market in China is obvious. Opium exporters might make high profits only if there was no competition, because competition would drive down the price paid in China. With this, we have to retell the story of Malwa opium from the beginning.

Bengal opium had been sold in China for a long time without competition. Small quantities of opium from Turkey and Persia had been sold there also. But they posed no threat to Bengal opium because, according to the taste of Chinese addicts, they were very inferior.[91] In 1803, however, the governor-general of India, Marquis Wellesley, first learned about a serious competitor – Malwa opium – and was greatly alarmed. He ordered an immediate inquiry and found that it was produced in the independent native states of central India and transported to the coastal ports for export. British Bombay was one such port.

Wellesley decided that steps had to be taken 'for the prevention of further growth of that commerce, and for its ultimate annihilation'.[92] The best solution would be to annex the independent states in central India and thereby control the source of Malwa opium in the same manner as Bengal opium was controlled. Being unable to do that for the moment, one remedial measure would be to forbid the passage of Malwa opium through Bombay. But Bombay was not the only port through which it was exported; Portuguese Daman was another. There were also several native entrepôts. The prohibition at Bombay simply drove the traffic through Daman and Diu.[93]

      by this view and defended the opium monopoly along the same lines in his book (see particularly pp. 25 and 34).
88. *Ninth Report*, 1783, App. 61, quoted in Owen, *British Opium Policy*, p. 23.
89. Bond, *Speeches in the Trial of Warren Hastings*, v. 2, p. 504.
90. Court of Directors to the Governor-General in Council (separate revenue), 5 May 1799, in India Office Despatches to Bengal, v. 33, quoted in Owen, *British Opium Policy*, p. 44.
91. In addition, small quantities of opium produced in north India also found their way via Nepal and Lhasa into remote Chinese Turkistan, but not into the main market of China. See Bakhala, 'Indian Opium', chapter 5.
92. India Office Bengal Consultations, Governor-General in Council to the Government of Bombay, 30 June 1803, quoted in Owen, *British Opium Policy*, p. 83.
93. Richards, 'Peasant Production of Opium', v. 15, p. 65; Owen, *British Opium Policy*, p. 101.

The economics of imperialism

Wellesley hastened to negotiate an agreement with the viceroy of Goa to stop Portuguese possessions in India being used as entrepôts. That done, he was confident that 'no Malwa opium will henceforward find its way to the China Market'.[94] He was wrong; the Portuguese authorities were not as cooperative as he had hoped.

The company changed its tactics and allowed unimpeded passage of Malwa opium through Bombay by charging fees on the export. This saw the establishment of the Malwa Opium Agency in 1823.[95] While the agency brought revenue to Bombay, it did not eliminate competition in the opium market in China. But already, another approach was being considered, which attempted 'to secure the command of the market by furnishing a supply in so enlarged a scale and on such reasonable terms as shall prevent competition'.[96]

The tactics were threefold. The first was to increase production in Bengal at all costs. Accompanied by members of the Board of Revenue, the new governor-general of India, Lord Bentinck, toured the upper Ganges to discover new fields.[97] Appropriations were made for experimental culture.[98] Enormous energy was spent on forcing the poppy into new areas,[99] and coercion was not spared.[100] Production was greatly augmented.[101] The second tactic was to buy up entire crops of Malwa to control its supply to China. But the moment this intention was made known, the acreage under poppy in the independent native states increased phenomenally,[102] so this tactic backfired. The third plan was to try to block Malwa's routes to the sea by signing treaties to this effect with the rulers of the pertinent native states, but not all of them obliged. Even those who

94. India Office Letters from Bengal, v. 49, Governor-General in Council to the Court of Directors (public general), 7 June 1806, quoted in Owen, *British Opium Policy*, p. 84.
95. India Office, Bengal Board of Revenue, Miscellaneous Proceedings (Opium), 27 June 1823, R. 102, v. 35, no. 3, paras. 34 and 40, quoted by Bakhala, 'Indian Opium', chapter 3, n. 36. Revenue from this source began to feature on a fairly regular basis in 1830 (Parl. Papers 1865, v. 40, pp. 85–7). Some revenue in this score was listed in Parl. Papers 1822, v. 17, p. 560, but apparently not as part of a centrally planned long-term policy.
96. India Office Letters from Bengal, v. 81, Governor-General in Council to the Court of Directors (territorial: salt and opium), 30 July 1819, quoted in Owen, *British Opium Policy*, p. 87.
97. Ibid., v. 114, Governor-General in Council to the Court of Directors (separate revenue), 8 February 1831, quoted in Owen, *British Opium Policy*, p. 106.
98. Ibid., v. 118, Governor-General in Council to the Court of Directors (separate revenue), 10 April 1832, quoted in Owen, *British Opium Policy*, p. 107.
99. India Office, Bengal Board of Revenue, Miscellaneous Proceedings (Opium), 3 August 1830, quoted in Owen, *British Opium Policy*, p. 107.
100. Ibid., 26 October 1830, quoted in Owen, *British Opium Policy*, p. 108. See also B. Chaudhuri, 'Regional Economy', p. 327.
101. By the time the *Arrow* War began in 1856, the production had increased to more than four and a half times that of 1830.
102. India Office, Bengal Board of Revenue, Miscellaneous Proceedings (Opium), 9 March 1824, Samuel Swinton to the Board of Customs, Salt, and Opium, 17 February 1824; Third Report from the Select Committee, App. 4, p. 28, Abstracts on Malwa Opium, Bengal Political Consultations, 25 October 1822; both quoted in Owen, *British Opium Policy*, p. 90.

The problem of India

signed decided not to honour them because of considerable opposition by powerful economic groups within their states: merchants, bankers, moneylenders cum small-traders, and a sizeable community of opium cultivators who had benefited from a 'free' trade in the drug.[103] Routes to Portuguese Daman by way of Karachi in Sind, though circuitous, laborious, and expensive, were still open, and 'private traders were not slow to shift their operations to territories where no restrictions interfered'.[104] It was estimated that, in 1834–5, 5,600 chests were exported from Daman, as compared with the 7,000 chests that went through Bombay.[105]

The ultimate solution came in 1843 when British India, under another governor-general, Lord Ellenborough, annexed Sind. Henceforth, all Malwa opium had to pass through British territory before it could be exported.[106] Furthermore, the selling price of Malwa opium in China could now be regulated by varying the fees charged on it when passing through Bombay.

This explains the variations in the pattern of the fees charged on Malwa opium in Table 16.10, column 2. From 1830 to 1835, the fee on each chest of Malwa was Rs. 175.[107] In 1835, it was discovered that much Malwa opium was diverted from Bombay to Daman, whence it was shipped by Parsees.[108] Consequently the fees at Bombay were lowered to Rs. 125 per chest.[109] This rate was maintained for about eight years, resulting in a marked increase in the quantities exported through Bombay.[110] Once Sind was annexed in 1843, Karachi become a British port, cutting off Rajputana and central India from

103. B. Chaudhuri, 'Regional Economy', p. 313
104. Third Report from the Select Committee, App. 4, p. 33, Abstracts on Malwa Opium, quoted in Owen, *British Opium Policy*, p. 93. Apparently the main route followed was from Malwa through Pali, Jesalmir, and Karachi to Daman. See Morse, *International Relations of the Chinese Empire*, v. 1, p. 177, n. 18.
105. India Office, Letters from Bombay, LXI, Government of Bombay to the Court of Directors, 2 July 1835, quoted in Owen, *British Opium Policy*, p. 101, n. 61. We must not use the Daman of today to gauge the Daman of 1835. Today at Merseyside, Liverpool, for example, there is hardly an oceangoing vessel to be seen. But when Sun Yatsen arrived there on 30 September 1896, the place was bustling with long-range vessels of all descriptions, passenger and cargo (see my *Heroic Image*).
106. Owen, *British Opium Policy*, p. 102.
107. Before this system of fees was instituted in 1830, there was a debate on how much to charge without driving the trade to Daman. Bombay thought it should be Rs. 250 per chest, while Calcutta regarded the safe rate to be between Rs. 175 and 200. In the end, the lowest rate of Rs. 175 was favoured. A standard chest of opium weighed about 140 pounds. For all this, see Owen, *British Opium Policy*, p. 101.
108. As mentioned, an estimated 5,600 chests of Malwa opium were exported from Daman in 1834–5 compared with the 7,000 chests that went through Bombay. Government of Bombay to the Court of Directors, 2 July 1835, India Office Letters from Bombay, LXI, quoted in Owen, *British Opium Policy*, p. 101, n. 61. See also Morse, *International Relations of the Chinese Empire*, v. 1, p. 177.
109. Owen, *British Opium Policy*, p. 101. See also Morse, *The International Relations of the Chinese Empire*, v. 1, p. 177.
110. Owen, *British Opium Policy*, p. 102.

access to the sea except through British territory. Thereupon the rate at Bombay rose to Rs. 200 per chest; within two years, to Rs. 300; and within another two years, to Rs. 400 per chest. The revenue collected amounted to just over £225,000 annually in 1840–3. By 1848–9, it had soared to £887,000.[111]

But it is the annual and steep rises in 1859–62 that deserve special attention. Table 16.9 showed that there was an acute shortage of Bengal opium in those years. If Malwa were allowed to oversupply the market, prices would tumble. Fierce competition can cut margins so severely as to make certain commodities unprofitable. But if Malwa opium were to be charged hefty transit fees to Bombay, two objectives might be achieved. One was to arrest the reckless flow of Malwa opium to China. The other was to push up the price of Malwa opium in China to the extent that buyers should find it unattractive. Figures 16.5 and 16.6 suggest that this strategy seems to have worked. Despite some fluctuations, the supply was stabilized to a level which might be regarded as acceptable. When the supply of Bengal opium increased again in 1863–4, the transit fees charged on Malwa was dropped by Rs. 100 (from Rs. 600 to Rs. 500) per chest.[112]

Thus, the British authorities in India were able to regulate the quantity of opium supplied to the China market partly by varying the transit fees charged on Malwa opium. They were able to dictate such fees because the annexation of Sind had made Bombay the only point of exportation for the landlocked independent states of central India. Gaining control over Malwa opium worked further wonders. Since Malwa opium was only about half the price of Bengal opium, its controlled export to China could undercut the development of major new sources from Persia or Turkey.[113] It was speculated that cheap Malwa might even reduce the possibility of the Chinese cultivating their own opium.[114]

XII. Justifying the annexation of Sind

How did the governor-general of British India, Lord Ellenborough, justify the annexation of Sind? He did so, in a secret capacity, on financial grounds, claiming that the annexation would provide an opportunity to recover the losses incurred by the wars in China and Afghanistan because he expected Sind to yield a net profit of £500,000 a year.[115] This justification has taken

---

111. Ibid., pp. 102–3.1830–1   112. See Table 16.10.
113. Richards, 'Peasant Production of Opium', v. 15, p. 66.
114. Ibid. This proved too optimistic. The Chinese did eventually produce opium cheaper than even Malwa and ultimately managed to take away the dominant position occupied by Indian opium.
115. Governor-General, Secret Consultations, Bengal Secret Letters (1) 28, 419; Ellenborough to Wellington (private), 22 April 1843, PRO 30/12/28/12; Ellenborough to Fitzgerald (private), 22 April 1843, PRO 30/12/77, all quoted in M. E. Yapp, *Strategies of British India: Britain, Iran and Afghanistan* (Oxford, Clarendon Press, 1980), pp. 488 and 624.

The problem of India

some historians by surprise, one of whom has tried to explain it away thus: 'But Ellenborough himself probably never set much store on his own arguments and rightly, for Sind lost money until the end of British India'.[116]

Historians have every reason to be surprised because Ellenborough expressed himself badly. He was telling only part of the truth. First, that alleged 'net profit' was not to be collected at Sind but at Bombay, and therefore would not be accrued to Sind. Second, according to Table 16.10 column 3, the amount of transit fees charged on Malwa opium passing through Bombay in the financial year 1842–3, the year immediately prior to annexation, was Rs. 2.42 million, or about £242,000. Ellenborough had good reason to expect that after annexation, when all of Malwa opium exported to China would pass through Bombay, the income from transit fees would be about doubled.[117] Indeed the plan exceeded his expectations. A couple of years later, that income was more than £600,000. Since the cost of collecting this revenue was close to nothing (see Table 16.10, column 4), Ellenborough was perhaps also entitled to describe this as 'net profit'. Thus, it seems that he had not manufactured his figures at all; that was the part of the truth which he had told.

What Ellenborough had not disclosed, even in an official and secret capacity, was that the net profit was to be derived from transit fees levied on Malwa opium destined for China and that these fees could be doubled and quadrupled so as to control the market in China in order to eliminate competition to Bengal opium, as well as to forestall possible competition from Persia and Turkey.

Throughout the fierce controversy consequent on the annexation, Ellenborough kept quiet on the subject of opium revenue, remaining silent until some ten years later.[118] He had good reason for reticence. When the company had taken steps in 1824 to monopolize the yield of Malwa opium by signing treaties to that effect with the local princes, there was a storm of protest in India even from British officials.[119] For example, Sir Charles Metcalfe, resident at Delhi, complained that 'those officers who ought to be the Instruments of protection and the representatives of a paternal supremacy become the mere subaltern agents of an opium monopoly, searchers and confiscators'.[120] Although Ellenborough had found a means of monopolizing Malwa

116. Yapp, *Strategies of British India*, p. 488.
117. In addition, there was always the possibility of raising those charges to increase revenue, as we have seen.
118. C. J. Napier, *Defects, Civil and Military, of the Indian Government* (London, Charles Westerton, 1853), p. 357. Later still, during the Parliamentary debate over the *Arrow* dispute in 1857, he was to elaborate on the importance of opium to the Indian revenues and British global trade (see Chapter 7). Naturally, historians who are convinced that Napier's vanity was the basic cause of the annexation, refused to believe Lord Ellenborough. See, e.g., H. T. Lambrick, *Sir Charles Napier and Sind* (Oxford, Clarendon Press, 1952), p. 365.
119. See Owen, *British Opium Policy*, pp. 92–101.
120. India Office Bengal Political Consultations, minute by Sir Charles Metcalfe, 10 October 1827, quoted in Owen, *British Opium Policy*, p. 95.

opium, it would have been politically unwise to go around trumpeting that achievement.

Many historians of India have attributed the annexation of Sind to the vanity and lust for personal glory of General Sir Charles Napier,[121] who was 'the agent of Ellenborough's policy in Sind'.[122] Such historians have refused to believe Ellenborough even though some ten years later he told the truth about opium being an important factor in the decision to annex Sind.[123] Other historians, while not overlooking Napier's personal ambitions, have argued that the annexation was part of a frontier defence strategy to safeguard British India against attack from the northwest.[124] While paying due regard to both interpretations, I wish to emphasize that the episode was related to British India's determination to monopolize the opium market in China through gaining control of the flow of Malwa opium. It was a classic case of British expansion into one place being a 'by-product of expansion into another',[125] in the same vein that the seizure of Lagos may be better understood in terms of British objectives in its hinterland, and of Aden in terms of its strategic importance, because Aden was of little value in itself.[126]

Let us put these three interpretations of the annexation of Sind in perspective. First, we must say that they are not mutually exclusive. Second, the episode may be interpreted as an act of 'economic imperialism' conceived by the government of India; while the activities of Napier and others may be seen as examples of 'subimperialism', motivated by the desire for glory or for more tangible personal benefits and justified by strategic fears.

I should repeat that the transit fees were collected at Bombay and not in Sind itself. A function of British-controlled Sind was merely to channel all

---

121. See, e.g., Lambrick, *Sir Charles Napier and Sind*. Lambrick has ably put the controversial annexation of Sind in due perspective. The question of opium, as introduced here, offers yet another perspective to that still-controversial subject. For an assessment of the scholarship up to the time of Lambrick, see Vincent A. Smith, *The Oxford History of India* (Oxford, Clarendon Press, 1958), p. 619.
122. Yapp, *Strategies of British India*, p. 485.
123. See, e.g., Lambrick, *Sir Charles Napier and Sind*, p. 365.
124. See, e.g., Yapp, *Strategies of British India*, pp. 1–2 and 484–5. His main thesis is that 'the concerns of British foreign policy were mainly in Europe and Indian strategies were viewed in the light of that preoccupation' (ibid., p. 19). Thus, the perceived French and then Russian threat to India was portrayed as part of the same threat to Britain. In addition, he finds that the deliberately cultivated opinion of British invincibility was the fundamental cause of many wars in India. 'If Indian enemies of British power believed that revolt was foredoomed to failure they would be less inclined to make the attempt. Accordingly, it was vital that the Raj should never be defied and never beaten but should always present an impression of confident, overbearing power. Essentially it was bluff, but it was a bluff which no one could be allowed to call and its maintenance was at the root of most of the wars of British India' (ibid., p. 12).
125. R. J. Gavin, 'Palmerston's Policy towards East and West Africa, 1830–1865'. Unpublished Ph.D. thesis, University of Cambridge, 1959, p. i.
126. Ibid.

Malwa opium to Bombay. For accounting purposes, therefore, this revenue would not appear in the balance sheets for Sind. This made it all the more awkward for the British Cabinet, which had to defend Ellenborough for fear of exposing the 'Government to criticism from within the Conservative Party as well as from without'.[127] Indeed, the government had to edit the Sind correspondence to remove Napier's stronger expressions before printing it for the parliamentary debate.[128] Not surprisingly, the pertinent statistics for Sind were not made available for public scrutiny. When it was considered safe to do so ten years later, in 1853–4, it was clear that Sind continued to run annual deficits (see Table 16.16).[129]

Even more detailed accounts for Sind appeared a year later. Not only gross revenue, but the net revenue as well as the actual cost of troops stationed there became available. A large number of troops had to be posted there because, after annexation, Sind had become the frontier of British India. In addition, the tribes of Sind actively resented the British occupation. Table 16.17 shows that, more often than not, the actual cost of troops alone exceeded the net revenue. But Sind was valuable and worth keeping not only in terms of the transit fees collected at Bombay, but also as an important tool in monopolizing the opium market in China. As regards the Sind deficit, if we compare Table 16.10, column 3, with Table 16.16, column 3, we find that the amount of transit fees collected at Bombay were sufficient to compensate for that deficit many times over.

The timing of the annexation is interesting. It took place in 1843, a year after the Treaty of Nanking was signed, which opened four more Chinese ports for foreign trade, increasing prospects for augmented sales of opium to China. In view of Ellenborough's elucidation of the commercial function of Indian opium worldwide,[130] it is interesting that he should have decided to annex Sind the very year after the treaty. This observation is made without underestimating in any way the importance of both the local political circumstances, such as the role of Napier, and British India's regional strategic considerations (and

127. Yapp, *Strategies of British India*, pp. 493–4.
128. Ibid., p. 495.
129. The deficit may be partly explained by the fact that under the Talpur Mirs (1782–1843), agriculture received scant attention from the rulers, who actually converted large tracts of arable land into hunting grounds even at the loss of revenue to the state. After British rule began in 1843, agricultural conditions improved and revenue increased. See V. D. Divekar, 'Regional Economy (1757–1857): Western India', in Kumar (ed.), *The Cambridge Economic History of India*, v. 2, p. 333. But as we have seen, even after ten years of British rule, Sind was still very much in the red. In Sind, rice was the principal crop, followed by jowar, bajri, and wheat (ibid., p. 337). The British tried to introduce the cultivation of U.S. cotton in Sind as in other places in Western India, but 'all government efforts failed miserably almost everywhere, except in the district of Dharwar' (ibid., p. 338). Small wonder that Sind continued to carry a deficit.
130. See Chapter 10, especially the treatment of Ellenborough's speech (Ellenborough, 26 February 1857, Hansard, 3d series, v. 144, col. 1363) therein.

Table 16.16. *Sind deficit, 1851–60 (£ million sterling)*

Year	Gross revenue 1	Expenditure 2	Deficit (col. 2 − col. 1) 3	Expenditure expressed as a percentage of revenue (col. 2 ÷ col. 1) 4
1851–2	—	—	—	—
1852–3	—	—	—	—
1853–4	0.23	0.51	0.28	221.74
1854–5	0.33	0.49	0.16	148.48
1855–6	0.31	0.55	0.24	177.42
1856–7	0.36	0.57	0.21	158.33
1857–8	0.43	0.74	0.31	172.09
1858–9	0.43	0.82	0.39	190.70
1859–60	0.46	0.88	0.42	191.30

Sources: Parl. Papers 1857, Session 2, v. 29, p. 78, for the years 1853–6; 1857–8, v. 42, p. 94, for 1856–7; 1859, Session 2, v. 23, p. 188, for 1857–8; 1860, v. 49, p. 228, for 1858–9; and 1861, v. 43, p. 112, for 1859–60. Cols. 3 and 4 are my calculations.

Table 16.17. *Actual cost of troops in Sind, 1851–60 (£ million sterling)*

Year	Gross revenue 1	Net revenue 2	Charges: Actual cost of troops 3	Actual cost of troops expressed as a percentage of revenue (col. 3 ÷ col. 2) 4
1851–2	0.24	—	—	—
1852–3	0.26	—	—	—
1853–4	0.25	—	—	—
1854–5	0.33	0.19	0.19	100.00
1855–6	0.31	0.13	0.18	138.46
1856–7	0.36	0.16	0.16	100.00
1857–8	0.43	0.23	0.21	91.30
1858–9	0.43	0.23	0.24	104.35
1859–60	0.46	0.26	0.29	111.54

Sources: Parl. Papers 1861, v. 43, p. 257. Col. 4 is my calculation.

London's perception thereof), such as the need to build up a viable frontier defence line.

Furthermore, it was not as though Ellenborough had no choice but to annex Sind, and to do so at this particular juncture. On the contrary, the relationship between the British political agent responsible for the region, James Outram, and the rulers of Sind, the Amirs (Emirs), was good. It was only with a view to putting pressure on the Amirs to favour his negotiations with them over Shikarpur that, in February 1842, Outram first notified his government of certain reports of disaffection among the Amirs.[131] The evidence was unreliable, related only to minor misdemeanours.[132] Ellenborough, though dissatisfied with the claim, gave Napier a strong hint to proceed on the assumption that the evidence was accurate.[133] Napier welcomed the chance and made sweeping demands on the Amirs. No discussion was permitted. 'The Khairpur Amirs agreed, but they were not prompt enough for Napier, who advanced his forces'[134] and defeated them. The Haidarabad Amirs panicked, signed the treaty, then took up arms only to be defeated too.[135]

As a soldier, Napier would probably have argued that the occupation of Sind was strategically essential.[136] But as a bitter and frustrated patriot,[137] Napier probably regarded the annexation as a means, at last, to wealth and honour.[138] But it was Ellenborough who had encouraged him to do so and who, like his predecessors Lords Wellesley and Bentinck, was in command of the wider picture, including the need to monopolize the opium market in China. Small wonder that in England the debate on Sind was conceived wholly on moral grounds, in terms of how unfairly the Amirs had been treated and so forth,[139] while Ellenborough kept quiet on the subject of opium.

XIII. Free trade versus imperial interests

Lord Ellenborough would have antagonized many people had he said anything about the annexation of Sind ensuring a British monopoly on the opium market in China. In the face of mounting criticisms of the company's monopoly of Bengal opium, Parliament had appointed a select committee to hold a public inquiry as early as 1830–2. The central issue then was whether a satisfactory alternative means of raising revenue might be found if the monopoly were abolished. Three alternatives were proposed: an increased assessment on poppy lands, an excise duty on opium, or an export duty on it.

131. Outram to Willoughby (private), 22 February 1842; Outram to Colvin (private), 27 February 1842, ESL 84, 86, and 89/25, 22 February 1842, all quoted in Yapp, *Strategies of British India*, pp. 482 and 623.
132. Yapp, *Strategies of British India*, p. 485.
133. Ellenborough to Napier, 24 November 1842, ESL 90, 64/62, 20 December 1942, quoted in Yapp, *Strategies of British India*, pp. 486 and 623.
134. Ibid., p. 486.
135. Ibid., p. 487.
136. Ibid., p. 485.
137. Ibid., p. 484.
138. Ibid., pp. 484–5.
139. Ibid., p. 492.

The economics of imperialism

In the end, the inquiry found that none of these would be as satisfactory as the profit from the monopoly. As James Mill testified, 'The revenue at present derived from opium is very large, and tolerably certain; and I should very much question whether government, by any duties they could impose, or any change of system, would levy a larger one or even so large'.[140] He also stressed that the profit from monopoly derived entirely from the foreign consumer, whereas all the alternatives fell squarely on British India itself.[141] The alternative was to impose 'additional taxes on India's overwhelmingly poor population'.[142]

James Mill was the father of the philosopher John Stuart Mill and mentor of the economist David Ricardo.[143] He was a founding member of the Political Economy Club and a dedicated believer in laissez-faire capitalism. He was also an employee of India House.[144] The position he took about the opium monopoly typifies the hard-headed economic view of many British politicians. In the end, the parliamentary committee found that the monopoly should be upheld: the monopoly thus survived two attempts at abolition. It was to survive a third attempt, in the 1890s, by a royal commission set up specifically to examine the opium monopoly in India, as we shall see later in this chapter.

The same public inquiry of 1830–2 also examined the company's monopoly of all British trade with China. The majority view was that prohibiting private traders to do business in Canton was in effect limiting the capacity of the British commercial world to compete with other Europeans. A typical opinion was that whatever good the company's monopoly was doing at Canton was done 'at the cost of England'.[145] Consequently, the monopoly was abolished.[146]

Thus, the overriding rationale for preserving a particular monopoly, or abolishing another, was clearly not free trade. Rather, it was British national interest in terms of the benefits a particular strategy might bring to the British Empire. Like the tea duty in the United Kingdom, the opium monopoly in India survived waves of attacks by the free-traders.

Again, I must stress the importance of distinguishing between the British policy makers and the British free-traders. Policy makers were determined to

---

140. J. Mill's evidence, 28 June 1832, in Parl. Papers 1831–2, v. 11, Q3040.
141. Ibid., Q3024.
142. Harcourt, 'Black Gold', p. 5.
143. David Ricardo (1772–1823) was the principal founder of what has been called the 'classical school of political economy'. His father was a Dutch Jew who settled in England. Ricardo had no classical training, but set up business in the London Stock Exchange and made a fortune. In 1799 he came across Adam Smith's *Wealth of Nations* and in 1817 wrote his famous *Principles of Political Economy and Taxation*. For a modern analysis of his work, see Samuel Hollander, *Ricardo, the New View: Collected Essays* (London, Routledge, 1995).
144. J. Mill's evidence, 28 June 1832, in Parl. Papers 1831–2, Q2991.
145. W. S. Davidson's evidence, 11 March 1830, in Parl. Papers 1830, v. 5, Q3049.
146. See my article 'Monopoly in India', pp. 79–95.

Table 16.18. *Major Indian exports: Indigo, cotton, and opium, 1813–61 (in Rs. millions)*

Year	Indigo 1	Cotton 2	Opium 3
1813–14	15.6	4.0	1.2
1820–1	11.3	5.6	12.1
1830–1	26.7	15.3	19.9
1850–1	18.4	22.0	59.7
1860–1	20.2	56.4	90.5

Note: Statistics for the year 1840–1 are not available in the original source, probably because of the Opium War.
Source: K. N. Chaudhuri, 'Foreign Trade', in Kumar (ed.), *Cambridge Economic History of Frdia*, v. 2, p. 844.

preserve the tea duty and the opium monopoly because both of them brought in significant revenue. No government survives without adequate revenue. Free-traders could argue that to replace the revenue from tea duty and opium, the government could cut expenditures or raise other taxes. But which expenditure to cut – the budget of the Royal Navy? This would jeopardize Britain's global interests and international standing. Which tax to invent, revive, or increase – the poll tax? This would make the government very unpopular.

Subsequently, income tax was permanently introduced in Britain in the 1840s.[147] But the hefty tea duty and the opium monopoly remained, partly because extra money was still needed for continual expansion and protection of the empire. Acquisition of new territories did not always bring added revenue. We have seen, for instance, how the annexation of Sind entailed a financial burden that was offset only by the revenue which came from the control of Malwa opium at Bombay. New cash crops could be developed and existing ones expanded in India, but up to the time of the *Arrow* War there was not a great deal of joy in this area either.[148] As Table 16.18 shows, by 1860–1

147. Income tax was first introduced by Pitt in 1797. This was later dropped by Addington, who had to revive it in 1803 on account of Britain's declaring war on Napoleonic France on 17 May 1803 (J. Steven Watson, *The Oxford History of England: The Reign of George III, 1760–1815* [Oxford, Clarendon Press, 1960], pp. 375, 413, and 414). It was dropped after 1816 when peace was restored, but reintroduced by Peel in 1842. See Henry Roseveare, *The Treasury: The Evolution of a British Institution* (London, Penguin, 1969), p. 188.
148. Encouraging the cultivation of U.S. strains of cotton as an export commodity was a good case in point. The Lancashire mills, for example, had been buying large quantities of cotton from the United States because Indian cotton had too short a staple for their purposes. Therefore the British authorities wanted 'to convert the whole of Bombay Presidency into one great cotton–field', according to evidence before the House of Commons Committee on East India

The economics of imperialism

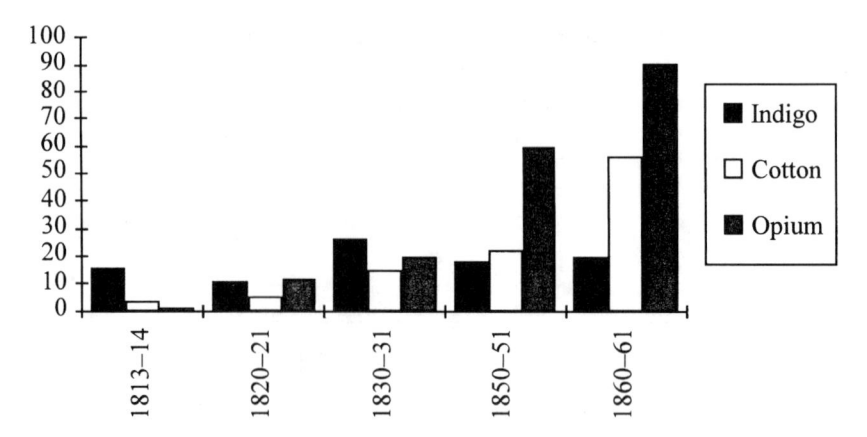

Figure 16.7. Major Indian exports: Indigo, cotton, and opium, 1813–61 (in Rs. millions; based on Table 16.17)

opium was still by far the most important export compared with the two other major Indian exports, cotton and indigo.[149] Figure 16.7 shows that, by mid-century, opium completely dwarfed the other two.

If opium continued to be the single most important cash crop for export from India, and if monopoly was the best means of ensuring its maximum return, one can understand why British policy makers wanted to protect it against the passionate free-traders within Britain. And one must remember that it was the policy makers, not the free-traders, who decided on war or peace with the major market for opium – China.

But convinced that free trade was the single most important cause of the Opium War, the author of the standard reference on that war wrote, 'Had there been an effective alternative to opium, say molasses or rice, the conflict

Produce in 1840. In 1836 the Bombay government had made concessions in land tax where cotton was grown, and even showed willingness to receive the rents in cotton instead of cash. In 1840 three U.S. planters were brought to the Bombay presidency to experiment in growing exotic cottons. But 'all governmental efforts failed miserably almost everywhere, except in the district of Dharwar, where the climate was almost like that of the cotton-growing regions of America'. See V. D. Divekar, 'Regional Economy (1757–1857): Western India', in Kumar (ed.), *Cambridge Economic History of India*, v. 2, pp. 338–9. Indian cotton was exported to China, but there was a demand only when the cotton crops in China had failed or been reduced by unfavourable conditions.

149. As we saw, experimental cultivation of tea in India was only beginning at this time. Ultimately, Indian tea was to become a major export, surpassing opium for the first time in 1900–1901. The importance of opium as an export had begun to decline since the Chinese started cultivating their own after the *Arrow* War. See K. N. Chaudhuri, 'Foreign Trade', in ibid., p. 844.

The problem of India

might have been called the Molasses War or the Rice War'.[150] But could molasses or rice ever have been effective an alternative to opium in terms of revenue for the British authorities in India and profits for the British merchants involved? I can scarcely imagine Britain selling rice to China, however coervice its methods. As for molasses – well, it is ridiculous.

While it is not unusual to use an idea to explain a phenomenon, in the case of Indian opium, the opposite approach might provide more food for thought. Without the revenue from opium, British expansion in India might not have been sustained – indeed, the company itself might not have remained solvent without the opium revenue as a 'bulwark against bankruptcy'.[151] By the time of the *Arrow* War, opium revenue had grown to almost 22 per cent of the gross revenue of the whole of British India.[152] Without the profit from opium, British merchants would not have been able to buy so much tea and silk from China. This tea and silk 'afforded a convenient, possibly even essential, method of transferring from India to London each year approximately two million pounds sterling in imperial tribute'.[153] And without that tea from China, paid for with Indian opium, British customs would have had a shortfall of about 21 per cent in import duties,[154] or an average annual shortfall of 8.68 per cent in the United Kingdom's gross revenue.[155]

I am not suggesting that the British passion to open up China for free trade did not contribute to the British decision to wage the *Arrow* War. I am merely saying that the author in question, by putting forward his 'Molasses War' theory, grossly underestimated the importance of opium. So did the inventor of the 'measles' paradigm, who insisted that the Opium Wars would have taken place even if no opium was involved, on the grounds that they were cultural wars, caused by the plague-like spread of European culture.[156]

Four decades later, the royal commission into Indian opium was still a whitewash.[157] India had to wait another ten years before a substantial increase in its general income made the opium revenue less important as a bulwark against bankruptcy than it had seemed in the past.[158]

150. Chang, *Commission Lin*, p. 15.
151. Owen, *British Opium Policy*, p. 330.
152. See Table 16.8, col. 3, for the financial year 1857–8.
153. Richards, 'Peasant Production of Opium', p. 66. These 2 million pounds constituted the approximate total of the heterogeneous collection of the so-called Home Charges, private profits, pension payments, and so on.
154. See Table 14.8, col. 5.
155. See Table 14.9, col. 8.
156. See Fukuzawa, 'Datsu–A–ron'; and Blacker, *Fukuzawa*, pp. 122–3.
157. See later in this chapter.
158. Owen, *British Opium Policy*, p. 330. This increase in India's general income, together with a massive production of opium in China, prompted a change of heart in both the Indian and Chinese governments in 1911, whereby they signed the Treaty of Tientsin, which stipulated the simultaneous suppression of poppy cultivation in China and progressive reduction in Indian exports in the following seven years. But in 1912, thousands of chests of Indian opium

XIV. 'Expansion by poison' and other interpretations

Another influential view needs to be considered. Pertinent Chinese experts share one conviction: for the purpose of imperial expansion in China, the British used opium to poison the Chinese.[159] Often quoted is the despatch Commissioner Lin sent to Queen Victoria, in which he pleaded with her not to drug the Chinese, as she would not have wished to drug her own subjects in the United Kingdom.[160] This moralistic approach has been extended to interpreting the *Arrow* War. Such an approach can lead people into thinking that the British had low moral standards, and further into thinking that therein lay the origin of the *Arrow* War. Hastings's attitude lends support to such an approach: he was fully aware that opium was a pernicious article, the consumption of which he would not permit in India; but he encouraged its export to China.[161]

Here, a distinction must be made between the Britons in the colonies and the Britons at home. The two had quite different priorities. Hastings's priority was to find money, any money, to keep his Indian administration afloat. To achieve this, he did not mind drugging the Chinese; but he was not poisoning them in order to take their country.

The Britons at home were a different story altogether. In England at the time, opium was not illegal, and certainly not regarded as immoral; and for medical purposes, doctors did not view it as dangerous, because it was seldom smoked and therefore its deleterious effects were not obvious. It was generally taken orally, which hardly made it addictive, and often cordials contained opium. Administered orally, opium was considered central to medicine because of its ability to relieve pain.[162] It was 'a medicament of surpassing usefulness which undoubtedly found its way into every home'.[163] It was sold openly, used freely, and imported through normal channels of trade. The main source of this medicinal opium was Turkey, 'where they prepare it much better than what comes from India, which is much softer and fouler than the Turkey'.[164]

---

were seized at Canton soon after the 1911 Revolution in China. This goaded the secretary of state for India to announce in 1913 that henceforth no more opium would be sold to China (ibid., pp. 311–54).
159. For the most recent views, see the essays collected in *Quru yu kangzheng*.
160. The full text has been translated in Ssu-yu Teng and John K. Fairbank (eds.), *China's Response to the West* (New York, Atheneum, 1963), pp. 24–7.
161. Letter from the President [Warren Hastings], Proceedings of the President and Council, 15 October 1773, *Ninth Report*, 1783, App. 59A, quoted in Owen, *British Opium Policy*, pp. 22–3.
162. In China, too, opium taken orally also had a long history of being used as a painkiller.
163. Berridge and Edwards, *Opium and the People*, p. xxv. This is a penetrating study of opium consumption in the United Kingdom.
164. Ibid., pp. 3–4, quoting 'W.B.E.', *A Short History of Drugs and Other Commodities, the Produce and Manufactory of the East Indies* (London, n.p., n.d.), p. 47.

The problem of India

The relevant statistics are set out in Table 16.19. It shows the amount of opium imported into the United Kingdom each year, for about twenty years until 1856, when – significantly, perhaps – the drug was no longer listed in the usual Parliamentary Papers which reported its annual importation. This table also shows the quantities entered for home consumption (and hence the amount of import duty paid) and the quantity reexported.

Furthermore, cultivation of the poppy in Britain was actively encouraged as a commercial enterprise that would bring economic benefits to the nation. The Society of Arts offered prizes and medals to successful growers. Other learned societies followed suit. The Caledonian Horticultural Society aimed to encourage the production of lettuce opium.[165] Some experiments were quite successful, but the precarious nature of the climate and marauding hares combined to prevent British opium from becoming a large-scale commercial proposition.[166] The point is that these experiments, too, demonstrate British society's acceptance of opium use – administered orally but not smoked.

Ironically, it was the Opium War which initiated the debate in the United Kingdom about the morality of opium smoking. During the debate in Parliament on the war, Gladstone condemned opium as a 'pernicious article'.[167] Although the government dismissed his attack as rhetoric, the message seems to have slowly sunk in. The quiet dropping of opium in the Parliamentary Papers as a legal import in 1856 (see Table 16.19) may suggest that steps were taken to control its use and spreading in the United Kingdom, and may explain why parliamentary opposition to it did not grow beyond Gladstone's remark. Outside Parliament, anti-opium organizations were formed but were short-lived and without much public impact,[168] principally because they were opposing opium smoking in Asia – something which was apparently of little concern to the average Briton. It is by this time, then, that Commissioner Lin began to have a case. If the British government had now became convinced about the dangers of opium smoking and started to take steps to control its use in Britain, then morally the government should no longer push legalization of opium in China, where the British knew only too well that opium was smoked.

The debate in Parliament on the *Arrow* War rekindled anti-opium feelings, as we have seen in Chapter 13. Later, on 10 September 1858, the Society of Friends appealed to Lord Derby, who had originally opposed the *Arrow* War in 1857[169] and had now become prime minister, not to pressure the Chinese government to legalize the opium trade.[170] It was very doubtful if Derby, now

---

165. Berridge and Edwards, *Opium and the People*, pp. 12–13.
166. Ibid., p. 16.
167. Gladstone, 8 April 1840, Hansard, 3d series, v. 53, col. 818.
168. Berridge and Edwards, *Opium and the People*, p. 175.
169. See Chapter 8.
170. Berridge and Edwards, *Opium and the People*, p. 175, quoting the Society's appeal, which is held in the Braithwaite Collection, Society of Friends.

Table 16.19. *Opium in the United Kingdom, 1837–55*

Year	Opium imported (pounds) 1	Home consumption (pounds) 2	Gross import duty received (£ sterling) 3	Opium reexported (pounds) 4
1837	79,651	37,616	1,881	67,476
1838	95,832	31,204	1,560	13,028
1839	196,246	41.671	2,084	10,193
1840	77,872	47,623	2,457	35,848
1841	155,609	39,161	2,038	61,104
1842	72,373	47,861	2,513	126,515
1843	244,215	32,160	1,730	302,947
1844	248,325	32,734	1,718	196,871
1845	259,626	39,880	2,094	238,243
1846	103,078	34,922	1,828	113,375
1847	118,332	45,766	2,402	68,521
1848	200,019	61,178	3,212	79,205
1849	105,504	44,009	2,311	113,154
1850	126,102	42,324	2,222	87,451
1851	106,003	50,368	2,645	65,640
1852	205,780	62,521	—	102,217
1853	159,312	67,038	—	87,939
1854	97,388	61,432	—	68,395
1855	112,865	56,067	—	50,143

Note: The financial years listed above sometimes ended on 31 December of the same year, and sometimes on 5 January of the following year: see Parl. Papers 1856, v. 55, p. 1. The figures for home consumption plus reexport do not tally with the quantity imported in specific years, presumably because some opium was stored. In other years, the amount reexported is far greater than the amount imported. Some of the difference might have been made up of opium produced in Britain. Unfortunately we do not have figures for the amount produced in Britain.

Sources: Parl. Papers 1839, v. 46, pp. 3 and 5, for the year 1837; 1840, v. 44, pp. 3 and 5, for 1838; 1840, v. 44, pp. 3 and 5, for 1839; 1841, v. 26, pp. 3 and 5, for 1840; 1843, v. 52, pp. 3 and 5, for 1841; 1843, v. 52, pp. 3 and 5, for 1842; 1845, v. 46, pp. 3 and 5, for 1843; 1846, v. 44, pp. 3 and 5, for 1844; 1846, v. 44, pp. 3 and 5, for 1845; 1847–8, v. 45, pp. 3 and 6, for 1846–7; 1850, v. 52, pp. 4 and 8, for 1848–9; 1852, v. 51, pp. 4 and 8, for 1850; 1854, v. 65, pp. 6 and 12, for 1851–2; 1856, v. 55, pp. 6 and 14, for 1853–5; 1857–8, v. 53, pp. 5 and 11, for 1865–7; and 1861, v. 59, pp. 5 and 11, for 1858–60.

in power, would do anything to jeopardize the Indian revenue. But he was lucky; he was saved from considerable embarrassment by the second tariff conference, held at Shanghai on 13 October 1858. As mentioned earlier, this conference fixed the tariff to be levied on opium, thus legalizing it by default.

Anti-opium agitation continued, led mainly by the Quakers. The best hope

The problem of India

of success came in 1892, when Gladstone became prime minister. A royal commission was established. The secretary of state for India, Lord Kimberley, was resolutely in favour of the opium trade, and he received tacit encouragement from Gladstone.[171] Thus, Gladstone's vehement denunciation of opium when he was not in office must not be taken at face value. The report of the royal commission concluded that the opium monopoly should continue.[172]

This episode reinforces the main argument in this and other chapters in Parts Five and Six of this book. Tangible national interest as perceived by the policy makers, not free trade or any such abstract ideas, was the driving force behind Britain's waging of the *Arrow* War. The politicians' grandstanding – whether it took the form of vehement denunciations of the opium trade, as was the case with Gladstone, or professions of unswerving support for free trade, as was the case with Clarendon – must be considered in the political context of the time.

Yet another accepted and influential interpretation of the Opium War and the *Arrow* War is that of the clash of two cultures.[173] While this approach has merits, it is too general to reconcile with the specific statistics and issues presented in this chapter. In this regard, perhaps one might mention two examples. The British authorities professed that the Chinese could not survive without opium. Commissioner Lin believed that the British could not live without Chinese rhubarb. Do these views represent differences in culture? Or does the British view merely reflect an attempt at rationalizing a profitable though unlawful trade? And does Lin's view mirror no more than sheer ignorance on his part? Both profit and ignorance could propel nations to war. But to avoid the specific issues by resorting to a vague reason such as 'the clash of two cultures' gives the impression of rationalizing an unpalatable war.

171. Ibid, p. 186.
172. Ibid.
173. See Morse, *International Relations of the Chinese Empire*, v. 1.

17
The balance sheet:
The Chinese are now buying more

I. Imports: Tea

By the Treaty of Tientsin, the British obtained their objective of direct access to the tea-producing areas of the Yangtze basin. Whether or not their expectations were fulfilled, however, requires some examination. Table 17.1 shows the quantity of tea imported from China before, during, and after the *Arrow* War. It extends to many years before the war in order to show a long-term pattern of development, covering thirty years in all. It ends in 1867, seven years after the conclusion of peace.

In those seven years of the postwar period, the average annual amount of tea imported from China was over 115 million pounds. Furthermore, the annual quantity remained fairly steady. During the four years of earnest hostilities, 1857-60, the annual average was about 72 million pounds. During the four years before just the war, 1853-6,[1] the annual average was about 79 million pounds. These figures suggest that there was a marked increase in the availability of tea after free access was obtained to the tea-growing area of the Yangtze. More important, these teas were bought much more cheaply than before, being now free from both the transit dues levied between the producing areas and the treaty ports, and the charges of Chinese middlemen.

The four years before the war, 1853-6, were marked by disturbances in China. By 1853, the Taipings had captured Nanjing on the Yangtze River.[2] The Taipings' occupation of the lower Yangtze area starved Shanghai of tea and silk for export.[3] By 1854 the Red Turbans were besieging Canton, seriously disrupting the export of tea and other goods.[4] But British and other foreign

1. The *Arrow* incident occurred on 8 October 1856, and localized hostilities started some time after. On this basis, 1856 is not counted here as a year of war.
2. See Franz Michael, *The Taiping Rebellion: History and Documents* (Seattle, University of Washington Press, 1966), v. 1, pt. 3.
3. For a vivid eyewitness account of the difficulties in obtaining tea for export from Shanghai, see Yung Wing, *My Life in China and America*, especially chapters 9-12.
4. See my, *Yeh Ming-ch'en*, chapter 6.

Table 17.1. *Tea imported into the United Kingdom direct from China, 1838–67 (millions of pounds)*

Year	Quantity	Year	Quantity
1838	39.00	1853	68.64
1839	37.19	1854	83.30
1840	22.58	1855	81.56
1841	27.64	1856	84.80
1842	37.41	1857	60.30
1843	42.78	1858	73.36
1844	51.75	1859	71.92
1845	50.71	1860	85.30
1846	54.53	1861	92.15
1847	55.36	1862	109.76
1848	47.35	1863	129.44
1849	53.10	1864	115.10
1850	49.37	1865	112.78
1851	69.49	1866	130.86
1852	65.30	1867	117.55

Sources: Parl. Papers 1859, Session 2, v. 23, p. 319, for the years 1838–58; 1863, v. 65, p. 292, for 1859–62; and 1867–8, v. 67, p. 305, for 1863–7.

merchants found an alternative supply in Fujian province.[5] This explains why the tea exported to the United Kingdom annually in these years was more than in any of the previous years, that is, 1843–52. But once direct access to the Yangtze area was obtained, the increase in supply was dramatic.

In terms of gaining more and freer access to Chinese tea, it is interesting to compare the effect of the *Arrow* War with that of the Opium War. Both are evident in Table 17.1. During the two years just before the Opium War, 1838 and 1839, the United Kingdom's annual average quantity of tea imported from China was about 38 million pounds. During the Opium War, 1840–2, the annual average was about 25 million pounds. Then for ten years afterwards, the annual average was about 52 million pounds. Here again, the consequences of greater access were quite remarkable. Unlike the *Arrow* War period, the Opium War period was free from domestic uprisings, and the question of other variables did not exist.

After the *Arrow* War was over and British access to the Yangtze granted, the

[5]. See Hao Yen-p'ing, *The Commercial Revolution in Nineteenth-Century China: The Rise of Sino-Western Mercantile Capitalism* (Berkeley and Los Angeles, University of California Press, 1986), chapter 6.

The economics of imperialism

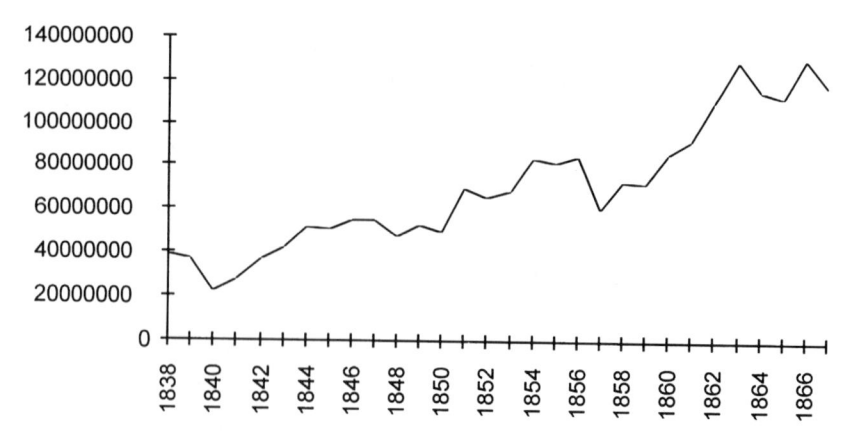

Figure 17.1. Tea imported into the United Kingdom direct from China, 1838–67 (millions of pounds; based on Table 17.1)

Taipings still occupied the lower Yangtze area, seriously disrupting trade. At one stage, they even threatened Shanghai. This explains why the British authorities subsequently helped the Chinese government fight the rebels.[6] The Taiping Rebellion was finally suppressed in 1864. A graph may convey more powerfully than a table the effect of direct access to the Yangtze basin on the supply of tea (see Figure 17.1).

However, the danger signs were already there in the United Kingdom market for Chinese tea. Tea cultivation in British India proved a great success and production was increasing rapidly. Furthermore, a new player, Japan, was entering the market, as Table 17.2 shows. Ultimately, Indian tea was to replace Chinese tea in the United Kingdom. But there was more immediate bad news for Chinese raw silk.

II. Imports: Raw silk

Like tea, raw silk in China was produced in large quantities in both the Yangtze River basin and the Canton delta. The difference was that the Canton delta was also infested with rebels, from 1854 up to the time of the *Arrow* War. In other words, there was no alternative supply to that from the Yangtze. What was the effect of the *Arrow* War on the importation of silk from China? Table 17.3 gives the relevant statistics for silk over the same thirty years as did Table

[6]. See G. S. Gregory, *Great Britain and the Taiping* (Canberra, Australian National University Press, 1969), chapters 7–9. See also R. J. Smith, *Mercenaries and Mandarins: The Ever-Victorious Army of Nineteenth Century China* (New York, KTO Press, 1978), chapters 8–9.

The balance sheet

Table 17.2. *Computed real value of tea imported into the United Kingdom from China, India and Japan, 1853–67 (£ million sterling)*

Year	China	Br. E. Indies	Japan
1853	—	—	nil
1854	5.38	0.03	nil
1855	5.12	0.03	nil
1856	5.12	0.08	nil
1857	4.31	0.19	nil
1858	5.04	0.09	nil
1859	5.53	0.15	nil
1860	6.60	0.24	nil
1861	6.50	0.17	0.10
1862	8.76	0.17	0.18
1863	10.05	0.31	0.25
1864	8.61	0.39	0.16
1865	9.33	0.34	0.26
1866	10.44	0.53	0.13
1867	9.18	0.70	0.11

Note: Computed real value began in 1854, hence the year 1853 was blank. British India was called British East Indies in those days.

Sources: Parl. Papers 1854–5, v. 51, p. 77, for the year 1853; ibid., p. 74, for 1854; 1856, v. 56, p. 77, for 1855; 1857, Session 2, v. 35, p. 99, for 1857; 1857–8, v. 54, p. 102, and 1859, v. 28, p. 105, for 1858; 1860, v. 64, p. 107, for 1859; 1861, v. 60, p. 106, for 1860; 1862, v. 56, p. 106, for 1861; 1863, v. 65, p. 92, for 1862; 1864, v. 57, p. 94, for 1863; 1865, v. 52, p. 99, for 1864; 1866, v. 68, p. 99, for 1865; 1867, v. 66, p. 103, for 1866; and 1867–8, v. 67, p. 105, for 1867.

17.1. Instead of a marked increase, as was the case with tea, there was a sharp decline in silk in the postwar period. The annual average quantity was only about 1.2 million pounds. That of the war years of 1857–60 had been more than 3.74 million pounds. That of the four years just preceding the war had been 4.29 million pounds. Thus, it seems that greater access was greeted by a dramatic decline in the quantity of silk imported from China. Visually, this decline appears even more striking, as Figure 17.2 shows.

By contrast, the previous war, the Opium War, seems to have fulfilled the expectations of the British policy makers. Again according to Table 17.3, the annual average quantity of raw silk imported from China for the two years just before the Opium War was about 0.54 million pounds. That for the

Table 17.3. *Imports of raw silk into the Untied Kingdom from China, 1838–67 (millions of pounds)*

Year	Quantity	Year	Quantity
1838	0.72	1853	3.00
1839	0.36	1854	4.95
1840	0.25	1855	5.05
1841	0.28	1856	4.20
1842	0.18	1857	7.19
1843	0.28	1858	2.52
1844	0.35	1859	3.19
1845	1.18	1860	2.09
1846	1.84	1861	2.75
1847	2.02	1862	3.27
1848	2.24	1863	1.70
1849	1.86	1864	0.46
1850	1.81	1865	0.14
1851	2.10	1866	0.11
1852	2.47	1867	0.04

Sources: Parl. Papers 1859, Session 2, v. 23, p. 319, for the years 1838–58; 1863, v. 65, p. 292, for 1859–62; 1867–8, v. 67, p. 305, for 1863–7.

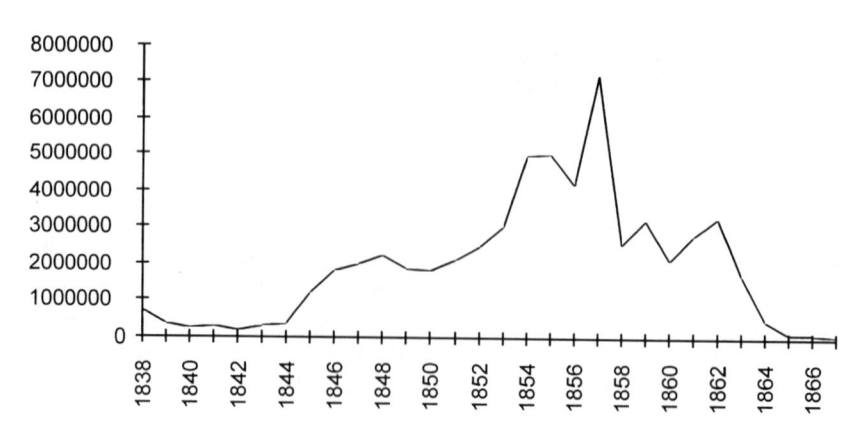

Figure 17.2. Import of raw silk into the United Kingdom from China, 1838–67 (millions of pounds; based on Table 17.3)

The balance sheet

war years of 1840–2 was about 0.23 million pounds. That for the postwar decade was about 1.61 million pounds. Why did the *Arrow* War not produce similar increases?

There are two plausible explanations. Again, the two main areas of sericulture in China were the lower Yangtze region (particularly around Suzhou) and the Canton delta (especially the county of Shunde). In 1853, as mentioned, the Taipings captured Nanjing. The silk-producing areas farther downstream remained unaffected for some years, but the strain was beginning to be felt. In 1854, the Small Sword rebels took over the walled city of Shanghai.[7] The commercial section of the city was successfully defended by foreign contingents, but the situation was not conducive to business confidence. At Canton, the Red Turban rebels besieged that city in the latter part of 1854 and into 1855. After their defeat, rebel discipline broke down quickly, and bands of marauders ravaged the countryside.[8] The instability cast doubt on the ability of the Chinese to maintain a steady supply of silk. Not surprisingly, British merchants began looking to alternative sources of supply.

There were already such alternative sources outside China. By the time of the *Arrow* War, India, Turkey, Egypt, and Holland had become substantial rivals to China as suppliers of raw silk to the United Kingdom.[9] Once a trading relationship had been consolidated with these alternative sources, businessmen would be reluctant to go back to the old supplier even after conditions in China returned to normal. Table 17.4 shows that by the time the Taiping Rebellion was suppressed in 1864, China had lost its dominant position as the major supplier of raw silk to the United Kingdom. Thus, the rebellion had done serious damage to China in more ways than one.[10]

The sharp decline continued unabated. By 1867, China's percentage of total raw silk imports to the United Kingdom had fallen to less than 1 per cent from nearly 60 per cent in 1855. Visually, the decline looks as in Figure 17.3.

The French had unexpected gains, however. Their production of raw silk had plummeted in 1852 as a result of pébrine (a contagious disease of the silk worm), and the major silk manufacturing centre of Lyon had been forced to

7. See my article entitled 'The Taipings' Distant Allies: A Comparison of the Rebels at Shanghai and at Canton', in *Austrina: Essays in Commemoration of the 25th Anniversary of the Founding of the Oriental Society of Australia*, ed. A. R. Davis and A. D. Stefanowska (Sydney, Oriental Society of Australia, 1982), pp. 334–50. The Small Swords were not a subgroup of the Taipings; they rose independently of each other. They tried to join, but were prevented from doing so by the government troops.
8. See my *Yeh Ming-ch'en*, chapter 6. The Red Turbans were not a subgroup of the Taipings. They rose independently, although the Red Turbans were greatly influenced by the Taipings.
9. For statistical information about the quantities of raw silk supplied by the various parts of the world to the United Kingdom in 1857, see Table 14.17.
10. The other damages were the catastrophic loss of lives – estimated at about 20 million – and the complete dislocation of people in the areas affected.

Table 17.4. *China's percentage of the total amount of raw silk imported into the United Kingdom, 1853–67*

Year	Percentage	Year	Percentage
1853	36.43	1861	31.77
1854	55.33	1862	30.11
1855	59.48	1863	18.47
1856	49.79	1864	8.32
1857	54.45	1865	1.69
1858	32.20	1866	1.99
1859	32.17	1867	0.68
1860	22.87		

Sources: Compiled from statistics in Parl. Papers 1854–5, v. 51, p. 64, for the year 1853; 1854–5, v. 51, p. 61, for 1854; 1856, v. 56, p. 65, for 1855; 1857, v. 35, p. 520, for 1856; 1857–8, v. 54, p. 89, for 1857; 1859, v. 28, p. 92, for 1858; 1860, v. 64, p. 94, for 1859; 1861, v. 60, p. 93, for 1860; 1862; v. 56, p. 93, for 1861; 1863, v. 65, p. 74, for 1862; 1864, v. 57, p. 76, for 1863; 1865, v. 52, p. 79, for 1864; 1866, v. 68. p. 79, for 1865; 1867, v. 66, p. 83, col. 2, for 1866; and 1867–8, v. 67, p. 83, col. 2, for 1867.

look elsewhere for supplies.[11] Thus, in 1854, Paul Chartron appointed a representative in Shanghai to purchase raw silk.[12] By this time *likin* (transit taxes) had been established in the Yangtze River area. Not having paid the lower prices of pre-*likin* days, the French had no complaints. Now they were delighted that the Treaty of Tientsin exempted from *likin* the raw silk they bought at the places of production. *Likin* was normally levied on goods in transit, for example, on their way to their port of embarkation. In 1860, therefore, the Chamber of Commerce of Lyon resolved to create a steamship line to China and to found a bank there. Accordingly, the Comptoir d'Escompte opened its first foreign branch in Shanghai later that year, and the next year the French government signed a contract with the Messageries Maritimes providing for a monthly departure to East Asia.[13] French enthusiasm was somewhat dampened in 1870 when the British, having greatly reduced their purchase of raw silk from China, agreed to revise the Treaty of Tientsin to allow for a modest increase in the Chinese duty on the export of raw silk.[14] Instantly the president

11. John F. Laffey, 'Roots of French Imperialism in the Nineteenth Century: The Case of Lyon', *French Historical Studies*, 6, no. 1 (Spring 1969), p. 81.
12. Ibid., p. 82.
13. Ibid.
14. See Art. 12 of the Alcock Convention, 1870.

Figure 17.3. China's percentage of the total amount of raw silk imported into the United Kingdom, 1853–67 (based on Table 17.4)

of the Chamber of Commerce of Lyon requested that the French minister in China be instructed to oppose the increase, since silk had formed 'the principal element of our commerce with China. Further, the use of Chinese silk is necessary to the work of our looms'.[15] Without the support of the British, French efforts were in vain. Nonetheless, the French continued to buy large quantities of Chinese raw silk, accounting for about 42.07 per cent of the total amount of raw silk received from all sources in the 1870s. By 1888, France, principally Lyon, took about two-thirds of the silks from China.[16]

It seems, therefore, that although British policy makers might have waged the *Arrow* War in part to acquire easier and greater access to the supply of Chinese raw silk, such access was not utilized by the British merchants when so obtained, because substitute supplies were found to be more secure, if not always cheaper.

III. British exports

Did the *Arrow* War fulfil British expectations in terms of exports to China? Table 17.5 provides the basis for such an assessment. It shows the value of U.K. exports to China (including Hong Kong)[17] for the years 1854–66. In 1854,

15. Louis Guetin to the Minister of Agriculture and Commerce, 3 May 1870, quoted in Laffey, 'French Imperialism', p. 83.
16. Laffey, 'French Imperialism', p. 83.
17. It is interesting that British statisticians took China and Hong Kong as one in their calculations. They did so with good reason. Hong Kong at this stage was still sparsely populated,

The economics of imperialism

Table 17.5. *Value of U.K. exports to China (including Hong Kong), 1854–66 (£ million sterling)*

Year	Exports to China (and Hong Kong)	Total U.K. exports	China's percentage of total U.K. exports (col. 1 ÷ col. 2)
1854	1.00	63.33	1.58
1855	1.28	69.14	1.85
1856	2.22	82.53	2.69
1857	2.45	84.91	2.89
1858	2.88	76.39	3.77
1859	4.46	84.27	5.29
1860	5.32	92.23	5.77
1861	4.85	82.86	5.85
1862	3.14	82.10	3.82
1863	3.89	95.72	4.06
1864	4.71	108.73	4.33
1865	5.15	117.63	4.38
1866	7.48	135.20	5.53

Sources: Parl. Papers 1859, Session 2, v. 28, pp. 6 and 335, for the years 1854–8; 1863, v. 65, pp. 6 and 292, for 1859–62; and 1867–8, v. 67, pp. 6 and 305, for 1863–6.

which was the third year before the *Arrow* incident of 8 October 1856, the United Kingdom exported about £1 million worth of products to China (including Hong Kong). This represented 1.58 per cent of the total value of U. K. exports in that year. In 1863, the third year after the *Arrow* War ended, the United Kingdom exported nearly £4 million worth of goods to China (including Hong Kong), representing 4.06 per cent of the already augmented total value of U.K. exports in that year. This fourfold increase was indeed phenomenal. If we look beyond 1863 for yet another three years, say until 1866, we shall find equally dramatic increases. In 1866, the value of U.K. exports to China (including Hong Kong) was about £7.5 million. This represented about 5.53 per cent of the total value of U.K. exports in that year. It must be noted that the total value of annual U.K. exports was itself rapidly increasing at the same time and that, therefore, exports to China formed an increasing proportion of the United Kingdom's globally expanding export trade. If the value of U.K. exports to China (including Hong Kong) in 1854 is used as a base-year figure, then that in 1863 was 388.71 per cent of that figure, and that in 1866 was

while much of the Kowloon peninsula was sandy plains. Most U.K. products shipped to Hong Kong were reexported to China.

The balance sheet

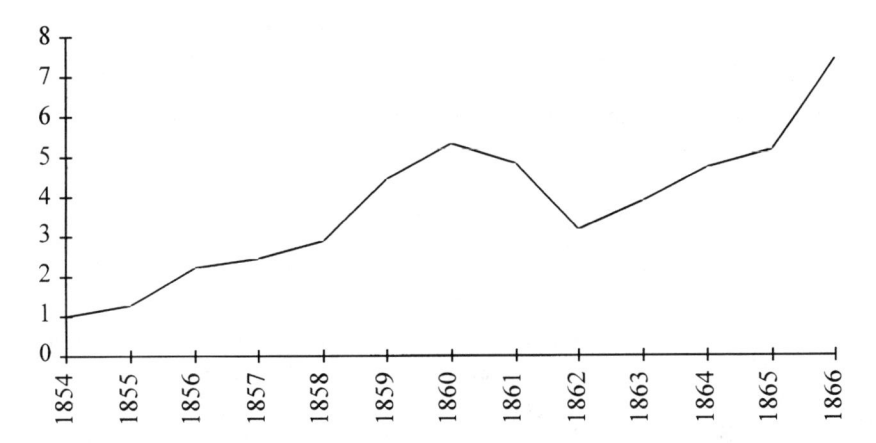

Figure 17.4. Value of U.K. exports to China (including Hong Kong), 1854–66 (£ million sterling; based on Table 17.5)

747.17 per cent. Visually, the value of U.K. exports to China (including Hong Kong) is presented in Figure 17.4.

However, looking at the total value of U.K. exports to China (including Hong Kong) leaves one somewhat uneasy. How much of this value was that of staple U.K. manufactures such as cottons and woollens? How much of it was that of arms and ammunition, for example, which would satisfy only a temporary need in China?

In 1854–5, as mentioned, the Red Turban rebels ultimately besieged Canton and were able to 'menace the City with a stoppage of all supplies'.[18] The Peninsula and Oriental Steam Navigation Company (P & O), among others, had done a roaring trade by using steamers to tow 'up the River to Canton, Chinese vessels and goods in the nature of supplies and munitions of war'.[19]

The rebels gave notice of a blockade of Canton.[20] This sparked off a fierce debate among the British authorities. The acting attorney-general in Hong Kong, W. T. Bridges, denied that the insurgents had any right by international law to institute a blockade, on the grounds that this could be lawfully done only by a sovereign power, while a blockade declared by individuals was unlawful respecting foreigners.[21]

18. Bowring to Clarendon, Desp. 19, 9 January 1855, FO17/226.
19. Stirling to Bowring, 12 January 1855, enclosed in Bowring to Clarendon, Desp. 31, 15 January 1855, FO17/226. Stirling was the British rear-admiral commanding the China station of the Royal Navy, and the predecessor of Sir Michael Seymour.
20. Ibid.
21. W. T. Bridges to Bowring, 14 January 1855, enclosed in Bowring to Clarendon Desp. 31, 15 January 1855, FO17/226.

The economics of imperialism

Sir John Bowring, for his part, regarded the right of Britons to trade in all articles not contraband – and munitions of war were not considered contraband by the Canton authorities when supplied to them – guaranteed by treaty. He required all Chinese subjects, including rebels, to respect the treaty.[22] Previously, Whitehall had deemed it 'proper and allowable that British vessels should, at the request of the Chinese, escort and convoy Junks from Port to Port and protect them from Pirates'.[23] The acting attorney-general in Hong Kong decided that there was no 'distinction between convoy by towing and convoy by escort'. He considered 'them both to be a lawful form of trading by British subjects in China'.[24]

Admiral Stirling disagreed: 'Until otherwise instructed I must decline to employ H. M. Ships of War in aiding or protecting Chinese vessels, whether in tow of British merchant vessels or otherwise, in the commission of a Breach of an Actual Blockade established either by Insurgents or Imperialists within the Territory and Jurisdiction of China'.[25] Bowring disclaimed any 'responsibility for the consequence' of the Admiral's views[26] and told P & O to carry on regardless.[27]

Apparently, the British merchants had their way. According to Table 17.5, the value of U.K. exports to China in 1856 almost doubled from that of the preceding year. How much of all this increased value may be attributed to the purchase of arms by the Chinese, and how much to the *Arrow* War having opened up more of China to British products?

Table 17.6 lists the major items of U.K. exports to China (including Hong Kong) for the years 1854-8.[28] Here, it will be seen that cottons and woollens remained the major commodities. Then came lead and shot, followed by iron and steel. Lead and shot were, of course, ammunition in those days. Interestingly enough, the value of this item doubled in 1856 and 1857, dropping back to its prewar level in 1858. Were the British selling the Chinese lead and shot that could be fired back at them? We should not be surprised. In recent decades, for example, the British sold war technology to Iraq up to the time of

22. Bowring to Stirling, 15 January 1855, enclosed in Bowring to Clarendon, Desp. 31, 15 January 1855, FO17/226
23. Foreign Office to Bonham, 19 September 1848, enclosed in Bowring to Clarendon, Desp. 64, 1 February 1855, FO17/226.
24. W. T. Bridges to Bowring, 21 January 1855, enclosed in Bowring to Clarendon, Desp. 64, 1 February 1855, FO17/226.
25. Stirling to Bowring, 20 January 1855, enclosed in Bowring to Clarendon, Desp. 64, 1 Febrauary 1855, FO17/226.
26. Bowring to Stirling, 2 February 1855, enclosed in Bowring to Clarendon, Desp. 73, 3 February 1855, FO17/226.
27. W. Woodgate to Walker, 3 February 1855, enclosed in Bowring to Clarendon, Desp. 73, 3 February 1855, FO17/226.
28. At this stage, British statisticians still did not separate the various items of export to China from those to Hong Kong, although they had done so, beginning with 1854 as mentioned, with the total value of such exports.

Table 17.6. *U.K. exports to China (and Hong Kong), 1854–8 (£ million sterling)*

Product	1854	1855	1856	1857	1858
Cottons	0.502	0.788	1.334	1.574	1.824
Woollens	0.157	0.134	0.269	0.287	0.391
Cotton yarn	0.139	0.096	0.210	0.158	0.266
Lead and shot	0.044	0.047	0.080	0.093	0.048
Copper	0.023	0.047	0.037	0.025	0.021
Iron and steel	0.016	0.022	0.067	0.074	0.064
Linens	0.012	0.011	0.051	0.018	0.015
Beer and ale	0.012	0.013	0.013	0.036	0.026
Coals etc.	0.011	0.018	0.021	0.046	0.029
Apparel etc.	0.008	0.008	0.016	0.014	0.018
Glassware	0.007	0.007	0.007	0.015	0.017
Cutlery etc.	0.004	0.006	0.009	0.012	0.012
Stationery	0.003	0.004	0.006	0.005	0.008
Earthenware	0.001	0.002	0.002	0.004	0.004
Tin plate	0.001	0.001	0.007	0.004	0.010
All other articles	0.595	0.073	0.088	0.086	0.123
Total	1.001	1.278	2.216	2.450	2.876

Source: Parl. Papers 1859, Session 2, v. 28, p. 335, for the years 1854–8.

the Gulf War (1991), technology which was then used against British and allied troops.[29] Their descendants in Australia did the same sort of thing, right up to the Pacific War. W. H. Donald lamented in 1939: 'It is almost pathetic to see Australia with its 7,000,000 people supplying Japan on the one hand with pig-iron and war materials and on the other hand, frantically preparing to resist an invasion by the Japanese'.[30]

The increase in the value of iron and steel sold was even more dramatic. It

29. For summaries of various reports on this saga, see U.S. Information Service, Ref. FF 11/10/92 NFS289, summary of Dean Baquet's article, 'Britain Drops Case against 3 with Arms Sales to Iraq', *New York Times*, 10 November 1992, p. A1 (TK 252750); FF 11/12/92 NFS 488, summary of Eugene Robinson's article, 'Britain to Probe Cabinet Role in Iraqi Arms Sales', *Washington Post*, 11 November 1992, p. A27 (TK 253026); FF 07/19/93 LFS108 and 07/19/93 NFS 198, summary of Douglas Jehl's article, 'Who Armed Iraq? Answers the West Didn't Want to Hear', *New York Times*, 18 July 1993 (TK295592). I am grateful to the librarian of the research centre of the U.S. Information Service in Sydney, Peter Gilbert, for his help in locating these reports.
30. Quoted in Frank Clune, *Sky High to Shanghai* (Sydney, Angus & Robertson, 1947), p. 363. W. H. Donald was Australian and made this comment in a letter to Clune. At the time he was an adviser to Chiang Kai-shek.

Table 17.7. *U.K. exports to China (and Hong Kong), 1859–62) (£ million sterling)*

Product	1859	1860	1861	1862
Cottons	2.759	3.160	3.180	1.277
Woollens	0.703	0.871	0.723	0.693
Cotton yarn	0.431	0.410	0.307	0.284
Iron and steel	0.115	0.145	0.086	0.109
Lead and shot	0.066	0.114	0.123	0.214
Beer and ale	0.046	0.099	0.022	0.040
Coals etc.	0.046	0.069	0.034	0.088
Copper	0.037	0.059	0.046	0.033
Linens	0.026	0.031	0.029	0.022
Apparel etc.	0.022	0.033	0.029	0.037
Cutlery etc.	0.022	0.026	0.028	0.027
Glassware	0.021	0.030	0.016	0.024
Tin plate	0.013	0.004	0.012	0.015
Stationery	0.008	0.011	0.016	0.014
Earthenware etc.	0.004	0.007	0.006	0.010
All other articles	0.140	0.249	0.193	0.251
Total	4.458	5.318	4.849	3.137

Source: Parl. Papers 1863, v. 65, p. 292, for the years 1859–62.

almost tripled in 1856–8. Iron and steel, of course, are raw materials for the manufacture of weapons. Thus, it seems that the Red Turban Rebellion and the *Arrow* War affected greatly, though temporarily, the pattern of Chinese imports from the United Kingdom.

Table 17.7 is a continuation of Table 17.6, and covers the years 1859–62. Here again, cottons and woollens dominated U.K. exports to China. But when the *Arrow* War ended in 1860, the sale of lead and shot to China in that year almost doubled that of 1859. In 1862, it almost doubled again. The import of iron and steel was also maintained at a high level. These phenomena may be explained by the fact that once the quarrel with the Chinese government was over, the British authorities began considering support for that government in their efforts to suppress the Taiping Rebellion. If the year 1861 was still one of 'indecision',[31] 1862–4 were years of active 'intervention'.[32] The most notable contribution of the British authorities was their training and arming of the so-called Ever-Victorious Army.[33] Thus, British assistance in putting the Manchu

31. Gregory, *Great Britain and the Taipings*, chapter 6.
32. Ibid., chapter 7.
33. See Smith, *Mercenaries and Mandarins*.

government's house in order also seems to have affected the pattern of Chinese imports from the United Kingdom.

The crucial issue now is to determine whether the increased quantities of woollens and cottons exported from the United Kingdom to China were due to the *Arrow* War having gained Britain greater access to Chinese markets. Let us begin our analysis with the year 1830, when His Majesty's government held a public inquiry into the British East India Company's trading monopoly in China. Giving evidence, numerous witnesses accused the company of having been singularly unsuccessful in selling woollens and cottons to the Chinese.

In fact, the company lost a good deal of money in the trade in these products, 'which was carried on rather to satisfy the people of England than for any profit to be derived from it'.[34] Even at greatly reduced prices, sometimes halved,[35] company employees still found it difficult to persuade their Chinese counterparts to buy. In the end the company had to resort to purchasing tea in proportion as woollens and cottons were taken.[36] The Chinese merchants, in turn, had to sell their woollens and cottons at a loss. They tried to make good that loss by raising the prices of tea sold to the company. This partly explained the higher price of tea in the United Kingdom than in the United States.[37]

Why was it difficult to sell woollens and cottons to China? In those days, the rich in China preferred padded silk garments to woollens in the winter. The poor could not afford woollens and wore padded cotton clothes. Thus, neither the rich nor the poor would buy British woollens. As for British cotton textiles, they were likewise unsaleable partly because of the strong Chinese rural tradition of spinning and weaving at home to clothe the whole family. Besides, British textiles manufactured from U.S. cotton and shipped to China with the additional margins for freight, insurance, and profit, were really not serious competitors for the Chinese homespun in terms of price. Furthermore, Chinese homespun was much more durable than the British manufactures.[38]

There is little reason to doubt that the situation was substantially the same in the *Arrow* War period. We have noticed a remarkable rise in the quantity of tea imported into the United Kingdom from China. The corresponding rise in the export of U.K. woollens and cottons to China most likely would have been a

---

34. J. F. Davis's evidence, 22 February 1830, in Parl. Papers 1830, v. 5, Q507. See also C. Majoribands's evidence, 18 February 1830, in ibid., Q182; and J. C. Melville's evidence, 11 May 1830, in Parl. Papers 1830, v. 5, Q5128.
35. Majoribands's evidence, 18 February 1830, in Parl. Papers 1830, v. 5, Q302 and Q318.
36. Ibid., Q574.
37. Ibid., Q509.
38. See Morse, *International Relations of the Chinese Empire*, v. 1, chapter 4.

Table 17.8. *U.K. imports of tea compared with its export of woollens and cottons, 1827–67*

Year	Tea: quantities (millions of pounds) 1	Percentage, using 1827 as the base-year figure 2	Value of woollens and cottons combined (£ million sterling) 3	Percentage, using 1827 as the base-year figure 4
1827	39.75	100.00	1.68	100.00
1828	32.68	82.21	1.58	94.05
1829	30.54	76.83	1.44	85.71
1830	31.90	80.25	1.78	105.95
1831	31.65	79.62	1.33	79.17
1832	31.71	79.77	1.45	86.31
1833	32.06	80.65	1.32	78.57
1834	32.03	80.58	1.17	69.64
1835	42.05	105.79	1.56	92.86
1836	48.52	122.06	2.29	136.31
1837	36.50	91.82	1.74	103.57
1838	39.00	98.11	1.99	118.45
1839	37.19	93.56	2.44	145.24
1840	22.58	56.81	3.19	189.88
1841	27.64	69.53	2.93	174.40
1842	37.41	94.11	2.65	157.74
1843	42.78	107.62	3.40	202.38
1844	51.75	130.19	4.01	238.69
1845	50.71	127.57	3.60	214.29
1846	54.53	137.18	3.42	203.57
1847	55.36	139.27	2.63	156.55
1848	47.35	119.12	2.50	148.81
1849	53.10	133.58	3.65	217.26
1850	49.37	124.20	4.46	265.48
1851	69.49	174.82	4.69	279.17
1852	65.30	164.28	4.49	267.26
1853	68.64	172.68	4.74	282.14
1854	83.30	209.56	6.25	372.02
1855	81.56	205.18	5.45	324.40
1856	84.80	213.33	5.75	342.26
1857	60.30	151.70	6.22	370.24
1858	73.36	184.55	9.88	588.10
1859	71.92	180.93	3.46	205.95
1860	85.30	279.31	4.03	239.88
1861	92.15	231.82	3.90	232.14
1862	109.76	276.13	1.97	117.26
1863	129.44	325.64	2.17	129.17
1864	115.10	289.56	3.35	199.40
1865	112.78	283.72	4.32	257.14

Table 17.8. (*cont.*)

Year	Tea: quantities (millions of pounds) 1	Percentage, using 1827 as the base-year figure 2	Value of woollens and cottons combined (£ million sterling) 3	Percentage, using 1827 as the base-year figure 4
1866	130.86	329.21	6.08	361.90
1867	117.55	295.72	5.86	348.81

Note: In col. 1, the quantity of tea is selected instead of the value. In the Parliamentary Papers, value was represented by 'official value' up to 1853 and by 'computed real ralue' thereafter. Such a change would have made col. 2, if presented in value, unworkable. Therefore in col. 2, the entry in each year after 1827 is represented as a percentage of that of 1827. In col. 3, value is selected because it is impossible to combine woollens and cottons in quantity – the quantity of cottons was not given in the original statistics, only value. Col. 4 follows the same format as col. 2.
Sources: Parl. Papers 1859, Session 2, v. 23, pp. 315 and 319, for the years 1825–58; 1863, v. 65, pp. 291–2, for 1859–62; 1867–68, v. 67, pp. 304–5, for 1863–7.

result of the kind of bargaining just mentioned, and not a result of greater access to the Chinese markets.

To test this hypothesis, Table 17.8 has been compiled. It covers thirty-one years, beginning in 1827, when the statistics in this regard became available. We shall use this as the base-year figure – 100 per cent. The table ends in 1867, seven years after the *Arrow* War. From this table, it seems that the oscillation in sales of woollens and cottons in China, generally speaking, follow those of tea there. It appears, therefore, that the sort of bargaining observed in the 1820s continued after the company's monopoly had been abolished.

This point is made even clearer in Figure 17.5. It shows that, using 1827 as the base-year figure (100 per cent) the rise and fall in these percentages follow each other quite closely during the days of the company, and for about two decades afterwards. Thus, it seems that the British merchants had to follow the company's practice of purchasing tea in proportion as woollens and cottons were taken.[39]

Then came a wild fluctuation in 1858, when the sale of woollens and cottons jumped at the same time as the purchase of tea actually fell. It is unclear how the British merchants managed this feat. However, one must remember that goods exported from Britain were not necessarily sold at their destination. The Treaty of Tientsin, which was signed in 1858 and promised to open up the interior of China to foreign trade, might have raised wild expectations for 'that

39. See Majoribands's evidence, 18 February 1830, in Parl. Papers 1830, v. 5, Q574.

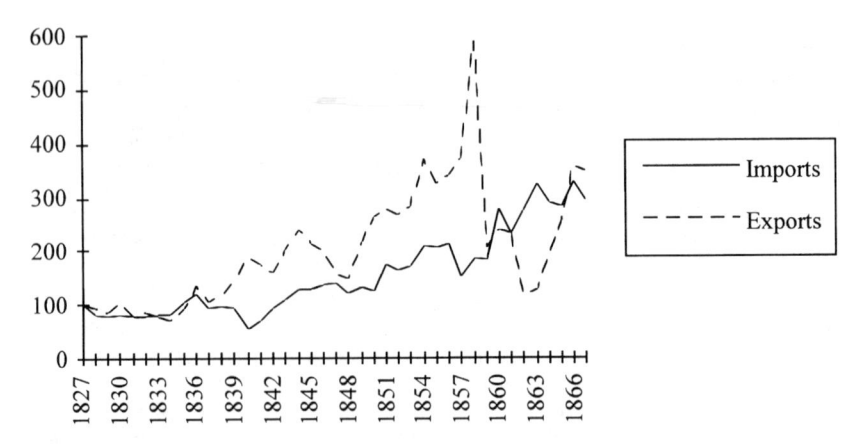

Figure 17.5. U.K. imports of tea compared with export of woollens and cottons, 1827–67 (using 1827 as the base-year figure of 100 per cent; based on columns 2 and 4, Table 17.8)

huge market of four hundred millions'.[40] Probably, the British merchants simply oversupplied the market.

The repercussions were quick to follow. The export of woollens and cottons slumped the next year and continued to fall sharply for some years to come. Even increased purchases of tea failed to improve the sale of woollens and cottons. In the case of cottons alone, the sharp decline may also be partly related to the cotton shortage caused by the U.S. Civil War, beginning in 1861.[41] In any case, it appears that there were sufficient surplus stocks in China to last many years; and when the Chinese merchants finally got rid of their stocks of British woollens and cottons by 1865 – five years after the *Arrow* War – these manufactures began to move again.

The inevitable conclusion is that the British policy makers were wrong in their assumption that opening more of China would improve the sale of British woollens and cottons. Again, the value of cotton exports alone to China in 1858–60 is said to have doubled that of 1855–7. In 1860, 43 per cent of the total value of British cottons exported was taken by four markets: 20.7 per cent by India, 8.7 per cent by the United States, 6.8 per cent by Turkey, and 6.5 per cent by China.[42] But 1860 was the peak year, from which a decline by 2 per

40. S. Osborn, *The Past and Future of British Relations in China* (Edinburgh, Blackwood, 1860), p. 10.
41. For the effect of the cotton shortage on the Lancashire mills, see Redford, *Manchester Merchants and Foreign Trade*, chapter 2. The Manchester Chamber of Commerce and Industries commented that the stagnation of the cotton trade in 1861, for example, was due as much to 'want of markets as to want of cotton' (ibid., p. 14, quoting the chamber's proceedings, 18 September 1861).
42. D. A. Farnie, *The English Cottoon Industry and the World Market, 1815–1896* (Oxford, Clarendon Press, 1979), p. 138.

The balance sheet

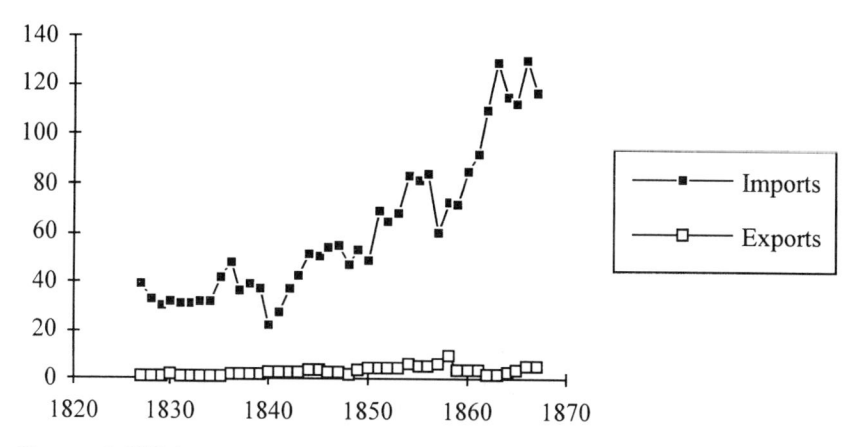

Figure 17.6. U.K. imports of tea compared with its export of woollens and cottons, 1827–67 (in millions of pounds for tea; £ million sterling for woollens and cottons; based on colums 1 and 3, Table 17.8)

cent was witnessed in 1861, and a further 5.5 per cent in 1862.[43] These figures corroborate my analysis. In sum, it seems that the *Arrow* War fulfilled the expectations of the British policy makers in so far as they gained greater access to supplies of tea (which was utilized) and silk (which became redundant).

However, they were wrong to expect that greater access to China's market per se would increase the sale of British woollens and cottons. In this sense, the validity of the Mitchell Report, and the case which Pelcovits has built on it, still stands. Pelcovits argues that the Foreign Office allowed itself to be persuaded by old China hands of the huge market for such British products. Mitchell, a colonial official in Hong Kong, realized by 1852 that no such market existed. The Chinese were self-sufficient, especially in clothing. Mitchell prepared a report to this effect. It was shelved by his superior, who did not wish the Foreign Office to know of it.[44] Had the senior British officials known and taken it seriously, they might not have waged the *Arrow* War with the same sort of enthusiasm.

This point is reinforced in Figure 17.6, which shows that tea imports after the *Arrow* War ascended higher and higher, but the British exportation of woollens and cottons to China went forward only very slowly.

The fact remains, however, that British exports to China did grow sharply after the *Arrow* War. This growth was due, as mentioned, partly to the British

43. Ibid., p. 140.
44. Pelcovits, *Old China Hands and the Foreign Office*, pp. 15–17.

451

Table 17.9. *U.K. exports to China (and Hong Kong), 1863–6 (£ million sterling)*

Product	1863	1864	1865	1866
Cottons	1.170	2.011	2.788	4.421
Woollens	1.003	1.337	1.532	1.662
Lead and shot	0.311	0.170	0.047	0.104
Cotton yarn	0.239	0.242	0.104	0.429
Iron and steel	0.221	0.182	0.133	0.121
Arms etc.	0.086	0.075	0.048	0.113
Beer and ale	0.079	0.047	0.046	0.059
Coals etc.	0.078	0.078	0.053	0.064
Apparel etc.	0.063	0.044	0.031	0.049
Copper	0.051	0.056	0.067	0.062
Linens	0.040	0.037	0.046	0.071
Cutlery etc.	0.039	0.031	0.021	0.016
Glassware	0.033	0.026	0.016	0.020
Pickles etc.	0.031	0.021	0.012	0.020
Provisions	0.031	0.022	0.013	0.018
Tin plate	0.026	0.045	0.009	0.005
Earthenware etc.	0.014	0.009	0.006	0.010
Paper of all sorts	0.011	0.009	0.010	0.010
Stationery	0.009	0.007	0.004	0.006
All other articles	0.354	0.262	0.164	0.218
Total	3.889	4.711	5.15	7.478

Source: Parl. Papers 1867–8, v. 67, p. 305, for the years 1863–7.

merchants' tactics of selling woollens and cottons in proportion to the greatly increased purchases of tea. The other factor was the extraordinary situation to be found in China at this time, as we shall see in the next section.

IV. Exports: War materials

The year 1863 was a watershed, as Table 17.9 shows. In this year, the item 'Arms etc.', in addition to 'Lead and shot' and 'Iron and steel', made its first appearance on the list of the U.K. exports to China. This is not surprising in light of the Taiping Rebellion. As mentioned, active intervention by the British authorities began in 1862, and sales of arms to the Chinese government followed quickly. The sale of arms ranked sixth in the order of value of U.K. exports to China and Hong Kong conjointly. Thus, arms and ammunition simply added to the value of trade to some extent, but by no means disrupted the pattern of British exports.

Table 17.10. *Export of U.K. products to China, 1854–66 (£ million sterling)*

Year	Exports to China	Total exports	China's percentage (col. 1 ÷ col. 2)
1854	0.53	63.33	0.84
1855	0.89	69.14	1.29
1856	1.42	82.53	1.72
1857	1.73	84.91	2.04
1858	1.73	76.39	2.27
1859	2.53	84.27	3.00
1860	2.87	92.23	3.11
1861	3.11	82.86	3.76
1862	2.02	82.10	2.47
1863	2.42	95.72	2.52
1864	3.09	108.73	2.84
1865	3.60	117.63	3.06
1866	5.09	135.20	3.76

Sources: Compiled from statistics in Parl. Papers 1859, Session 2, v. 28, p. 6, for the years 1854–8; 1864, v. 57, p. 6, for 1859–63; 1867–8, v. 67, p. 6, for 1864–6.

V. In sum

Until 1854, statistics for the exportation of British products to China were mingled with those for Hong Kong. But for the period of the *Arrow* War, it is possible to gauge the effect of the conflict on the exportation of British products directly to China. For this purpose, Table 17.10 has been compiled. The year 1854, not 1855, has been selected as the starting point because, although 1855 was the year immediately before the *Arrow* War, it was also when abnormal purchases of British war materials took place because of the siege of Canton. In this respect, 1854 was a more normal prewar year. With regard to the cut-off point for Table 17.10, 1866, not 1860, has been chosen because, as mentioned, the British began shipping even larger quantities of arms to China after 1860, to help the Chinese government fight the Taipings. That rebellion was finally suppressed in 1864, so allowing a year or so for things to settle down, 1866 would have been a more normal postwar year.

According to Table 17.10, the United Kingdom exported about £0.53 million worth of goods to China in 1854. In 1866 the figure was £5.09 million, a nearly tenfold increase. Globally, the United Kingdom exported £63.33 million worth of goods in 1854. In 1866, these were worth £135.2 million – just over twice their earlier level. Thus, exports to China went up tenfold while total U.K. exports only doubled in the same period. In relative terms, China's share of the United Kingdom's total exports grew from a mere 0.84 per cent in 1854 to 3.76 per cent in 1866 – an almost fivefold increase.

It goes without saying that the export of Indian opium to China also increased with the opening of areas hitherto closed to foreign trade. By 1865, its demand had augmented 'in a very satisfactory manner at the Yangtze and northern ports, and there is every prospect of the trade at the former becoming more and more important . . . [and] extending to all the ports and provinces.'[45] Statistical information on the postwar sharp rises of the export of Indian opium to China has been provided in Chapter 16.

In view of all these remarkable increases, Palmerston's cabinet, in opposition in 1858–9, could congratulate themselves for having decided to use the *Arrow* quarrel as a pretext for coercion. And the opposition, briefly in power in 1858–9, could feel equally vindicated for having continued that war until Palmerston returned to power in June 1859 to bring it to a successful conclusion in 1860.

45. 'Commercial Report . . . China, 1865', Parl. Papers, 1866, v. 71, p. 84. For later developments, see Owen, *Opium Policy*; and Harcourt, 'Black Gold'.

Part VII
The dynamics of imperialism

The final decision to wage war on China was made in London. The pivotal consideration was to make the Chinese government legalize the contraband opium trade and to expand legitimate British trade in China. A peaceful means to this end having been rejected by the Chinese authorities three months earlier, the British government resorted to violence. This was the ultimate origin of the *Arrow* War. Why has it been so difficult to come to this conclusion? – the dynamics of imperialism, so dynamic that it has proved exceedingly hard to track down, in the words of Professor Wang Gungwu, 'the beast'. Let us now condense these findings to see how we have come to pinpoint the real origins of the war and if we have provided a logical framework within which to explain this phenomenon.

18
Conclusion

I. The confusion of imperialism

Much of the confusion surrounding the origins of the *Arrow* War arose because the *Arrow* incident was regarded as the casus belli by Britain at the time, and by historians generally since. It was such a flimsy excuse that I could hardly believe the British authorities were serious; they did not tell the truth. Lord Ellenborough was an exception. In censuring Bowring for having acted 'throughout with no motive whatever but that which is denounced – general covetousness and the desire of making money by the misfortunes of mankind', he revealed the pivotal cause of the war.[1] Others in the House of Lords preferred to keep quiet. This is not surprising. Would any government in any age admit pubicly to the motives Ellenborough ascribed to Bowring?

Members in the House of Commons were similarly restrained. Nonetheless the debate there developed in such a way as to unravel the real intentions of the government: the fearless Palmerston accepted Russell's challenge and gave material justification for the military measures which Bowring had taken against China.[2] This episode began with Richard Cobden[3] and Erskine Perry[4] complaining about the imbalance of trade with China; the lord advocate proposing, for the sake of the grave interests involved, to fight the war to the end;[5] and Sidney Herbert highlighting the importance of the opium trade for Indian finance;[6] whereupon Palmerston defended the opium trade by saying that it helped to balance the trade deficit with China. He regretted that the Chinese had rejected the British appeal for treaty revision, for otherwise opium would have been legalized and British trade expanded. He wondered what

1. Ellenborough, 26 February 1857, Hansard, 3d series, v. 144, col. 1364.
2. Palmerston, 3 March 1857, Hansard, 3d series, v. 144, col. 1826.
3. Cobden, 26 February 1857, Hansard, 3d series, v. 144, col. 1412.
4. Perry, 26 February 1857, Hansard, 3d series, v. 144, col. 1460.
5. The lord advocate, 27 February 1857, Hansard, 3d series, v. 144, col. 1517.
6. Herbert, 2 March 1857, Hansard, 3d series, v. 144, col. 1677.

Britain was supposed to do under the circumstances.[7] Thereupon Disraeli spelled out what Palmerston did not wish to say publicly: to use force to increase British economic interests in China.[8]

The British press perceptively observed that most members of Parliament preferred to dwell on numerous issues other than this single most important one, because no minister would dare stand up and frankly say, 'I have acted in this matter for the extension of British power'. Whoever did so would be frozen by the silence of a shocked assembly.[9] The result was 'that we have not the honest opinion of the British Parliament upon the justice or expediency of our proceedings in China'.[10] Underneath the official silence, however, were general principles in which everybody concurred – the commercial interests of the world's greatest trading nation. 'Like many of the wars in which England has engaged, this is a merchants' war'.[11] In pursuit of commercial interests, the merchants were unabashed in calling a spade a spade. It is the sophistry that pervaded most of what was said in Parliament and elsewhere that has confused the issue to this day.

This particular merchants' war has caused confusion among not only diplomatic but British political and economic historians. It is generally believed that mid-Victorian England was gripped by free-trade ideology and that British expansion overseas in this period is best interpreted within the framework of free-trade imperialism. If so, how does one square these views with the fact that the major leaders of free-trade ideology – Richard Cobden, John Bright, and Thomas Milner-Gibson, the most prominent members of the Manchester school – were all thrown out of Parliament during the Chinese Election which was fought to a large extent over the issue of war with China? Accepted explanations of the expulsion include the school's pacifism during the Crimean War and its support for franchise reform.[12] Both are far-fetched. One must remember that the mass meeting held on 29 January 1857, initially called to hear Bright's offer of resignation on the grounds of ill health, for example, had ended as a great demonstration of his 'firm hold on the constituency'.[13] If his pacifism and radical views had been the key factors for his rejection two months later, these grievances would have revealed themselves at that meeting. Another received explanation is that the electors had been swayed by the government's jingoism. But merchants, generally hard-nosed, are not so readily swayed by empty slogans. Rather, they would have been more easily excited

7. Palmerston, 3 March 1857, Hansard, 3d series, v. 144, col. 1828.
8. Disraeli, 3 March 1857, Hansard, 3d series, v. 144, col. 1836.
9. *Morning Star*, 6 March 1857.
10. *Spectator*, 7 March 1857.
11. *Manchester Guardian*, 11 March 1857.
12. Arthur Silver, *Manchester Men and Indian Cotton, 1847–1872* (Manchester, Manchester University Press, 1966), p. 82.
13. Ibid., p. 83.

Conclusion

by the prospects of gain or tipped off balance by threats of bankruptcy. I have found (see Chapter 10) that the Manchester business people had become hysterical as a result of the adverse vote in the House of Commons.[14] Their concerns were not just those of manufacturers keen to expand the China market, but also those of exporters of goods to India, where the interruption of the opium trade could cause serious problems since their Indian customers depended on that illicit trade for their funds.[15] Thus, the phenomenon 'Manchester had cut off its nose to spite its face'[16] can be explained – the electorate there wanted to squash all opposition to the *Arrow* War.

II. The pretext for imperialism

Reluctant to speak their minds, government members of Parliament concentrated on sensational charges about the alleged insult to the British flag, which they insisted was the fundamental casus belli. Walter Bagehot once divided the English constitution into two classes: the *dignified* parts, which excited and preserved the reverence of the population; and the *efficient* parts, by which it worked and ruled.[17] Thus, alleged compromises to national honour could be very inflammatory to the general public. That is why the British government so freely exploited that allegation, and the British public so readily believed it.

However, the evidence suggests overwhelmingly that the British flag was unlikely to have been flying, let alone hauled down. British nautical practice required that no ship fly its flags while at anchor. The *Arrow* was at anchor at the time of the incident, and had been so for five days. These factors make Parkes's claim that the boat was 'lying with her colours flying'[18] read inconsistent and incredible. One has to remember that Parkes blurted out this claim in a state of great agitation. To make amends, Parkes subsequently alleged that two of the sailors were 'unmooring the lorcha at the moment when the mandarins boarded',[19] so as to give the impression that the boat was about to set sail and the flags were accordingly, albeit prematurely, up. In making that allegation, Parkes seems to have forgotten that the captain of the *Arrow* was not on board, but was away breakfasting in another boat. It is inconceivable that

---

14. See Bazley to Clarendon, 5 March 1857, FO17/280, p. 37.
15. Chang, *Commissioner Lin*, pp. 192–3, quoting Parl. Papers 'Memorials Addressed to Her Majesty's Government by British Merchants Interested in the Trade with China' (1840).
16. Silver, *Manchester Men and Indian Cotton*, p. 84.
17. Walter Bagehot, *The English Constitution* (London, Thomas Nelson, 1872), p. 74.
18. Parkes to Bowring, Desp. 150, 8 October 1856, para. 1, FO228/213.
19. Parke's account of his interrogation of Leang A-yung, 9 October 1856, enclosed in Parkes to Bowring, Desp. 155, 9 October 1856, FO228/213. Again, this claim about unmooring the *Arrow* was not corroborated by any other evidence; one also wonders why the account had to take the form of a short declaration by Parkes himself, rather than the usual statement by a witness, as happened with all the other evidence.

the captain could have commanded his sailors to lift anchor and then gone away for breakfast; or that the sailors could have lifted anchor without orders, amounting to mutiny. Parkes also seems to have forgotten that the incident had happened around 8 A.M. and that the sailing papers of the *Arrow* were still deposited in his consulate, which would not open until 10 A.M. How dared any boat leave port without its papers?

Thus, even Lord Clarendon called the *Arrow* incident 'a miserable case'.[20] Lord Elgin considered it 'a scandal to us'.[21] The journalists on the spot omitted any mention of the alleged insult to the flag,[22] while those in England similarly omitted it.[23] In Parliament, the opposition bombarded the government with questions about the flag, most of which remained unanswered.[24] A year later, a journalist in Hong Kong wrote: 'The *Arrow* subject has been exhausted – its defenders left the field long ago'.[25] Nonetheless, the British government insisted that the *Arrow* incident was *the* origin of the war. Hence, Chapter 2 assumes an importance which it may not have otherwise had. In that chapter it was discovered that in all probability the Union Jack had not been insulted. Even in the most unlikely event[26] that there had been such an affront, we have seen that the law lords argued quite convincingly that the affront had not been intended.[27]

In this context, Chapter 3 is just as important, discovering that it was Parkes who turned the *Arrow* affair into an international incident. He kept first Bowring and then Seymour in the dark about the expiry of the ship's register until it no longer mattered, and manipulated the two into launching an undeclared war on China. He might not, from the start, have cold-bloodedly chosen to make an issue of the incident. But after his heated exchange of words and then blows with the Chinese officers, he was certainly determined to turn it into one. Thereupon, personal grievance and his perception of public duty seem to have prompted him to change his attitude towards Captain Kennedy's story about the insult to the flag from one of disbelief to one of total support. Kennedy would have had every reason to fabricate such an insult because I found that his ship had been guilty of at least receiving stolen goods from pirates. Anxious to stop the exposure of such a crime by preventing his sailors from being examined by the Chinese authorities, he must have thought the only way was to have them claimed back by the British consul immediately.

20. Clarendon, 24 February 1857, Hansard, 3d series, v. 144, col. 1196.
21. Walrond (ed.), *Letters and Journals of Elgin*, p. 209.
22. *The Times*, 29 December 1856.
23. Ibid., 2 January 1857.
24. See Chapters 8–9.
25. *Daily Press* (newspaper clipping, Hong Kong), 6 January 1858, Ryl. Eng. MSS 1230/67.
26. It will be remembered that independent Portuguese eyewitnesses, aboard lorcha no. 83, confirmed the Chinese assertion that no flags were flying on the *Arrow*. Derby, 24 February 1857, Hansard, 3d series, v. 144, col. 1166.
27. See Chapter 8.

And the most prompt and effective way to mobilize the consul was to allege that the Chinese had insulted the flag. Young Parkes disbelieved and then believed him, not because of Kennedy's powers of persuasion, but because of Parkes's own impetuosity which led to his scuffles with the Chinese officers.

An eminent Chinese historian has asserted that 'Palmerston's government needed a war with China, as a result of which there was an *Arrow* incident'.[28] In other words, the incident was deliberately manufactured in order to create a casus belli. Who was the manufacturer? Specifically, it would have to be Parkes. That historian did not substantiate his claim, but we have to commend his imagination.

Thus, in many ways Parkes's actions in this affair may be compared with those of such empire builders as the French officers in Africa,[29] the Russian officers at the capture of Bokhara and Khiva,[30] the junior Japanese officers involved in the murder of Zhang Zuolin in Manchuria,[31] or even Parkes's own compatriot Sir Charles Napier in the annexation of Sind in India.[32] However, Parkes's own vision of empire was not territorial. He commented, 'I do not myself recognise any very defined line between our political and our commercial interests; the two are so intimately woven together, that one leads to the other'.[33] So his political actions during the *Arrow* dispute had a commercial objective – an informal empire in the Gallagher–Robinson mode.

III. The personalities of imperialism

Neither the majority of the British government members nor those of the opposition seemed to recognize fully that in Consul Parkes might be found an origin of the *Arrow* War. Neither party had any means of knowing Parkes's personal humiliation at the hands of the Chinese officers, his love of war games, and what Palmerston might have insinuated to him at 10 Downing Street early in 1856. As a result, although the opposition denounced Parkes's behaviour as 'grotesque',[34] it could not understand why he had behaved in this manner. Nor

---

28. Hu, *Cong Yapian zhanzheng dao Wusi yundong*, p. 190. Again, Professor Hu is perhaps the most influential historian in China, being the president of the Chinese Academy of Social Sciences.
29. See, e.g., A. S. Kanya-Forstner, *The Conquest of the Western Sudan: A Study in French Military Imperialism* (Cambridge University Press, 1969).
30. See, e.g., Richard A. Pierce, *Russian Central Asia, 1867–1917* (Berkeley and Los Angeles, University of California Press, 1960).
31. See John Hunter Boyle, *China and Japan at War, 1937–1945* (Stanford, Calif., Stanford University Press, 1972), p. 330.
32. See Chapter 16; and also Lambrick, *Sir Charles Napier and Sind*.
33. Quoted in Platt, *Finance, Trade and Politics*, p. 271.
34. This is the word used by Malmesbury; see Malmesbury, 26 February 1857, Hansard, 3d series, v. 144, cols. 1350–1.

could many in the government. Furthermore, not even the government appeared to realize that Parkes had put words into Bowring's mouth, manipulated Admiral Seymour, and deliberately misrepresented Yeh's letters to escalate the dispute, as we have found in Chapter 3. Parkes may have been overzealous in carrying out what he may have perceived as the government's wishes, but it would have been virtually impossible for the prime minister to admit that a serious mistake had been made.[35] Thus, Palmerston was obliged to support Parkes at all costs. He could not be expected to concede that an origin of the *Arrow* War might be attributed to his Achilles. In this context, it seems that the tail wagged the dog.

Nor could Palmerston disavow Bowring, whom he had selected personally, first as consul to Canton and later as plenipotentiary, and whom he must have understood had acted in support of Parkes's scheme. The opposition said that Bowring was possessed with a monomania. The monomania lay in his private thirst for glory and his public concern over British trade in China. His desire to win glory might be traced to the Chinese victory over the Canton City question in 1849. His public concerns were related to the expansion and legalization of the opium trade in China. This monomania was a very dangerous state of mind. 'It made a man more dangerous in every single relation of life than almost any other constitution of mind', said the bishop of Oxford, for a man so possessed by 'one fixed fancy . . . seemed never to have appreciated the crime and evil of the bloodshed and misery he was causing'.[36] Vivid examples of this were unearthed in Chapter 4. Among them, his lie to Commissioner Yeh 'that the lorcha *Arrow* lawfully bore the British flag under a register granted by me',[37] when he knew perfectly well that the *Arrow*'s register had expired; and, of course, his conspiracy with Parkes to hide that expiry from the admiral in his attempt to get the admiral to take coercive action against China, in the course of which he concealed not only from the admiral but from his superior in London, Lord Clarendon, that he had had detailed discussions with Parkes *before* the conference on 20 October, in which the admiral, Bowring and Parkes participated.

Instead of blaming his own agents, Palmerston reproached that 'insolent barbarian Yeh'[38] who, 'in order to keep the English out of Canton, ordered the people to insult them, while the people outside treat the English

---

35. A recent example of something similar was the air raids on Libya ordered by President Ronald Reagan in retaliation for the alleged Libyan involvement in the terrorist bombing of a German nightclub frequented by U.S. servicemen. Subsequently, the German authorities discovered that Syria, and not Libya, had been the guilty party. The United States has never apologized for the wrongful punishment of Libya, and one almost suspects that later U.S. actions through the UN against Libya over the explosion of a Pan Am plane over Lockerbie in Scotland were attempts to justify the earlier mistake.
36. Wilburforce, 26 February 1857, Hansard, 3d series, v. 144, col. 1382.
37. Bowring to Yeh, 14 November 1856, Parl. Papers 1857, v. 12, pp. 143-4.
38. *The Times*, 28 March 1957.

respectfully'.[39] Thus, despite Cobden's demolition of the government's ploy inside Parliament to attribute the origins of the war additionally to the so-called insults allegedly meted out by the Cantonese people,[40] outside Parliament Palmerston reformulated that ploy to assert that Yeh had ordered such insults, an assertion which, as we have seen in Chapters 5–6, is false.

So what about Palmerston himself as one of the key personalities of British imperialism at this time? On the basis of an analysis of his speeches and private letters, Robert Gavin has shown that Palmerston conceived of every human society as an aggregate of conflicting economic and political interest groups held together by the power of its government.[41] Thus, Palmerston attributed Commissioner Lin's suppression of opium in 1839–40 to the alleged machinations of local poppy growers,[42] which were nonexistent in China at this time. And he wrote in 1860 that Britain had just concluded the *Arrow* War with 'a third of the human race but the greater part of whom have seen our success with almost as much pleasure as those successes have afforded to ourselves'.[43] Palmerston's powers of manipulation were indeed remarkable, and he seems to have been able to get away with it through sheer charisma and a somewhat risqué humour.

In his own mind, Palmerston perceived it to be his duty to plan on a grand scale, trusting that his 'restless activity encircled the globe'.[44]

IV. The rhetoric of imperialism

Given Palmerston's world, understandably he refused to blame his agents, and even vigorously defended them. After he had appointed Elgin the new plenipotentiary, he still said publicly that the appointment was no disparagement to Bowring. 'When special difficulties arise special men are sent out to settle them. Lord Elgin has thus gone out without superseding Sir John Bowring, who will continue to be what he is'.[45] But by this time he had stripped Bowring of his powers, although he allowed him to continue as governor of Hong Kong. Such was the rhetoric of imperialism.

This rhetoric also involved the press. Naturally, the *Arrow* quarrel caused enormous controversy in the newspapers as in Parliament. But the journalists were much more honest than the politicians about saying frankly where real British interests lay, as we found in Chapter 7.

39. Palmerston's speech on Friday, 27 March 1857, at Tiverton immediately after the election. See *The Times*, 30 March 1857.
40. See Chapter 9.
41. Gavin, 'Palmerston's Policy towards East and West Africa, 1830–1865', p. 25.
42. Palmerston, 9 April 1840, Hansard, 3d series, v. 53, col. 940, quoted in ibid.
43. Palmerston to Panmure, 22 December 1860, Panmure Papers, quoted in ibid., p. 26.
44. Palmerston, 1 March 1843, Hansard, 3d series, quoted in ibid., p. 32.
45. Palmerston's speech as reported by *The Times*, 30 March 1857.

Thus, *Punch* said that nothing could have surpassed the eloquence of Lord Derby's speech, but believed that he would have made an even more enthusiastic address if the rupture at Canton had occurred under a government led by him, and therefore obliged to speak on the other side of the question.[46] *Punch* scarcely gave more credit to Gladstone, saying that he was merely playing a deep game of chess.[47] *The Times* even addressed this homily to Yeh: 'If Parkes, Bowring, Seymour, Palmerston, Labouchere and their colleagues have beaten you with rods, Derby, Ellenborough, Russell, and Graham humbly hope that they may live to give you a taste of scorpions'.[48] Superbly these passages distil the essence of the debate in the House of Lords as set out in Chapter 8.

The *Spectator* was equally perceptive. Commenting on the vote in the House of Commons, it wrote: 'And that vote will have no influence on the course of events in China; will neither undo what has been done, nor stay the employment of force till force has bent the stubbornness of the Chinese to our Western will'.[49] It concluded that the vote was really on the question of whether Palmerston should continue in office or not, because the members knew that how they cast their ballot papers would have no practical effect in China. Had the situation been different, had the members known that their votes would affect the course of events they were nominally discussing, there would always have been too much patriotism and good sense to allow the interests of the country to be made a mere stalking-horse for the party.[50] All this was revealed in Chapter 9.

What ultimately gave Palmerston strength, and the strength to support his agents, however reckless, was the public passion of imperial Britain at this time, as we discovered in Chapter 10. It was his unerring feeling for the popular pulse that carried the day. He was acutely aware of his own popularity as the winner of the Crimean War. He probably also shared the general sentiment of the time that peace was dull. Thus, he enjoyed speaking out in a tone that deliberately echoed the patriotic fervour of Trafalgar and Waterloo. It was a tone not much resorted to in politics of his era, though later in the century it was to become commonplace, until it was sullied in the mud of Flanders.[51]

This is not to suggest that all Victorian Britons were preoccupied with jingoism or material interests to the exclusion of other considerations. To the radical Cobden, for example, commerce was a means of promoting peaceful

46. *Punch*, 7 March 1857, p. 98.   47. Ibid.
48. *The Times*, 28 February 1857.
49. *Spectator*, 7 March 1857.
50. Ibid.
51. Beeching, *The Chinese Opium Wars*, p. 225. Flanders was the front line of the British army in continental Europe during the Great War, during which about one million British soldiers died.

collaboration among nations, and any attempt to extend it by violence was a contradiction.[52] His speech in the House of Commons was 'closely argued, full of matter, without an accent of passion, unanswerable on the special case, and thoroughly broad and statesmanlike in general views'.[53] It won the hearts of even some of Palmerston's supporters. It sent the Liberal Party scurrying to woo its own members during the weekend break in the debate. It obliged the government to manipulate the press. Despite all these efforts the government lost the debate.

In the House of Lords, the government had better luck. Hereditary peers were not so easily persuaded. Nonetheless, Derby's powerful appeal to justice and humanity caused the government to circulate rumours about the ill health of the Archbishop of Canterbury and about vacancies in the Order of the Garter in an attempt to reduce the number of members being swayed.[54]

The phenomena in both houses of Parliament may be attributable to the Victorian liberal conscience. The Parliament of 1857, elected on a limited franchise, was dominated by the British upper class. As gentlemen of means and generally well educated, they could exercise their independent judgement and vote according to their conscience. Ten years later, the Second Reform Bill widened the franchise further. This was followed by the Liberal Party's reforms that echoed the U.S. caucus system, binding all M.P.s of the party to the same vote at pains of expulsion. Early in the twentieth century the Labour Party came into being and introduced a system of payments to M.P.s, further reducing their independence. So, even democratization has a price attached to it. Indeed liberal England died a strange death.[55] In this sense, the *Arrow* War debate – so obviously cogent and sober except for some government members – was a watershed at which, once passed, even radicals became jingoistic.

V. The mechanics of imperialism

When we probe behind the rhetoric of imperialism, we discover a new world. The Cabinet decided to wage war on China and for that purpose actively sought French and U.S. allies, even before the *Arrow* incident occurred. This may be regarded as corroborative evidence to support the theory that Palmerston had secretly tipped Parkes early in 1856 to watch for a chance to pick a quarrel with China. The British authorities necessarily concealed their intentions about opium. In this respect the French pretended they were blind, while the Americans deliberately kept their eyes wide open. Even the untrust-

52. Hine, *Richard Cobden*, p. 266.
53. Morley, *Richard Cobden*, p. 654.
54. See Chapter 8.
55. These words are borrowed from Dangerfield's *Strange Death of Liberal England*.

worthy Russians had to be considered possible allies. All this was unveiled in Chapter 11.

Commercial interests had to square with the liberal conscience in the politics of imperialism, as we found in Chapter 12. And when the clouds of war began to gather, the energies of pressure groups were released in what I have termed the 'lobbies of imperialism', as highlighted in Chapter 13. All these groups obtained the ear of the government about their major concerns. The exceptions were the anti-opium lobby led by Lord Shaftesbury, and the few with territorial ambitions who cast a covetous eye on Shanghai and Taiwan.

VI. The economics of imperialism

Members of Parliament were able to obtain general perceptions of the importance of British interests involved because annual statistical returns prepared by various government departments were tabled in Parliament. Thus, Bowring, for many years a member of Parliament before his appointment to China, was made aware that £3 million or £4 million of Indian revenue depended on the opium trade.[56] Palmerston was able to say that the import of Chinese tea had increased from 42 million pounds in 1842 to 80 million in 1856.[57] Grey could remark that British duty on Chinese tea was 'one of the main items of support to the revenue'.[58] Albemarle could specify that this revenue was worth 'between £5,000,000 and £6,000,000, to say nothing of upwards of £3,000,000 to the Indian revenue, being one-sixth of the whole of the revenue of that country'.[59] Small wonder that even a supporter of Cobden's motion, Erskine Perry, took the view that the war had to go on for the sake of British interests.[60] Hence, British perceptions of the importance of their vested economic interests played a pivotal role in the decision to widen hostilities into a full-scale war.

How accurate were those perceptions? Chapter 14 quantified the perception that the Chinese *should* buy more British manufactures; Chapter 15, that the Chinese *could* buy more; and Chapter 16, that the Indian economy depended on treaty revision to legalize opium in China. Chapter 17 showed that the Chinese increased their purchase of British (including Indian) commodities after the *Arrow* War. Such increases were made possible by throwing open the entire Chinese market and legalizing opium de facto. Permission was also obtained for British merchants to purchase tea at the places of production and to claim exemption from its transit dues, enabling them to buy larger quantities

---

56. Bowring to Clarendon, 4 October 1855, MSS. Clar. Dep. C37 China.
57. Palmerston, 3 March 1857, Hansard, 3d series, v. 144, col. 1828.
58. Grey, 24 February 1857, Hansard, 3d series, v. 144, col. 1236.
59. Albemarle, 26 February 1857, Hansard, 3d series, v. 144, col. 1354.
60. Perry, 26 February 1857, Hansard, 3d series, v. 144, col. 1462.

of tea at cheaper prices than ever before, not least for their industrial workers at home. All this fulfilled British expectations and, from the viewpoint of British commercial interests, justified the war.

Here, I must repeat that I am not suggesting that members of the British Parliament and bureacracy ever reached the clarity of perception which the statistics presented here convey. Rather, the aim of these chapters is to verify and quantify the general perception of the importance of British mercantile interests in the origin of the *Arrow* War.

The same kind of reasoning has led me to reopen the investigation into the annexation of Sind in India. Consequently, I found that in addition to the political and strategic dimensions, there were overwhelming economic arguments for the British to take such a step. The aim was to monopolize the all-important opium market in China, as we have discovered in Chapter 16.

VII. Ascertaining the origins of the *Arrow* War

Historians generally regard the *Arrow* incident itself as the origin of the war.[61] In the limited sense that it was used as a casus belli, this was so. Chapters 2–4 illustrated clearly how that incident had been exploited as an excuse for hostilities. In this case, the exploiters (Parkes and Bowring) rather than the respondents to their provocations (Yeh and the Cantonese populace) were the originators of the war.

However, some historians are inclined to attribute the genesis of the war to so-called Chinese xenophobia, both popular and official, at Canton. Chapters 5–6 showed that certainly there was hostility among the Cantonese people towards bullies such as Charles Compton for whom not even Palmerston had sympathy. No doubt there was also hostility among the Chinese officials at Canton towards Bowring's relentless attempts to crash the city gates. But in both cases the hostility was not xenophobic, because it was not occasioned by 'morbid dread or dislike of foreigners'. Even Bowring testified to the normally friendly disposition of the Cantonese.[62] Some members of Parliament also regarded Yeh's behaviour throughout as exceedingly civil.[63] Thus, the hostility in both cases was merely a reaction to an origin, rather than the genesis itself, of the *Arrow* War. That origin was 'Rule, Britannia', as we have seen in Chapter 6. If we free ourselves from the preoccupation of making and answering the charges of *Cantonese* xenophobia, we find that shoe was on the other foot. Because the same evidence produced by both sides indicates that, instead,

61. See, for example, the works by Costin (*Great Britain and China*) and Graham (*China Station*).
62. See, e.g., Bowring to Palmerston, 12 May 1849, Broadlands MSS, GC/BO/84; see also Bowring to Palmerston, 7 July 1849, Broadlands MSS, GC/BO/87.
63. See the debate in both houses of Parliament in Hansard, 3d series, v. 144.

'the strangers at the gate'[64] were xenophobic, and were certainly responsible for causing the war.

In the same vein, Yeh's refusal to receive Bowring at his official residence inside the walled city was regarded as a termination of friendly relations by Britain,[65] if not by other nations such as the United States (which had not yet imposed the 'Pax Americana'). Understandably some British historians have interpreted the *Arrow* War as a war for diplomatic recognition.[66] In terms of tracing the origins of the war, however, British determination to batter down the gates of Canton to get recognition was merely a means to an end. The end was to have opium legalized and to open the interior of China to British trade. This could not be achieved until Chinese resistance, epitomized in the closed city gates, was demolished. This discovery was made in Chapter 6. The end was an origin of the war, not the means. The fact remains, of course, that although London seized the advantage when hostilities broke out, it had not plotted to enter the city through a hole blasted in the wall.

The actions and demands of Parkes and Bowring were hot topics in the parliamentary debates. The business of politicians was to get power and keep it, not to play at being historians and to investigate the origins of the war. Consequently, the pretext for imperialism and the personalities of imperialism received a great deal of attention in the British press and parliament. What happened behind the scenes, in terms of the mechanics of imperialism, with respect to its diplomacy, politics, and lobbies, has remained obscured until today.

During the subsequent election, Palmerston was forthcoming on economic matters only when he was dealing with the merchants. Did he need to say any more to merchants who had openly demanded that their government insist on the right of access to all coastal and river ports by civilian and naval shipping?[67] Here, the politics of imperialism boiled down to a public defence of Bowring's actions, including his monomania to enter Canton, and thereby defending British national interests in China. To trace the origins of the *Arrow* War, therefore, we have had to go beyond the pretext, personalities, rhetoric, and mechanics of imperialism, and finally arrive at the economics of imperialism.

The economics of imperialism, as revealed in Part Six, were dynamic indeed. We saw in Chapter 14 how the perception of a British trade deficit with China, and the perception of China as a huge market for British exports, fuelled the imagination of British policy makers, diplomats, and merchants alike. We have also seen how the import duty on Chinese tea alone enabled the

64. Here, I am borrowing an expression originally used by Frederic Wakeman, Jr., who adopted this term as the title of his first book.
65. *The Times*, 2 January 1857.
66. See, e.g., Hurd, *Arrow War*, p. 27.
67. Cobden, 26 February 1857, Hansard, 3d series, v. 144, col. 1410.

Conclusion

British government to derive a revenue equivalent to a fair part of the Royal Navy's annual budget. The strong desire to augment both exports to and imports from China propelled the Foreign Office to instruct Bowring to seek revision of the Treaty of Nanking in order to open up the Chinese interior.

In addition, we saw Chapter 15 how the benefits derived from the sale of Indian opium to China kept the Lancashire mills supplied with U.S. cotton, kept labour force of the British Industrial Revolution supplied with tea, and provided the medium of return for British exports to India.

In Chapter 16, we saw how the opium smokers in China helped keep the Indian government afloat, helped finance British expansion in India, and assisted the growth of Bombay. The perception that even larger sales of opium to China, and hence greater benefits to the British imperial economy, might be achieved by throwing open the interior of China was a great incentive for war. Conversely, the fear that the opium trade might once again be suppressed in China created a powerful impulse to force the Chinese government to legalize opium after all persuasion had failed. In the China trade lay significant British national interests, which were to be protected at all costs and extended whenever possible.

Treaty revision for the legalization of opium and extension of trade to the interior of China are valuable pointers to the underlying rationale of the war, which, as we saw in Chapter 17, achieved phenomenal increases in British (including Indian) exports to and imports from China. Again, the war fulfilled British expectations.

Although members of the opposition might have been in general agreement with the government about the need to expand the China trade, some of them also believed that it was not in Britain's best interest to have blundered into war with China in the way that Bowring had. But once in government in 1858, they decided that as Britain was already at war, the war would have to be won. In other words, they did not consider it in the national interest to accept or to propose withdrawal at that stage, for fear that this might have serious repercussions for the empire elsewhere and for Britain's international standing generally.

When Palmerston regained office in 1859, and Lord John Russell joined Palmerston's cabinet, Russell confessed: 'It seems strange that I who objected so much to Bowring's proceedings about the lorcha should be so ready to support Bruce – but so it is'.[68]

In tracing the genesis of the *Arrow* War, therefore, we have found not a single origin but many, so closely woven that the absence of any one might have changed the war's timing and manifestation. First, there was the *Arrow* inci-

---

68. Russell to Palmerston, 19 September 1859, G. D. 22/30, quoted in Costin, *Great Britain and China*, pp. 296–7. Bruce was the now British minister plenipotentiary in the Far East, after Elgin.

dent, without which a different casus belli would have had to be found. Second, there was Parkes; had he not wanted to exploit the incident to avenge a personal insult, and perhaps to carry out what he perceived as Palmerston's implication, there would not have been an *Arrow* quarrel. Third, there was Bowring; had he not wanted to use the quarrel to resolve the Canton City question, he might not have connived with Parkes to get the admiral to wage an undeclared war on China. Fourth, there were the British economic interests in China and elsewhere; had these not existed, there would not already have been preparations for war in London and Paris even before the *Arrow* incident.

VIII. Reassessing some entrenched interpretations

Some writers have argued that the Opium War must not be so-called. A. J. Sargent has contended thus on the grounds that the Treaty of Nanking did not mention opium.[69] Peter Fay has maintained that the war was fought 'to recover the value of certain property plus expenses'.[70] Frank Welsh has pleaded that the responsibility for having allowed the opium trade to continue for thirty years must be shared by the rapacious British merchants and the corrupt Chinese officials.[71]

These arguments cannot stand. First, want of mention does not necessarily mean that something does not exist. Second, the property the value of which the British tried to recover was opium. Third, collaboration by Chinese officials in an illegal act does not make the act any more legal. To crown all, even these arguments pale into insignificance if we consider the vast British economic interests involved in the opium trade right up to the time of the *Arrow* War and beyond. The *Arrow* War, like the Opium War before it, had to be fought to safeguard such interests.

The China trade was a matter of such importance to the national interests of Britain that, to defend it, the politicians and even James Mill had shown themselves capable of acting against free-trade principles. The preservation of the opium monopoly in India is a case in point. The attempt to monopolize the free opium market in China was another. In view of this, interpreting the causation of the *Arrow* War purely in terms of the 'imperialism of free trade'[72] now appears too general to be adequate. To be sure, broadly speaking Britain *did* want to achieve free trade with China through the war; but as we have seen,

---

69. Sargent, *Anglo-Chinese Commerce and Diplomacy*, p. 87.
70. Peter Ward Fay, *The Opium War, 1840–1842* (Chapel Hill, University of North Carolina Press, 1975), pp. 194–5.
71. Welsh, *History of Hong Kong*, p. 98.
72. This influential theory was originally espoused in the famous article written jointly by John Gallagher and Ronald Robinson, 'Imperialism of Free Trade', and was subsequently much refined by Platt in his *Finance, Trade, and Politics*.

Conclusion

more specific reasons for the war had to do with a strong desire to monopolize the opium market in China and to gain direct access to the tea-producing regions and thereby cut out the role of the Chinese merchants and avoid paying the transit dues. Indeed, historians who insist that the *Arrow* War was chiefly about free trade must have found it hard to explain why the champions of free trade – Cobden, Bright, and Milner-Gibson – opposed the war, as we saw in Part Four.

On the other hand, the attempt by Chinese historians to interpret it as a second opium war gains a great deal of credibility – not because of their moralistic rationale – but because of the new-found importance of opium as set out in Part Six. In view of this, I am just as prepared to call it the Second Opium War as I am to label it the *Arrow* War. However, I still prefer the latter because it does not carry with it nationalistic or moralistic overtones.

Similarly, the theory about the events in the 'periphery' heavily influencing the decision-making in the 'centre'[73] holds water in so far as the pretext, personalities, and mechanics of imperialism are concerned. But we need to look beyond all these, to examine the economics of imperialism, before we can begin to understand its dynamics, which were the driving force behind the *Arrow* War.

As for the theory of the 'clash of two cultures',[74] it can be feeble and ineffective as an explanation for the origins of the *Arrow* War unless we set it in concrete terms as detailed in Part Three. Further concrete terms may be found in a point raised in Part Four, namely the distinction between Confucian ethical and British legal thinking in our study of modern international relations in general, and the *Arrow* War in particular. Lawyers were the largest professional group in the House of Commons, and several of the career politicians in the Lords had legal backgrounds, while all Chinese officials were Confucian scholars.[75] The rule of law and the rule of virtue are opposing concepts. They proved irreconcilable in the past. As the world is getting smaller every day, let us hope that there will be a healthy combination of the two in our dealings with each other, if only to reduce the number and scale of world conflicts. We must

---

73. See D. K. Fieldhouse, *The Colonial Empires: A Comparative Survey from the Eighteen Century* (London, Weidenfeld & Nicolson, 1965); and Eric Stokes, *The Peasant and the Raj: Studies in Agrarian Society and Peasant Rebellion in Colonial India* (Cambridge University Press, 1978), chapter 5.
74. This theory, which has influenced generations of China experts, was originally put forward by the sixth president of the United States, John Quincy Adams, who said in December 1841, 'The cause of the Opium War is the *kotow*', in a lecture delivered before the Massachusetts Historical Society (see *Chinese Repository*, 9 [May 1842], p. 281). This theory was later developed by Morse to cover the *Arrow* War as well (see Morse, *International Relations of the Chinese Empire*, v. 1). The theory was given even greater currency by Li Chien-nung in his textbook, originally written in Chinese and later translated into English and published under the title *The Political History of China, 1840–1928*; see especially p. 45.
75. All Chinese officials had to pass the civil service examinations, of which the syllabus consisted exclusively of Confucian classics. See, e.g., my *Yeh Ming-ch'en*.

also bear in mind that there is something called a 'European superiority complex' in addition to the 'middle kingdom mentality', that the former is far less widely acknowledged than the latter in Western literature, and consequently the latter has been made to carry the cane far more regularly than the former. On the other hand, I find it very encouraging that recent Chinese publications are much more critical of the 'middle kingdom mentality' than ever before.[76] In view of all this, the extreme form of the theory of the 'clash of two cultures', namely the 'measles' paradigm, is clearly irrelevant to the causes of the *Arrow* War despite the claims of its originator.[77] And metaphors such as a 'Molasses War' or 'Rice War'[78] entirely lack conviction.

In conclusion, it was not 'Monster' Yeh, nor Cantonese xenophobia, nor free trade, nor periphery–centre tensions, nor the clash of cultures generally, and certainly not kowtow, molasses, or measles as claimed, respectively, by a U.S. ex-president, a historian of Chinese decent, and a Japanese philosopher, however widely they may have been quoted – but national interests as perceived by British policy makers which provide an adequate basis to interpret the genesis of the *Arrow* War.

There are grave dangers in studying certain topics in nineteenth-century China, India, Britain, or indeed any country in isolation from the rest of the world. We have seen how imperfectly we may understand the China trade without reference to the wider picture that includes India, other British colonies, the United States, the United Kingdom, and the United Kingdom's global trade. We have also seen how the existing explanations for the acquisition of Sind in India remain inadequate unless we relate it to the British desire to control Malwa opium destined for China. And indeed we have seen how the epoch-making rejection of leading members of the Manchester school in the Chinese Election could not be properly understood if we restrict ourselves to the confines of British domestic politics.

IX. The wider picture: Some theories on the working of imperialism

Let us put these issues in a wider context. David Fieldhouse writes, 'The second expansion of Europe', which began in 1815, 'was a complex historical process in which political, social and emotional forces in Europe and on the periphery were more influential than calculated imperialism'.[79] In this respect, Parkes's overweening desire to avenge a personal grievance suffered during the *Arrow*

---

76. See, e.g., Mao Haijian, *Tianchao de bengkui* (The collapse of the celestial empire: A reexamination of the Opium War) (Beijing, Joint Publishing Co., 1995).
77. See Fukuzawa, 'Datsu-A-ron'; and Blacker, *Fukuzawa*, pp. 122–3.
78. Chang, *Commissioner Lin*, p. 15.
79. Fieldhouse, *Colonial Empires*, p. 381.

incident and Bowring's obsession with entry into Canton City both substantiate Fieldhouse's view about emotional forces on the periphery. The fiery debates in the British press and in Parliament, as well as the Chinese Election, all reinforces his position concerning the political, social, and emotional forces at home. In this, Fieldhouse's perceptiveness is admirable.

However, his further claim that these forces, both on the periphery and at home, were 'more influential than calculated imperialism' raises immediate problems in interpreting the causation of the *Arrow* War. It is quite possible that what happened at the periphery in the case of Parkes's engineering an undeclared war had actually been instigated by Palmerston at the centre, so to speak, as we have seen in Chapters 3–4. More important is the calculated imperialism revealed in Part Five: Whitehall had been coolly scheming for war well before the emotional *Arrow* incident erupted in faraway East Asia.

In addition, Fieldhouse has argued that 'the myth of imperial profit-making is false'.[80] The economics of imperialism, however, as unveiled in Part Six, suggest that imperial profit-making is not a myth, certainly not in the short term. One characteristic feature of British expansion in this period in China and India was indeed imperial profit-making. In China, gaining direct access to the tea-growing areas by means of the *Arrow* War to reduce the cost of tea and thereby enhance the profits is evidence of this. In India, annexing Sind so that fees on the export of Malwa opium might double, triple, and quadruple, is also proof. The relentless efforts to gain complete control of Malwa opium as well as Bengal opium, in order to monopolize and even manipulate the Chinese market to ensure steady and high returns, are yet further evidence of this profit-making.[81] Indeed, we must not lose sight of the national interests as perceived by the policy makers – Palmerston himself had said so in as many words. They knew very well the general structural importance of the triangular trade to the British economy. The export surplus from India, made possible by opium and fostered by the persistently low value of the rupee, greatly helped Britain's balance of payments with Asia and the rest of the world; otherwise an average of about £10 million would have to be added to the United Kingdom's annual trade deficit in visible goods.[82] This was presumably what the lobbyists of 1857 perceived when they made their comments about China bills being used to buy U.S. cotton and to pay for British manufactures destined for India.[83]

---

80. Ibid.
81. The profit-making priority of this period, of course, is distinctly different from the purely land-grabbing fever in Africa towards the end of the nineteenth century, when 'the acquisition of colonies itself became a status symbol irrespective of their value'. See E. J. Hobsbawm, *The Age of Empire, 1875–1914* (London, Weidenfeld & Nicolson, 1966), p. 67.
82. See Chapter 16, especially Table 16.14. See also next note.
83. See Part Five. It will be remembered that, previously, Britain had been in deficit in its bilateral trade with China. That was the time before Indian opium was sold to China. Now, this opium

It must be added that those who provided the profit were not just the Chinese or the Indians. The duties on tea which yielded so much government revenue in Britain, for example, came out of the pockets of British tea-drinkers, the great majority of whom were relatively poor or of very modest means. But in this particular case, gaining direct access to the tea-producing areas in China and thus avoiding the payment of multifarious transit dues, as well as cutting out the role of the Chinese merchants, could lower tea's cost considerably, and thereby also its sale price to the benefit of tea-drinkers in Britain. This was particularly important to the British manufacturers, whose workers drank large quantities of tea with sugar which gave them energy. More expensive tea could mean higher wages and less competitive industrial products. Thus, the specific groups in Britain that benefited from the advancement of imperial interests in this particular field included the British government, manufacturers, merchants and their associates, and to a lesser extent the British public.

By 'merchants and their associates' I mean those involved in trading and the range of service, financial, and professional interests that worked hand in glove with the traders. With this, I find myself joining the latest debate in the wider picture of empire (if only to put my own work into perspective), where the pertinent literature is mountainous and the debate so diverse as to defy ready comprehension.[84]

This latest debate centres on a new concept called 'gentlemanly capitalism' and has been advocated by P. J. Cain and A. G. Hopkins in their two-volume work *British Imperialism*.[85] The authors have argued that 'gentlemanly capitalism', rather than industrial or commercial capitalism, was mainly responsible for British overseas expansion from the late seventeenth to the early twentieth centuries. Gentlemanly capitalism encompassed landed and commercial wealth as well as service, financial, and professional interests, notably in the City of London, and is said to have exercised a dominant influence over government and policy making.

In so far as my study is partly concerned with opium, tea, and other commodities in which British traders, bankers, financiers, brokers, accountants, insurers, lawyers, shippers, and other 'gentlemanly capitalists' were deeply involved, and for the promotion of which the British government was

---

money was used to pay for not only Chinese tea and silk, but also U.S. cotton and Indian produce.

84. Andrew Porter, ' "Gentlemanly Capitalism" and Empire: The British Experience since 1750' *Journal of Imperial and Commonwealth History*, 18, no. 3 (1990), p. 265. Fieldhouse has remarked, 'Imperial history has grown beyond the competence of any one man: there can no longer be a complete imperial historian'. See his article, 'Can Humpty Dumpty Be Put Together Again? Imperial History in the 1980s', *Journal of Imperial and Commonwealth History*, 22, no. 2 (1984), pp. 9–23.
85. Cain and Hopkins, *British Imperialism*.

prepared to go to war with China, I have independently lent support to this new concept in a general way. However, when this gentlemanly influence is gauged in specific instances such as those examined in Part Five, I find that it was not so pervasive as it might appear. To begin with, it was the government that took the initiative for treaty revision and, when that failed, plotted for war. The merchant princes began to put forward their bids only when they saw that the clouds of war were gathering. Even then, not all their demands were favourably received in Whitehall – some were rejected. Thus, to a fair extent I find myself in the company of Robert Gavin, who has discovered that most of Palmerston's policy in Africa 'was put into action despite rather than because of the merchants' pressure'.[86]

Furthermore, my findings go beyond the gentlemanly capitalists in London. They extend to other cities in Britain, including those in the industrial north and, more important, to the colonial masters in India and the British officers and merchants in China. This analysis reveals a close working relationship between the metropolis and the periphery which cannot be explained merely within the context of the gentlemanly capitalists in the City of London.

Economic opportunism is only one of many interpretations of British overseas expansion. Others include strategic and political explanations. With respect to the annexation of Sind, for example, we have seen that Lambrick[87] has presented his political case and that Yapp has advanced strategic arguments.[88] To these I have added an economic dimension. In the case of the *Arrow* War itself, strategic considerations, in a military sense, have been examined and dismissed in Chapter 11. Political explanations (pretext, personalities, and politics) have also been explored and found to be insufficient to clarify the origins of the war, whereupon I have attempted economic answers as well. In doing so, I have also discovered that some hegemonic ideology such as the imperialism of free trade is by itself inadequate to elucidate the specific origins of the *Arrow* War.

Let me put my work in the context of the history of imperial theories.

Apparently the first attempt at explaining how the British Empire 'happened' was made by Sir John Seeley, who, lecturing in 1882, suggested that it all occurred in a 'fit of absence of mind'.[89] The implication was that the Britons, like the Romans long before them,[90] were intrinsically fitted by fate for world

---

86. Gavin, 'Palmerston's Policy towards East and West Africa, 1830–1865', p. 350.
87. See Lambrick, *Sir Charles Napier and Sind*.
88. Yapp, *Strategies of British India*.
89. J. R. Seeley, *The Expansion of England* (London, Macmillan, 1883), pp. 8–10.
90. We should not forget that until the nineteenth century most British historians accepted the unhistorial claims of the medieval writer Geoffrey of Monmouth, who traced the descent of the Britons from the Romans. For Monmouth's views, see his *The History of the Kings of Britain*, trans. by Lewis Thorpe (London, Penguin, 1966).

dominance[91] – an extension of the rhetoric of invincibility we saw at work in British India. History has shown that neither the Romans nor the Britons were invincible. Furthermore, by tracing the origins of the *Arrow* War from Canton to Hong Kong, Calcutta, Bombay, London, back to Nanjing, then Paris, Washington, and St Petersburg, I have shown that Britons certainly did not wake up one morning to find that 'they had sleepwalked their way to dominion over palm and pine'.[92]

Next came J. A. Hobson and V. I. Lenin, who interpreted modern European imperialism as the highest stage of capitalism, being the result of late-nineteenth-century developments in industry, business, trade, and finance.[93] In other words, they concentrated on what I call the 'economics of imperialism' to the exclusion of its personalities, politics, diplomacy, and other factors, all of which, we have seen, made their own significant contributions towards imperial expansion.

Then Joseph Schumpeter adopted a sociological approach, attributing European expansion in general to a traditional aristocracy who felt threatened socially by domestic developments in industry, urbanization, and democracy, and who therefore sought consolation by going out to conquer.[94] If applied to Britian, recent scholarship shows that the British aristocracy did not actually do the physical work of empire-building,[95] and therefore such an application may show 'dismaying ignorance of the social structure and social history of nineteenth-century Britain'.[96] In the specific case of the *Arrow* War, neither Bowring nor Parkes came from aristocratic families; but here Schumpeter's other theme comes into the spotlight. He made a distinction between Britain's generally 'pacific and mercantilist' expansion and the militaristic expansion of the continental European powers. There was nothing pacific about the *Arrow* War, and one cannot assume that economic imperialism is somehow pacific.

91. 'The poet of the *Aeneid* has Jupiter forecast a Roman rule that will know no bounds of time or space. And Anchises' pronouncement from the underworld previews Augustus extending imperial power to the most remote peoples of the world. Livy characterises his city as *caput orbis terrarum* and its people as *princeps orbis terrarum populus*. Horace asserts that the *maiestas* of the *imperium* stretches from one end of the world to the other.' E. S. Gruen, 'The Imperial Policy of Augustus', in Kurt A. Raaflaub and Mark Toher (eds.), *Between Republic and Empire: Interpretations of Augustus and His Principate* (Berkeley and Los Angeles, University of California Press, 1990), pp. 395–416: p. 395.
92. I very much agree with David Cannadine, whose words I am here quoting from his 'The Empire Strikes Back' (review article), *Past and Present*, no. 147 (May 1995), p. 183. My analysis in this part of the Conclusion has benefited greatly from his lucidly expressed views.
93. J. A. Hobson, *Imperialism: A Study* (London, Allen & Unwin, 1902); and V. I. Lenin, *Imperiaism: The Highest Stage of Capitalism* (Moscow, 1947).
94. J. A. Schumpeter, *Imperialism and Social Classes*, translated by Heinz Nordon and edited with an introduction by Paul M. Sweezy (New York, A. M. Kelley, 1951). The original version was published in 1919, three years after Lenin's thesis first appeared.
95. David Cannadine, *The Decline and Fall of the British Aristocracy* (New Haven, Conn., Yale University Press, 1990).
96. Cannadine, 'The Empire Strikes Back', p. 183.

Conclusion

Schumpeter's assumptions highlight the dangers of imposing a European model on other environments, even if it were environments just across the English Channel.

Next came Gallagher and Robinson, who proffered a political-diplomatic-strategic argument, suggesting that the British Empire in Africa, for example, was the result of a persistent desire by the 'official mind' to safeguard the essential sea routes to India.[97] One major criticism of this theory has been its sidestepping the whole question of who the policy makers were and what they were supposed to have been doing, by subsuming them under the vague term the 'official mind'. By detailing the mechanics of imperialism in Part Five, I have given the official mind flesh and blood. However, I have also shown that strategic arguments did not apply to the *Arrow* War, reducing the validity of the Gallagher–Robinson thesis as a general interpretation of imperialism.

There followed Galbraith and Fieldhouse, who emphasized the importance of events at the periphery of the British Empire forcing the hands of decision makers in the imperial metropolis.[98] In the case of the *Arrow* War, I have found, instead, that events in the periphery actually provided the decision makers with exactly the pretext they needed for a measure that was already in the making – London had been spoiling for a fight even before the *Arrow* incident occurred. Moreover, that pretext had been faked by Palmerston's Archilles[99] and sanctioned by Bowring,[100] whom Palmerston had hand-picked and on whom he had deliberately slackened the rein.[101] In this context, the way for what happened at the periphery had been paved by the centre. True, Palmerston could not have foreseen something like the *Arrow* incident. But the fact that he had encouraged Parkes to be tough shortly before the incident was apparently taken by the consul as licence to do what he subsequently did.

Most recently, Cain and Hopkins have put forward their 'gentlemanly capitalists' theory, concentrating almost solely on the role of the City of London in the creation of the British Empire over three centuries.[102] One major criticism of this interpretation, like that of the 'official mind', is its failure to delineate who these gentlemanly capitalists were. While identifying the bosses of the leading firms in the City that had substantial China interests, and by highlighting their lobbying and electioneering activities in Parts Four and

---

97. R. Robinson and J. Gallagher, *Africa and the Victorians: The 'Official Mind' of Imperialism* (London, Macmillan, 1961).
98. J. S. Galbraith, 'The 'Turbulent Frontier' as a Factor in British Expansion', *Comparative Studies in Society and History*, no. 2 (1960); and D. K. Fieldhouse, *Economics and Empire* (London, Weidenfeld & Nicolson, 1973).
99. See Chapter 3.
100. See Chapter 4.
101. Cobden, 26 February 1857, Hansard, 3d series, v. 144, cols. 1416–17.
102. Cain and Hopkins, *British Imperialism*.

Five, I have found that the pressure groups included not only gentlemanly capitalists, but also industrialists, missionaries, and other sections of the wider British community at home and abroad. More important, Palmerston's cabinet decided to wage the *Arrow* War in spite, and not because, of the gentlemanly capitalists and other lobby groups.

As David Cannadine has pointed out, each and every one of these theories is monocausal and mutually exclusive, and it is difficult to believe that a phenomenon so complex and long-lasting as British imperialism can have had only one single, all-encompassing explanation.[103] Instead of covering an extensive period of time and focusing on one central theme, I have concentrated on one episode and explored the conceivable causes. I have found these causes to be complementary to each other. Their importance varied according to specific situations. What was true of the *Arrow* War might not be true in other imperial incidents. Rigorous examination of the evidence in the case of the *Arrow* War has revealed that life is a messy business and that historians must resist the temptation to tidy it up. Monocausal theories succumb to that temptation. Nevertheless, such theories may contain valuable insights, and historians who reject any or all of them out of hand do so at their peril. Let us take from all the theorists whatever seems to be genuinely useful for the matter in hand, and be grateful for it.

Still with regard to the wider picture, let us look at the receiving end of British imperialism, in this case China.

X. The wider picture: Some theories on the working of Chinese foreign policy

What was the driving force behind Chinese foreign policy in the mid-nineteenth century? Reviewing the major interpretations, James Polachek has found two divergent lines. One, advocated by John King Fairbank in his *Trade and Diplomacy*, concentrated 'on the persisting influence of imperial Confucianist notions of statecraft'.[104] The other, which I put forward in my *Yeh Ming-ch'en*, emphasized the 'displacement or distortion of a "rational" foreign policy as a consequence of the onset of the great wave of mid-century rebellions'.[105] On balance, Polachek seems more inclined towards my view, agreeing that Yeh, 'usually offered up as exemplary of the spirit of Sinocentric ideological arrogance', was in fact 'a harassed administrator, too preoccupied with the day-to-day problems of securing and funding his inland outposts to have time left for soothing British petitioners'.[106] Professor Fairbank has also acknowledged the

103. Cannadine, 'The Empire Strikes Back', p. 182.
104. Polachek, *Inner Opium War*, pp. 3–4.
105. Ibid., p. 4, summarizing my views.
106. Ibid.

Conclusion

validity of this interpretation.[107] Indeed, the two views are complementary to each other, and not mutually exclusive; it is only a matter of emphasis in regard to particular circumstances.

Polachek continues, 'This is perhaps further than Wong would be willing to go, but here too we see the seeds of local control setting the tone of Ch'ing [Qing] diplomacy, pushing it in a direction it might not have taken had there been no rebellion to worry about'.[108] Having completed this study, I am still unwilling to go that far. Local passion might have distorted Qing diplomacy on parochial issues such as the Canton City question, but Qing foreign policy in general, especially that concerning grave national interests such as opium legalization, or perceived national security such as opening the interior of China to foreigners, does not seem to have been affected in any way by the views of the gentry in either Canton or its environs. In any case, the gentry were not supposed to have had access to such 'classified' information.

Polachek, having made a pioneering study of the factional politics at Beijing, thinks that 'little can be learnt by focusing upon events in the distant southeast', because 'until 1850, at least, it was Peking that made the critical decisions on foreign and domestic policy'.[109] Here, Polachek contradicts himself (see his other view as quoted in the previous paragraph). His second view additionally merits reconsideration as a result of my findings in Chapters 5–6. Therein, it has been discovered, for example, that the emperor had to approve the suspension of the prefect of Canton in 1846 on the grounds of animosity felt by the Cantonese towards him. Such animosity originated from the rumour that the prefect had foreign guests in his yamen, which was situated inside the walled city. Also in Chapter 5 we learned that in 1849, the emperor was obliged to eat his words because his mandarins in Canton had already issued a false edict refusing the Britons entry. It was again clearly a case of the tail wagging the dog.

Acknowledging that this was indeed the case, Polachek attributes it to Beijing's 'loose supervision over policy enforcement in peripheral Canton'.[110] Why should the absolute monarch's supervision be tight elsewhere and loose in Canton? In all pertinent memorials to the throne, whether authored by the conciliatory Manchu Qiying, or the firm Han Chinese Xu and Yeh, the concern had always been for the danger of imminent rebellion should the tail not be allowed to wag the dog on these specific issues. The emperor invariably bowed to this argument. Polachek's own meticulous research has shown that the emperor in the 1810s and again the 1830s was obliged to loosen the time-

---

107. See Fairbank's review in *Pacific Affairs*, 49, no. 4 (Winter 1976–7), pp. 701–2.
108. Polachek, *Inner Opium War*, p. 5.
109. Ibid., p. 9.
110. Ibid., p. 245.

The dynamics of imperialism

honoured tight control over criticisms of the bureaucracy by the literati because of the rebellions of the time.[111]

Thus, the present study reinforces and extends my earlier interpretation of the effect of domestic rebellions on Chinese foreign policy. Not only did the onset of the great rebellions of the 1850s affect the diplomacy of the mandarins at Canton, but the mere reference in the 1840s to possible rebellions was sufficient to alter certain aspects of the foreign policy pursued by Beijing, especially on issues such as the Canton City question which, though initially parochial, ultimately led to a war that saw the sack of the national capital.

Polacheck holds Yeh 'responsible for provoking' the *Arrow* War.[112] This interpretation appears to be based on Yeh's reckless fabrication in 1849 of the false edict, in collaboration with Commissioner Xu.[113] Yeh's motive is believed to be 'glory-seeking',[114] something perhaps related also to Yeh's brother Mingfeng being a member of an anti-treaty political faction active in the South City of Beijing.[115] Certainly, Yeh was reckless in that affair. But as we found in Chapter 5, Yeh acted out of desperation to save his own career and life. More important, Chapters 3 and 5 showed that Yeh's handling of the *Arrow* incident some eight years later, far from being provocative, was as conciliatory as it possibly could be at every stage of the negotiations.

For decades some historians have been regaling their readers with concepts of popular and official xenophobia at Canton, as if China's international relations in the mid-nineteenth century were cast by a rabble and by a no less irrational imperial commissioner in charge of China's foreign affairs. Chapters 5–6 will have provided readers with alternative food for thought. Indeed, it seems that the term 'Chinese xenophobia' gained most currency when the Cold War was running hottest and may have reflected the attitudes of the authors at the time, rather than those of the subjects of their historical research.

There is a theory, widely accepted in China, that an important origin of the *Arrow* War may be found in the Taiping, Red Turban, and other rebellions that simultaneously ravaged central and southern China. The argument is that the Qing government was exhausted by these upheavals, thus presenting a golden opportunity for the British again to wage war on China, a war they could expect to win easily.[116] Such a consideration makes strategic sense, and may have swayed Parkes and Bowring when they reported the unrest to London.[117] But the pivotal consideration in London, made obvious by Palmerston and Clarendon, was Yeh's final rejection of the British demand for

111. Ibid., pp. 41, 43–4, 80–1, and 109.
112. Ibid., p. 5.
113. Ibid., pp. 242–54.
114. Ibid., p. 252.
115. Ibid., p. 251.
116. I have encountered this view regularly during my various lecture tours in China.
117. See Parkes to Bowring, Desp. 157, 13 October 1856, FO228/213.

treaty revision and not the domestic pressure he was under. As a result, the theory under review must be qualified accordingly.

With regard to Parkes and Bowring reporting to London about Yeh's crushing domestic burdens, they had expected him to yield readily when they added foreign coercion to such problems. They were wrong. They failed to fathom the domestic politics as outlined in Chapter 6 and, thereby, grossly underestimated Yeh's determination to resist. Thus, yet another dimension might be added to the earlier interpretation of Qing foreign policy advocated in my *Yeh Ming-ch'en*. Foreign coercion, however enormous, did not outweigh in Yeh's mind the importance he attached to domestic forces such as the military, the gentry, and the militia, who had helped him quash the rebellions and on whose loyalty he continued to rely for the survival of his administration.

Let us finish by looking again at the Chinese paradigm in which British imperialism in general, and the *Arrow* War in particular, have been interpreted. This paradigm is couched in terms of the British determination to 'conquer, enslave, plunder and slaughter' the Chinese.[118] Such a judgement can easily be formed on the basis of the behaviour of thugs such as Charles Compton and other British merchants like him, as we saw in Chapter 6; on the basis of the ransacking of Yeh's official residence by that idle and curious throng who followed the official British party, as we saw in Chapter 5; and on the basis of the Royal Navy's pounding of forts surrounded by human dwellings at Canton, as we saw in Chapter 4.

But the *intentions* of the British government and Britons in general are a different matter. The rest of this book has shown that neither the British government agents on the spot, however reckless, nor the British prime minister, however bellicose, nor the British public, however passionate, had specific objectives of this kind in mind. Parkes's overwheening desire was to avenge a personal insult to begin with. Bowring's plan was to enter Canton City and thereby to protect and expand British trade. Palmerston's objective was to stay in office, while the British public chanted 'Rule, Britannia'. But all these desires, plans, and objectives combined seem to manifest a general intention, conscious or subconscious, to establish British dominance in China – not to build a formal empire by conquest as in India, but to set up an informal one which Britain could exploit without having to carry administrative, defence, or other burdens.[119] In this context the use of the word 'conquer', let alone 'enslave', seems inappropriate; 'plunder and slaughter', they did.

118. As mentioned, these words seem to be a direct quotation from the Chinese version of the 'Communist Manifesto' by Marx and Engels. See Wang Di, 'Minzu de zainan yu minzu de fazhan', p. 36.
119. In fact, some have argued that the acquisition of formal empire was a sign and ultimately a source of weakness. See Bernard Porter, *The Lion's Share: A Short History of British Imperialism, 1850–1970* (London, Longman, 1975).

XI. The still wider perspective: The rise and fall of great powers

It is hoped that this work has also shed new light on great power diplomacy and a complex historical phenomenon called 'appeasement', especially on the long-standing love–hate relationship between Great Britain and France. We have seen in Chapter 11 how accommodating Britain was towards France when it wanted the latter to be one of its allies against China in the pending war. Even after the alliance had been agreed upon, the Quai d'Orsay appears to have continued to make life difficult for Whitehall. As we saw in Chapter 12, Lord Clarendon told Greville he 'wished to Heaven he could be delivered from office; everything went wrong, the labour, anxiety, and responsibility were overwhelming'. What was the problem? The difficult state of Britain's relations with France was 'more than could be endured' – he could not depend on the French government and never knew from one day to another what the consequences of its conduct might be.[120] Nonetheless, Clarendon endured. If his endurance were some form of appeasement, then Paul Kennedy's thesis about British appeasement emerging upon the death of Lord Palmerston in 1865[121] will have to be extended to include Palmerston's tenure as prime minister, when British diplomacy, dominated by the firebrand, was supposedly anything but appeasing.

Appeasement was necessary because Britain needed allies, who were important in more ways than one. Morally, it wanted them to share the responsibilities of war, in much the same way that the United States subsequently dragged the United Nations into the Korean War[122] and more recently the Gulf War. Financially, it would have liked them to share the expenses. Militarily, nobody could be absolutely certain of victory, and having allies would greatly enhance the prospects of success. Holding its own imperial interests close to its chest, Britain could afford to be humble to its Western partners when it wanted them to help achieve that success.

This work delineates and contrasts the different kinds of imperialism, which is a term too often taken for granted because it is familiar or avoided because it is vague and elusive. A crucial element which we must consider while studying imperialism is the role of war in the rhythm of rise and decline of great powers, as a mechanism by which new equilibria are achieved. This is an issue which Kennedy appears to have deliberately put on one side. In many ways the *Arrow* War may be compared to a world war, in which all the major powers,

---

120. Greville diary, 17 February 1857, as reproduced in Greville, *Leaves from the Greville Diary*, pp. 781–2.
121. See Paul Kennedy, 'The Tradition of Appeasement in British Foreign Policy, 1865–1939', in his *Strategy and Diplomacy*, pp. 13–39.
122. Later the United States wanted the same moral justification for the Vietnam War, but did not get it.

except the Austro-Hungarian Empire, were involved. This war met all of Britain's objectives as we have seen in Chapter 17, contributing to its continued global predominance. Russia also got what she wanted: a huge tract of land and a seaport which General Muraviev proceeded to name Vladivostok. But the Russian aim seems to have been more vainglorious than economic – its Far Eastern acquisitions, very poorly linked to the metropolis, became the classic burdens of an overextended empire. The British strategy was to create an informal empire in China,[123] which brought economic benefits but involved no acquisition of territory and the burden thereof – a strategy so well conceptualized by the Gallagher–Robinson theory of free-trade imperialism.[124] This British approach contrasts sharply not only with the Russian design of the time, but also with the subsequent Japanese scheme for their Greater East Asia Co-Prosperity Sphere during World War II.[125] Indeed Britain objected to the dismemberment of China because British strategy was based on the calculation that it would gain the predominant share of China's wealth via free trade throughout the whole of that country.

Great power rivalry was an important part of imperial history, having generated a good many colonial wars. However, in the constant process of revision, younger revisionist historians tend to forget this important feature because it has already been dealt with by the first generation of imperial historians.

Due attention must be paid to the external, and not just the internal, economic dimensions of a nation in the balance of power worldwide. Paul Kennedy has estimated that in 1815–85, Great Britain defended her global position at the cost of a mere 2 or 3 per cent of GNP.[126] If we look beyond the national boundary of the British Isles and cast our eyes further than its GNP, we shall find that neither the millions of pounds sterling fetched by selling Bengal opium to China nor the millions of pounds sterling derived from duty on Chinese tea were counted as part of Britain's GNP. Once opium had been legalized as demanded by Britain, the Chinese began cultivating opium locally, and Britain lost an important source of revenue, which might have contributed to some extent to Britain's decline after 1885.

We should also remember that opium revenue was a significant link in the chain of British global trade, so the loss was far more than that of revenue

123. See my article 'The Building of an Informal British Empire in China in the Middle of the Nineteenth Century', *Bulletin of the John Rylands University Library of Manchester*, v. 59, no. 2 (Spring 1977), pp. 472–85.
124. Gallagher and Robinson, 'The Imperialism of Free Trade'.
125. See B. Hashikawa, 'Japanese Perspectives on Asia: From Dissociation to Co-prosperity', in A. Iriye (ed.), *The Chinese and Japanese: Essays in Political and Cultural Interactions* (Princeton, N.J., Princeton University Press, 1980). See also Paul Kennedy, 'Japanese Strategic Decisions, 1939–45', in his *Strategy and Diplomacy, 1870–1945* (London, Allen & Unwin, 1983), pp. 179–95.
126. Paul Kennedy, *The Rise and Fall of the Great Powers* (New York, Random House, 1987), p. 153.

alone. Thus, Kennedy's major thesis on the rise and fall of world powers, namely that the changing balance of domestic productive forces correlates closely with the ebb and flow of hegemony, should be extended to include a power's external economic activities. Besides, we have noted in Chapter 16 the United Kingdom's serious trade deficit in visible commodities, which must have been made up by invisible ones such as financial services and shipping. In addition to the domestic productive power of a nation, therefore, its overseas financial strength must also be included in our interpretation of the rise and fall of great powers. It is here that the theory of Cain and Hopkins on gentlemanly capitalism comes into play.[127]

Paul Kennedy thinks that the bid by the Hapsburg family for hegemony in Europe failed because its debt-servicing consumed about two-thirds of its revenue.[128] In terms of British expansion in India, we have seen in Chapter 16 that debt-servicing was not a problem because Bengal opium revenue was sufficient for that purpose. This reinforces the point about looking beyond the domestic productivity of a nation when we try to explain the fortunes of a great power.

With respect to cultural conflicts, as recently conceptualized by Samuel Huntington,[129] the alleged insult to the British flag aboard the *Arrow* assumes a new significance in the study of historical causation. After all, it was used as the casus belli. Behind this flimsy excuse was an earnest British desire to be treated as equals by the celestials, a desire that dated back to Lord Macartney's Mission to China in 1792–4[130] if not before. Defeating China in the Opium War had not raised the esteem of Britons among the Chinese elite; in fact quite the reverse. This is made amply clear by the despatches from the Chinese authorities,[131] which the British diplomats could read in translation, but more so by the private correspondence among the Chinese elite, whose cursive script and classical Chinese language have put it beyond the reach of most modern scholars.[132] Words in the diplomatic despatches could be translated, but often not the concept behind them. The result has been a series of misunderstand-

127. See their *British Imperialism*. See also D. C. Coleman and Christine MacLeod, 'Attitudes to New Techniques: British Businessmen, 1800–1950', *Economic History Review*, 2d series, v. 39, no. 4 (1986), pp. 588–611.
128. Kennedy, *Great Powers*, chapter 2.
129. See his *The Third Wave: Democratisation in the Late Twentieth Century* (Norman, University of Oklahoma Press, 1991).
130. See Robert A. Bicker (ed.), *Ritual and Diplomacy: The Macartney Mission to China, 1792–1794* (London, British Association of Chinese Studies and Wellswepp, 1993).
131. See my *Anglo-Chinese Relations*, passim; see also the observations by Professor Wang Gungwu in his review of my book in the *Journal of the Oriental Society of Australia*, 15–16 (1983–4), pp. 198–9. The language of the mandarins was even less restrained in their memorials to the emperor and in private correspondence than the diplomatic despatches; for details, see *Shilu*, passim.
132. I am referring to the documents in the so-called Canton Archive, captured from Commissioner Yeh's yamen during the war and now deposited in the Public Record Office in London. Neither translators of the time, nor most other recent scholars, have had the skills

ings on both sides. The role of cultural differences in the making of war and peace is a rich area for systematic exploration, witness Chapters 2–6, but one must not repeat the mistake of casting it in a vague general concept and then using it as an excuse to ignore economic and other imperial realities, as so many historians have done.

With regard to methodology, we must look at international relations through the multiple lenses of different national viewpoints and divergent disciplines. Until we approach the *Arrow* War in this way, its true nature of approximating a world war will remain obscured by national preoccupations. At a time when the world is getting smaller every day, national and even regional objectives cannot be safely pursued in isolation from activities in the rest of the globe. Even in the nineteenth century, we have found, for example, that the parochial instituting of one-thousandth ad valorem of transit dues by local Chinese officials desperate for funds to fight the Taipings contributed to the outbreak of the *Arrow* War. Conversely, Paul Kennedy's admirable broad sweep of world history, in which he cannot possibly pay sufficient attention to specific local issues as factors of historical causation, can lead to generalizations that are not always well sustained.[133]

On the other hand, local issues cannot be understood properly without due reference to the wider picture. As mentioned, for example, the British annexation of Sind in India could not be explained satisfactorily if we were to restrict our views only to political and strategic considerations. And to appreciate the importance of the opium revenue to the United Kingdom's balance of payments, we have to cast our eyes beyond even the Indian subcontinent: to China to examine the opium market; to global trade patterns; and, of course, to the palaces of the colonial masters to appreciate the British desire, against loudly professed free-trade principles that are said to have been 'near the realms of religion',[134] to monopolize that opium market.[135] The annexation of Sind, like the seizure of Lagos and Aden,[136] reminds us of Ranke's dictum that 'there is no national history in which universal history does not play a great role'.[137]

---

to decipher these documents. My first book, on the commissioner, relied heavily for its information on that archive. Twenty years after its publication, I am not aware that the archive has been systematically used by any other scholar.
133. See his *Great Powers*. In his section on Ming China, for example, a greater depth of understanding of Chinese history could have strengthened his thesis.
134. See Gavin's doctoral thesis, 'Palmerston's Policy Towards East and West Africa, 1830–1865', p. 4.
135. For more details, see my article 'British Annexation of Sind in 1843: An Economic Perspective', *Modern Asian Studies* (Cambridge University Press), 31, pt. 2 (May 1997), pp. 225–44.
136. For an analysis of the seizure of Lagos and Aden, see Gavin, 'Palmerston's Policy towards East and West Africa, 1830–1865'.
137. Quoted in Theodore H. von Laue, *Leopold Ranke: The Formative Years* (Princeton, N.J., Princeton University Press, 1950), p. 85.

We can specialize no more in one discipline than in the affairs of one country. To acquire a good understanding of the world around us, we must not lock ourselves up in any particular cage, but should rise above all boundaries that separate national histories, political priorities, economic preoccupations, diplomatic wrangles, legal arguments, and strategic schemes. In this respect, even the 'periphery–metropolis'[138] interpretation of imperial history now looks parochial.

Finally, how far may we call the *Arrow* War a world war? In terms of great power involvement, global economic entanglement, and worldwide diplomatic intrigue, it was indeed something on a world scale. However, in this war the great power interests were aligned (against China), the military balance was one-sided (against China), and the conflict was geographically contained (within China), all of which are factors not associated with the concept of world war. But there is one fundamental element which underpins the *Arrow* War and the two world wars – the massive destruction of lives and property with modern weaponry to satisfy the perpetrators' 'general covetousness and the desire of making money by the misfortunes of mankind'.[139] No, it was not a world war, only deadly dreams, bearing shades of things to come.

138. See D. K. Fieldhouse, *The Colonial Empires: A Comparative Survey from the Eighteen Century* (London, Weidenfeld & Nicolson, 1965).
139. Ellenborough, 26 February 1857, Hansard, 3d series, v. 144, col. 1364.

Chronology of major events

The dates are represented by six-digit numerals. The first two digits represent the year. Thus, 42 means 1842. The second two digits represent the month. Thus, 08 means August. The third two digits represent the day. Thus, 420829 means 29 August 1842. All dates refer to the nineteeth century.

420829 Treaty of Nanking was signed.
540213 Clarendon instructed Bowring to revise the Treaty of Nanking.
550927 The *Arrow* was registered in Hong Kong.
560202 (approx. date) Palmerston gave Parkes a special audience in Downing St.
560606 (approx. date) Parkes returned to China as acting consul at Canton.
560630 Yeh formally rejected Bowring's official request for treaty revision.
560830 News of Yeh's rejection of treaty revision reached London.
560924 British approached French for joint military action against China.
560927 The *Arrow*'s register expired and was not renewed.
561003 The *Arrow* entered the harbour of Canton and lowered her flags.
561008 Around 8 A.M., harbour police boarded the *Arrow*. Parkes claimed the *Arrow*'s flags had been flying, wrote to Yeh, Commodore Elliot, and Bowring.
561009 Parkes took depositions from Kennedy, Leach, and two Chinese sailors.
561010 Parkes received Elliot's positive answer. Yeh returned nine sailors, keeping two pirate suspects and one key witness. Parkes refused to receive them, increased his demands to include an apology from Yeh. Elliot arrived at Canton.
561011 Parkes proposed to Bowring the seizure of one or more Chinese war junks.
561012 Parkes sent Yeh a forty-eight-hour ultimatum. Yeh ordered all his war junks to leave Canton waters to avoid an escalation of the conflict.
561013 Parkes wrote to Bowring emphasizing threats of rebellions to Yeh.
561014 Elliot and Parkes seized a merchant vessel chartered by the Chinese government.
561016 Bowring secretly instructed Parkes to tell Yeh that he wished to visit him '*at his yamun in the City*' – 'a stepping-stone' for more important things to come.
561019 Without warning or sanction, Parkes left Canton to call on Bowring.
561020 Tripartite conference among Parkes, Bowring, and Seymour, at which Parkes proposed a specific plan for military action. His plan was accepted.

487

561021 Parkes told Yeh that continued retention of the twelve sailors signified his violation of treaty; he gave Yeh twenty-four hours to accede to his demands.
561022 Yeh returned all twelve sailors. Parkes refused them. The French government welcomed the British initiative for a joint military expedition against China.
561023 Seymour destroyed the four barrier forts between Whampoa and Canton.
561024 Bowring officially requested Seymour to demand entry into Canton City.
561025 Parkes conveyed to Yeh a thinly veiled demand for entry into Canton City.
561026 Sunday, Yeh turned down Parkes's unrelated demand to enter Canton City.
561027 Seymour began bombarding the City of Canton at ten-minute intervals.
561028 Yeh offered $30 for every British head taken. Seymour concentrated his fire on Yeh's residence, causing fire to break out, from which the Royal Navy tried to protect the foreign factories by pulling down the adjoining Chinese houses.
561029 Royal Navy blasted a hole in the city wall, stormed the city, and visited Yeh's residence. Keenan planted the U.S. flag atop the city wall and Yeh's residence.
561030 Seymour threatened still more bombardment unless Yeh agreed to receive him.
561031 Yeh continued to dwell on the rights and wrongs of the *Arrow* incident.
561101 Seymour declined any further argument on the case of the *Arrow*.
561102 Thereafter Royal Navy threw 'shot and shell' every day into the city.
561106 Royal Navy captured the French Folly Fort.
561108 Bowring proposed that the Bogue forts be destroyed.
561112 Royal Navy captured the Bogue's Hengdang Islands forts.
561113 Royal Navy captured the Bogue's Anianxie forts. Yeh still would not yield.
561114 Parkes wrote, 'Our position is certainly an embarrassing one'.
561115 U.S. naval, consular, and business communities evacuated Canton. Chinese soldiers guarding the barrier forts fired on U.S. warship by mistake.
561116 Commodore James Armstrong retaliated by destroying the barrior forts. The French left Canton.
561117 Bowring arrived at Canton and requested Yeh to receive him in Yeh's yamen.
561117 Yeh still tried to argue about the rights and wrongs of the *Arrow* incident.
561118 Bowring declared that it was 'useless to continue correspondence' and left.
561201 Whitehall received Bowring's despatch about the *Arrow* incident.
561204 Royal Navy resumed shelling Canton.
561214 A mysterious fire broke out in the foreign factory area at Canton, destroying U.S., French, and other foreign possessions, but not those of the British.
561215 The English factory itself caught fire and was burned down.
561216 Britain and France reached complete agreement on joint naval expedition.
561229 *The Times* printed a telegraphic despatch from Trieste about the *Arrow* incident.
561230 The *Thistle* was attacked by Chinese soldiers disguised as passengers.
570103 Bowring called on Seymour to strengthen the defence of Hong Kong.
570105? Seymour went back to Hong Kong and found 'great uneasiness' there.
570106 The *London Gazette* published Seymour's report on his operations in Canton.
570110 The British Cabinet met to discuss the *Arrow* crisis.
570112 Seymour set on fire the suburbs on each side of the Factory Gardens.
570114 Seymour withdrew from the Dutch Folly and the Factory Gardens.
570115 An attempt was made to poison the European community in Hong Kong.

570202 William Marcy disapproved of the actions by Keenan and Armstrong.
570203 The Queen opened Parliament.
570212 Seymour was compelled to withdraw from Canton altogether.
570224 Tuesday, Lord Derby opened the *Arrow* debate in the House of Lords.
570225 No debate in the House of Lords.
570226 Thursday, *Arrow* debate resumed in Lords. When the vote was taken, the Opposition lost: 110 to 146. *Arrow* debate began in the House of Commons.
570227 Friday, *Arrow* debate continued in the House of Commons.
570228 Saturday, weekend break for Parliament. Palmerston wooed members.
570301 Sunday, weekend break for Parliament. Palmerston wooed members.
570302 Monday, *Arrow* debate resumed in Commons.
570303 Government lost *Arrow* debate in Commons by 16 votes – 247 to 263.
570310 Elgin's appointment was reported in the press.
570314 Britain approached the United states for a tripartite expedition against China.
570321 Parliament was prorogued. Chinese Election campaigning began.
570407 Votes of the general election were counted: Palmerston was returned to office.
570410 United States rejected the British approach for a tripartite expedition against China.
570401 Britain approached Russia for a tripartite expedition against China, in vain.
570420 Elgin formally appointed plenipotentiary.
570521 Yeh tried to sound out Bowring's disposition towards a peaceful settlement.
570724 Yeh despatched two officials to Hong Kong again to try starting negotiations.
571021 Yeh exhorted Elgin to resume peaceful relations.
571214 Allies gave Yeh forty-eight hours to surrender.
571228 Allies began bombarding Canton.
580101 Canton fell. Yeh was taken prisoner.
580216 Some Hong Kong journalists visited Yeh and concluded that the artist who had sketched him as a monster must have eaten 'raw beef steaks and raw onions'.
580626 Anglo-Chinese Treaty of Tientsin was signed.
580627 French-Chinese Treaty of Tienstin was signed.
581106 Anglo-Chinese tariff agreement on taxing opium at 30 tales per 100 catties.
600918 Harry Parkes et al. were taken prisoner by Sengkelinqin.
600922 Emperor Xianfeng fled Beijing.
601006 French forces sacked the Summer Palace (Yuan Ming Yuan) in Beijing.
601007 British joined French in the sack of the Summer Palace in Beijing.
601008 Parkes et al. were released.
601018 Fritish forces set fire to the Summer Palace and burned it down.
601024 Anglo-Chinese Convention of Peking was signed.
601025 French-Chinese Convention of Peking was signed.

Word list

Amoy (Xiamen) 夏門
Allum – see Zhang Peilin
Aniangxie 阿娘鞋
Banno Junji 阪野潤治
Beijing (Peking) 北京
Bogue, the (Humen) 虎門
Canton (Guangzhou) 廣州
Canton River (or Pearl River, Zhujiang) 珠江
Cao Lütai 曹履泰
Chapoo (Zhapu) 乍浦
Ch'in Hsiao-i (Qin Xiaoyi) 秦孝儀
Chen Weidong 陳衞東
Chiang Kai-shek (Jiang Jieshi) 蔣介石
Chiang Pai-huan (Jiang Baihuan) 蔣百幻
Cho Lee-jay (Zhao Li-ji) 趙利濟
Chü Mi (Ju Mi) 居蜜
Chusan (Zhoushan) 舟山
Commissioner Lin (Lin Zexu) 林則徐
Commissioner Xu (Xu Guangjin) 徐廣縉
Commissioner Yeh (Ye Mingchen) 葉名琛
dao 道
Daoguang 道光
Deng Xiaoping 鄧小平
Dong Zhongshu 董仲舒
Dutch Folly Fort (Haizhu Paotai) 海珠砲台
Eight Banners (Ba Qi) 八旗
fangui 番鬼
fazhi 法治
Foo-chow-foo (Fuzhou Fu) 福州府
Foochow (Fuzhou) 福州
Fujian 福建
Fukuzawa Yukichi 福澤喻吉
gangkou 港口

Word List

Gaozhou 高州
governor (*xunfu*) 巡撫
governor-general (*zongdu*) 總督
Green Standard (Lü Ying) 綠營
Guangdong 廣東
Guangxi 廣西
Guangyin Hill 觀音山
Guangzhoufu 廣州府
Hengdang 橫擋
Honan (Henan) 河南 (south of Canton City)
Hong Kong (Xianggang) 香港
Hoppo (Yuehaiguan jiandu) 粵海關監督
Howqua (Wu Chongyue) 伍崇曜
Hu Shouwei 胡守為
Huang Entong 黃恩彤
Huang Yen-yü (Huang Yanyu) 黃延毓
Huangzhuqi 黃竹歧
Hubei 湖北
Hubu 戶部
Hunan 湖南
imperial commissioner (*qinchaidachen*) 欽差大臣
Jiangsu 江蘇
Jiangxi 江西
Jilong 基隆
Kaou-chow (Gaozhou) 高州
Koay Shiaw-chian (Guo Xiaoqian) 郭孝謙
laocheng 老城
Leang-gwo-ting (Liang Guoding) 梁國定
Li Chien-nung (Li Jiannong) 李劍農
Li Peng 李鵬
Li Yuzheng 李玉貞
Liang Guang 兩廣
Liang Guoding 梁國定
Liang Jiang 兩江
Liang Mingtai 梁明太
liang shouxian 兩首縣
likin 釐金
Liu Guilin 劉桂林
Liu Zhongdong 劉中東
Lu Guoxin 陸國新
Lu Ping 魯平
Luo Baoshan 駱寶善
Macao (Aomen) 澳門
Magdalen Lee (Li Wu Miaoling) 李吳妙玲
magistrate (*zhixian*) 知縣

Word List

Manchuria (Manzhou)　滿州
Mu-ke-de-na　穆克德訥
Muzhanga　穆彰阿
Nanhai　南海
nanjue　男爵
Nanking (Nanjing)　南京
Ningpo (Ningbo)　寧波
Niulangang　牛欄岡
Ou Hong　區鈝
Panyu　番禺
Patten, Christopher　彭定康
Peiho (Baihe)　白河
Peking (Beijing)　北京
Prince Kung　恭親王
Qianlong　乾隆
Qin Esheng　秦咢生
Qing　清
Qiu Jie　丘捷
Qiying　耆英
ren　仁
Renxin Mansion　仁信樓
renzhi　人治
Sanyuanli　三元里
Schevelyoff, Konstantin v.　石克強
Shameen (Shamian)　沙面
Shanghai　上海
Shunde　順德
Suzhou　蘇州
Taipei (Taibei)　台北
Taku (Dagu)　大沽
Tan Boon Chiang (Chen Wenzhang)　陳文章
Tianjin (Tientsin)　天津
Tsang Chiu-lin – see Zeng Zhaolion
Wangxia　望廈
Wei Hsiu-mei (Wei Xiumei)　魏秀梅
Whampoa (Huangpu)　黃埔
Wu Deduo　吳德鐸
Wuzhou　梧州
Xia Li　夏笠
Xianfeng　咸豐
xincheng　新城
Xu Guangjin　徐廣縉
yamen　衙門
Yang Guoxiong　楊國雄
Yang Tianshi　楊天石

Word List

Yangtze (Changjiang)　楊子江（長江）
Yangzhou　楊州
Ye Mingchen (Yeh Ming-ch'en)　葉名琛
Ye Mingfeng　葉名豐
Yilibu　伊里布
Yishan　奕山
Yiu Ngar-shui (Yao Yasui)　姚雅穗
Yu Baoshun　余葆純
Yuen Chuk-nang (Ruan Zhuneng)　阮祝能
Zeng Zhaolian　曾昭蓮
Zhang Peilin　張霈霖
Zhang Zuolin　張作霖
Zhao Huifang　趙惠芳
Zhao Huizhi　趙惠芝
Zhao Ziyang　趙紫揚
Zhongnanhai　中南海
Zhou Xingliang　周興樑
Zhou Yumin　周玉民
zhujiuzu　誅九族

Abbreviations

Adm.	Admiralty
B2; B4	Classifications in the Matheson Archive of Jardine Matheson and Co., University Library, Cambridge
BL	British Library, London
BMP	*Who's Who of British Members of Parliament*
Broadlands MSS	Palmerston Papers, National Register of Archives
DG	Daoguang period
DNB	*Dictionary of National Biography*
FO	Foreign Office
CO	Colonial Office
MSS Clar. De.	Manuscripts, Clarendon Deposits, Bodleian Library, Oxford
PRO	Public Record Office, London
QSLZ	*Qingshi liezhuan*
Ryl. Eng. MSS	Rylands English manuscripts, John Rylands University Library of Manchester
XF	Xianfeng period
YWSM	*Chouban yiwu shimo*

Bibliography

Archives

British Foreign Office Archives: Public Record Office, London
1. FO17, General correspondence, China
2. FO228, Embassy and consular reports, China
3. FO230/74-5, Copybooks of Chinese language documents
4. FO233/183-4, Copybooks of Chinese language documents
5. FO677/26-7, Copybooks of Chinese language documents
6. FO682, Chinese language diplomatic correspondence and other documents
7. FO931, Canton Archive (originally belonging to FO682)

British Admiralty Records: Public Record Office, London.
Adm. 1
Adm. 125/1

British Museum Holdings of the Beijing Gazette 京報: British Museum, London

Chinese Records: First National Archives, Beijing, China 中國第一歷史檔案館
1. Grand Council copies of edicts 軍機處上諭檔
2. Grand Council copies of memorials 軍機處錄副奏摺
3. Grand Council register of edicts and memorials 軍機處隨手登記檔

National Palace Museum, Taibei, Taiwan 故宮博物院
1. Grand Council monthly logbook of imperial edicts 上諭檔方本

French Records: Quai d'Orsay, Paris
China despatches to and from the Ministère des Affaires Étrangères, as contained in volumes numbered 4 to 34

Indian Records: India Office Library, London
1. Bengal Board of Revenue, Miscellaneous Proceedings (Opium)

495

2. Bengal Consultations: Governor-General in Council to the Government of Bombay
3. Despatches to Bengal: Court of Directors to the Governor-General in Council (separate revenue)
4. Governor-General, Secret Consultations, Bengal Secret Letters
5. Letters from Bengal: Governor-General in Council to the Court of Directors (territorial: salt and opium)
6. Letters from Bombay: Government of Bombay to the Court of Directors
7. Proceedings of President and Council, 15 October 1773, *Ninth Report from the Select Committee, 1783*

United States Records: Division of Manuscripts, Library of Congress, Washington, D.C. (all of the following are on microfilm)
1. Cushing Papers: Caleb Cushing
2. Foote Papers: Captain Andrew Hull Foote
3. Marcy Papers: William L. Marcy
4. Pierce Papers: Franklin Pierce
5. Reed Papers: William R. Reed, Private Diary of Mission to China, 1857–9.
6. United States Department of State, Consular Despatches
7. United States Department of State, Diplomatic Despatches
8. United States Department of State, Diplomatic Instructions

Company papers

Baring Papers: Guildhall Library, London
(By kind permission of Baring Brothers and Co.)
HC 6.1.1–20 House Correspondence, 1828–76

Matheson Papers: University Library, Cambridge
1. B2 General correspondence, Jardine Matheson and Co.
2. B4 Personal letters, Jardine Matheson and Co.

Private papers

Alabaster Papers: In the possession of Mr David St Maur Sheil, Lamma Island, Hong Kong
1. Alabaster diary
2. Alabaster papers

Bowring Papers: John Rylands University Library of Manchester
1. Ryl. Eng. MSS 1228, Sir John Bowring's letters to his son Edgar
2. Ryl. Eng. MSS 1229, Sir John Bowring's letters to his son Lewis
3. Ryl. Eng. MSS 1330, Letters to Sir John Bowring, filed newspaper clippings, and so forth

Cobden Papers: British Library, London
BL Add. MSS

Clarendon Papers: Bodleian Library, Oxford
(By kind permission of the seventh earl of Clarendon)
1. MSS Clar. Dep. C8 China (1853)
2. MSS Clar. Dep. C19 China (1854)
3. MSS Clar. Dep. C37 China (1855)
4. MSS Clar. Dep. C57 China (1856)
5. MSS Clar. Dep. C69 China (1857)
6. MSS Clar. Dep. C85 China (1858)

Davis Papers: Cambridge (privately owned by a descendant of Sir John Francis Davis who wishes to remain anonymous)

Granville Papers: Public Record Office, London
Granville MS PRO 30

Graham Papers: Bodleian Library, Oxford
Graham MSS (on microfilm)

Palmerston Papers: Royal Historical Commission, London
Broadlands MSS GC/BO/83
Broadlands MSS GC/BO/84
Broadlands MSS GC/BO/85 (with some Chinese-language documents)
Broadlands MSS GC/BO/86
Broadlands MSS GC/BO/87 (with some Chinese-language documents)
Broadlands MSS GC/BO/88
Broadlands MSS GC/BO/89

Parkes Papers: University Library, Cambridge
(By kind permission of Sir John Keswick)

Russell Papers: Public Record Office, London
PRO 12G

Wodehouse Papers: British Library, London
BL Add. MSS

Printed primary sources: In Chinese

Chouban yiwu shimo 《籌辦夷務始末》 (An account of the management of foreign affairs).
1. Imperial edicts and memorials of the Daoguang period pertaining to foreign affairs. 10 vs. Beiping, 1930. Taipei reprint, 1963.
2. Imperial edicts and memorials of the Xianfeng period pertaining to foreign affairs. 8 vs. Beijing, Zhonghua shuju edition, 1979.

Da Qing lichao shilu《大清歷朝實錄》(Veritable records of the successive reigns of Qing emperors). Taipei reprint, Wenhai, 1970.
1. Daoguang period, 10 vs.
2. Xianfeng period, 8 vs.

Daoguang Xianfeng liangchao chouban yiwu shimo buyi《道光咸豐兩朝籌辦夷務始末補遺》(Supplements to *Chouban yiwu shimo*, Daoguang and Xianfeng periods). Taipei, Institute of Modern History, Academic Sinica, 1966.

Di'erci yapian zhanzheng《第二次鴉片戰爭》(Source materials on the Second Opium War). 6 vs. Compiled by Qi Sihe 齊思和 et al. on behalf of the Chinese Historical Society. Shanghai, Renmin chubanshe, 1978. Cited as *Er ya* after first mention in notes.
v. 1, The attack on Canton, Taku and Tientsin: Extracts from contemporary private records, writings, and local gazetteers – 682 pages
v. 2, The attack on Peking: Extracts from contemporary private records, writings, and local gazetteers – 643 pages
v. 3, Chinese archival material (1853–8) – 608 pages
v. 4, Chinese archival material (1859) – 547 pages
v. 5, Chinese archival material (1860) – 549 pages
v. 6, Translations of selected non-Chinese materials – 573 pages

Institute of Modern History, Academia Sinica (comp.). *Jindai Zhongguo dui xifang ji lieqiang renshi ziliao huibian*《近代中國對西方及列強認識資料彙編》(A collection of materials reflecting modern Chinese perceptions on the West and the powers). 10 vs. Taibei, Institute of Modern History, Academia Sinica, 1972–88.

Institute of Modern History, Chinese Academy of Sciences (comp.). *Yapian zhanzheng shiqi sixiangshi ziliao xuanji*《鴉片戰爭時期思想史資料選輯》(Sources reflecting the thinking current during the Opium War). Beijing, Joint Publishing Co., 1963.

Qingdai Zhong-E guanxi dangan shiliao xuanbian《清代中俄係檔案史料選編》(Selected sources on China–Russia relations during the Qing period, 3d series [1851–62]). 3 vs. Compiled by the Ming-Qing section of the Palace Museum. Beijing, Zhonghua shuju, 1979: v. 1, 1851–7; v. 2, 1857–9; v. 3, 1859–62.

Siguo xindang《四國新檔》(New archives on China's relations with Great Britain, France, America and Russia). 4 vs. Taibei, Institute of Modern History, Academic Sinica, 1966.

Printed primary sources: In English

British Documents on Foreign Affairs: Reports and Papers from the Foreign Office Confidential Print, Part 1, Series E, Asia, v. 16, Chinese War and Its Aftermath, 1839–1849, ed. Ian Nish. Frederick, Md., University Publications of America, 1994.

British Documents on Foreign Affairs: Reports and Papers from the Foreign Office Confidential Print, Part 1, Series E, Asia, v. 17, Anglo-French Expedition to China, 1856–1858, ed. Ian Nish. Frederick, Md., University Publications of America, 1994.

British Parliamentary Papers
Pertinent volumes from the year 1800 to 1898

British Parliamentary Debates
1. Hansard, 3d series, v. 53 (1840)
2. Hansard, 3d series, v. 65 (1842)
3. Hansard, 3d series, v. 144 (1857)
4. Hansard, 3d series, v. 159 (1860)

Correspondence Relative to the Earl of Elgin's Special Mission to China and Japan, 1857–59. Reprinted by the Chinese Materials Center, San Francisco, 1975.

Greville, Charles Cavendish Fulke. *The Greville Memoirs: A Journal of the Reign of Queen Victorian from 1852 to 1860.* 6 vs. London, Longmans, Green, 1887.

United States Congressional Documents
1. Sen. Exec. Doc., No. 22, 35th Congress, 2d Session,
   pp. 1–495: Robert McLane Correspondence
   pp. 495–1424: Peter Parker Correspondence
2. Sen. Exec. Doc., No. 30, 36th Congress, 1st Session,
   pp. 1–569: William B. Reed Correspondence
   pp. 569–624: John E. Ward Correspondence

British newspapers

(British Library, Newspaper Division, Colindale, London)
Chronicle
Daily News
Globe
Guardian
Manchester Guardian
Morning Post
Morning Star
News
News of the World
Nonconformist
Press
Punch
Reynolds Newspaper
Spectator
The Times

Other newspapers

China Mail (daily), Hong Kong, 1845–9
  (Public Record Office, Hong Kong)

Chinese Repository (monthly), 20 vs., Canton, 1832–51 (reprinted in Japan)
North China Herald (weekly), Shanghai, 1850–61 (St Antony's College, Oxford)

Works in Western langauges

'A Field Officer'. *The Last Year in China to the Peace of Nanking: As Sketched in Letters to His Friends*. London, 1843.
A Draft Agreement between the Government of the United Kingdom of Great Britain and Northern Ireland and the Government of the People's Republic of China on the Future of Hong Kong. Hong Kong, 1984.
Abbot, Charles, Second Baron Colchester (ed.). *History of the Indian Administration of Lord Ellenborough, in his correspondence with the Duke of Wellington. To which is prefixed . . . Lord Ellenborough's letters to the Queen during that period*. London, 1874.
Abeel, David. *Journal of a Residence in China and the Neighbouring Countries from 1830 to 1833*. London, 1835.
Abstract of British Historical Statistics. Comp. B. R. Mitchell, with the collaboration of Phyllis Deane. Cambridge, 1962.
Adams, John Quincy. 'Lecture on the War with China'. *Chinese Repository*, v. 11 (1842) pp. 274–89.
Adams, William Y. *Nubia: Corridor to Africa*. London, 1977.
Akita, Shigeru. 'British Informal Empire in East Asia, 1880s–1930s: A Japanese Perspective'. In Janet Hunter (ed.), *Japanese Perspectives on Imperialism in Asia*. London, London School of Economics, 1995, pp. 1–29.
Alcock, Rutherford. *The Capital of the Tycoon*. 2 vs. New York, 1863.
Allen, G. C., and A. G. Donnithorne. *Western Enterprise in Far Eastern Economic Development – China and Japan*. London, 1954.
Allgood, G. *China War, 1860: Letters and Journal*. London, 1901.
Anderson, Flavia. *The Rebel Emperor*. London, 1958.
Anderson, M. A. 'Edmund Hammond: Permanent Under-Secretary of State for Foreign Affairs, 1854–73'. Ph.D. thesis, University of London, 1956.
Archer, Thomas, and A. H. Stirling. *Queen Victoria: Her Life and Reign*. 4 vs. London, 1901.
Argyll, Duke of. *George Douglas, Eighth Duke of Argyll, KG. K.T. (1823–1900): Autobiography and Memoirs*. Ed. dowager duchess of Argyll. 2 vs. London, 1906.
Australian Dictionary of Biography, v. 2, 1788–1850. Ed. A. G. L. Shaw and C. M. H. Clark. Melbourne, 1967.
Ayerst, David George. *Guardian Omnibus, 1821–1971: An Anthology of 150 Years of Guardian Writing*. London, 1973.
Bagehot, Walter. *The English Constitution*. London, 1872.
Bagehot, Walter. *The Collected Works of Walter Bagehot*. Ed. F. Morgan. London, 1995.
Bagenal, Philip Henry Dudley. *The Life of Ralph Bernal Osborne, M.P.* London, 1884.
Bakhala, Franklin. 'Indian Opium and Sino-Indian Trade Relations, 1801–1858'. Ph.D. thesis, University of London, 1985.
Ball, Alan R. *British Political Parties: The Emergence of a Modern Party System*. London, 1981.

Banno, M. *China and the West, 1858–1861: The Origins of the Tsungli Yamen.* Cambridge, Mass., 1964.
Baquet, Dean. 'Britain Drops Case Against 3 with Arms Sales to Iraq'. *New York Times*, 10 November 1992, p. A1 (USIS TK 252750).
Bartle, G. F. 'The Political Career of Sir John Bowring (1793–1872) between 1820 and 1849'. M.A. thesis, University of London, 1959.
Bartle, G. F. 'Sir John Bowring and the *Arrow* War in China'. *Bulletin of the John Rylands Library*, 43, no. 2 (1961), pp. 293–316.
Bartle, G. F. 'Sir John Bowring and the Chinese and Siamese Commercial Treaties'. *Bulletin of the John Rylands Library*, 44, no. 2 (March 1962), pp. 286–308.
The Basic Law of the Hong Kong Special Administrative Region of the People's Republic of China (April 1990). Hong Kong, 1990.
Bayly, C. A. *The New Cambridge History of India, v. 2, pt. 1, Indian Society and the Making of the British Empire.* Cambridge, 1988.
Beal, Edward. *The Origins of Likin, 1853–1864.* Cambridge, Mass., 1958.
Beasley, W. G. *The Meiji Restoration.* Stanford, Calif., 1973.
Beeching, Jack. *The Chinese Opium Wars.* London, 1975.
Bell, H. C. F. *Palmerston.* 2 vs. London, 1936.
Bentley, Michael. *Politics without Democracy, Great Britain, 1815–1914: Perception and Preoccupation in British Government.* Oxford, 1984.
Berridge, Virginia, and Griffith Edwards. *Opium and the People: Opiate Use in Nineteenth-Century England.* New Haven, Conn., 1987.
Bevington, Merle Mowbray. *The Saturday Review, 1855–1868: Representative Educated Opinion in Victorian England.* New York, 1941.
Biaggini, E. G. 'The Coercion of China, 1830–1860: A Study in Humbug'. D.Litt. thesis, University of Adelaide, 1944.
Biagini, Eugenio F., and Alastair J. Reid (eds.). *Currents of Radicalism: Popular Radicalism, Organised Labour, and Party Politics in Britain, 1850–1914.* Cambridge, 1991.
Bickers, Robert A. (ed.). *Ritual and Diplomacy: The Macartney Mission to China, 1792–1794.* London, 1993.
Bingham, J. Elliott. *Narrative of the Expedition to China from the Commencement of the War to the Present Period.* London, 1842.
Blacker, Carmen. *The Japanese Enlightenment: A Study of the Writings of Fukuzawa Yukichi.* Cambridge, 1969.
Blainey, Geoffrey. *The Tyranny of Distance: How Distance Shaped Australia's History.* Melbourne, 1982.
Blake, Clagette. *Charles Elliot, R.N.: A Servant of Britain Overseas.* London, 1960.
Bonner-Smith, D., and E. W. B. Lumby (eds.). *The Second China War, 1856–1860.* London, 1954.
Boot, H. M. *The Commercial Crisis of 1847.* Hull, 1984.
Booth, Charles (ed.). *Labour and Life of the People in London.* London, 1891–1902.
Bourne, K. *Palmerston: The Early Years, 1784–1841.* London, 1982.
Bowen, James. 'Education, Ideology and the Ruling Class: Hellenism and English Public Schools in the Nineteenth Century'. In G. W. Clarke (ed.), *Rediscovering Hellenism: The Hellenic Inheritance and the English Imagination.* Cambridge, 1989, pp. 161–86.

Bowring, Sir John. *Autobiographical Recollections of Sir John Bowring, with a Brief Memoir by Lewin B. Bowring*. 8 vs. London, 1877.
Boyle, John Hunter. *China and Japan at War, 1937–1945*. Stanford, Calif., 1972.
Brewer's Dictionary of Phrase and Fable. London, 1963.
Briggs, Asa. *The Age of Improvement*. London, 1959.
Briggs, Asa. *Victorian People*. London, 1965.
Brown, Lucy. *The Board of Trade and the Free Trade Movement, 1830–1842*. Oxford, 1958.
Brown, Lucy. *Victorian News and Newspapers*. Oxford, 1985.
Bruce, H. A. *Letters of the Rt. Hon. H. A. Bruce, G.C.B., Lord Aderdare of Duffryn*. 2 vs. Oxford, 1902.
Brunnert, H. S., and V. V. Hagelstrom. *Present Day Political Organization of China*. Trans. A. Beltchenko and E. E. Morgan. Shanghai, 1963.
Burke's Genealogical and Heraldic History of the Peerage, Baronetage, and Knightage. Ed. Peter Townsend. 104th ed. London, Burke's Peerage, 1967.
Buxton, Sydney Charles. *Finance and Politics: An Historical Study, 1783–1885*. London, 1888.
Cady, J. F. *The Roots of French Imperialism in Eastern Asia*. New York, 1954.
Cahill, Justin. 'From Colonisation to Decolonisation: A study of Chinese and British Negotiating Positions with Regard to Hong Kong'. History IV honours thesis, University of Sydney, 1995.
Cain, P. J., and A. G. Hopkins. 'Gentlemanly Capitalism and British Expansion Overseas: I. The Old Colonial System, 1688–1850'. *Economic History Review*, new series, 39, no. 4 (1986), pp. 501–25.
Cain, P. J., and A. G. Hopkins. 'Gentlemanly Capitalism and British Expansion Overseas: II. New Imperialism, 1650–1945'. *Economic History Review*, new series, 40, no. 1 (1986), pp. 1–26.
Cain, P. J., and A. G. Hopkins. *British Imperialism: Crisis and Deconstruction, 1914–1990*. London, 1993.
Cain, P. J., and A. G. Hopkins. *British Imperialism: Innovation and Expansion, 1688–1914*. London, 1993.
Caloner, W. H. 'Currency Problems of the British Empire'. In Barrie M. Ratcliffe (ed.), *Great Britain and Her World, 1750–1914: Essays in Honour of W. O. Henderson*. Manchester, 1975, pp. 179–207.
Cambridge History of India, v. 5, 1497–1858. Ed. H. H. Dodwell. Cambridge, 1929.
Cannadine, David. 'The Context, Performance and Meaning of Ritual: The British Monarchy and the "Invention of Tradition", c. 1820–1977'. In Eric Hobsbawn and Terence Ranger (eds.), *The Invention of Tradition*. Cambridge, 1983, pp. 101–64.
Cannadine, David. *The Decline and Fall of the British Aristocracy*. New Haven, Conn., 1990.
Cannadine, David. 'The Empire Strikes Back' (review article). *Past and Present*, no. 147 (May 1995), pp. 180–94.
Cassels, N. G. 'Bentinck: Humanitarian and Imperialist – The Abolition of Suttee'. *Journal of British Studies*, 5, no. 1 (November 1965), pp. 77–87.
Cecil, Algernon. *Queen Victoria and Her Prime Ministers*. New York, 1953.
Chan, M. K., and David J. Clark (eds.). *The Hong Kong Basic Law: Blueprint for 'Stability and Prosperity' under Chinese Sovereignty?* Hong Kong, 1991.

Bibliography

Chang, Hsin-pao. *Commissioner Lin and the Opium War*. Cambridge, Mass., 1964.
Chang, Nien. *Life and Death in Shanghai*. London, 1986.
Chao, Tang-li. 'Anglo-Chinese Diplomatic Relations, 1858–70'. Ph.D. thesis, University of London, 1956.
Chaudhuri, B. 'Agrarian Relations: East India'. In Dharma Kumar (ed.), *The Cambridge Economic History of India, v. 2, c. 1757–c. 1970*. Cambridge, 1983, pp. 86–177.
Chaudhuri, Binay Bhushan. 'Growth of Commercial Agriculture in Bengal, 1859–1885'. *Indian Economic and Social History Review*, 7, nos. 1 and 2 (1970), pp. 25–60.
Chaudhuri, K. N. 'Foreign Trade and Balance of Payments (1857–1947)'. In Dharma Kumar (ed.), *The Cambridge Economic History of India, v. 2, c. 1757–c. 1970*. Cambridge, 1983, pp. 804–77.
Cheong, W. E. *Mandarins and Merchants: Jardine Matheson & Co., a China Agency of the Early Nineteenth Century*. London, 1979.
Chiang, Pei-huan. 'Anglo-Chinese Diplomatic Relations, 1856–60'. Ph.D. thesis, University of London, 1939.
Choi, Chi-chueung. 'Cheung Ah-lum: A Biographical Note'. *Journal of the Hong Kong Branch of the Royal Asiatic Society*, v. 24 (1984), pp. 282–7.
Chowdhury, Benoy. *Growth of Commercial Agriculture in Bengal*. Calcutta, 1964.
Clarke, P., and Jack S. Gregory (eds.). *Western Reports on the Taiping: A Selection of Documents*. Canberra, 1982.
Clune, Frank. *Sky High to Shanghai*. Sydney, 1947.
Coates, Patrick D. *The China Consuls: British Consular Officers, 1843–1943*. Hong Kong, 1988.
Cohen, Paul. *China and Christianity: The Missionary Movement and the Growth of Chinese Antiforeignism, 1860–1870*. Cambridge, Mass., 1963.
Coleman, D. C., and Christine MacLeod. 'Attitudes to New Techniques: British Businessmen, 1800–1950'. *Economic History Review*, new series, 39, no. 4 (1986), pp. 588–611.
Collet, C. D. *History of the Taxes on Knowledge: The Origin and Repeal*. 2 vs. London, 1899.
Conacher, J. B. *The Aberdeen Coalition, 1852–1855: A Study in Mid-Nineteenth-Century Party Politics*. Cambridge, 1968.
Conacher, J. B. *The Peelites and the Party System, 1846–1852*. Newton Abbot, 1972.
Cooke, George Wingrove. *China: Being 'The Times' Special Correspondent from China in the Years 1857–8, with Corrections and Additions*. London, 1858.
Cordier, Henri. *L'expedition de Chine de 1857–1858: Histoire diplomatique. Notes et documents*. Paris, 1905.
Cordier, Henri. *L'expedition de Chine de 1860: Histoire diplomatique. Notes et documents*. Paris, 1905.
Correspondence Relative to the Earl of Elgin's Special Missions to China and Japan, 1857–59. San Francisco, 1975. (This is a reproduction of a set of Parliamentary Papers bearing the same name.)
Costin, William Conrad. *Great Britain and China, 1883–1860*. Oxford, 1937.
Cox, Gary W. *The Efficient Secret: The Cabinet and the Development of Political Parties in Victorian England*. Cambridge, 1987.
Crosby, Travis L. *Sir Robert Peel's Administration, 1841–1846*. Newton Abbot, 1976.
Crouzet, Francois. 'Trade and Empire: The British Experience from the Establishment

of Free Trade until the First World War'. In Barrie M. Ratcliffe (ed.), *Great Britain and Her World, 1750–1914: Essays in Honour of W. O. Henderson*. Manchester, 1975, pp. 209–35.

Cunynghame, Arthur. *The Opium War, Being Recollections of Service in China*. Philadelphia, 1845.

Dangerfield, George. *The Strange Death of Liberal England*. New York, 1961.

Daniels, Gordon. 'Sir Harry Parkes: British Representative in Japan, 1856–83'. D.Phil. thesis, University of Oxford, 1967.

Dasent, Arthur Irwin. *John Thaddeus Delane, Editor of The Times: His Life and Correspondence*. 2 vs. London, 1908.

Davis, Michael C. *Constitutional Confrontation in Hong Kong: Issues and Implications of the Basic Law*. London, 1989.

Davis, Ralph. *The Industrial Revolution and British Overseas Trade*. Leicester, 1978.

Davis, Sir John. *The Chinese; A General Description of the Empire of China and Its Inhabitants*. 2 vs. London, 1836.

Davis, Sir John. *China during the War and since the Peace*. 2 vs. London, 1852.

Dennett, Tyler. *Americans in Eastern Asia*. New York, 1922.

Dictionary of National Biography. Editors vary. 22 vs. Oxford: Since 1917.

Divekar, V. D. 'Regional Economy (1757–1857): Western India'. In Dharma Kumar (ed.), *The Cambridge Economic History of India, v. 2, c. 1757–c. 1970*. Cambridge, 1983, pp. 332–52.

Downing, C. Toogood. *The Fan-Qui in China, 1836–37*. 3 vs. London, 1838.

Drescher, Seymour. *Econocide: British Slavery in the Era of Abolition*. Pittsburgh, Pa., 1977.

Dunn, Wie T. *The Opium Traffic in Its International Aspects etc*. Thesis (degree unspecified), Columbia University, 1920.

Durand, H. M. *Life of Major-General Sir Henry Marion Durand*. 2 vs. London, W. H. Allen, 1883.

Durand, Sir Henry Marion. *The First Afghan War and Its Causes*. 2 vs. London, 1879.

Eames, James Bromley. *The English in China: Being an Account of the Intercourse and Relations between England and China from the Year 1600 to the Year 1843 and a Summary of Later Developments*. London, 1909.

Edsall, Nicholas C. *Richard Cobden: Independent Radical*. Cambridge, Mass., 1986.

Edwardes, S. M. *The Rise of Bombay: A Retrospect*. Bombay, 1902.

Edwards, E. W. *British Diplomacy and Finance in China, 1895–1914*. Oxford, 1987.

Elliot, Sir George. *Memoir of Admiral the Honourable Sir George Elliot*. London, 1863.

Eminent Chinese of the Ch'ing Period (1644–1912). Ed. Arthur W. Hummel. Washington, D.C., 1943–4.

Etherington, M. D., and Keith Forster. *Green Gold: The Political Economy of China's Post-1949 Tea Industry*. Hong Kong, 1993.

Evans, Richard John. *Rethinking German History, Nineteenth-Century Germany and the Origins of the Third Reich*. London, 1990.

Fairbank, J. K. 'The Legalization of the Opium Trade before the Treaties of 1858'. *Chinese Social and Political Science Review*, 17, no. 2 (July 1933), pp. 215–63.

Fairbank, J. K. 'Tributary Trade and China's Relations with the West'. *Far Eastern Quarterly*, 1, no. 2 (1942), pp. 129-49.
Fairbank, J. K. *Trade and Diplomacy on the China Coast: The Opening of Treaty Ports, 1842-54.* Cambridge, Mass., 1953.
Fairbank, J. K. 'Synarchy under the Treaties'. In Fairbank (ed.), *Chinese Thought and Institutions*. Chicago, 1957, pp. 204-31.
Fairbank, J. K. 'The Early Treaty Port System in the Chinese World Order'. In Fairbank (ed.), *The Chinese World Order*. Cambridge, Mass., 1968, pp. 257-75.
Fairbank, J. K. 'The Creation of the Treaty Port System'. In Fairbank et al. (eds.), *The Cambridge History of China*, v. 10, pt. 1. Cambridge, 1978, pp. 213-63.
Farnie, D. A. 'The Cotton Famine in Great Britain'. In Barrie Ratcliffe (ed.), *Great Britain and Her World, 1750-1914: Essays in Honour of W. O. Henderson*. Manchester, 1975, pp. 153-78.
Farnie, D. A. *The English Cotton Industry and the World Market, 1815-1896*. Oxford, 1979.
Fay, Peter Ward. *The Opium War, 1840-1842: Barbarians in the Celestial Empire in the Early Part of the 19th Century and the War by Which They Forced Her Gates Ajar*. Chapel Hill, N.C., 1975.
Fieldhouse, D. K. *The Colonial Empires: A Comparative Survey from the Eighteenth Century.* London, 1965.
Fieldhouse, D. K. *Economics and Empire*. London, 1973.
Fieldhouse, D. K. 'Can Humpty Dumpty Be Put Together Again? Imperial History in the 1980s'. *Journal of Imperial and Commonwealth History*, 12, no. 2 (May 1984), pp. 9-23.
Finlay, James, and Co. *Manufacturers and East India Merchants, 1750-1950*. Glasgow, 1951.
Fitzmaurice, Edmond George, Lord. *Life of Granville George Leveson Gower, Second Earl Granville*. 2 vs. London, 1905.
Forbes, F. E. *Five Years in China: From 1842 to 1847 – With an Account of the Occupation of the Islands of Labuan and Borneo by Her Majesty's Forces*. London, 1848.
Forbes, Robert B. *Personal Reminiscences*. Boston, 1878.
Forrest, Denys. *Tea for the British: The Social and Economic History of a Famous Trade.* London, 1973.
Fortune, Robert. *Three Years Wandering in the Northern Provinces of China.* 2d ed. London, 1847.
Fortune, Robert. *A Journey to the Tea Countries of China*. London, 1852.
Fortune, Robert. *A Residence among the Chinese*. London, 1857.
Foster, John Watson. *American Diplomacy in the Orient*. New York, 1903.
Galbraith, J. S. 'The "Turbulent Frontier" as a Factor in British Expansion'. *Comparative Studies in Society and History*, no. 2 (1960), pp. 150-68.
Gallagher, John, and Ronald Robinson. 'The Imperialism of Free Trade'. *Economic History Review*, new series, 6, no. 1 (1953), pp. 1-15.
Gardella, Robert. *Harvesting Mountains: Fujian and China Tea Trade, 1757-1937*. Berkeley and Los Angelos, 1994.
Garnsey, P. D. A., and C. R. Whittaker (eds.). *Imperialism in the Ancient World*. Cambridge, 1978.
Gatrell, V. A. C. *The Hanging Tree: Execution and the English People, 1770-1868*. Oxford, 1994.

Gavin, R. J. 'Palmerston's Policy towards East and West Africa, 1830–1865'. Ph.D. thesis, University of Cambridge, 1959.
Gerson, J. J. *Horatio Nelson Lay and Sino-British Relations, 1854–1864*. Cambridge, Mass., 1972.
Gladstone, W. G. *The Gladstone Diaries, v. 5, 1855–1860*. Ed. M. R. D. Foot and H. C. G. Matthew. Fourteen vs. Oxford, 1978.
Gooch, G. P. (ed.). *The Later Correspondence of Lord John Russell, 1840–1878*. 2 vs. London, Longmans, Green, 1925.
Gordon, Arthur. *The Earl of Aberdeen*. London, 1894.
Gordon, Arthur Hamilton, First Baron Stanmore. *Sidney Herbert, Lord Herbert of Lea: A Memoir*. 2 vs. London, 1906.
Gordon, Barry. *Economic Doctrine and Tory Liberalism, 1824–1830*. London, 1979.
Graham, Gerald S. *The China Station: War and Diplomacy, 1830–1860*. Oxford, 1978.
Grant, James Hope. *Incidents in the China War of 1860*. Compiled from the private journals of Sir Hope Grant by H. Knollys. London, 1875.
Greenberg, Michael. *British Trade and the Opening of China, 1800–42*. Cambridge, 1951.
Gregory, G. S. *Great Britain and the Taiping*. Canberra, 1969.
Greville, Charles Cavendish Fulke. *Leaves from the Greville Diary*. Arranged by Philip Morrell. London, 1920.
Griffin, Eldon. *Clippers and Consuls: American Consular and Commercial Relations with Eastern Asia, 1845–1860*. Ann Arbor, Mich., 1938.
Grimsted, Patricia Kennedy. *Archives and Manuscript Repositories in the USSR: Moscow and Leningrad*. Princeton, N. J., 1972.
Gros, Jean Baptiste Louis, Baron. *Négotiations entre la France et la Chine en 1860*. Paris, 1864.
Gruen, Erich S. 'The Imperial Policy of Augustus'. In Kurt A. Raaflaub and Mark Toher (eds.), *Between Republic and Empire: Interpretations of Augustus and His Principate*. Berkeley and Los Angeles, 1990, pp. 395–41.
Gruen, Erich S. *The Image of Rome*. Eaglewood Cliffs, N.J., 1969.
Guha, Amalendu. 'Raw Cotton of Western India: 1750–1850'. *Indian Economic and Social History Review*, 9, no. 1 (1972), pp. 1–42.
Gulick, Edward V. *Peter Parker and the Opening of China*. Cambridge, Mass., 1973.
Hamilton, C. I. *Anglo-French Naval Rivalry, 1840–1870*. Oxford, 1993.
Hao, Yen-p'ing. *The Comprador in Nineteenth Century China: Bridge between East and West*. Cambridge, Mass., 1970.
Hao, Yen-p'ing. *The Commercial Revolution in Nineteenth-Century China: The Rise of Sino-Western Mercantile Capitalism*. Berkeley and Los Angeles, 1986.
Harcourt, Freda. 'Black Gold: P&O and the Opium Trade, 1847–1914', *International Journal of Maritime History*, 6, no. 1 (June 1944), pp. 1–83.
Harnetty, Peter. *Imperialism and Free Trade: Lancashire and India in the Mid-Nineteenth Century*. Vancouver, 1972.
Harris, James Howard, third earl of Malmesbury. *Memoirs of an Ex-Minister: An Autobiography*. 2 vs. London, 1884.
Hart, Jennifer. *Proportional Representaton: Critics of the British Electoral System, 1820–1945*. Oxford, 1992.

Hawkins, Angus. *Parliament, Party and the Art of Politics in Britain, 1855–59*. London, 1987.
Hay, Sir John. *The Suppression of Piracy in the China Sea, 1849*. London, 1889.
Haynes, William G. *The Economics of Empire: Britain, Africa and the New Imperialism, 1870–95*. London, 1979.
Headrick, R. Daniel. *Tools of Empire: Technology and European Imperialism in the Nineteenth Century*. New York, 1981.
Headrick, R. Daniel. *Invisible Weapon: Telecommunications and International Politics, 1851–1945*. New York, 1991.
Hetherington, Alastair. *Guardian Years*. London, 1981.
Hilton, Boyd. *Corn, Cash, Commerce: The Economic Policies of the Tory Governments, 1815–1830*. Oxford, 1977.
Hilton, Boyd. *The Age of Atonement: The Influence of Evangelicalism on Social and Economic Thought, 1795–1865*. Oxford, 1988.
Hinde, Wendy. *Richard Cobden: A Victorian Outsider*. New Haven, Conn., 1987.
Hindler, Wilfrid. *The Morning Post, 1772–1937: Portrait of a Newspaper*. London, 1937.
Hinsley, Francis Harry. *Sovereignty*. 2d ed. Cambridge, 1986.
The History of The Times, 1841–1884: The Tradition Established. London, 1939.
Ho, Ping-ti. *Studies on the Population of China, 1368–1953*. Cambridge, Mass., 1959.
Hobsbawm, E. J. *The Age of Empire, 1875–1914*. London, 1966.
Hobson, J. A. *Imperialism: A Study*. London, 1902.
Hodder, Edwin. *Life and Work of the Seventh Earl of Shaftesbury*. 3 vs. London, 1886.
Hollander, Samuel. *Ricardo, the New View: Collected Essays*. London, 1995.
Hollis, M., and S. Smith. *Explaining and Understanding International Relations*. Oxford, 1990.
Holt, E. *The Opium Wars in China*. London, 1964.
Howe, Anthony. *The Cotton Masters, 1830–1860*. Oxford, 1984.
Hsiao, Kung-ch'üan. *Rural China: Imperial Control in the Nineteenth Century*. Seattle, Wash., 1960.
Hsü, Immanuel C. Y. *China's Entrance into the Family of Nations: The Diplomatic Phase, 1858–1880*. Cambridge, Mass., 1960.
Hsü, Immanuel C. Y. *The Rise of Modern China*. Fourth ed. New York, 1990.
Huang, Yen-yü, 'Viceroy Yeh Ming-ch'en and the Canton Episode, 1856–1861'. Ph.D. dissertation, Harvard University, 1940 (subsequently published in full with the same title in *Harvard Journal of Asiatic Studies*, no. 6 [1941], pp. 37–127).
Huc, Évariste Régis. *Christianity in China, Tartary and Tibet*. 3 vs. London, 1857–58.
Hudson, G. F. *Europe and China: A Survey of Their Relations from the Earliest Times to 1800*. London, 1931.
Hunt, Freeman. *Lives of American Merchants*. 2 vs. New York, 1858.
Hunt, William. *Then and Now; or, Fifty Years of Newspaper Work, with an Appendix*. Hull, 1887.
Hunter, William C. *The 'Fan Kwae' at Canton before Treaty Days, 1825–1844*. London, 1882.
Huntington, Samuel P. *The Third Wave: Democratisation in the Late Twentieth Century*. Norman, Okla., 1991.
Hurd, Douglas. *The 'Arrow' War: An Anglo-Chinese Confusion, 1856–60*. London, 1967.
Hurley, R. C. *The Opium Traffic: Historical, Commercial, Social, and Political Aspects etc*. Hong Kong, 1909.
Hurst, Michael (ed.). *Key Treaties for the Great Powers, 1814–1914*. Newton Abbot, 1972.

Ilyushechkin, V. P. *The Taipings' Peasant War*. Moscow, 1967.
Inglis, Brian. *The Opium War*. London, 1976.
Inglis, Brian. *The Forbidden Game: A Social History of Drugs*. London, 1977.
Ingram, Edward. *The Beginning of the Great Game in Asia, 1828–1834*. Oxford, 1979.
Iriye, Akira (ed.). *The Chinese and the Japanese: Essays in Political and Cultural Interactions*. Princeton, N.J., 1980.
Jackson, C. E. 'The British General Elections of 1857 and 1859'. D.Phil. thesis, University of Oxford, 1980.
Jardine Matheson and Co. *An Outline of the History of a China House for a Hundred Years, 1832–1932*. Hong Kong, 1934.
Jehl, Douglas. 'Who Armed Iraq? Answers the West Didn't Want to Hear'. *New York Times*, 18 July 1993 (USIS TK295592).
Jennings, John M. 'The Forgotten Plague: Opium and Narcotics in Korea under Japanese Rule, 1910–1945'. *Modern Asian Studies*, 29, no. 4 (1995), pp. 795–815.
Johnson, Robert Erwin. *Far China Station: The U.S. Navy in Asian Waters, 1800–1898*. Annapolis, Md., 1979.
Johnston, James D. *China and Japan: Being a Narrative of the Cruise of the U.S. Steam Frigate Powhatan, in the Years 1857, '58, '59, and '60*. Philadelphia, 1861.
Jone, Michael Wynn. *George Cruikshank: His Life and London*. London, 1978.
Jones, Ray. *The Nineteenth-Century Foreign Office: An Administrative History*. London, 1971.
Jones, Walter S. *The Logic of International Relations*. 7th ed. New York, 1991.
Jones, Wilbur Devereux. *Lord Derby and Victorian Conservatism*. Oxford, 1956.
Kanya-Forstner, A. S. *The Conquest of the Western Sudan: A Study in French Military Imperialism*. Cambridge, 1969.
Kavanagh, Dennis. *Thatcherism and British Politics: The End of Consensus?* Oxford, 1987.
Keay, John. *The Honourable Company: A History of the English East India Company*. New York, 1994.
Keir, David Lindsay. *The Constitutional History of Modern Britain since 1485*. 9th ed. London, 1969.
Kennedy, Paul. *The Realities behind Diplomacy: Background Influences on British External Policy, 1865–1980*. London, 1981.
Kennedy, Paul. *Strategy and Diplomacy, 1870–1945*. London, 1983.
Kennedy, Paul. *The Rise and Fall of the Great Powers: Economic Change and Military Conflict from 1500 to 2000*. New York, 1987.
Kennedy, Paul. *Preparing for the Twentieth-First Century*. London, 1993.
Kessinger, Tom G. 'Regional Economy (1757–1857): North India'. In Dharma Kumar (ed.), *The Cambridge Economic History of India*, v. 2, c. 1757–c.1970. Cambridge, 1983, pp. 242–70.
Kiernan, V. G. *The Lords of Human Kind: European Attitudes towards the Outside World in the Imperial Age*. London, 1969.
King, Frank H. H. *Money and Monetary Policy in China, 1845–1895*. Cambridge, Mass., 1965.
Kissinger, Henry. *A World Restored: The Politics of Conservatism in a Revolutionary Era – A Detailed Study of Diplomacy and Political Manoeuvre, 1812–22, with Particular Reference to Metternich and Castlereagh*. Boston, 1957.
Kissinger, Henry. *Diplomacy*. New York, 1994.

Koay, Shiaw-chian. 'British Opinion and Policy on China between the First and Second Anglo-Chinese Wars, 1842–1857'. M.A. thesis, University of Leeds, 1967.
Koss, Stephen. *The Rise and Fall of the Political Press in Britain, v. 1: The Nineteenth Century*. London, 1981.
Kuhn, Philip A. *Rebellion and Its Enemies in Late Imperial China: Militarization and Social Structure, 1796–1864*. Cambridge, Mass., 1970.
Kumar, Dharma (ed.). *The Cambridge Economic History of India, v. 2: c. 1757–c.1970*. Cambridge, 1983.
Kurland, Philip B. *Watergate and the Constitution*. Chicago, 1978.
Lambrick, H. T. *Sir Charles Napier and Sind*. Oxford, 1952.
Lane-Poole, Stanley. *The Life of Sir Harry Parkes, v. 1, Consul in China*. London, 1894.
Langer, William. *The Diplomacy of Imperialism, 1890–1902*. 2d ed. Cambridge, Mass., 1956.
Laumann, Maryta M. *The Secret of Excellence in Ancient Chinese Silks*. Taipei, 1984.
Lay, Horatio Nelson. *Note on the Opium Question, and Brief Survey of Our Relations with China*. London, 1893.
Layard, Austen Henry. *Nineveh and Its Remains*. 2 vs. London, 1850.
Layard, Austen Henry. *Discoveries in the Ruins of Nineveh and Babylon*. London, 1853.
Leader, R. E. *Life and Letters of John Arthur Roebuck, PC, QC, MP with Chapters of Autobiography*. London, 1897.
Leavenworth, Charles. *The Arrow War with China*. London, Low, Marston & Co., 1901.
Lee, Alan J. *The Origins of the Popular Press, 1855–1914*. London, 1976.
Lees-Milne, James. *Prophesying Peace*. London, 1977.
Lenin, V. I. *Imperialism: The Highest Stage of Capitalism*. Moscow, 1947.
Little, R., and M. Smith (eds.). *Perspectives on World Politics*. 2d ed. London, 1991.
Louis, William Roger. *Imperialism at Bay, 1941–1945: The United States and the Decolonization of the British Empire*. Oxford, 1977.
Louis, William Roger (ed.). *Imperialism: The Robinson–Gallagher Controversy*. New York, 1976.
Lucas, Reginald. *Lord Glenesk and the Morning Post*. London, 1910.
Lynn, Martin. 'The "Imperialism of Free Trade" and the Case of West Africa, c. 1830– c. 1870'. *Journal of Imperial and Commonwealth History*, 15, no. 1 (October 1986), pp. 22–40.
MacCarthy, D., and A. Russell, *Lady John Russell: A Memoir*. London, 1926.
Macdonagh, Oliver. *Early Victorian Government, 1830–1870*. London, 1977.
MacGregor, David R. *The Tea Clippers: An Account of the China Tea Trade and of Some of the British Sailing Ships Engaged in It from 1849–1869*. 2d ed. London, 1972.
Machin, G. I. T. *Politics and the Churches in Great Britain, 1832–1868*. Oxford, 1967.
McKenzie, R. T. *British Political Parties: The Distribution of Power within the Conservative and Labour Parties*. London, 1955.
Maier, Charles S. *The Unmasterable Past: History, Holocaust, and the German National Identity*. Cambridge, Mass., 1988.
Maitland, F. W. *The Constitutional History of England: A Course of Lectures Delivered*. Cambridge, 1909.
Mandler, Peter. *Aristocratic Government in the Age of Reform: Whigs and Liberals, 1830–1852*. Oxford, 1990.
Mann, Michael (ed.). *The Rise and Decline of the Nation State*. Oxford, 1990.

Mao Tse-tung. 'The Chinese Revolution and the Chinese Communist Party'. In *The Selected Works of Mao Tse-tung*. Beijing, 1967, v. 2, pp. 305–34.
Mao Tse-tung, 'Talks at the Yenaenan Forum on Literature and Art'. In *The Selected Works of Mao Tse-tung*. Beijing, 1967, v. 3, pp. 69–98.
Martin, Kingsley. *The Triumph of Lord Palmerston: A Study of Public Opinion in England before the Crimean War*. Revised ed. London, 1963.
Martin, W. A. P. *A Cycle of Cathay or China, South and North*. New York, 1897.
Marx, Karl. *Marx on China: Articles from the 'New York Daily Tribune', 1853–1860* (with an introduction and notes by Dona Torr). London, 1968.
Matheson, J. *The Present Position and Prospects of the British Trade with China*. London, 1836.
Matthew, Henry Colin Gray. *Gladstone, 1809–1874*. Oxford, 1986.
Matthew, Henry Colin Gray. *Gladstone, 1875–1898*. Oxford, 1995.
Maxwell, Sir Herbert. *The Life and Letters of George William Frederick, Fourth Earl of Clarendon*. 2 vs. London, 1913.
McPherson, D. *Two Years in China: Narrative of the Chinese Expedition from Its Formation in April 1840 till April 1842*. London, 1842.
Meadows, T. T. *Desultory Notes on the Government and People of China, and on the Chinese Language*. London, 1847.
Miall, A. *The Life of Edward Miall, Formerly Member of Parliament for Rochdale and Bradford etc*. London, 1884.
Michael, Franz. *The Taiping Rebellion: History and Documents*. Seattle, Wash., 1966.
Michie, Alexander. *An Englishman in China during the Victorian Era: As Illustrated in the Career of Sir Rutherford Alcock . . . Many Years Consul and Minister in China and Japan*. Edinburgh, 1900.
Misra, B. B. *The Central Administration of the East India Company, 1773–1834*. Manchester, 1959.
Moges, Marquis de. *Recollections of Baron Gros' Embassy to China in 1857–8*. London, 1900.
Monmouth, Geoffrey. *The History of the Kings of Britain*. Trans. Lewis Thorpe. London, 1966.
Monypenny, W. F., and G. E. Buckle. *The Life of Benjamin Disraeli*. 6 vs. London, 1910–20.
Moore, D. C. *The Politics of Deferemce: A Study of the Mid-Nineteenth-Century Political System*. Hassocks, 1976.
Morley, John. *The Life of Richard Cobden*. 6th ed. London, 1883.
Morley, John. *The Life of William Ewart Gladstone*. London, 1908.
Morse, Hosea Ballou. *The Chronicles of the East India Company Trading to China, 1635–1843*. 4 vs. Oxford, 1926.
Morse, Hosea Ballou. *The International Relations of the Chinese Empire*. 3 vs. Shanghai, 1910–18.
Mui, Hoh-cheung, and Lorna H. Mui (eds.). *William Melrose in China, 1845–1855: The Letters of a Scottish Tea Merchant*. Edinburgh, 1973.
Myers, Ramon H. *The Chinese Peasant Economy: Agricultural Development in Hopei and Shangtung, 1890–1949*. Cambridge, Mass., 1970.
Napier, C. J. *Defects, Civil and Military, of the Indian Government*. London, 1853.

New History of China. Ed. S. L. Tikhvinsky. Moscow, Nauka, 1972.
Newbury, Colin. 'The Semantics of International Influence: Informal empires reconsidered'. In Michael Twaddle (ed.), *Imperialism, the State and the Third World*. London, 1992, pp. 23–66.
Newman, R. K. 'India and the Anglo-Chinese Opium Agreements, 1907–14'. *Modern Asian Studies*, 23, no. 4 (1989), pp. 525–60.
Newman, R. K. 'Opium Smoking in Late Imperial China: A Reconsideration'. *Modern Asian Studies*, 29, no. 4 (1995), pp. 765–94.
Nichols, Roy Franklin. *Franklin Pierce, Young Hickory of the Granitic Hills*. Philadelphia, 1958.
Nolde, John J. ' "The Canton City Question", 1842–1849: A Preliminary Investigation into Chinese Antiforeignism and Its Effect upon China's Diplomatic Relations with the West.' Ph.D. dissertation, Cornell University, 1956.
Nolde, John J. 'The False Edict of 1849. *Journal of Asian Studies*, 20, no. 3 (1960), pp. 299–315.
Nolde, John J. 'Xenophobia in Canton, 1842 to 1849'. *Journal of Oriental Studies*, 13, no. 1 (1975), pp. 1–22.
Northcote, Stafford Henry, earl of Iddesleigh. *Twenty Years of Financial Policy: A Summary of the Chief Financial Measures Passsed betweene 1842 and 1861, with a Table of Budgets*. London, 1862.
Nye, Gideon. *Tea and the Tea Trade*. New York, 1850.
Nye, Gideon. *Rationale of the China Question*. Macao, 1857.
Nye, Gideon. *The Gauge of the Two Civilizations: Shall Christiandom Waver? Being an Inquiry into the Causes of the Rupture of the English and French Treaties of Tientsin; and Comprising a General View of Our Relations with China* . . . Macao, 1860.
O'Brien, Patrick K. 'The Costs and Benefits of British Imperialism, 1846–1914', *Past and Present*, no. 120 (1988), pp. 163–200.
O'Brien, Patrick K. 'The Imperial Component in the Decline of the British Economy before 1914'. In Michael Mann (ed.), *The Rise and Decline of the Nation State*. Oxford, 1990, pp. 12–46.
Oliphant, Laurence. *Narrative of the Earl of Elgin's Mission to China and Japan in the Years 1857, '58, '59*. 2 vs. London, 1859.
Opie, Iona, and Peter Opie (eds.). *The Oxford Book of Nursery Rhymes*. Oxford, 1951.
Osborn, S. *The Past and Future of British Relations in China*. Edinburgh, 1860.
Ouchterlony, John. *The Chinese War: An Account of All the Operations of the British Forces from the Commencement to the Treaty of Nanking*. London, 1844.
Owen, David. *British Opium Policy in India and China*. New Haven, Conn., 1934.
Palmer, Sarah. *Politics, Shipping and the Repeal of the Navigation Laws*. Manchester, 1990.
Parker, Charles Stuart. *Life and Letters of Sir James Graham, Second Baronet of Netherby, 1792–1861*. 2 vs. London, 1907.
The Parliamentary Diaries of Sir John Trelawny, 1858–1865. Ed. T. A. Jenkins. Camden fourth series, v. 40. London, 1990.
Parry, J. P. *Democracy and Religion: Gladstone and the Liberal Party, 1867–1875*. Cambridge, 1986.
Patten, Christopher. *Our Next Five Years – The Agenda for Hong Kong*. Hong Kong, 1992.

Pearson, Hesketh. *Dizzy: The Life and Nature of Benjamin Disraeli, Earl of Beaconsfield.* London, 1951.
Pelcovits, Nathan A. *Old China Hands and the Foreign Office.* New York, 1948.
Peterson, W. J. 'Early Nineteenth Century Monetary Ideas on the Cash-Silver Exchange Ratio'. *Papers on China*, no. 20. Cambridge, Mass., 1966.
Peyrefitte, Alain. *The Collision of Two Civilisations: The British Expedition to China in 1792–4.* Trans. from the French by Jon Rothschild. London, 1993.
Philips, Cyril Henry. *East India Company, 1784–1834.* 2d ed. Bombay, 1961.
Pierce, Richard A. *Russian Central Asia, 1867–1917.* Berkeley and Los Angeles, 1960.
Platt, D. C. M. *Finance, Trade, and Politics: British Foreign Policy, 1815–1914.* Oxford, 1968.
Platt, D. C. M. 'The Imperialism of Free Trade: Some Reservations'. *Economic History Review*, new series. 21, no. 2 (1968) pp. 296–306.
Platt, D. C. M. *The Cinderella Service: British Consuls since 1825.* London, 1971.
Platt, D. C. M. 'Further Objections to an "Imperialism of Free Trade", 1830–1860'. *Economic History Review*, new series, 26, no. 1 (1973), pp. 77–91.
Polachek, James M. *The Inner Opium War.* Cambridge, Mass., 1992.
Porter, Andrew. ' "Gentlemanly Capitalism" and Empire: The British Experience since 1750'. *Journal of Imperial and Commonwealth History*, 18, no. 3 (October 1990), pp. 265–95.
Porter, Bernard. *The Lion's Share: A Short History of British Imperialism, 1850–1970.* London, 1975.
Prest, John. *Lord John Russell.* London, 1972.
Pritchard, Earl H. 'The Origins of the Most-Favored Nation and the Open Door Policies in China'. *Far Eastern Quarterly*, 1, no. 2 (February 1942), pp. 161–72.
Quested, Rosemary K. I. *The Expansion of Russia in East Asia, 1857–1860.* Kuala Lumpur, 1968.
Rajevari-Prasada. *Some Aspects of British Revenue Policy in India, 1773–1833: The Bengal Presidency.* New Delhi, 1970.
Rankin, Mary B. ' "Public Opinion" and Political Power: Qingyi in Late Nineteenth Century China'. *Journal of Asian Studies*, 41, no. 3 (1982), pp. 453–84.
Ratcliffe, Barrie M. (ed.). *Great Britain and Her World, 1750–1914, Essays in Honour of W. O. Henderson.* Manchester, 1975.
Redford, Arthur. *Manchester Merchants and Foreign Trade, v. 2: 1850–1939.* Manchester, 1956.
Richards, J. F. 'The Indian Empire and Peasant Production of Opium in the Nineteenth Century'. *Modern Asian Studies*, 15, no. 1 (1981), pp. 59–82.
Ridley, Jasper. *Lord Palmerston.* London, 1970.
Roberston, William. *The Life and Times of the Right Honourable John Bright.* London, 1884.
Robins, Keith. *John Bright.* London, 1979.
Robinson, Eugene. 'Britain to Probe Cabinet Role in Iraqi Arms Sales'. *Washington Post*, 11 November 1992, p. A27 (USIS TK 253026).
Robinson, R., and John Gallagher. *Africa and the Victorians: The 'Official Mind' of Imperialism.* London, 1961.
Rosen, Steven J., and Walter S. Jones. *The Logic of International Relations.* 2d ed. Cambridge, Mass., 1974.
Roseveare, Henry. *The Treasury: The Evolution of a British Institution.* London, 1969.

Bibliography

Rowat, R. B. *The Diplomatic Relations of Great Britain and the United States.* London, 1925.
Russell, Lord John. *Recollections and Suggestions, 1813–1873.* London, 1875.
Sabin, A. K. *The Silk Weavers of Spitalfields and Bethnal Green.* London, 1931.
Sanders, Lloyd C. *Life of Viscount Palmerston.* London, 1888.
Sargent, A. J. *Anglo-Chinese Commerce and Diplomacy.* Oxford, 1907.
Scarth, John. *Twelve Years in China: The People, the Rebels, and the Mandarins.* Edinburgh, 1860.
Schrecker, John E. *Imperialism and Chinese Nationalism: Germany in Shangtung.* Cambridge, Mass., 1971.
Schumpeter, J. A. *Imperialism and Social Classes.* Trans. Heinz Nordon and ed. with an introduction by Paul M. Sweezy. New York, 1951.
Scott, J. M. *The Great Tea Venture.* New York, 1965.
Seeley, J. R. *The Expansion of England.* London, 1883.
Selden, Mark. *The Yenan Way in Revolutionary China.* Cambridge, Mass., 1971.
Semmel, Bernard. *The Rise of Free Trade Imperialism: Classical Political Economy, the Empire of Free Trade and Imperialism, 1750–1850.* Cambridge, 1970.
Sen, Sunil Kumar. *Studies in Industrial Policy and Development of India, 1858–1914.* Calcutta, 1964.
Sen, Sunil Kumar. *Studies in Economic Policy and Development of India, 1848–1926.* Calcutta, 1966.
Sen, Sunil Kumar. *The House of Tata, 1839–1939.* Calcutta, 1975.
Shaw, Samuel. *The Journals of Major Samuel Shaw, the First American Consul at Canton.* Boston, 1847.
Shorter Oxford English Dictionary: On Historical Principles. Oxford, 1983.
Siddiqi, Asiya. 'The Business World of Jamsetjee Jejeebhoy'. *Indian Economic and Social History Review*, 19, nos. 3–4 (July–December 1982), pp. 301–24.
Silver, Arthur. *Manchester Men and Indian Cotton, 1847–1872.* Manchester, 1966.
Skidelsky, Robert (ed.). *Thatcherism.* London, 1988.
Smith, Francis Barrymore. *The Making of the Second Reform Bill.* Cambridge, 1966.
Smith, R. J. *Mercenaries and Mandarins: The Ever-Victorious Army of Nineteenth Century China.* New York, 1978.
Smith, Tony. *The Pattern of Imperialism: The United States, Great Britain, and the Late-Industrializing World since 1815.* Cambridge, 1981.
Smith, Vincent A. *The Oxford History of India.* Oxford, 1958.
Smith, Woodruff D. 'Complications of the Commonplace: Tea, Sugar and Imperialism'. *Journal of Interdisciplinary History*, 23, no. 2 (Autumn 1992), pp. 259–78.
Somervell, David Churchill. *Disraeli and Gladstone: A Duo-Biographical Sketch.* New York, 1926.
Spence, Jonathan D. 'Opium Smoking in Ch'ing China'. In Frederic Wakeman, Jr., and Carolyn Grant (eds.), *Conflict and Control in Late Imperial China.* Berkeley and Los Angeles, 1976, pp. 143–73.
Spence, Jonathan D. *The Search for Modern China.* New York, 1990.
Spicer, Michael. 'British Attitudes towards China, 1834–1860, with Special Reference to the *Edinburgh Review*, the *Westminster Review*, and the *Quarterly Review*'. M.A. thesis, University of Sydney, 1985.

Stanley, C. J. 'Chinese Finance from 1852 to 1908'. *Papers on China*, no. 3. Cambridge, Mass., 1949.
Steele, E. D. *Palmerston and Liberalism, 1855–1865*. Cambridge, 1991.
Steinberg, Jonathan. *Why Switzerland?* Cambridge, 1976.
Stelle, Charles C. 'Americans and the China Opium Trade in the Nineteenth Century'. Ph.D. dissertation, University of Chicago, 1938.
Stephenson, F. C. A. *At Home and on the Battlefield: Letters from the Crimea, China and Egypt, 1854–1888*. London, 1915.
Stewart, Robert. *The Politics of Protection: Lord Derby and the Protectionist Party, 1841–1852*. Cambridge, 1971.
Stokes, Eric. *The Peasant and the Raj: Studies in Agrarian Society and Peasant Rebellion in Colonial India*. Cambridge, 1978.
Stuart, Richard H. *The Pictorial Story of Ships*. London, 1977.
Sturgis, James L. *John Bright and the Empire*. London, 1969.
Sun, E-tu Zen. 'The Board of Revenue in Nineteenth-Century China'. *Harvard Journal of Asiatic Studies*, no. 24 (1963), pp. 175–228.
Swinhoe, Robert. *Narrative of the North China Campaign of 1860* . . . London, 1861.
Swisher, Earl. *China's Management of the American Barbarians: A Study of Sino-American Relations, 1841–1861, with Documents*. New Haven, Conn., 1951.
Swisher, Earl. *Early Sino-American Relations, 1841–1912: The Collected Articles of Earl Swisher*. Ed. Kenneth W. Rea. Boulder, Colo., 1977.
Tan, Chung. 'The Britain–China–India Trade Triangle (1771–1840)'. *Indian Economic and Social History Review*, 11, no. 4 (December 1974), pp. 412–31.
Tan, Chung. *China and the Brave New World: A Study of the Origins of the Opium War, 1840–42*. New Delhi, 1978.
Tarling, N. 'The Mission of Sir John Bowring to Siam'. *Journal of the Siam Society*, 50, pt. 2 (December 1962), pp. 91–118.
Tarling, N. 'Harry Parkes' Negotiations in Bangkok in 1856'. *Journal of the Siam Society*, 53, pt. 2 (July 1965), pp. 412–31.
Taylor, A. J. P. *Essays in English History*. London, 1976.
Taylor, Miles. *The Decline of British Radicalism, 1847–1860*. Oxford, 1995.
Taylor, Robert. *Lord Salisbury*. London, 1975.
Teiwes, Frederick Carl. *Politics and Purges in China: Rectification and the Decline of Party Norms, 1950–1965*. 2d ed. New York, 1993.
Temple, Henry John, Third Viscount Palmerston. *Letters of the Third Viscount Palmerston to Laurence and Elizabeth Sulivan, 1804–1863*. Ed. Kenneth Bourne. Camden fourth series, v. 23. London, Royal Historical Society, 1979.
Teng, Ssu-yü, *The Taiping Rebellion and the Western Powers: A Comprehensive Survey*. Oxford, 1971.
Teng, Ssu-yü, and J. K. Fairbank (eds.). *China's Response to the West*. Cambridge, Mass., 1954.
Tennyson, Alfred Lord. *The Princess: A Medley*. In *The Poetical Works of Alfred, Lord Tennyson*. London, 1908, pp. 165–217.
Thomas, Peter D. G. *Tea Party to Independence: The Third Phase of the American Revolution, 1773–1776*. Oxford, 1991.

Thorold, Algar Labouchere. *The Life of Henry Labouchere.* London, 1913.
Thurston, Anne F. *Enemies of the People.* New York, n.d. (c. 1987).
Tong, Te-kong. *United States Diplomacy in China, 1844–1860.* Seattle, 1964.
Treaties, Conventions, etc., between China and Foreign States. Shanghai, 1908.
Trevelyan, George Macaulay. *The Life of John Bright.* London, 1913.
Tripathi, Dwijendra. 'Opportunism of Free Trade: The Lancashire Cotton Famine and Indian Cotton Cultivation'. *Indian Economic and Social History Review*, 4, no. 3 (1967), pp. 255–63.
Tsiang, T. F. 'Difficulties of Reconstruction after the Treaty of Nanking'. *Chinese Social and Political Science Review*, no. 16 (1932), pp. 317–27.
Turner, F. S. *British Opium Policy.* London, 1876.
Twaddle, Michael (ed.). *Imperialism, the State and the Third World.* London, 1992.
Ukers, William Harrison. *All about Tea.* 2 vs. New York, 1935.
van der Linden, M. H. *The International Peace Movement, 1815–1874.* Amsterdam, 1987.
Victoria, Queen. *The Letters of Queen Victoria: A Selection from Her Majesty's Correspondence between the Years 1837 and 1861.* Ed. Arthur Christopher Benson and Vicount Esher. 3 vs. London, 1908.
Vincent, John. *Pollbooks: How Victorians Voted.* Cambridge, 1967.
Vogel, Robert C. *Railways in American Economic Growth.* Baltimore, 1964.
Vogler, Richard A. *Graphic Works of George Cruikshank: 279 Illustrations, Including 8 in Full Colour.* New York, 1979.
von Laue, Theodore H. *Leopold Ranke: The Formative Years.* Princeton, N.J., 1950.
Wakeman, Frederic, Jr. *Strangers at the Gate: Social Disorder in South China, 1839–1861.* Berkeley and Los Angeles, 1966.
Wakeman, Frederic, Jr. 'The Canton Trade and the Opium War'. In John King Fairbank et al. (eds.), *The Cambridge History of China, v. 10, pt. 1.* Cambridge, 1978, pp. 163–212.
Wakeman, Frederic, Jr., and Carolyn Grant (eds.). *Conflict and Control in Late Imperial China.* Berkeley and Los Angeles, 1976.
Walpole, Spencer. *The Life of Lord John Russell.* 2 vs. London, 1889.
Walrond, Theodore (ed.). *Letters and Journals of James, Eighth Earl of Elgin.* London, 1872.
Ward, John Manning. *Earl Grey and the Australian Colonies, 1846–1857: A Study of Self-Government and Self-Interest.* Melbourne, 1958.
Wardroper, John. *The Caricatures of George Cruikshank.* London, 1977.
Waterfield, Gordon. *Layard of Nineveh.* London, 1963.
Watson, J. Steven. *The Oxford History of England: The Reign of George III, 1760–1815.* Oxford, 1960.
Watt, George. *A Dictionary of the Economic Products of India.* Six vs. Delhi, 1889–96.
Welsh, Frank. *A History of Hong Kong.* London, 1993.
Wesley-Smith, Peter, and Albert Chen. *The Basic Law and Hong Kong's Future.* Hong Kong, 1988.
White, William. *The Inner Life of the House of Commons.* London, 1898.
Who's Who of British Members of Parliament: A Biographical Dictionary of the House of Commons, Based on Annual Volumes of 'Dod's Parliamentary Companion' and Other Sources. Ed. Michael Stenton. Four vs. Hassocks, 1976.

Williams, Frederick Wells (ed.). *The Life and Letters of Samuel Wells Williams, LL.D., Missionary, Diplomatic Sinologue*. New York, 1889.
Williams, Hugh Noel. *The Life and Letters of Admiral Sir Charles Napier, KCB*. London, 1917.
Wilson, Andrew. *The 'Ever-Victorious Army': A History of the Chinese Campaign under Lt.-Col. C. G. Gordon, CB, RE, and of the Suppression of the Tai-Ping Rebellion*. Edinburgh, 1868.
Wilson, Derek. *Rothschild: A Story of Wealth and Power*. London, 1988.
Winter, James. *Robert Lowe*. Toronto, 1976.
Witmer, Helen Elizabeth. *The Property Qualification of Members of Parliament*. New York, 1943.
Wolffe, John. *The Protestant Crusade in Great Britain, 1829–1860*. Oxford, 1991.
Wolseley, G. J. *Narrative of the War with China in 1860*. London, 1862.
Wong, J. Y. 'The "Arrow" Incident: A Reappraisal'. *Modern Asian Studies*, 8, no. 3 (1974), pp. 373–89.
Wong, J. Y. 'Harry Parkes and the *Arrow* War in China'. *Modern Asian Studies*, 9, no. 3 (1975), pp. 303–20.
Wong, J. Y. 'Sir John Bowring and the Question of Treaty Revision in China'. *Bulletin of the John Rylands University Library of Manchester*, 58, no. 1 (Autumn 1975), pp. 216–37.
Wong, J. Y. *Yeh Ming-ch'en: Viceroy of Liang-Kuang, 1852–58*. Cambridge, 1976.
Wong, J. Y. 'The Building of an Informal British Empire in China in the Middle of the Nineteenth Century'. *Bulletin of the John Rylands University Library of Manchester*, 59, no. 2 (Spring 1977), pp. 472–85.
Wong, J. Y. 'Monopoly in India and Equal Opportunities in China, 1830–33: An Examination of a Paradox'. *South Asia: Journal of South Asian Studies*, new series, 5 (1982), pp. 81–95.
Wong, J. Y. 'The Taipings' Distant Allies: A Comparison of the Rebels at Shanghai and at Canton'. In A. R. Davis and A. D. Stefanowska (eds.), *Austrina: Essays in Commemoration of the 25th Anniversary of the Founding of the Oriental Society of Australia*. Sydney, 1982, pp. 334–50.
Wong, J. Y. *Anglo-Chinese Relations, 1839–1860: A Calendar of Chinese Documents in the British Foreign Office Records*. Oxford, 1983.
Wong, J. Y. *The Origins of an Heroic Image: Sun Yatsen in London, 1896–1897*. Hong Kong, 1986.
Wong, J. Y. (ed.). *Australia–China Relations, 1987: Business and Management, with Messages from Prime Minister Robert James Lee Hawke and Premier Zhao Ziyang*. Canberra and Beijing, 1987.
Wong, J. Y. (ed.). *Sun Yatsen: His International Ideas and International Connections, with Special Emphasis on Their Relevance Today*. Sydney, 1987.
Wong, J. Y. (ed.). *Australia and China 1988: Preparing for the 1990s, with Messages from Prime Minister Robert James Lee Hawke and Premier Li Peng*. Canberra and Beijing, 1988.
Wong, J. Y. 'New Light on China's Foreign Economic Relations in the Nineteenth Century' (review article). *Harvard Journal of Asiatic Studies*, 48, no. 2 (December 1988), pp. 521–34.
Wong, J. Y. 'The Rule of Law in Hong Kong: Past, Present and Prospects for the Future'. *Australian Journal of International Affairs*, 46, no. 1 (May 1992), pp. 81–92.

Wong, J. Y. 'British Annexation of Sind in 1843: An Economic Perspective'. *Modern Asian Studies*, 31, Part 2 (May 1997), pp. 225–244.
Wood, Herbert John. 'Prologue to War: Anglo-Chinese Conflict, 1800–1834'. Ph.D. dissertation, University of Wisconsin, 1938.
Woodward, Ernest Llewellyn. *The Age of Reform, 1815–1870*. Oxford, 1954.
Wrong, Edward Murray. *Charles Buller and Responsible Government*. Oxford, 1926.
Yapp, M. E. *Strategies of British India: Britain, Iran and Afghanistan*. Oxford, 1980.
Young, G. M. *Victorian England: Portrait of an Age*. London, 1953.
Yudkin, John. *Pure, White and Deadly: The Problem of Sugar*. London, 1972.
Yung, Wing. *My Life in China and America*. New York, 1912.
Zaretskaya, S. I. *China's Foreign Policy in 1856–1860: Relations with Great Britain and France*. Moscow, 1976.

Works in Chinese and Japanese

Anon. '王茂蔭與咸豐時代的新幣制' (Wang Maoyin and the new currency system in the reign of Xianfeng). In《中國近代史論叢》(Essays on modern Chinese history). Taibei, 1958, v. 3, pp. 49–70.
Bo Jun 伯鈞 and Shi Bo 世博. '第二次鴉片戰爭中的葉名琛評價管見' (Our views on Ye Mingchen's role in the Second Opium War). *Tianjin shifan daxue xuebao* 《天津師范大學學報》(Tianjin Normal University Journal), no. 3 (1984), pp. 64–8.
Chen Jiang 陳絳 and Yang Surong 楊蘇榮. '論辛酉政變' (On the 1861 coup). 《復旦學報》(Fudan University Journal), no. 5 (1987), pp. 35–40.
Chen Shenglin 陳勝璘. '香港地區被逼"割讓"和"租借"的歷史真象' (Historical facts about the 'cession' and 'lease' of Hong Kong).《學術研究》(Academic Research), no. 2 (1983), pp. 89–94, and no. 3, pp. 85–95.
Chen Xulu 陳旭麓. '炮口下的震憾：鴉片戰爭與中國傳統社會崩裂' (The roar of the cannon: The Opium War and the collapse of traditional Chinese society).《近代史研究》(Modern Historical Studies), no. 6 (1990), pp. 13–19.
Chen Zhigen 陳志根. '如何理解第二次鴉片戰爭是第一次鴉片戰爭的繼續和擴大' (How to appreciate that the Second Opium War was the continuation and expansion of the First Opium War).《中學歷史教學》(Teaching History at Secondary Schools), no. 4 (1984), pp. 36–8.
Chu Dexin 褚德新 et al. (comps.).《中外舊約章匯要》(A collection of old treaties). Harbin, 1991.
Commercial Press, Taiwan.《中國國際貿易史》(A history of China's international trade). Taibei, 1961.
Da Qing huidian《大清會典》(Collected statutes of the Qing period). Guangxu period.
Da Qing huidian shili《大清會典事例》(Precedents for the collected statutes of the Qing period). Guangxu period (1875–1908).
Di'erci yapian zhansheng《第二次鴉片戰爭》(The Second Opium War). Written by a collection of anonymous and officially chosen historians. Shanghai, 1972.
Ding Mingnan 丁名楠 et al.《帝國主義侵華史》(The invasion of China by imperialism). V. 1, Beijing, 1958; v. 2, Beijing, 1986.

Ding Mingnan 丁名楠. '英國侵占香港地區的經過' (How Britain occupied Hong Kong). 《近代史研究》 (Modern Historical Studies), no. 1 (1983), pp. 149–62.
Du Weiming 杜維明. '儒家論說的現代涵義' (The contemporary meaning of Confucianism). 《九十年代》 (The Nineties), no. 308 (September 1995), pp. 93–5.
Fan Kezheng 樊克政. '關於龔自珍生平事蹟中的幾個問題' (On the timing of Xuannan Poetry Club's acquiring its name and related issues). 《清史論叢》 (East China Normal University Journal), no. 4 (1980), pp. 92–4.
Fang Chang 方長. '再談龍涎及我國吸食鴉片始於何時' (Further discourse on dragon saliva and the beginning of opium smoking in China). 《文史》 (Literature and History), no. 25 (1985), pp. 348–9.
Fang Shiguang 方式光 '"祺祥政變"剖析' (An analysis of the 'Qixiang coup'). 《學術月刊》 (Academic Monthly), no. 2 (1986), pp. 67–72.
Fang Shiming 方詩銘. 《第二次鴉片戰爭史話》 (Popular history of the Second Opium War). Shanghai, 1956.
Feng Tianyu 馮天瑜. '試論道咸間經世派的"開眼看世界"' (On the 'global perspective' of the pragmatists at the time of Emperors Daoguan and Xianfeng). 《近代史研究》 (Modern Historical Studies), no. 2 (1991), pp. 18–30.
Fu Qixue 傅啟學. 《中國外交史》 (A diplomatic history of China). Taibei, 1966.
Fu Yiling 傅衣凌. 《明清農村社會經濟》 (Rural economy and society of the Ming and Qing periods). Beijing, 1961.
Fu Zhenlun 傅振倫. 《中國方志學通論》 (On Chinese local gazetteers). Shanghai, 1935.
Gong Shuduo 龔書鐸 et al. '建國三十五年來鴉片戰爭史研究綜述' (A survey of the works on the Opium War published during the thirty years since the establishment of the People's Republic of China). 《近代史研究》 (Modern Historical Studies), no. 3 (1984), pp. 148–66.
Guangdong tongzhi 《廣東通志》 (Local gazetteer of Guangdong province). Guangzhou, 1822.
Guangzhou fuzhi 《廣州府志》 (Local gazetteer of Guangzhou prefecture). Guangzhou, 1879.
Guo Binjia 郭斌佳. '咸豐朝中國外交概觀' (A survey of Chinese diplomacy during the reign of Emperor Xianfeng). 《武大社會科學季刊》 (Wuhan University Social Sciences Quarterly), 5, no. 1 (1935), pp. 81–126.
Guo Hanmin 郭漢民 and Chi Yufei 遲雲飛. 《中國近代史實正誤》 (Correcting factual errors in the writing of modern Chinese history). Changsha, 1989.
Guo Tingyi 郭廷以 (ed.). 《近代中國史事日誌》 (A daily chronology of modern Chinese history). Taibei, 1963.
Guo Weimin 郭衛民. '何桂清與咸豐帝的對外政策之爭及其影響' (The disagreement between He Guiqing and Emperor Xiangeng on foreign policy). 《近代史研究》 (Modern Historical Studies), no. 6 (1993), pp. 77–89.
Hamashita Takeshi 濱下武志. 《中國近代經濟史研究》 (Studies on modern Chinese economic history). Tokyo, 1989.
He Yikun 何貽焜. 《曾國藩評傳》 (A critical biography of Zeng Guofan). Taibei, 1964.
He Yuefu 賀躍夫. 《晚清士紳與近代社會變遷—兼與日本士族比較》 (The gentry in late Qing and social change – With a comparison with the samurai in Japan). Guangzhou, 1994.

Hu Bin 胡濱.《英國檔案有關鴉片戰爭資料選譯》(Translations of selected British documents about the Opium War). 2 vs. Beijing, 1993. (The documents translated appear to include those in the Parliamentary Papers, as well as FO881/75A and FO881/75B, up to the year 1841.)

Hu Sheng 胡繩.《從鴉片戰爭到五四運動》(From the Opium War to the May Fourth Movement). Shanghai, 1982.

Hu Shiyun 胡世芸. '葉名琛被俘日期考辨' (Pinpointing the date at which Ye Mingchen was captured).《上海師院學報》(Shanghai Teachers' College Journal), no. 2 (1983), pp. 112–14.

Hu Shiyun 胡世芸. '第二次鴉片戰爭時期的一篇主戰奏疏—僧王奏稿' (A hawkish memorial at the time of the *Arrow* War – That by Prince Seng).《內蒙古師院學報》(Inner Mongolia Teachers' College Journal), no. 2 (1985), pp. 94–9.

Hua Tingjie 華廷杰. '觸藩始末' (An account of contacts with foreigners), now collected in *Er ya*, v. 1, pp. 163–96.

Huang Guangyu 黃光域. '第二次鴉片戰爭中為英軍掠走的廣州各衙門檔案的下落' (The whereabouts of the Canton Archives captured by the British forces during the Second Opium War).《歷史研究》(Historical Studies), no. 3 (1980), pp. 191–2.

Huang Huaqing 黃樺青. '近代中國茶葉對外貿易衰落原因初探' (A preliminary investigation into the decline of Chinese tea exports).《泉州師專學報》(Quanzhou Teachers' College Journal), no. 2 (1985) pp. 46–53.

Huang Yifeng 黃逸峯 and Jiang Duo 姜鐸 (eds.).《中國近代經濟史論文集》(Essays on modern Chinese economic history). Nanjing, 1981.

Institute of Modern History, Fujian Academy of Social Sciences (ed.).《林則徐與鴉片戰爭論文集》(Essays on Lin Zexu and the Opium War). Fuzhou, 1985. (This is a collection of twenty papers selected from those presented to a conference held in August 1982 at Fuzhou to commemorate Lin Zexu. A similar conference was held in August 1985, in which I participated. But the papers do not seem to have been similarly published.)

Jia Shoucun 賈熟村. '僧格林沁其人' (On Senggelinqin).《文史知識》(Literature and History), no. 12 (1984), pp. 92–148.

Jia Zhifang 賈植芳.《近代中國經濟償社會》(The economy and society of modern China). Shanghai, 1949.

Jiang Mengyin 蔣孟引.《第二次鴉片戰爭》(The Second Opium War). Beijing, 1965.

Lai Xinxia 來新夏.《林則徐年譜》(A chronology of Lin Zexu's life). 2d ed. Shanghai, 1985.

Li Enhan 李恩涵.《曾紀澤的外交》(The diplomacy of Zeng Jize). Taibei, 1966.

Li Fengling 李鳳翎.《洋務續記》(A supplementary account of foreign affairs). Collected in *Er ya*, v. 1, pp. 222–6.

Li Guoqi 李國祁.《張之洞的外交政策》(The foreign policy of Zhang Zhidong). Taibei, 1970.

Li Jiannong 李劍農.《中國近百年政治史》(Chinese history of the past hundred years). 2 vs., 2d ed. Taibei, 1962.

Li Liling 李力陵.《曾，左，胡》(Zeng Guofan, Zuo Zongtang, Li Hongzhang). Gaoxiong, 1962.

Li Taifen 李泰棻.《方志學》(On local gazetteers). Shanghai, 1935.
Li Yongqing 酈永慶, '關於道光二十九年的"偽詔"考析' (An investigation of the 'False Edict' of 1849).《歷史檔案》(Historical Archives), no. 2 (1992), pp. 100–106. Reprinted in《中國近代史》(Modern Chinese History), K3, no. 6 (1992), pp. 79–85.
Liang Jiabin 梁嘉彬.《廣東十三行考》(The *hong* merchants of Guangdong). Shanghai, 1937.
Liang Rencai 梁仁彩.《廣東經濟地理》(The economic geography of Guangdong). Beijing, 1956.
Liang Tingnan 梁廷楠.《粵海關志》(The Canton customs office). Taibei reprint, 1968.
Lie Dao 列島 (ed.).《鴉片戰爭史論文專集》(Essays on the Opium War). Beijing, 1958.
Lin Chongyong 林崇墉.《林則徐傳》(Biography of Lin Zexu). Taibei, 1967.
Lin Dunkui 林敦奎 and Kong Xiangji 孔祥吉. '鴉片戰爭前期統治階級內部鬥爭探析' (An exploration into the conflicts within the ruling class prior to the Opium War).《近代史研究》(Modern Historical Studies), no. 3 (1986), pp. 1–19.
Lin Zengping 林增平. '廣州羣眾"反河南租地"事件年代辯誤' (Clarifying the time of the Cantonese opposition to British lease of Henan).《近代史研究》(Modern Historical Studies), no. 2 (1979), pp. 250–5.
Liu Yan 劉彥.《中國外交史》(A diplomatic history of China). Taibei, 1962.
Lu Qinchi 陸欽墀. '英法聯軍佔據廣州始末' (An account of the Anglo-French occupation of Canton). In《中國近代史論叢》(Essays on modern Chinese history). Taibei, 1958, v. 1, pp. 74–109.
Lü Shiqiang 呂實強.《中國官紳反教的原因，一八六零——一八七四》(Reasons why the Chinese official-gentry were anti-Christian, 1860–74). Taibei, 1966.
Luo Yudong 羅玉東.《中國釐金史》(A history of *likin*). Shanghai, 1936.
Makesi Engesi 馬克斯，恩格斯.《馬克斯恩格斯論中國》(Marx and Engels on China). Beijing, 1950.
Mao Haijian 茅海建. '第二次鴉片戰爭中清軍與英法軍兵力考' (A comparasion between the Chinese and Anglo-French forces during the Second Opium War).《近代史研究》(Modern Historical Studies), no. 1 (1985), pp. 196–217.
Mao Haijian 茅海建. '第二次鴉片戰爭中清軍指揮人員雛論' (A preliminary discussion of the commanders of the Qing forces during the Second Opium War).《歷史教學》(Teaching History), no. 11 (1986), pp. 12–18.
Mao Haijian 茅海建. '關於廣州反入城鬥爭的幾個問題' (Some problems related to the Canton City question).《近代史研究》(Modern Historical Studies), no. 6 (1992), pp. 43–70.
Mao Haijian 茅海建.《天朝的崩潰》(The collapse of the celestial empire: A reexamination of the Opium War). Beijing, 1995.
Meng Xianzhang 孟憲章.《中國近代經濟史教程》(A text on modern Chinese economic history). Shanghai, 1951.
Mou Anshi 牟安世. '從鴉片戰爭看勝敗的決定因數是人不是武器' (From the Opium War one can see that what decided victory and defeat was men and not weapons).《人民日報》(The People's Daily), 11 October 1965.
Ning Jing 寧靖 (ed.).《鴉片戰爭史論文專集續編》(Essays on the Opium War, second series). Beijing, 1984.

Pan Zhenping 潘振平. '鴉戰爭後的"開眼看世界"思想'(The idea of a 'global perspective' after the Opium War).《歷史研究》(Historical Studies), no. 1 (1896), pp. 138–53.

Qian Tai 錢泰.《中國不平等條約之緣起及其廢除之經過》(The beginning and end of the unequal treaties imposed on China). Taibei, 1961.

Qingchao yeshi daguan《清朝野史大觀》(A review of the apocryphal history of the Qing dynasty). Shanghai, 1930.

Qingshi liezhuan《清史列傳》(Biograpies of Qing history). Ed. Zhonghua shuju 中華書局. Shanghai, 1928.

Qixianhe shang diaosou (pseud.) 七絃河上釣叟.《英吉利廣東入城始末》(An account of the British entry into the city of Canton), 1929. Collected in *Er ya*, v. 1, pp. 211–21.

Quru yu kangzheng《屈辱與抗爭》(Humiliation and resistance). Beijing, 1990. (Collected therein are papers originally presented to a conference held to mark the 150th anniversary of the Opium War.)

Sasaki Masaya 佐佐木正哉.《鴉片戰爭口研究》(Sources on the Opium War). Tokyo, 1964.

Sasaki Masaya 佐佐木正哉.《鴉片戰爭口中英抗爭：資料編稿》(Anglo-Chinese conflict after the Opium War: Documents). Tokyo, 1970.

Shi Nan 石楠. '略論港英政府的鴉片專賣政策' (On the opium monopoly in Hong Kong).《近代史研究》(Modern Historical Studies), no. 6 (1992), pp. 20–42.

Sun Jinming 孫金銘.《中國兵制史》(A history of the Chinese military systems). Taibei, 1960.

Sun Yanjing 孫燕京. '近五年鴉片戰爭史研究述評' (A survey of works on the Opium War in the past five years).《近代史研究》(Modern Historical Studies), no. 1 (1991), pp. 133–42.

Taiping tianguo《太平天國》(Sources on the Taiping Heavenly Kingdom). 8 vs. Shanghai, 1952.

Tang Xianglong 湯象龍. '道光時期的銀貴問題' (The problem of the rising price of silver in the Daoguang period). In《中國近代史論叢》(Essays on modern Chinese history). Taibei, 1958, v. 3, pp. 9–39.

Tao Chengzhang 陶成章. '天地會源流考' (The origins of the Heaven and Earth Society). In Luo Ergang 羅爾綱 (ed.),《天地會文獻錄》(Documents relating to the Heaven and Earth Society). Chongqing, 1943.

Tao Wenzhao 陶文釗. '美國國家檔案館（總館）所藏有關中國檔案材料簡介' (An introduction to the Chinese materials in the National Archives and Records Service of America).《近代史研究》(Modern Historical Studies), no. 5 (1985), pp. 190–226.

Wan Anan 王亞南.《中國半封建半殖民地經濟形態研究》(A study on the semifeudal and semicolonial economy of China). Beijing, 1980.

Wang Di 王笛. '民族的災難與民族的發展' (The nation's catastrophe and the nation's development). In《屈辱與抗爭》(Humiliation and resistance). Beijing, 1990, pp. 31–44.

Wang Fangzhong 王方中.《中國近代經濟史稿》(A draft of modern Chinese economic history). Beijing, 1982.

Wang Junyi 王俊義. '龔自珍，魏源"參加宣南詩社"說辨正' (A reappraisal of the

view that Gong Zizheng and Wei Yuan 'joined the Xuannan Poetry Club').《吉林大學學報》(Jilin University Journal), no. 6 (1979), pp. 104-7.

Wang Junyi 王俊義. '關於宣南詩社的幾個問題' (Several questions concerning the Xuannan Poetry Club)'. In《清史研究集》(Essays on Qing history), no 1 (1980), pp. 216-42.

Wang Kaixi 王開璽. '黃爵滋禁煙奏疏平議' (On Huang Jüezi's memorial on opium prohibition).《近代史研究》(Modern Historical Studies), no. 1 (1995), pp. 1-13.

Wang Ping 王平. '論鴉片戰爭前後中國社會政治思想的變向' (On the changes in political ideas before and after the Opium War).《南京大學學報》(Nanjing University Journal), no. 4 (1994), pp. 56-9.

Wang Xiaoqiu 王曉秋. '鴉片戰爭在日本的反響' (Japan's reaction to the Opium War).《近代史研究》(Modern Historical Studies), no. 3 (1986), pp. 20-45.

Wang Zengcai 王曾才.《中英外交史論集》(Essays on Anglo-Chinese diplomacy history). Taibei, 1979.

Wang Zhongmin 王重民 et al. (eds.).《太平天國》(Sources on the Taiping Heavenly Kingdom). 8 vs. Shanghai, 1952.

Water Division of the Ministry of Hydraulic Electricity 水力電力部水管司 (ed.).《清代淮河流域洪澇檔案史料》(Flood and waterlogging data on the Huai River in the Qing period). Beijing, 1988.

Water Division of the Ministry of Hydraulic Electricity 水力電力部水管司 (ed.).《清代珠江韓江洪澇檔案史料》(Flood and waterlogging data on the Pearl and Han Rivers in the Qing period). Beijing, 1988.

Wei Hsiu-mei 魏秀梅.《清季職官表》(Table of officials of the late Qing). 2 vs. Taibei, 1977.

Wei Jianyou 魏建猷.《中國近代貨幣史》(A history of the currency system in modern China). Shanghai, 1955.

Wei Jianyou 魏建猷.《第二次鴉片戰爭》(The Second Opium War). Shanghai, 1955.

Wei Yuan 魏源.《聖武記》(A military history of the Qing). Fourteen *juan*. Completed 1842. 2 vs. Taibei reprint, 1962.

Wei Yuan 魏源.《海國圖志》(Illustrated gazetteer of the maritime countries). Sixty *juan*. 1847. 7 vs. Taibei reprint, 1967.

Wei Yuan 魏源.《魏源集》(Collected works of Wei Yuan). 2 vs. Beijing, 1976.

Wong, J. Y. 黃宇和. '太平軍初起是北上還是東進的問題初探' (Why did the Taipings go north at the beginning of their rebellion when they should have gone east?'. In《太平天國史譯叢》(Taiping studies: Translation series), no. 1 (1981), pp. 258-80.

Wong, J. Y. 黃宇和. '帝國主義新析' (A new interpretation on imperialism).《近代史研究》(Modern Historical Studies), no. 4 (1997), pp. 22-62.

Xiao Yishan 蕭一山.《清代通史》(History of the Qing). Taibei reprint, 1963.

Xin Fenglin 刑鳳麟 and Hai Yang 海陽. '關于馬神甫事件' (On the M. Chadelaine incident).《社會科學戰線》(Frontline Social Sciences), no. 3 (1983), pp. 151-6.

Xiong Yuezhi 熊月之. '一八四二年至一八六零年西學在中國的傳播' (The spread of Western learning in China, 1842-1860).《歷史研究》(Historical Studies), no. 4 (1994), pp. 63-81.

Xu Shuofang 徐朔方. '鴉片輸入中國之始末及其他' (The importation of opium, and related questions).《文史》(Literature and History), no. 25 (1985), pp. 343-7.

Xue Fucheng 薛福成. '書漢陽葉相廣州之變' (Grand Secretary Ye and the Canton episode),《庸盦續編》(Yongan collection), 1898. Now collected in *Er ya*, v. 1, pp. 227–35.

Yang Guozhen 楊國楨.《林則徐傳》(Biography of Lin Zexu). Beijing, 1981.

Yang Guozhen 楊國楨. '宣南詩社與林則徐' (Lin Zexu and the Xuannan Poetry Club).《夏門大學學報》(Xiamen University Journal), no. 2 (1994), pp. 107–17.

Yang Yusheng 楊玉聖. '鴉片戰爭時期中國人的美國觀' (Chinese perception of America at the time of the Opium War).《史學月刊》(History Monthly), no. 1 (1994), pp. 51–4.

Yao Tingfang 姚廷芳 (ed.).《鴉片戰爭與道光皇帝，林則徐，琦善，耆英》(The Opium War and Emperor Daoguang, Lin Zexu, Qishan and Qiying). 2 vs. Taipei, 1970.

Yao Weiyuan 姚薇元. '論鴉片戰爭的直接原因' (The direct cause of the Opium War).《武漢大學學報》(Wuhan University Journal), no. 4 (1963), pp. 104–15.

Yao Weiyuan 姚薇元.《鴉片戰爭史實考》(An appraisal of the various facts related to the Opium War). Beijing, 1984. (In fact, this is an assessment, paragraph by paragraph, of an unpublished treatise entitled《道光洋艘征撫記》[An account of war and peace made by foreign ships in the Daoguang period] by Wei Yuan 魏源, who completed it in August 1842.)

Yao Xiangao 姚賢鎬. '兩次鴉片戰爭後西方侵略勢力對中國關稅主權的破壞' (Western encroachment on Chinese customs sovereignty in the wake of the Opium Wars).《中國社會科學》(Chinese Social Sciences), no. 5 (1981), pp. 1–24.

Yi Tingzhen 易廷鎮. '第二次鴉片戰爭初期美國對華軍事行動始末' (American military action against China at the beginning of the Second Opium War).《南開學報》(Nankai University Journal), no. 3 (1984), pp. 18–25.

Yu Shengwu 余繩武. '殖民主義思想殘餘是中西關系史研究的障礙' (Residual colonial ideas are an obstacle to the research on Sino-Western relations).《近代史研究》(Modern Historical Studies), no. 6 (1990), pp. 13–19.

Yu Shengwu 余繩武 and Liu Cunkuan 劉存寬 (eds.).《十九世紀的香港》(Nineteenth-century Hong Kong). Hong Kong, 1994.

Yu Shengwu 余繩武 et al.《沙俄侵華史》(A history of Russian aggression against China). 3 vs. Beijing, 1976–80.

Yu Zongcheng 郁宗成. '法國檔案館有關英法聯軍侵略中國的史料' (French archival holdings on the invasion of China by the Anglo-French forces).《歷史研究》(Historical Studies), no. 1 (1983), pp. 123–30.

Yuan Qing 元青. '鴉片戰爭前後經世派人士西洋觀變遷的文化局限' (The limitations of the worldview of the pragmatists before and after the Opium War).《中州學刊》(Zhongzhou Journal), no. 3 (1994), pp. 122–4.

Zhai Houliang 翟厚良. '一八五九年大沽之戰爆發原因再探' (A further examination of the reason for the outbreak of hostilities at Taku).《史學月刊》(History Monthly), no. 5 (1985), pp. 51–8.

Zhang Hailin 張海林. '論"天津條約"簽訂後咸豐帝對英法的外交政策' (Emperor Xianfeng's foreign policy towards Britain and France after the signing of the 'Treaty of Tianjin').《南京大學學報》(Nanjing University Journal), no. 3 (1987), pp. 133–46.

Zhang Hailin 張海林. '傳統文化與咸豐帝對外政策' (Traditional culture and Emperor Xianfeng's foreign policy).《江海學刊》(Jianghai Journal), no. 6 (1987), pp. 58–61.

Zhang Hailin 張海林. '第二次鴉片戰爭中清政府"輯民攘夷"政策述論' (On the Qing policy of 'involving the people in a war of resistance' during the Second Opium War).《蘇州大學學報》 (Suzhou University Journal), no. 2 (1988), pp. 28–31.

Zhao Erxun 趙爾巽 et al. (eds.).《清史稿》(A draft history of the Qing dynasty). Shenyang, 1937.

Zhao Huirong 趙蕙蓉. '恆祺與一八六零年北京議和' (Hengqi and the peace negotiations in Beijing in 1860).《歷史檔案》(Historical Archives), no. 2 (1986), pp. 92–8.

Zhao Jing 趙靖 and Yi Menghong 易夢虹.《中國近代經濟思想史》(A history of modern Chinese economic thinking). Beijing, v. 1, 1980; v. 2, 1982.

Zhao Jing 趙靖 and Yi Menghong 易夢虹 (eds.).《中國近代經濟思想資料選輯》(Selected materials on modern Chinese economic thinking). 3 vs. Beijing, 1982.

Zhao Zhongfu 趙中孚.《清季中俄東三省界務交涉》(Sino-Russian negotiations over the Manchurian border issue, 1858–1911). Taibei, 1970.

Zhu Jinfu 朱金甫. '鴉片戰爭前道光朝言官的禁煙論' (The anti-opium views of the censors before the Opium War during Emperor Daoguang's reign).《近代史研究》 (Modern Historical Studies), no. 2 (1991), pp. 57–66.

Zhu Jinfu 朱金甫 and Li Yongqing 酈永慶. '第一次鴉片戰爭期間禁煙問題初探' (New inquiry into the question of opium prohibition during the First Opium War).《人民日報》(The People's Daily), 6 January 1986, p. 5.

Zhu Qingbao 朱慶葆. '論清代禁煙的舉措與成效' (On the effectiveness of opium prohibition in the Qing period).《江蘇社會科學》(Jiangsu Social Sciences), no. 4 (1994), pp. 82–7.

Zuo Shunsheng 左舜生 (ed.).《中國今百年史資料初編》(Source materials for the study of modern Chinese history in the last hundred years, part one). Taibei, 1958.

Zuo Shunsheng 左舜生 (ed.).《中國今百年史資料續編》(Source materials for the study of modern Chinese history in the last hundred years, part two). Taibei reprint, 1966.

Zuo Yufeng 左域封. '第二次鴉片戰爭中英軍侵占大連灣始末' (British occupation of Dalian Wan during the *Arrow* War).《遼寧師院學報》(Liaoning Normal College Journal), no. 1 (1981), pp. 44–7.

Index

Aberdeen, fourth earl of (George Hamilton Gordon, 1784–1860), 138, 238, 300
Achilles, 82, 462, 477
Adams, John Quincy (6th U.S. president, 1825–8), 33
Addington, Henry Unwin (1790–1870), 85 (and n. 14), 108, 307
Aden, 422, 485
Admiralty, 28, 153, 154, 267, 268, 286, 287, 289–90, 302, 307, 309
advances, 393 (and n. 13)
adverse vote, 216, 218, 220, 221, 222, 223, 234, 242, 245; condemned, 252; gave Palmerston a stronger hand, 300–1; made Manchester hysterical, 218, 222, 254, 255, 310, 408, 459
Afghan Wars, 279
Afghanistan, 184, 420
Africa, 461, 475, 477
agitation, 229–32
Alabaster, Chaloner., 110
Albermarle, sixth earl of (George Thomas Keppel, 1799–1891), 180 (and n. 53), 181 (and n. 55); opium not pernicious, 325
Albert, Prince, 250
Alcock, Rutherford, 147, 263
Allum, *see* Zhang Peilin
American Civil War, 450
American demands, 271
Amirs (Emirs), 425; Khairpur, 425; Haidarabad, 425
Amur, 276, 280
Anglo-French Allied Forces, 37
Anglo-French naval rivalry, 267, 290–1
Aniangxie (Annung-hoy), 98–9
animus, 206, 228

Anstey, Chisholm (attorney-general of Hong Kong), 228
anti-English, 201, 202, 221
anti-opium lobby, 322–8, 466; short-lived and without much public impact, 431; reactivated, 431
anti-foreignism, 53, 128, 129, Canton safest city with no, 134–6; foreign provocations causing, 136–40, 196
apology, 72, 104, 206, 230, 232
apparent British trade imbalance with China, 335–7, 366–9
appeasement, 482
Arabs, 360
Archbishop of Canterbury, 293, 465
argumentum baculinum, 306
Argyll, duke of (George Douglas, 1823–1900), 107 (and n. 196), 178–9; praised Russell, 244–5; on Gladstone, 247; on the attorney-general, 291–2; on Bowring, 304, 306
Armstrong, Commodore James, 7; criticised by President Pierce, 177; went to Japan, 273; criticised by Secretary of State William Marcy, 275
Arrow incident, 4, 14, 23, 24, 26, 28, 29, 32, 37, 41, 44ff, 55, 57, 69, 75, 80, 84; animus of, 206; attitudes of *The Times* on, 156; 'contemptible', 207; Elgin not instructed to obtain reparation for, 328; even the attorney-general shook his head ominously on, 292; faked, 72, 83, 159, 477; flimsy excuse, 457; incidental to British government's scheme of things, 214; 'justified', 203; a manufactured excuse (*The*

525

Times), 160; 'mean and paltry', 161; a 'miserable affair' (Russell), 241; 'a miserable case' (Clarendon), 63; not the cause of war, 199; quickly displaced, 93, 97, 98, 99–100, 104, 105, 106, 107, 156; Rev Piercy on, 319–20; 'a scandal' (Elgin), 63; sensational, 459; 'of small moment', (*The Times*) 156; 'unfortunate aggression' (*Daily Press*), 63; a varnish (*Morning Chronicle*), 159; war without, 330

Arrow War, 11, 12, 13, 14, 16, 19, 21, 27, 31, 32, 33, 34, 36, 37, 39, 67; ascertaining the origins of, 467–70, 470–2; debate a watershed in British politics, 465; increased British imports from China, 434ff; increased British exports to China, 441ff; represented many firsts in British politics, 297 (and n. 86), 297–8, 321–2

Arrow, 3, 41, 43, 44, 47, 48; arrived at Canton on 3 October 1856, 57; history of, 177 (n. 23); left Hong Kong on 1 September 1856, 57; lying with her colors flying, 56, 61, 62, 63, 64; Lyndhurst's principle re, 178; nationality of, 175, 176, 177, 178, 179; ownership of, 43, 53, 73, 164, 166; trading in rice, 57; transactions with pirates, 58

arsenic, 11, 226, 227, 230
Ashburnham, Major-General, 227, 308
assessed taxes, 348
'at sea', 181–3
atoms, 234, 297
attorney-general of Hong Kong, 178, 228
attorney-general, 213; *Punch* on, 299; summoned to cabinet meeting, 291–2
auctions, 399; changed from six monthly to monthly, 410
Aurora, 279
Australia, 317, 318, 445; needed Chinese labourers to develop the resources of, 318; needed Chinese women to keep the men in, 317–18
Austro-Hungarian Empire, 483

Bagehot, Walter, 459
Baines, Thomas, 219
bale (of silk, weighed about 90 lbs.), 362 (and n. 55)
Bank of Western India, 411
Baring, Sir Francis Thornhill (1796–1866), 212 (and n. 125), 213, 224, 244

barrier forts, 7, 77, 91
Bate, Commander, 78, 83
Beijing Gazette, 267
Beijing, 79, 309; foreign residence in, 29, 271, 303, 315; intentions unclear to London, 286; sack of, 1
Benares, 392 (and sources for Table 16.4)
Bengal, 391; decline in supply of opium, 402; opium, 392 (and n. for Table 16.4)
Bentham, Jeremy (1748–1832), 86 (and n. 18)
Bentinck, Lord (governor-general of India, 1831), 418
betel nuts, 369
Bethell, Richard (1800–73), 291; as attorney-general since 1856, 291(n. 50); had a 'retaining fee', 213, 291; *Punch* on, 299; summoned to cabinet meeting, 291–2
Bihar, 392 (and sources for Table 16.4)
bills of exchange, 374; from China, 374–6
bird's nests, 369
Bird's–Nest Fort, 101, 113
Blandford, second marquis of (1822–83), 228 (and n. 76)
Blenheim (forts), 289
blockade, 433; of Canton by rebels, 443
Blue Peter, 51
Board of Revenue (Indian), 418
Board of Trade, 333, 339, 376
Bogue, the, 16; forts, 98–9, 114
Bokhara, 401, 461
bombardment of Canton City, 95–6, 98, 100, 153; 'bad and base', 160, 166; cost MP seats, 252; 'loss of life enormous', 283; a 'massacre', 196, 288; a 'terrible punishment', 198
Bombay, 390, 411; Bank of, 411; experiential cultivation of U.S. strain of cotton in, 427 (and n. 148); opium passes at, 394–6, 405–6; renamed Mumbai, 390 (n. 6); rise and prosperity of, 411
Bonham, Sir George (1803–63), 6 (and n. 26), 15, 117ff, 122, 137; declared entry in abeyance, 140
Borthwick, Peter (editor of the *Morning Post*), 169
Boston, 355
Bowring, Edgar J. (son of Sir John), 304
Bowring, Lady, 102
Bowring, Sir John (British minister plenipotentiary in the Far East and

concurrently governor of Hong Kong, 1854–9), 4 (and n.10), 18, 20, 22, 23, 24; appealed to Peter Parker, 273; argued against Granville's instructions, 141–2; argued against Malmesbury's instructions, 142–3; became a political sacrifice, 302–6; cautioned by Clarendon, 143; character of, 85ff; Clarendon approved conduct of, 302; Clarendon's relations with, 87, 262–3; commercial experience of, 87, 262–3; conduct conformed to government policy, 301; conspiracy of, 89, 90, 104, 106, 462; consul at Canton, 121ff, 136; contravened Clarendon's instructions, 144, 146; contravened instructions, 95, 103, 105, 106, 194; in defence of, 104, 105, 106, 107, 203–4; dragon boat, 136; early career of, 87; encouraged by end of Crimean War, 199–200; full of regret, 84; full of self importance, 122; given free rein, 304; humiliated, 122–3, 126; insulted national honour, 104; learnt some Chinese, 86–7; lied to Clarendon, 89, 462; lied to Seymour, 89, 91, 106; lied to Yeh, 88, 103; 'made such a fool of himself', 293; 'most mischievous man', 188; nowhere to hide, 94; was obsessed with entering Canton City, 88–95, 95–7, 99–100, 103, 106, 107, 108, 124–5, 126–7, 462; 'over the Great Wall', 85, 307; Palmerston's relations with, 87, 108, 122, 123, 140, 262–3, 462; perceptions of the opium trade and Indian revenue, 125–6, 462, 466; possessed by a monomania, 106, 107, 185, 462; repeatedly restrained, 306, 307; severely criticised by Cobden, 194; 202; slackening of the rein on, 108; spread rumours about Peter Parker, 273; to be superseded, 304–5; and undeclared war, 95–7, 98, 99
bravery, 98, 99
bread poisoning (in Hong Kong), 11–12, 21, 26, 102–3, 205, 206, 226, 227–8 (and n. 74); allegedly by baker Allum, *see* Zhang Peilin; Palmerston's manipulation of, 230, 295
Bridges, W. T. (acting attorney-general of Hong Kong, 1855), 443, 444
Bright, John (1811–88), 36 (and n. 238); at bottom of the poll, 250, 254, 298; election postmortem for, 255–6; nervous breakdown of, 255

Bristol, 221
British Chamber of Commerce at Canton, 115
British East India Company, 317, 324, 369; complete records of, 380; end of monopoly of, 369 (and ns. 8–9), 380; lost a great deal of money trading in cottons and woollens, 447; parliamentary inquiry into, 425–6, 447; purchased teas in proportion to cottons and woollens taken, 447
British West Indies, 317; needed industrious Chinese labourers to grow cotton, 318
British, resources, 280–2; exports to China, 333–7; imports from China, 337–9
Brodie, Benjamin, 325
Bruce, the hon. Frederick (Elgin's brother), 307, 470
Buchanan, James (U.S. president-elect), 275
Byzantium, 360

Cabinet, 29, 212, 222, 230, 267, 270, 454; met to discuss the *Arrow* incident, 284–5, 286; and penal dissolution, 298; prepared to go to war alone, 290; sought French allies even before *Arrow* incident, 465; uneasy about the *Arrow* incident, 284–5, 286; what to do with Bowring?, 306
Cain, P. J., 474, 477
Calcutta, 399; opium auctions at, 399 (and n. 30), 401, 414
Caledonian Horticultural Society, 431
Cambridge House (Palmerston's London residence), 219
Cannadine, David, 476 (and n. 92), 478
Canning, Stratford, 105
Canton Archive, 19, 119
Canton City question, 10, 15, 17, 26, 27, 86, 88–97, 108; grafted onto the *Arrow* dispute, 93–97, 98, 99–100, 104, 105, 106, 107, 156, 241; history of, 114ff; no material advantage to be gained, 106, 115ff; Parker dissociated U.S. government from, 274; Sanyuanli spirit and, 130l–31; 1849 a watershed in, 139; a writer from Shanghai on, 287. *See also* Bowring, Sir John
Canton City: forced entry of, 96–7; ransom of, 129, 131
Canton prefect, 117, 132–3, 479
Cao Lütai, 131
Cape of Good Hope, 22

527

captain of convenience, 3–4, 55, 57, 59; *see also* nominal captain

Cardwell, Edward (1813–86), 169 (and n. 79), 215, 223; joined Palmerston's cabinet, 299–300

Carnarvon, fourth earl of (Henry Howard Molyneux, 1831–90), 61 (and n. 107), 104, 179

cash crops, 427–8

Cass, Lewis, 275

casus belli, 29, 32, 37–8, 72, 83, 104; Cobden's bewilderment over, 270; contemptible, 207; faked a, 72, 83, 159, 477, 477; flimsy, 457; Graham's bewilderment over, 256, 269–70; look out for a, 82, 87, 269; a manufactured excuse (*The Times*), 160, 199; motives behind, 193–6; sensational, 459; of small moment (*The Times*), 156; stumbled into, 193; a varnish (*Morning Chronicle*), 159

Catholic Party, 169

caucus, 215, 465

Cecil, Robert (1830–1903), 199; succeeded as third marquis of Salisbury, 199 (n. 36)

censure, 211, 293, 294, 295, 301

Ceylon, 308

Chapdelaine, M. Père (French missionary), 267 (and n. 267), 271

Chapoo, 309

Charleston, 194

Charton, Paul, 440

chest of opium, 390; weighed 140 lbs in India, dried out to become 133.3 lbs (1 Chinese pecul) in China, 390 (n. 7)

Chester, 247

Chiang Kai-shek, 445 (n. 30)

Chiang Pai-huang, 13

Chichester, earl of, 320 (and n. 66)

Chin A-shing, 51

China: firms, 220, 221; growth of, 285; place in the United Kingdom's imports globally, 339–43; trade, 188–9, 207–9, 208, 221; war, 307

Chinese Coalition, 225, 238–40, 244, 295; combination of 'all the scrabs and debris', 299; universally condemned, 252;

Chinese Election, 25, 26, 152 (and n. 5), 171, 172, 225, 247; in British politics, 253; created permanent landmarks, 298; threw out champions of free trade, 298, 458; unprecedented, 250–1

Chinese export duties, 343

Chinese foreign policy, 478–81; interpretations of, 120, 147–8, 478–81

Chinese import duties, 343

Chinese Repository, 33

Chinese women, 229; needed in Australia, Singapore, straits settlements, and West Indies, 316–19

Christianity, 185–6, 191, 195; effect of opium on, 324

Church Missionary Society, 320

Chusan (Islands), 116–17, 267, 268; reports of Russian intentions on, 277 and Sir John Davis, 278; and Clarendon, 278; and Palmerston, 278; Clarendon ordered occupation of, 309

Chusan, 45

City of London Liberal Registration Association, 245

City of London, 219, 224, 230, 241, 242, 253, 311, 474, 477

civil establishment, 355

civil service examination (Chinese), 132–3; British adoption of, 161

Civis Romanus sum, 134, 137 (and n. 57), 138–9; 'not a very attractive motto', 197

Clarendon, fourth earl of (George Frederick Villiers, 1800–70), 10 (and n. 63), 20, 28, 55, 61; described the *Arrow* incident as 'a miserable case', 63; and law of force, 81, 189; *The Times*'s relations with, 155; on insult, 175; threw in a good word for Russell, 243; became target of public attention, 290; was 'low, worn, and out of sorts', 290; supported the cause of missionaries, 321–2 (and n. 73)

clash of two cultures, 32, 33, 433, 471, 484

Clerkenwell News, 168

Cobden, Richard (1804–65), 30 (and n. 195), 34, 36, 70, 82, 69, 193; severely criticised Bowring, 194, 202; demolished 'insults' ploy, 196–7, 463; on trade, 207, 464–5; censure motion carried by 16 votes, 211; criticised by *Punch*, 235; satirised by *Punch*, 238; 'peacemonger', 132, 248; fought election on the 'Chinese question', 249; on the *Arrow* question, 249; motion doctored, 293–4; defeated, 298; annoyed by submission of East India and China Association of Liverpool, 312

Index

Cochrane, Baillie (d. 1890), 224 (and n. 56)
Cochrane, Read-Admiral Sir Thomas (1789–1872), 135 (and n. 47), 197
Colchester, Lord, 184
Cold War, 480
Coldstream Guards, 314
colonial expansion, 316–19
colonial ordinance (of Hong Kong), 43 (n. 4); invalid, 177, 178; materially altered the supplementary treaty, 178; facilitated smuggling, 189–90, 205; under which 'Sir John Bowring has made such a fool of himself', 293
'commercial candidates', 245
commercial interests, 284, 302; vs liberal conscience, 283–4, 285, 286; vs territorial ambition, 316
commercial shock, 283
Commissioner Lin, *see* Lin
Commissioner Yeh, *see* Yeh
commodity trade gap, 366
commonsense approach, 292, 301
Communist Manifesto, 11 (n. 70), 151
Commutation Act of 1784, 343
Comptoir d'Escompte, 440
Compton, Charles, 34, 136, 138, 139, 467, 481
computed real value (of imports), 332
Confucius, 183, 186, 187, 191, 204, 229
conscience vote, 214
Conservative Party (Tory), 30 (n. 200), 80 (n. 76), 168, 221, 230; split in 1846, 168–9
conspiracy, 88, 89, 91, 104–5, 154, 202, 273, 274, 275, 462
Constantinople, 105, 276
constitutional power to make war, 282, 296, 308, 309
Corporation of London, 220
corps diplomatique, 230
Costin, W. C., 53, 54, 55, 56, 60
cotton, 427; experimental cultivation of U.S. strain of, 427 (and n. 148); in United States, 190, 409–10
cottons, 255, 333, 444, 446, 447; sold in proportion to teas purchased in China, 447–52
covetousness, 189, 208, 457
Cowley, Lord (British ambassador to France), 266ff
Crawford, Colvin, and Co., 220

Crawford, Robert Wigram (1813–89), 220 (and n. 26), 242, 245, 251
Crawfurd, John, 325
Crimean War, 28, 276; concluded in March 1856, 199; how Britain financed the, 280–1; and John Bright, 254, 255; and Lord John Russell, 240 (n. 140); and Palmerston, 200–1, 235–6, 238, 252, 289, 464; and Seymour, 273
Crompton, T. B. (owner of the *Morning Post*), 169
Cruikshank, George (1792–1878), 216–7, 228
Currie, Raikes (1801–81), 242 (and n. 148), 243, 245; could only address the reporters, 246
customs revenue, 347
cutlery, 263

D'Aguila, Major-General, 197
Daily News, 159, 160, 167, 170; 'pious and pedagogic', 171; 'served the Liberalism of conviction', 171
Daily Telegraph, 168 (and n. 68); 'served the Liberalism of convention', 171
Daman, 417, 419 (and n. 105)
Dart, 45
Davies, Lloyd (1801–60), 24, 195–6 (and n. 15)
Davis, Sir John, 82, 94, 114–15, 116, 130, 138–9, 196–7, 278
de Bourboulon (French minister in China, 1857), 291, 302
de Courcy, Count René (French minister in China, 1856), 271
de Montalembert, Count, 187
debt-servicing, 390–1
declared value (of exports), 332
Delane, John (editor of *The Times*), 154, 169
Delhi, 421
demystification, 234
Deng Xiaoping, 38
Dent, Lancelot, 220
Derby, fourteenth earl of (Edward George Geoffrey Smith Stanley, 1799–1869), 80 (and n. 76), 103, 105–6, 169; tried to buy *John Bull*, 171; founded the *Press*, 171; re the flag, 175; patriotic, 184; miscalculated, 252; hoped to dislodge Palmerston, 288–9; approached Gladstone, 289; gave notice in House of Lords, 290; appealed to by Society of Friends against legalisation of opium, 431

Index

Dillon, Edward, 319
diplomatic recognition, 31, 33, 34, 149, 468
Disraeli, Benjamin (1804–81), 30 (and n. 200), 169; cautioned Derby against dislodging Palmerston, 289; founded the *Press*, 171; miscalculated, 252; re-elected, 251–2; resisted approached to buy *Reynold's Newspaper*, 237; responded to Palmerston's speech, 208, 295; tried to buy *John Bull*, 171
Diu, 417
Don Pacifico (1851), 213
Donald, W. H., 445
Dracos, 198
Duke, Sir J., 245, 246 (and n. 176)
Dutch Folly (Haizhu Fort), 8, 45 (and n. 17), 47, 96, 100, 162
duty of care, 180
duty on tea, 343, 347–50; on wine, 385
dynamics of imperialism, 352, 455, 471

Earl, Charles (captain of the *Chusan*), 45, 52, 59, 88
East India and China Association of Liverpool, 207, 292, 304; annoyed Cobden, 312
East India and China Association of London, 210, 285, 292; on Chinese emigration, 317; offered local information to Clarendon, 285 (and n. 15); submission forwarded to Bowring, 303
East India House, 376, 426
economic causation, 28
economic imperialism, 422
economic interests, 270, 466–7
Edict of Nantes, 360
Education, Department of (established 1856), 167–8
election perspectives, 252–7
election postmortem, 252–3
electioneering, 230
electoral reform, 288
Elgin, eighth earl of (1811–63), 39 (and n. 251); appointment announced, 222; appointment announced to Bowring, 305; considered for appointment, 222 (and n. 39); a deeply sensitive man, 413; forwarded Mitchell's report, 263; found it repugnant to impose on a defeated government so deleterious a change in its law, 413–14; to leave England on 26 April 1857, 308;

Palmerston on, 306; reduce Canton first, 149; 'wretched question of the *Arrow*', 63
Ellenborough, earl of (Edward Law, 1790–1871), 105 (and n. 181), 107; annexed Sind, 419; criticised Bowring for 'general covetousness', 189, 208, 457; on global trade, 190, 409–10; justified annexation of Sind, 420–5; patriotic, 184
Ellice, Edward the younger (1810–80), 249 (and n. 200)
Elliot, Captain Charles (1801–75), 134 (and n. 40); on opium profits, 406
Elliot, Commodore, 47, 75, 76, 77, 78, 80, 112
Elmslie, A. W., Consul, 123
embargo, 352
emigration (from China), 29, 303, 308, 317–19
Engels, Friedrich (1820–95), 151, 195
English version (of treaty), 303, 308
Enlightenment, 183
enslavement, 11, 38, 151, 481
Ever-Victorious Army, 446
Executive Council (of Hong Kong), 102
expansion by poison, 430–3
expiry, 181–3, 252, 460
export duties (Chinese), 343
export of British manufactures to China, 333–5
extradition, 53 (and n. 58), 74
extraterritorial rights, 58 (and n. 92)
extraterritoriality, 308

fabrication, 227; *see also* Parkes, Bowring
Factory Gardens, 26, 100
Fairbank, John King, 478
false edict, 5, 6, 118ff, 134, 140, 479, 480; Chinese original of, 119; English translations of, 118–19
fangui, 136
Fay, Peter Ward, 470
fertile land, 392 (and n. 12)
Fieldhouse, David K., 472–3, 477
Fielding, Colonel George, 313–14
Fielding, Lieutenant-Colonel Percy, 314
filibusterer, 167
fire engines, 26, 101
firebrand, 209, 229, 230, 295, 482
fires, caused by Royal Navy's bombardment, 100; deliberately lit by order of Seymour, 101; mysterious, 100, 274

530

Flanders, 464
Flint, 247, 248
Fong Ah-ming, 43
Foreign Office, 309; *see also* Whitehall
Formosa, 313; *see also* Taiwan
Fortune, Robert, 316; advocated occupation of Chusan, 316; made secret cuttings of Chinese tea plants, 316
franchise reform, 254
Free Trade, Home, and Foreign Affairs Association of Manchester, 288
free press, 300
free trade ideology, 384–5; at its climax, 385 (and n. 40); gripped England, 458
free-trade principles, 470; was 'near the realms of religion', 485
free-traders, 426–7, 428
freights and other services, 408
French Folly (Fort), 8, 98, 100, 289
French, allies, 282; demands, 267, 271; personnel, 7; treaty, 320, 321
Fujian, 313; as an alternative source of tea, 435
Fukuzawa, Yukichi, 33

Galbraith, J. S., 477
Gallagher, John, 461, 477, 483
Ganges, 418
gangkou, 115
Garrett, Major-General Sir Robert, 227
Garter, Order of the, 293, 465
Gavin, Robert, 463, 475
General Consular Instructions, 10
general election, 152 (and n. 5), 237, 241, 206 (n. 250)
general law of nations, 175–6
gentlemanly capitalism, 36–7, 253, 408; assessment of, 474–5, 484; at the time of the *Arrow* War, 311, 312; at the time of the Opium War, 311; war without, 330; in which merchants offered local information, 285 (and n. 15)
Gibralta, 178
Gladstone, William Ewart (1809–98), 159 (and n. 35), 197; on technicalities and generalities, 204–7; viewed division as having done 'more honour to the HC', 211; a raging 'Jesuit', 247–8; and the Midlothian campaign (1878–80), 247; responded to Derby's approach, 289;

caught between liberal conscience and naked interests, 295; joined Palmerston's cabinet as chancellor of the Exchequer (1859), 296; taken to task by Roebuck, 296; taken to task by Grey, 296–7; joined Palmerston's cabinet as chancellor of the Exchequer (1855), 299; 'power of speaking', 299; described opium as 'pernicious', 431; became prime minister, 433; tacitly encouraged continuation of opium monopoly in India, 433
Glasgow, Chamber of Commerce and Manufactures of, 304, 317
global trade (of U.K), 190, 219, 406–10, 416, 473 (and n. 83), 483; deficit, 408–10
Globe, the, 170 (and n. 91), 222; fabricated story, 227; Palmerston's relations with, 170, 242, 244; about-turn of, 244, 245
Glynne, Sir Stephen, 247–8
GNP, 483
Goa, 418
Goderich, Lord, 248
Gourley, Dr W., 216, 217
Graham, Gerald, 277
Graham, Sir James (1792–1861), 24 (and n. 176); on Bowring, 256, 269–70; re-elected, 251
Grand Canal, 158, 263, 268, 309
Granville, second earl of (Granville George Leveson-Gower, 1815–91), 62 (and n. 113), 81, 105; foreign secretary appointing Bowring acting plenipotentiary, 141; announced dissolution of Parliament, 212; uneasy about the *Arrow* incident, 284; repeatedly confused the opium issue, 325–6
Great Seal, 307
Great War, 215
Greater East Asia Co-Prosperity Sphere, 483
Greenberg, Michael, 376, 412
Gregson and Co., 220, 253
Gregson, Samuel, 210, 220, 253, 285; offered local information to Clarendon, 285 (and n. 15)
Greville, Charles Cavendish Fulke (1784–1865), 170, 206, 207, 232, 237, 482
Grey, Earl (Henry George, third Earl Gray, 1802–94), 61 (and n. 105), 81, 107, 175, 325
Guangdong, 71, 111, 116
Guangxi, 140
guerrilla warfare, 205

Index

Guildhall, 220, 242, 243, 246
Gulf War (1991), 445 (and n. 29), 482
Gutzlaff, Rev Charles, 69

Hamelin, Admiral (French), 266, 268
Hammond, Edmund (permanent under-secretary for foreign affairs), 287, 299, 304, 312, 315, 317, 319; dealt with opium papers, 327; on the ill health of the Archbishop of Canterbury, 293; 465; on vacant Garters, 293, 465
Hansard, 191
Hanse Towns, 355
Hapsburg, 391, 484
Hastings, HMS, 16
Hastings, Warren, 416, 430
Hawarden (Gladstone's property), 247
Hayter, Sir William Goodenough (1792–1878), 242 (and n. 154)
He Guiqing, 415
head price, 12, 95–6, 110 (n. 8), 225, 228, 230
Headrick, Daniel, 22
hegemony, 391, 475, 484
Hengdang (Wangtung), 98–9
Hephaistos, 82
Herbert, Sidney (1810–61), 103, 169 (and n. 78), 199, 211; joined Palmerston's cabinet, 299
Higgings, Alfred, 219
Hobson, J. A., 476
hongs, 158
Hoole, Rev E., 321
Hopkins, A. G., 474, 477
Hoppo, 56
Horse Guards, 314
Howqua, 107, 122, 123
Huang Entong, 117, 133
Huang Liankai, 44
Huang Yen-yü, 118
Huangzhuqi, 136–7
Huddersfield, 248
Huguenots, 360
Huntington, Samuel, 484
Hurd, Douglas, 2, 12, 52, 66
hustings, 233
hysteria, 218, 222, 254, 255, 310, 408, 459, 473

imperial, 474; interests, 474, 482; law, 179; profit-making, 473; tribute, 429

imperialism of free trade, 34–5, 36, 256; evaluation of, 365, 380–5, 416–7, 417–20, 425–9, 440–1, 458; holds a lot of water, 314; Parkes's views on, 461; too general to be adequate, 470–1, 475; substantiated the 'official mind' of, 477; well conceptualized, 483
imperialism, 1; calculated, 473; the confusion of, 1ff, 457–9; diplomacy of, 261ff, 468; dynamics of, 451ff, 478, 471; economics of, 331ff, 466–7, 468; lobbies of, 310ff, 468; mechanics of, 259ff, 465–6, 468; personalities of, 67, 461–3, 468; politics of, 283ff, 468; pretext for, 41ff, 459–61, 468; rhetoric of, 15ff, 463–5
import duties (Chinese), *see* Chinese import duties
income and property taxes, 347
income tax, 280–2 (and n. 128), 288–9; introduced in 1840s, 427
Independent Irish Party, 169
India Board, 317
India House, 376, 426
India, 386; debt-ridden, 386–90, 396; extension of British rule in, 386–9; finances, 20, 188–9, 211; indigenous rebellions in, 389; insolvent, 389, 429; new banks in, 411
Indian debt, 386–90; serviced by opium revenue, 390
Indian Mutiny, 39 (and n. 257), 389
Industrial Revolution, 358, 410
Inflexible, HMS, 8
insult to the flag, 31, 32, 40, 45, 55, 62, 63, 64, 65, 111, 114, 232; attorney-general shook his head ominously at, 292; Elgin not instructed to obtain reparation for, 328; fabricated, 59; intended?, 175–7, 185; transposed by Parkes, 47, 48, 72, 75, 76, 78; war without, 330
insults in China, 16, 17, 31, 34, 196–8, 230, 463
international law, 291; made attorney-general shake his head ominously, 292
Iraq, 444
iron and steal, 444, 445–6
Ironson, Robert, 318
Ishan, 132
Italy, 255, 360

532

Index

Japan, 436; entered tea market, 436; supplied with iron and war materials, 445
Jardine Matheson and Company, 210, 220, 362, 376
Jardine, David, 114, 116
Jardine, William, 210; masterminded the Opium War, 210, 285 (n. 15), 311
Jeejeebhoy, Jamshetji (1783–1859), 411
Jiang Mengyin, 152
jingoism, 27, 172 (and n. 116), 200–3, 226, 240, 248, 254, 458, 464
John Bull, 171
joint military action, 266
judges of the realm, 323
junior ministers, 213
junk (Chinese vessel), 181
justice and equity towards the Chinese, 325
justice and humanity, 185–7, 465

Karachi, 419
Keenan, James (U.S. consul at Canton), 6, 64; Secretary of State William Marcy ordered inquiry into, 274
Kendall, Nicholas (1800–78), 200–1 (and n. 42)
Kennedy, Paul, 391, 482, 483, 484, 485
Kennedy, Thomas (Captain of the *Arrow*), 3, 4, 43, 51; fabricated an insult, 460–1; ordered to give up his credentials, 58 (n. 89)
Khiva, 461
Kimberley, Lord (secretary for India), 433
Kinnaird, Arthur Fitzgerald (1814–87), 211 (and n. 112)
Kisseleff, General (Russian ambassador in Paris), 276
Korean War, 482
Kowloon (47 sq. km), 11, 280, 314
kowtow, 31, 33
Kung, Prince, 39

Labouchere, Henry (1798–1869), 194 (and n. 8), 203, 315
Lagos, 422, 485
Lancashire, 254
land and assessed taxes, 347, 348, 349, 350
landed aristocracy, 161
Lane, O.T., 100
Lao Zi, 229
lascars, 137

law lords, 60, 174, 184–5
law of force, 81, 189, 195
Layard, Austen Henry (1817–94), 223 (and n. 42), 298
Leach, John (captain of the *Dart*), 45, 51, 59
lead and shot (as sold to Chinese), 40, 444, 446
Lenin, V. I., 476
lettuce opium, 431
Leung A-yung, 51, 52
Lewis, Sir George Cornwall (chancellor of the Exchequer), 280; uneasy about the *Arrow* incident, 284; 'sober-minded', 284; 'cold-blooded as a fish', 284; on income tax, 289
Lhasa, 401 (n. 32), 417 (n. 91)
Li Mingtai, 44
Li Yuzheng, 18
Liang Jianfu, 44
Liang Jiang, 145, 183, 415
Liang Kuoding, Captain (*shoubei*), 44, 47, 111
liang shouxian, 123
Liberal Party (Whig), 168, 230, 295, 300
liberal conscience, 187, 191, 193, 199, 209, 212, 213, 214, 215, 288, 465; vs commercial interests, 283–4, 285, 286, 290; conscience-stricken, 290; exploitation of, 300; as played out in politics, 292–7; of *The Times*, 283
Libya, 462 (n. 35)
likin, see transit dues
Lin, Commissioner, 221, 232, 378, 401; began to have a case, 431; letter to Queen Victoria, 430; Palmerston's allegation about, 463; *see also* rhubarb
Lindsay, William Shaw (1816–77), 224 (and n. 49)
Liverpool Chamber of Commerce, 318
Liverpool, 213, 218–19, 247; the Exchange in, 219
Lloyds, 219
local constituencies, 252–7
local poppy interest, 232, 463
Lockerbie (Scotland), 462 (n. 35)
London Gazette, 153, 154, 194, 222, 285, 286, 304, 330
London Tavern, 241, 243
London, 219; City of, 219; Corporation of, 220; lord mayor of, 220, 230
long ells (a form of British textiles), 370 (and table note)

533

lorcha, 3, 43
lord advocate, 30, 203, 207, 261, 262
lord chancellor, 60 (and n. 102), 61, 106; dealt with Shaftesbury's request, 327; first to speak against Shaftesbury's anti-opium motion, 324
lord mayor (of London), 220
Louis Napoleon, 208
Lowe, Robert (1811–92), 200 (and n. 40), 235
Ludgate Hill, 217
Lyndhurst, Lord (John Singleton Copley, 1772–1863), 9 (and n. 58), 60, 88, 104, 106, 175, 188; 'in high force', 290; patriotic, 184; 'sense of justice', 290
Lyon, 439, 440, 441; Chamber of Commerce of, 440, 441
Lytton, Edward George Bulwer (1805–70), 198 (and n. 27)

Macao Passage Fort, 101, 113
Macao, 58, 69, 273, 319
Madras, 308
Malabar, 178
Malacca, 178
Malmesbury, third earl of (James Howard Harris, 1807–89), 81 (and n. 88), 104, 107, 169; described Parkes's action as grotesque, 462; rejoinder to Palmerston, 232–3
Malta, 178
Malwa Opium Agency, 390; established in 1823, 390, 394 (ns. 23–4), 418 (and n. 95)
Malwa opium, 390, 402; British endeavours to control, 417–20; compensated for shortfalls in Bengal opium, 405; half the price of Bengal, 420; route to the sea, 419 (n. 104); undercut competition, 420 (and n. 114)
Mammon, worship of, 251
Manchester Chamber of Commerce and Manufactures, 115, 218
Manchester Commercial Association, 289; advocated British rule of Shanghai, 289, 312–13
Manchester Guardian, 171 (and n. 105); shame-faced, 256
Manchester Peace Party, 169
Manchester school, 254
Manchester, Free Trade, Home, and Foreign Affairs Association of, 288
Manchuria, 276, 461

Mansion House, 230, 232, 233
marauding hares, *see* lettuce opium
Marcy, William (U.S. secretary of state), 274; disapproved of Armstrong's attack on the barrier forts, 275; ordered inquiry into Keenan's abuse of U.S. flag, 274
marine police, 53
Martin, R. Montgomery (former colonial treasurer of Hong Kong), 315 (and n. 32); pushed for the occupation of Chusan and the whole of China, 315–16
Marx, Karl, 25, 27, 37, 38, 151, 165ff, 191, 195
Matheson and Co., 220
Matheson, James, 210–11
Mauritius, 1, 308
measles paradigm, 32, 33, 429, 472
Medhurst, W. H., 144–5
Mercantile Bank of India, London, and China, 411
merchants' war, 218–20, 222, 302, 458
Mersey, 213
Merseyside, 419 (n. 105)
Messageries Maritimes, 440
Metcalfe, Sir Charles (Resident at Dehli, 1827), 421
Methuen, Lord (Frederick Henry Paul), 24, 104 (and n. 173), 176
metropolis, 22, 471, 475, 477, 486
Miall, Edward (1809–81, founder and editor of the *Nonconformist*), 237 (n. 119), 298 (and n. 93)
Michie, Alexander, 376
Middle East, 411
middle kingdom mentality, 33, 472
Midlothian campaign (1878–80), 247
'might is right', 195
military budgets, 281
military flags, 111
Mill, James, 426, 470
Mill, John Stuart, 426
Milner-Gibson, Thomas (1806–84), 36 (and n. 237); lost his seat at Manchester, 250, 254, 298; seconded Cobden's motion, 202–3
Minto, Lord, 209
missionary expansion, 319–22
missionary freedom, 320
Mitchell Report, 263, 451
Moffatt, George, 294
Molasses War, 31, 35–6, 428–9, 472

Index

Molesworth, Sir William, 155
Moncreiff, Rt. Hon. James (1811–71), 30 (n. 193); *see also* lord advocate
monomania, 106, 107, 185, 462
monopoly, and revenue, 327; by agency, 416; by contract, 416; and Chinese opium market, 417–20
morality, 183, 187, 431; on the part of the Chinese, 183–5, 191, 430, 431, 471; on the part of the British, 425, 431
Morning Chronicle, 159ff, 170
Morning Post, 26, 156ff; abused the Chinese people, 229; on the bread poisoning, 26, 226–8; on the Commons debate, 215; history of, 169–70; laurels for Palmerston, 236, 238; Palmerston's paper, 170; relations with the government, 158
Morning Star (paper of Cobden and Bright), 172, 240
Morse, H. B., 135; claimed opium had to be used to balance the books, 411 (and n. 64); denied that opium had anything to do with the two Opium Wars, 415–16 (and n. 82)
Moscow, 312
most-favoured-nation, 264, 320
Mostyn, Thomas E. (1830–61), 248 (and n. 188)
Muzhanga, 124

Nanhai, 123
Nanjing, 69, 125, 135, 137, 145; captured by the Taipings, 359, 434, 439
Napal, 401 (n. 32), 417 (n. 91)
Napier, General Sir Charles, 422, 461
Napier, Lord (British ambassador to Washington), 275; told U.S. government everything except demand to legalise opium, 275
Napoleon Bonaparte, 205, 343
Napoleonic Wars, 343
national honour, 104, 153, 154, 185, 200, 201, 206, 215, 223, 225, 230, 231, 233, 240, 242, 244, 252; cast to the dust (Roebuck), 251; effect of opium on, 324; freely exploited, 459; missionaries on, 320, 321; viz-a-viz treaty revision, 270
national interest, 251, 300, 301, 302, 426–7, 428, 433, 468, 468, 470, 473
national scandal and reproach, 234
nationalism, 183, 191

natural allegiance, 178, 179
nautical practice (British), 9, 44, 54, 166, 459
nemine contradicente, 244
Newcastle-upon-Tyne, 221–2
Nicaragua, 167
nobodies, 250; needed a 'microscope' to see the, 251; one-sixth of the most conspicuous men replaced by, 250
Nolde, John, 17, 118ff
nominal captain, 26, 43; *see also* captain of convenience
Nonconformist, 237
North Carolina, 355
North China Herald, 125
Northcote, Sir Stafford (1818–87), 161 (and n. 86)

official value (of imports), 332
Opium War, 11 (and n. 70), 27, 31, 32, 33, 34, 37, 39, 67, 69, 110, 116, 128, 129, 136, 153, 378, 413; decline in sale of opium during, 401; indemnities, 116–7, 132; and the Indian debt, 390; initiated debate in U.K. about morality of opium, 431; lobbies, 311; masterminded by William Jardine, 210, 311
opium cultivation, 393; expansion of, 418
opium legalization, 27 (and n. 182), 28, 29, 35, 38, 141, 221; achieved, 415; Elgin instructed to obtain, 275, 308, 413; Elgin refused to pressure China for, 412–3; immoral, 431; Palmerston's views on, 413; Reed lobbied Elgin for, 414–15; United Kingdom kept France in the dark about, 275, 466; United Kingdom kept United States of America in the dark about, 275, 466
opium monopoly, 35, 393, 417; in China market, 417–20, 473; Gladstone tacitly encouraged continuation of, 433; parliamentary inquiry (1830–2) into, 425–6, 447; received tacit encouragement from Gladstone, 433; royal commission (1890s) on, 426, 429, 433; royal commission decided continuation of, 433; 'scandalised the public conscience', 324; 'single-minded determination of an autocratic state to sustain', 394
opium revenue, 394; British India's second largest source of revenue, 396; cheaper than salt to produce, 392; Derby would not jeopardize, 431–2; most valuable of all

535

revenues, 396; parliamentary inquiry, 425–6; relative to other charges, 396; 'single-minded determination of an autocratic state to sustain', 394; ten times cheaper than salt to collect, 394, 396; '22 per cent of Indian revenue', 429; viz-a-viz India's revenues, 396

opium, 27, 33, 34, 35, 36, 37, 39, 322–8; abominable, 211; almost every British merchant in China was involved, 210; auctions of, 399, 401, 414; 'bulwark against bankruptcy', 429; and British expansion in India, 390–1; channel of remittance, 412, 469; cheaper to produce than salt, 392; cost of production of, 391–2; cultivation in India 'negligible before British rule', 390; cultivation in United Kingom actively encouraged, 431; decline in supply from Bengal, 402; deleterious, 211; end of Indian, 429 (n. 158); English cordials had plenty of, 430; fear of renewed suppression of (in 1851), 125–6, 141–2, 413–16; growth in British India, 390 (and n. 8); helped Britain balance the books, 412; imported into United Kingdom until 1856, 431; jeopardised Chinese ability to buy British manufactures, 378; legalised, 415; and Manchester, 255; as a medium in global trade, 190, 219, 406–10, 416, 423; monopoly, 394; more than paid for tea and silk, 408; most fertile land requisitioned to grow, 392 (and n. 12); not illegal in England, 430; not pernicious, 325; opium trade, 189–91, 209–11, 255, 299; Palmerston's frank admission, 211, 214; Palmerston's view on illegality of, 413; passes, 394–6, 405; pernicious, 416, 430, 431; Persian, 401; profits, 406–10; profits at least 'fourteen times the prime cost', 394 (and n. 21); prohibition against, 413; *Punch* on, 328; revenue, 394; scandalised the public conscience', 324; serviced the Indian debt, 390; sharp rise in sale of, 401; size of land requisitioned to grow, 392 (and n. 12); single most important cash crop in India, 428; sold mainly to China, 399–401; suppression of (in 1839), 375, 378, 401, 413; thousands of chests burnt in 1911, 429 (n. 158); three-fifths at Canton, 210; transported under armed guard, 394;

Turkish, 401; value in China, 408; value in India, 408; Warren Hastings on, 416, 430; worth $30 million p.a., 210

Oriental Bank, 411

Osborne, Ralph Bernal (1808–82), 201 (and n. 44)

Outram, James (political agent for Sind, 1843), 425

Owen, David, 376

Oxford City, 223

Oxford, bishop of, 187, 190, 462

Oxford, University of, 247

Oxley, Dr, 325

P&O (Peninsular & Oriental Steam Navigation Company), 22; introduction of service in 1848 led to sharp rise in sale of opium in China, 401; supplied Canton government with arms, 443–4

Pacific War, 445

pacifism, 255, 298, 458

Pakenham, Adjutant-General, 227

Palmer, McKillop, Dent, and Co, 220

Palmerston, third viscount (Henry John Temple, 1784–1865), 8 (and n. 49), 24, 70; relations with Parkes, 82, 87, 269, 461, 462, 465, 477; relations with Bowring, 87, 108, 122, 123, 140, 462, 463; thundered over 1849 entry crisis, 140; relations with *The Times*, 154ff, 284; used the *Morning Post*, 170; used the *Globe*, 170; used the *Morning Chronicle*, 170; 'full of arrogance and jactance', 170; manipulated the provincial press, 172; appealed to patriotism, 201; abused Yeh, 201–2, 231–2, 462; defended Bowring, 203–4, 463; 'pale, anxious, unnerved', 205; suffered from a bad cold, 25, 206; on trade expansion, 206, 295; accepted Russell's challenge, 208, 241; dismissed by Russell in 1851, 208; brought down Russell's government, 208; sent Russell to Vienna, 208; frank admission concerning opium, 211; defeated in the House of Commons by 16 votes, 211; merchant support for, 218–23; electioneering, 230–2; made up stories, 231; at Tiverton, 231–2; 'full of deception and falsehood', 232; risqué joke, 232; and the Crimean War, 184, 200–1 (and n. 45), 235–8, 252; national idol, 237;

'Palmerstonian mania', 235–8, 238; 'strike another blow', (1851) 264; manipulated MPs, 294–5; never had parliamentary consent for the *Arrow* War, 296; manipulation of the *Arrow* issue, 297; and penal dissolution, 211–2, 223, 298, 307; contrived his own defeat?, 305; on illegality of opium, 413; alleged local Chinese poppy interest, 232, 463; alleged Chinese pleasure with defeat, 463

Palmerstonian mania, 237, 238

Panmure, second baron (Fox Maule, 1801–74, secretary for war), 281 (and n. 124)

Panyu, 123

Paris, 273, 308

Parker, Dr Peter, 1, 265; appointed minister to China, 272; saw Clarendon, 272; saw Walewski, 273; saw Bowring, 273; avoided Bowring, 273; disapproved of bombardment of Canton, 273; beaten to Washington by the French, 274

Parkes, Harry (acting British consul at Canton, 1856), 4 (and n. 8), 10, 22, 23, 26, 45; early career, 69ff; relations with Palmerston, 82, 87, 269, 461, 462, 465, 477; manipulated correspondence, 49, 50, 73; manipulated witnesses, 51ff, 59ff, 75, 77, 78; manipulated Bowring, 70, 72, 73, 76, 162, 460; manipulated Seymour, 77, 78, 113, 460; faked a casus belli, 72, 83, 159, 459–60, 465; demanded apology, 72, 112, 164; warmongering, 75; unauthorised visit to Hong Kong, 77 (and n. 51), 89; proposed a northern expedition, 80; proposed occupation of Canton, 80; possible understanding with Palmerston, 82, 86; 'impersonification of the *Arrow* case', 83; 'blue eyes', 83; one of three commissioner to rule Canton, 83; fell out with Bowring, 84–5; conspiracy, 89–90, 91, 462; covered Bowring, 93; sought cover, 94; *Civis Romanus sum*, 137 (and n. 157), 139; irritated pride of, 160; superior to Chinese law, 163; 'if you *would* read a little international law', 163; conduct approved by Clarendon, 302; attached to Elgin's mission, 307; on Britain's political and commercial interests, 461; 'grotesque', 461

Parliamentary Papers, selective publication of, 315

Parliament, 4; parliamentary inquiry, 425–6, 447

Parsees, 411–12, 419

party loyalty arguments, 294

party politics, 187, 297–300; fluidity of, 297

Patna, 390

patriotism, 132–4, 184, 201, 215, 230, 301; of addicts, 401; of Bowring, 305; of Lyndhurst, 184; of MPs, 464

Pax Americana, 148, 468

Pax Britannica, 148

Peace Party, 250; *see also* Cobden

Pearl River, 75, 98, 359

pébrine (a disease of the silk worm), 439

pecul (or picul, a Chinese unit of weight equal to about 133.3 pounds), 370

Peel, Sir Robert (1788–1850), 169 (and n. 75), 323

Peelites, 298, 300

Peiho, 79, 80, 146, 184, 265, 273; Clarendon ordered blockade of, 289, 309

Pelcovits, Nathan, 330, 451

penal dissolution, 211–2, 223; worked wonders for Palmerston, 298, 307

Penang, 401

perceptions, 332, 406

periphery, 22, 471, 475, 477, 486

Perry, Sir Erskine (1807–58), 30 (and n. 197), 207, 209–10; suffered vote of no confidence, 223

Persia, 39, 352, 417, 420, 421; and opium, 401; question of, 288

Persian War, 288, 296, 352

Persigny, Count, 266–72

phantom enemy, 277

Philimore, Robert Joseph (d. 1885), 198 (and n. 30)

Pierce, President, 272; refused to join Anglo-French expedition, 282

Piercy, Rev Geoffrey, 319

Pigeard, Captain (French), 267, 268, 269

piracy, 29, 308

Pitt, William, 296

Platt, D. C. M., 35

plunder, 11, 38, 151, 187, 191, 481

Polachek, James, 120, 478–80

Political Economy Club, 426

political conspiracy, 202, 244

political press, 167ff; party alignments, 172; statistics about, 171

political sacrifice, 302
Portugal: and Daman, 417, and possessions in India, 418
Portuguese lorcha (no. 83), 55, 63
Pottinger, Sir Henry (1789–1856), 69 (and n. 69), 102, 116, 131, 134, 137
pragmatism, 154, 202, 273, 274, 275, 292, 293, 327
Presidency Bank of Bengal, 411
Presidency Bank of Bombay, 411
Press, 171, 227–8
press, manipulation of the, 172
Privy Council, 62, 29
protonationalism, 129ff
provincial press, 172; statistics about, 172
provocations, 136–40, 196
public duty, 296, 305, 414–15
public expenditure, 353, 356
Punch, 161–5, 167, 225, 235, 236; on Derby, 464; on the legality of the opium traffic, 328; 'microscope', 251
punishment, 198; British, 198-200, 226–9; Chinese, 216
putchuck (or putchuk, a Kashmir root plant), 370 (and n.)
Putiantin (Russian plenipotentiary to China), 280; demanded Chinese territory, 280

Qiying, 94, 115, 116–17, 133; conciliatory, 479; convention with Davis on Chusan, 278; severely punished, 124
Quai d'Orsay, 18, 482
Quakers, 432
Queen Victoria, 70, 105, 196, 430; letter to Chinese emperor, 307; opened Parliament with a 'microscope', 251; and Palmerston, 298; speech by, 288, 297

racism, 109, 157, 158, 195, 213, 217, 228, 229, 236, 286
Radicals, 169, 230; split, 298
Raj, 376
Rajputana, 419
ransom, *see* Cauton City
Rattler, 265
re-elected members, 251
reality, 332ff, 406
rebellions, 71, 111, 140, 142, 406; as an alleged origin of the *Arrow* War, 480; effect on foreign policy, 479–480; strategic value,
71–2, 262, 480–1; Xu and Yeh preoccupied with, 142–3; Yeh preoccupied with, 144, 145
Red Fort, 113
Red Guards, 53
Red Turban Rebellion, 146–7, 406, 434, 439; affected British exports, 446; as an alleged origin of the *Arrow* War, 480; besiege Canton, 443, 453
Reed, William (U.S. minister to China, 1857), 414
register, 3, 4, 5, 17, 43, 55, 57, 59, 63, 70, 71, 74, 87–8; facilitated smuggling, 189–90, 205; expiry of, 181–3, 252, 460; Marx on, 166; *Punch* on, 162, 163, 164; Seymour kept in the dark about, 91, 154
reinforcements, 226–7, 286, 287
remittance, 27, 190, 409, 412, 429, 469
Renxin Mansion, 107, 122, 123, 144, 147
renzhi, 183–5, 191
Reynold's Newspaper, 237
rhetoric, 38, 184, 300, 301–2
rhubarb, 433
Ricardo, David (1772–1823), 426 (and n. 143)
Rice War, 36, 369
rise and fall of great powers, 482–6
Robinson, Ronald, 461, 477, 483
Roebuck, John Arthur (1801–79), 211 (and n. 114); re-elected, 251; took Gladstone to task, 296
Rogers, Frederick (permanent under-secretary for the colonies), 293
Rolfe, Robert Monsey (1790–1868), *see* lord chancellor
Romans, 475, 476 (and n. 91)
Rothschild, baron, 245 (and n. 170)
Royal Navy, 27, 34, 469
royal commission, 35, 385
rule of law, 183–5, 193, 199, 214, 215, 262; disregarded by Palmerston, 282; 'shaking their heads very much about it', 291; Shaftesbury argued his anti-opium case on, 323; Palmerston's view on, 413; viz-a-viz opium legalisation, 413
rule of virtue, 183–5, 191
'Rule, Britannia', 67, 140ff, 467, 481
rupee, 391; equal to 2 shillings, 391 (sources to Table 16.3); low value of, 473
Russell, Lord John (1792–1878), 95 (and n. 82), 168; relied on the *Daily News*, 170, 171;

538

challenged Palmerston, 207–8, 209, 241; dismissed Palmerston in 1851, 208; sent to Vienna, 208; seriously talked to, 209; seduced Palmerston's supporters, 209; City constituency, 224; 'on his knees', 240–6; help from Clarendon, 243; help from Hayter, 243; 'Jahn', 243, 245; about-turn, 245; self-defence, 245; joined Palmerston's cabinet, 299, 469
Russian Academy of Sciences, 18
Russian allies, 276–80
Russian ecclesiastical mission, 28, 277
Russian threat, 18, 28, 29, 276–8
ryots, 393; interest-free advances to, 393 (and n. 13); contracted to grow opium, 393; required to deliver entire produce at a fixed rate, 393 (and n. 15); left with 'only the cost of production', 393 (and n 16); with traditional skills, 393

salt, 391–4; more expensive to produce than opiumm, 392; smuggling of, 56
Sanyuanli, 129, 133, 134, 135; spirit, 130–1
Sargent, A. J., 470
Schevelyoff, Konstantin v., 18
Schumpeter, Joseph, 476
Second China War, 1
Second Opium War, 10, 11, 13, 14, 37, 39, 151, 191, 471
Second Reform Bill (1867), 465
Secret Service, 171
sedition, 132
Seeley, Sir John, 475
self-interest, opposition to naked, 290
sensation, 225, 226, 228
sericulture, 360
services (about 20 per cent of value of commodities), 366
Seymour, Rear-Admiral Sir Michael (commander of the China Station, 1856–60), 5 (and n. 16), 7, 8, 26, tripartite conference, 89–91; kept in the dark, 91, 154; used as a shield, 94; destruction of forts, 113; reduced Canton first, 149; in the eyes of *Punch*, 164; no case, 164, 166; U.S. perspective on, 273; lost an eye in the Baltic, 273; first report to Admiralty published in the *London Gazette*, 285; second report, 286, 287; third report, 289–90; to continue under Elgin, 308; made an idol, 330 (n. 122)

Shaftesbury, seventh earl of (Anthon Ashley Cooper, 1801–85), 189, 238, 322 (and n. 74); raised question of opium trade, 299, 466; motion on opium, 322–8; opium 'scandalised the public conscience', 324; *Punch* on, 327
Shameen, 113
Shanghai intendant, 125
Shanghai, 145, 146, 273; fallen to Small Sword rebels, 439; French opened a bank in, 440; proposed occupation of, 289, 312, 313
Sheffield, 251
Shikarpur, 425
shoubei, 47
Shunde, 439
Siam, 70, 84
siege of Canton, 111, 443, 453
silk, 27, 284; bale of, 362 (and n. 55); British silk weaving industry, 360–1; in Canton area, 436; exempted from import duty since 1845, 361; French increased purchases of, 439–41; generated revenue, 361; history of, 360–1 (and n. 47); increased purchases of, 285; price of raw, 362; price rise, 284; rival suppliers of, 439; sharp decline in U.K. purchases after *Arrow* War, 437, 439; sharp rise in U.K. purchases after Opium War, 437; silks, 361 (and n. 50); in southern Europe, 284; in Yangtze area, 436
silkworm eggs, 360
silver, drain of, 374; Indian scarcity of, 411; role in Indian economy, 401–2; smuggling of, 374; surplus of, 410–12
Sind, 419; annexation of, 419, 472; deficit, 423 (and n. 129); edited correspondence of, 423; interpretations of annexation of, 475; justification for annexation of, 420–5; timing of annexation of, 423
Singapore, 1, 102, 178, 303, 305, 308; '50,000 Chinese males but no Chinese women', 317; opium sold to, 401
slaughter, 11, 38, 151, 187, 191, 481
Sleigh, Alexander, 219
Small Sword, 439
Smith, Dr George (first Anglican Bishop of Victoria, Hong Kong), 320
Smith, John Abel, 311
Society of Arts, 431
Society of Friends, 431

539

sophistry, 222, 458
South City (Beijing), 480
Spanish dollar (worth about 5 shillings), 362 (and n, 54)
Spanish vice-consul, 109
Spartan, 165
Spectator, 160, 464
St Leonards, Lord (Edward Burtenshaw Sugden, 1781–1875), 61 (and n. 109), 81, 104, 107, 176, 179; demolished the 'at sea' argument, 182
St Petersburg, 276, 279
Stamp Act (repealing the stamp duty, 1855), 154, 167
stamp duty, 167, 172
steam, 22, 57, 181; impact on opium traffic, 401
Stirling, Rear-Admiral Sir James (1791–1865), 18 (and n. 138), 28, 146; proposed occupation of China, 276–7; argued with Bowring re rebel blockade, 444
Stock Exchange, 219
Straits of Malacca, 318
straits settlement, 318, 401
strategic interpretation, 18, 28, 276–8, 422 (and n. 124), 475, 485
Stratford de Redcliffe (Stratford Canning), 105
Straubenzee, Major-General, 227
Su Acheng, 43
sub rosa, 415
sub-imperialism, 422
sugar, 221; as a body fuel, 358; consumption of, 358 (and n. 38); refiner, 221
Summer Palace, 401
Sun Yatsen, 217–18 (n. 12), 419 (n. 105)
superiority complex, 33, 472
Supplementary Treaty, 69, 264, 321
Suzhou, 439
Sybille, HMS, 76
Syria, 462 (n. 35)

Taiping Rebellion, 71, 140, 144, 311 (and n. 12), 352; captured Nanjing, 359, 434, 439; twenty million people perished in, 406; opium taxed to finance suppression of, 415; occupied lower Yangtze, 436; threatened Shanghai, 436; Britain helped suppress, 436, 446–7, 452; as an alleged origin of the *Arrow* War, 480

Taiwan, 313; proposed occupation of, 313
Tan Chung, 376
tea duty, 343–7; and British drinkers, 474; importance of, 347–50, 469; rates, 343; and the Royal Navy, 350–5
tea market, 284; near consternation in, 284
tea, 27, 93, 207, 188; Act (1773), 355; British shipping engaged in, 357; a daily necessity, 284, 357, 358–9; direct access to, 434–5; Dutch smugglers of, 356; Fujian offered alternative supply of, 434; growth of, 285; healthy aspects of, 357; history of, 355; increased purchase of, 285; Indian cultivation of, 356 (and n. 31), 360, 436; purchased in proportion to cottons and woollens taken, 447–9; re-exporting of, 357; related services, 357; revenue, 93, 192; supplemented the poor diet, 358–9; thrown into Boston harbour, 355; U.S. cultivation of, 355
telegraph, 22, 23, 48, 63
temperance, 216–17
Tenant Party, 169
Tennyson, Alfred Lord, 236 (and n. 117)
territorial ambitions, 274; of U.S., 274; of France, 274; of England, 274, 312–16; on Shanghai, 312–13; on Taiwan, 313, 314; on Chusan, 313, 314, 415, 416; on the whole of China, 276–7, 314–15, 316; vs commercial interests, 316
Texas, 355
The Times, 153ff, 283; controlled by the government?, 154, 155; attitudes towards the *Arrow* incident, 156, 160; homily on Yeh, 300; relations with Palmerston, 154ff, 284; proposed occupation of Chusan, 314–15
Thistle, 109
Thornton, Richard, 219
Tianjin (Tientsin), 146, 414, 265, 273
Tiverton, 231–2
trade expansion, 206
trade imbalance, 335–7, 366–9; an alarming 913 per cent of, 366; Britain absolutely dominated China's maritime trade, 383–4; Cobden's complaint about, 457; deficit, 372–4; in fact a trade surplus of, 371–2
transit dues (*likin*), 303, 304, 308, 440; at

Index

Bombay, 417–20, 420–3; contributed to the *Arrow* War, 485; origin of, 359
Treaty of Nanking, 25, 28, 29, 30, 38, 115, 153, 165, 262, 265, 335, 378; signed on 29 August 1842, 69; exchange of, 116; raised unbounded expectations, 208; British dissatisfaction with, 263; defunct, 306; did not legalise opium, 413; and annexation of Sind, 423; revision of, *see* treaty revision
Treaty of Tientsin (1858), 413; signed on 26 June 1858, 413; did not legalise opium, 413; dismayed opium smugglers, 414; granted access to Yangtze basin, 434; raised wild expectations, 449–50
Treaty of Tientsin (1911), 429 (n. 158)
treaty obligation, 73–4
treaty ports, 320
treaty revision, 25, 28, 29, 146, 149, 153, 207, 209, 214, 262–6, 302; history of, 263; law officers' views on, 264 (and n. 22), 270, 307; Bowring's views on, 265; Chinese emperor's views on, 265; Yeh's refusal to consider, 265–6, 335; Clarendon's explosion over, 266; British approach to France over, 266; British approach to U.S.A. over, 266; viz-a-viz *Arrow* incident, 270; French views on, 271; U.S. views on, 272, 274; *The Times*'s support for, 284; *Arrow* incident offered new excuse for, 303, 307; to avoid transit dues, 359–60; to legalise opium, 27 (and n. 182), 28, 29, 35, 38, 141, 221, 275, 308, 378
Trevelyan, Sir Charles (1807–86), 161 (and n. 86)
triangular trade, 21, 36, 365, 375, 376–9, 412
Trieste, 23, 153, 259, 283
tripartite intervention, 266, 267, 271, 272; French welcomed (22 October 1856) British approach for, 266; U.S. rejected (10 April 1857) British approach for, 275; Russia sought participation in, 276; U.K. sought Russian participation in, 279; Russia rejected (April 1857) British approach for, 279; British Cabinet now prepared to go to war without, 290, 291
Turkey, 255, 312, 417, 420, 421
Turkish opium, 401, 417, 420, 421; considered inferior by Chinese smokers, 401; considered superior by British drinkers, 430; imported into U.K. until 1856, 431
turncoats, 225, 299–300
tyranny of distance, 67

United States: allies, 266, 267, 271, 272–5; flag insulted, 7, 24, 64–5, 107, 176–7; merchants, 414; strain of cotton, 427 (and n. 148)
unmooring, 51 (and ns. 48 and 49), 54, 459
Utilitarian, 86

Vallancey, Major G., 279, 313
varnish, 159, 195; (deluxe), 196
Vavasseur, James, 317–18
vessels of light draft, 266
vexata quaestio, 92, 97, 132
Vienna, 208
Vladivostok, 1, 483
volte-face, 5, 244, 245
'*vox populi, vox Dei*', 134, 137, 147

Wade, Thomas, 10
Wakeman, Frederic, 12, 120
Walewski, Count, 208, 266–72, 291
Walker, General William, 167
Wangxia, 264
War Department, 307
war: expenditures, 280–2; materials, 452; undeclared, 53, 64, 80, 81, 84, 233, 308, 309; unpalatable, 433; unsanctioned, 297, 308, 309
Washington, 194
Watergate, 173 (and n. 117)
Wei Jianyou, 7, 13
Wellesley, Marquis (governor-general of India, 1803), 417
Welsh, Frank, 470
Wensleydale, Lord (James Parke, 1782–1868), 61 (and n. 111), 180, 182
Wesleyan Methodist Mission, 321
West India Committee, 318
West Indies, 317; needed industrious Chinese labourers to grow cotton, 318
West Riding, 248–9
Western Australia, 28
Westminster, 215, 255
Wetheral, Quartermaster-General, 227

541

Whampoa, 77, 109, 114, 139, 273
Whitehall, 4, 28, 29, 251, 253-4, 262, 475; took up the cause of missionaries, 321-2 (and n. 73)
wine duty, 385
Wodehouse, Lord (British ambassador at St Petersburg), 276, 279
Wood, Sir Charles (first lord of the Admiralty), 281 (n. 124); uneasy about the *Arrow* incident, 284
Woodgate, W., 90 (and n. 49), 92
woollens, 333, 444, 446, 447; sold in proportion to teas purchased in China, 447-52
world war, 1, 486
worship of Mammon, 251
worsted, 263
Wortley, Stuart (solicitor-general, 1857), 299

xenophobia, 9, 17, 31, 34, 128, 148-9, 467, 480; British, 9, 34, 137-9, 140, 141, 148-9, 226 (and n. 67), 468; official, 17, 34, 128ff, 140ff, 148-9, 467; virulent, 136; disappeared in 1849, 139-40; turned friendship at Canton in 1849, 142
Xia Li, 14
Xiamen (Amoy), 84, 85, 380
Xiangfeng, Emperor (reg. 1851-61), 6 (and n. 32)

Xie Fucheng, 15
Xu Guangjin, Commissioner (d. 1858), 6 (and n. 29), 16, 117ff

Yangtze, 29, 184, 263, 268, 309, 359, 434
Yangzhou, 359
Ye, Mingfeng, 480
Yeh (Ye Mingchen, 1809-59), Imperial Commissioner, 6 (and n. 31), 7, 8, 10, 16, 21, 26, 38; half-apologized, 50, 74, 80, 112, 160, 163, 166, 199; offered no resistance, 79, 112, 113; offered resistance, 79; a monster?, 8, 109-110, 127, 226; conciliatory, 112ff; opposed British entry into Canton City in 1849, 119ff; reasons for intransigence, 120-1, 124, 312; made a baron, 121; preoccupied with rebellions in five provinces, 144; sought Bowring's aid, 146-7; 'Give them anything', 147; abused by Palmerston, 201-2, 231-2; defended in England, 235; views on Chapdelaine's case, 267 (n. 267); homily on, 300
Yeh's residence, bombardment of, 78, 79, 95; pillaged, 114
Yellow River, 309
Yorkshire, 248

Zhang Peilin (Allum), 227 (n. 70), 228
Zhang Zuolin, 461